POPULAR MUSIC
IN
America
FORGING THE AMERICAN SPIRIT

Second Edition

STAN L. BRECKENRIDGE
California State University, Fullerton

Kendall Hunt
publishing company

Cover images © Shutterstock, Inc.

Kendall Hunt
publishing company

www.kendallhunt.com
Send all inquiries to:
4050 Westmark Drive
Dubuque, IA 52004-1840

Copyright © 2006, 2012 by Stan L. Breckenridge

ISBN 978-0-7575-9760-2

Printed in the United States of America

10 9 8 7 6 5 4 3 2 1

CONTENTS

Chapter Fourteen

Chapter Fifteen

Chapter Sixteen

Chapter Seventeen

ABOUT THE AUTHOR

Stan Breckenridge is a teacher, author, composer, singer and pianist, recording artist, and performer, and holds a Ph.D. in Musicology from the prestigious Claremont Graduate University in Claremont, California. Selected as a United States Fulbright Scholar, Dr. Breckenridge possesses a proven track record of educational excellence. Over the years his teaching assignments have spanned the curriculum: World Music, History of Jazz, Afro-American Music Appreciation, Western Music Appreciation, History of Rock, Basics of Music, Computer Applications in Music, Musicianship, Classical Piano, Pan-African Dance and Movement, Jazz/Commercial Keyboard Studio, Music Literature, Jazz Traditions, and various performance ensembles.

As a specialist in American music, he has presented papers at numerous conferences. Some of these include "Le Texte Dans La Musique Populaire Afro-Américaine" in Metz, France; "Grooving Body Movements: Rhythm as Language" at the Hungarian Society for the Study of English conference, in Debrecen, Hungary; and a presentation, titled "African American Music as a Representation of American Identity" at The Fryderyk Chopin Academy of Music in Warsaw, Poland. This presentation was sponsored by the joint efforts of the U.S. Embassy in Poland and the Music Academy in presenting the Embassy's ongoing program titled "America Presents."

In addition to Dr. Breckenridge's experience as an academician, he is continually involved in music as a professional musician. Performing as a singer and pianist abroad and domestically for many years, he has delighted audiences in Western and Eastern Europe, Japan, Hong Kong, and many cities throughout the United States. Local performances include venues such as The Dorothy Chandler, The Greek Theater, The Los Angeles Forum, The Los Angeles Sports Arena, The Embassy Hotel, The Hollywood Bowl, The Watts Summer Festival (West Coast equivalent of Woodstock on the East Coast), Capitol Records, T.V. Channels 5, 11 and KOCE, Maverick's Flats, Dooto's, and many others. Stan Breckenridge has appeared with and/ or performed for personalities such as Scott Baio, Bobby Blue Bland, Bill Cosby, The Five Blind Boys of Alabama, Rosie Grier, Merv Griffin, Mahalia Jackson, Jerry Lewis, Moms Mabley, Greg Morris, Martha Reeves (of the Vandellas), Sam Riddle, Rowan & Martin, David Ruffin (of the Temptations), Avery Schriber, Nancy Sinatra, O. C. Smith, The Stylistics, John Travolta, John Wayne, The Young Hearts, and many others.

As a recording artist, Stan Breckenridge has released an album every other year since 1999. In addition to his current single release titled "Love Sign" (from the soon to be released album *Humanity*), other recordings include *Reflections* (released October, 2009), *A Soulful Christmas* (2008), *This is My Song* (2007), *Live in Poland* (2005), *Solo* (2003), *Meditations* (2001), and *Expositions* (1999). Most albums and songs are available on ITunes, Rhapsody, Amazon, and through many other music download companies.

Over the years, Dr. Breckenridge has gained a wide knowledge of creative and innovative approaches to learning, particularly for people of varied intellectual, cultural, and economic levels. With a strong background in music performance, the integration of performance is one of his strongest contributions to student learning. As a matter of course, he presents his performances as well as the performances of others, and perhaps more pertinent to an educational institution, the students themselves are encouraged to perform, as an adventurous approach to teaching and learning.

In closing, Dr. Breckenridge is a member of the American Society of Composers, Authors, and Publishers; active member of the Disney Resorts Advisory Board; the United States Fulbright Alumni Association; the Phi Mu Alpha Music Fraternity; and sits on the Board of Directors of Fun with Drums.

ACKNOWLEDGMENTS

With this book now in its second edition, I am even more thankful to the many people who have helped to make it possible. First, I am deeply grateful to my wife, Glennis, for spending countless hours reading and editing, and for many conversations about how this book might be beneficial to everyone. I wish to express my thanks to Valerie Gardner for the many hours spent reading and editing the first edition of this book. A significant portion of the initial manuscript was the result of her insightful comments and recommendations. My graduate mentor, Dr. Nancy Van Deusen at Claremont Graduate University, instilled in me the confidence to write about my passion for music. I owe her continued gratitude. To my thousands of students over the years, it is because of you I began my journey to write about and hopefully contribute to the knowledge of popular music in America. Your inspiration is greatly appreciated. I am appreciative to the editing staff at Kendall Hunt Publishing, Inc. Without their openness to listening and helping to form my many ideas about this book it would have taken longer to complete. Finally, I want to thank all musicians over the years for their creative abilities, dedication, and contributions to one of God's greatest gifts—music.

LIST OF SONG NAVIGATORS

INTRODUCTION

There exists great interest in those music styles that have become a part of the American music scene. Some of these include American-born styles such as punk, folk, rhythm & blues, bluegrass, thrash, disco, jazz, and blues, soul, country, hip-hop, honky-tonk, heavy metal, and styles from abroad now nestled in American culture such as reggae, polka, Latin music, and classical music.

Since the late 19th century, America remains to be a place where different musical styles and traditions are welcomed. Attributable to its diverse population and musical tastes, there exists, more so than in any other country, numerous styles of music in America. Resulting in an American ideology, the music industry in America continues to identify, probe, and market many styles of music that, in effect, reveals its music scheme, or what I refer to as its "idea" of music.

Ideologically, every culture has its identifiable substances of music. As part of its philosophy and social mores, these substances may be based on specific sounds, instruments, purpose/functionality, communicative properties, therapeutic qualities, and so on. America's musical ideology is the result of its many ethnic, cultural, and gender based influences that have contributed to the early formation of the American spirit. As stated in the book *Natives and Strangers: Blacks, Indians, and Immigrants in America*:

> America evolved from a colonial society into a modern industrial-urban nation not only because of its Anglo-Saxon enclaves but also because people of both sexes and differing backgrounds contributed ideas, skills, and especially labor to the building of the nation (p. vii)

THE FORGING OF THE AMERICAN SPIRIT

Without question there continues to be a certain attitude, personality, or aura about many individuals nurtured in the social, political, and cultural context of American society. Furthermore, finding a constitutional agreement of ideals and desires to forward a way of living that could put in place principles that would endure for centuries is something that cannot be overstated. A new order, if you will, forged ahead that set out to distinguish itself from the continent across the Atlantic. This New World brought forth dreams and new, or different, goals; it was smothered with people of many different ethnicities and nationalities all residing on its eastern seashores. And out of this emerged, to our knowledge thus far, a community that built itself on pride, individualism, a work ethic that ensured success for many, though not all, and a peculiar "spirit" that separates it from other countries. Subtle, yet powerful enough to demand worldwide respect this, what I refer to as "American Spirit", now influences all things in America. Though most specific traditions, with respect to cultures and ethnicities, are transplantations from other places, it is the American Spirit that shaped, and continues to shape these traditions that manifest as American.

Music, in my humble opinion, exemplifies this idea as people from Africa, England, France, Germany, Holland, Italy, Hungary, Ireland, Mexico, Norway, Russia, Scotland, Spain, Jewish people immigrating from Germany, Poland, and Russia, and, of course, Native Americans all have their unique music traditions. They have their folk music, worship music traditions, and some, not all, brought their remembrances of celebrated composers who were regularly engaged in music activities for the elite. This could not be truer. Though America is not a pluralistic society, though not at the moment, it at least respects, by and large, the many different cultural folk music traditions. With regard to composers from the aforementioned countries whose main task was to provide music for artistocracy, the music of individuals such as Bach, Haydn, Mozart, Beethoven, Chopin, Verdi, Brahms, Mendelssohn, just to name a few, have without question become the cornerstone for music universities, conservatories, and musicological consortiums nationwide. But what is interesting is that in addition to the many folk music traditions and the urge to retain the performance traditions of classical music, there arose a new music, or at least, non-distinguished music, that is without doubt identifiably American. Whether one is referring to the Negro spiritual, rock, blues, jazz, bluegrass, hillbilly, metal, punk, emo, to name some, they all were in some way influenced by the very nature of the American spirit.

Beginning with British immigration and the inception of American colonies in as early as 1607, America's ideology was being instituted from a particular European culture that viewed itself as superior to others. Moreover, its Protestant religious beliefs helped to establish certain moral and social guidelines that, in their view, distinguished them from others.[1] Embedded in the culture, these views were transplanted to North American soil. It soon became evident that nationality, ethnicity (and racism) and gender would play a major role in sociopolitical and, musical ideology in America.

The confrontation of British ideology with Native American and other European cultures–and eventually with African slaves through agricultural labor and commercial enterprises, contributed to the underpinning of the American spirit. Indeed, for the first two and a half centuries of its existence, the spirit of America was shaped by many sociopolitical structures and conditions. Some of these include the following:

Transatlantic Slave Trade (1619–1863)
Tolerance for religious difference
French and Indian War in 1754
The American Revolution in 1775 and the subsequent Declaration of Independence in 1776
Freedom of speech
Pennsylvania Packet and General Advertiser in 1784 (1st daily newspaper)
Bill of Rights, effective 1791
Philadelphia to Washington, D.C. in 1800 (transfer of the nation's capitol)
War of 1812
Abolitionist Movement
Indian Removal Act of 1830
First telegraph message (Washington to Baltimore in 1844)
United States' war on Mexico in 1846
Civil War in 1861–1865

Despite some viewpoints of the United States as a dispassionate driving machine that destroys everything in its path for capitalistic and political gains, its striving for freedom for all as evidenced by the 13th Amendment, and its current promotion of ethnic, gender, and religious tolerance resonates its commitment to community and justice. It is from this voice that a spirit unlike any other has emerged and radiates an eternal beacon of tolerance, opportunity, and democracy. Reflected in

---

[1] Protestantism was the result of the Reformation of the 16th century. Its goal was to reform certain practices of the Roman Catholic Church.

the social structure of American society, the American spirit continues to appeal to the human soul. Whether natives or from abroad, composers, performers, producers, and music industry professionals are inspired by the American spirit and the nation's truly diverse culture.

I believe this to be central to the foundation of the American Spirit. No other geographical place boasts the diversity of cultural heritage present in America. Albeit principally of European origin with regard to politics and social mores, American culture is far richer in terms of diversity than those cultures that are etymologically bound to one place. The great strength of American culture is that it is inclusive of different beliefs and heritages.

THE AMERICAN SPIRIT GIVES BIRTH TO AMERICAN MUSIC

With music of indigenous Native Americans, Europeans beginning in the 15th century, and Africans in the early 1600s, one can argue that American music is an amalgamation of many cultural influences, ideologies, and musical traditions. The process of acculturation and/or assimilation by and within these cultures combined with philosophies of America's founding fathers has given rise to musical styles and traditions that reflect undeniable attitudes and social mores of the American spirit. Freedom of speech is one resounding attribute of this spirit. Embedded within society, a composer/lyricist is instinctively empowered, not to mention sanctioned by the First Amendment, to express himself or herself with minimal textual restrictions. Such an enormous empowerment should not be taken lightly, as personal expression helps to define and understand who we are as individuals and as a culture. The spirit of American society consciously embodies freedom of speech, unlike some cultures where this freedom is stifled. The musician, whom I often regard as the "historian via musical rhetoric," captures and then regurgitates everyday life situations through musical rhetoric, which, by and large, reflects attitudes and social behaviors of the American spirit.

ORGANIZATION OF THIS BOOK

Generally the subject of music is organized chronologically and is thus placed within historical parameters, thereby creating a framework for the discussion of artistic and stylistic tendencies, as well as specific influential musicians. Consequently, the initial issue for me as I wrote this book dealt with the identification and use of specific temporal parameters or epochs that seem to represent quite distinctive social, political, cultural and economic environments. Having contemplated this since the first edition of this book, I still believe that a viable youth culture as a targeted consumer for marketing popular music has played and continues to play a major role in the scheme of popular music and the business of music. As a result, the 1940s (as the first occurrence of marketing to the youth culture) is used as the principal dividing line for examining popular music in America.

In looking at popular music in America before the 1940s, some profound influential circumstances are evident that relate to the country's social, political, cultural, and economic fabric. This provided additional analytical periods for examining music: the American Colonial Period–Civil War to Post-Civil War and WWI; and WWI to WWII.

After WWII, the popular music scene was, for the first time in American history, significantly affected by the youth culture as well as by advancements in technology. (Prior to this time, adolescent through pre-adult-aged individuals were not considered a viable market with respect to sheet music and record sales in the music industry.) With a booming economy and increased family sizes, the 1940s were a time of youth investments. With the advent of technological advancement, an interest in artificial intelligence, and consequent computer applications in music, the process of composing music today using these technologies, which first flourished in the 1970s, creates yet another turning point in the popular music scene in America. In the previous edition the 1970s became the final parameter. Since then, however, music analyses from the turn of the 21st century and slightly before then show, due to an ample amount of time for music to adjust, the need to frame and discuss music characteristics in an additional period. Thus, the temporal parameter "21st Century" is added in this edition.[2]

Over the years in teaching the subject of music, I have discovered that a general discussion of the "nature" or meaning of music proved to be useful to students of diverse musical understanding, social and cultural backgrounds, gender, and age. Notwithstanding the fact that the description of music is based on perspective, class discussions began with considering two viewpoints: (1) What is music? and (2) What is music to them [students]? In the first inquiry, students began their essay response with, "Music is . . ." while the words "to me". . . were added in the second instance. Although a few students segregated the two considerations by articulating on music's substances (e.g., tones/pitches, rhythm, harmony, etc.), and by describing its functionality (e.g., communication, therapeutic, emotional, etc.), the majority found it difficult to isolate these viewpoints. Having now experienced this exercise, students became more cognizant of the fact that they possess more knowledge about different stylistic approaches that distinguish music styles than they do about the very "nature" of music. Consequently, a section of this book is dedicated to that topic — the nature of music.

The nature or spirit of music influences and reflects certain aspects of society. In other words, because music contains inherent qualities that represent natural/logical truths and principles about life, such as symbols, shape, sound, emotion, and so on, it possesses certain appealing qualities that, by nature, speak to the mind, body, and soul, and as a result is threaded into the social, cultural, political, and economic fabric of society. Lodged in society, music has become an extremely viable commodity that has engendered a capitalistic medium with enormous sociopolitical and economic staying power. Rightly so, the business of music also receives a separate chapter within this book.

---

[2] This book provides pertinent information about the popular music scene in America beginning with the American Colonial Period. However, the last half of the 20th century to present day is the focus.

PART ONE

Woodstock. © Warner Bros. Pictures/Photofest

GENERAL ASPECTS OF POPULAR MUSIC

- CHAPTER ONE: What is Popular Music?
- CHAPTER TWO: The Business of Music
- CHAPTER THREE: Getting Music to the People

OVERVIEW

The daunting task of revealing the idiosyncratic aspects of the many styles of popular music in America might best be approached first with an understanding of music's nature, music as a profession or industry, and its proliferation. In doing so, an acknowledgement of facts, truisms, and colloquialisms will hopefully provide an understanding of what popular music is all about. For instance, an important aspect addressed in Chapter One is the use of the phrase "popular music" in 19th century American society. People often use this phrase interchangeably when referencing music which is neither classical nor folk music, or regardless of the genre, music which is simply popular. Chapter One also offers the reader analytical categories that can be used to buttress his or her own meaning of popular music.

Chapter Two continues the discussion of popular music and music in general by furnishing the reader with information about significant components of the music industry. Under the heading "Business of Music," it conveys the infrastructure of the profession as it relates to the creation, performance, recording, and legal issues of music. Information presented is emboldened by quotes from leading authors in the field of entertainment attorney representation.

Chapter Three looks at the proliferation of music, beginning with performance and touring. It continues with an examination of the importance of sheet music as the first main mechanism for encapsulating music that can be later shared among future generations. Following this, the significance of radio, sound recording, and television are argued for which seemed more beneficial to the proliferation of music. While each of these offer advantages over another and may indeed be ideal when pursuing mass audiences, music festivals, particularly of popular youth-culture music, have become seasonal occasions that can draw tens of thousands of people. The cadre of music festivals cited reveal not only music artists and their performances, but also perhaps a phenomenon, emboldened by the success of the Monterey Pop Festival and Woodstock, 1967 and 1969 respectively, that has brought the initial vehicle–touring–for the proliferation of music full circle.

Information garnered in these three chapters will unsparingly impart deeper knowledge, and thus will be a liberating experience on the General Aspects of Popular Music.

CHAPTER ONE

WHAT IS POPULAR MUSIC?

INTRODUCTION

The goal of this chapter is a survey of the music that was popular in America prior to the period following WWII. A subsequent goal is to qualify colloquial usages of the phrase "popular music." The term"popular music" is neither indigenous to America nor is it solely a 20th or 21st century term. As eloquently stated in the *New Harvard Dictionary of Music*, the phrase "popular music" first appeared, with regard to Western culture, in the 18th century:

> "The 18th and 19th centuries saw the development, chiefly in Europe and America, of a genre distinct from both folk and classical or art music. It differed from the former in being composed and notated and in developing a musical style not distinctive of a certain region or ethnic group. Though many early pieces of popular music shared general features with classical music of the day, they were briefer and simpler, making fewer demands on both performer and listener."[1]

Interpreted from this quote, popular music today is still being used to distinguish that music which is neither classical, with some exceptions, nor folk music. Specifically this could mean theatrical music, and the plethora of stylistic and categorical names such as bluegrass, blues, country, disco, folk, jazz, metal, rhythm & blues/rock & roll, zydeco, and many others. In any event, the usage of "popular music" as a term that references non-classical or folk music is still widely used. Examples include "After the Ball" (1891, written by Charles Harris), "Ol' Man River" (from the musical *Show Boat*, 1927) "Hound Dog" (recorded 1953 by Willie Mae Thornton; and by Elvis Presley in 1955), "Born This Way" (2011, by Lady Gaga). Today, other usages of this term refer to music that is popular regardless of style, and songs that are popular within "popular" music. Examples of the former include *Prelude in C Minor* (1841, by Frederick Chopin). This piece also became popular among audiences in the 1970s due to Barry Manilow's song "Could It be Magic" (1973), which uses an excerpt from Chopin's work incorporated at the beginning and ending of the song. *Symphony No. 5 in C Minor* (1808) by Ludwig Van Beethoven also received some notoriety during the 1970s from the popularity of the disco song "A Fifth of Beethoven" (1976). With regard to the latter; the meaning of popular songs of popular music is the primary basis for this book. In other words, the focus of this book is a discussion of popular songs of blues, country, jazz, rock, hip-hop, and so on. It is noteworthy to mention that, unlike the *New Harvard Dictionary* definition stated above, folk songs from the 1950s as well as other stylistic and categorical songs will be considered as popular music.

---

[1]Randel, *The New Harvard Dictionary of Music*, p. 646.

We begin here with exploring the meanings of music within the context of three general headings: substance, function, and quality. Clearly the meanings of these will bleed into another, but this unintentional circumstance helps to negate any doubt about music's inter connectedness.

SUBSTANCE AS A CONTRIBUTING FACTOR TO A SONG'S POPULARITY

Substance is the essential "stuff" that makes what we call music.

Sound

A term with broad usage, *sound* is regularly understood by many as the audible character of a voice or instrument. Distinguishing substances include pitch and timbre. In that a specific voice or instrument indeed has its own character, it would be feasible to assume a critical argument exists for the appropriateness of an instrument's usage. In other words, is there aesthetic value in hearing the cello, for example, play the same melodic line in the hip-hop song "The Breaks" (1980) that is rapped by Kurtis Blow? Conversely, would it be reasonable to assume there is worth in hearing the main theme to the first movement of *Symphony No. 5 in C Minor* by Ludwig van Beethoven be performed by an orchestra and singer Grace Slick? Perhaps these are unfair comparisons as we have already grown accustomed to hearing these performed with their respective instrumentations. We should nonetheless realize a song's popularity could indeed be based in large part to an instrument's or singers' specific sound. (Also see *timbre,* discussed below.)

Consonant and dissonant harmonies

As a result of harmony, consonance entails the agreement, with respect to sound frequencies, of different pitches through time and space. Most individuals have the proclivity to favor songs with consonant harmonies over those that are dissonant. While this is true, the existence of dissonant harmonies that pervade every aspect of a piece can even generate an appealing effect. For instance, the song "Free Jazz" (1960) by Ornette Coleman possesses an untraditionally performative character that is exemplified by an unidentified structure or form, using seemingly "unorganized" or unorthodox music approaches such as numerous dissonances, non-measurable durations, and nontraditional timbres.

Organization

As an example of substance, the popularity of a song can be based on its organization. Ragtime music, for example, gained popularity in part due to its structure of different movements or sections—a compositional practice in classical music. Often organized in an AABBACCDD format, the performer or listener could eventually learn how to melodically and harmonically distinguish the different sections, thus gaining a fuller understanding of the piece and consequently make it more appealing. Some examples include Scott Joplin's "Maple Leaf Rag" and "The Entertainer." Art rock (a.k.a. progressive rock) in the 1970s is known for its highly organized performances and recordings. In addition to entertainment, its goal was also intended to raise the level of rock music to that music which deserves critical analysis for its display of progressive development akin to America's progressive society. To many in America's civil society, rock music seemed to have a lack of musical or aesthetic acumen. That its existence was still permeating mainstream society was, to many, a formidable outlook of for possible future. As a way to justify rock as a viable form of art, composers and performers in the late 1960s/early 1970s found it useful to apply various admirable features of classical music, such as multi-movement works and the many compositional techniques of a symphonic orchestra, to the core of rock music's typical orchestration: lead singer, guitar, bass, and drums (and maybe a keyboard). Soon works like *Days of Future Passed* (1969) by The Moody Blues, *Space*

Oddity (1969) by David Bowie, and *Dark Side of the Moon* (1973) by Pink Floyd helped catapult rock music to critical acclaim.

Lyrical Content

Does all music have a lyrical content? Certainly not, but we cannot ignore those that do. A song's lyrical content can have a tremendous impact on its popularity. With today's craving for staying in touch as evidenced by the many social networking institutions like Facebook, Twitter, and LinkedIn, it seems many take stock in building relationships. This manner of comforting is illustrated in the song "I Won't Let Go" (2011) by Rascal Flatts. Even a song title can spark interest among consumers. Take, for instance, Michael Jackson's song "Bad" (1987). Many listeners' interpretation of the word *bad*, perhaps unwittingly, fell somewhere between "a bad or naughty person" and the more common euphemistic meaning of *bad* as "good." Since it was spoken in the first person during the song's chorus, many presumed Jackson to be a conceited individual whose arrogance had gone too far. In actuality, Jackson was singing from the viewpoint of a gang member who thinks he is bad. Some people accused Jackson of ". . .the audacity to say he's bad [good]." This presumption, and other anecdotes about him (such as his using skin whitener and sleeping in a pure-air, coffin-like bed) made Jackson a controversial figure. Controversy, particularly negative or spectacular, is extremely effective in contributing to a song's popularity and is utilized as an incidental marketing strategy.

Timbre

The quality of sound can be identified using words that fall under the term *timbre*. Descriptive words include full-throated, whisper, guttural, nasal, spoken-like, and so on. It can be used to describe the quality of a voice or instrument. Often, consumers use this term, perhaps unwittingly, as a means of selecting their favorite artist. For example, singers Harry Connick, Jr. and Michael Bublé receive favorable remarks due in part to their similar *timbre* as the popular singer and actor Frank Sinatra (1915–1998). Other singers, like Axl Rose (metal), Norah Jones (easy listening), Bob Dylan (folk), Ella Fitzgerald (jazz), Jimmie Rogers (hillbilly), Billie Holiday (blues), Ricky Martin (Latin), Madonna (mainstream), Willie Nelson (country), Lady Gaga (pop), and James Brown (soul), can all be distinguished from others by their vocal *timbre*. In the song "Papa Don't Preach" (1986), Madonna's vocal *timbre*, plus the song's danceable rhythm and its orchestrated and "organized" arrangement, helped to induct it into the cast of mainstream popular music. Because timbre deals with the ability to manipulate one's instrument (or voice), those instruments or non-vocal utterances that can affect its sound include *aerophones* (air) and *chordophones* (string). Aerophones include brass and woodwind instruments, while violin, viola, cello, guitar, bass, mandolin, and banjo are all categorized as chordophones. Generally, it is what one does with his or her instrument that produces a unique or different sound. Often this involves playing an instrument in an untraditional manner such as positioning one's mouth on a mouthpiece (trumpet, saxophone, and trombone) differently from what a player generally does; or unconventionally playing a given pitch or chord on a string instrument. Specific instrumentalists who have distinguishing characteristics with *timbre* include Miles Davis vs. Stan Kenton (trumpet players), B.B. King vs. Albert King (guitarists), Lester Horton vs. Ben Webster (tenor saxophonists). Still, an instrumentalist's *timbre* can differ based on the construction of the instrument, such as Dizzy Gillespie's trumpet.

Rhythm

While syncopated rhythms are an indisputable feature of bluegrass, they are also an undeniable aspect of gospel music. Occurring as a combination of weak and strong (accents) beats and/or a combination of uneven beats (a.k.a. syncopation) is in essence, a complex rhythm. In gospel music, the tempo may be slow, but the rhythmic figures are often extremely syncopated. Such complexity is the result of the propensity to "fill up" the space of time. Without doubt, rhythm is the main feature in hip-hop music. It is regularly considered to be the determining factor for a song's success. Albeit words and phrases are a primary component, the rhythmic phraseology governs the "rap."

Tempo

The tempo of a song can also influence its level of popularity. The fast banjo-picking style of Earl Scruggs is one of the most gripping and intriguing aspects of bluegrass music. Often performed *allegro*, bluegrass can encourage the body to move in ways unknown to its executor. Like bluegrass, other styles with the intention to encourage dancing, the tempo generally needs to be at least *allegretto* (moderately fast) such as what is heard in the songs "Till the World Ends" by Britney Spears, "Party Rock Anthem" by LMFAO featuring Lauren Bennett & GoonRock, "Run the World (Girls)" by Beyonce, "On the Floor" by Jennifer Lopez featuring Pitbull, and "Fade" by Christine W (all in mid-2011).

FUNCTIONALITY AS A CONTRIBUTING FACTOR TO A SONG'S POPULARITY

The functionality of music can be understood through its utilitarian qualities.

Communication

Functionality as a contributing factor to a song's popularity is evident in the song "Mean" (2011) by Taylor Swift. Here she speaks about situations where the underclassman is often picked on, but in the end will prevail and be a successful individual. These words are functional in that they provide encouragement for the many young individuals who are bullied. Music can be used as an effective way to convey messages that otherwise may be overlooked. This is illustrated in the song "Ohio" (1970) by Crosby, Stills, Nash, and Young, which references the shooting of four students during a Vietnam anti-war demonstration at Kent State University. Another example of song as a functional device with respect to communication is well documented among the singing of songs by African slaves. Known as Negro spirituals, songs within this repertoire are frequently used as a didactic way to teach about the functionality of these songs among the slave community. Also called telegraph songs, there was a hidden message for fellow slaves to, for example, escape their plantation such as in the song "Steal Away", or to instruct where to travel as heard in the song "Follow the Drinking Gourd."

Dance

A song's dance appeal also functions as a contributing factor to its popularity. In the second decade of the 21st century dance songs encompass a wide spectrum of lyrical meanings. Some of these include a religious connotation as heard in "Judas" by Lady Gaga; or songs that encourage people to keep on dancing like "Till the World Ends" (2011) by Britney Spears and "Dancing Tonight" (2011) by Kat DeLuna featuring Fo Onassis; and Chris Brown's declaration that of always seeing "Beautiful People" (2011) In the "The Hustle" (1975) by Van McCoy and the Soul City Orchestra, the even subdivisions within a quadruple meter combined with a particular orchestral arrangement (which was typical of the disco movement), provided inviting dance rhythms for even the novice dancer.

Entertainment

- *Comedic Parody*—"Mother-in-Law" (1961) by Ernie K-Doe functions as both a communicative device in speaking about a common topic among people (mothers-in-law) and entertainment as a comedic parody.

- ***Visual Presentation***—The popularity or success of a song can also be based on its function and/ or purpose within the larger scheme of visual presentations such as theatre, opera, dance, or an art show, and other social occasions such as a social dance, holiday gathering, poetic recitation, or an athletic event. In theatre productions, in addition to its eventful or momentary emotion, music plays a vital role as a continual contributor to the unification of disjunctive scenes, characters, staging, and plots. At the same time, theatrical productions such as *Shuffle Along* (1921), *Show Boat* (1927), *Porgy & Bess* (1935), *Sweet Charity* (1966), *Godspell* (1971), and *Phantom of the Opera* (1986) facilitate a song's popularity. For example, the song "I'm Just Wild About Harry" gained popularity through the musical *Shuffle Along*. The 1926 novel *Porgy* by Du Bose Heyward was later adapted into the musical *Porgy and Bess*, which premiered in Boston in 1935. One of the musical's songs, "Summertime", became a standard in theatre, jazz, and vocal repertoires. The novel *Sweet Charity* was the inspiration for a musical comedy about a woman employee at the Fan-Dango Ballroom in New York, who because of her past, can't marry a particular Italian film star; This musical popularized the song "Big Spender." The musical *Godspell*, which presented Jesus Christ's Last Seven Days on earth musically *vis-à-vis* rock songs, greatly contributed to the popularity of the song "Day by Day." Richard Stilgoe and Andrew Lloyd Weber's book and subsequent musical play *Phantom of the Opera* (1987) boast songs that remain popular today, such as "All I Ask of You" and "Music of the Night." Operatic works such as *Aida* in 1871 by Giuseppe Verdi, *Die Fledermaus* (*The Bat*) in 1874 by Johann Strauss, and *Le Nozze de Figaro* (*The Marriage of Figaro*) in 1786 by Wolfgang Amadeus Mozart all gave rise to several songs that, after their premieres, became popular throughout Europe as well as among audiences in America. In ballet, the song "Dance of the Sugar Plum Fairies" became popular via Tchaikovsky's ballet *The Nutcracker Suite*.

Marketability

Without doubt a song's marketability plays a major role in the success of a product, and consequently the song's success. In a New York Times article about Lady Gaga in 2011, regarding the release of *Born This Way* the author writes, "Once an artist's biggest source of income, recorded music now plays second fiddle to touring, endorsements, merchandise sales and an array of other revenue streams . . . Lady Gaga, who has lined up more branding and promotional deals in the last six months than most artists will in a lifetime."[2] It should be noted that Gaga's marketing team allowed a one-day sale of $.99 cents for a MP3 digital download, through Amazon, of the entire album. In addition to Lady Gaga's "image" as a marketable commodity, messages in her songs of self-acceptance and having an attitude of compassion for others is evident in the songs "Hair" and "Born This Way" (both in 2011).

Popular music's marketability as an important component of gaming is due to its ability to add audible drama to a game's visual action. As a result, selecting well-known songs for the gaming industry's player age range was found to be a marketable expense. For instance, the song "Helter Skelter" (1968) from The Beatles album of the same name (frequently referred to as The White Album), is used to advertise the next title in the *Red Fraction* series.

"On March 10, 2011 President Obama and first lady Michelle Obama host students, parents, and teachers, and others at the White House Conference on Bullying Prevention."[3] With such an important and public announcement on a topic that permeates many parts of America's civil society, and the world for that matter, institutions and individuals who embrace this campaign do so by publically denouncing

---

[2] Ben Sisario, (June 1, 2011), In Lady Gaga's Album, Evidence of a New Order, *New York Times*.

[3] David Jackson, March 10, 2011, Obama's day: Campaign against bullying, *USA Today*.

this unacceptable behavior using their specific medium. Of particular note here is the social network giant Facebook. In an article in *The Wall Street Journal* writer Michael Hickins states,

> "Facebook is throwing its social networking clout behind the Obama Administration's anti-bullying campaign. The social networking company participated in a series of discussions about both online and offline bullying hosted by the White House and webcast throughout the day, and announced several expanded safety features on its website."[4]

Music Television or MTV is another giant that certainly has relations with the music industry, it joined forces with the campaign by making a movie ". . . based on a true story of cyberbullying victim Abraham Biggs . . . a 19-year-old Florida college student who suffered from bipolar disorder."[5] The movie deals with ". . . the lives of four teens whose paths cross unexpectedly on one eventful night."[6] Other institutions who joined the anti-bullying movement include *Nickelodeon* (viewers from ages 2–14), and the popular T.V. program *Glee*. Noteworthy artists who embrace the campaign include Britney Spears, Ke$ha, and Ann Hathaway. The song "Mean" (2011) by Taylor Swift helped to disseminate, though unintentionally tied to the campaign, the anti-bullying campaign to an extremely wide and large audience as, during the month following the campaign announcement, "Mean" was listed on country music's Top 10 chart.

QUALITY AS A CONTRIBUTING FACTOR TO A SONG'S POPULARITY

Quality is that inherent substance that outwardly illuminates and beautifies a distinguishing character.

Style

The quality or character of a song, such as its recognized style, also lends a helping hand to its success. For example, songs composed and arranged in the manner of rhythm & blues of the 1940s were often favored over other styles of the day, such as big band jazz.[7] Consequently, these songs became the popular hits of the day. The antithesis of this would be, for example, the unpopularity among the industry's general buying consumer of the style known as punk. Due to lyrical messages that often focused on anti-government, disgust with society, and so on, punk during the late 1970s was not recognized as a popular style of music.

Character

Another quality of popular music has to do with a song's specific artist such as Bob Dylan, Natalie Cole, Britney Spears, or Michael Jackson. Due to Dylan's uncanny ability to convey messages of personal sentiment on behalf of farmers, women's rights, civil rights, and other social issues, he, due to his character, continues to be recognized as a beacon for helping to raise people's level of social consciousness. Even though many of his fans became angry as a result of his transition from folk to folk rock, he nonetheless inspired many folk rock artists such as the Byrds and The Turtles. Many would agree that Natalie Cole's recording of "Unforgettable" probably received initial attention as the result of her deceased father Nat King Cole's voice on the recording as well. Even so, both voices add to the song's unmistakable character. Britney Spears was one of the most popular musical artists of 2002. Even though her later songs may be somewhat musically inferior to her earlier releases, Ms. Spears' character greatly contributed to the continuation of high record sales. Also due to his controversial

---

[4] Michael Hickins, March 10, 2011, Facebook Backs Obama Anti-Bullying Campaign, *The Wall Street Journal*.
[5] Sterling Wong, March 10, 2011, MTV Joins Obama's Anti-Bullying Campaign With New Movie, MTV.com/
[6] *Ibid.*
[7] 1946 denotes the end of the big band jazz era.

personal life, Michael Jackson's character on and off-stage has garnered more attention that most artists to date. The musical character of his recordings, beginning with the album *Off the Wall* (1977) and through *Thriller* (1983), motivated other artists during the 1980s and 90s to explore new ways of developing popular music.

A song's character can also be attributed to the maturity (age) of the performer. In the 1950s, marketed as "Teen Pop Idols" artists include Elvis Presley, Pat Boone, Connie Francis, and Frankie Avalon, to name some. The notion of Teen Pop Idols has continued to present day.

Justin Bieber. © DENNIS M. SABANGAN/epa/corbis

Here is a list of some of the most popular artists and their debut singles who, although quite dissimilar stylistically, are/were popular during the second decade of the 21st century.

Jennifer Love Hewitt (age 15) - "Let's Go Bang" (1995)
NSYNC (ages 14–19) - *NSYNC* (1998)
Aaron Carter (age 12) - *Aaron Carter* (1998)
Christina Aguilera (age 19) - *Christina Aguilera* (1999)
Britney Spears (age 18) - *Baby One More Time* (1999)

Michelle Branch ` (age 14) - "The Spirit Room" (2001)
Avril Lavigne (age 17) - "Let Go" (2002)
Hillary Duff (age 16) - *Metamorphosis* (2003)
Miley Cyrus (age 15) - *Meet Miley Cyrus* (2007)
Justin Bieber (age 15) - *My World* (EP) (2009)

Still another category of performers who can impact a song's popularity is family groups.[8] Some popular performers include: Aly and A.J., The Allman Brothers, The Beach Boys, The Carter Family, The Five Stairsteps, The Jackson Five, The Jonas Brothers, Menudo, and The Osmonds.

Radio-Friendly Appeal

Quality as a contributing factor to a song's popularity can also be understood by examining its radio-friendly appeal. It must be noted that a less radio-friendly appeal is not limited to what some would call bad music, because of a song's lyrical content, and/or the ethnicity of the artist. For instance, some people believed hillbilly music, frequently heard on the WSM radio beginning in the 1920s, was not a desirable sound as it used folk-type instruments such as the banjo and mandolin. In addition, the notion of playing the violin (aka fiddle) in a different manner was not conducive, among some people, in contributing to the advancement of American music. Even though artists such as Bill Monroe, Fiddlin' Joe Carson, The Carter Family, Uncle Dave Macon, and Jimmie Rodgers were very popular among southern whites, and even some blacks, they were not the taste for others in the northern and western part of the U.S. At the same time, blues music was not considered radio friendly because the lyrics of artists like Son House, Blind Lemon Jefferson, Bessie Smith, and Gertrude "Ma" Rainey, to name some, generally talked about and thus appealed to African Americans. Indeed, because people were by law segregated prior to the Civil Rights Act of 1964, radio was consequently also segregated. Stations whose intent was to market its advertisers' products mainly to white audiences played music by white artists, while black and some white advertisers' products were relegated to black audiences, who subsequently preferred black artists. Music by rhythm & blues African American artists such as Louis Jordan, Clyde McPhatter, Willie Mae Thornton, Dinah Washington, and many others were generally played more on stations with an intended black audience. What was favored, however, were the recordings of singers who were accompanied by big bands that were becoming popular and provided the bulk of radio-friendly sounds. This included artists like Frank Sinatra, Bing Crosby, Kate Smith, and Morton Downey. William S. Paley, the operator of CBS records, realized that having artists like these would help to increase his listening audience and ultimately lead to his ability to acquire more advertisers, thus generating more revenue and prestige for CBS Records. As a result of this success, the trend was set among radio programmers, directors, and board members to seriously consider an artist's radio friendly appeal.

Beginning in the 1960s, and certainly by the 1970s, radio-friendly appeal was less about an artist's ethnicity, but rather more about mainstream society's acceptance of a song's lyrical content. After the turn of the recent millennium artists such as Shania Twain, Jennifer Lopez, Red Hot Chili Peppers, and Justin Timberlake received much airplay, while others such as Moby, Cinder, and The Foo Fighters were heard less frequently as a result of their less friendly appeal or mainstream marketability. Presently, radio-friendly appeal is all over the spectrum with regard to lyrical content, style, and ethnicity, as evidenced by artists like Lady Gaga, Rihanna, Justin Bieber, Michael Buble, Black Eyed Peas, and many others. Because of the seemingly infinite number of Internet radio stations, and social networks like Facebook and MySpace, there presently exists a very fine line between whether or not an artist will receive airplay.

---

[8] I consider family groups those where at least half the group is related.

Crossover Appeal

Popular music today is also determined by a song's crossover appeal with respect to chart categories. That is to say a song's ability, whether musically or market-driven, to appear on different charts representing distinct markets (e.g., stylistic categories, demographics, etc.), thus gaining a wider audience. Today a song's crossover appeal is almost also guaranteed to reach the platinum status, or at least gold.[9] We can also assume that most, if not all, Top 10 artists on *Billboard's* Hot 100 chart will reach the gold, and probably the platinum mark. Examples are provided below listing artists and their different chart ratings (See Figure 1).

Marketability

Often times, the popularity of a song is due, in part, to the performer's being of a different culture than what is usually associated with a given style. For example, African Americans are generally not popular country music artists. Even so, Charlie Pride became the first African American performer to have numerous country music hits. The Number One song on *Billboard's* Country Songs chart during the week of April 25, 2011, was "This" by Darius Rucker, an African American. In both cases, it is this author's opinion that their popularity is partly due to their unexpected ethnicity where country music is concerned. Generally, hip-hop music is associated with African American artists; however, the artist known as Eminem, a white American, has become a staple among hip-hop artists. The group known as Living Colour, which includes some African American members, is regarded as a metal band—a style not popular among the African American community. The white English artist Adele topped the charts with the song "Someone Like You" (from the album *Adele 21*) using characteristics similar to what one would find among African American singers, and the song "Rolling in the Deep" (same album) uses characteristics of country music. It is interesting to note that Adele was influenced by country

Artist	Song	Charts
Adele	"Rolling in the Deep"	Hot 100, R&B/Hip-Hop, Rock Songs, Pop Songs, Dance/Club Play, Radio Songs
Pitbull Featuring Ne-Yo, Afro Jack & Nayer	"Give Me Everything"	Hot 100, Pop Songs, Latin Songs, Dance/Club Play, Radio Songs, Digital Songs,
Katy Perry Featuring Kanye West	"E.T."	Hot 100, R&B/Hip-Hop, Pop Songs, Digital Songs, Ringtones
Bruno Mars	"The Lazy Song"	Hot 100, Pop Songs, Digital Songs, Ringtones, Latin Pop Songs
Lady Gaga	"The Edge of Glory"	Hot 100, Pop Songs, Radio Songs, Digital Songs, Ringtones, Canadian Hot 100

Figure 1.1 Songs, and their representative artist, that crossed over to other *Billboard* charts during the week of June 18, 2011.

---

[9] In general, "gold" means the sale of 500,000 singles or albums; while 1,000,000 is for platinum.

music during her visit to the American south. When many consumers heard the re-recording of Percy Sledge's "When A Man Loves A Woman" recorded by Michael Bolton, they were surprised to find he was a white American. But before Adele there was another white English artist who sounded even more African American, and thus became popular due in part to this reason. Known as Joss Stone, some of her popular songs include "Tell Me What We're Gonna Do Now," "Tell Me 'Bout It," and "Cry Baby Cry" with Santana and Sean Paul.

CHAPTER TWO

THE BUSINESS OF MUSIC

INTRODUCTION

Music has developed into a multi-billion dollar industry. To be successful in the music industry, one must have organization and structure, management and legal representation, and an excellent sense of business-related matters. The business of music consists of many components: contracts, publishing, copyright, royalties, licensing, marketing and artist management, sound recordings, record labels, distribution, producers, trade journals, music marketing system, and media types. It is also an industry that is focused on free enterprise. The intention of this chapter is to provide a general overview to demonstrate the significance of the "business of music" within the music industry. By no means does this information furnish a complete discussion of all facets of the music business. For a more complete understanding of the workings and business of the music industry, one can consult the following sources:

> *All You Need to Know About the Music Business*, Seventh edition (2010) by Donald Passman
> *The Musician's Business & Legal Guide*, Fourth edition, (2008) by Mark Halloran
> *This Business of Music: The Definitive Guide to the Music Industry*, Tenth edition, (2007) by William Krasclovsky and Sidney Shemel
> *The Guerilla Guide to the Music Business*, Second Edition (2006) by Sarah Davis and Dave Laing
> *The Music Business (Explained in English)* (2006) by David Naggar, Esq.
> *A Music Business Primer* (2003) by Diane Rapaport
> *The Music Business: Career Opportunities and Self-Defense*, (2003) by Dick Weissman
> *Navigating the Music Industry: Current issues and Business Models* (2003) edited by Dick Weissman and Frank Jermance

THE RECORDING INDUSTRY: A HISTORY

The invention of the phonograph (a cylinder device) by Thomas Edison (1847–1931) in 1877 marked the beginning of sound recordings. The process involved speaking or sounding into a diaphragm, which triggered a stylus (needle) that then placed marks on the tinfoil that engulfed the cylinder. When recorded, the sound was played back on yet a different diaphragm and stylus. The problem with Edison's system was that making copies of these recordings was quite an arduous task. Ten years later, German-born Emile Berliner (1851–1929) invented the gramophone, which became the favored recording device abroad and in America. Its recording process involved a stylus that actually cut spiral grooves onto a flat wax record.[1] Consequently, this process was economically feasible for making copies. Consumers soon began to take advantage of the notion of hearing an artist perform a song the same way each time, and doing so in the comfort of their homes. A couple of early well-known artists and their songs include Billy Murray and his hit songs "Meet Me in St. Louis" in 1904 and "Take Me Out to the Ball Game" in 1908; Sophie Tucker, who recorded what became her most memorable song, "Some of These Days" in 1910/11; and Ada Jones, who recorded "Come, Josephine, in My Flying Machine" in 1911.

Unfortunately, like radio broadcasting, the momentum in further advances of sound recording slowed as the result of WWI. Even though America didn't enter the war until 1917 (near its end), the conflict nonetheless caused a diminishing of record manufacturing and buying. Fortunately, by the end of the war productivity in America was again flourishing, as there was great interest in recordings of jazz, blues, and hillbilly (which became country music). The first jazz recordings were made by the Original Dixieland Jazz Band in 1917 and the Creole Jazz Band in 1918. The first blues and hillbilly recordings were made during the early 1920s. At this time, vinyl record buying was at an all-time high with slightly over 100 million units sold (reported in 1921).[2]

Here are some pertinent facts regarding the recording industry.

1. Columbia, Edison, and Victor were the earliest major recording labels both pre- and post-WWI.
2. Vinyl Record: The speed began at 78 RPM, but by the 1930s, 33 RPM became the standard.
3. Long playing (LP) recordings began in 1948; Columbia became the first successful label to use the LP.
4. 45 record: The end of WWII saw the rise of the 45-RPM record that featured two songs, one on each side of the record. 78-RPM records became obsolete.
5. Stereo records were first introduced in 1958; RCA was one of the first to succeed in this venture.
6. The four-track tape system appeared in 1963; the eight-track in 1965.
7. Quadraphonic sound appeared in the early 1970s.
8. Sony and Phillips were successful in introducing digital (versus analog) recording and the CD (compact disc) in 1982.
9. In 1983, consumers purchased more cassette tapes than LPs.
10. Today, CDs make up 95% of record sales, followed by 4.5% in cassettes, and .5% for DVD sales.
11. In 1987, DAT (digital audio tape) appeared.

RECORD LABELS—PRE WWII

The earliest record labels were recording sound on cylinders (circa 1890s). The Columbia Phonograph Company was one of the first major labels, as it recorded favored styles and artists of the day. Some of these are ". . . recordings by the U.S. Marine Band, which included Sousa marches, Strauss waltzes, and such popular Irish favorites as 'Little Annie Rooney' and 'Down Went McGinty.'[3] Edison and Victor Talking Machine Company were other noted companies during this time.

By the early 20th century, flat discs were emerging as the standard for sound recordings among the three major labels: Edison, Victor, and Columbia. In addition to Bill Murray and Ada Jones, other early artists and their songs included barbershop vocal groups such as the Haydn Quartet and the

---

[1] Alexander Graham Bell (1847–1922) invented a machine called a *graphophone* that made wax recordings.
[2] Soon after, however, the record industry suffered a dramatic decline in sales as commercial radio broadcasting began delivering live music performances of favored artists to consumers in the comfort of their own home.
[3] Reebee Garofalo. *Rockin' Out: Popular Music in the USA*. Second Edition. New Jersey: Prentice Hall, 2002.

Peerless ("Sweet Adeline," 1904). After WWI, there surfaced numerous recording companies such as Okeh, EMI (Electrical and Musical Industries), RCA (Radio Corporation of America, same as Victor), Vocalion, Melontone, Oriole, and Brunswick.

The stock market crash in 1929 and the subsequent Great Depression had a comparably devastating effect on the record industry, and sales declined dramatically.[4] President Roosevelt's order to close all U.S banks for 100 days further compounded businesses' woes. Two major labels continued producing recordings (albeit minimally in comparison to previous years) as well as acquiring records from other labels, particularly big band jazz/swing and blues. RCA recorded some of the more prominent artists such as Tommy Dorsey, Benny Goodman, Glenn Miller, Artie Shaw, and Fats Waller. Columbia's artists included Bessie Smith, Bing Crosby, The Carter Family, Duke Ellington, Fletcher Henderson, Robert Johnson, Ted Lewis, and Paul Whiteman.[5]

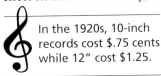

In the 1920s, 10-inch records cost $.75 cents while 12" cost $1.25.

To help unemployed Americans both with and without occupational trades, President Roosevelt established the Works Progress Administration (WPA) in 1935. Although record manufacturing and consumer spending on records was still declining, the WPA provided various musical groups with opportunities for performance. Such an endeavor helped fuel musical creativity, which continually fulfilled public tastes as well as functioned as an effective social diversion during those economically catastrophic years. Consumer confidence appeared to be rising by the discontinuation of the WPA in 1939, and as Germany invaded Poland that same year, America entered a new era: WWII. The United States was drawn into the war when Pearl Harbor was attacked by Japan in 1941. Along with other factors, this event brought about some major changes in the music industry.

RECORD LABELS—WWII THROUGH THE 1960s

A decline in big band performances was one of the major changes in the music industry attributed to the war. As many men and women were engaged in the war effort, there was a gradual decline in patrons at those venues that regularly hosted big bands.

Although not directly attributed to the war but nonetheless occurring in tandem with the decline of big band performances (a favored medium for the previous 20 years), the National Academy of Broadcasters' (NAB) went on strike against the American Society of Composers, Authors, and Publishers (ASCAP) in 1939. This precipitated a void of live broadcast music, and gave rise to vocalists becoming "pop" stars. Many vocalists–who generally did not have union and association ties as did instrumentalists– were already singing with big bands, and at this juncture were now able to satisfy consumer tastes of big-band-type music while at the same time filling the void of live broadcast music performances. Some of the most notable singers of RCA/Victor included Bing Crosby, Frank Sinatra, Dinah Shore, and Perry Como.[6]

The growing taste among certain consumers for rhythm & blues and country music was another change in the recording industry with respect to record labels that was also attributed to WWII and the NAB strike against ASCAP. During and after WWII, there was a massive migration of blacks and southern whites to northern urban centers (like Chicago), in response to the increased demand

---

[4] Records were selling for just under a dollar during the Depression.

[5] The Great Depression caused the merging of several notable companies such as Banner, Oriole and Perfect, and Romeo to the American Record Corporation (ARC) in 1929. Consolidated Film Industries, who also had stock in ARC, acquired BRUNSWICK; Melotone and Vocalion established the Brunswick Record Corporation in 1930. In 1931, in the UK, Columbia and HMV merged and formed EMI (Electrical Musical Industries). It is important to note that many recordings may have occurred under these and a few other label names; however, during this time, RCA and Columbia were the root companies.

[6] Bing Crosby recorded the most successful single of all time "White Christmas," for Decca records in 1942.

for workers. This influx of people brought blues and country music with it, resulting in both greater exposure and increased popularity of these styles with existing urban dwellers. Driven by the need and desire to fill the void of live broadcast music to supply these enormous demands, new labels and a call for new or unrecorded seasoned artists ensued. Moreover, with the introduction of 45RPM records over the economically inferior 78RPM, labels reclaimed their status as a viable component of the music industry. Because the major labels at this time (RCA and Columbia) were reluctant to invest in these new musical styles, a surge of independent companies (a.k.a. indie), some of which became major forces in the industry, materialized as the recording labels that distributed rhythm & blues and country music to America and abroad. Here is a list of some of the more prominent indie companies, including a few of their artists that became well known during the 1950s and 60s.

1. **Atlantic** (formed in New York, 1947)–Chuck Willis, Clyde McPhatter, The Drifters, Joe Turner, LaVern Baker, Little Esther, Ray Charles, Ruth Brown, Stick McGhee, The Chords, and The Clovers
2. **Chess** (formed in Chicago, 1947; Checker subsidiary label formed in 1953)–Bo Diddley, Chuck Berry, Elmore James, Etta James, Howlin' Wolf, Muddy Waters, Rosco Gordon, and The Moonglows
3. **Capitol** (formed in Hollywood, 1942)–Art Tatum, Beach Boys, Buck Owens, Duke Ellington, Ella Mae Morse, Frank Sinatra, Freddie Slack, Kingston Trio, Gene Vincent, Nat King Cole, Peggy Lee, Stan Kenton
4. **Decca** (formed as UK label in 1929; USA Decca formed in 1934)–Bill Haley, Ernest Tubb, Louis Jordan, The Four Aces, and The Weavers
5. **Imperial** (formed in Los Angeles, 1947)–Fats Domino, Ricky Nelson, Slim Whitman, Smiley Lewis, and the Teddy Bears
6. **King** (formed in Cincinnati, 1945; subsidiary labels include DeLuxe, Federal, and Queen, featuring hillbilly and R&B music)–James Brown, Homer and Jethro, Bradley Kincaid, Bull Moose Jackson, Delmore Brothers, Hawkshaw Hawkins, Ivory Joe Hunter, Lonnie Johnson, The Five Royales, and Wynonie Harris.
7. **Mercury** (formed in Chicago, 1945)–The Penguins and The Platters
8. **Specialty** (formed initially under the name Juke Box Records, Los Angeles, 1946)–Little Richard, Sam Cooke, Lloyd Price, The Swan Silvertones, and The Soul Stirrers
9. **Sun** (formed in Memphis, 1952)–In 1950, under the name Memphis Recording Service, Sam Phillips (owner/operator) recorded artists such as Bobby Blue Bland, B.B. King, Howlin' Wolf, and Rosco Gordon. Establishing his own label–SUN Records–Sam Phillips's artists included Rufus Thomas, the Prisonaires, Carl Perkins, Elvis Presley, Jerry Lee Lewis, and Roy Orbison
10. **Vee-Jay Records** (formed in Gary, Indiana, 1953)–Jerry Butler, The Four Seasons, John Lee Hooker, Little Richard, Memphis Slim, and Jimmy Reed

Instead of complying with popular music tastes among southern whites and blacks, RCA and Columbia (a.k.a. CBS-Columbia Broadcast System) opted to continue recording its established artists, who, by and large, appealed to the over-30 and conservative listener. From the 1930s through the 1950s, Columbia acquired, at varied times, recording artists such as Louis Armstrong, Dave Brubeck, Duke Ellington, Johnny Mathis, Miles Davis, Orrin Tucker, Percy Faith, Ray Price, Rosemary Clooney, and Thelonious Monk.[7] Despite the fact that these artists were producing large revenues for Columbia's regime, they could not compete with

---

[7] Some of these labels' popular film soundtracks have included *Kiss Me Kate* and *South Pacific*, both in 1949, and the classic *My Fair Lady* in 1956.

the magnitude of new and younger listeners, which frankly meant even greater revenues. Perhaps the most significant example is RCA's purchase of Elvis Presley's contract from Sun records in 1955. No longer could the major labels ignore the viability of country, rhythm & blues, and rock & roll music.

With issues of civil rights, advancements in technology, the emergence of new musical styles, and a greater understanding of music's global attraction, new recording companies as well as numerous mergers have occurred since post-WWII. Many of these labels continue to thrive on the business of selling records and have developed into major corporations, becoming integrally woven into America's capitalistic system. As we examine some of the more recent successful labels and artists, it is important to be aware of the fact that labels and artists will change, but the business of music, particularly the selling of recorded sound, will continue.

RECORD LABELS—PRESENT DAY

Currently, when considering record labels, there exist the "big four": Sony, Universal Music Group, EMI, and Warner Music Group. Within these four are subsidiary labels; some of these and their respective artists include the following:

1. **Atlantic**–Matchbox Twenty, Phil Collins, Sean Paul, Taproot, and The Donnas
2. **Arista**–Alan Jackson, Avril Lavigne, Kenny G, Pacifier, Pink, Santana, Whitney Houston
3. **Capitol**–Coldplay, Keith Urban
4. **Columbia**–Barry Manilow, Chris Botti, Dixie Chicks, Five for Fighting, James Taylor, John Mayer, Miles Davis, Nas, System of A Down, Tony Bennett
5. **Def Jam**–Ja Rule, Jay —Z, LL Cool J, Stone Sour
6. **Elektra**–Missy "Misdemeanor" Elliott, Socialburn
7. **Epic**–B2K & P. Diddy, Celine Dion, Chevelle, Jennifer Lopez, Korn, Mudvayne, Pearl Jam, Shakira, Tori Amos
8. **Interscope**–Audioslave, Counting Crows, Enrique Iglesias, Eminem, Eve, Herb Alpert, Nirvana, No Doubt, Puddle of Mud, Queens of The StoneAge, Sheryl Crow, Vanessa Carlton, 50 Cent, 2Pac
9. **Island/Def Jam**–Bon Jovi, CKY, Def Leoppard, Mariah Carey, Saliva, Sum 41
10. **Jive**–Justin Timberlake, R-Kelly
11. **Mercury**–Shania Twain
12. **MCA**–Field Mob, George Strait
13. **RCA**–Christina Aguilera, Dave Matthews Band, Foo Fighters, Fourplay, Kelly Clarkson
14. **Sony**–India, Jon Secada, Ricardo Arjona, Victor Manuelle
15. **Verve**–Charlie Haden, Diana Krall, Herbie Hancock, Joe Sample, Michael Brecker, Natalie Cole
16. **Virgin**–Norah Jones
17. **Warner Bros.**–Boney James, Faith Hill, Kirk Whalum, Luis Miguel, Madonna, Mana, Michelle Branch, Norman Brown, Olga Tanon, Red Hot Chili Peppers

RECORD LABELS—DIVISIONS

There are ten general divisions in the infrastructure of a typical record label, according to David Naggar, Esq. in his book *Music Business (Explained in English)*:[8]

1. **Artists and Repertoire**–Finds marketable songs for its artist(s)
2. **Sales**–Sells a product to various wholesale (distribution) and retail businesses

---

[8] Naggar, David, esq. *The Music Business: Explained in English*. Revised. San Francisco, CA: DaJe Publishing, 2006.

3. **Promotion**–Maintains personal contact with various media people such as radio music directors, disc jockeys, and various executives
4. **Marketing**–Creates specific advertisements tailored to an artist
5. **Production**–Records the work of an artist
6. **Finance**–Handles the financing of given artists' projects
7. **Product Management**–Manages all the contributing divisions of an artists' project
8. **International**–Deals with the global concerns of an artist/record
9. **Business and Legal Affairs**–copyrights, royalties, contracts, and manages other related issues
10. **Artist Development**–Prepares the musicality and presentation of an artist for recording and live performances

RECORD LABELS—DISTRIBUTION

The sale of recordings is one of the record label's primary concerns. Consequently, methods for the distribution of its records are of paramount interest. Some recent statistics disclose the following:

In 2002, Nielsen Soundscan (discussed herein under "Music Charting System") reported the following through November of that year:

- 528.9 million albums (CDs) sold
- 11 million singles
- By far, CDs outsold cassette tapes, 501.7 million CDs to 25.6 million cassette tapes
- Weekly sale of albums–14.5 million; singles–336,000
- Chain stores represented the greatest number of album sales (271.2 million) followed by Mass Merchant[9] (171.1 million), Independent (68.4 million), and Nontraditional (18 million).[10]

Distribution plays a major role in the overall plan of record selling and purchasing. Without wholesale and retail distribution and strategic marketing schemes, the information above would be substantially less. Presently, there are four methods of distributing recordings:

1. Wholesale distributors (the largest and most significant)
2. One-stops
3. Rack jobbers
4. Licensees

Wholesale distributors purchase records in large quantities from record labels and sell them, in bulk, to large chain record stores. While these distributors buy directly from record labels, "One-Stops buy from the major distributors and sell them [records] to Mom and Pop record stores. . ."[11] in small quantities. Rack Jobbers also buy from the major distributors, but they set up racks of music in other types of retail stores, such as bookstores and general consumer product stores. While the one-stops and rack jobbers purchase records from the major distributors, the "licensee is someone who signs a license agreement with a record company, which allows them to *actually manufacture* and distribute records, as opposed to merely buying and distributing goods manufactured by the record company."[12] According to David Naggar ". . . there are now only five major national wholesale distributors left in the U.S.,

---

[9] Mass Merchants are stores with numerous types of merchandise. Examples include Wal-Mart, Costco, K-Mart, etc.).
[10] Nielson Soundscan, November 2002.
[11] Passman, *All You Need to Know About the Music Business*, p. 166.
[12] *Ibid*. 167.

and all of them are owned by conglomerates that also own the major label record companies." These are illustrated below:

MAJOR NATIONAL WHOLESALE DISTRIBUTOR	2002 % OF TOTAL RECORD SALES	RECORD LABELS DISTRIBUTED
BMG	14.8%	Arista, BMG, RCA
EMI	8.3%	Capital, Virgin
Sony	15.7%	Columbia, Epic, Sony
Universal Music Group	28.9%	Interscope, Island/Def Jam, MCA
WEA	15.9%	Atlantic, Elektra, Warner Bros.
Independent Sector	16.4%	

Record label executives continue to investigate new and innovative ways to distribute recorded sound to consumers. Today's consumers can choose from CDs, the Internet, IPODs, DVDs, and the recent Cloud. The goal is to create increasingly smaller sizes with the capacity to store more data. Who knows? Tomorrow's music might be transmitted via subcutaneously implanted transceivers! Whatever form media dissemination takes, artistic creations will still need to be captured (recorded) and placed in a particular mode of delivery for the listener. Since the late 19th century, the advantages of capturing sound far outweighs its disadvantages, and therefore the need to develop new technologies of harnessing and disseminating sound will more than likely continue.

COPYRIGHT

A copyright is what is needed to "stake a claim" for your creative work in order to receive monetary rewards. Without proof of ownership it can be a daunting task to get paid for your work. Victor Herbert, a well-known operetta composer, appeared before the United States Congress regarding reforming copyright issues. Sometime following his appearance the United States Supreme Court (then known as the United States American Court) ruled in favor of protecting copyright ownership for original songs.

Record labels, publishers, distributors, and artists have yet another vehicle for disseminating their songs with the expansion of music marketing, via the Internet. Presently, consumers have the opportunity to download digital music using various e-commerce sources. Peer-to-peer, commonly known as P2P, entails music sharing among consumers. To do this, consumers purchase software that enables them to download music files from one another's computer systems via file sharing. This practice has caused much concern among record label executives and songwriters with respect to issues surrounding copyright infringement. Copying music in any form, whether to CD, cassette, or downloading to a computer, without the consent of the copyright owner is illegal. According to Billboard, "the Recording Industry Association of America (RIAA) reports that an estimated 2.6 billion copyrighted files are traded over P2P networks every month."[13] In an effort to combat declining record sales as the result

---

[13] *Billboard*, July 5, 2003, p. 1.

Form SR
For a Sound Recording
UNITED STATES COPYRIGHT OFFICE

REGISTRATION NUMBER

_____

SR   SRU

EFFECTIVE DATE OF REGISTRATION

_____
Month   Day   Year

DO NOT WRITE ABOVE THIS LINE. IF YOU NEED MORE SPACE, USE A SEPARATE CONTINUATION SHEET.

1   TITLE OF THIS WORK ▼

PREVIOUS, ALTERNATIVE, OR CONTENTS TITLES (CIRCLE ONE) ▼

2

a   NAME OF AUTHOR ▼

DATES OF BIRTH AND DEATH
Year Born ▼   Year Died ▼

Was this contribution to the work a "work made for hire"?
❏ Yes
❏ No

AUTHOR'S NATIONALITY OR DOMICILE
Name of Country
OR { Citizen of ▶ _____
Domiciled in ▶ _____

WAS THIS AUTHOR'S CONTRIBUTION TO THE WORK
Anonymous? ❏ Yes ❏ No
Pseudonymous? ❏ Yes ❏ No

If the answer to either of these questions is "Yes," see detailed instructions.

NATURE OF AUTHORSHIP   Briefly describe nature of material created by this author in which copyright is claimed. ▼

NOTE

Under the law, the "author" of a "work made for hire" is generally the employer, not the employee (see instructions). For any part of this work that was "made for hire" check "Yes" in the space provided, give the employer (or other person for whom the work was prepared) as "Author" of that part, and leave the space for dates of birth and death blank.

b   NAME OF AUTHOR ▼

DATES OF BIRTH AND DEATH
Year Born ▼   Year Died ▼

Was this contribution to the work a "work made for hire"?
❏ Yes
❏ No

AUTHOR'S NATIONALITY OR DOMICILE
Name of Country
OR { Citizen of ▶ _____
Domiciled in ▶ _____

WAS THIS AUTHOR'S CONTRIBUTION TO THE WORK
Anonymous? ❏ Yes ❏ No
Pseudonymous? ❏ Yes ❏ No

If the answer to either of these questions is "Yes," see detailed instructions.

NATURE OF AUTHORSHIP   Briefly describe nature of material created by this author in which copyright is claimed. ▼

c   NAME OF AUTHOR ▼

DATES OF BIRTH AND DEATH
Year Born ▼   Year Died ▼

Was this contribution to the work a "work made for hire"?
❏ Yes
❏ No

AUTHOR'S NATIONALITY OR DOMICILE
Name of Country
OR { Citizen of ▶ _____
Domiciled in ▶ _____

WAS THIS AUTHOR'S CONTRIBUTION TO THE WORK
Anonymous? ❏ Yes ❏ No
Pseudonymous? ❏ Yes ❏ No

If the answer to either of these questions is "Yes," see detailed instructions.

NATURE OF AUTHORSHIP   Briefly describe nature of material created by this author in which copyright is claimed. ▼

3

a   YEAR IN WHICH CREATION OF THIS WORK WAS COMPLETED
_____ ◀ Year
This information must be given in all cases.

b   DATE AND NATION OF FIRST PUBLICATION OF THIS PARTICULAR WORK
Complete this information ONLY if this work has been published.
Month ▶ _____ Day ▶ _____ Year ▶ _____
_____ ◀ Nation

4

a   COPYRIGHT CLAIMANT(S) Name and address must be given even if the claimant is the same as the author given in space 2. ▼

b   TRANSFER If the claimant(s) named here in space 4 is (are) different from the author(s) named in space 2, give a brief statement of how the claimant(s) obtained ownership of the copyright. ▼

See instructions before completing this space.

APPLICATION RECEIVED

ONE DEPOSIT RECEIVED

TWO DEPOSITS RECEIVED

FUNDS RECEIVED

DO NOT WRITE HERE
OFFICE USE ONLY

MORE ON BACK ▶
• Complete all applicable spaces (numbers 5-9) on the reverse side of this page.
• See detailed instructions.   • Sign the form at line 8.

DO NOT WRITE HERE
Page 1 of _____ pages

EXAMINED BY	FORM SR
CHECKED BY	
CORRESPONDENCE ❑ Yes	FOR COPYRIGHT OFFICE USE ONLY

DO NOT WRITE ABOVE THIS LINE. IF YOU NEED MORE SPACE, USE A SEPARATE CONTINUATION SHEET.

PREVIOUS REGISTRATION Has registration for this work, or for an earlier version of this work, already been made in the Copyright Office?

❑ Yes ❑ No If your answer is "Yes," why is another registration being sought? (Check appropriate box) ▼

a. ❑ This work was previously registered in unpublished form and now has been published for the first time.

b. ❑ This is the first application submitted by this author as copyright claimant.

c. ❑ This is a changed version of the work, as shown by space 6 on this application.

If your answer is "Yes," give: **Previous Registration Number** ▼   **Year of Registration** ▼

5

DERIVATIVE WORK OR COMPILATION

Preexisting Material Identify any preexisting work or works that this work is based on or incorporates. ▼

a

Material Added to This Work Give a brief, general statement of the material that has been added to this work and in which copyright is claimed. ▼

b

See instructions
before completing
this space.

6

DEPOSIT ACCOUNT If the registration fee is to be charged to a deposit account established in the Copyright Office, give name and number of account.

Name ▼   **Account Number** ▼

a

CORRESPONDENCE Give name and address to which correspondence about this application should be sent. Name/Address/Apt/City/State/Zip ▼

b

Area code and daytime telephone number   (   )   Fax number   (   )

Email

7

CERTIFICATION* I, the undersigned, hereby certify that I am the

Check only one ▼

❑ author   ❑ owner of exclusive right(s)

❑ other copyright claimant   ❑ authorized agent of _____

Name of author or other copyright claimant, or owner of exclusive right(s) ▲

of the work identified in this application and that the statements made by me in this application are correct to the best of my knowledge.

Typed or printed name and date ▼ If this application gives a date of publication in space 3, do not sign and submit it before that date.

_____   Date _____

Handwritten signature ▼

8

Certificate will be mailed in window envelope to this address:	Name ▼
	Number/Street/Apt ▼
	City/State/Zip ▼

YOU MUST:
· Complete all necessary spaces
· Sign your application in space 8

SEND ALL 3 ELEMENTS
IN THE SAME PACKAGE:
1. Application form
2. Nonrefundable filing fee in check or money order payable to Register of Copyrights
3. Deposit material

MAIL TO:
Library of Congress
Copyright Office-SR
101 Independence Avenue SE
Washington, DC 20559-6238

9

*17 U.S.C. §506(e): Any person who knowingly makes a false representation of a material fact in the application for copyright registration provided for by section 409, or in any written statement filed in connection with the application, shall be fined not more than $2,500.

Form SR-Full   Rev: 01/2009   Print: 01/2009 — 20,000   Printed on recycled paper

U.S. Government Printing Office: 2009-349-387/80,018

of P2P file sharing, the RIAA on behalf of major record labels has filed lawsuits against companies as well as some individuals.[14] One of the more recent suits involves four college students from Princeton University, Rensselaer Polytechnic Institute, and Michigan Technological University. The law allows up to $150,000 fine/penalty for each pirated song; it's reported that the defendants have ". . . offered between 27,000 and 1 million songs each for free trading."[15] To further combat music piracy, the RIAA issued this warning on April 29, 2003, to "about 200,000 users of the Grokster and Kazaa file-sharing services . . ."[16] who were engaged in downloading music files:

> "COPYRIGHT INFRINGEMENT WARNING: It appears that you are offering copyrighted music to others from your computer. Distributing or downloading copyrighted music on the Internet without permission from the copyright owner is ILLEGAL . . ."[17]

Moreover, the Phoenix-based SunComm Technologies "has developed a technology that ". . . enables the secure transfer of music to a computer but blocks the ability to burn copies or share files via peer-to-peer networks."[18] Finally, new legislation has appeared that will help to protect copyrighted material from P2P networking. Known as the Piracy Deterrence and Education Act (HR 2570X), this legislation engages the Department of Homeland Security's Bureau of Customs and Border Protection, which has the authority to confiscate copyrighted material from any individual or business. Also, on April 29, 2004 the Senate Judiciary Committee approved the Protecting Intellectual Rights Against Theft and Expropriation Act (PIRATE). Previously, the Department of Justice (DOJ) could only bring to trial and prosecute criminal cases; PIRATE allows the DOJ to prosecute civil cases, such as copyright infringement.

Perhaps these and other efforts used to combat copyright infringement are paying off, as the RIAA reported an increase of CD album sales from January through June of 2004. It is reported that nearly 330 million CD albums were sold during this period. In lieu of the inevitability of digital downloads, the RIAA is now reporting on digital download sales (58 million songs during this same period) that are offered legally through online music services.

Record groups and e-commerce businesses are working to establish agreements that satisfy all parties concerned. In an article in *Billboard*, writer Brian Garrity states: "In a move that analysts are billing as a significant indicator of the gathering momentum for legitimate online music services, AOL launched its version of the MusicNet subscriber service."[19] In a previous issue, Garrity states: "While at launch, MusicNet on AOL is offering only 50% of the Billboard 200 and asking $17.95 per month for the ability to burn 10 songs . . ."[20] This clearly shows an effort being made to accommodate the copyright owner, the record label, and the consumer. Collaborations continue as Microsoft and Sony are currently working on a deal that will probably be the largest contender in the music digital download industry. Presently, however, Apple's iTunes appears to be the most popular music digital downloading service for general consumers. April 28, 2004 marks iTunes's one year anniversary. In another article, Garrity states: "Apple claims a current sales of 2.7 million songs per week, or 140 million per year."[21] Even though iTunes

---

[14] The major record groups include Universal Music Group, AOL Time Warner Inc.'s Warner Music Group, and Sony Music Entertainment.
[15] Frank Ahrens, "Four Students Sued Over Music Sites: Industry Group Targets File Sharing at Colleges," *Washington Post*, April 4, 2003.
[16] Sue Zeidler, "Music Industry Sends Warning to Swappers," *Reuters*, April 30, 2003.
[17] RIAA press release, April 29, 2003
[18] *Billboard*, July 12, 2003.
[19] *Billboard*, March 8, 2003.
[20] *Billboard*, February 26, 2003.
[21] *Billboard*, May 8, 2004.

(or any other company, for that matter) doesn't own most songs in the history of recorded music, it nevertheless ". . . features more than 700,000 songs from all five majors and 450-plus independents."[22]

Simultaneously, components of the music industry are pursuing new ways to offer music. As stated in a *Billboard* article March 3, 2003:

"In addition to recording artists/labels, film, T.V., and commercial publishers are finding new sources as the result of diminished record sales—attributed to the internet—they include music for videos, cell phone tunes, hip-hop samples, and karaoke machines."[23]

Perhaps the best solution for this to date is the unveiling of Apple's new creation. On Monday, June 6, 2011 Apple's iCloud customers will be able to hear their music using. . .

". . . any device free of charge as long as the files were purchased through iTunes . . . [the] company plans to charge users a $25 flat-rate to stream music not purchased through iTunes . . . Apple will keep 30 percent, while labels receive 58 percent, and publishers the remaining 12"[24]

MUSIC CONTRACTS AND PUBLISHING

Contracts are needed to provide a framework for a working relationship between the various parties within the music industry. A list of some of the more common music entities that require some form of contractual agreement follows:

1. Songwriter and publisher
2. Publisher and record label/producer/film/TV/theatre
3. Artist and manager/agent
4. Artist and record label
5. Record label and distribution company
6. Record label and tour management company

The term *songwriter* refers to a person who creates both music (i.e., sound) and lyrics. If a song is created by means of collaboration between individuals who create the music and lyrics separately, the terms *composer* and *author* (or *lyricist*), respectively, are most appropriate. Once a song is created and before a publisher is pursued, it is imperative that its writer secure a copyright from the Library of Congress.[25] Even though the U.S. Copyright Act of 1976, in essence, states that a work is automatically protected by copyright when it becomes "fixed"—music notation or recorded (i.e., a tangible substance)—it is highly recommended that the songwriter wait until the official copyright is received before contacting a publisher or, for that matter, anyone in the music business.[26]

Once the copyright is received from the Library of Congress, the songwriter can pursue a publishing company.[27] Making a song available to the various media is the job of the publisher, as he/she is the

---

[22] *Ibid.* The reference to the five majors refers to distributing companies: BMG, EMI, Sony, UMG, WEA. See information later in this section.

[23] *Billboard*, March 3, 2003.

[24] Matthew Calmia, Cloud Services May Help Curb Piracy, Retrieved on June 24, 2011 from http://www.mobiledia.com/news/93159.html

[25] There is a small fee for each copyright; presently this is $35.00 (online only). You can visit the U.S. Copyright office at http://www.copyright.gov/forms/.

[26] I don't purport that most people in the music industry are dishonest; it just makes good business sense.

[27] In today's music industry, like during the Tin Pin Alley era, many established songwriters have their own publishing company. Also, a publishing firm may have many writers on contract within its organization.

middle person between the writer (composer and/or lyricist) and, ultimately, the performer/recording artist. The publisher has either personal contact with performers and various media or the ability to get a song to them–a task that is often impossible for the unknown writer.

SONGWRITER AND PUBLISHER

The purpose of the contract between the songwriter and the publisher is to establish a working relationship with regard to royalty payments should the song be used by an individual or institution. It is understood that the songwriter's ultimate goal is to have his/her song performed so that royalties can be received. (Types of royalties such as mechanical and performance rights will be discussed later within the chapter.) Issues addressed in the contract may include exclusive or non-exclusive agreement, duration of contract, and royalty percentage. The exclusive contract implies that the songwriter writes "exclusively" for the publisher and therefore cannot publish a song with another publisher during the duration of the contract. The contractual agreement generally lasts for a number of years, and the songwriter is obligated to create a certain number of songs each year. The non-exclusive contract is generally a one-time agreement. With regard to royalty payment, the contract stipulates the songwriter's and publishers' agreed-upon percentages.

Similar to the procedure of "plugging" that occurred during the Tin Pan Alley days, the publisher's principal task is to get its songwriter's song to an artist, the Artist and Repertoire person of a record label, musical director or director of a stage play, or film/TV music director/consultant. If successful, a contract is drawn between the publisher and the interested party.[28] Here is an example of the process from song creation to royalty payment (performance right only):

> Chelsea the songwriter receives a copyright from the Library of Congress for the creation of her song titled "My Song." She engages in contract negations with AAA Publishing Company. Their contractual agreement states an agreed-upon percentage of royalty payments. Chelsea's song is recorded by John the singer. Incrementally throughout the year, AAA Publishing Company receives a royalty payment from a performance licensing agency such as ASCAP, BMI, or SESAC for performances of "My Song." AAA Publishing Company sends a royalty payment to Chelsea as stipulated in their contract.

PRODUCER

While the recording engineer tracks all the instruments and voices and places these recorded parts on tape and/or hard drive, the producer is most responsible for the specific sound results for his or her artist(s). Often this entails vocal and/or instrumental coaching on the performance of parts, song structure, tempo, and making primary decisions on how all the parts work together—or mix (a.k.a. mixdown). As the liaison between the artist and consumer, the producer must be aware of what is needed from the artist that musically and even visually in many cases, appeals to consumers. Because in most situations the producer is a musician as well, and he or she is quite capable of articulating, by demonstration, what is desired from the artist(s).

ARTIST AND MANAGER

The contract between an artist and his/her manager is one of the most intimate relationships in the music business. A manager's responsibility goes beyond the typical business relationship, as he/she is privy to personal information about the artist. Therefore, the best working relationship is based on trust. In this

---

[28] The publisher acts on behalf of the songwriter.

relationship, the manager knows the musicality and abilities of his/her artist and represents the artist in a manner that is uncompromisingly professional. M. William Krasilovsky and Sidney Shemel point out:

> ". . . personal managers are responsible for day-to-day career development, personal advice and guidance, and planning the long range direction of the artist's career. Because of the broader nature of their responsibilities, managers usually have a much smaller number of clients than agents. Their responsibilities include:
>
> - Choosing literary, artistic, and musical material
> - Handling matters relating to publicity, public relations, and advertising
> - Adopting the proper format for the best representation of the artist's talents
> - Selecting booking agents to secure engagements for the artist
> - Determining (in conjunction with the booking agent) the types of employment most beneficial to the artist's career
> - Selecting and supervising the artist's accountants and attorneys"[29]

A significant number of new artists may not have the advantage of a professional manager before signing with a record label. In fact, the manager may be a band member or even a relative (such as the father of a member of The Beach Boys) or friend of the band or artist. Even though the manager may be well-suited for the artist, he/she may not be the best person to conduct contract negotiations with a record label.[30] If this is the case, it is highly recommended that the artist consult an entertainment attorney before signing any contracts.

With regard to agents, many record labels have their own in-house tour management department, and there are even more labels that hire a talent agent firm or an individual agent to handle their artists' live performances. According to Krasilovsky and Shemel ". . . the leading talent agencies are the William Morris Agency, International Creative Management (ICM), and Creative Artists Associates (CAA)."[31] With regard to individual agents:

> An agent finds or receives offers of employment and usually negotiates the terms of the contract. An agent works on a commission basis, normally 10 to 15 percent of the artist's earnings for a given engagement. The rate depends on state regulations, the particular talent union involved, and the duration of the engagement negotiated[32]

Additionally ". . . agents in the music industry are involved almost exclusively in booking live personal appearances (concerts). Music agents are sometimes involved in commercials, tour sponsorship, television specials, and other areas . . ."[33]

MARKETING AND ARTIST MANAGEMENT

The music industry today is often understood as being market driven. As a result, a performer's visual appeal and charismatic nature play a significant part in how he/she is marketed. Therefore, record labels and consequently producers, composers and performers/entertainers—concerned with increasing their

---

[29] M. William Krasilovsky and Sidney Shemel. *This Business of Music: The Definitive Guide to the Music Industry*. NY: Billboard Books, 2002, pp. 351–352.

[30] Record executives are seasoned business personnel who employ specific strategies for attaining their label's desired objectives. It would therefore be in the artist's best interest to secure similar representation.

[31] Krasilovsky and Shemel, p. 351

[32] *Ibid.*, p. 351.

[33] Passman, p. 74.

chances of success—regularly produce songs most suited to consumer tastes. In view of this fact, artists are of two general types: entertainers and performers.[34]

Entertainers tend to be more market-driven than performers. While the entertainer has a tendency to focus more on mass appeal, the performer on the other hand is apt to nurture his/her specific talent/gift and is therefore less driven by audience appeal/approval. This is not to suggest that performers are not concerned with the effect of their presentation. On the contrary, one of their principal goals lies in the "effect" of a song and its aesthetic character. In addition, one should not delegate a given artist to only one category, as there are numerous artists who simultaneously perform and entertain. For instance, Michael Jackson exhibits virtuoso dancing and therefore is regarded as a performer, yet he is indeed entertaining. Joni Mitchell's artistic phrase stylizations combined with lyrics that engage and provoke thought, with emotions and memories, display her remarkable talents as a performer. Yet the playfulness of her staple melodic contours and yodel-like vocal nuances are rather entertaining.

Because major music labels are generally market-driven (rather than artist-driven), label executives have found it advantageous, through proven results, to groom an artist based on consumer tastes rather than the artist's inherent talent or personal preferences. The point is that executives, producers, and A & R (named artist repertoire, one who finds material for his/her artist) people of the music industry are in the business for business (i.e., monetary gain).

Television is still the most effective way to market an artist, as music is used not only for sources such as MTV and VH1, but also as theme songs for various programs such as *The David Letterman Show*, the *Jay Leno Show*, Disney programs, and so on. Even more effective than these is the Grammy Awards. For example, the 45th Grammy Awards[35] show featured artists such as Simon & Garfunkel (singer/guitarist and singer), No Doubt (an Orange County pop-punk group featuring a woman singer), Norah Jones (singer and pianist), Vanessa Carlton (singer and pianist), John Mayer (singer and guitarist), James Taylor (singer and guitarist), Yo Yo Ma (cellist), the Dixie Chicks (singers and instrumentalists), Coldplay (band), and Ashanti (singer). The outcome for these artists is generally favorable with respect to airplay and record sales; thus allowing them a greater level of popularity and/or longevity.

Talent agencies and record labels are constantly thinking of ways to disseminate their artists to the consumer. One creative marketing endeavor is called "12 to 20." This is a "teen marketing firm [that] bundles together fledging talent with anti-drug messages into mandatory school assemblies; each package may travel for two to eight weeks."[36] The Rayne and TG4 are two recent groups that have recently participated in this endeavor.

The Latin market is also engaged in various teen marketing schemes. For example, in 2002 albums were made from a popular soap opera titled *Cómplices al Rescate*, aired in Puerto Rico and the United States. The show, translating to *Accomplices to the Rescue*, "features 13-year-old actress Belinda Peregrín playing the role of twin sisters Silvana, who sings pop, and Mariana, who sings *grupera* music."[37] Two albums were released titled *Silvana: Cómplices al Rescate* and Mariana: *Cómplices al Rescate*.

Sony has embarked on yet another innovative way to market its conglomeration of technology products and music ideas. As of February 2003 it has:[38]

---

[34] As will be explained, an artist can be both.

[35] This year marks the first time the Grammy Awards were broadcast live using 5.1 Surroundsound.

[36] Susanne Ault, *Billboard*, 2003, p. 18.

[37] Lelia Cobo, *Billboard*, 2002, p. 34.

[38] To date, America spends approximately $20 billion dollars each year on toys.

". . . signed licensing deals with Blink-182, P.O.D., Mekon, Freezepop, and Dieselboy to showcase their music in the game . . .Amplitude, an update version of the Sony Play Station 2 music game Frequency, allows players to mix and remix hit songs during both offline and online game play."[39]

Labels and management personnel are considering tour events such as the Vans Warped Tour, which celebrated its 10th anniversary in August 2004. Its founder, Kevin Lyman, has organized nightly band performances on different stages at various venues throughout the country. Bands perform simultaneously on different stages with titles like North Stage, South Stage, Volcom Stage, Maurice Stage, Lyman Says, Smartpunk, and Ernie Ball. Performing in noted venues such as the Reliant Center in Houston, Texas, the Verizon Wireless Amphitheatre Lot in New Mexico, the Cal State Fullerton Amphitheatre in California, Desert Breeze Skate Park in Las Vegas, Nevada, and the Central Florida Fairgrounds in Orlando, Florida, bands receive exposure among people with many musical tastes and band preferences. Some bands include Yellowbird, New Found Glory, ASG, Guttermouth, The Casualties, Thursday, Rise Against, Senses Fail, Melee, Rolling Blackouts, The Matches, Brazil, Ghetto Lust, Last Collapse, and many others. With the resounding success of this touring and band-marketing format, Lyman has organized an additional tour titled "Taste of Chaos," which began in February 2005. Similar to the Vans Warped Tour format that occurs in the summer, this multi band, multi venue venture provides exposure opportunities for bands and entertainment for consumers during the winter. The band named The Used, with their successful album titled *In Love and Death*, was one of the highlights of the inaugural Taste of Chaos tour.

LICENSING

Licensing is the "bread and butter" for composers and songwriters, as it leads to royalty payments for many decades. On behalf on composers and songwriters ". . . ASCAP, BMI, and SESAC . . . negotiate licenses (permissions) with radio and TV stations, nightclubs, cabarets, discos and the like, that enable them to perform publicly the musical compositions contained in the performing rights organizations' catalogs" (Halloran, p. 123).

ASCAP, or the American Society of Composers, Authors, and Publishers was founded in 1914 and is the first and one of the most widely used music licensing organizations in the United States. The formation of ASCAP is the result of a lawsuit initiated by Victor Herbert ". . . against Stanley's Restaurant [NYC] which led to the historic decision by Justice Oliver Wendell Holmes in the American Supreme Court in 1915 that a composer's works could not be publicly performed for profit without his permission.[40] Herbert felt that others were profiting from his efforts, and therefore filed a lawsuit that sparked litigation that was eventually decided by the United States Supreme Court.[41]

BMI, or Broadcast Music Incorporated, was founded in 1939. Initiated by the National Academy of Broadcasters (NAB), BMI was created to oppose ASCAP's seemingly unfair royalty rates and continued price increases. Given that most songs aired by broadcasters were from ASCAP's music catalog, radio stations had to either "pay for play" or not play music at all. In January 1941, a boycott by NAB members ensued, leading to no music from ASCAP's catalog of songs being aired for most of the year.

In a strategic move to position itself as a competing licensing agency, BMI decided to be more sensitive to the emerging groups of whites and blacks, often migrating from rural environments, who

---

[39] *Billboard*, February, 2003, p. 49.
[40] P. Hardy and D. Lang. *The Farber Companion to 20th-Century Popular Music*. Boston, MA: Farber and Farber, 1990, p. 357.
[41] See the U.S. Copyright Act for detailed information regarding copyrights and royalties.

favored country and urban blues/rhythm & blues. ASCAP was partial to the post-vaudeville way of doing business, and as such its marketing strategy generally didn't consider the musical tastes of southern whites, and blacks in general. BMI soon found its niche by catering to these two groups, which consequently created a flood of new as well as seasoned country and urban blues/rhythm & blues artists.

SESAC is the European Society of Stage, Authors and Composers. It is the European equivalent to the licensing agencies in the United States. Other performing rights agencies include PRS, IMRO, and SOCAN. Additional types of music collection agencies will be discussed in the ensuing paragraphs on royalties.[42]

ROYALTIES

A *royalty* is a payment to a writer, publisher, performer, or record label for the use of their work in one or more of the following categories:

1. Performance-Based Income Sources
   a. Radio
   b. TV
   c. Cable
   d. Satellite
   e. Live and recorded performances
   f. Internet
2. Mechanical
   g. Record sales
3. Synchronization
   h. A sound recording that is synchronized in a film or TV program

There are three corresponding types of collection societies and rights organizations: performing rights, mechanical rights, and performing rights for recording artists and record companies.[43] *Performing Rights Agencies* collect monies for licensing writers' songs from various media types such as radio, TV, film, the Internet, concert halls, and so on. In other words, every form of media (as well as business) that pursues capital growth must get a license, which includes a fee, to play music with a copyright. The fee amount is based on the weight of the medium, which is determined by its music usage (e.g., number of songs or background music vs. featured songs) and consumer market aspects. For instance, a radio talk show that uses songs as background music would pay a smaller fee than a radio show that broadcasts "top 40" songs twenty-four hours a day. As an example, according to their Web site, "BMI surveys include more than 450,000 hours of radio airplay, 6 million local TV program hours, and 6.5 million network TV program hours."[44] In addition to this, ASCAP and BMI give licenses to various businesses. Some of these include restaurants, night clubs, hotels, Web sites, and so on. The fee is typically based on revenue. An unprecedented fee was negotiated in October 2004, when ASCAP and the Radio Music License Committee (representing the radio industry) agreed that the latter would pay $1.7 billion as a flat fee for the air performances and streaming files of nearly 8 million songs played on over 12,000 commercial radio stations.

---

[42] In America, ASCAP and BMI are the most popular. Most songwriters, publishers, performers, and record labels belong to one of these two agencies.

[43] As you can imagine, it would be in the writer's, artist's, publisher's, or label's best interest to be registered with one or all of these agencies, as they collect monies on their behalf.

[44] BMI at www.bmi.com/about

Collected fees from the various media types by all the aforementioned performance rights agencies are paid, minus administrative costs (which are comparatively minimal) to writers and publishers. (Please see Contracts and Publishing for the discussion of writer/publisher fee disbursements.) The six major performing rights agencies include the following:

The United States
American Society of Composers, Authors, and Publishers (ASCAP)
Broadcast Music Incorporated (BMI)
Society of European Stage, Authors, and Composers (SESAC)

Britain
Performing Right Society (PRS)

Ireland
Irish Music Rights Organization (IMRO)

Canada
(SOCAN)

A relatively new practice that is increasing in popularity is listening to music via the Internet. The advantage here is that consumers can scan thousands of radio stations on a global scale. This means of listening to music has resulted in diminished royalties for record labels, publishers, and songwriters. To prevent future losses, and to obtain compensation for this lost revenue, copyright owners and music industry executives have instigated litigation. With the passage of the Small Webcasters Settlement Act in December 2002, royalty payments to artists have become a reality for certain Webcasters.[45] The WSA has created the following fees for webcasters:

For October 28, 1998 through December 31, 2002, eligible small Webcasters pay royalties of 8% of revenue or 5% of expenses, whichever is higher, with minimums of $500 for 1998 and $2,000 for 2001 and 2002.

For 2003 and 2004, the rate rises to 10% of a Webcaster's first $250,000 in revenue and 12% thereafter or 7% of expenses, whichever is higher, with minimums of $2,000 for Webcasters that gross less than $50,000 and $5,000 for those with revenue of $50,000 or more (*Radio & Records*, December 2002, p. 3).

Mechanical Rights Agencies collect fees from record labels for record sales and distribute the monies to publishers, who in turn pay their writer(s). The Harry Fox Agency in New York is by far the most widely used mechanical rights agency in the United States.

Performing Rights Agencies For Recording Artists And Record Companies collect royalties on their behalf. SoundExchange is the most widely used agency in the United States. Although fees vary from company to company, here is an excerpt from a book written by an experienced attorney regarding this area:

"For a new artist who has never had a record deal or a signed artist who has never sold more than say 100,000 albums of any record, a typical royalty rate will be 12% to 14% of the SRLP if he or she is signed to a major label record company. The spread is a bit wider if signed to an independent label. The typical range for an independent label is 10% to 14% of SRLP" (Naggar, p. 35).

Here is a common scenario: Your recently formed band is hired (for a fee) to play for four hours for someone's 21st birthday. Because you've only had two opportunities to rehearse, and you've only been

---

[45] In 2002, the FCC selected HD Radio as the technical standard for digital radio. *SRLP* refers to the Suggested Retail List Price.

working on four original songs, a decision needs to be made quickly. You have four choices: (1) Play each original song for about 45 minutes; (2) Play the same four songs continually until the end of the four-hour engagement; (3) Don't play; or (4) Play songs recorded by other artists. If you're like me when I was in my late teens and early twenties, money was needed. Therefore, option 3 was not even considered. Unless guests at the engagement enjoy an artist's improvisational talents, or your originals are stylistically analogous to psychedelic rock or free jazz, the first option is probably not the best idea. Number 2 might work if people in attendance have plugs stuffed in their ears. Option number 4 is the best choice for the following reasons:

1. Listening and learning pre-recorded songs is the quickest way to expand a band's repertoire.
2. There are times when an artist will want to make money, and playing a number of "popular songs" is one way to get re-hired.[46]
3. Playing songs of other artists gives an artist compositional ideas, whether similar or dissimilar.

Before playing the engagement, it is important and fair that the copyright owner, not the original performer (unless he/she is the owner), be paid for the performance of his/her song. (Wouldn't you want to be paid if you were entitled to a royalty?) To be protected from possible litigation if you intend to receive money by playing a copyrighted song, you should inquire about a performance license. There are ". . . two alternatives: you may negotiate a 'mechanical license' from the copyright owner; or you may use the 'compulsory mechanical license' provision of the copyright law . . ." (Krasclovsky, p. 65). I also recommend that each band member join the musicians union and pay what is known as "work dues" for playing copyrighted songs.

MUSIC UNIONS

In 1896 the American Federation of Musicians (AFM) considered a professional to be an individual who gets paid for their services. Like any other union, the AFM protects the working person, in this case musician, in a number of circumstances — performances, touring, and recording — related to receiving rightful financial compensation. Moreover, the union seeks to offer its membership valuable qualities of life including health benefits and retirement (e.g., the AFM Employer's Pension Welfare Fund, formed in 1959). Although various union-type efforts were made to help the working musician in the mid-1800s, it wasn't until 1896 that something was established and charted by the American Federation of Labor. In 1900 it officially became known as the American Federation of Musicians. Through its 115 years of existence on the music scene in America and Canada, the AFM continues to be instrumental in staying abreast of new technologies that in some way or another affect its memberships' creative works and due royalties.

TRADE JOURNALS

Trade journals are divided into two basic categories: popular and professional.

Popular Trade Journals

Some of the better-known popular trades include *Rolling Stone*, *Musician*, *Circus*, *Down Beat*, *Spin*, and *Hit Parade*. While professional trades are directed toward all aspects that encompass the professional artist, popular trades focus on a more broader circulation of subscribers and readers.[47] Topics in these publications include both information about and suggestions for professional and amateur songwriters, plus articles on musical instruments and recording technology.

---

[46] I realize that some listeners prefer to hear a cover version played in the same manner as that of the original performer. This is the exception, not the rule. My experience shows that most people generally appreciate a cover version with the new artist's personal touch. Believe in yourself, and people will appreciate you.

[47] Readers also include professional artists.

Professional trade journals

Some of the most widely known professional trades over the years include *Billboard*, *Cash Box*, *Record World*, *Gavin*, *CMJ* [*Country Music Journal*] *New Music Project*, and *Radio & Records*. Presently, *Billboard* is by far the most comprehensive professional music trade journal published in the United States, as well as in some countries abroad. *Radio & Records* is second, and leads the professional journals in information relevant to radio broadcasting and broadcasters. The reading of professional trade journals is essential for professional artists, music business executives, music retailers, radio and television executives, and others in the business. Information provided includes, but is not limited to, popular music charts, popular artists, music reviews, recording technology, and numerous articles on various topics associated with music (such as music styles, censorship, and legislation). These publications ". . .have great influence in the record and broadcast industries."[48]

MUSIC CHARTS

A *music chart* is a list of songs that are identified by style (such as country and rhythm & blues) or a descriptive marketing category (such as Top 40 or Pop). The latter can contain different styles as well; it refers to the most popular songs across a broad market. In both cases, songs are on a given chart based on record sales and airplay. Stylistic chart names, which may have separate album and single categories, include:[49]

Bluegrass
Classical
Country
Jazz
Latin
Rhythm & blues/hip-hop
New Age
Rock (a.k.a. rock mainstream)
Alternative (a.k.a. rock modern)
(Blues, contemporary Christian, gospel and reggae appear periodically)

While the "style" category listed above is easily understood, identifying specific music features of what is "market-driven" are not as obvious, and therefore warrant further explanation. Market-driven charts have, by and large, industry or market-enthused categories.[50] Today market-driven chart names include the following:[51]

Pop (a.k.a. Hot)
Adult Contemporary
Adult Top 40
Christian Albums
Christian Songs

---

[48] David Baskerville, *Music Business Handbook & Career Guide*. Sixth Edition (CA, Thousand Oaks: Sage Publications, Inc., 1995), 226.

[49] This list is a synthesis of chart names used by *Billboard* and *Radio & Records*, magazines that weekly rank the most popular songs based on sales and airplay.

[50] One could certainly argue the point that most of the general pop names could in fact entail the use of specific music characteristics, which help to contribute to its distinction as one of the said pop names. Perhaps the difference is the fact that the stylistic chart names were artist-inspired as opposed to market- enthused.

[51] Chart names that appear periodically in this type include Music Video and World Music.

Dance/Club Play Songs
Dance/Electronic Albums
Heatseekers
Independent Albums
Internet
Kid Albums
Soundtracks
Tastemaker Albums
Top 40 Tracks
Tropical Albums
Tropical Songs
Urban
World Albums

Each market-driven chart caters to a certain consumer group. For instance, below is a list of the 10 most popular singles, as reported by *Billboard* in November 2002 and May 2011, that are listed under the chart names Adult Contemporary and those listed under Hot 100:[52]

(2002)		(2011)	
Title	**Artist**	**Title**	**Artist**
"Cry"	Faith Hill	"Just the Way You Are"	Bruno Mars
"A Thousand Miles"	Vanessa Carlton		
"Can't Stop Loving You"	Phil Collins	"Firework"	Katy Perry
		"September"	Daughtry
"A Moment Like This"	Kelly Clarkson	"Marry Me"	Train
"The Game of Love"	Santana feat. Michelle Branch	"Mine"	Taylor Swift
		"Rhythm of Love"	Plain White T's
"Superman (It's Not Easy)"	Five For Fighting	"F**kin' Perfect"	Pink
"Hero" Enrique Iglesias "Soak Up the Sun"	Sheryl Crow	"King of Anything"	Sara Bareilles
		"Secrets"	OneRepublic
		"Raise Your Glass"	Pink
"A New Day Has Come"	Celine Dion	"E.T.	Katy Perry feat. Kanye west
"Do It For Love"	Daryl Hall & John Oates	"Rolling in the Deep"	Adele
		"Till the World Ends"	Britney Spears feat. Minaj and Kei$ha
"Die Another Day"	Madonna		
"A Moment Like This"	Kelly Clarkson	"Just Can't Get Enough"	The Black Eyed Peas
"Ignition"	R. Kelly		

Figure 2.1 Billboard Top 10 Singles in November 2002 and May 2011.

---

[52] As previously mentioned, ratings are based on record sales and radio airplay. Also, Adult Contemporary markets to a specific age range (approx. 25–35 years of age), while Hot 100 is marketable to a wide audience, but primarily young listeners.

(2002)		(2011)	
Title	**Artist**	**Title**	**Artist**
"Don't Mess With My Man"	Nive feat. B.B. Casey	"The Lazy Song"	Bruno Mars
"Virginity"	TG4	"S & M"	Rihanna
"All the Things She Said"	T.A.T.U.	"On the Floor"	Jennifer Lopez feat. Pitbull
"Gimme the Light"	Sean Paul	"Blow"	Kei$ha
"When I Get You Alone"	Thicke	"Down On Me"	Jeremiah feat. 50 Cent
"A New Day Has Come"	Celine Dion	"Look At Me Now"	Chris Brown feat. Lil Wayne & Busta Rhymes
"Don't Stop Dancing"	Creed		

Figure 2.1 (continued)

The Adult Contemporary chart (for listeners from their mid-20s) includes certain styles that are normally associated with particular artists: country artists such as Faith Hill and Sheryl Crow, and Latin artists such as Santana and Enrique Iglesias. Styles evidenced by the above Hot 100 chart (wide audience) include R & B/ Hip-Hop (R. Kelly, Nive, TG4, Sean Paul) and rock (Pearl Jam and Creed). Because of the type of listener with respect to age, these results suggest that a greater number of adults (mid-20s and above) favor country and Latin styles more than they do R & B/hip-hop and rock styles. Because adults are generally less concerned with those social trends favored by teens and young adults we could conclude that country and Latin styles must offer something different than do R & B/hip-hop and rock styles. Since R & B/hip-hop and rock styles appear on the Hot 100 (or Pop) chart, which represents all ages including preadolescents, one could generally conclude that these styles:

1. Are most popular among a diverse audience
2. Probably are less lyrically challenging
3. Have been within the popular realm for a longer time than other styles
4. Represent mainstream culture
5. May be more dance oriented

Another type of market-driven chart is named "Eventful: Most Demanded", which means just that—those artists who are in high demand with regard to performances. In May of 2011 these included (listed beginning with the most demanded):

1. Justin Bieber
2. Mana
3. Go For It!
4. Shane Dawson
5. Eminem
6. Yanni
7. Digitour
8. Grave Encounters
9. Big Time Rush
10. Shakira

Eminem. © MTV/photofest

MUSIC CHARTING SYSTEM

Charting the progress of songs is one of the main features of professional trade journals. The music charting system identifies popular songs and numerically ranks them by virtue of record sales and radio airplay.[53] Reasons for a song's appearance on the "charts" is based largely on marketing techniques and strategies, popular artist appeal, creative recording techniques, and ". . . the most current musical taste of the public."[54] Music charts identify specific styles or types of music such as classical, country, jazz, Latin, pop (under the guise of Hot 100), new age, rhythm & blues/hip-hop and rock, and record type (such as single and album). They also recognize those ". . . records that are the most widely programmed and/or the biggest sellers throughout the country."[55]

A song is placed on a chart(s) as the result of its conspicuous showing ". . . from a national sample of top 40 radio airplay monitored by broadcast data systems, top 40 radio playlists, and retail and rack singles sales . . ."[56] The current method and procedure in which *Billboard* monitors and tabulates recordings is gathered by its Broadcast Data System (BDS) and the company named Nielson

---

[53] With regard to record sales, unit is the term used to describe the product (i.e., CD, cassette, LP, etc.). Charts identify those songs that are gold (500,000 units), platinum (million units), and multi platinum (2x = 2 million, 3x = 3 million, 5x = 5million, and so on).

[54] Baskerville, 75.

[55] Harvey Rachlin, *The Encyclopedia Of The Music Business* (N.Y.: Harper & Row, Publishers, Inc., 1981), 73.

[56] *Billboard.* (N.Y.: Billboard Magazine, 1992), 74.

Soundscan. The *Music Business Handbook & Career Guide* provides an excellent explanation of each of these:

> Billboard's Broadcast Data System (BDS) enables computers in major and secondary markets to "listen" to radio stations 24 hours a day. The BDS technology monitors broadcasts and recognizes songs and/or commercials aired by radio and TV stations. Records and commercials must first be played into the system's computer, which, in turn, creates a digital "fingerprint" of that material. The fingerprint is downloaded to BDS monitors in each market. Those monitors can recognize that fingerprint or "pattern" when the song or commercial is broadcast on one of the monitored stations. Once a song pattern has been recognized by the remote computer, it updates its records, identifying the exact time, date, and station. Each evening, the pattern library is updated and the day's detection history is transmitted from the remote sites to the BDS central operations facility where the equipment spews out relative chart positions for the recordings that particular week.

> Whereas BDS monitors airplay, Soundscan tabulates sales of record products. Soundscan's sales tabulations are generated by a computer network linked to retail outlets and rack jobbers nationwide, representing more than 65% of the nation's record sales. Previously, record companies were forced to estimate sales based on the number of records they manufactured and shipped to retailers. Even approximately accurate sales figures were not available until the retailer shipped unsold product back to the label. Known as "returns," this product wasn't received by a label until sometimes months after the initial shipment. Soundscan's sales data are used by Billboard to compile its Top 200 Album, Top Country Album, and Top Catalog Album charts as well as its Top Point-of-Sale Singles charts.[57]

Prior to the implementation of Soundscan (before May 1991), *Billboard* and other professional trade journals' methods of tabulating data with regard to sales and airplay involved personal contact with retailers and radio stations. The following information regarding Billboard's Hot 100 pop singles chart is an example showing the process by which songs were tabulated and placed on the charts and subsequently became popular hits: Each week *Billboard* placed between 180–200 songs, in alphabetical order, on a Sales Check Sheet. These sheets were distributed to selected retailers (dealers and sub-distributors)[58] for their ". . . sales data on a qualitative basis . . . Very Good, Good, and Fair, and to name their top 15 selling items."[59] Retailers were selected on the basis of ". . . recommendations made by the sales departments of record companies . . .".[60] All data were collected and processed by computer. With regard to the tabulation of airplay, approximately 150 radio stations were contacted daily by *Billboard* personnel. Data collected included feature songs or background music on their playlists (each station had a list of songs it intended to play on a given day), and their relative importance or significance to the industry of the given station. Similar to retailers, selected radio stations were the result of ". . . recommendations made by the promotions departments of labels and retailers in one-stops . . .".[61] Data from both Sales Check Sheets and radio playlists (with other pertinent data) were processed, and *Billboard* printed a Hot 100 chart.

---

[57] Baskerville, 72.
[58] Subdistributors are also known as "rack jobbers" and "one-stops." Also, retailers are personally contacted by *Billboard* chart personnel to collect requested data.
[59] Rachlin, 77.
[60] *Ibid.*, 77.
[61] *Ibid.*, 77.

The tabulation of airplay and sales reports, particularly prior to Soundscan, has received criticism over the years, often involving accusations of manipulation with regard to airplay and record sales inputs that subsequently affected the charts. An example, known as the "payola scandal," involved radio disc jockeys who were accused of accepting payment from record labels in exchange for airing their artist's song.[62] With regard to sales, the inaccuracy and/or exaggeration of reports could have taken place among record stores. While these are relevant and legitimate criticisms, a lack of collaborative evidence suggests that the earlier method of tabulation is most probably credible.

As previously mentioned, professional trade journals such as *Billboard* and *Radio & Records* sequentially rate songs based on information received from BDS and Soundscan, and place songs on various charts.

---

[62] Perhaps the most widely known example of this practice involves the disc jockey Alan Freed. Mr. Freed, among others, was under investigation, and convicted by a congressional committee during the late 1950s for accepting such "payoffs." Also, Mr. Freed is known for disseminating the phrase "rock & roll" over the airwaves to a wider and larger audience during a radio broadcast in 1951.

CHAPTER THREE

GETTING MUSIC TO THE PEOPLE

U2. © Lynn Goldsmith/Corbis

INTRODUCTION

The popular group U2 with their 360 Tour in 2011 is to date the highest grossing tour in history. This landmark was achieved during the group's performance in Sao Paulo, Brazil. Interestingly though, it seems we have come full circle with the notion of "touring" as the most effective way to market one's music to the people at a time when radio, recordings, and social media appear to be the norm. The word "marketing" is indeed the operative word. Today's strategic planning for gaining large revenues involves not only earnings from ticket sales, but from merchandising as well. Merchandising includes

39

CDs, T-shirts, pens, hats, buttons, hoodies, posters, key rings, to name some. With CD sales on the decline in light of digital downloads, and unfortunately, piracy, artists and their record labels are using merchandising as a way to recoup lost revenue of CD sales. Fortuitously however, touring, with its merchandizing booths is one of the best ways to sell CD's as well as increasing their popularity for future ventures. Consumers often want something to bring home, and CDs along with T-shirts are two popular items. So how have we come full circle with regard to touring? Prior to YouTube, Facebook, the Internet, sound recording, and radio, touring was the only way to get music to the people. (An exception to this, of course, is people "traveling" to see their favorite artists.)

Without question, touring allows artists the opportunity to make a personal connection with their fan base in an effort to draw them closer to their creativity and music. With the advent of radio, artists could promote their music to an even larger audience without having to endure the sometimes arduous ordeals that touring can create. And for the consumer it seemed reasonable, as having to get dressed up, perhaps finding a date, and, of course, having ample money which may not have been readily available. Consequently, now one could listen to some of his or her favorite artists in the comfort of their home. A problem with radio in this regard nevertheless was consumers' inability to only hear artist(s), as disc jockeys and program directors were beholding to their sponsors — whose music selections were more market-driven. Soon after radio, however, sound recordings would fill this void as they allowed consumers to listen to their favorite artist(s) repeatedly. Though sound recordings seemed to be the most popular vehicle for disseminating music, television–sound and visual–became the norm, though not at first, for promoting music.

Television was the "next big thing" in the 1940s and 50s, it was not, however, a welcome environment for promoting the new music at that time called "rhythm & blues"/"rock & roll." In fact, this was the underground music of the 1950s and therefore needed to be promoted by word of mouth and most significantly here, touring. Through the socially challenging time leading up to the 1950s and continuing through the early 1960s, mainstream Americans' (i.e., dominant culture) confrontation with the youth's, particularly white teens, interest in African American community and their music left black and white artists of "rhythm & blues"/"rock & roll" to seek other ways to promote their music other than by radio and television. Though there were radio stations during this time like WLAC, WJW, WINS, to name a few, who regularly played this music, these efforts were minimal compared to what could be accomplished by touring. Consequently, touring remained the best way to get music to the people. For both black and white artists public appearances of their rhythm & blues and/or rock & roll music occurred either by touring, by dance shows like *American Bandstand*, and as incidental music in films like *Beach Blanket Bingo*. In order to compete for consumer interests, artists needed to stay abreast of these and other appearances as well as maintain a touring schedule every one or two years. Just around the corner, the feasibility of holding an event where artists from diverse music styles could congregate and individually perform their music in front of tens of thousands of fans became a reality with the Monterey Pop Festival in 1967, and Woodstock in 1969.

Following the 1960s with styles of music like art rock, funk, disco, and early hard rock in the 1970s, touring seemed to be favored among consumers as artists of these styles began to incorporate theatricalism with grandiose stages into their performances. This is particularly true as record sales of albums plummeted again during the 1970s. Though popular music at the time was gaining more acceptance on television it still was not an environment where artists felt welcomed to do what they believed their fans desired. Nonetheless,music executives believed television was the most cost effective way to market their artists, so they forged ahead with plans of finding new ways that accompanied touring to get the music to the people.

MTV logo. © MTV/Photofest

On August 1, 1981, Music Television or MTV had the promise of becoming the best way to market music—much the same as radio did in the 1920s, but now with the ability to see the artists. And indeed, MTV did what music executives and artists hoped it would do, providing a vehicle for promoting music within a platform designed solely for music. Following the success of MTV, the internet began to gain momentum in the 1990s and consumers became captivated by its possibilities of improving life on a number of fronts, including music. Then once again we see hard copy CD sales—the music industry's, composers' and artists' bread and butter—slowly beginning to diminish as many consumers began getting their music via P2P (or file to file) sharing (i.e., free). At the turn of the 21st century there was no question technology was going to be a major player in getting music to the people. With Facebook, MySpace, Twitter, and YouTube, artists and music executives realized that being rightfully compensated for the creativity, time, and hard work that goes into making music recordings was going to be a long and arduous task. At the same time, artists and music executives knew that touring and its complimentary merchandizing was more than ever a necessity for survival in this continual evolution of technology.

Consequently, we see seasoned and new, mature and young, and expert and novice artists embarking on tours. Music festivals like Lollapalooza, Warped Tour, Coachella Valley Music and Arts Festival, and the Bonnaroo Music and Arts Festival allowed artists the opportunity to perform live in front of tens of thousands people. Touring is becoming realistic for seasoned artists as well. What we see happening is an increase of performers coming out of semi-retirement and embarking on performance touring, as well as recording projects. Examples include The Cars, a late 1970s–80s new wave band emerging from a 24-year hiatus (new album: *Move Like This*), and Aretha Franklin (age 69), the "queen of soul", on tour for several dates in 2011.

In addition to touring there exists other means for getting music to the people. For instance, though music can stand on its own, it is frequently used anywhere from minimally to being the featured component within another medium. "Minimal" implies the music accompaniment functions mainly as incidental music. Examples include a theatrical, film or television production depicting a scene at a restaurant or nightclub where a soloist or band is performing (which may or may not be visible in the program). Moderate usage of music in a theatrical, television or film production would be, for instance, the existence of various dance scenes that require music accompaniments. Programs that feature musicians, styles of music, and music events are considered those with maximum music subjects. A few of these include American Bandstand, Soul Train, the Country Music Awards, the Grammy Awards, the Grand Ole Opry television show, and many others. Television commercials also provide another vehicle for disseminating music. Today, a specific song is often used as accompaniment for a product. The following paragraphs discuss ways to get music to the people.

In the United States, music as a business became highly recognized during the latter part of the 19th century as the result of music publishing firms. Certainly music performances as business ventures were evident prior to this time—impresarios, artist managers, producers, and so on had to deal with contracts, marketing, accounting, and other business-related variables. However, music as an entrepreneurial venture, particularly among a large number of non-performers, did not occur until the proliferation of publishing firms and sheet music publications. Known by the moniker of "Tin Pan Alley", these firms enjoyed the profitable market of the music/entertainment industry without any competition for a little more than a quarter of a century. Shortly thereafter, the emergence of two new disseminating mediums of music would forever affect the "business of music"—namely, radio and sound recordings.

After WWI, transmitting sounds through electromagnetic waves, more commonly referred to as radio, and the production of sound recordings were fast becoming the two new methods of disseminating music to consumers. The potential of both technologies was known for some time prior to WWI, but the necessities of war precipitated a hibernation period, postponing both the proliferation of radio broadcasting as well as what would soon be an explosion of sound recordings. Following the war, the business of music quickly arose as a free enterprise that spawned professions, occupations, legislative acts, and the like, which were greatly attributed to these new media. Although the business of publishing sheet music continued to be a successful venture, it no longer monopolized the business of music.

While sheet music continues to play a major role in the dissemination of music, there exist other mechanisms that are responsible for getting music to the people. These include radio, record labels, television programs, video games, music societies, music festivals, music conservatories, educational institutions, athletic events, and, of course the ubiquitous internet. First, however, we begin with sheet music.

SHEET MUSIC

The sale of sheet music of popular songs from television programs, theater and film, and recorded songs is big business.[1] For many songs, though not all, a sheet music publication adds to their lasting popularity. No device is needed other than an instrument to play the music. Even today, in an era where consumers have turned to conveniences such as digital music downloads, there still exists a market for sheet music sales of popular songs from TV, theater and film, and various recordings from a diversity of styles.

---

[1] This is discussed in greater detail in Chapter Two, The Business of Music.

West Side Story Poster. © United Artists Corporation/Photofest

Popular television programs in 2011 featuring music performances that resulted in sheet music publications included *Glee, American Idol*, and *The Voice*. The weekly sitcom *Glee*, now in its third season, features a group of aspiring teenage singers who perform various songs set in a choral, madrigal-like manner. The show also presents various storylines concerning the relationships, competitions, and academic issues typical of most American high schools. The focus of the show is the performance of songs by a 14-member cast, who regularly perform popular songs from current as well as past recording artists. Following each episode, certain songs are published in the form of sheet music. Some titles among current artists include "Rolling in the Deep" by Adele, "Firework" by Katy Perry, "Forget You" by Cee-Lo Green, "Baby" by Justin Bieber, "You Raise Me Up" by Josh Groban, "Born This Way" by Lady Gaga, and "Jar of Hearts" by Christina Perri. Songs such as "Don't Stop Believin'" (1981) by Journey and "Smile" (1936) by Charles Chaplin are among the repertoire of earlier artists.

American Idol. © Fox Broadcasting/Photofest

As America's top vocal competition television show in 2011, contestants on *American Idol* have drawn songs from countless popular artists, and those not so popular, during its history of over a decade. Some popular songs sung by the many contestants over the years that resulted in published sheet music include "1+1" by Beyonce, "(You Want To) Make a Memory" by Bon Jovi, "Home Sweet Home" by Carrie Underwood, "Do I Make You Proud" by Taylor Hicks, and many more.

Competing with *American Idol*, the program *The Voice* sets out to reveal virtuoso vocal performances in a televised competition format. Some popular songs performed by its contestants that resulted in published sheet music include songs and their respective performers such as "Set Fire To the Rain" by Adele, "Here Comes the Sun" by The Beatles, "The Voice Within" by Christina Aguilera, "America the Beautiful" by Samuel Augustus Ward, "Over the Rainbow" by Judy Garland, and "The Edge of Glory" by Lady Gaga.

With regard to sheet music from theater and film productions, music plays a crucial role in "sound painting" the visual canvas with dramatic inferences that can have long lasting effects on the consumer. Published sheet music from theater productions is a result of several factors: 1) songs that are effective in evoking meaning from the text 2) nicely composed compositions that are tuneful and somewhat easy to sing, and 3) songs that become popular due to the actor/singer's vocal performance. (See Figure 3.1 for some selections.) Regarding the film category, songs that become published sheet music are of two types: 1) theme songs; and 2) songs with specific titles. Those of the first type are often titled with (or without) the word "Theme" or "Main Theme." Examples include "Star Wars (Main Theme)", "Theme From Jaws", "Ghostbusters", "Theme From Star Trek", "The English Patient", "Chariots of Fire" "Taxi Driver", "Gone With the Wind", "Theme From Jurassic Park", Theme From Lawrence of Arabia", "Mission Impossible Theme", and "Breakfast at Tiffany's." For the second type, the list below includes published sheet music of today's and yesterday's film productions.

THEATER	FILM
"Maria," "Here Come the Jets," "I Like To Be in America" from *West Side Story* (1961)	"Circle of Life" and "I Just Can't Wait To Be King" from *The Lion King* (1994)
"You're the Top," "I Get a Kick Out of You," and "Anything Goes" from *Anything Goes* (1934)	"Tomorrow," "It's the Hard-Knock Life," and "You're Never Fully Dressed Without a Smile" from *Annie – The Movie* (1982; musical in 1977)
"Shine," "Electricity," and "The Letter" from *Billy Elliot* (2005; film in 2000)	"The Godfather (Love Theme)" and "Speak Softly Love" from *The Godfather* (1972)
"Man Up," "Hasa Diga Eebowai" from *The Book of Mormon* (2011)	"When I Look At You" and "A Different Side of Me" from *The Last Song* (2010)
"I Believe in You," Rosemary," and "Happy to Keep His Dinner Warm" from *How To Succeed in Business Without Really Trying* (1961)	"The John Dunbar Theme" from *Dances With Wolves* (1990)
"All That Jazz" and "Chicago" from *Chicago* (1975; play opened in 1926)	"His Eye is on the Sparrow," "Dancing in the Streets," and "Ain't No Mountain High Enough" from *Sister Act* (1992; musical in 2009)
"Sherry" and "Big Girls Don't Cry" from *Jersey Boys* (2005)	"Dead Man's Chest" and At World's End" from *Pirates of the Caribbean* (2003)
"I Just Can't wait to Be King," "Hakuna Matata," and "Circle of Life" from **The Lion King** (1997; film 1994)	"Raiders March" *from Raiders of the Lost Ark* (1981)
"Supercalifragilisticexpialidocious" and "Chim-Chim-Cheree" from *Mary Poppins* (2006; film 1964)	"You've Got a Friend in Me" from *Toy Story* (1995)
"Music of the Night" and "All I Ask of You" from *The Phantom of the Opera* (1976; film 1925)	"Hedwig's Theme" and "Harry's Wondrous World" from *Harry Potter* (2001)
"For Good" and "Defying Gravity" from *Wicked* (2003)	"Beyond The Sea" from *Finding Nemo* (2003)
"Easy to Be Hard" and "Aquarius" from *Hair* (1967; film in 1979)	"Almost There," "Down in New Orleans," and "Gonna Take You There" from *The Princess And The Frog* (2009)

It is important to note that in addition to popular theater and film productions, popular sheet music sales occur around specific holidays, such as Independence Day and Christmas. For instance, just before and after Independence Day in 2011 sales of popular sheet music songs included "God Bless America" (Irving Berlin), "God Bless the U.S.A." (Lee Greenwood), "The U.S. Armed Forces Medley" (The United States Military Band), "Statue of Liberty" (Neil Enloe), "The Star Spangled Banner" (John Stafford Smith), and "You're a Grand Old Flag" (George M. Cohan). Popular Christmas publications include "O Holy Night," "Ave Maria," "The Little Drummer Boy," "Silent Night," "Jingle Bells," "Deck the Halls," "The Twelve Days of Christmas," "Angels We Have Heard On High", and many others.[2]

RADIO

That music is mainly about listening to the radio is one of the most effective ways of "getting music to the people." During its early proliferation, radio, unlike records that need to be purchased or venues that require costs for various services, was quite a novel way for consumers to enjoy different styles of music without having to pay for it.

Radio broadcasts (as was also the case with sound recordings) began during the late 19th century. By the early 20th century, radio broadcasting using wireless technology made headway as Reginald Fessenden demonstrated the first wireless broadcast in 1906. Broadcasting became solidified several years later with Lee de Forest's (1873–1961) spectacular transmissions from the top of the Eiffel Tower, and from the Metropolitan Opera featuring the famous opera singer Enrico Caruso. Born in Council Bluffs, Iowa, de Forest had been encouraged to follow in his father's footsteps as a minister. Following the family's move to Alabama, where his father became president of Talladega College (an all-black institution), young de Forest became immersed in an upper-class environment combined with the formality of the South. After graduating from high school, he attended Yale University's Sheffield Scientific School and became fascinated with electronics. During his stay there, his fascination got the best of him as an experiment caused a power outage throughout the entire University. Following a suspension, he was permitted to continue his studies, and by 1899 Lee de Forest earned a Ph.D. As evidenced by the title of his dissertation, "The Reflection of Hertzian Waves at the End of Parallel Wires," de Forest, now regarded as an inventor, wanted to apply Heinrich Hertz's (the person after whom *hertz* is named) theories to wireless telephony.

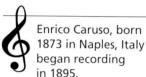

Enrico Caruso, born 1873 in Naples, Italy began recording in 1895.

Throughout the years, de Forest received over 180 patents for various inventions. Two of these stand out with regard to the music industry: the audion (or vacuum tube) and sound for film. The audion, which amplifies a signal, was invented by Lee de Forest in 1906. By 1922 he had invented Phonofilm, a recording process that placed sound and video on film as parallel lines. The development of the Phonofilm process had been delayed by the patriotic commitment to combine resources for the war effort, which effectively curtailed all further advancements in wireless broadcasting for the general public. After the war, de Forest and many others paved the way for wireless telephony, which became the basis for today's broadcasting and sound recording. At this same time, with American radio owned and operated mainly by American companies[3], the Radio Corporation of America (RCA) was formed as a holding company for distributing patents. Very few, however, were afforded its stock. Those that did included American Telephone and Telegraph (AT&T), General Electric (GE), and Westinghouse. By 1920, the broadcast of the results of the presidential race between Warren Harding and James M. Cox on KDKA radio illustrated how useful broadcasting could be.[4]

Soon hundreds of stations were operating throughout the country, offering news, literature, drama, and music. In 1926, RCA developed a subsidiary named the National Broadcasting Company (NBC) that operated two networks: the Red Network and the Blue Network. With regard to music, the former

---

[2] Popular digital sheet music downloads, retrieved July 3, 2011 from http://www.musicnotes.com/
[3] This was the result of acquiring the American Marconi company, which was primarily owned by British investors.
[4] Warren Harding was elected U.S. President and served from 1921–1923.

broadcasted more conservative styles and genres such as opera and light classical, while the latter favored songs popular with Americans such as jazz, marching band music, and, to some extent, blues.

With the success of NBC and the possibilities of radio becoming a viable force in America's economy, after a rough start Columbia Broadcasting Station (CBS) became a rival of NBC in 1927. One major difference between the two networks was their philosophy as to the focus of radio in general. At NBC, headed by David Sarnoff, the focus was placed on using radio to enlighten people through news, literature, drama, and music. Although CBS offered similar broadcasts, its driving force, as set forth by its operator, William S. Paley, was placed on its advertisers.

Here are some pertinent facts about the recording industry.

1. 1919: General Electric (GE) bought the assets of American Marconi from British investors.
2. October 11, 1919: Radio corporation of America (RCA, 1919–1986) was incorporated.
3. 1920: American Telephone and Telegraph (AT&T) and Westinghouse acquired assets from RCA and jointly owned RCA.
4. 1926: RCA formed the National Broadcasting Company (NBC).
5. 1927: United Independent Broadcasters was formed by Arthur Judson, a musician turned talent agent; Columbia Phonograph Broadcasting Company was formed, which later (1929) became Columbia Broadcasting Station. (CBS ceased to exist as an independent company in 1995.)
6. 1932: RCA acquired complete ownership of itself, including NBC, following the Justice Department's antitrust suit.
7. Mid-1930s: RCA expanded its broadcast to advancements in television technology.
8. March 13, 1937: The establishment of forerunner to what is now called CBS World News Roundup.
9. 1938: RCA implemented its own standard to television and sought approval first from the Radio Manufacturers Association (RMA), then the Federal Trade Commission (FTC).
10. April 30, 1939: RCA inaugurated its televised broadcasting, by airing the opening of the World's Fair in New York.
11. 1940: The National Television Standard Committee (NTSC) was formed by RMA.
12. 1941: The FCC finally approved RCA's television standard: 525-line, 60-seconds per field.
13. 1946: CBS began serious efforts to implement television programming, with eventual shows such as *I Love Lucy*, *Gunsmoke*, and *Ed Sullivan*.
14. 1948: CBS gained momentum against its rival NBC as Jack Benny, Grace Burns and Steve Allen, and Red Skelton were signed as personalities.
15. Early to mid-1940s: RCA and others (such as CBS) proposed standards for color television.
16. 1953: Following numerous debates even to the United States Supreme Court, the FCC adopted RCA's color television standard.
17. 1974: CBS was incorporated as its interest included radio, television, music (Columbia Records), a magazine (*Woman's World*), and publishing (Holt, Reinhart, and Winston).

POPULAR MUSIC AND THE VINYL RECORD INDUSTRY

Prior to the vinyl record industry in the 1920s, songs in America became popular mainly through musical theatre productions (minstrelsy and vaudeville), and less significantly by traveling bands, popular dance halls, and supper clubs. Most influential was musical theatre and the subsequent publications of sheet music by numerous publishing houses. Indeed, furnishing music scores for the general consumer was by far the most successful business venture of the music industry prior to the emergence of radio and vinyl records–both in the 1920's. Numerous publishing firms, collectively known as "Tin Pan Alley" supplied music books and sheet music for the growing number of people who were skilled in the art of reading musical notation. With the composition and publication of vaudeville-inspired songs, and the publishing of individual songs of favorite theatrical productions, publishers satisfied the musical tastes of many Americans.

Although many road shows traveled to different areas where people were distinguished by socio-economic class and ethnicity, much of America's early music prior to the vinyl record industry was regional. In other words, music played and performed was generally the result of a region's traditions, needs, and specific tastes. For instance, hillbilly music was generally appealing to southern rural whites, while blues was often more predominant among southern rural blacks. When records and radio were accessible to these two groups, they became aware of musical differences that influenced their musical tastes.

Just before and shortly after WWI, new ways of marketing music to the consumer (radio and sound recordings) began threatening the sheet music publishing business. Although early radio performances and sound recordings involved musical theatre songs and performers, sheet music publishing firms did not benefit. Despite the fact that publishing companies used radio and sound recordings as ways to market their song holdings, they never fully embraced these new technologies. In reality, rather than having to attend a live performance, (which was not possible to do as often as one would like) or play the music oneself, (which often produced inferior results compared to a professional presentation), consumers could now experience their favorite artists at their leisure via radio broadcasts and/or sound recordings.

After WWI, radio broadcasts and sound recordings (regularly manufactured on vinyl records by this time) became the principal methods for disseminating a composer's/publisher's music to the general consumer. With the advent of the vinyl record industry, songs became popular as the result of record sales and radio airplay.[5] Soon after, various record labels executed certain strategies to effectively market their music to the general public. Because these strategies still play a significant role in the music industry today, it behooves the reader to understand the following terms relative to society with respect to music marketing: *culture, youth culture, popular youth culture,* and *popular* or *mainstream culture.*[6]

Culture

Culture is defined as certain traits that are shared by a group of people. These may include language, values, philosophy, ideology, religion (or lack thereof), musical tastes, body movement, eating tastes, and so on.

Youth Culture

As mentioned in the introduction, youth culture did not become a viable market until post-WWII. The term *youth culture* further identifies a specific sub-culture distinguished by a certain age range. Because music-playing devices greatly affect people's access to music (and with today's technological advancements, this access seemingly evolving on a monthly basis) the standard age range constantly shifts. We must also consider civil society's social norms and accepted behavior for members of the youth culture, including their impact on having the means to not only purchase music, but also to attend public performances. Although conjecture and debate still exists regarding an agreeable standard for the youth

---

[5] See Chapter Two, Business of Music, for information regarding the procedure used to tabulate popular records.
[6] Also, see Chapter Two.

culture's specific age range, it generally encompasses ages fifteen through twenty-five, the ages which will also be used in this text.[7]

Popular Youth Culture

Young people have extreme differences in musical tastes.[8] Consequently, it becomes necessary to further distinguish a "popular" youth culture. Rampaging emotions that are often associated with self-identification are typical among teenagers. As an expression of personal sentiments, music facilitates the progress of these teenage psychological stages. Bearing this in mind, there exist three general categories of teenage listening tastes:

1. Those that favor popular or mainstream music,
2. Individuals who favor music only from their generation, who either consciously or unwittingly oppose the previous generation's musical tastes, and
3. Youth that tend to favor certain classic songs of various rock styles from previous generations.[9]

The first category has by far the highest percentage of youth culture listeners.

Popular or Mainstream Culture

Popular or mainstream culture encompasses the widest range of individuals, including people of every age, gender, social status, and nationality. The music of popular culture tends to be less complex musically as well as less politically charged.[10]

TELEVISION PROGRAMS

Without question music performances that appear on television programs (competition shows, sitcoms, and commercials) gain much notoriety and consequently experience a boost in revenue. Programs that incorporate a significant amount of music include *Glee*, *The Voice*, *American Idol*, *So You Think You Can Dance*, *Hannah Montana*, and *A.N.T. Farm*, to name a few. *Glee*, as previously mentioned (see sheet Music section), helps to disseminate previous and current popular songs by performing these in madrigal-like manner (vocal ensemble with instrumental accompaniment). Some songs performed have included (Listed alphabetically) "Born This Way" by Lady Gaga, "Dancing Queen" by ABBA, "I Feel Pretty" from *West Side Story*, "Isn't She Lovely" by Stevie Wonder, "Rolling in the Deep" by Adele, "Try a Little Tenderness" by Otis Redding, and many others. In addition, the performance of these and other songs appear on *Glee*, and recordings are offered on iTunes as digital downloads. With much success, the creators of *Glee* have now started a competition called "The Glee Project" where candidates, on camera, are housed together in Los Angles where they ". . . learn song-and-dance numbers, fine-tune their acting chops . . . As it airs, hopefuls are cut from the competition . . . In the end, the winner will have a seven-episode role on the next season of Fox's *Glee*."

---

[7] At fifteen, one can get a permit to work and therefore earn money to purchase recordings. By 25, one has either completed college and/or is seriously considering settling down (career, marriage, family). In other words, this age represents another stage of maturity.

[8] This observation is based on my personal experience of teaching thousands of students over the years.

[9] There exist other categories such as youth who favor classical music and those that oppose secular music in favor of religious music only.

[10] Trends of popular or mainstream culture are forever changing, and therefore it should be understood that today's underground or non-popular culture could be tomorrow's popular culture.

Kelly Clarkson. © NBC/Photofest

American Idol, as previously mentioned (see sheet Music Section), is one of today's popular televised programs where singers perform songs of varied styles. With millions of viewers every week during its competition period, (which has occurred between eight and twelve weeks), *American Idol* has been one the most watched television program for a number of consecutive years, and therefore is ideal for promoting music. To keep viewers on the edges of their seats, the audience nominates his or her favorite artists by voting, either by text message or phone. The singer with the least amount of votes is eliminated from the show and sings his or her farewell song. Also, a little controversy doesn't hurt the show's rating, as there is often an argument over the wrong person being eliminated. With more women watching American Idol, it is interesting to note that genderism may play a role in seemingly talented women being eliminated from the show. In an article titled "American Idol: 5 Theories Why Pia Toscano Was Eliminated," the author, Shirley Halperin, offers certain theories why girls get cut. She states,

> "Girls don't like girls: It's a longstanding trend on 'American Idol,' whose audience is overwhelmingly female—girls don't vote for the female contestants. Blame it on same-gender envy or the crush factor . . . girls get . . . plucked like the petals of a flower."[11]

---

[11] Shirley Halperin, American Idol: 5 Theories Why PiaToscano Was Eliminated, *Hollywood Reporter*, April 8, 2011.

The Voice is a vocal competition where contestants go through various levels of performance in front of judges who eventually, along with a televised studio audience, determine the best singer. The winner is crowned "The Voice" and receives $100,000 and a recording contract. Most importantly to this discussion is the show's performance of popular songs, past and present. Some of these include "Dog Days Are Over" recorded by Florence and the Machine, "I Will Always Love You" recorded by Whitney Houston, "The Man Who Can't Be Moved" recorded by The Script, and "The Thrill is Gone" recorded by B.B. King. Like *Glee*, performance of these and other songs appear on the televised program and are followed by recordings that are offered as digital downloads on iTunes.

Although not focused on music performance, *So You Think You Can Dance* nevertheless uses music from a diverse number of artists to accompany the different styles and types of dances performed by the competitors. Some of these dance styles and types include tango, hip-hop, jazz, ballet, theatrical, waltz, cha-cha, and several others. Consequently, these dances require music that is most suitable for each dance's inherent rhythmical pattern.

Television commercials provide another vehicle for disseminating music. Often, the music used to draw viewers to the commercial is from a previous generation. As mentioned previously, this is due to the targeted group being those who have greater buying power, usually late 30s and above. That said, some popular songs among the 30-something and above ages include "What I Like About You" (1980) by the Romantics, used in a Raging Waters (water theme park) commercial;the songs "Willie and the Hand Jive" (1958) by Johnny Otis and "Car Wash" (1976) by Rose Royce are used in advertisements for Delta faucets; and "Helter Skelter" (1968) by The Beatles is used in a commercial for the new series of *Red Fraction* video game.

MUSIC FESTIVALS

Music festivals are generally events that occur over an extended period of time, usually two to four days on a given weekend. An exception to this is Coachella, which presently occurs for two-weekends of three days each. Some, but not all, of these festivals include mainly music and other activities such as interactive games, art exhibitions, and, of course, merchandising. There are many music festivals that focus on performances of diverse styles of music, specific styles of music, or those specific to cities and/or counties. The focus here will be on the former. Some noted music festivals include the Newport Jazz Festival (started in 1954), the Monterey Pop Festival (1967), Woodstock (1969), the Monterey Bay Blues Festival (1986), Lollapalooza (1991), Warped Tour (1995), Coachella Valley Music and Arts Festival (1999), Bonnaroo Music and Arts Festival (2002), the NYC Winter Jazzfest (2005), Stagecoach California's Country Music Festival, and the Undead Jazzfest (2010). Music festivals are an effective vehicle for promoting new artists and introduce audiences of varied tastes to other styles and types of music. Some of these festivals generate significant sums of money. For example, an average ticket price of $230 to attend Bonnaroo in 2011 times 85,000 guests equals $19,550,000. Due to earned gate receipts combined with sharing profits from artists merchandising, festival products, food, and so on, if festivals are planned properly they can be quite a lucrative venture as well as an effective way to "get music to the people."

The Newport Jazz Festival, advertised as the First Annual American Jazz Festival, began in 1954in the city of Newport, Rhode Island. Initially, the festival offered an interested audience a lkineup of both old and new jazz artists. During the latter part of the 1960s, festival promoters and business executives wanted to reach a larger audience by bringing together what was actually happening socially and culturally in the music scene in America—namely, music diffusion. Musicians of different styles were borrowing from each other and jazz was not excluded from this approach to music. Consequently artists representing styles such as jazz rock (Blood, Sweat & Tears), blues (B.B. King), funk (James Brown and Sly & The Family Stone), fusion (Miles Davis), hard rock/early metal (Led Zeppelin), and others were included in the 1969 festival. Having undergone a number of changes over the years with respect to location, sponsorship, and issues surrounding some unruly crowds, the festival following a return to Newport in 1981, has seemingly returned to its status as the premier jazz festival in America. Presently, the festival occurs within a three-day period at the beginning of August. Some artists over the years have included (listed alphabetically) Brubeck Brothers, Regina Carter, Ravi Coltrane, Miles Davis, Joey DeFrancesco, Duke Ellington, Michael Feinstein, Ella Fitzgerald, Dizzy Gillespie, Giovanni Hidalgo, Hiromi, John Hollenbeck Large Ensemble, Mario Castro Quintet, Wynton Marsalis, Nina Simone, Esperanza Spalding, Trombone Shorty, Muddy Waters, Randy Weston, and many others.

In 2011 the **Monterey Jazz Festival** celebrated its 54th anniversary. Located on the same property as the well-known Monterey Pop Festival in Monterey, California, the festival in 2011 featured over 500 performing artists on 8 different stages. Unlike most other music festivals, stages for this 3-day event are equally divided between indoor and outdoor venues. Nearly every singer and instrumentalist of jazz music beginning in 1954 has performed at what is frequently regarded as the premier west coast jazz festival in America, or the world for that matter. Only a small handful are noted here (listed alphabetically) Geri Allen, Louis Armstrong, Count Basie, Dave Brubeck, Benny Carter, John Coltrane, Chick Corea, Miles Davis, Joey DeFrancesco, Duke Ellington, Tia Fuller, Dizzy Gillespie, Benny Green, Herbie Hancock, Hiromi, Billie Holiday, Bobby Hutchinson, India. Arie, Modern Jazz Quartet, Thelonious Monk, Carmen McRae, Gerry Mulligan, John Pizzarelli, Joshua Redman, Dianne Reeves, Sonny Rollins, Poncho Sanchez, Esperanza Spalding, Henry Threadgill, Sarah Vaughn, Gerald Wilson, and many more.

The **Monterey Folk Festival** of 1963 opened with prominent performers like Joan Baez, Bob Dylan, Peter, Paul and Mary, and Pete Seeger. It soon became known as the **Monterey Pop Festival** and was held on June 16–18, 1967 in Monterey, California. The sojourn of rock music festivals, this three-day event brought together some of the earliest innovators of rock music like Jimi Hendrix, Janis Joplin, and The Who. Like other festivals of "popular" music, it included artists from a number of different styles such as (listed alphabetically) The Association, Booker T. & The M.G.'s, Big Brother and the Holding Company, Buffalo Springfield, Eric Burdon and The Animals, The Butterfield Blues Band, The Byrds, The Grateful Dead, Canned Heat, Jefferson Airplane, Hugh Masekela, The Mamas & The Papas, Steve Miller Band, Quicksilver Messenger Service, Lou Rawls, Otis Redding, Ravi Shankar, Simon and Garfunkel, and others.

Lollapalooza celebrated its 21st anniversary in 2011 at its yearly location in Grand Park, Chicago, Illinois. A 3-day, multi-stage event that began in 1999, it usually occurs on the first Friday, Saturday, and Sunday of August, and currently boasts over 130 performers. It features a variety of music styles and types and their representative artists. It is interesting to note that the billing for Lollapalooza 2007 displayed Lady Gaga in small print, against those with top billings such as The Black Keys, Daft Punk, Ben Harper & The Innocent Criminals, Iggy & The Stooges, Interpol, Kings of Leon, Modest Mouse, Muse, My Morning Jacket, Pearl Jam, The Roots, Satellite Party, Patti Smith, Snow Patrol, Regina Spektor, and Yeah Yeah Yeahs. Three years later in 2010, however, it was a different story, and Lady Gaga received top billing with artists such as Arcade Fire, The Black Keys, Jimmy Cliff, Cut Copy, Cypress Hill, Devo, Green Day, Hot Chip, MGMT, The National, Phoenix, Soundgarden, Spoon, and The Strokes. Furthermore in 2011, according to an article in Forbes magazine Lady Gaga tops The Celebrity 100 list.[12] Over its 21-year history other performers have included (listed alphabetically) Jane's Addiction, Beastie Boys, Cage the Elephant, The Black Crows, Dashboard Confessional, Billy Idol, Fishbone, Green Day, Ice T, Body Count, Kasabian, The Killers, Living Colour, Los Amigos

---

[12] Dorothy Pomerantz, *Forbes*, May 18, 2011.

Invisibles, Nine Inch Nails, Primus, Sioxsie & The Banshees, Smashing Pumpkins, A Tribe Called Quest, The Verve, Weezer, and many others.

The Warped Tour, also known as the Vans Warped Tour due to its sponsorship by the Vans (shoes) corporation, is a multi-stage music event that began in 1995. Unlike Bonnaroo, which remains in the same location each year, the Warped Tour does just what its name says—it tours. Furthermore, where Bonnaroo occurs over four days, the Warped Tour occurs in one day, but in approx. 44 different locations for its U.S. performances, from the end of July to mid-August. Though initially a domestic-touring event, the Warped Tour is now touring internationally to places in Australia and Europe. In its early years, it focused on young teens that enjoyed skating, BMX biking, snowboarding, and punk music. Currently, performances are from a diverse number of styles and their representative artists. Some performers over the years have included (listed alphabetically): AFI, Anti-Flag, Asking Alexandria, August Burns Red, Big B, Blink-12, Campaigning For Zeros, CIV, Columbyne, Dance Gavin Dance, The Devil Wears Prada, D-12, Electric Touch, Eminem, Face to Face, Flogging Molly, Foxy Shazam, Gatsby's American Dream, Gym Class Heroes, Ice-T, Incubus, Jurassic 5, Katy Perry, Less Than Jake, Limp Bizkit, NOFX, Reel Big Fish, Sun 41, Weezer, and many others.

Coachella Valley Music and Arts Festival, commonly referred to as simply Coachella, began as a two-day event in 1999 held in Indio, California, featuring mainly music, and secondarily sculpture and installation art. Initially it was held in October. Currently, however, it occurs in mid. April. Beginning in 2007, the event spawned over three days and has become an extremely successful event for international and domestic artists alike. Offering a wide array of styles, some performers have included (listed alphabetically) Arcade Fire, Beastie Boys, Björk, Black Keys, Coldplay, Depeche Mode, DJ Shadow, Iggy Pop, Jay-Z, Jurassic 5, The Killers, Kings of Leon, LCD Soundsystem, Madonna, Massive Attack, Paul McCartney, Morrissey, M.I.A., Mumford & Sons, Nine Inch Nails, Pearl Jam, Portishead, Prince, Rage Against the Machine, Red Hot Chili Peppers, Siouxsie and the Banshees, Tool, Kanye West, and many others.

Bonnaroo Music and Arts Festival, which celebrated its 10th anniversary in 2011, is a 4-day multi-stage (9 stages in 2011) music festival that features artists of varied styles. Located on an approximately 750-acre farm in Manchester, Tennessee, the festival also includes (as stated on its official webpage):

> ". . . dozens of epic performances . . . the festival's 100-acre entertainment village buzzes around the clock with attractions and activities including a classic arcade, on-site cinema, silent disco, comedy club, theater performers, a beer festival, and a music technology village."[13]

Over the years styles have included country, blues, funk, gospel, hard rock, hip-hop, pop, metal, punk, rock, traditional rock & roll, and others. Considering the price of $210–$250 for all four nights to listen to numerous performers each day, Bonnaroo is one of today's favored music festivals. Noted performers have included Beastie Boys, The Allman Brothers, The Black Keys, Five Blind Boys of Alabama, James Brown, Cage the Elephant, J. Cole, Bootsy Collins, Old Crow Medicine Show, The Dead, Death Cab for Cutie, De La Soul, Bob Dylan, Eminem, Béla Fleck & The Flecktones, Trevor Hall, Hackenshaw, Herbie Hancock's Headhunters, Nora Jones, Jurassic, Wiz Khalifa, B.B. King, Kings of Leon, Miranda Lambert, Los Lobos, Loretta Lynn, Dave Matthews Band, Mumford & Sons, Neville Brothers, Pearl Jam, Tom Petty & The Heartbreakers, The Police, Preservation Hall Jazz Band, RAQ, Bonnie Raitt, The Roots, Scissor Sisters, Earl Scruggs & Friends, Bruce Springsteen and

---

[13] Bonnaroo, retrieved from www.bonnaroo.com/about.aspx on June 18, 2011.

the E Street Band, Mavis Staples, The Strokes, Toots and the Maytals, Tortoise, Kanye West, The White Stripes, Lucinda Williams, Steve Winwood, Yonder Mountain String Band, and many others.

The NYC Winter Jazzfest began as a one-day event in 2005 during early January. Seven years later it occurred over a two-day period featuring numerous performers at five different venues in New York City. Noted artists have included Aethereal Base–3rd Eye, Amina Figarrova, Bad Touch, Tia Fuller, Charles Gayle Trio, Chico Hamilton & Europhia, The In-betweens, TinekePostma, The Respect Sextet, Matana Roberts, Marcus Strickland Quartet, Dan Tepfer Trio, Doug Wamble, and many others.

Stagecoach California's Country Music Festival marked its fifth year on April 30 and May 1, 2011. The event takes place following the Coachella festivaland has included contemporary (like Kenney Chesney, Rascal Flatts, and Carrie Underwood) and some past country music artists (such as Wanda Jackson, Loretta Lynn, and Earl Scruggs). Artists over its five-year history have included (listed alphabetically) The Gatlin Brothers, Glenn Campbell, Rodney Crowell, Charlie Daniels Band, Eagles, Whiskey Falls, John Fogerty, Kris Kristofferson, Tim McGraw, Reba McEntire, Miranda Lambert, Nitty Gritty Dirt Band, Brad Paisley, Kid Rock, Darius Rucker, Leon Russell, Secret Sisters, Ricky Scaggs, Ralph Stanley and the Crinch Mountain Boys, Sugarland, Josh Turner, Rhonda Vincent, Sara Watkins, and Lucinda Williams.

The Undead Jazzfest is a fairly new event that began in 2010 for jazz musicians and listeners alike. The music generally consists of jazz traditionalists and experimentalists, as well as introducing "new jazz" musicians 2011's event boasted over fifty performers spread out in eleven venues across four boroughs in New York City. Specific areas include Manhattan, and the Park Slope, Gowanus, and Williamsburg neighborhoods in Brooklyn. Some artists appearing within the eleven venues included Aperiodic, Dean Bowman, The Claudia Quintet, Gerald Clayton, Erik Friedlander, Graffito, Marika Hughes, Dave King Trucking Company, Mary Halvorson Trio, ZeenaParkins and The Adorables, Marc Ribot, Jamie Saft New Zion Trio, Satoko Fujii ma-do, and many others.

YOUTUBE AND SOCIAL MEDIA NETWORKS

Founded by Chad Hurley and Steven Chen on September 11, 2005, YouTube is perhaps the most powerful vehicle for disseminating music to the international stage. In an article written by Steve Knopper he asserts that "... YouTube . . . over the past six years has helped break pop superstars from Lady Gaga to Justin Bieber. . ." He goes on to say that Eric Garland ". . . believes YouTube is the number one source for music in the world. . .nearly half of adults listen to music online for free, and 58 percent of those via YouTube . . ."[14] Presently a song's popularity, regardless of its musicality, can be attributed to the number of hits it receives on YouTube. As to why certain songs receive more hits over others, there are several factors that govern this. One, millions of people of all ages and countries are afforded the opportunity, via the internet, to communicate their views about nearly anything without much scrutiny on social networks like Facebook and Twitter. Each user has any number of friends (Facebook) or followers (Twitter) who in turn have their own friends and followers and so on. TA single individual can upload a video or audio of someone singing in their kitchen and (if it's appealing in some way) the video or audio may go "viral." Another factor that may govern why a song goes viral is an individual's remarkable talent. An example would be the video showing Justin Bieber at age four or five standing in his kitchen playing rhythms with his hands on a chair. It is indeed quite extraordinary for an individual at this age to play the types of syncopated rhythms that Bieber is demonstrating. Sometimes a song goes viral because it is"disliked" for one reason or another. An example is the song by the then-13 year-old Rebecca Black titled "Friday" (March 2011). As of June 15, 2011 it has received 166,434, 503 million views on YouTube, with an 88% "thumbs down" disapproval rating. Imagine if the video displayed some

---

[14] Steve Knopper, *Rolling Stone*, March 31, 2011 issue, p. 17).

sort of advertisement? Regardless of the song's like ability, the viewer is exposed to the advertisement, which makes good business. The song has created such a stir that the popular singer Katy Perry includes a significant part of Ms. Black's song in her June 14, 2011 video titled "Last Friday Night (TGIF)."

Not only is YouTube a great mechanism for the listening public, it is also a way to politicize one's message. For example, in 2009 President Lee of the American Federation of Musicians used YouTube,

". . . to carry a message . . . urging interested individuals to sign onto the AFM petition for a legislative fix for musicians to carry their instruments on board planes . . . The new strategies of using YouTube to carry the AFM's message [was] an overwhelming success.[15]

More on the topic of social media, Lady Gaga has gone from minor billing in Lollapalooza 2007 to a major billing in her appearance at the music festival in 2010, to *Forbes* magazines' top entertainer in their Celebrity 100 list of 2011. "The Queen Monster's $90 million in earnings and mastery of social media pushed her past perennial winner Oprah Winfrey."[16] The article goes on to say,

"Gaga is there not just because of the $90 million she earned with a Monster tour, but also because of her 32 million Facebook fans and 10 million Twitter followers . . . who helped move 1 million digital downloads of her recent single "Born This Way" in only five days."[17]

ATHLETIC EVENTS

Music performances at athletic events are yet another way in which songs may become popular, particularly in a major sporting event such as the Super Bowl. Because this event hosts spectators who possess a wide array of musical tastes, it is crucial that music performances be "pop" or diverse as a way to appeal to that wide audience. For example, in Super Bowl XXXIV (2002), Shania Twain, No Doubt, and Sting were three of the featured halftime performers. Shania Twain's crossover marketability is partly due to the use of many different instruments (vocals, fiddle, drums, bass, guitar, and keyboard synthesizer formed and played in the fashion of a guitar), lively danceable music, and lyrical content that does not offend the audience. No Doubt (the Orange County, California punk group who also performed that same year at the 45th Grammy Awards), appeals to both teen and young adult audiences. Consisting of a woman vocalist, drummer, bass, guitar, and synthesizer, No Doubt presents some features of punk music in a "pop" or non-threatening manner (with respect to older spectators). Sting has wide musical appeal and is noted for his lyrical sentiments toward issues concerning humanity.[18] After the performance of Janet Jackson and Justin Timberlake at the halftime show of Super Bowl XXXVI (2004), with the widely discussed and controversial episode of Ms. Jackson's bare breast being revealed on national television, her record label executed a marketing strategy by releasing her new CD earlier than the scheduled date. Inadvertent or not, this exploit undoubtedly generated significant additional revenue for her newly released products (e.g., new CD and a Janet Jackson doll showing a star on her nipples).

A song's particular function can also be attributed to its use in other types of media. In many cases this is an advantage for the composer/artist wanting to sell more CDs. Not all, however, always agree with this strategy. For example, The Kings of Leon rejected the use of their song "Use Somebody" on the popular television sitcom *Glee*. A band member stated they were unfamiliar with the sitcom and the song was being over-marketed at the time.

---

[15] American Federation of Musicians retrieved June 17, 2011 from http://www.afm.org/about/our-history/2000–2009.

[16] Dorothy Pomerantz, *Forbes*, May 18, 2011.

[17] *Ibid.*

[18] In this performance, Sting is accompanied by the instrumentalists of No Doubt.

VIDEO GAMES

Although video games with music accompaniment have been in existence since the 1970s, it wasn't until the 1990s that games like *DJ Hero, Guitar Hero, Karoke Revolution, Red Fraction, Rock Band, Rock Smith, Tap Tap Revenge,* and *Tommy Hawk* included a diversity of either well-known recordings from various artists (such as "Helter Skelter" by The Beatlesin the *Red Fraction* video game series) or featured songs composed for the game which became popular subsequent to the game's popularity. *Guitar Hero* (2005) and *Rock Band* (2007) are two of the most popular video games to incorporate numerous well-known songs of diverse styles, including "Spanish Castle Magic" (1967) by Jimi Hendrix, "Crossroads" (1968) by Cream, "Iron Man" (1970) by Black Sabbath, "Suffragette City" (1972) by David Bowie, "Next To You" (1978) by The Police, "Smoke On the Water" (1972) by Deep Purple, "Killer Queen" (1974) by Queen, "Ace of Spades" (1980) by Motörhead, "I Love Rock and Roll" (1982) by Joan Jett and The Blackhearts, "Should I Stay or Should I Go" (1981) by The Clash, "Cowboys From Hell" (1990) by Pantera, "Symphony of Destruction" (1992) by Megadeth, "Cochise" (1992) by Audioslave, "In Bloom" (1990) by Nirvana, "Learn To Fly" (1999) by Foo Fighters, "Reptilla" (2004) by The Strokes, "When You Were Young" (2006) by The Killers, and "Take Me Out" (2004) by Franz Ferdinand. With the release of *The Beatles:Rock Band* in 2009, sales of *Rock Band* have greatly increased.

THE CLOUD

The second decade of the 21st century offers yet another innovative way to get music to the people. Known as the "cloud", it makes keeping hard copies (vinyl, CDs, DVDs, etc.) of recordings seem like something that may one day be a thing of the past. In the future you can access your entire music collection, residing in a spatial environment, and listen to a selection on any playing device at any time. Amazon, Apple, and Google are all offering services that allow consumers to listen to their music on any device (as long as they have an internet connection). As with any new approach to listening to music, not everyone is sold on this seemingly "green" technology. For instance, those without an internet connection will not be afforded this new approach to storing and listening to music. Also, in order to listen to music already ripped and burned, or purchased another way (other than from iTunes for instance) a monthly service fee (currently approx. $25) will be charged to upload the customer's music to the cloud. Furthermore, failed internet connections, unwanted viruses, or hacked servers, not uncommon today, will undoubtedly cause some frustration. Obvious advantages include the ability to store all music in one location including no physical merchandise, the ability to listen to music on a number of different devices, and contributing to green technology. Another advantage from the viewpoint of the artist, record label, and publisher is that this new approach to listening and purchasing music will help to recoup deserved royalties as the result, in part, of illegal digital music downloading. Perhaps even more stirring from a creative viewpoint is the ability to incorporate smartphone/tablet applications with the recorded music. For example, Björk's album *Biophilia*, is regarded as the first album to include a smartphone/tablet application:

> ". . . built around every song: apps that diagram the song in both conventional music notation and invented graphic notation, that remap the songs as scientific phenomena like (among other things) planetary systems and crystal structures, that encourage to toy with components of the music to create of their own . . ."[19]

---

[19] Jon Pareles, The Cloud That Ate Your Music, *The New York Times*, June 22, 2011.

PART ONE

GENERAL ASPECTS OF POPULAR MUSIC: SUMMARY

Key Terms
- Popular music
- Operettas
- Classical music
- Folk music
- Style
- Sound
- Consonance
- Dissonance
- Form (Organization)
- Timbre
- Rhythm
- Tempo
- Crossover Appeal
- Copyright
- P2P
- Producer
- Licensing
- Royalty
- Performance Rights
- Mechanical Rights
- Music Charts
- Billboard Magazine
- Popular Youth Culture
- Mainstream

Music and Business
- Recording Industry
- Music Licensing Agencies
- Radio Industry
- Recording Industry Association of America
- Music Unions
- Music Festivals
- Social Media

Discussion Questions:
- What is popular music?
- Discuss the two ways people use the term "popular music"?
- How is popular music shaped today? What are some significant factors?
- How is music marketed in today's social climate? Does gender and ethnicity play a crucial role in an artist's level of popularity? If so, how?
- Do music charts represent the best qualities of a style of music? Is there a need to categorize music by ethnicity, e.g. Latin pop songs or Mexican regional?
- In your opinion, what are a few of the most important aspects of the business of music every artist should know?
- Is there an advantage to an artist's offering selected songs for free to entice consumers to purchase their music?

Learning Beyond the Classroom:
Popular music in America is represented by many genres, styles and types, genders, ages, cultures, ethnicities, socio-economic classes, political affiliations, and from moderate to virtuoso composers and performers. Here are some activities one can do beyond the classroom to reinforce learning:

- Attend a live performance anywhere from a singer accompanying him/herself on guitar in a public setting such as a coffee shop or pianist at a shopping mall, to a concert at a major entertainment venue. You might be amazed by your ability to hear music characteristics of the performance based on the knowledge gained from Chapters One, Two, and Three.
- Offer to assist a friend or family member with selecting music for an event. Your understanding of the many different genres and styles of music will be invaluable.
- Most people know of a friend, friend of a friend, sibling, child, or neighborhood band that could benefit by your knowledge of the importance of the business of music. Suggest some resources, or offer to identify components of the music business for their edification.
- As a college student pursuing a career in Communication, Entertainment Studies, Advertising, and Entertainment Law, to name some, visit or apply for an internship at a reputable business among these professions. Perhaps you have interest in managing a friend who is a singer/songwriter/performer or a neighborhood band. Information garnered from Chapters One, Two, and Three will greatly assist in learning about the duties of a manager and/or agent.
- If you are a user of Facebook or Twitter or other social media, perhaps you'd like to conduct your own survey of friends' favorite artists, songs, performance venues, and so.

PART TWO

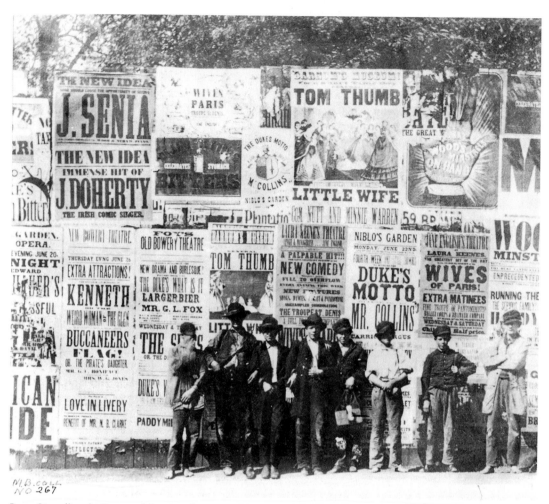

Boys Standing in Front of Posters from Bamum's Museum, Theater, and Minstrel Show.
© The Mariners' Museum/CORBIS

MUSIC AND EARLY AMERICAN SOCIETY

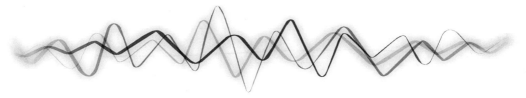

- CHAPTER FOUR: European Origins of Popular Music
- CHAPTER FIVE: African American Origins of Popular Music
- CHAPTER SIX: Popular Entertainment (Minstrelsy, Traveling Road Shows, Vaudeville)

AN OVERVIEW

AMERICAN COLONIAL PERIOD—CIVIL WAR

There is minimal disagreement among scholars as to the time period of the beginning of the American Colonial Period (1607–1783).[1] Most scholars also concur that Europeans from England, Ireland, and Scotland, Africans, and to some extent Native Americans were most instrumental in laying down the foundation of the American spirit. Providing an account of experiences through the written word or by oral tradition, these and eventually people's statements have provided today's scholar and general consumer with a wealth of knowledge about the distant past. Written accounts through newspapers such as the *Boston News-Letter* and the *Virginia Gazette*, town and court records, and information from personal diaries[2] provide early evidence of lifestyles among colonial Americans. Also, the validity of oral traditions can be substantiated from the wealth of information that now exists in written descriptions, musical notation, and representative recordings. These resources continue to be instrumental in piecing together the musical activities of colonists, African slaves, and indigenous peoples. Even though recording devices were not available during the colonial period, we know a great deal about the context of music and its subsequent lyrical themes. A more comprehensive understanding of music's context and place in society can be derived by examining the reasons for European expansion into the New World, with a subsequent focus on early settlements, including the people who lived in them and their lifestyles.

The *Boston News-Letter* was America's first continuously-published newspaper. The first issue appeared on April 24, 1704.

With greater opportunities and prosperity for many Europeans, U.S. population grew from a quarter of a million to nearly three million between the years 1770–1780. Just prior to the American Revolution (1775–1783), the New World was quickly becoming a land where its people were looking to

---

[2] Though numerous testaments about music mainly illustrate the writers' personal biases and limited musicality, they nonetheless are helpful in demonstrating music's function and purpose.

sever their ties from European imperialistic dominance and ideology. Although still greatly influenced by European society, these Americans set out to solidify a truly "American Spirit," first by writing the Declaration of Independence (1776), and then by selecting their first President, George Washington. By the turn of the 19th century, America was progressing in leaps and bounds. At this time, more than ever before a distinction grew between two music traditions: high art and popular. H. Wiley Hitchcock calls these traditions "cultivated" and "vernacular," respectively:

> I mean by the term 'cultivated tradition' a body of music that America had to cultivate consciously, music faintly exotic, to be approached with some effort, and to be appreciated for its edification, its moral, spiritual or aesthetic values. By the 'vernacular tradition' I mean a body of music more plebeian, native, not approached self-consciously but simply grown into as one grows into one's vernacular tongue; music understood and appreciated simply for its utilitarian or entertainment value.[3]

Whether one calls it high art or cultivated, vernacular or plebeian (blue-collar), the meaning is the same. With the Romantic Period nearing (beginning in the 1820s), much of the high art music in America was fashioned after the German tradition of such composers as Beethoven, Liszt, Mendelssohn, Schubert, and Schumann. This chapter focuses on vernacular or popular music between 1784 and 1900: minstrelsy, traveling road shows, vaudeville, theatre, ragtime, early blues, and marching band music.

In addition to these two categories, one could argue in favor of adding "folk music" as a third genre. However, during the majority of the 1800s, this music was generally viewed as ethnic music that grew out of the many different cultures in America—German, Scotch-Irish, Jewish, and African, to name some. It is difficult to generalize about this music as it is strictly related to each individual culture's language, and moral, spiritual, and social behavior.

By the second decade of the 19th century, there arose political, social, economic, and cultural differences between people in the northeast and the southeast. In addition, advances in technology spawned America's Industrial Revolution. The term "Antebellum Period" exemplifies the growing clash between Northern and Southern American ideologies that eventually led to America's Civil War in 1861.

The Confederate surrender in Virginia to the Union in 1865 marked the end of the Civil War, which helped to shape new attitudes, ideologies, and social proposals for the American spirit. In that same year, the Emancipation Proclamation of 1863 (first issued by President Lincoln on September 22, 1862) became the 13th Amendment. The Civil Rights Act of 1866 gave citizenship to black men. By 1869, the establishment of the National Women's Suffrage Association by Susan B. Anthony and Elizabeth Cady to promote women's voting rights empowered women such as Victoria Woodhull, who in 1870 became the first woman to announce her candidacy for the office of the president of the United States. Clearly America was becoming the haven it had longed to become, with states being united on issues concerning race, gender, equality, tolerance and opportunity. Social structures of the Antebellum Period were being substituted with mores that centered on freedom, a rising middle class, and further expansion of the United States.

The population in America increased from 40 million before the Civil War to nearly 80 million just after it and through the turn of the century. With the annual per capita income rising to nearly $1,200.00 after the war (a 50% increase from before the war), a decrease of daily work hours

[3] H. Wiley Hitchcock, *Music in the United States: A Historical Introduction*, (NJ: Prentice-Hall, Inc, 1969), pp. 43–44. It is important to note that Hitchcock also identifies a third tradition, namely folk music, in a footnote, but chooses not to discuss this genre in his book.

(from 12 to 10 hours), and a surge to rebuild the country created a great need for leisure activities, including social and public entertainment.

To accommodate this burgeoning population and expand on these idealistic conditions, America also needed to contend with the indigenous peoples and its former African slaves. During the 1880s, Native Americans began the arduous forced migration to Oklahoma to reside on reservations. The occasion known as the pow-wow became a major social event for the congregating of many different tribes. Described by some as an intertribal get-together and by some as a picnic, the pow-wow included song, dance, drumming, games, and other forms of social entertainment. These activities attracted producers of traveling western shows, who incorporated various Native American singing styles and dances into their programs. The most famous one, *Buffalo Bill's Wild West Show*,[4] opened July 4, 1882, in North Platte, Nebraska, and continued for twenty-five years, touring throughout America and Europe. Consisting of dramatizations of conflicts between natives and pioneers, Pony Express races, General Custer's last stand, and stagecoaches running from bandits, these shows put the producers' concept of the American West on display.[5]

With regard to the free slaves, in 1866 Congress passed the first Civil Rights Act for recognizing and treating African American men as U.S. citizens. All African American men were now able to pursue educational goals as a means for progress and success. In addition to colleges and universities for blacks, such as Wilberforce University in Ohio (1856)[6], Fisk University in Tennessee (1866), and Hampton Institute in Virginia (ca. 1870), various private and government-funded foundations emerged to assist blacks in achieving their goals. Some of these included the Peabody Education Fund (1867), the John F. Slater Fund (1892), the General Education Board (1902), and the Julius Rosenwald Fund (1912).

In New York's cosmopolitan environment, "Immigrants and an urban setting had produced a highly fragmented culture . . ."[7] With the entertainment industry being centered in New York, musical tastes were just as diverse. To suit the many musical tastes, the most popular types of public theatrical entertainment during the last third of the 19th century included blackface minstrelsy (a.k.a. blackface), burlesque shows, traveling road shows, variety shows, and vaudeville. The components of blackface included skits, dances, and songs that were performed as exaggerated representations of black culture. Burlesque shows were generally the same, but with women performing double entendres through turns and high kicks. Traveling road shows included medicine shows, gillies, and carnivals. Variety shows were a hodgepodge of entertainment that evolved into vaudeville, which was developed for family entertainment. Popular music styles during this period included ragtime, country or folk blues, and New Orleans jazz. By the turn of the century, patriotic marches by John Philip Sousa, the theatrical songs of Tin Pan Alley, and the beginning of a distinct American theatre took residence in the hearts of Americans.

---

[4] The *Wild West Show* was created by William Cody, a.k.a. Buffalo Bill.

[5] Another famous act was performed by Bill Pickett, born Willie M. Pickett on December 5, 1870 in Austin, Texas (died 1932 from a head injury caused by a kick from his horse). He was known for creating the "bull-dogger," meaning he could bring down a steer with his teeth. This was done in much the same way bulldogs did, by grabbing the snout.

[6] Wilberforce has the distinction of being the first college for African Americans in the United States.

[7] Henderson and Bowers, *Red Hot & Blue*, p. 7.

CHAPTER FOUR

EUROPEAN ORIGINS OF POPULAR MUSIC

INTRODUCTION

DATE	TITLE	COMPOSER	STYLE
1722	Prelude and Fugue in C Minor from the *Well-Tempered Clavier*, Book I	Johann Sebastian Bach (1685–1750)	Classical
1741	*The Messiah*	George Friedrich Handel (1685–1759)	Classical
1750s	"Yankee Doodle"[1]	Dr. Richard Shuckburg	Folk
1750s	"Barb'ry Allen" (Barbara Allen)	Anonymous (maybe Scottish origin)	Folk
1786	*Le Nozze di Figaro* (*The Marriage of Figaro*)	Wolfgang Amadeus Mozart (1756–1791	Classical
1808	Symphony No. 5 in C Minor	Ludwig van Beethoven (1770–1827)	Classical
1820s	"Turkey in the Straw"	George Washington Dixon (ca. 1800–1861) and/or Robert Farrell	Folk
1857	"Jingle Bells"	James Pierpoint (1822–1893)	
1880s	"Polly-Wolly Doodle"	Anon	Folk

EIGHTEENTH CENTURY POPULAR MUSIC

By the first third of the 18th century, all thirteen colonies were established, but there was still much work to accomplish, and music was not the colonists' primary concern. Still, diversion from the many arduous tasks was desired and folk music generally remedied this circumstance, at least for a while. In a way, the folk music sung and played was distinctive among the many different ethnic and

---

[1] See information later in this chapter regarding the recognition of "Yankee Doodle" as an American song.

enclave communities. Each of these groups sang songs relative to their homeland experiences and, now, in a New World they sang about circumstances encountered while forging a new home, namely America.

America gained its independence from the British Empire in 1776 and soon it needed to get an account of the number and types of people that then resided in its territories. The first U.S. Census in 1790 recorded the following:

English - 48.3%
African - 18.9%
German - 6.9%
Scots - 6.6%
Scots-Irish - 4.8%
Irish - 2.9%
Dutch 2.7%
Native American - 1.8%
French and Swedish - 1.8%

Each of these groups had their own language, religious beliefs (similar and dissimilar), and thus cultural distinctions. Because of these differences, along with the desire to live among those who shared similar beliefs and customs, many lived in segregated communities. Therefore, each community had its own music to use as entertainment, diversion from daily work tasks, socializing and dancing, remembrances of their homeland, and so on. If there was a sense of popular music that was shared by these cultures, it would be that of the dominant British culture. Certainly so, the English controlled those institutions that bound people together as Americans such as government and politics, commerce, education, Protestantism, business, land, social events, and so on. And with these came their dominance of what was deemed American patriotic music; songs children sang in school, and Protestant religious hymns found in hymnals throughout the many different cultural communities. In a sense, one could regard this as being popular music, in that it was music that many people, regardless of their cultural and ethnic traditions, heard at some time or another within and by the aforementioned institutions.

Near the turn of the next century, people's musical taste began to deviate from the typical folk songs of the day in that they favored both as listeners and as performers, more challenging and stimulating music that they perceived as being suitable to their sociopolitical upward mobility. Although their socioeconomic status afforded them greater chances of attaining the necessary musical skills for adequately performing classical music, they lacked the cultural heritage normally associated with aristocrats (i.e., elites or entitled lifestyle, a true desire to play "high art" music). Consequently, there arose a great need for newly composed music as well as for simplified classical pieces for home enjoyment. At this time, opera was also becoming more appealing to the middle class, as its subjects and topics had broadened in content rather than remaining limited to earlier themes of aristocratic society and events.

Comic and ballad operas with their humorous and less serious subject matter were well suited to the musical taste of the emerging middle class. For example, *Le Nozze di Figaro (The Marriage of Figaro)* composed by Wolfgang A. Mozart in 1786, focuses on love and the interweaving of emotions of a servant couple, namely Figaro, the valet of Count Almaviva, and Susanna, the maid servant of Countess Almaviva. One particular comedic scene of the operetta deals with three men who accidentally spy on each other regarding each one's fondness for Susanna.

People in America during the 18th century fashioned their musical tastes around the English culture's two-tier system. In other words, classical music was favored among the more affluent American colonists, while the less fortunate colonists, immigrants, indentured servants, and African slaves favored folk music. America gradually abandoned this practice, particularly after gaining independence from British government. The absence of an imperialistic sociopolitical structure in America created a different way in which people viewed themselves with respect to sociopolitical and economic class. There soon emerged an influx of new ideas among the middle class. (As a matter of fact, America was–and still is–a land of opportunity, an environment where all free people had the right, by law, to pursue any legal endeavors to improve their quality of life.)

Nineteenth Century Popular Music

Consumer interest in more developed music during the 18th century ushered in an even greater desire for this music in the 19th century. Because the Industrial Revolution caused people to move from agrarian-based communities to urban cities, a social culture emerged and set the standard for many others migrating from rural environments. Though many people continued to favor music enjoyed in their former rural environment, it soon became evident that if they were to be successful assimilating, and being aware of the social and cultural mores of the urban cities would be quite beneficial. And certainly developing a taste for classical music was understood to be more conducive to this new environment.

> 1842–New York Philharmonic Society was established.

Lighthearted comic operas (or operettas), with their spoken (rather than recitative and sung) dialogue, remained popular throughout the 19th century. For instance, Richard Wagner's *Die Meistersinger von Nürnberg* (*The Mastersingers of Nuremberg*) premiered in Munich on June 21, 1868. A music drama presented in three acts, three men (knight Walter von Stolzing, Beckmesser, and Hans Sachs) are in love with Eva, the daughter of Velt Pogner, a wealthy goldsmith of Nuremberg. Pogner promises the hand of his daughter to the winner of a song contest. A drama with love, jealously, and unselfish emotions, this opera is woven within the German mastersong tradition.[2]

In America during the last third of the 19th century, a stable middle class was recognized by the music industry as a viable marketing community. Many people frequented comic and ballad opera performances, and in addition there were a growing number of people who could afford other forms of regular music recreation, including both music instruction and subsequent performance for oneself and attendance at nightly professional performances. A significant number of people of varying social classes during the late 19th century and into the 20th century were viewing and listening to the same entertainment presentations on a regular basis. Some of these included theatrical shows such as blackface minstrelsy, operettas, vaudeville, and American theatre; and specific styles of music such as blues, ragtime, and New Orleans jazz (a.k.a. Dixieland jazz). Some popular minstrel songs included "Camptown Races," "Jump Jim Crow," "Old Folks at Home," "Oh! Susanna," "All Coons Look Alike to Me" (formerly known as "All Pimps Look Alike to Me)," "I'm in the Right Church but the Wrong Pew," the already mentioned "Turkey in the Straw", and the popular stage production *The Mulligan Guard*. Popular operettas include *The Mikado* (1885) by Gilbert and Sullivan, *The Wizard of the Nile* (1895), written by Harry B. Smith with music by Victor Herbert; it featured the song "Starlight, Star Bright"), *Babes in Toyland* (1903) by Victor Herbert, *Naughty Marietta* (1910), written by Rida J. Young with music by Victor Herbert; it featured songs such as "Ah, Sweet Mystery of Life" and "I'm Falling in Love with Someone." Ragtime songs became popular due in part to sheet music publications, which allowed even intermediate individuals studying music the chance to entertain his or her guests in private parlors. Some popular songs included "Mississippi Rag" (1897) by William Krell, "Harlem Rag" (1897) by Thomas Turpin, "Maple Leaf Rag" (1899)

---

[2] "German mastersong" is a tradition of lyric poetry from previous centuries.

by Scott Joplin, and "The Entertainer" (1902) by Scott Joplin. The preference and eventual popularity of Vaudeville songs over-shadowed minstrel songs and gave rise to favorites such as shows "After the Ball" (1892) by Charles Harris, "Shine on Harvest Moon" (ca. 1907) performed by Nora Bayes, "Marie from Sunny Italy" (ca. 1910) Irving Berlin, and "Some of These Days" (1911) performed by Sophie Tucker.

In light of this growing common experience, popular music in America became regarded as those particular pieces that were most widely known by the general public, often introduced by professional, amateur, and itinerant performers.

The dissemination of popular music was not as we know it–by recordings–but rather by:

"... live performance. People streamed into vaudeville houses, theatres, and concert halls for their musical entertainment ... Streetside life in the late nineteenth century nourished a musical theatre that spoke for the new American mosaic. The result was a celebration of diverse urban cultures, including the Irish-tinged vaudeville routines of Harrigan and Hart, the Dutch acts of Weber and Fields, and the minstrelsy of Williams and Walker[3]

However, the end of WWI was threatening the lucrative business of sheet music publications and the emerging vinyl record industry. In this context, people did not necessarily need to attend live performances to listen to some of their favorite singers—they were made readily available by sound recordings.

EUROPEAN EXPANSION INTO THE NEW WORLD

Disappointed by the limited amount of potential trade goods discovered in North America–particularly gold and silver–enterprising individuals soon conceived the possibility of colonizing areas in an effort to produce a viable agricultural system that could compete with

In 1587 in Roanoke, Virginia, Virginia Dare (of English descent) was the first American-born child.

European markets. Such a capitalistic venture called for people (European migrants, Africans, and the indigenous peoples) to cultivate the land. To lure people to the New World, early colonists offered free land, particularly to those of humble beginnings in Europe, in exchange for a five-to seven-year service of work (a.k.a. indentured servitude). Many individuals willingly migrated to the New World with the hope of opportunity and good fortune.[4]

An attempt was also made to force the indigenous peoples into slavery. As pointed out by Robert Blauner, this was not an easy task:

North American colonists made several attempts to force Indians into dependent labor relationships, including slavery. But the native North American tribes, many of which were mobile hunters and warrior peoples, resisted agricultural peonage and directly fought the theft of their lands. In addition, the relative sparsity of Indian populations north of the Rio Grande limited

---

[3] Amy Henderson and Dwight Bowers, *Red, Hot & Blue: A Smithsonian Salute to the American Musical.* Washington: Smithsonian Institute Press, 1996, pp. 1, 3.

[4] It should be understood that not all poor migrants became indentured servants, as a significant number of people paid for their passage and found some means of survival once they settled in the New World. In Dinnerstein, Nichols, and Reimers' book, *Natives and Strangers: Blacks, Indians, and Immigrants in America,* NY: Oxford University Press, 1990 the authors state, "... the English occasionally kidnapped laborers and sent them to America. They also used the colonies as a dumping ground for convicts, and between 1718 and 1775 the courts banished at least 50,000 people to the colonies."

their potential utility for colonial labor requirements. Therefore Native American peoples were either massacred or pushed out of the areas of European settlement and enterprise. South of the Rio Grande, where the majority of Native Americans lived in more fixed agricultural societies, they were too numerous to be killed off or pushed aside, though they suffered drastic losses through disease and massacre. In most of Spanish America, the white man wanted both the land and the labor of the Indian. Agricultural peonage was established and entire communities were subjugated economically and politically. Either directly or indirectly, the Indian worked for the white man.[5]

Despite the captivity of a large number of Native Americans, the colonists still needed more people to cultivate the land. It became feasible to establish a system for bringing African slaves to the New World. Unlike indentured servants, slaves were property for life. Resulting from the South's need for physical farming as opposed to the north's "more diverse economy . . ."[6], slaves were a more common sight in the South.

With the combination of the migration of people (primarily male) from many European countries, the African slaves, and the indigenous peoples; the root of the American spirit was being forged in ways only some envisioned, into what subsequently would become one of the greatest nations. Out of this combination of diverse peoples, ideologies, traits, and customs emerged as what is now regarded as America—a globally distinctive culture.

Despite the fact that St. Augustine, Florida—founded in 1565—is the oldest European settlement in America, the early 1600s is recognized as the beginning of the Colonial Period. In 1606, the London Company—a charter of entrepreneurs approved by King James I—sponsored an expedition to Virginia and Jamestown was established in 1607. Although only 32 of the original 101 settlers survived the brutal winter that year, people were determined to make this "New World" their home. In January of the following year, 110 new colonists arrived in Jamestown, and by 1609 people had planted and harvested tobacco—Virginia's primary crop. In 1619, the first legislative assembly occurred in Jamestown, Virginia. Not only did the British pave the way for the eventual establishment of the American colonies, but the Dutch did as well. They occupied what is now Albany, New York, following an expedition headed by Henry Hudson in 1609. Other countries such as France, the Netherlands, Portugal, Russia, and Sweden at some point in time pursued "the establishment of . . . trading posts and colonies around the world."[7] Among the many countries involved, Scotch-Irish and German immigrants represent the two largest cultures that followed the British in colonizing the New World. By the 18th century, immigrants from other countries—among them Jews, French-Protestant, and Irish—also came to America in search of a better life and/or greater opportunities.

By the end of first third of the 18th century, the original thirteen colonies had been established along the eastern seaboard. Beginning with Virginia, founded in 1607, and ending with Georgia, founded in 1732, the other eleven colonies include Massachusetts, New Hampshire, Maryland, Connecticut, Rhode Island, Delaware, North Carolina, South Carolina, New Jersey, New York, and Pennsylvania.

---

[5] R. Blauner, in "Colonized and Immigrant Minorities" in *From Different Shores: Perspectives on Race and Ethnicity in America*, edited by Ronald Takaki, Second Edition, (NY: Oxford University Press, 1994), p. 150.

[6] Dinnerstein, p. 27.

[7] Dinnerstein, Nichols, and Reimers. *Natives and Strangers: Blacks, Indians, and Immigrants in America*, NY: Oxford University Press, 1990, p. 3.

MUSICAL STYLES AND DANCING ACTIVITIES DURING THE COLONIAL PERIOD—OVERVIEW

109th CONGRESS

1st Session

H. CON. RES. 51

Expressing the sense of Congress regarding the primary author and the official home of "Yankee Doodle".

IN THE HOUSE OF REPRESENTATIVES

February 9, 2005

Mr. McNulty submitted the following concurrent resolution; which was referred to the Committee on Government Reform

CONCURRENT RESOLUTION

Expressing the sense of Congress regarding the primary author and the official home of "Yankee Doodle".

Whereas the song "Yankee Doodle" is humorous, patriotic, and dates back to the colonial period of America;

Whereas "Yankee Doodle" was popular from its inception, spreading throughout New England and the Middle Atlantic States, where it was sung at parades, in taverns, and beside campfires;

Whereas the British soldiers, known as Redcoats, began singing the song at the beginning of the American Revolution as a means of deriding the rag-tag Continental Army;

Whereas, after the Battle of Lexington, "Yankee Doodle" became an anthem and a source of pride among the rough-hewn Americans who were taking on the polished British Redcoats;

Whereas, while the tune of "Yankee Doodle" originated in Europe as a common air, many claims as to the authorship of the lyrics have been made;

Whereas, despite the other claims, Dr. Richard Shuckburgh, a British Army surgeon who served on America's frontier for most of his adult life, is today generally considered to be the primary author of the lyrics to "Yankee Doodle"; and

Whereas Dr. Shuckburgh is believed to have written almost all, if not all, of the lyrics for "Yankee Doodle" at Fort Crailo in the present-day city of Rensselaer, New York, after viewing the provincial forces gathered there during the 1750's for an attack on Fort Ticonderoga: Now, therefore, be it

Resolved by the House of Representatives (the Senate concurring), That it is the sense of Congress that—

(1) Dr. Richard Shuckburgh should be recognized and honored as the primary author of "Yankee Doodle"; and

(2) Fort Crailo, located in the city of Rensselaer, New York, should be recognized as the "Home of Yankee Doodle".

The purpose of exhibiting the 51st Resolution by the U.S. Congress is to offer a time frame of what many believe is an American song, and music's transnational character that can occur in two or more countries, and here between Europe and the New World at the time of the Colonial Period.

Just prior to the colonists' arrival in the New World, music genres and styles in Europe included opera, polyphonic sacred and secular music, madrigal singing, concertos, preludes, fantasies, suites, waltzes, and so on. These and other styles and types of music are attributed to composers such as Johann Sebastian Bach, William Byrd, John Dowland, Joseph Haydn, Claudio Monteverdi, Thomas Morley, and Thomas Welkes.

But for the early colonists music activities can be segregated into folk songs (secular) and religious songs. Because most people lived in rural environments during early colonization, music activities often occurred informally. People sang songs or listened to others while working or relaxing, and these songs were accompanied by violin (fiddle), flute, Jews harp, hautboy (oboe), bugles, and/or drums.[8] Albert Stoutamire provides an excellent report of "advertisements concerning musical instruments found in the *Virginia Gazette* from 1751 through 1779. . .": An excerpt is provided here.

September 5, 1751 ....To be sold . . . "A spinet"
June 25, 1752 ....Meeting to consider the church "organ to be sent for."
February 12, 1762 ....For sale–Jew's harps & violins
(PD) April 11, 1766 ....For sale–fiddles & Roman strings
(PD) July 25, 1766 ....For sale–violins, German flutes, violin bows, bridges, pegs, and strings (in Norfolk)
(PD) June 4, 1767 ....For sale–bugles, Roman strings, and long fiddle sticks
(PD) January 8, 1767 ...."Spinets and harpsichords made and repaired"
(PD) September 17, 1767 ...For sale–"A very neat hand organ"
(PD) December 3, 1767 ..For sale–hunting horns, Roman fiddle strings, and long fiddle sticks
(R) July 14 , 1768 ....Lottery for raising money to build a new church and the purchase of an organ (in Fredericksburg)[9]

It is probable that singing occurred as soon as humans expressed (whether in sung, spoken, or uttered nuances) personal sentiments about their surroundings. Unfortunately, the absence of recording devices cannot support this claim, so musicologists and anthropologists have relied on artifacts left behind, and oral tradition to identify songs of long ago. We can safely assume, however, that songs were frequently passed from generation to generation through oral tradition, and therefore are fairly accurate. Such an assumption is based on the notion that music played a vital role in people's lives, whether as social commentaries and/or personal expressions concerning issues of the frontier, personal sentiments about the homeland, or merely for entertainment. Indeed, singing is one of the most remarkable modes of expression that is characteristically human. One can presume that people, particularly during the American Colonial Period, utilized words that were unique to their socioeconomic and sociopolitical situations. And because of one's sociocultural and/or maternal ties, within this new environment songs were learned and sung without the relevance or potency experienced by previous generations, which were in their homeland across the Atlantic. Nevertheless, the same tunes (with perhaps some variation) and similar words were sung and handed on to the next generation.

---

[8] Most colonial ships were not large enough to frequently transport large instruments such as the pianoforte and harpsichord.
[9] Albert Stoutamire, (1972). *Music of the old South: Colony to confederacy.* Rutherford, NJ: Fairleigh Dickinson University Press, p. 30

Dancing was another pastime that occurred as a diversion from arduous agricultural duties. Particularly in the South, people enjoyed classic French dances such as the *cotillion* and *quadrille* as well as country dances, all in the same evening. By the end of the first third of the 18th century, dancing schools appeared in the South to smooth the progression of men into gentleman status.[10] Whether among the colonists, indentured servants, or slaves, dancing was generally favored as it proved to be an effective social function that required minimal planning. Depending upon their status (i.e., free or slave), colonists often set aside Friday and/or Saturday nights for socializing, using dancing as a means to divert their minds from their daily responsibilities. The fiddle provided the initial accompaniment at these dances, with the eventual addition of guitar and banjo.

SINGING DURING THE COLONIAL PERIOD

While dancing was quite a common activity during early colonization, singing was even more ubiquitous, as this activity encouraged camaraderie among individuals. The songs that developed expressed the personal concerns of the "folk," and are generally regarded as folk songs. During early colonization, a large body of folk songs existed among both Europeans and African slaves.[11] For both groups, music served many purposes: social comfort, diversion from daily work, and entertainment. The repertoires, particularly the lyrics, differed with each group's social environment. Freedom was the dividing line for the Europeans: opportunities abounded for moderate to wealthy colonists and provided numerous subjects for music making. Even though a significant number of indentured servants were treated not much better than slaves, they were mobile and consequently found themselves in a wide variety of environments. Moreover, hope as a motivational stimulus surely endured, as their servitude was not interminably lengthy. Although moderate to wealthy colonists and indentured servants were of two different sociopolitical/economic classes, they shared some of the same songs with respect to memories of the mother country. For the African slave, on the other hand, music activities were restricted to three social contexts: work, recreation, and worship. As a result, specific lyrics that were expressed in these contexts encapsulated the emotions of oppression and despair.

Exploring the work habits and responsibilities of both indentured servants and slaves, one finds some similarities in their singing practices:

1. People sang songs as a means of diversion from physical labor.
2. Singing proved to be one of the most comforting modes of expression concerning personal feelings.
3. *A cappella* singing happened more frequently than singing with instrumental accompaniment.
4. Vacillating between the major and minor third is one of the most salient practices used by both folk singing groups.[12]
5. There exist certain metaphysical modes of expression, albeit articulated from different cultures and sociopolitical/economic classes, when emotions of melancholy, hope, recreation, and sanctification are expressed by the human voice.

---

[10] In the South, ballroom dance occasions frequently followed the evening's music concert or performance.

[11] This is not to ignore the possible musical contributions of the indigenous people to American folk singing, but since language was a barrier and confrontational matters were unresolved between them and the Europeans, it is difficult to confirm specific contributions.

[12] The recording of "House Carpenter" illustrates this idiosyncratic practice of folk music, and consequently country and blues.

Even though indentured servants and slaves were socially segregated, one can't ignore the similarity of their singing practices.[13]

The inescapable influence of musical ideas between whites and blacks, which occurred primarily through agricultural employment, was rapidly diminishing by the beginning of the 18th century. It soon became evident among many people that country music was for whites, while blacks were the only ones who experienced the blues. Although this opinion still lingers today, one can't deny the crossover-appeal of the stylistic qualities of artists like Shania Twain, Willie Nelson, and Ray Charles, to name just a few. In any case, the reader should be aware of similarities between country and blues music, and furthermore be cognizant of their shared roots—namely, folk songs.

SINGING AMONG THE COLONISTS

Beginning in the early 1600s, songs by the British and Scotch-Irish represented one of the largest bodies of musical repertoire that had a sustaining effect on the lyrics, function, and manner in which folk songs were presented in America. Transmitted orally from generation to generation, these songs were used to:

1. Entertain,
2. Educate,
3. Pacify, and
4. Express personal sentiments.

Personal sentiments are represented in the largest percentage of songs. Typical themes include:

1. Love,
2. Death,
3. Infidelity,
4. Morality, and
5. Religion.

A number of songs incorporate several themes within their content. For example, the song titled "The House Carpenter"[14] speaks about a woman who leaves her husband and baby for another man who promises her a "better life," which is referring to the New World. She departs with him, leaving her husband and baby, but mourns en route to the New World because she'll never see her baby. Something causes a leak in the ship and it sinks, killing all aboard. A similar story is told in the song titled "The Gypsy Davy,". Here, a woman leaves her aristocratic husband and baby for a seemingly free-spirited gypsy named Davy. Upon discovering his wife with the gypsy at a campfire, the husband asks if she will abandon her family. Her poignant response in essence says she will forsake her husband but not her baby.

Because men represented the majority of white settlers, songs, whether sung by men or women, often tell the story from the male viewpoint. Such is case in the song titled "The Rich Old Farmer." In the song a man speaks of a rich farmer who has an only daughter who is beyond comparison to other women. Mesmerized by her tall, slender, and delicate body, a certain young man desires to marry her, but first

---

[13] This continued well into the early 20th century, as evidenced by country musicians who worked alongside blacks. Around 1913, Bob Wills, for example, was influenced by black blues music as the result of working in the cotton fields alongside blacks in Hall County, Texas.

[14] This and the following songs are on the album titled *Anglo-American Ballads* edited by Alan Lomax. Library of Congress, Division of Music, Recording Laboratory, AAFSL1, 1956.

needs to cross to Missouri in search of work. Prior to his leaving, they vow to stay together until death. After kissing and shaking hands, he sets out for Two Pikes, Missouri where he finds plenty of work as well as an abundance of whiskey. One day, while walking in the public square, he comes upon the mail boat. Even before receiving a letter from the postman, he becomes apprehensive. Upon reading the letter the postman gives him, he discovers that his true love has married another man. Broken-hearted, he goes around rambling on about his misfortune and alluding to the possibility of never seeing his parents again, there is no need to return home. Even though the song's lyrical content deals with despair, it is interesting to note that it is sung in a 6/8 meter at a moderate tempo. Generally, this type of rhythmic character would be used for more festive occasions. Perhaps it shows that singers or practitioners at this time made attempts to present songs in a rhythmically interesting manner despite their lyrical content.

The song titled "One Morning in May" is about the death of a young woman. We can presume she is young, as there is a passage where she asks her "parents" to come and visit her dying body. The song tells the story of a woman who likes pleasure and drinking. Too much of this causes her to end up in jail, and soon she is on her deathbed. She asks her mother and father to come and pity her soul. She is bedridden with headaches, heartaches, and knows she is about to visit death. The next part of the story is interesting, as she sends for the preacher, knowing she is bound to die, but also calls for the doctor to come heal her wounds. Such hope quickly fades, and she makes the statement that she, perhaps intuitively, knows her body is doomed for hell. Finally, she asks for three young ladies to seal her coffin, and requests four young ladies to hold white roses while they carry her to the grave.

A favorite song among many titled "Barbara Allen" recounts the story of a man named William who is lying on his deathbed and asking to see his beloved Barbara Allen. So consumed are they with love for each other, the lyrics reveal that after William's death on Saturday, Barbara Allen dies on Sunday, and they were both buried on Easter Monday.

A common experience among frontiersmen that was expressed through song was their confrontation with the indigenous peoples. The song titled "The Sioux Indians" describes frontiersmen and their seemingly hopeless success of prevailing over the indigenous peoples with only a limited number of colonists against hundreds of Sioux. Songs such as this left an irrevocable hatred for the indigenous peoples in the hearts of many colonists and frontiersmen, especially when such experiences frequently death through bows and arrows.

The devil is also a common character in these songs. The song titled "The Farmer's Curst Wife" is a tale about a farmer who offers his mean-spirited wife to the devil. Upon the devil's acceptance, it is quickly discovered that the wife will kill everyone in hell. She is returned to the farmer—who is on his deathbed—and kills him. The moral of the story, although flawed, is that women can be as evil as the devil. Another story about the devil is the song titled "The Devil's Nine Questions." Clearly a song to encourage religious and spiritual morality, the devil poses questions that, if answered incorrectly, will result in his owning the person's soul. (Biblical questions are not posed here, but rather general inquiries.) Although songs specifically naming the devil are not as frequent, the use of the word hell appears in numerous folk ballads.[15] The song titled "Pretty Polly" is about a man who kills his true love Polly and leaves her lying dead and alone. Eventually his actions replay in his mind so many times that he finally comes to the point of accepting the fact that he is going to hell.

A sense of conviction is one of the most appealing aspects of these and other folk songs. The listener is quickly drawn into the song as the result of the singer's apparently testimonial performance. The attention is quickly placed on the lyrics and not the singer because the singing is performed without vocal virtuosity, with imperfections in pitch, and is often sung *a cappella*. Indeed, this focus on lyrics is

---

[15] A fuller discussion of religious music activities among the colonists is provided in a separate section.

one of the most traditional and appealing qualities of folk singing. To solidify this, folk songs generally entail a simple melody that is set to a number of verses. The simplicity of the melody with its accompanying rhythm makes it easy both to listen to and sing.

Over the years, some of the more popular folk songs sung by the English, Scottish, and Irish have become a part of America's musical heritage. These include "O Dear, What Can the Matter Be," "God Save Great Washington," "Soldier's Joy," "What a Beau Your Granny Was," and the well-known "Yankee Doodle." Even "The Star Spangled Banner" is European in origin. While Francis Scott Key wrote the lyrics in 1814, the melody of "The Star Spangled Banner" came from a British drinking song. In 1931, it was adopted as the U.S. National anthem.

18TH CENTURY: POPULAR MUSIC ACTIVITIES

With colonization well under way, people had more time for cultivating the arts. Performances by professionals and those seeking professional careers in music became more commonplace during the 18th century. The first concert took place in Boston during the first third of the century, and in Charlestown the first opera (the ballad opera *Flora: Or The Hub and the Well* by Colley Cibber) was performed in the courtroom on February 18, 1735.[16]

People from many walks of life began to show interest in performing as well as composing and selling their own songs. As seen in the following quote, Benjamin Franklin (1716–1790), at about 16 years old, began taking an interest in ballad writing. The quote also illustrates several points about music activities and ideas among the colonists concerning social singing and songs:

> I now took a fancy to poetry, and made Some little pieces; my brother, thinking It might turn to account, encouraged me, and put me on composing occasional ballads. One was called The Lighthouse Tragedy, and contained an account of the drowning of Captain Worthilake, . . . the other was a sailor's song, on the taking of Teach (or Blackbeard) the pirate. They were wretched stuff, in the Grub-street-ballad style; and when they were printed he sent me about the town to sell them. The first sold wonderfully, the event being recent, having made a great noise. This flattered my vanity; but my father discouraged me by ridiculing my performances, and telling me verse-makers were generally beggars.[17]

HIGH ART MUSIC ACTIVITIES: 18TH CENTURY

These musical activities included operettas, sacred music concerts, and various genres that fall under classical music idioms such as symphonic/orchestral concert, concerto, and opera. Musical activities such as these were particularly intended for European aristocrats or those among the upper class, hence the designation "high art."

Because early settlers were preoccupied with colonization, they did not initially have the facilities or professional musicians suited to the production of high art music. By the late 17th century, cities such as Boston, Philadelphia, New York, and Charleston had large populations, and consequently entertainment first appeared in those colonies. With the migration of more music professionals and the subsequent construction of accommodating facilities, music performances ensued with works by notable composers such as J. S. Bach, Beethoven, Mozart, Handel, and Haydn.

---

[16] This and the ensuing section–18th and 19th centuries respectively–provide information on popular or non classical music styles. Classical or Western music styles are discussed under the heading "High Art Music Among the Colonists."

[17] Benjamin Franklin, *The Autobiography of Benjamin Franklin*, (NY: Macmillian Press), 1962, p. 9–10.

As previously mentioned, *Flora: Or The Hub and the Well* by Colley Cibber was the first opera performed in the New World (February 18, 1735). It was not until 1750, however, that opera was well received in America. John Gay's *The Beggar's Opera* was performed in New York and was a great success. First performed in 1728 in England, Gay's work surpassed all expectations by playing for an unprecedented sixty-two weeks.[18] Regarded as the first ballad opera–often a parody on some serious aspect of the popular Italian opera tradition and society–Gay's comedy delivered the story utilizing dialogue and singing organized in three acts rather than the typical five acts. Furthermore, Gay utilized familiar tunes, called *ballads*, including a few from noteworthy composers like Handel in an effort to appeal to a broad audience. As is the case with many operas, *The Beggar's Opera* is a love triangle between Macheath (highwayman), Polly (Macheath's fence's daughter), and Lucy (the jailer's daughter). Somehow it is revealed that Macheath is married to his daughter, Peachum–an action that will land him in jail. Polly warns him, and Macheath, determined to avoid going to jail, flees to an area where he frolics with whores who eventually betray him. Now in jail, Macheath is confronted by Lucy (the jailer's daughter), who helps with his escape. Before long he is captured and returns to jail. The story winds down as the jailer brings in four other wives of Macheath, each with a child. Macheath finally concedes his lascivious lifestyle and is sentenced to be hung. The Beggar–who also introduced the story–appears in an adjacent scene with people "begging" him to change this sad scene to a happy one. Agreeing to this, the Beggar asks Macheath to select one wife.

With such great success, by the mid-to-late 18th century two opera houses were established in the United States: The American Company (a.k.a. The Old Company) in New York, founded in 1752; and The New Company in Philadelphia, founded in 1792. With these and other performance venues doing well, there emerged a demand for sheet music. It is reported that over 15,000 songs were published in the years following the American Revolution to the beginning of the Antebellum Period (circa 1920). Although full-time employment as a musician was not feasible, the possibility of earning money by composing songs for possible sheet music revenue combined with performing and giving music lessons encouraged European musicians to migrate to the New World.

POPULAR MUSIC ACTIVITIES: 19TH CENTURY

Prior to the Civil War, composers such as Stephen Foster wrote songs with the intent of capturing the American spirit. Songs such as "Beautiful Dreamer" and "Oh, Susanna" have left an indelible impact on the music scene in America.

The singing of holiday music was also a favorite pastime among people at this time:

> In an era of hard work, rural isolation and monumental inhibition holidays were liberating occasions. . . . So strongly felt was the need for this kind of lusty communalizing that many U.S. holidays got their start as national institutions in the decade just after the Civil War.[19]

Memorial Day was the most significant holiday after the war. Initiated by John A. Logan, this holiday celebrated the living and dead veterans of the Civil War, Mexican War, and the War of 1812. The significance of this holiday to music is the fact that the brass band–the most favored type of band during the late 19th century–accompanied the many parades that honored the men and women who fought in these wars.[20]

---

[18] It is reported that *The Beggar's Opera* inspired the development of Covent Garden–London's most famous opera house.

[19] Editors of Time-Life Books. (1999). *Prelude to the century: 1870–1900*. Alexandria, Virginia: Time-Life Books. Arbor Day, started on April 22, 1875 by J. Sterling Morton, was another holiday that began after the Civil War. Arbor Day was established in an effort to plant trees around the countryside.

[20] Independence Day, although a holiday that began before the Civil War, was also celebrated with parades and brass bands.

Some popular Civil War songs included "Abolitionist Hymn," "Davy Crockett," "Santa Ana," "Battle Hymn of the Republic," "Lincoln and Liberty," "Bonnie Blue Flag," "Lorena," "When This Cruel War Is Over," "Farewell Mother," "There Was an Old Soldier," "General Patterson," "The Cumberland's Crew," "Cumberland Gap," "When Johnny Comes Marching Home," "In Charleston Jail," "All Quiet Along the Potomac," "Longstreet's Rangers," "Roll, Alabama, Roll," "Abe Lincoln," and "Old Rebel."

Over the centuries, people have expressed their emotions through music about seemingly every historical event and most common situations. Organized by the audio collection titled *Celebrate America [sound recording]: An American Folksong Archive*, some examples of the many categories of folk music that have occurred over the years include:

Colony days
Revolutionary War
Songs of battle
Play parties/courting
Westward movement
Civil War
Political campaigns
Cowboy songs
Bad men ballads
Tall tales and nonsense
Railroad songs
Rivers and lakes
The open road
Loggers and miners
Sea shanties
Farm songs/city songs
Imported folk songs
World War I
More American voices
World War II

Some familiar folk songs in America include "Yankee Doodle," "John Henry," "The Blue-Tail Fly," and "Frankie and Johnnie."

Children's songs are also considered to be folk songs. After all, folk songs are not only used for expression, but also for:

Education	– "Alphabet Song" and "Counting Song"
Religion	– "He's Got the Whole World in His Hands"
Celebration	– "Happy Birthday"
Camaraderie	– "Clap Hands"

RELIGIOUS MUSIC ACTIVITIES

In addition to secular songs, the colonists also brought their religions and religious beliefs to the New World. Indeed, many of them left Europe to escape religious persecution. In many ways, America was a religious refuge, as many Europeans experienced numerous religious battles in their homelands:

1. Catholics persecuted Mennonites in the mid-16th century.
2. In 1555, John Rogers–a Catholic priest who converted to Protestantism–was burned alive by the authority of Queen Mary and thus became the first Protestant martyr.
3. In 1562, Catholics killed many Huguenots/French Protestants. Ten years later in Paris on St. Bartholomew's Day, August 24th, thousands of Huguenots were massacred by Catholics. It is reported that by the end of the next century, some 400,000 Huguenots had immigrated to the New World.
4. An early 17th century engraving shows Huguenots mutilating a Catholic priest by tearing out his insides and forcing one priest to eat another one's grilled genitals. Engravings also show priests being buried alive[21]
5. Jesuit John Ogilvie was hanged and then mutilated in 1615.
6. In 1641, Irish Catholics forced one hundred Protestants from Loughgall Parish, County Armagh, to their death by drowning them in the River Bann near Portadown, Ulster.
7. Jesuits Brian Cansfield and Ralph Corbington died at the hands of English Protestant authorities. The former died in Yorkshire in 1643, while the latter was hung by London authorities in 1644.
8. In 1731, some 20,000 Lutherans were expelled from Austria by the Catholic Archbishop Leopold von Firmian.

These examples of religious persecution clearly show that people had different religious beliefs, and were willing to resort to violence to defend those beliefs. Immigrating to the New World was one way Europeans could, to some extent, escape persecutions and be able to freely worship without conflict.

In the early 1600s, religious fervor was not compromised by having to deal with the many arduous tasks of daily life in the New World. Colonists strove to make their religious beliefs the cornerstone for acquiring peace, worth, and success in their new world. Indeed, striving for religious perfection was the main agenda for many. As pointed out by Barlow and Dates, the British considered the Quakers to be the truest of religious people who based their life on a Puritan values.[22] It was this particular ideology that greatly influenced early religious musical practices. For instance, songs were frequently sung *a cappella* as a way to focus more on the words, as for many, any instrumental accompaniment would cause people to lose the true essence of God's Word. Nonetheless, singing encouraged religious camaraderie among the congregation and consequently the community, as Martin Luther states:

"Next to the Word of God, Music deserves the highest praise. The gift of language combined with the gift of Song was given to man that he should proclaim the Word of God through Music."[23]

Early religious music among the colonists included psalms and hymns.[24] Psalms were most frequently sung during religious days as well as on various sacred and secular occasions. Among the early colonists, particularly the Dutch and English in the North, psalm singing occurred at Sunday worship services, funerals, weddings, holidays, and family prayer meetings in the home. In those settings where a congregation was present, a person generally known as a *precentor* would sing a phrase of a psalm,

---

[21] Engraving from Richard Verstegen, *Théâtre des Cruautez des Hérétiques de notre temps* Antwerp: Adrien Hubert, 1607, Folger Shakespeare Library, Washington, D.C. (3)
[22] See Barlow and Dates, *Natives and Strangers: Blacks, Indians, and Immigrants in America.*
[23] Martin Luther (1483–1546)
[24] Although religious songs were not considered to be popular during this time, certain songs were favored by people of particular religious sects, geographical areas, and ethnic groups.

and the congregation would respond with some variation. Congregations read the responses scripturally (i.e., word for word) from the Book of Psalms in the *Holy Bible* or from a book called a *psalter* that contained favorite psalms. The *Bay Psalm Book* (published in 1640), which only contained text, is the earliest psalter reported in the English colonies.[25] Because most people at this time were unskilled in the art of reading musical notation, there was no need for it. Instead, the precentor would apply a favorite tune to a particular psalm. In general, songs were sung in unison with either a *rubato* (no distinct tempo) or slow tempo.[26] It should be pointed out that although psalms were frequently sung in unison, some occurrences of harmonic psalmody were also done.

> "[It] should not surprise us that polyphonic arrangements of psalm tunes, for enjoyment at home, were soon forthcoming. In England, Damon's psalter of 1579 contained four-part settings, and in 1592 Michael East (Este) enlisted the aid of prominent composers of the day (John Dowland, Giles Farnaby, Michael Cavendish, and others) to provide polyphonic settings for his psalter. Two later and very popular collections of harmonized psalm tunes were Richard Alison's of 1599 and Thomas Ravenscroft's of 1621. . ."[27]

Many people, however, held a similar view to John Calvin (Swiss-French protestant leader) regarding the singing of religious music. He believed that music for congregational singing or even music sung by trained choirs should not be difficult, as is the case with polyphonic music. To encourage singing among the congregation, stout Calvinists produced a psalter in 1562 that contained people's favorite popular melodies, and altered Catholic melodies and other hymns.

The singing of psalms functioned as liturgical music and was most suitable to the Puritan way of worship. It gradually became outdated as interest grew in hymnal singing. Prior to the growth of hymnody, music instruction in note reading was encouraged by some churches to help people sing with greater accuracy.

As early as March, 1722, Boston had a Society for Promoting Regular Singing, with a core of about ninety who had learned to read music. From that time on, the singing school, convened to learn, practice, and demonstrate the skill of reading music at sight, became an important institution in the colonies, social as well as musical.[28]

Because music has always been a crucial component of religious liturgies and because Protestantism was experiencing a renovation, if you will, religious music practices were also affected. Rather than continue the traditional congregational singing of psalms, congregations in many colonies expressed a desire to reform singing practices. The slow, monophonic, and scriptural singing of psalms was becoming outdated in favor of the livelier, tuneful, homophonic, and poetic (religious) singing of hymns. Although congregational hymn singing was still common, some churches began instituting choirs who rehearsed songs specific to the church liturgy. The 1707 publication titled *Hymns and Spiritual Songs* by Dr. Issac Watts was one of the favored hymnals among the colonies. Regarded highly, this hymnal gave a clear direction of singing that helped to substantiate the reforming of religious music practices during the Great Awakening.[29]

---

[25] The 9th edition of the *Bay Psalm Book* contained thirteen melodies in addition to text.

[26] In the North, it is reported that on numerous occasions slaves would accompany their masters to the "meetinghouse" (worship location) and participate (seated in separate pews in the rear of the room) in the singing of psalms.

[27] H. Wiley Hitchcock, *Music in the United States: A Historical Introduction*, (New Jersey: Prentice-Hall, Inc, 1969), p. 3.

[28] Hitchcock, p. 8.

[29] In 1729, Boston hosted the first public concert. In 1735, Charles Town (later Charleston) hosted the first performance of an opera: *Flora: Or Hob in the Well.*

CHAPTER FIVE

AFRICAN AMERICAN ORIGINS OF POPULAR MUSIC

AMERICAN COLONIAL PERIOD–CIVIL WAR

INTRODUCTION: MUSICAL ACTIVITIES DURING THE AFRICAN DIASPORA

While British-influenced songs were more functional for free people, songs dealing with oppression and bondage were more prevalent among African slaves. Fixed in three social contexts–work, recreation, and worship–songs among the slaves were interchangeable.

Today, scholars often ponder whether African American music would have been more exuberant if Africans had journeyed to the New World of their own accord rather than as slaves. Were it not for the hideous conditions that Africans faced during the transatlantic slave trade, would styles such as spirituals, blues, and soul even exist? Perhaps not, since vocal expressions such as field hollers/cries, moaning, and groaning as protestations of harsh working conditions are all embedded in spirituals, blues, and soul. On the other hand, these sorts of expressions were commonplace in Africa. For instance, it was a common practice to invoke similar vocal articulations as a way to communicate emotions of great intensity. So whether Africans arrived in the New World on their own accord or through slavery, these vocal articulations would probably have occurred. This quandary will perhaps never be answered. It is a fact that the early formation of American folk music was affected by the inheritance of African culture, dance, and musical activities during the African Diaspora.

The African Diaspora refers to the dissemination of native Africans to other parts of the world.[1] The New World and subsequently the transatlantic slave trade (1619–1863) will be our focus, as they both provide a framework for examining folk songs among African slaves on American soil.

The conditions slaves endured during the voyage from Africa to the West Indies had a significant impact on the development of African American music. The following condensed narration of Olaudah Equiano's (b. 1745) experiences as a captured slave at the age of ten or eleven provides some insight into this pivotal relationship:

> *The first object which saluted my eyes when I arrived on*
> *the coast was the sea, and a slave ship. . . . I was*
> *immediately handled and tossed up to see if I were*
> *sound by some of the crew. . . . When I looked round the*

---

[1] Africans were also transported to countries such as Brazil.

ship too and saw . . . a multitude of black people of
every description chained together . . . I no longer
doubted of my fate. . . . I fell motionless on the deck and
fainted . . . When I recovered I found some black people
about me . . . I asked them if we were not to be eaten by
those . . . They told me I was not. . . . I was soon put
down under the decks, and there I received such a
salutation in my nostrils . . . so that with the
loathsomeness of the stench and crying together, I
became so sick and low that I was not able to eat . . . but
soon two of the white men offered me eatables, and on
my refusing to eat, one of them held me fast by the
hands . . . and tied my feet while the other flogged me
severely . . . could I have got over the nettings I would
have jumped over the side . . . into the water: and I have
seen some of these poor African prisoners most severely
cut for attempting to do so, and hourly whipped for not
eating . . . In a little time. . . . I found some of my own
nation. . . . I inquired what was to be done with us . . .
we were to be carried to these white people's country to
work for them. . . . At last she came to an anchor . . . we
were all put under deck. . . . The stench of the hold
while we were on the coast was so intolerably loathsome
that it was dangerous to remain there for any time. . . .
The closeness of the place and the heat of the climate,
added to the number in the ship, which was so crowded
that each had scarcely room to turn. . . . This produced
copious perspirations . . . and brought on a sickness
among the slaves, of which many died . . . This situation
was aggravated by the galling of the chains, and the filth
of the tubs . . . into which the children often fell and
were almost suffocated. The shrieks of the women and
the groans of the dying rendered the whole a scene of
horror almost inconceivable . . . At last we came in sight
of . . . Barbados . . . many merchants and planters . . .
came on board . . . and examined . . . They also made us
jump, and pointed to the land, signifying we were to go
there. . . . Soon after we landed there came to us Africans
of all languages. We were conducted . . . to the
merchant's yard, where we were all pent up together like
so many sheep in a fold without regard to sex or age . . .
We were not many days in the merchant's custody before
we were sold after their usual manner, which is this: On a
signal given, the buyers rush at once into the yard where
the slaves are confined, and make choice of that parcel
they like best . . . In this manner, without scruple, are
relations and friends separated, most of them never to
see each other again . . . there were several brothers who

. . . were sold in different lots; and it was very moving. . .
to see and hear their cries of parting . . .[2]

Over five hundred years ago African slaves were brought to the Americas by Portuguese explorers. This practice continued as Spanish, French, Dutch, and British merchants entered the slave trade over the next two hundred years selling slaves to plantation and mine owners in the West Indies for importation to North America.[3] A slave trade distribution pattern based on the nationalities of sellers soon developed. The pattern was even more clearly defined by the fact that each nation procured slaves from specific areas in West Africa. For example, the Portuguese purchased slaves from black rulers in Senegal and sold them in Brazil, and the English did their trading with the Ashanti off the Gold Coast and sold their slaves in North America. The French bought slaves in Dahomey and sold them in Haiti and the Louisiana Territory. Indeed, the trading of humans for various goods from the Europeans was a common occurrence among African chiefs and merchants during the 17th and 18th centuries. Exploiting captives of tribal wars, disorderly tribesmen or servants from other tribes, or for selfish gain, Africans bargained away other Africans in exchange for exotic European goods to increase their sociopolitical and economic power among their own people as well as other tribes and nations.

To prevent the slaves from communicating with one another as tribal societies after they were bought or bartered, slave traders and plantation owners stripped these Africans[4] of their many customs and intentionally placed them together, without consideration for their distinctive heritages. This process deprived these Africans of their traditional customs in many areas including religion, and most significantly, their languages. Africans, just as Europeans, belong to a number of different linguistic groups, each of which has its own language and music tradition. Richard Ligon writes: "The Negres . . . are fetch'd from severall parts of *Africa,* who speake severall languages, and by that means, one of them understands not another . . ."[5]

Although the Portuguese, Spanish, and Dutch were procuring slaves before the British and French, our focus will be the on the latter, as they are most relevant to the connection that exists between Africa and the New World, via the African Diaspora, and ultimately folk songs sung by slaves.

Crammed on board ships en route to the West Indies, men and women were often separated by being placed on different decks. Men were generally placed in the ship's hull and harnessed with ankle and wrist chains, thus affording only limited movement. The women were not physically secured in the same manner as the men because they were less physically intimidating to their captors. Nonetheless, they were maintained in chains during certain times of the voyage.

The arduous journey from West Africa to the West Indies (where the majority of slaves were sold prior to coming to the New World) required keeping the slaves physically healthy to prevent deaths as well as rheumatism and other diseases resulting from these repugnant conditions. "Dancing the slaves" (exercising) was a frequent occurrence on these slave ships since no profit was the reward for unhealthy "human cargo." It entailed moving the slaves onto the deck of the ship and coercing them to dance. Records indicate that a fiddle, banjo, or in some cases, the drum was

---

[2] Equiano, pp. 25–32.

[3] In 1619, the English imported the first shipment of Africans to their colonies in Jamestown, Virginia. See Eileen Southern's book *The Music of Black Americans: A History,* 2d ed. (W. W. Norton & Company, Inc., 1983), 1.

[4] It is important to understand that African slaves in the New World were much farther removed from Africa than those Africans who were enslaved in the West Indies. Richard Dunn writes: "The West African slave, barred from the essentials of European civility, was free to retain as much as he wished of his West African cultural heritage. Here he differed from the Negro in Virginia or New England, who was not only uprooted from his familiar tropical environment but thrown into close association with white people and their European ways. It is not surprising, therefore, that blacks in the sugar islands preserved more of their native culture than blacks in North America. The West Indian slaves learned enough broken English to communicate with their overlords, but they were always bilingual and retained their tribal dialects." (See. R. Dunn, *Sugar & Slaves,* p. 250.)

[5] See R. Ligon. *True & Exact History of the Island of Barbados, 1657,* pp. 46, 50.

used as accompaniment. The "cat" or cat-o-nine-tails (a common term referring to the whip) forced those slaves who were reluctant to dance. This occurrence became a custom for one or all of the following reasons:

1) The activity was believed to keep the slaves physically healthy.
2) The "dance" provided entertainment for the slaves' captors.
3) As perceived by some captains, it was a way to release tension.
4) To some, it was viewed as an activity (i.e., dancing) similar to what the slaves did in their homeland.
5) It was believed to diminish insurrection, which, to some, justified this hideous behavior.

For African slaves, it became necessary to develop communication strategies if they were to progress as a people. Music became the first and most effective communication system for the plantation slave, whether in the West Indies or on the American mainland. This happened for several reasons:

1) In Africa, music served as a form of communication; it conveyed textual information, personal expression or sentiment, and announcements.[6]
2) Although Africans were generally prohibited from communicating using their native languages, they were allowed to use their own languages while singing, particularly for the custom known as "dancing the slaves."
3) In general, music is non threatening. This was particularly important to the slaves, as their captors generally perceived their musical activities as anything but a way to communicate secret messages.

For these reasons alone, many stylistic fashions soon developed and expanded into a myriad of rhetorical and poetic customs. Retrospectively, some of these include metaphoric recitations (such as "Crossroads," 1925 by Robert Johnson), songs with double meanings (such as the traditional spiritual "Steal Away"), and numerous vocal articulations such as *melisma*, bending, guttural sounds, full-throated voice, and blue notes, all of which were used to evoke a greater meaning of the text or context. These musical as well as lyrical customs have become conventional features needed for the composition and performance of styles within the realm of folk songs by slaves, and ultimately of African American music.

In the seventeenth century, colonies governed by Britain include Antigua, Barbados, Jamaica, South Carolina, and Virginia; French territories included Guadeloupe, Louisiana, Matrinique, and Saint Domingue.

Fortunately, there has been great interest over the years that has generated numerous research projects aimed at chronicling the music practices of the common folk by means of identification and musical notation. One of the earliest projects was the Port Royal Experiment that occurred during the Civil War. Here, in an effort to preserve songs of the slave, as there was much concern about their survival during the war, the government secured a team of individuals (Allen, Garrison, and Ware) to identify and notate those songs that were commonly sung by the slaves. The result of this effort produced the collection titled *Slave Songs of the U.S.* (published in 1867), which contains 136 songs with musical notation and lyrics. The works of John and Alan Lomax (father and son) has divulged some of the most significant bodies of American folk music that has been captured on record through voluminous field recordings.[7] Recorded during the early 1930s and 1940s, these songs are organized in various

---

[6] In addition to drums being used as a form of communication, Bowdich notes that "It has been mentioned in the Military Customs of the Ashantees, that peculiar sentences are immediately recognized by the soldiers, and people, in the distinct flourishes of the horns of the various chiefs. . ." (Bowdich, p. 362).

[7] In March, 1939, John Lomax (1867–1948) and Ruby Lomax (1886–1961), husband and wife, embarked on a three-month, 6,502-mile trip throughout the South with the intention of capturing, via recording devices, songs of the folk. The American Folklife Center at the Library of Congress holds these and other sound recordings of folkloric music.

collections. Some of these include *Anglo-American Ballads; Anglo-American Shanties, Lyric Songs, Dance Tunes and Spirituals;* and *Afro-American Spirituals, Work Songs, and Ballads.*[8]

To better understand the music activities of slaves on the mainland, a closer examination of African music traditions during the voyage from Africa, their lifestyles, and conditions in the West Indies is recommended. As noted by Pomfret and Shumway, "The colonists in the two areas [West Indies and mainland] were the same sorts of people, and the same kinds of men provided the planning and financing. In fact, entrepreneurs in England frequently had simultaneous interests in Virginia, Bermuda, and the West Indies."[9] "Moreover the two areas shared close commercial ties and a constant interchange of populations, both black and white. In the seventeenth and eighteenth centuries both Britain and France regarded all their colonies in the New World as part of the same colonial structure."[10]

Upon their arrival at the colonies in the West Indies, slaves were auctioned–as individuals, families, or in lots–and sold primarily to plantation owners.[11] Deprived of their culture, slaves had to adjust to a different lifestyle. A few of these changes included perspectives regarding religious activities and liturgical music, spirituality, the significance of dance within a religious context, and distinctions between sacred and secular occasions and music. For example, in a significant number of regions in Africa, the distinction between sacred and secular was not so evident. Many believed that all things experienced in nature are of the Creator, and therefore are sacred. Further, because men and women reside in and are nourished by nature, their activities are sacred. This perspective posed a problem for Africans with respect to dancing during religious activities within a dominantly European society. While Europeans regarded dance within the context of religious occasions as sacrilegious, many Africans, believed it to be for the glorification of the Creator.

Specific instrument use within religious contexts is another example of changes made by slaves. For example, slaves used the banjo or drum for religious activities, but among European clergy these same instruments were prohibited. The African had to face these and other changes on a daily basis. Once transported to the plantation, whether in the West Indies or on the mainland, slaves endured these changes within three principal social contexts: work, recreation, and worship.

OCCASIONS FOR MUSIC ACTIVITIES AMONG THE SLAVES: WORK, RECREATION, AND WORSHIP

In his autobiography, Frederick Douglas's (1818–1895) writes with regard to the singing of songs:

> "... they would make the dense old woods, for miles
> around, reverberate with their wild songs, revealing at
> once the brightest joy and the deepest sadness. They
> would compose and sing as they went along,
> consulting time nor tune. The thought that came up,
> came out—if not in the word, in the sound; and as
> frequently in the one as in the other. They would
> sometimes sing the most pathetic sentiment in the
> most rapturous tone, and the most rapturous

---

[8] It is interesting to note that these and other collections include songs that became a part of the early professional folk, country and blues singers' repertoire.

[9] Pomfret and Shumway, *Founding the American Colonies*, p. 304.

[10] Epstein, *Sinful Tunes and Spirituals: Black Folk Music to the Civil War*, p. 22.

[11] In the mid-19th century, the cost for an adult male could range from $1,000.00 to $1,250.00, while $850.00 to $1,000.00 would be paid for an adult female.

> *sentiment in the most pathetic tone . . . Every tone*
> *was a testimony against slavery, and a prayer to God*
> *for deliverance from chains. The hearing of those wild*
> *notes depressed my spirit and filled me with ineffable*
> *sadness. I have frequently found myself in tears while*
> *hearing them . . . Those songs still follow me, to*
> *deepen my hatred of slavery, and quicken my*
> *sympathies for my brethren in bonds. If one wishes to*
> *be impressed with the soul-killing effects of slavery,*
> *let him go to Colonel Lloyd's plantation, and on*
> *allowance day, place himself in the deep pine woods,*
> *and there let him, in silence, analyze the sounds that*
> *shall pass through the chambers of his soul, —and if*
> *he is not thus impressed, it will only be because there*
> *is no flesh in his obdurate heart . . . Slaves sing most*
> *when they are most unhappy. The songs of the slave*
> *represent the sorrows of his heart; and he is*
> *relieved by them, only as an aching heart is*
> *relieved by its tears.*[12]

WORK: AN OCCASION FOR SLAVE MUSIC ACTIVITIES

Because agriculture was the avenue for becoming wealthy and powerful among the colonists, the slaves' time was chiefly centered on work. It is through the examination of slaves' daily work tasks such as plantation maintenance/harvesting, black-smithing, and domestic duties that an ameliorative understanding of the significance of musical practices will become evident. Generally, slaves worked Monday through Friday from sunrise to sunset, and many plantation owners even worked their slaves a half a day on Saturday.[13]

Fieldwork was by far the most common duty of the African slave on both West Indian and American soils. Agricultural crops such as rice, tobacco, and cotton were grown on large plantations, which were, by and large, maintained by slaves. Planting, plowing, weeding, administering of insect repellants, and harvesting were common duties needed to ensure a successful plantation. As noted by the slaves through various post-Emancipation research projects and numerous accounts by whites, singing regularly accompanied the aforementioned duties. Despite the fact that no musical notation of slave singing exists before 1861,[14] various singing practices are fortunately substantiated by many written descriptions.

RECREATION: AN OCCASION FOR SLAVE MUSIC ACTIVITIES

Recreational activities often occurred on Saturday evening, as many slaves worked most of the morning and afternoon.[15] In general, activities were often centered on dancing, music, eating, and

---

[12] F. Douglas. (1968). *Narrative of the life of Frederick Douglas: An American Slave.* NY: Signet Classic.

[13] It is important to note that the success of large agricultural plantations in America was partly due to the result of their success in the West Indies prior to the importation of slaves to America.

[14] This year marks the first song in America, created and sung by blacks, to be noted with musical notation and text.

[15] Consequently, Saturday evening socializing was a tradition in African American culture throughout the 17th-19th centuries. Vestiges of this activity are present today as youth often congregate for dancing, music, and socializing. Louis Jordan ("father" of rhythm & blues) makes reference to this occasion in his 1949 song titled "Saturday Night Fish Fry."

socializing.[16] Because dancing and music were interrelated, it is important to know the various dances that called for instrumental accompaniment. Some of the more popular dances include the calenda, chica, juba, buck and wing, cakewalk, buzzard lope, and the pigeon wing.[17] Four dances worth mentioning, as they entailed both dancing and music, are the calenda (or calinda), chica, juba, and cakewalk. These were accompanied by drums, banjo, fiddle, or hand clapping/foot stomping.

According to Emery, "The calenda seemed to be the favorite of the blacks."[18] In his book, published in 1724, titled *Nouveau Voyage Aux Isles de l'Amerique*, Père Labat describes this dance.

> *The dancers are arranged in two lines, facing each*
> *other, the men on one side and the women on the*
> *other. Those who are tired of dancing form a circle*
> *with the spectators around the dancers and the drums.*
> *The ablest person sings a song which he composes on*
> *the spot on any subject he considers appropriate. The*
> *refrain of this song is sung by everyone and is*
> *accompanied by great handclapping. As for the*
> *dancers, they hold their arms a little like someone*
> *playing castagnettes. They jump, make swift turns,*
> *approach each other to a distance of two or three feet*
> *then draw back with the beat of the drum until the*
> *sound of the drums brings them together again to*
> *strike their thighs together, that is, the men's against*
> *the women's. To see them it would seem that they were*
> *striking each other's bellies although it is only the*
> *thighs which receive the blows. At the proper time they*
> *withdraw with a pirouette, only to begin again the*
> *same movement with absolutely lascivious gestures;*
> *this, as many times as the drums give the signal, which*
> *is many times in a row. From time to time they lock*
> *arms and make several revolutions always slapping*
> *their thighs together and kissing each other.*[19]

The chica, described here by Moreau de St.-Méry in his book titled *Danse* (published in 1796), was another dance favored by blacks in the West Indies and on the mainland.

> *When one wants to dance the Chica, a tune,*
> *especially reserved for that type of dance, is played*
> *on crude instruments. The beat is very pronounced.*
> *For the woman, who holds the ends of a kerchief or*
> *the sides of her skirt, the art of this dance consists*
> *mainly in moving the lower parts of her loins while*
> *maintaining the upper part of her body practically*

---

[16] Socializing was a time for love, friendship, courting, education, planning possible escapes or insurrections, expressions of personal sentiments, and so on.

[17] Depending on the slave master and general customs, certain dances may have occurred either in the West Indies or on the mainland.

[18] L.F. Emery, *Black Dance: From 1619 to Today*, p. 21.

[19] Père Labat, *Nouveau Voyage Aux Isles de l'Amerique*, Volume II, 52.

> *immobile. Should one want to enliven the Chica, a*
> *man approaches the woman while she is dancing,*
> *and, throwing himself forward precipitously, he falls*
> *in with the rhythm, almost touching her, drawing*
> *back, lunging again, seeming to want to coax her to*
> *surrender to the passion which engulfs them. When*
> *the Chica reaches its most expressive stage, there is in*
> *the gestures and in the movements of the two dancers*
> *a harmony which is more easily imagined than*
> *described.*[20]

The remaining two dances, juba and cakewalk, are also noteworthy because of their occurrence in minstrel shows. Sometimes referred to as *djouba,* the first originated in Africa and was also brought to the West Indies and the New World during American colonization. Most reports describe the juba as a competitive dance where an individual would do various physical antics in the center of a ring of people/dancers. The dance involved a shuffle-like step while patting a particular rhythmic pattern against one's body. It is interesting to note that the rhythmical pattern was performed more regularly by the bystanders in those locations where drums were prohibited.[21] (See discussion of blackface minstrelsy for more detailed information.)

The cakewalk was by far the most celebrated dance during the 19th and early 20th century. Its origin stems from slaves' mockery of whites attending formal dances. To begin, the formal march opened the ball as couples dressed in formal wear walked ceremoniously (i.e., with an erect upper torso) from their carriage to the ballroom floor. Finding humor in this manner of walking, slaves developed the cakewalk dance and used it as one of their competitive dances. The name *cakewalk* derives from the word *cake,* as it was the prize given for the best cakewalk dancer. In formal attire, slave couples would perform their best moves with kicks and special gestures to an engrossed audience. Ironically, Europeans were unaware of the slaves' motivation for creating this dance and soon adopted it as one of their favorite dances.

Other dances and their accompanying songs existed throughout the Antebellum Period and are recorded in Thomas Talley's *Negro Folk Rhymes.* Because of his personal knowledge through observation and oral tradition, this book is an invaluable resource and is therefore noteworthy for the reader with respect to attaining an ameliorative understanding of the nexus that exists between music and dance.

> *There are Negro Folk Rhyme Dance Songs and Negro*
> *Folk Dance Rhymes. An example of the former is*
> *found in "The Banjo Picking," and the latter, "Juba,"*
> *. . . The reader may wonder how a Rhyme simply*
> *repeated was used in the dance. The procedure was as*
> *follows: Usually one or two individuals "star" danced*
> *at a time. The others of the crowd (which was usually*
> *large) formed a circle about the individual(s) who were*
> *to take their prominent turn at dancing. I use the*
> *terms "star" danced and "prominent turn" because . . .*
> *all those present engaged sometimes at intervals in*

---

[20] Moreau de St.-Méry, *Danse,* pp. 51–52.
[21] At this particular time, the term "pattin' juba" was referenced to juba.

the dance. But those forming the circle, for most of
the time, repeated the Rhyme, clapping their hands
together, and patting their feet in rhythmic time with
the words of the Rhyme being repeated. It was the
task of the dancers in the middle of the circle to
execute some graceful dance in such a manner that
their feet would beat a tattoo upon the ground
answering to every word, and sometimes to every
syllable of the Rhyme being repeated by those in the
circle. There were many such Rhymes. "'Possum Up
the Gum Stump," and "Jawbone" are good examples.
The stanzas to these Rhymes were not usually limited
to two or three, as is generally the case with those
recorded in our collection. Each selection usually had
many stanzas. Thus as there came variation in the
words from stanza to stanza, the skill of the dancers
was taxed to its utmost, in order to keep up the
graceful dance and to beat a changed tattoo upon the
ground corresponding to the changed words.[22]

With regard to Negro folk dance rhymes, Talley continues:

There is a variety of Dance Rhyme to which it is
fitting to call attention. This variety is illustrated in
our collection by "Jump Jim Crow" and "Juba." In
such dances as these, the dancers were required to
give such movements of body as would act the
sentiment expressed by the words while keeping up
the common requirements of beating these same
words in a tattoo upon the ground with the feet and
executing simultaneously a graceful dance.

WORSHIP: AN OCCASION FOR SLAVE MUSIC ACTIVITIES

Despite the fact that Saturday was generally accepted as the day for recreation and that on many plantations Sunday was regularly viewed as a day for worship, Sunday was also a time for recreation.[23] It is interesting to note, as mentioned by Richard Ligon (17th century), that on Sunday men and women generally danced separately.

On Sunday they rest, and have the whole day at their
pleasure . . . on Sundaies in the afternoon, their
Musick plaies, and to dancing they go, the men by

---

[22] Thomas Talley. *Negro Folk Rhymes*, pp. 235–236. Edited, with an Introduction and Notes, by Charles K. Wolfe. New Edition copyright 1991, Thomasina T. Greene.

[23] It must also be understood that many frowned upon dancing, music, and general merrymaking. In 1665 Reverand Morgan Godwyn, of England, visited Virginia and commented on blacks and Indians: "Nothing is more barbarous, and contrary to Christianity, than their Idolatrous Dances, and Revels; in which they usually spend the Sunday . . ." – Godwyn, *Negro's & Indians Advocate*, p. 331.

themselves, and the women by themselves, no mixt
dancing. . . . They may dance a whole day, and neer
heat themselves. . ."[24]

Sunday was set aside as a day of worship among the colonists who regarded religion as an important part of their life. Consequently, many slaves (but not all) were given the opportunity to participate in Christian worship as well, but could not hold their own religious services. In the North and South, slaves regularly accompanied their masters to worship services.[25] For the slave, the singing of religious songs was not only relegated to worship services, but occurred in all three societal settings (work, recreation, and worship). This can be attributed to several reasons:

1) The slaves utilized religious words for developing communication strategies.
2) The slave master favored the singing of these words, as he felt less threatened by possible insurrection.
3) To many slaves, these words provided faith and hope for a better life and therefore were sung in all settings.

The significant number of slaves who accompanied their masters to Sunday worship services participated in the singing of psalms, and eventually hymns.[26] Like the colonists, slaves also favored Dr. Watts's *Hymns and Spiritual Songs.* The most significant collection of religious songs favored by slaves was Richard Allen's *A Collection of Spiritual Songs and Hymns Selected From Various Artists,* published in 1801. Recognized as one of the first blacks to become an ordained minister of the Methodist faith (late 18th century), Mr. Allen collected 136 favored songs among black congregations. More important is the establishment of the African Methodist Episcopalian (AME) church as the result of Mr. Allen's innovations. Here was created the AME hymn: a style of singing that involved the embellishing of "regular" hymns. Characterized by the singing of a number of verses that are spontaneously interspersed with a refrain, separate parts sung by men and women, and syncopated rhythms, the AME hymn was a precursor of the popular repertoire commonly known as Negro spirituals.

Negro spirituals are defined as spontaneous religious songs–a definition that describes the character of the AME hymn. These songs were functional for the slaves as they provided lyrics of salvation and ultimately of hope. As emancipation approached, this repertoire became even more significant as the first true Negro spiritual, titled "Go Down Moses" (1861), was published with text as well as musical notation. As the result of this publication, it became clear how these songs were to be sung, which consequently generated interest among musical groups to perform this music for audiences in America and abroad. To ensure their acceptability, it became common to perform those songs as they were composed and arranged within the rules of Western musical standards. Interestingly, many blacks, particularly those in pursuit of upward mobility, were also in favor of restructuring these, in essence, slave songs. Consequently, there arose a tradition known as "concertizing." Essentially, this entailed a particular manner of vocal production and vocal control, harmonic textures, rhythmic propensities, and other performance practices conducive to Western standards rehearsed for the concert stage. In addition, performance practices such as hand clapping, call and response phrasing, lyric improvisation, and a seemingly wandering refrain were employed to produce the engaging spirit that

---

[24] See Richard Ligon, *True and Exact History of the Island of Barbados,* 1657.

[25] Records also indicate that, beginning in the 18th century, some slave masters allowed their slaves, with written permission, to attend worship services outside of the plantation.

[26] It must be understood that religious activities among the slaves during the 17th and 18th centuries were not governed by any common law, but rather by each plantation owner.

was typical of Negro spirituals. Singing that was governed by concertizing made the performance more aesthetic than its original liturgical context. Two early African American groups that disseminated this music worldwide include the Fisk Jubilee Singers (formed in 1871) and the Hampton Institute Choir (formed in 1873).

FESTIVAL AND HOLIDAY ACTIVITIES AMONG THE SLAVES

In both the North and South during the late 18th and into the 19th centuries, large numbers of slaves congregated for various festival/holiday activities. Even though slaves were bound to their plantations (particularly in the South), there were nonetheless some occasions for singing, dancing, and general merrymaking activities. Pinkster Day (in states such as New York and Maryland) and Place Congo (now called Beauregard Square in New Orleans) were the two major festivals.[27] Both of these are very significant to the study of Africans in the New World, as they provide evidence of African celebratory traditions. Unlike the regimented social structure of most slaves where African celebratory customs and traditions were generally forbidden, Pinkster Day and Place Congo were two occasions where such customs and traditions were commonplace. It is reported that people came from both within and from neighboring regions to view the many entertaining activities. Numerous colonists who came to observe on these occasions often commented on the slaves' ability to endure long hours of nonstop playing of instruments for dancing and general merry-making.[28] Thus, these festivals provided entertainment for both blacks and whites while at the same time preserving some remembrance of the slaves' African heritages.

Pinkster Day, which referred to Pentecost Sunday, was celebrated by the Dutch and eventually the English. First occurring in Albany, New York, Pinkster lasted for nearly one week, with the whites celebrating the first day or so and the blacks the remaining days. In addition to dancing and singing by blacks that took place in the center, around ". . . the perimeter of the square were erected stalls, booths, and tents that featured exhibitions of wild animals, rope dancing, bareback riding, and other attractions common to a fair."[29] Without a doubt, dancing was the most enjoyable activity during Pinkster Day. Accompanied by drums, banjo, fiddle, and fife (flute), dancing seemed to have occurred nonstop.

Unlike Pinkster Day, which celebrated a particular religious holiday, Place Congo was more of an occasion that occurred on Sundays, among the slaves, at an area that became known as Place Congo. Now known as Beauregard Square, New Orleans, slaves would gather on Sundays after religious services to participate in various dancing activities. Groups of people would form circles according to their tribe and would dance those dances (accompanied by singing, drums, banjo, and rattles) unique to their tribe.

CONCLUSION

One can draw the conclusion that folk songs sung among Europeans influenced the early development of "country" music (initially known as hillbilly), while folk songs sung by the African slave were the inspiration for "blues" music. Both genres–country and blues–are folk-based. The differences between country and blues music, while rooted in slavery, were exacerbated by the striations of society resulting from social, political, cultural, and economic patterns that developed during the Reconstruction Era, which consequently affected both musical lyrics and performance styles of the groups that developed.

---

[27] Other festivals among the slaves included 'Lection Day, John Conny Festivals, and Voodoo.

[28] This occurs because, as one player becomes tired, another quickly resumes his place as the instrumentalist.

[29] Eileen Southern, *Music of Black Americans*. W.W. Norton, NY. Third Edition. 1997, p. 53.

During the late 19th century, free blacks were disengaging from their previously coerced ties with Whites in favor of black separatism, which precipitated a movement of minimal sharing of social and (most significantly in this context) folk music activities. For whites, the industrial revolution hastened the desire to avail themselves of the many opportunities for success in entrepreneurial endeavors, tradesmanships, and (noteworthy here) other no farming professions.

CHAPTER SIX

POPULAR ENTERTAINMENT

MINSTRELSY

> *"If I could have the nigger show back again in its*
> *pristine purity and perfection I should have but little*
> *further use for opera."*[1]
> Mark Twain

Like many others during his time, Mark Twain was amused by various forms of social entertainment such as variety shows, operas, operettas, circus acts, and burlesque shows. Above all, both he and his contemporaries enjoyed the American minstrel show.

The 1850s marks the crowning years of the minstrel era, but its foundation began as early as the 1820s. Prized as America's indigenous entertainment, minstrel shows continued to be popular through the late 19th century. Although a fascination with and consequent portrayal of Negro characterizations through spoken and sung black dialect on stage existed in Great Britain during the late 1700s, it is in America that the "minstrel show" evolved. The British actor Charles Mathews (1776–1835) introduced staged entertainment centered on black lifestyles to America during the 1820s. Intrigued by black people's humor, dialect, and their proclivity for music and dancing, Mathews presented comedic lectures (as they were called in Europe) on stage to amuse his audience. Inspired by the popularity of Mathews's comedic act, George Washington Dixon (1808–61) became the first American to perform comedic skits of black culture on stage. By the late 1820s, Dixon and eventually other performers such as George Nichols and J.W. Sweeney were regularly doing solo acts, primarily in the Northeast, between other stage entertainments. The most celebrated early American minstrel performer was Thomas Dartmouth Rice (1808–60), who became known as the "daddy" of minstrelsy. Noted for his depiction of a plantation stable boy with ragged clothing who walked and danced in a certain way while singing, Rice amused audiences beginning in the Midwest and ending on the east coast. Performing this black characterization between other entertainment productions with great success, Rice embarked on an entrepreneurial endeavor performing an imitation of this stable boy singing a song titled by Rice as "Jim Crow Song," (a.k.a. "Jim Crow"). This eventually led to the establishment of the Jim Crow characterization, which crowned him the "father"/ "daddy" of minstrelsy.

Although with solo acts, it was the minstrelsy "troupe" or group of four to six performers that became the craze. Groups have an advantage over soloists in that they can provide a more diverse program due to their ability to perform both as an ensemble and as soloists. Members of groups frequently

---

[1] *Autobiography*, 59.

played instrumental numbers together using the banjo, fiddle/violin, bone castanets, and tambourine. They also performed conversational skits and polyphonic textures using spoken black dialect. The Virginia Minstrels was the earliest popular troupe that emerged using these and other performance practices. Featuring Frank Bower, Daniel Emmett, Dick Pelham, and William Whitlock, four white males. The Virginia Minstrels first performed in 1843 at the well-known Chatman Theatre in New York. Mimed through exaggerated music, dance, and speech patterns, the group's depictions of black slaves as illiterate and lazy plantation workers and/or urban blacks as womanizers and street-wise men helped to establish the format of the minstrel show for the many groups that followed.

George Thatcher's Greatest Minstrels Poster. © Corbis

Commonly known as Ethiopian minstrelsy or blackface, this traveling comedic stage show–initially composed exclusively of whites–portrayed aspects of black culture through characterizations that eventually became known as Jim Crow and Zip Coon. In addition to these two characterizations, female impersonation was also popular. Performers such as Fred Malcom, The Great Eugene, and Burt Shepard mimed exaggerated antics as a ballerina or the frequently used wedding scene. Mimicking these acts contributed to a performer's success. Though there were some women performers, the public stage, especially for this type of lascivious thematic material, was still not considered an appropriate environment for respectable women, and thus the presence of female performers was comparatively minimal.

Recognizing the profitability of this stage performance, other white minstrel companies and performers soon emerged. Some of these included Cohan and Harris's Minstrels, Kelly and Leon's Minstrels of New Zealand, the George Christy Minstrels, John Diamond, Morris Brothers Pell and Trowbridge's Minstrels of Boston, the brothers Dick and Joe Sweeney, and the Ethiopian Serenaders. Some black minstrels, particularly after 1865, included Charles Hicks, Ernest Hogan, Billy Kersands, George Walker, and Bert Williams, and earlier the famous William Henry "Juba" Lane. Although a male-dominated industry, some female minstrels who also "blackened-up" included Sally Cohen, Trixie Friganza, Artie Hall, Beverly Sitgreaves, Edna May Spooner, and Jennie Yeamans.

Essentially, performers would "blacken-up" (even black performers), which entailed placing dark or burnt cork on the face and white paste on the lips in an effort to visually portray blacks in an exaggerated manner. Situating themselves in a half circle on stage, on one end sat the interlocutor, or announcer (master of ceremony), who often also sang and/or played an instrument, while the others, in addition to singing, dancing and reciting comedic dialogue, played typical instruments: fiddle, banjo, tambourine, and bone castanets.[2] In many songs the fiddle played the melody, the banjo furnished the harmony, while the tambourine and bone castanets concentrated on complimentary rhythms while maintaining the tempo. The tempo was such that it accompanied some of the more typical dances such as the cake-walk, juba, buck and wing, Virginia Essence, two-step, and the plantation stick dance.

Greatly inspired by E.P. Christy (a member of the celebrated Christy Minstrels formed in 1844), a typical minstrel show entailed a tripartite format: overture, olio, and finale.

Overture	An instrumental introduction that set the mood for the performance.
Olio	The specialty act in which a member or several members performed their particular "special" presentation. It could be singing, playing an instrument, dancing, telling jokes, or a skit (via Jim Crow or Zip Coon characterizations).
Finale	Also known as the "walk around," this was the final song during which the troupe would engage the audience in singing and dancing while walking "around" and through them.

With regard to the musical material, in its early stage a number of minstrel songs, albeit with slave themes, were not melodically and lyrically characteristic of music in black culture. Rather, they were adaptations of what white performers perceived to be both "black" in character as well as ideal for white audiences. One particular aspect of these songs was the phonetically exaggerated spellings of song titles such as "Lubly Fans Would You Cum Out Tonight" and "Whar Did You Cum From." Lyrical themes for the skits often centered around black stupidity, animalistic behavior, uncontrollable sexual urges (among men and women), infidelity, behavior that bordered on heathen-like, and the ". . . gastromical delights of chicken, pork chops, and watermelon."[3] Songs such as "All Pimps Look Alike to Me" (a.k.a. "All Coons Look Alike to Me", written by the black comedian-dancer Ernest Hogan) and "Coon, Coon, Coon," while entertaining among black and white audiences, underscored whites' belief in black inferiority and thus deepened the scar of racism.

[2] As was discussed with regard to folk songs, the fiddle and eventually the banjo were favored instruments among the colonists, indentures, and African slaves nearly two centuries before the minstrel period.
[3] Morgan and Barlow, *From Cakewalks to Concert Halls*, (Washington, DC: Elliott and Clark Publishing, 1992), p. 18.

Female impersonations included female ballerinas with, of course, male physiques; depictions of black women with facial, leg, and chest hair, as well as earrings through their noses, which portrayed them as savage-like;[4] or skits that portrayed men being forced to the alter by overwhelmingly powerful women who were taller, more sensible, and who possessed a great desire for families.

As minstrelsy became more popular, many performers sought to improve the quality of their performances as well as to diminish the overt references to black illiteracy and slave lifestyles. As a result, noted composers such as Stephen Foster, Dan Emmett, and James Bland were regularly commissioned to compose songs that best suited this new approach to minstrel shows. Some of Foster's most popular songs included "My Old Kentucky Home" and "Old Folks at Home." Dan Emmett wrote "Dixie" (a.k.a. "Dixie's Land"), which became essential to every performer's repertoire, James Bland wrote the song "Carry Me Back to Old Virginny," which Virginia eventually adopted as its state song. Other popular songs from this later period included "Oh! Susanna" and "Camptown Races." These and other songs have become a part of America's cultural heritage.

While whites were commonly commissioned by publishers to write new songs, with the exception of James Bland, blacks were generally regarded as performers: first as amateurs and then eventually as professionals. One particular black performer that stood above others and claimed the crown "The Greatest Dancer in the World" was none other than Master William "Juba" Lane. While on a visit to America, Charles Dickens (1812–1870) wrote:

> *Single shuffle, double shuffle, and cross-cut: snapping*
> *his fingers, rolling his eyes, turning in his knees,*
> *presenting the backs of his legs in front, spinning*
> *about on his toes and heels like nothing but the man's*
> *fingers on the tambourine; dancing with two left legs,*
> *two right legs, two wooden legs, two wire legs, two*
> *spring legs–all sorts of legs and no legs-what is this*
> *to him? And in what walk of life, or dance of life,*
> *does man ever get such stimulating applause as*
> *thunders about him, when, having dances his partner*
> *off her feet, and himself too, he finishes by leaping*
> *gloriously on the bar counter, and calling for*
> *something to drink, with the chuckle of a million*
> *counterfeit Jim Crows, in one inimitable sound?*[5]

Despite the fact that some black performers were also seen performing during the mid-19th century, the majority of black minstrel performers, with the exception of Master William "Juba" Lane, did not become popular until after the Civil War–the time of the 13th Amendment. In 1865, Charles Hicks became the first African American to organize an all-black minstrel show with his group, the Georgia Minstrels–a name claimed by several. As the result of racism and discrimination practices, he sold the company to a white producer named Charles Callendar and the group became Callendar's Georgia Minstrels, but not before experiencing national and international success. Hick's Georgia Minstrels performed for audiences in the United States, and more comfortably (as the result of less racism) for international audiences in countries like Germany, the British Isles, Great Britain, and Australia. The following quote from Tom Fletcher in his book *100 Years of the Negro in Show*

---

[4] An interesting anecdote: Many contemporary people, particularly teens through young adults, wear nose, navel, upper ear, eyebrow, and/or lip earrings.

[5] Charles Dickens, *American Notes*, (First printed in 1842, reprint published by NY: Modern Library, 1996).

Business allows us to get a glimpse of minstrelsy for black performers. The year was 1888, and Fletcher was 15:

> *We rehearsed in Portsmouth and opened in Mayville, Kentucky. The name of the show was Howard's Novelty Colored Minstrels. . .The show consisted of fourteen people including an "orchestra" composed of Eddie Cross, banjo player, and Ed Wilson, a piano player out of Lexington, Kentucky, who doubled on the guitar. . .The two Eddies would play a few tunes and we would sing a few songs and give out the handbills. A colored man with a banjo would draw almost as big a crowd as an elephant in a circus. My place in the first part was just like the boy in the A. G. Fields Minstrels. The first part was the regular semi-circle, the Interlocutor slightly elevated in the center with five men (three singers and two endmen) on each side. The banjo and guitar were just a little behind the Interlocutor. Nat Lucas was the Interlocutor. End men, Tambos, were Bill Reid and Tom Gales; Bones, Henry Derring and Frank Green. In addition the Bayou Quartet and Frank and Willie Jackson, dancers, were also featured. The show lasted around one hour and forty-five minutes. Everybody in the show appeared at least twice, and the entire company appeared in the afterpiece. The songs were the regular tunes of the period, spirituals, original songs and songs by Sam Lucas, Stephen Foster and Jim Bland. The places we played had nothing but town halls. In a number of these towns, the halls were only used a few times a year. Mr. Howard would rent the hall, or he would get the use of the hall in some way, and we would have to clean and dust the place and make our own footlights because when the school or the townspeople had their infrequent occasions to use the hall they would bring their own lamps from home. . .Most of the halls seated less than four hundred people and there were times when the audience would have to stay outside until we were dressed for the show. Admission prices were from 15 cents to 50 cents for matinees and at night, 25, 50 and $1.00, according to the crowd. . .Since the towns we played were mostly small ones, getting lodgings was pretty tough. The colored people where we had to lodge were not well equipped to take care of anybody outside their own families. Being on their own only a short time, very few of them could offer*

> *outsiders a place to sleep. Meals were okay because*
> *nearly all of the people had their own farms and*
> *smoke houses. . .During the winter, in many towns,*
> *we were compelled to sleep in the halls, opera houses*
> *and railroad stations. There wasn't any steam heat in*
> *those days, but all of the places had a big coal or*
> *wood stove. We would all sit around the big hot fire*
> *and get what few winks we could.*[6]

It was considered more entertaining for many white audiences to experience blackface minstrelsy by "blackened-up" black performers, but eventually many black performers discontinued performing in blackface. Some of the most popular black performers during the post-antebellum era and into the new century included Billy Kersands,[7] Bert Williams, George Walker, Charles Hicks, Whistling Rufus, and Sam Lucas.[8]

Black performers entertained both white as well as black audiences, with the same performance taking on a different meaning based on the audience's (black or white) interpretation. For instance, among black audiences it was a common practice to satirically imitate white performers imitating blacks. The difference is that white audiences weren't aware of the satire. In any case, the genie was out of the box, and a significant contribution to America's popular taste had unknowingly come to rest on the shoulders of black culture. As J. Kinnard wrote in 1845:

> *Who are our true rulers? The Negro poets, to be sure.*
> *Do they not set the fashion, and give laws to the*
> *public taste? Let one of them, in the swamps of*
> *Carolina, compose a new song, and it no sooner*
> *reaches the ear of a white amateur, than it is written*
> *down, amended (that is, almost spoilt), printed, and*
> *then put upon a course of rapid dissemination, to*
> *cease only with the utmost bounds of Anglo-*
> *Saxondom, perhaps with the world.*[9]

The Minstrel era was by far the most popular entertainment medium just before and slightly after the Civil War. In fact, it is regarded as America's first entertainment presented on stage in front of a public audience. Its overall character, demeanor, and charismatic nature permeated other entertainment venues such as medicine shows, gillies, carnivals, early American Theatre, vaudeville, and Black Musical Theatre. By far, it was the most influential entertainment in which most performers of the popular stage got their start. Al Jolson's successful career was largely based on his eccentric performances in blackface (see American Theatre). W.C. Handy and Gertrude Rainey (the "father" and "mother", respectively, of the blues) and Bessie Smith (the "empress of the blues") all performed in blackface during the beginning of their careers. A renowned singer and exotic dancer, and at one point one of the wealthiest of black women, Josephine Baker performed in blackface as a teen before her tour in Paris, where her career blossomed. And even performers such as Judy Garland, Mickey Rooney, and Frank Sinatra "blackened-up" at some point during their career. The fact remains, the minstrel era was a

---

[6] See Tom Fletcher, *100 Years of the Negro in Show Business*, (New York: Da Capo Press), 1984.
[7] It is reported that Kersands received $100.00/week, the highest pay among black performers during this time.
[8] Bert Williams and George Walker began as a duo, namely Williams and Walker. In 1865, Charles Hicks became the first black person to organize and produce an all-black minstrel show.
[9] See J. Kinnard, "Who Are Our National Poets?" *Knickerbocker Magazine* 26, 1845.

vibrant period of entertainment, and was one of the most frequented venues for hearing popular songs. In principle, a song's popularity was largely based on the success it received in a particular minstrel show. As is the case today, theatrical performances create a forum in which numerous songs are introduced, and some become treasured memories.[10]

TRAVELING ROAD SHOWS

Medicine shows, gillies, circuses, and carnivals were types of traveling road shows that occurred between the decline of the minstrel period (1870s) and the beginning of vaudeville (1890s). Medicine shows consisted of men posing as doctors or pharmaceutical experts who traveled by covered wagon from town to town, proclaiming their ointments and potions to be cures for any ailment. In an effort to lure prospective buyers to their goods and merchandise, particularly since town officials generally expressed their opposition to these salesmen "setting up shop" in town, one to several performers regularly accompanied this type of show and performed various attention-getting activities as the wagon hurriedly went through the town. Because of the popularity of minstrelsy, some Jim Crow and Zip Coon characterizations, as well as acrobatic and theatrical antics, permeated these and other road shows. Unlike the minstrel show prior to the Civil War where mainly white performers took the stage, by this time white America was becoming more intrigued by seeing black performers. Consequently, in addition to minstrel shows, black performers were frequently seen in various traveling road shows. For instance, it is reported that George Walker of the Williams and Walker team came to the entertainment business via a medicine show.

> When quite young, George Walker traveled from his hometown of Lawrence, Kansas, to California by working with medicine shows. Used as an attention-getter, Walker would sing, dance, and play the tambourine and bones until enough people gathered so that the quack doctor could profitably make his sales pitch.[11]

As previously noted, various dances and instruments were nearly identical to those used in the minstrel show, whether by black or white performers. As pointed out by Edward Thorpe, a noted author of *Black Dance:*

> The dances ranged from the Buck and Wing, the Strut, the Soft-shoe shuffle, jigs, reels, jumps, twists, and any step or acrobatic maneuver the executant could do best. Sometimes they accompanied themselves on the tambourine or banjo, sometimes the music or rhythm was provided by a colleague.[12]

Where the medicine show was often a performer's indoctrination to the entertainment industry, aside from blackface, the gillie was the graduation toward attaining some sort of security in the business. Often regarded as a fair or small-scale circus/carnival, the gillie was an entertainment venue that

---

[10] For example, "Memories" from *Cats,* "The Circle of Life" from *The Lion King,* or "All I Ask of You" from *Phantom of the Opera.*

[11] Lynne Fauley Emery, *Black Dance: From 1619 to Today,* p. 211.

[12] Edward Thorpe, *Black Dance,* p. 50.

traveled in several covered wagons. (The name *gillie* derived from name of the wagon "wheel.") Where remedies were the commodities for medicine shows, an environment of broad-reaching entertainment was the focus of the gillie. These shows included group-rehearsed performances of singing, dancing, acrobatic stunts, and dramatic skits performed under tents, one or two amusement rides, and games. Again, vestiges of the minstrel era were the underpinnings of the entertainment. Most evident is the tripartite format that was performed under the tent. To begin, a comedian would get the audience roaring in laughter and would be followed by ". . . specialty acts such as jugglers or acrobats and some eccentric dancing."[13] Group singing and dancing would follow, ". . . and the show would close with an Afterpiece, a favourite sketch and dance number affectionately known as Eph and Dinah."[14] The most striking difference between the medicine show and the gillie is the fact that the latter was strictly for entertainment purposes. The term *gillie,* however, was not as popular as its successor, namely *carnival.* There were probably numerous carnivals or circuses that were in fact gillies, but perhaps the word *gillie* had associations with a past that most people wanted to forget. In any case, for many entertainers the carnival, which frequently traveled by train, was the epitome of road shows if one's goal was to be involved in a more established venue. Carnivals consisted of animal shows, a number of mechanical thrill rides, games, and singing, dancing, and theatrical performances. Similar to the gillie, customers were drawn to small tents by performers doing certain attention-getting antics. Once inside the tent, the audience was thrilled with music and dance that most often included vestiges of the minstrel period.

These and other road shows became the training ground for many future performers and entrepreneurs of the entertainment business. As we move forward, numerous variety shows of all sorts became a favorite pastime for many Americans. Eventually, these shows found a home in the most entertaining venue of the early 20th century to vaudeville. Despite the fact that radio and sound recordings showed promise as a contributor to the tapestry of American entertainment, live performances were still the principle vehicle used to nurture a performer's talents as well as to satisfy consumer musical tastes.

VAUDEVILLE

The end of the minstrel period, with the various aforementioned traveling road shows intervening, marks the beginning of vaudeville. The term's meaning derives from the French word for "burlesque" or "cabaret"–light entertainment.[15] Unlike the minstrel show, where an entire troupe or company would travel to an engagement, vaudeville performers became individuals, a team of generally two people, or groups with a featured performer (such as Sissieretta Jones and her Black Patti Troubadours) whose engagements were arranged by booking agents. Though vestiges of minstrelsy through songs, dances, and skits were still being used, vaudeville performances (many still containing performers in blackface) consisted of a variety of acts—singing, dancing, comedy skits, jugglers, ventriloquist, animal antics, acrobatics—intended for the entire family. Initially under the auspices of "variety show," these antics became the foundation for vaudeville.

Tony Pastor is given much of the credit for the transformation of the variety show to vaudeville. Born in New York, ca. 1835, Mr. Pastor learned a great deal about America's tastes for entertainment at an early age. His experiences included minstrel shows and circuses as an acrobat, comedian, and/ or singer. As is the case with many entertainers, constant touring for Pastor eventually became a least-desired activity. Consequently, he nestled into the cosmopolitan environment in New York where he performed as a comic singer. Because of the success of previous experiences, his shows also included a

---

[13] *Ibid.*, p. 51.

[14] *Ibid.* (Eph and Dinah portrayed an old couple dancing with increasing agility, ending with phenomenal movements.)

[15] Opera, cantata, and musical theatre were all considered major entertainment.

variety of entertainment, even the incorporation of racially/ ethnically different perf
and black performers on the same stage). Seeing the success of this venture, and ha>
family-oriented entertainment, in 1865 he opened Tony Pastor's Opera House, l(
District of New York.[16]

Due to his success, numerous theatres commonly referred to as vaudev..
emerged by the late 19th century.[17] Unlike minstrelsy, where theatre owners rarely encou..
mixed audiences, a significant number of vaudeville houses made an attempt to appeal to a..
isfy blacks and whites, different social classes, and different ethnicities. As stated by Henderson and
Bowers:

> "... while some theatre aimed at only a single ethnic
> element, most of the major houses tried to offer the
> broadest range of acts to attract the largest audience.
> Leading teams of the era likewise presented
> themselves not simply in the guise of one particular
> ethnicity but cheerfully changed from 'Dutch' to
> blackface minstrel to Irish."[18]

Performers had to be able to present African American, Irish, and German cultural characteristics
to a variety of audiences, both mixed and segregated. A number of performers gathered their material
by viewing characteristics of various cultures and presented them on stage in front of diverse audiences.
Presented in exaggerated comedic skits and songs and dances, their performances helped to desensitize
the fear of racial or ethnic ambiguities. In spite of the socioeconomic and cultural status of African
Americans, Irish, Germans, and Jews, these same cultures represented the largest body of vaudeville
performers. Among the many successful performers, two-man teams such as Williams and Walker,
Harrigan and Hart, and Weber and Fields were a frequent occurrence. This two-mann team was often
composed of a "straight guy" and a "confused guy," (one who possessed intelligence therein), or a tall,
slim man and a short, chubby fellow. The two-man team allowed three layers of humor: two separate
characterizations; and the result of combining the two.

The most popular African American two-man team of early vaudeville was Bert Williams and
George Walker of the Williams and Walker team. In 1872, Edward Harrigan and Tony Hart formed the
most successful team among early Irish vaudevillians. Beginning in the last decade of the 19th century,
Lew Fields and Joe Weber (of Jewish descent) formed the most successful early team that focused
on German/Dutch culture. Even though performers were quite capable of presenting characteristics
of various cultures, each had their own niche. For example, Williams and Walker, billed as the "Two
Real Coons," were more appealing to audiences for their blackface minstrel performances. Williams
played the Zip Coon type character while Jim Crow was characterized by Walker. Moreover, capitalizing on the attention to the dancing antics of blacks as expressed by whites, Williams and Walker took
advantage of this and were frequently billed as the best black comedic and dancing team of vaudeville.
Without a doubt, the cakewalk was their most successful dance presentation. Following the team's
disbandment in 1909 as a result of Walker's serious illness, Bert Williams became a popular solo artist.
Some of his most successful songs include "I'm in the Right Church But the Wrong Pew," "Come After
Breakfast, Bring Along Your Lunch and Leave Before Suppertime," and "Woodman Spare That Tree."

---

[16] Prior to vaudeville, variety shows were regularly performed in saloons–an environment considered by many to be unsuitable
for ladies and children.
[17] Tony Pastor's Opera House was one of the most successful vaudeville houses during the late 19th century.
[18] Henderson and Bowers, *Red Hot & Blue*, p. 11.

910, three years after the opening of the first *Ziegfeld Follies,* Bert Williams became the only black performer in an all-white group of performers.

Harrigan and Hart's 1873 skit of *The Mulligan Guard* greatly influenced the heroic nature of Irish immigrants as perceived by Americans, and consequently they are noted for their contributions to the foundation of Irish humor. Through this "musical," as it was called, Harrigan and Hart became one of the first major acts to present characteristics of different cultures on the American stage. Their goal was to explicitly exploit images of New York's cultural metropolis, which included Jewish, English, Chinese, Black, Italian, Polish, Irish, and German ethnicities. The sociocultural backdrop of their performances included cultural images of various ethnic situations and lifestyles, particularly regarding people in the Bowery district. The Harrigan and Hart team disbanded after twelve years, but left an indelible tradition in American entertainment. Harrigan continued as a solo performer/producer, and, like Pastor, became a central figure in the development of what eventually became American theatre.

In 1896, Weber and Field started on a path that placed them among the greatest comedians whose material focused on the Dutch and German peoples. As noted by Henderson and Bowers:

> *Their (Field and Weber) act combined "Dutch*
> *knockout"—that is, slapstick—and burlesque. Not as*
> *"striptease" but as parody or comic imitation. It was a*
> *rambunctious, physical act, involving a lot of pushing*
> *and shoving, and, in what is said to be original with*
> *them, custard pies in the face.*[19]

In addition to two-man teams, vaudeville was a haven for solo performers as well.[20] Some of the more popular soloists were Sophie Tucker, Nora Bayes, Lillian Russell, Victor Herbert, and Sissieretta Jones. For each of these performers, singing was the area of expertise. Given the sociocultural climate at the time, opportunities for black performers were limited. Sophie Tucker, of Jewish ancestry, was one of the first successful non-black performers of the 20th century to disseminate black music to white American audiences. (In future years, Elvis Presley and Vanilla Ice would fulfill the same function for rhythm & blues/rock & roll, and hip-hop/rap, respectively.) The performance of black-sounding music by non black performers, as evidenced as early as the minstrel era, was rather fashionable–certainly through WWI. By 1910, Ms. Tucker, after bouts with Yiddish theatre, presentations, and sentimental ballads of the Tin Pan Alley-style, fashioned her vocal stylizations in the ragtime and blues idioms. Her first recording with the Edison company titled "The Lovin' Rag" was followed by her staple song, titled "Some of These Days." Billed as a "red-hot mama," Sophie Tucker was scheduled, in 1920, to become the first person to record a blues song. But due to an unsubstantiated reason, this honor was bestowed upon a new rising star, Bessie Smith, who sang and recorded "Crazy Blues" (1920). Another performer who eventually found success as a vaudeville singer was Nora Bayes. As a member of the initial *Ziegfeld Follies* in 1907, Ms. Bayes is best known for her song, co-written with her husband Jack Norworth, "Shine on, Harvest Moon." Ten years later, as America entered WWI, she popularized George M. Cohan's patriotic song titled "Over There." Although minstrel, Tin Pan Alley, ragtime, and blues comprised the staple singing styles of vaudeville, some singers received notoriety by performing light opera or operettas. Under the banner "of French opera bouffe, British comic opera, and Viennese operetta-of Offenbach, Gilbert and Sullivan, and Lehár . . ."[21] these performance traditions rivaled other popular entertainment in America, particularly among those partial to and/or in pursuit of

---

[19] Henderson and Bowers, p. 15.

[20] It should be noted that solo performers were also the result of the disbanding of a two-man team.

the high arts. The singer Lillian Russell, billed as the "Queen of Broadway," Victor Herbert, a composer of light opera music, and Sissieretta Jones, billed as "Black Patti,"[22] were all recognized performers of light opera.

The cultural metropolis of New York–the birthplace of vaudeville–was not the norm of American communities with respect to an environment of ethnic tolerance. Though physically segregated with respect to living environments, there nevertheless was greater diversity, and, consequently, a forum for building a more ethnically forbearing environment. This was not the case in other states, cities, and towns across America that also favored vaudeville performances. While it is true that a number of theatre houses catered to and subsequently encouraged performers to appeal to a broad audience, there were two different circuits: black and white. Consequently, most black and white performances of early vaudeville that occurred outside of New York were booked through separate circuits-theatre houses that were mainly distinguishable by the environment and color of one's skin, audience and performer alike. The Keith Orpheum's, Loewe's, and Pantages were popular white vaudeville circuits while the T.O.B.A. (Theatre Owners Booking Agency)[23] was the most prestigious agency that booked black performers. While white performers were booked through the white circuit, and the black circuit catered to black audiences for black performers, there were some exceptions to the latter. For instance, performers such as Bert Williams, the Nicholas Brothers (a famous tap dancing brother team), and Pigmeat Markham (a comedian) also performed on the white circuit. Another interesting event that led to the appearance of more black performers on the white vaudeville circuit was a strike in 1901 against the white circuit. Instigated by the performing group known as the White Rats, this strike created the need for theatre houses to solicit performers who would, in, in essence, cross the picket line.[24] Since many white performers banded together to oppose unfair practices, the white circuit began to employ more black performers.

Vaudeville became the venue where artists polished their area of expertise prior to becoming a part of the more established musical theatre on Broadway, and eventually the radio and sound recording industries. Unlike today's pop or teen idol performer whose virtuoso talent is not the norm, the success of a vaudevillian was primarily adjudicated on sheer talent. Vaudeville became passè by the close of WWII. However, it did not end without creating a legacy. The new entertainments-American theatre, radio, and TV/film-were all drawing from the thicket and wealth of performance traditions established by vaudevillians and their predecessors. Theatrical plays such as *Shuffle Along* (1921) and *Showboat* (1927), albeit containing vaudeville-inspired scenes and attitudes, diminished the popularity of vaudeville shows. The *Amos and Andy* radio program became an all-American favorite, yet displayed comedic rhythm and rhyme schemes of popular vaudevillians. The *Ed Sullivan Show* in the 1950s was, in effect, vaudeville on television. Most people recognize the names of performers such as Abbott and Costello, Amos and Andy, George Burns, Gracie Allen, Jack Benny, W.C. Fields, Bob Hope,[25] Al Jolson, Jackie "Moms" Mabley, the Three Stooges, and Ethel Waters. Each began as a vaudeville performers.

---

[21] Henderson and Bowers, p. 30.

[22] The heading "Black Patti" made reference to the white Italian-American singer, Adelina Patti. Although she gained notoriety as a singer of light opera, a greater level of success, due to her being black, was attained through typical vaudeville songs.

[23] Among black performers, the T.O.B.A. acronym was also translated as "Tough on Black Actors."

[24] A similar occurrence happened in 1941, when the National Association (Academy) of Broadcasters (NAB) instigated a strike against ASCAP for monopolizing an important segment of the music industry.

[25] Bob Hope died at age 100 on July 27, 2003, at his home in Taluca Lake, CA. He was one of the great performers of the vaudeville era.

PART TWO

MUSIC AND EARLY AMERICAN SOCIETY: SUMMARY

Key Terms

- 13 original colonies
- Industrial Revolution
- Slavery
- A cappella
- Comic and ballad operas
- High art music
- Antebellum Period
- Precentor

- Rubato
- African Diaspora
- Dancing the slaves
- Melisma
- Juba dance
- Cakewalk dance
- Jim crow
- Zip coon

Featured Genres/Styles

- Folk music
- Operettas
- Classical music
- Psalm and hymn singing
- Minstrelsy
- Vaudeville

Music and Society

- Music was used as a social diversion from work.
- Segregated communities shaped what and how people used music.
- One's socioeconomic status affected their chances of receiving formal music training.
- The transnational nature of "Yankee Doodle" and its subsequent recognition by the 109th Congress of the U.S.
- Types of musical instruments used during the Colonial Period were based on availability, cost, and one's musical skills.
- Dance, like music, created a diversion from arduous agricultural duties.
- Music and society were not segregated but rather worked in tandem, thus fueling, for instance, the types of topics people sang about.
- Religious beliefs affected one's music circumstances.
- Slaves' music activities can be examined based on the social context they were afforded, namely work, recreation, and worship.

Discussion Questions:

- What were some of the first cultures to contribute to the formation of American music?
- What is meant by Old Immigration and New Immigration?
- Are there any vestiges of minstrelsy in today's entertainment business?
- Why did people choose to perform music using certain instruments?
- Why did people choose to live in segregated communities, and did this affect their music activities?

- Offer reasons why some people regard secular music as sacrilegious while others do not.
- How did African slaves use music as a means to persevere in a hostile environment? Identify specific music practices, including lyrical usages.

Learning Beyond the Classroom:

- Attend a circus or carnival and determine if any remnants of minstrelsy, traveling road shows, or vaudeville still exist.
- Go to an ethnic festival (other than your own ethnic group) to examine the dissimilarities as well as similarities to your own group.
- Search the web to learn how to construct and play a recorder instrument. If possible, purchase an inexpensive harmonica and search YouTube to learn how to play it.
- Play a game with family or friends to see who can identify and sing some of America's early folk songs.
- Attend several places of worship to examine the following:
  - Styles of music sung and/or played
  - Instruments used
  - Do the singers and instrumentalists appear to be trained?
  - Is there congregational singing?
- Research your family's heritage(s) for types of music (and dances) and instruments used in their lives.

PART THREE

Bourbon Street in the French Quarter. © Jerry Cooke/CORBIS

A NEW CENTURY AND TWO WORLD WARS

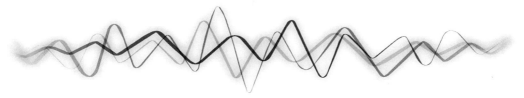

1900-WORLD WAR I
- CHAPTER SEVEN: Popular Entertainment (Ragtime, Marching Band Music, Tin Pan Alley, Mainstream Musical Theater, Black Musical Theatre)
- CHAPTER EIGHT: New Orleans Jazz

WORLD WAR I – WORLD WAR II
- CHAPTER NINE: Blues (Folk and Classic styles)
- CHAPTER TEN: Country (Hillbilly and Bluegrass styles)
- CHAPTER ELEVEN: Chicago Jazz, New York Jazz, and Big Band Jazz

OVERVIEW

The phenomenal feat of human flying achieved by the success of Orville and Wilbur Wright's flight at Kitty Hawk, North Carolina, in December 1903 demonstrated that Americans were progressing exponentially at a pace that exceeded many expectations. Without question, the turn of the 20th century inspired hope for a brighter future for Americans. Reflecting this hope for a greater America, the now-established middle class engaged in social entertainment such as ragtime and marching band music, which appealed to people's popular tastes. Tin Pan Alley–an entrepreneurial aspect of the music business–helped to fuel these growing tastes and spawn the eventual proliferation of sheet music publications.

Into the middle of the second decade of the new century, America's momentum was stifled somewhat with worldwide confrontations over territorial, national, political, and cultural issues as a number of countries engaged in a world war. In 1917, the United States entered WWI when it declared war on Germany. As vaudevillian inspired performances were becoming passé by the end of the war (1918), new approaches to entertainment were taking hold, particularly an "American" musical theatre that embraced the importance of story, music, and dance to a successful production.

Events leading up to, during, and just after WWI, which ended in 1918, fostered new ideas and attitudes about the American spirit, and these new perspectives permeated the entertainment industry. For instance, in 1908 the first major automobile–the Model T. Ford–was sold, favorably affecting how consumers viewed the emergence and use of technologies such as radio and sound recordings. The National Organization for the Advancement of Colored People (NAACP) was founded the following year.

The music industry, as well as other business sectors, seriously began to consider the marketability of products to the rising African American community. America was not only concerned about domestic problems, but also about its interests and resources abroad. Its disagreement with Nazism and related issues in Europe opened the door for its declaration of war against Germany. The American entertainment world, beginning with musical theatre, reflected the segregation from European socialistic ideals as thematic material for productions by gradually establishing a truly American theatre. In 1927, the production of *Showboat* launched a plethora of American theatricalism. That same year, the film titled *The Jazz Singer* starring Al Jolson inspired a flurry of films with songs and dialogue. A cascade of events concerning the rights of women and other feminist issues occurred in record numbers. Some of these included:

1. A demonstration in New York against sweatshops and child labor in 1908.
2. In 1911, 146 people, mainly women, were killed in a fire at the Triangle Shirtwaist Company sweatshop in New York.
3. In 1915, the Women's International League for Peace and Freedom was founded.
4. In 1916, the National Women's Party was founded; the first birth control clinic (Brooklyn, New York) was opened;[1] and Jeannette Rankin (of Montana) became the first woman elected to the House of Representatives.
5. In 1917, women protested at the White House for the right to vote.

For the first time in the Unites States, women were coming to the forefront with regard to public entertainment. Certainly women had been a part of public stage entertainment during the last third of the 19th century, but the numbers rarely rivaled those of their male contemporaries. In general, women were more accepted in sociocultural entertainment such as operettas, theatre, and music concerts, and less appreciated for their musicality in burlesque shows, minstrelsy, and vaudeville. Even though women were just as talented as men, opportunities for them were curtailed as the result of gender discrimination. Theatre houses and booking agents either personally discriminated against women or socially discriminated against them in fear of repercussion. The surge of women's protests for equal rights during this time brought rightfully needed attention to their concerns, and brought other possibilities to light with regard to entertainment. Sound recordings (to be discussed later in this chapter) were one such opportunity.

Black Migration

Near the close of and slightly after WWI, thousands of African Americans had migrated from Florida, Alabama, Louisiana, Tennessee, and Mississippi to areas such as Chicago and New York for better opportunities. For many, the boll weevil (insect) was destroying most opportunities for agricultural jobs. Perhaps just as important, many desired to get away from the relentlessly oppressive southern racial prejudices that were an inescapable part of their daily lives.

In Chicago, black neighborhoods sprang up in the south and west sides. Many of the migrants worked in meat packing factories and steel mills, and at various domestic jobs. With regard to music influences in Chicago, notable performers included Eddie Boyd, Big Bill Broonzy, Blind Lemon Jefferson, Memphis Minnie, Tampa Red, Washboard Sam, Roosevelt Sykes, and John Lee "Sonny Boy" Williamson. Those who migrated from the Mississippi Delta such as Bill Broonzy, Tampa Red,

---

[1] While the first public birth control clinic opened at this time, Margaret Sanger was arrested for opening one. In 1921, Ms. Sanger formed the American Birth Control League.

Memphis Minnie, and Blind Lemon Jefferson were the most influential. They brought their recitative country blues style of singing and playing, and fused it with urbanized conditions to create a distinct "Chicago blues" sound.

Jazz musicians from New Orleans also migrated to the big cities after the closing of the red-light district in New Orleans known as Storyville, and to take advantage of the many economic opportunities in the North. Musicians from New Orleans who migrated to Chicago brought with them the excitement of the New Orleans jazz sound, which spawned the development of Chicago jazz. The urbanized city of Chicago was flourishing in terms of the nightclub scene; it demanded the best quality music, with an even greater focus on dance music. In New York, the sound of New Orleans jazz was greatly influenced by the Original Dixieland Jazz Band, featuring Bix Beiderbecke, which spawned what some regard as New York Dixieland. At the same time, different approaches to instrumentation, texture, harmony, rhythm, and dynamics in jazz were being incorporated by artists such as Fletcher Henderson, Paul Whiteman, Duke Ellington, and Jean Goldkette. Noted as the entertainment capital of the world, New York's cosmopolitan environment also demanded diversity, skill, musicianship, and class for its many entertainment sources.

Jazz was being heard not only in America, but in Europe as well. The Original Dixieland Jazz Band had traveled to Europe as early as 1919, and others soon followed. In 1924, Saw Wooding and his group recorded in Berlin and played in Copenhagen. His band consisted of piano (Wooding), banjo, drums, trumpets (3), trombone, tuba, and woodwind players (3), all of whom played several instruments. Noble Sissle and His Orchestra performed in Paris in 1929. European venues were integrated with regard to black and white bands as well as audiences, but it was a different story in the United States.

By the 1920s, the vinyl record boom was occurring, and in addition to male country blues songsters, female vocalists were also being recorded. Resulting from the spread of blues to so many geographical areas, performers who were nurtured in environments quite dissimilar to those of the early southern bluesmen began to perform this marketable music, but with their own personal lyrical and somewhat melodic inflections. Here, a window of opportunity gave rise to women performers, particularly African American women. Known as the classic blues era, certain performance traditions of the early bluesmen had become "classic." Some of these included maintaining a strict performance of the AAB song form and 12-bar blues progression, and, for women, lascivious lyrics aimed at male listeners. Many of the songs were conversations between a man and a woman expressed from a woman's viewpoint, presented for the enjoyment of men. Some of these titles include "Wayward Girl Blues" (ca. 1925) by Lottie Kimbrough, "I Hate That Train Called the M & O" (ca. 1930) by Lucille Hogan, "Dead Drunk Blues" (ca. 1930) by Lillian Miller, and "Stranger Blues" (ca. 1928) by Rosie Mae Moore.

In addition to recording country and classic blues, popular songs among people in the Appalachian region as well as working class white citizens were also sought after by record companies. This music was referred to as "hillbilly." Both blues and hillbilly styles were referred to as "specialty" music and thus were promoted as race and hillbilly music, black music and rural white music respectively.

Women Singers

Blues was not the only style of secular music sung by women. Women became a regular fixture with big bands. Catering to the diverse musical tastes in New York, women sang blues, ballads, Tin Pan Alley, and vocal jazz songs. Some of the most popular singers include these:

Ivie Anderson (Duke Ellington's band, 1930s)
Mildred Bailey (Paul Whiteman's Orchestra, 1930s)
Ella Fitzgerald (Chick Webb's band, 1935)

Helen Ward, Martha Tilton, and Helen Forrest (all three sang for Benny Goodman's Orchestra at some point during the 1930s)

Edythe Wright (Tommy Dorsey's band, 1930s)

Helen O'Connell (Tommy Dorsey's band, late 1930s/40s)

Sister Rosetta Tharpe[2] (Lucky Millinder's band during the 1940s)

Billie Holiday, Lee Wiley, Ella Fitzgerald, and Mildred Bailey were recognized recording artists during the 1930s/40s, and in retrospect, helped to set the stage for the "popular singer" tradition that began in the 1940s. At the same time, women were being recognized for their instrumental skills. Some noted instrumentalists included Shirley Clay, a trumpeter who played with Claude Hopkins (1930s); Mary Lou Williams, a pianist who played with Andy Kirk's Twelve Clouds of Joy (1930s); and the pianist Lovie Austin. As a result of the war effort and other social conditions, by the end of WWII blues music was frequently performed in big cities where it functioned more as dance and entertainment music than as sociocultural commentary on black lifestyles. Thus *urban* or *city blues* became a more appropriate designation for this particular manifestation of the blues.[3]

Big Band Jazz

While black bands in New York from the 1920s through mid-1930s played in small to moderately large venues that were primarily intended for black audiences, white bands "were catering to a much wider and more generalized audience: big ballrooms, hotel dance floors, [and] major vaudeville and movie theatres were their usual settings."[4] Consequently, white bands were generally larger–hence the term "big bands."[5] The music played by these bands was not strictly jazz, as performances frequently included various styles of dance music–jazz, waltz, marches, ragtime, and even polkas. To suit the musical tastes of the general audience, other instruments were added that corresponded to stylistic preferences. For instance, Paul Whiteman's Orchestra in 1928 included 2 pianos, accordion, drums (also chimes, gong, plus other percussion instruments), bass, banjo, 2 tubas, 5 violins, 6 woodwinds, 4 trumpets, and 4 trombones. Violins were most suitable for waltzes; the accordion sound pleased polka enthusiasts of different nationalities; the tuba helped maintain the strict rhythm needed for marches; and the remaining instruments were typical among jazz bands. Because jazz was more marketable than waltzes, marches, and polkas, "jazz" denoted the overall flavor of these bands.

Big bands were not the only type of bands in Chicago and New York. In Chicago, the "south side style" called for small, 3- to 4-piece bands, and in New York small bands were ideal for the New York Dixieland and jam-session styles of playing. In addition to bands, there was a solo piano tradition of playing boogie-woogie, stride, and blues throughout these and other cities that permeated and influenced jazz styles as well as gospel music. Some pianists who played as a soloist as well as with a small combo (e.g., piano, bass, and drums) include Nat King Cole, Meade "Lux" Lewis, Fats Waller, James P. Johnson, Eubie Blake, Willie "the lion" Smith, and later players such as Art Tatum, Oscar Peterson, Dave Brubeck, and many others. Still other pianists during the 1920s, such as Thomas Dorsey and Perry Bradford (who often played organ as well) were also incorporating elements of the aforementioned piano styles in black religious music. Adding the 6/8 meter of blues, extended and altered chords

---

[2] Sister Rosetta Tharpe is most noted as a gospel singer beginning in the 1950s.

[3] A distinction will later be made between urban blues and rhythm & blues.

[4] Keepnews, *A Pictorial History of Jazz*, p. 117.

[5] The term big band, whether black or white bands, was a general term used for bands that were larger than the typical 6-piece or 9-piece band of New Orleans jazz and Chicago jazz respectively.

of jazz, and rhythmic tendencies of ragtime, blues, and jazz to religious hymns, contributed to characteristics and the subsequent rise of gospel music.

In addition to blues, jazz, and gospel, the folk singing tradition among white communities in the development of hillbilly music. Characterized by lyrics that centered on people's lifestyles, and instrument usages of fiddle and banjo, hillbilly music is the foundation of what we now regard as country (or country & western) music.

Country And Blues Music

What is now regarded as country music emerged from the folk singing traditions of the 17th century. At that time, it was not called "country" but rather "folk" or more appropriately, "hillbilly" (sung by people in the hills) music. In fact, the term *country/country & western* did not become a recognized stylistic category until the 1940s when, as a marketing scheme, it became an encompassing term for hillbilly, bluegrass, and western swing. The term *hillbilly* remained the same during the 1920s, while the latter two, as appellations for distinctive styles, did not surface until the 1940s.

In America the word *country* is used in a number of ways. It can refer to a body of land, a rural setting, a colloquial expression denoting a type of, by some perceptions, inferior dialect and social character, and lastly, a style of music.

Based on my exposure to the opinions of thousands of people of many demographic types, it seems that a number of people, particularly teens through college-age students, initially possess a somewhat negative attitude toward country music. They profess that country songs often consist of whining, references to one's dog, and the singing of tales of lost love and rural lifestyles–all of which do not relate to their own lifestyles. But how does this differ from the blues? In fact, the expression of whining is often characterized by the usage of bending notes and *melismatic* singing or by numerous vocal utterances, both of which are evident in blues music. Tales of lost love and rural lifestyles are also common in the blues. The word *dog*(s) is an African American euphemism used to refer to one's disgust with a particular person, such as what is heard in Big Mama Thornton's 1953 recording titled "Hound Dog" and Louis Armstrong and His Orchestra's (ca. 1932) song titled "You Rascal You,"[6] Yet I hear mostly favorable opinions of the blues. Notwithstanding the fact that, among many, blues singing is more rhythmically diverse and thus interesting, but also a word such as "dog" is used metaphorically in blues while in country the word's meaning refers to an animal. Although it should be understood that this is tied to culture and region, it nonetheless demands some attention. This said, I invite you to explore the several different types of country music so that your opinion is not based solely on assumptions of a song's demographics or social settings. The various types of country music addressed in this text section include hillbilly and bluegrass.

The popularity of hillbilly music grew as musicians traveled to various venues such as county fairs, tent shows, and even medicine shows around the turn of the 20th century. Radio was perhaps the most significant disseminating vehicle, as it eventually broadcasted hillbilly along with blues, jazz, classical, and religious lectures to people all over the country. People who would not normally listen to hillbilly were now able to formulate an opinion of it based on personal experience. As the demand for this music grew, string bands consisting of banjo, guitar, mandolin, and Hawaiian guitar became commonplace. Demand precipitated radio shows such as WWVA to market barn dances–a favorite pastime–to rural people. In 1925, WSM[7] radio in Nashville, Tennessee sponsored a Saturday Barn Dance that included

---

[6] Here is an interesting anecdote: Presently among youth, the word *dog* is used to reference one's friend.

[7] WSM reflects the station's motto, "We Shield Millions."

burlesque comedy and hillbilly music with artists such as the Fruit Jar Drinkers, the Possum Hunters, and Uncle Dave Macon. WSM radio became, and continues to be the most career-turning venue for country singers. Today it is known as the Grand Ole Opry.

By WWII, another migration of about 50,000 African Americans from the South influenced the style of music that was performed in the urban areas of Chicago. Again, musicians from the Mississippi delta region predominated: Chester "Howlin' Wolf" Burnett, Riley "Blues Boy" King (a.k.a. B.B. King), Jimmy Reed, and Muddy Waters. These musicians received their inspiration and nurturing via the singing mannerisms they heard on plantations. For instance, Howlin' Wolf was born in 1920 and lived on a plantation in the delta region before migrating to Chicago. B.B. King was inspired by the many blacks he encountered while working on a plantation in Mississippi. Singing stylizations of gospel and other forms of religious singing heard in black churches influenced blues artists such as Bill Broonzy and John Lee Hooker. Finally, the street corner was another forum where talents were honed, like those of blues artists Bo Diddley and Blind Lemon Jefferson.

Similar to the negative implications that resulted from identifying black music as a "race series," country music was also unfairly misunderstood, leading to further stereotypes of the music. To improve its image, the term *hillbilly*, which was used by musicians, was replaced with *country* or *country & western* during the 1940s by the music industry. In addition, the same events that contributed to the eventual dissemination of rhythm & blues during the 1940s–the creation of BMI and subsequent boycott of ASCAP–caused country music to gain further recognition.[8]

In the 1940s, to help disassociate the label "hillbilly" from country & western in people's minds as well as to accommodate a growing interest in the music, record labels opted to produce mainstream-type or "pop" songs using certain effective musical techniques. To accomplish this, singers performed love songs in a vocally dramatic manner–a typical technique of mainstream music–but with a southern or country-type accent. Record labels found it even more advantageous to have already established "pop" artists (not country & western) record a country song in the manner of country & western stylizations.[9]

MUSICAL THEATRE AFTER WWI: EUROPEAN AMERICAN AND AFRICAN AMERICAN SHOWS AND TRADITIONS

European American

Following a slowing down of theatrical productions during WWI, the quest for a truly American theatre was fulfilled through the plethora of shows under the guise of revues, musical comedy, and eventually musical theatre. *Ziegfeld's Follies* in 1917, 1918, and 1919 capitalized upon the talented and popular Isidore Itzkowitz, better known as Eddie Cantor. Cantor also worked with the Schuberts (Ziegfeld's archrival) in their productions titled *The Midnight Rounders* (1920) and *Make it Snappy* (1922). These productions all took place along the Great White Way, a nickname for Broadway, located in midtown Manhattan between 42nd and 53rd Streets. Alternative theatre productions with black themes starring African American performers such as *Shuffle Along* (1921), *Put and Take* (1921), and *Strut Miss Lizzie* (1922) also gained ground after the war. Because of the social segregation that existed between European Americans and African Americans, each group will be considered separately.

---

[8] See Chapter Three.

[9] This was particularly evident in the 1950s with country songs recorded by artists such as Tony Bennett, Frankie Laine ("Hey, Good Lookin'"), and Mitch Miller ("Cold, Cold Heart").

Composers and lyricists who contributed to a distinct American Theatre had already been involved in the tradition of Tin Pan Alley. In addition to Florenz Ziegfeld, the Schuberts, and Irving Berlin, others included George and Ira Gershwin, Oscar Hammerstein II, Lorenz Hart, Jerome Kern, Cole Porter, and Richard Rodgers. The American spirit was solidified as these and other figures were writing and producing shows for an even broader audience through the slowly emerging film scene.

What distinguished American theatre from the previous fascination with European imperialism was the advent of the "talkies." Although *The Jazz Singer* (1927) starring Al Jolson was not the first film to use sound throughout, it was the first to include talking/singing with sound.[10] Jolson's success with the performance of "Mammy" sparked great interest among impresarios, composers, and performers leading to a flurry of musicals with sound. Although the list of songs below is by no means conclusive, it does furnish the reader with some of the most successful songs of American theatre from WWI through WWII.

"Till the Clouds Roll By"	1917	*Oh Boy!*
"Manhattan"	1925	*Garrick Gaieties*
"Ol' Man River"	1927	*Show Boat*
"Let's Do It"	1928	*Paris*
"I Got Rhythm"	1930	*Girl Crazy*
"Lover"	1932	*Love Me Tonight*
"Night and Day"	1932	*The Gay Divorcee*
"I Get a Kick Out of You"	1934	*Anything Goes*
"Summertime"	1935	*Porgy and Bess*
"They Can't Take That Away from Me"	1937	*Shall We Dance*
"Let's Call the Whole Thing Off"	1937	*Shall We Dance*
"A Foggy Day"	1937	*Damsel in Distress*
"Love Is Here to Stay"	1937	*The Golden Follies*
"Isn't It Romantic"	1937	*The Golden Follies*
"The Lady Is a Tramp"	1937	*Babes in Arms*
"My Funny Valentine"	1937	*Babes in Arms*
"I Wish I Were in Love Again"	1937	*Babes in Arms*
"Bewitched"	1940	*Pal Joey*
"Oklahoma"	1943	*Oklahoma*
"Oh, What a Beautiful Morning"	1943	*Oklahoma*
"Bali Ha'i"	1949	*South Pacific*

As American theatre drew upon its precursor, vaudeville, so did the film industry (particularly in Hollywood) draw upon the traditions established by American theatre for its foundation. Beginning with *The Jazz Singer* in 1927, starring Al Jolson, this film inspired some of the most notable composers and lyricists of American theatre (most of those previously mentioned) to move to Hollywood for a more lucrative career. Many of them continued to write for both Broadway and film. While attendance at Broadway-styled theatre shows was still good during the Depression and throughout WWII, particularly in New York (where attendance was quite the fashion), "going to the theatre" for many Americans came to mean seeing and hearing their favorite personality on film. The suave dancing of Ginger Rogers and Fred Astaire, the cute singing and dancing of Shirley Temple (the girl with curls), and the

---

[10] *The Broadway Melody* in 1929 was the first musical to include speaking and singing with sound "throughout" the production.

inspirational vocalizations of Judy Garland in the *Wizard of Oz* (1939) became so popular that film emerged as the new entertainment media for the dissemination of music. With the additional impetus of improvements in sound recordings and radio, consumers began to favor records over sheet music as their means of enjoying music from their favorite visual productions. In the 1960s, the postwar baby boomers by virtue of their sheer numbers had ushered in an era in which the desire was to be entertained by rhythm & blues, rock & roll, and country music performers. Live Broadway shows could not compete with the advent of television as the main medium for promoting popular music stars and their music. Advertisers soon began to invest their dollars in radio and television, which impacted the diminishing popularity of American theatre.

African American

Heralded as the first all-black musical to achieve "major success on Broadway," *Shuffle Along* combined the efforts of Flournoy Miller and Aubrey Lyle (authors of the book of the same name), with those of Eubie Blake (composer) and Noble Sissle (librettist). The storyline involved two characters, Steve Jenkins and Sam Peck (who performed in blackface) as candidates for mayor of "Jimtown." As partners in a grocery store business, each candidate succumbs to unscrupulous acts of embezzlement, deceit, and trickery in an effort to win the highly esteemed office. Each promises the other that, if triumphant, he will elect the other as chief of police. Steve Jenkins wins the race, and elects Sam Peck as chief of police. A fight ensues between these two characters and a reform candidate, Harry Walton, unseats Steve Jenkins as mayor.

Despite the fact that *Shuffle Along* continued the display of derogatory, stereotypical images of African Americans as untrustworthy, with a propensity for engaging in unscrupulous activities and savage behavior such as fighting, the major focus was on the music and dancing. With regard to dancing, the final number, titled "Baltimore Buzz," was the "show stopper" in many people's view, which is probably why it was the final number. In any event, "nothing short of incomparable," outstanding, and "superb dancing" is how many described it. In fact, as the result of reviews and consumer comments, some advertisements highlighted the phrase "Baltimore Buzz" more prominently than the musical's title in either large and/or bold type to draw attention to "what all the shouting was about." Other advertising phrasing that illuminated the dancing aspect include "the world's greatest dancing show," and "*Shuffle Along* is the Negro Lightnin'!"

With regard to the music, the outline below provides song titles, recording dates, and bands for the musical numbers.

"How Ya' Gonna Keep 'Em Down on the Farm" (1919)–Noble Sissle (singer) and Lt. James Europe's 369th U.S. Infantry ("Hell Fighters") Band
"On Patrol in No Man's Land (1919)–Noble Sissle (singer) and Lt. James Europe's 369th U.S. Infantry ("Hell Fighters") Band
"Mirandy" (1919)–Noble Sissle (singer) and Lt. James Europe's 369th U.S. Infantry ("Hell Fighters") Band
"Gee, I'm Glad I'm from Dixie" (1920)–Noble Sissle (singer) and Orchestra
"Baltimore Buzz" (1921)–Noble Sissle (singer) and His Sizzling Syncopators
"Bandana Days"/"I'm Just Wild About Harry" (1921)–Eubie Blake and the Shuffle Along Orchestra
"In Honeysuckle Time" (1921)–Noble Sissle (singer) and His Sizzling Syncopators
"Love Will Find a Way" (1921)–Noble Sissle (singer), Eubie Blake (piano)
"Bandana Days" (1921)–Noble Sissle (singer), Eubie Blake (piano)
"Daddy, Won't You Please Come Home" (1921)–Gertrude Saunders (singer) and Tim Brymm and His Black Devil Orchestra

"Baltimore Buzz/In Honeysuckle Time" (1921)–Eubie Blake (solo piano)
"Gypsy Blues" (1921)–Paulo Whiteman and His Orchestra
"I'm Craving for That Kind of Love" (1921)–Gertrude Saunders (singer) and Tim Brymm and His
      Black Devil Orchestra
"The Fight" (1924)–Dialogue by Flournoy Miller and Aubrey Lyle

The proliferation of sheet music sales of songs such as "I'm Just Wild About Harry," "Bandana Days," and Baltimore Buzz" was another corroboration that impacted the importance of *Shuffle Along* to black musical theatre. At sixty cents per song, sheet music sales were very beneficial to composers' and lyricists' annual income. More significant to African American culture, the lyrics in these and songs that followed gradually diminished pejorative black stereotypes. Instead, songs became more akin to general American culture. In other words, subject matter was centered on the experiences of most Americans. Some examples include love as in "Love Will Find a Way" and "I'm Craving For That Kind of Love"; nostalgia as in "Bandana Days"; and matrimony as in "In Honeysuckle Time," "Gypsy Blues" and "Mirandy."

In closing, *Shuffle Along* surpassed expectations as a musical production that displayed true aspects of the African American community. As eloquently stated by Robert Kimball–author, researcher, and producer–in the liner notes of a recording under the auspices of Recorded Anthology of American Music:

> The show restored authentic black artistry to the mainstream of the American theatre. A daring synthesis of ragtime and operetta, it had an enormous impact on the development of the Broadway musical during its most vibrant years. It featured jazz dancing, was the first black musical to play white theatres across the United States, and was a vital part of the black cultural renaissance of the 1920s.[11]

The success of Shuffle Along ushered in a number of productions under the guise of black musical theatre. Furthermore, it set the stage for current trends in the field of American musical theatre. The list below includes some of the more successful black musical theatre productions that followed *Shuffle Along*.

Oh Joy (1922)
Plantation Review/From Dixie to Broadway (1922/1924)
Runnin' Wild (1923)
Chocolate Dandies (1924)
Rang Tang (1927)
Bottom Land (1927)
Keep Shufflin' (1928)
Blackbirds (1928)
Deep Harlem (1929)
Hot Chocolates (1929)
Messin' Around (1929)
Porgy and Bess (1935)
Cabin in the Sky (ca. 1942)
St. Louis Woman (ca. 1947)
Green Pastures (1936)

---

[11] Robert Kimball, [Producer]. *Shuffle Along*. Recorded Anthology of American Music, Inc. Library of Congress Card No. 75-751056, 1976.

CHAPTER SEVEN

POPULAR ENTERTAINMENT

RAGTIME

While traveling road shows and vaudeville were some of the most popular forms of entertainment for much of America during the late 19th century, ragtime was becoming a favorite type of music for social gatherings and entertainment. Its dissemination is attributed both to sheet music publications by various publishing houses throughout the country, including Tin Pan Alley (discussed later in this chapter) and to performances by piano players and various groups: brass bands, New Orleans jazz bands, and marching bands. Consequently, ragtime was frequently heard in cafes, supper clubs, political rallies, publishing firms, theatre houses (for eventual silent movies, including intermission music, and vaudeville shows), and lascivious venues such as those found in New Orleans's tenderloin district, namely Storyville (1897–1917).

Many consumers' first contact with this "proper" dance music was by way of social dance occasions. Taking pleasure in these songs, novice to highly-well-literate readers of piano scores sought out their favorite ragtime pieces to please their guests for listening to and–more important here–for dance music in the home. (It is important to note that a Victorian-type lifestyle still existed for many, in which case it was appropriate to entertain guests in one's parlor rather than consorting with them at commercial venues.) Composers and publishers alike shared an interest in producing ragtime music that catered to this musical taste. As pointed out by William Kenney:

> *The composition of scores and arrangements for*
> *social dance music had long offered an area of*
> *interracial cooperation between black*
> *musician/composers and white social dance*
> *instructors. Such musicians as J. R. Conner, James*
> *Hemmenway, Issac Hazard, and Edward De Roland in*
> *Philadelphia; William Brady and Walter F. Craig in*
> *New York; Henry E. Williams in Boston; and Joseph*
> *W. Postlewaite in St. Louis organized orchestras and,*
> *allying themselves with white social dancing teachers,*
> *composed dance music for publication.*[1]

---

[1] William H. Kenney. (1991). "James Scott and the Culture of Classic Ragtime," *American Music*, p. 10.

Although often featuring instruments like the banjo, the fiddle, and even the harmonica, ragtime music is most closely associated with the piano, largely due to sheet music publications, which are primarily arranged for piano. In addition, the piano can perform the principal components of music–melody, harmony, and rhythm–while most instruments only perform one of those functions. Finally, the piano was socially favored because of its economic value as a barometer of social status. So-cioculturally (i.e., among high-culture afficionados), playing ragtime (or any music) on the piano by reading sheet music was an admired achievement as well as often required for attaining upward mobility. Ragtime was exciting and exhilarating music that incited dancing, encouraged joyous emotions, and/or provided musical challenges for performers/composers.

Popular ragtime pieces were also orchestrated for larger bands. In general, ragtime pieces that were orchestrated for a small band or an ensemble did not play in the fashion of brass bands–the bands responsible for the proliferation of New Orleans jazz/Dixieland jazz style. Instead, pieces were orches-trated in the style of standard marching band music. As pointed out by William Kenney with refer-ence to James Scott's experiences in Carthage, Missouri, marching band type orchestrations permeated throughout America:

> [the] "... concert/military band still functioned as
> both concert groups and dance orchestras. As a
> concert band ... [bands] played marches, waltzes,
> and light classics ... When playing for the militia and
> citizens as a dance band [bands] established
> nineteenth century social dance music with the more
> rhythmically heated early twentieth century steps. ...
> At the turn of the century, wind ensembles featured
> the two-step, a fast ballroom dance introduced in the
> late 1880s ... The step was performed to standard
> marches like Souza's 'The Washington Post, (1889). ...
> Scott's 'The Fascinator–March and Two-Step, and 'On
> the Pike, were arranged for wind ensemble, and were
> performed both at dances and in concert.[2]

In addition to functioning as marching band music, ragtime was the favored accompaniment for dance occasions. For instance, beginning in the last third of the 19th century, an event known as a "cut-ting contest" consisted of two piano players, each with their own piano (placed side by side or back to back), attempting to outperform the other. Although no recordings were made of this practice, one can imagine all sorts of antics. These may have included playing the entire piece or a passage faster; different interpretations and/or improvisations; playing standing as opposed to sitting; a greater use of syncopations, and so on. The recording of "The Entertainer" as performed by Katia and Marielle LaBeque illustrates this exciting performance practice.[3]

Several theories exist as to the origin of ragtime with respect to its use as an identification of a specific style of music. Some say it derived from the syncopated rhythms that were produced by shoeshine boys slapping "rags" on customer shoes, while others believe it was inspired by the cutting contest–a common dance activity involving rhythmic dance steps that was regularly seen on many plantations before the Civil War–where the winner would receive the most "rags" raised in the air by

[2] *Ibid.*, pp. 8–9.
[3] Angel Records, Hollywood, CA, *Gladrags: Katia and Mariella LaGeque Performing on Two Pianos.*

dancers or ecstatically appreciative bystanders. In both cases, rhythm is the common denominator, and thus the word *ragging* was commonly used with reference to playing any song that was syncopated. Accordingly, the production of syncopated rhythms became the staple of traditional ragtime.[4] While syncopated rhythms were commonplace, particularly for dance occasions, it was not uncommon for a composer of ragtime music during the late 19th and early 20th centuries to compose a piece with less syncopation, in slower tempo, and in a triple meter. Furthermore, some pieces consisted of different tempi, thus displaying ragtime's ability to function as listening as well as dance music. All of this is evident in Joplin's piece titled "Bethena" as performed by Marvin Hamlisch in a 1974 recording. Another example of a relatively minimal use of syncopation is heard in the piece titled "Solace" (1908) as recorded in 1975 by Itzhak Perlman and André Previn. In this performance, the timbre of the violin exhibits yet another sound quality.

As is the case regarding temporal parameters of previous styles and genres, there can be no marginalization of ragtime. Scott Joplin once stated that syncopation–the very foundation of ragtime–was heard as long as the Negro race has been here. Alluding to the practice of rhythmic complexity, Joplin, born in 1868, heard syncopated rhythms on the banjo as played by local and itinerant black musicians. Furthermore, Louis Moreau Gottschalk (1829–1869) is generally accepted in scholarly circles as the first American composer to fuse elements of European and African slave music in his work titled "La Bamboula," which foreshadowed the beginnings of ragtime. This music was heard in cafes, minstrel shows, wine bars, vaudeville shows, parlors, music halls, brothels, and/or publishing houses well before 1897. During the early 1900s, ragtime grew in popularity as sheet music publications helped to disseminate the music to a growing middle class. The first publications include William Krell's composition titled "Mississippi Rag" (January 1897) and Thomas Turpin's (1873–1922) piece titled "Harlem Rag" (December, 1897).

The musical development of ragtime stems from certain characteristics and performance practices among African slaves combining with traditions of Western music. The syncopated rhythm in African-based music used by slaves is the most noticeable feature evident in ragtime. Form and structure, melodic, harmonic, and rhythmic counterpoint, and the use of standard rules of Western harmony are all characteristics of ragtime that were inspired by the Western music tradition. With respect to form, numerous ragtime pieces often consist of three or four different sections that are organized in a certain manner, most often AABBACCDD. Each section contains a distinct melodic theme and a pertinent harmonic progression. Take, for example, the piece "Maple Leaf Rag" (1899) by Scott Joplin. Its form is typical of many ragtime pieces. Moreover, each section contains an equal number of measures. Although this is the original form as established by Mr. Joplin, the sections may be organized differently by other artists. Jelly Roll Morton's version of "Maple Leaf Rag" illustrates this point.[5] The New England Conservatory Ragtime Ensemble's recording of "Maple Leaf Rag" demonstrates yet another way of performing the piece.[6] Here, dynamics are created by combining contrasting sounds, sparse and thick textures, and different volume levels.

Currently most people view ragtime as an instrumental style of music, but a general historical study of ragtime clearly demonstrates that songs from the minstrel period influenced its melodies. Performed by various minstrel and vaudeville performers, some songs included Ben Harney's "You've

---

[4] Scott Joplin makes reference to the notion that syncopation is a common African music tradition. Since Africans were brought to American soil during the transatlantic slave trade of the 1600s, and since syncopation is a common musical element of ragtime, one could argue that the beginnings of ragtime existed during the 1600s.

[5] See *Smithsonian Collection of Classic Jazz* [sound recording] Washington, D.C. : CBS Records, 1987.

[6] See *Jazz* [sound recording]. Opus Musicum OM128–130. 1980.

Been a Good Old Wagon But You've Done Broke Down," Ernest Hogan's "All Coons Look Alike to Me" (which was originally titled "All Pimps Look Alike to Me"), and W.T Jefferson's "My Coal Black Lady." Indeed, ragtime melodies derived from "coon songs" of the minstrel period.[7] In the context of minstrelsy, thematic material was centered on satires of rural and urban black lifestyles. One can apply a syllogism here: since syncopated rhythms were characteristic of black slave music, and minstrel, road show, and vaudeville performances drew heavily on black rural and urban lifestyles, then "coon songs" and their syncopated rhythms (a.k.a. ragtime) stood at the forefront as musical material for a performer's repertoire. Despite the fact that there was little distinction between the melodic character of "coon" and, in retrospect, a number of ragtime melodies just after the close of the Civil War, a concerted effort to disassociate the two arose by the late 19th century. To boost the demand for ragtime (as well as other) compositions, music publishing houses (e.g., in Boston, Chicago, St. Louis, and New York) employed strategies to market ragtime music to the growing middle class who desired to depart from music compositions with plantation themes and undertones of slavery. To suit the educated and musically literate public's demand for "good" and proper music (i.e., music generally not performed in "commercial" venues such as brothels and wine bars), publishing houses marketed ragtime pieces that combined musical elements of marching music and classical styles.

The "classic" tradition of ragtime is of great social and historical importance, as the factors underlying its development manifest significant social mores among black and white, albeit segregated, communities. In general, the classic tradition implied that the composer did not subject himself to the capricious and bawdy emotional character of "commercial" songs. Commercial music was enjoyed both as a middle class leisure activity and by migrants moving from southern rural areas to urban environments who needed social diversion from the arduous and frequently dangerous working conditions in factories and mines. During the late 19th century, various venues emerged that abetted in creating emotional and physical release from the daily work responsibilities of both groups. Largely attributed to the popularity of minstrel and vaudeville type entertainment, leisure activities included vaudeville theatres, silent movie theatres, saloons, supper clubs or dance halls, and amusement parks. These venues needed to appeal to a wide variety (i.e. socio-economically and culturally) of musical tastes. Frivolous music, which became regarded as commercial music, pleased most people's appetite for social diversion. Ragtime music was at the helm, as its rhythmic and exuberant vitality in many people's minds bore minimal reference to the past and seemed to illuminate a spirit of better times ahead. While these songs afforded job opportunities for many ragtime piano players, publishers, and composers, Joplin, Scott, and Boone also sought to present their music in the Victorian-like mannerism of pride and gentility for the middle and upper classes. Accordingly, they published/composed ragtime that combined musicological aspects of both classical and African American music styles. To accomplish this, composers notated in sheet music form the normally free, improvisational nature of ragtime pieces, allowing the performer to exhibit a more "controlled" emotional performance–a typical performance practice of classical music. These composers were well aware of the traditions of classical music as they frequently demonstrated the ability to include both classical and ragtime music on the same program performed in front of both black and/or white audiences.

---

[7] The word *coon* is generally regarded as a derogatory term, much like the word *nigger*, as both have the connotation of black inferiority. It is interesting to note that the term *coon* may not have had the same pejorative meaning in the late 19th century as it does today. See Edward A. Berlin's *Understanding the Language*, p. 6.

Labels like "ragtime" and "classical music" actually
obscured a far more fluid musical reality. James
Scott, Scott Joplin, and Blind Boone all mixed
ragtime with other genres in concert. Blind Boone,
swaying constantly at the keyboard, played everything
from Liszt's Hungarian Rhapsody no. 6, Gottschalk's
"Last Hope," "Imitation of a Train," and "Ragtime
Melody No. 1," to "old darky songs".[8]

With much attention given to ragtime during the late 19th and early 20th centuries, a number of other composers either composed ragtime songs and/or incorporated characteristics of it in works of varying genres. Regarded as the second of two great ragtime composers (Joplin being the first), James Scott (1885–1938) fused elements of marching music, classical, and African American songs contributing to the establishment of the "classic" ragtime tradition. Some of Scott's noted works include "Great Scott Rag" (1909), "Efficiency Rag" (1917), "New Era Rag" (1919), and "Modesty Rag–A Classic" (1920). Jelly Roll Morton was most noted for his ragtime piece titled "Grandpa's Spell" (1926). Other ragtime composers included Eubie Blake (1883–1983), John W. "Blind" Boone (1864–1927), George Botsford (1874–1949), Louis Chavin (1881–1908), Scott Hayden (1882–1915), Charles L. Johnson (1876–1950), Joseph Lamb (1887–1960), Arthur Marshall (1881–1968), Artie Matthews (1888–1958), Lucky Roberts (1887–1968), and Percy Wenrich (1887–1952). Although the majority of notable ragtime pieces were composed by men, women composers such as May Aufderheide (1890–1972) and Irene Giblin (1888–1974) were of great importance as well.

Works that also exhibit certain characteristics of ragtime include Joplin's *Treemonisha*. Although the first successful performance of this opera did not come to pass until the 1970s in Atlanta, Georgia, a rehearsal performance did occur in 1915 at the Lincoln Theatre, Washington D.C. *Treemonisha* is not a ragtime opera, but rather an "opera" that incorporates elements of ragtime. Its theme centers on education and its vital importance to blacks, particularly in America. Treemonisha, a young African American woman in a community of former slaves, is unlike much of her community. Her distinction, as conveyed in the opera, is based on her ability to articulate in ways similar to those of educated people rather than illiterates–whose decisions are often influenced by fallacies. Scholars have commented on the notion that the heroine in *Treemonisha* mirrors Joplin, as ". . . He wanted to free his people from poverty, ignorance, and superstition. . ."[9] It is evident by the music that Joplin was consciously portraying black people as more than worthy of the rights and citizenship bestowed upon all Americans. Indeed, many of his scores feature similar aurally favorable combinations of musical elements blending western European classical music, marching band music, folk music (black and white influences), and various African American music styles. Some of his celebrated ragtime pieces include "The Entertainer" (1902), "Bethena" (1905), "Ragtime Dance" (1906), "Pineapple Rag," and "Solace," (1908), and "Sugar Cane Rag" (1909). Eubie Blake was another composer who demonstrated an uncanny ability to incorporate ragtime with other genres. His musical score to *Shuffle Along*—the first successful musical theatre production to be written and performed by an African American–includes a number of songs that employ ragtime features. Irving Berlin's "Alexander's Ragtime Band" (1911) though not a ragtime piece, nevertheless illustrates the preponderance of ragtime as a viable, and thus marketable, style of music. In fact, Berlin's first full score to the musical *Watch Your Step* in 1914 was indeed a ragtime work.

---

[8] Kenney, p. 16.
[9] Kay C. Thompson. (1949). Lottie Joplin. *Record Changer 9* (October):8, p. 18.

MARCHING BAND MUSIC

As an important element of American music, the marching band tradition dates back to the Revolutionary War era, as bands were a "detail" of military platoons. Firmly established in the British tradition of duple and cut-time meters, an American marching band tradition did not become apparent until the late 19th century. Initially through the efforts of Patrick Gilmore (1829–1892), band music other than symphonic band music gradually became popular in America. Reflecting the American spirit and a truly American sound expressing patriotism and a voice for American nationalism, the work of John Philip Sousa (1854–1932) rises above all others. Appointed as the bandmaster of the elite Marine Band in 1880, Sousa quickly organized one of the most proficient bands of the time. Able to play for various occasions such as religious events, ballroom dancing, and social entertainment, his band's repertoire included various styles and music forms of the day such as marches, ragtime, hymns, patriotic songs, and even New Orleans jazz. Sousa is most memorable for his work titled "Stars and Stripes Forever" (1897). This work and others such as "The Revival" (1876), "El Capitan" (1886), "Washington Post" (1889), and "The Liberty Bell" (1893) helped to promote and firmly establish the American marching band tradition.

TIN PAN ALLEY

New York's commercial music district in Manhattan on 28th Street–known as Tin Pan Alley[10]–was the place where publishers and songwriters "plugged" their songs. The environment resembled an alley packed with numerous small rooms, each with a piano and a publisher and/or songwriter. The main objective of publishing companies was to plug, or advertise, their songs for a musical production, a well-known singer or stage performer, or the general consumer. Some rooms in Tin Pan Alley were occupied by the songwriter himself who plugged his songs for possible publishing contracts. For both the publisher and songwriter, this developed into a main source of income, as a growing number of consumers were becoming skilled in the art of reading music, particularly for piano. These consumers expressed a great desire to purchase sheet music of favorite songs from musicals, minstrelsy, or vaudeville in an effort to entertain themselves and guests during their leisure times. Such a demand engendered a lucrative business for many songwriters and publishers. For example, in 1892 Charles Harris (1867–1930) is credited for having the "first million seller" with his song "After the Ball." Other early notable songwriters included Paul Dresser, Harry Von Tilzer, Kerry Mills, George Evans, Egbert Van Alstyne, and George M. Cohan. Later notable songwriters included Irving Berlin and George and Ira Gershwin.

The publisher (and there were many) made the songs available to the general public through various marketing strategies. The most effective strategy entailed the dissemination of music through various live productions. Vaudeville and musical theatre were particularly favored because they appealed to all social classes, especially the middle and upper classes. Because the effect of radio and sound recording was minimal from the beginning of the 20th century through WWI, consumer attendance at live productions was at an all time high. Publishers paid close attention to those songs that received the

---

[10] William Taylor's book *Inventing Time Square: Commerce and Culture at the Crossroads of the World* (New York: Russell Sage Foundation, 1991) seems to be the earliest reference to the term "Tin Pan Alley." The author points out that Monroe Rosenfeld made reference to the combination of musical styles in three areas of New York–lower Broadway, Bowery, and Union Square–as sounding similar to musical dissonance.

most applause from audiences. While other factors such as the singer's popularity, the instrumentation, the specific scene, or the story may have contributed to a song's appeal, its consumer-friendly character was the overriding determinant of its popularity.

Tin Pan Alley's effect on the popular music scene at the turn of the 20th century was much more important than its notoriety as a geographic location. An increasingly large number of people began to purchase pianos, as this instrument enabled them to more effectively play the many new and exciting songs of vaudeville (including minstrel songs), arias from well-known operas, ragtime, and musical theatre. The piano served a dual purpose by displaying one's upward socioeconomic and consequent sociopolitical mobility, and by allowing for a more complete performance of the song, as it could simultaneously produce (depending upon one's musicality) the melody, harmony, and rhythm.

The task of the composer/lyricist was to create simple but tuneful music and supportive lyrics that would capture the heart of America's sociocultural population. An example is Irving Berlin's lyrics to "Marie from Sunny Italy" (1907), which was an appealing song that spoke to immigrants from Italy while at the same time creating an enchanting image of Italy for non-Italians. Berlin's "Play a Simple Melody" (1914) was a ". . . partner song . . . designed to be sung simultaneously in duet with a second song. . . ."[11] Irving Berlin, born Israel Baline in Russia, 1888, was one of the most recognized composers of this musical era. Emigrating to America with his family in 1893, little Irving was nurtured in New York's cosmopolitan environment of Italians, Jews, blacks, German's, and Irish. At an early age he began to teach himself piano and soon became a performer and composer of the popular style of the day, namely ragtime. His musical experience was broadened by working as a singing waiter and as a plugger[12] for the Von Tilzer Music Publishing Company. Consequently, he became familiar with the musical tastes of a wide variety of people. Soon after the turn of the century, at age 19, Berlin wrote his first songs: "Yiddle on Your Fiddle, Play Some Ragtime," "Sadie Salome, Go Home," and My Wife's Gone to the Country (Hurrah! Hurrah!) (all in 1909), "Alexander's Ragtime Band" (1911), and "When I Lost You" (1912). The latter song referred to the death of his young bride, Dorothy Goetz. While on their honeymoon Mrs. Berlin took ill and died a few months after their return to New York. In 1914, Berlin composed his first full score for the musical *Watch Your Step*. His next memorable music moment in American history occurred when he joined the armed services during America's entrance into WWI (1917), and composed one of America's most noted patriotic songs, "God Bless America."[13] This song came to fruition as the result of Berlin's interest in producing and directing a musical program for his fellow comrades. It is reported that he spoke to the Army General of his company about the possibility of producing such a show as a fund raiser. The results were "God Bless America" (1940) and "White Christmas" (1942). His music has been recorded and/or performed by a wide a variety of artists, including Louis Armstrong, Fred Astaire, Eddie Cantor, Bing Crosby, The Drifters, Billie Holiday, Judy Garland, Al Jolson, The Mills Brothers, Ethel Merman, Bill Murray, Frank Sinatra, Bessie Smith, Ethel Waters, and Lawrence Welk.

With the emerging focus on interest in sound recordings beginning in the 1920s, the significance of Tin Pan Alley gradually diminished and had all but disappeared by WWII.

---

[11] A. Henderson and D. B. Bowers. *Red Hot and Blue: A Smithsonian Salute to the American Musical*. Washington: Smithsonian Institute, 1996, p. 70.

[12] A plugger is a publishing firm employee who creates excitement for the firm's song during a live performance in hopes of encouraging people to buy the sheet music. A plugger is somewhat like a "groupie."

[13] What is interesting at this juncture in Berlin's life is the fact that he did not become a U.S. citizen until a few months prior to serving in the U.S. army.

MAINSTREAM MUSICAL THEATRE

As previously mentioned with regard to theatre in the United States before WWI, there was not an established tradition of thematic material that was distinctly American. A truly "American Theatre" come into its own until a few years before the Great Depression. Before this, theatre involved either the production of European plays–which were based on European society–or stage productions under the guise of minstrelsy, variety shows, and vaudeville.[14] The latter types of stage productions were becoming out-of-date, as there was a growing interest among Americans for entertainment that had little to do with images of slavery, negative cultural and immigrant stereotypes, and to some extent, European imperialism. It is important to note that such interest was apparent in both white and black communities. Because of the continuance of segregated communities, there were some performance traditions in each of them. In light of this, the following information includes a discussion of music for theatre among White and Black performers and their respective audiences.

As the industrial revolution became firmly established by the late 19th century and people found themselves in a stronger position to shape America's entertainment tastes, three changes occurred with regard to stage productions that created a significant difference between vaudeville, as previously discussed, and American theatre performances in the ensuing years:

1) A variety of performances moved from the Bowery district to uptown Broadway.
2) Exaggerated humor that was based on various ethnic groups was noticeably minimized.
3) A greater interplay developed between the music, the choreographed dance routines, and the story line.

At the turn of the 20th century, theatrical performance moved from the Bowery, Union Square, and lower Broadway districts to uptown Broadway–an area that was quickly dubbed "The Great White Way." Productions became more sophisticated and suited to increasingly diverse musical tastes. American theatre houses and various dining and hospitality businesses migrated to the area between 39th and 45th Streets; resulting in an explosion of electrical signs and billboards. It was also during this time that the heart of Broadway was duly named Times Square.

During the 1890s, thematic material for skits moved away from humor that was based on exaggerations of the cultural idiosyncrasies of urban immigrant societies in America to story lines that dealt with politics and general social issues. The popular two-man vaudevillian team of Fields and Weber made the transition from a variety show entertainment to a more selective musical of razzmatazz and a high-stepping revue of music. Unfortunately their association with the past rendered them less effective than newcomers like Victor Herbert, Florenz Ziegfeld, George M. Cohan, and the Schuberts. Even though Fields continued as a producer of several successful shows after the Weber and Fields disbandment in 1904, new ideas had taken hold.

More than any other theatrical entertainment of the time, the *Ziegfeld Follies* inspired the establishment of specific traditions that laid the foundation for American theatre. Furthermore, it was the culmination of ideas, geographical location, and more importantly here, the symbiosis of story, dance, and music that led to the success of Florenz Ziegfeld's *Ziegfeld Follies,* and thus an ideology for American

---

[14] Regarded as one of the most significant productions that facilitated the many musical tastes, *The Black Crook* appealed to New York's diverse population. Opening one year after the end of the Civil War and continuing with yearly productions into the 1880s, this production entailed a melodrama/ ballet adapted from *Der Freischütz* (1821) by Carl Maria von Weber. The work titled "Transformation Polka" (written by Thomas Baker) was one of the major songs. Nearly seventy-four years later, a musical revue titled *The Passing Show* clearly marked the beginning of theatre in America.

theatre. Ziegfeld's productions were a hodgepodge of musical selections from popular Broadway musicals banded together by a central theme.

One could certainly argue the point that American musical theatre is a product of the culmination of minstrelsy, variety shows and vaudeville, and operettas. Even though minstrelsy and its association and remembrance of slave plantation lifestyles continued to influence popular music and dance, its ideology and performance traditions were not about to be inducted into America's "hall of fame" theatre. Vaudeville, with its plethora of humor based on the many different immigrants and former black slaves, was not in line with America's desired image. Even though a number of operettas had been written by Americans, they were heavily influenced by European culture. There was a genuine need for something that was truly American; an ideology with minimal European vestiges that beyond doubt represented the American spirit. Four central figures stand out as the major contributors to the furtherance of uniquely American entertainment that began with minstrels and vaudevillians and ultimately culminated in the ideology of American Theatre: Victor Herbert, George M. Cohan, Florenz Ziegfeld, and the Schuberts.

Victor Herbert was a composer of light opera who produced a number of successful stage shows. These included *Babes in Toyland* (1903) and *Naughty Marietta* (1910). As previously mentioned, however, for many Americans operettas were generally viewed as extensions of European lifestyle produced on American soil. Herbert's greatest contribution to American theatre was the emphasis he placed on the music. In many of the vaudeville shows at the time, music, albeit good, was not the central ingredient of the skits or musicals. Herbert brought a sense of reverence to the notion that all parts of a production should revolve around or at least correlate to the music. Other productions at this time that premiered eventually popular songs included *The Wizard of Oz* (1903), *The Merry Widow* (1907), and Eugene Walter's *The Easiest Way* (1908).

George Cohan took the vibrancy of the immigrant-based humor of Harrigan and Hart and Weber and Fields and delivered his performances in a manner resonant of the operetta. As evidenced by his song "Give My Regards to Broadway" (1904), his focus was an idealistic persona of Broadway–the path to the America spirit. Broadway was also a facade that symbolized the success of urban America and all of its triumphs over seemingly insurmountable obstacles. The musical titled *Little Johnny Jones,* where "Give My Regards to Broadway" was debuted, featured another American song that evoked emotions of righteousness and American morality, namely "Yankee Doodle Boy."[15]

Florenz Ziegfeld and the Schuberts were America's first major impresarios–producers who organize all the components of a production. In addition to organizing the director, talent, general idea of musical selections, musicians, marketing, and staging, Ziegfeld and the Schuberts were able to project grandeur. Their innovatively creative grandiose productions transformed American theatre to the level of high art.

The *Ziegfeld Follies* were basically performances that combined music from popular American musicals into a story or narration. Commonly referred to as a "musical revue," the first follie premiered in 1907 as an advertisement strategy for the Jardin de Paris nightclub in New York.[16]

> *"The script was peppered with topical satire, poking*
> *fun at the foibles of such notables as Teddy*
> *Roosevelt, John D. Rockefeller, grand opera producer*
> *Oscar Hammerstein, and grand opera divo Enrico*
> *Caruso."*[17]

---

[15] "Yankee Doodle Boy" derived from the traditional tune titled "Yankle Doodle Dandy."
[16] The *follies* became the *Ziegfeld Follies* in 1911.
[17] Henderson and Bowers, p. 41.

As the *Ziegfeld Follies* continued throughout the years, its stories, costumes, staging, talent, and repertoire became increasingly sophisticated. Some of the earliest performers who became stars include Fanny Brice, Eddie Cantor, Bessie McCoy Davis, W.C. Fields, Marilyn Miller, Will Rogers, and Bert Williams. Some Follies songs that have remained popular throughout the years are "A Pretty Girl Is Like a Melody," "Mandy," "Second-Hand Rose," "Shine On, Harvest Moon," "You Can't Make Your Shimmy Shake on Tea," and many others.

Throughout his career, Ziegfeld produced such noted musicals as *"Sally* (1920), *Rio Rita* (1926), *Show Boat* (1927), and *Whoopee* (1928). . .His final shows were the musical comedies *Show Girl* (1929), *Smiles* (1930), and *Hot-Cha!* (1932).[18] After his death in 1932, Ziegfeld's follies lived on through 1943 as the result of performance rights of his musicals. *Show Boat* was by far the most successful production during the late 1920s. With its major creators Jerome Kern and Oscar Hammerstein, the musical production entailed an amalgamation of romance, costumes, music, and a distinct plot that truly represented the American spirit.

The Schuberts, contemporaries of Florenz Ziegfeld, also had a flair for extravagance. Consisting of brothers Sam, J.J., and Lee, the Schuberts did it all. They leased and managed theatres, wrote *libretti,* and composed musical compositions for a number of productions. Their involvement with musical theatre wasn't as creators at first, but rather as business entrepreneurs. In fact, their initial productions were imports from British comedy/entertainment, the first of which was secured by Sam Schubert as early as 1902. It has been intimated that the turn from British imports to more American-inspired themes and social mores caused the untimely death of Sam in 1905.[19] Some of the Schuberts' more memorable American-inspired musicals include *The Mimic World* (1908), *The Passing Show* (1912), *The Honeymoon Express* (1913), *Robinson Crusoe, Jr.* (1916), and *Sinbad* (1918). Their most notable performer was Al Jolson. Born in 1886 as Asa Yoelson in Lithuania, the name change to Al Jolson occurred following his family's migration to America in the 1890s. His first noteworthy success occurred in the Schuberts' production *La Belle Paree* (1911), which was a typical variety show. Appearing in blackface, Al Jolson wooed the audience with his baritone voice and animated mannerisms of black people. "Rockabye Your Baby with a Dixie Melody" (1918), written by Jean Schwartz, Sam Lewis, and Joe Young, is perhaps Al Jolson's most memorable song.

BLACK MUSICAL THEATRE

In 1921, *Shuffle Along,* became the first major black musical with a distinct storyline to appear "on" Broadway that was written and produced by African Americans, and performed by an all-black cast. Without the efforts of previous authors, composers, librettists, instrumentalists, and singers, however, such a monumental feat would probably not have occurred until much later. To attain a greater understanding of the complexity of black musical theatre within the context of mainstream culture and, of course, African American culture, some discussion of black productions prior to WWI is beneficial to the reader.

We have already explored what at this point can be viewed as vestiges of black musical theatre, namely Blackface Minstrelsy, traveling shows, and vaudeville. Specific characteristics of these types of productions such as performing in blackface, Jim Crow and Zip Coon-type characterizations,

---

[18] *Ibid.*, p. 48.

[19] Conjecture and debate still exist regarding Sam Schubert's death. Some believe it was the result of the Schubert's opposition to the Syndicate–the booking agency that monopolized American theatre.

savage-like images, infidelity, and /or deceit were apparent in an number of early black productions. Beginning in the early 1890s, however, a number of black theatrical presentations were slowly moving away from the stain of blackface minstrelsy to shows labeled as musical comedy, musical revue, or variety show. Some of the more popular early productions included *The Creole Show* (1890), *The Octaroons* (1896), *The South Before the War* (1896), *Oriental America* (1896), *A Trip to Coontown* (1892), *Clorindy: or the Origin of the Cakewalk* (1898), and *In Dahomey* (1903).

Most shows included a fairly large cast, at least for that time, that featured one to several favored individuals performing comedic skits, tuneful songs, and popular and/or new dances of the day. Staged with props, lighting, and often colorful costumes, these shows were also a venue for hearing popular African American styles of the day: ragtime, blues, and ballads (i.e., love songs). Consequently, there arose a number of composers, writers, and librettists that helped shape the ideology of black musical theatre. To better understand black musical theatre after WWI, an examination of the aforementioned productions is warranted.

The Creole Show, produced by Sam Jack's Creole Burlesque Company, was the first to exhibit this practice. With an all-black cast of men and women, this show set the stage for what was to follow. Its star, Sam Lucas, who later became the first black male in a major film *(Uncle Tom's Cabin,* 1915), fused his experiences of the minstrel period with those new trends. What *The Creole Show* initiated, John Isham (a white producer) and his production titled *The Octaroons* took further. This and his following productions frequently featured a finale of operatic arias. Of notable mention, that same year, is Sissieretta Jones, the star of the white-managed production titled *Black Patti's Troubadors.*[20] Conceived by Bob Cole, an African American writer and producer, the show's finale featured Ms. Jones singing arias from operas such as *Carmen, Il Travatore,* and *La Bohème.* The two former titles make reference to ethnicity. These terms–Creole and Octaroon–indicate that some variant of black ethnicity was still a useful marketing strategy for American entertainment. Moreover, it also shows that the notion of "light-skinned" blacks was indeed a marketing strategy designed to appeal to mainstream white America. Although not referencing fair complexion, *Oriental America,* credited as the first production with an all-black cast to appear on Broadway, another Isham production, draws attention to black people with the word *oriental.* In this context, black people are referred to as "orientals" in America.[21] While the aforementioned two productions featured all-black casts, *The South Before the War,* a predominantly black cast, was one of the first integrated productions in this category of musical comedy/variety show. Activities specific to slaves on the plantation (singing in the field, attendance at a religious or "camp meeting," and a social gathering that featured the cake-walk dance) were the basis of the show. *A Trip to Coontown,* by Bob Cole and Billy Johnson, with an all-black cast starring Sam Lucas, is noted as the first musical that was written, produced, and managed by African Americans. Performed in three acts, the story takes place in San Francisco at the home of Ben Gay, a wealthy bachelor. The second act is set in a restaurant named "The Riche," while the third act takes place at Plaza of Cliff House. The undercurrent of its seemingly litigious storyline is analogous to the Jim Crow and Zip Coon characterizations, namely a vagrant and con artist. Nonetheless, the show made its "off" Broadway debut in 1898, running for several years. Three eventual song favorites included "The Bowery," "After the Ball," and "Reuben, Reuben." That same year (1898) Will Marion Cook, a graduate of Oberlin College, Ohio, conceived, produced, and composed the music to *Clorindy: or the Origin of the Cakewalk.* With lyrics by the African American poet Paul Lawrence Dunbar, the show was destined for success. The production was written for and to star Cook's favored performers: Bert Williams and George Walker

---

[20] Sissieretta Jones was nicknamed Black Patti in reference to Adelina Patti–a popular Italian opera singer of the day.

[21] The word *oriental* means "out of one's homeland."

(two minstrel stars). In fact, the story was conceived as Cook expressed to them his ideas about how Louisiana came to know the cakewalk in the 1880s. Due to Williams's and Walker's success in the show *Hyde and Behman* they could not appear. Instead, Ernest Hogan,[22] a popular comedian who was appearing with Black Patti's Troubadours, became the featured performer. Hogan's performances of Cook's songs titled "Who Dat Say Chicken in Dis Crowd," and "Hottes' Coon in Dixie" helped make the show a success. Appearing at the Casino Roof Garden, this musical comedy with twenty-six cast members became the first black-conceived production to appear "on" Broadway. Although Williams and Walker were not able to work with Will Cook for this show, they did join forces during the production titled *In Dahomey*. With a conscious effort to diminish the preponderance of musicals centered on pejorative images of black culture, this production focused on the dignity and pride of Africans in Dahomey, Africa. Indeed, this was a story of a number of African Americans who, after discovering gold, went back to Africa–a movement of the same title that was stirring in some African American communities at this time. Williams's and Walker's triumphant character of autonomy from American-ization and political and economic success portrays the ideology of African Americans musically in the song "Evah Darkey Is King." Other popular songs included "I'd Like to Be a Real Lady" and "Molly Green." In 1906, Williams, Walker, and Cole produced a similar show titled *In Abyssinia*–whose theme was similar to that of *In Dahomey*: two African Americans win the lottery and tour Ethiopia. A few popular songs include "I'll Keep a Warm Spot in My Heart for You," "Let it Alone," and "I Thought My Troubles Were Over." Two years later, the production titled *Bandana Land* became their most famous Broadway musical. Some popular songs included "You're in the Right Church but the Wrong Pew," "I'm Just Crazy About You," "Just the Same," and "Kinky."

These and other shows and their creators laid the foundation for black musical theatre in the ensuing years. By the turn of the century, other composers and writers emerged and continued telling the story of the plight of the African American. Of notable mention are the brothers John Rosamund Johnson and James Weldon Johnson, composer and poet respectively, and James Reese Europe. The Johnson brothers collaborated with Bob Cole and produced two highly acclaimed musicals: *Shoo-Fly Regiment* (1906) and *The Red Moon* (1908). Drawing on the experiences of a people with a past rich in dignity, suffering, faith, and triumph, and capitalizing on his musical training at the New England Conservatory of Music, J. Rosamund Johnson was able to capture the spirit of black culture and regurgitate its essence through music composition. The Johnson brothers further diminished the stigma of blackface minstrelsy in American entertainment, and more significantly on black culture. The poetic recitations of James Weldon Johnson resounded with the "back to Africa" impetus that fueled the Harlem Renaissance. Featuring a musical score by his brother, the lyrics in *Lift Every Voice Sing* (regarded by many as the black national anthem) summon all to expect and appreciate liberty and freedom, and to remain faithful to one's Creator and homeland. John Rosamund Johnson was involved in other musical genres and subsequent activities. In 1911, he wrote the songs and conducted a revue titled *Hello Paris,* and subsequently became the first African American to conduct a white orchestra that accompanied a white cast in a New York venue. He was also active in composing for chorus and orchestra, and authored the work *Walk Together, Children* (1915).[23]

James Reese Europe, born into a family of musicians, was involved in music activities at an early age. Like J Rosamund Johnson, he was trained in Western standards of music theory and composition.

---

[22] As previous mentioned, Ernest Hogan (a.k.a. Rube Crowders) composed the popular ragtime song titled "All Pimps/Coons Look Alike To Me" (published in 1896).

[23] After WWI, he was responsible for editing works for Negro spirituals such as *The Book of American Negro Spirituals* (1925), and folksongs such as *Rolling Along in Song* (1937).

His relevance to black musical theatre began in 1903, at age twenty-two, while playing in a floor show or *cabaret,* as they were commonly known as in New York. Five years later he Europe became the musical director of *The Shoo-Fly Regiment.* Perhaps his most significant contribution to the advancement of musical activities for blacks was his founding of the Clef Club. This was an organization that functioned like a fraternity; it was professionally known, however, as a booking agent for black entertainment. With Europe as its first president, the Clef Club had its own symphony orchestra, which debuted at Carnegi Hall on May 2, 1912 at a time when many black and white performers were still performing in blackface. As imagined, this feat brought notoriety to the organization, which in turn affected how people viewed black entertainers. While conducting the orchestra at a function, Europe met Vernon and Irene Castle–two white popular dancers at the time. Impressed with his musicianship, they soon hired him as their band leader. James Europe entered the army when the United States entered WWI (1917) and, by request, formed a military band of African Americans. The following year, his unit of musicians became the first African American military group to come into France. Playing marching band-type music with jazz articulations, Europe's band received rave reviews from many in Western Europe. Returning to the states the following year (1919), his band toured many cities throughout the country. Other notable African American songwriters who continued the legacy include Shelton Brooks (noted for his 1916 song titled "Walking the Dog," which popularized the dance of the same name, and his song "Dark-town Strutters' Ball," 1917), and Joe Jordan, who was noted for writing for the Memphis Students who played jazz, and was instrumental in establishing Chicago as the jazz center from WWI to the mid-twenties.

In December of 1909, *Mr. Lode of Koal,* starring Bert Williams, was the last black-conceived musical to appear on Broadway. Nearly twelve years passed before the next musical appeared on Broadway, namely *Shuffle Along,* which will be discussed later.

CHAPTER EIGHT

NEW ORLEANS JAZZ

Louis Armstrong. © Photofest

INTRODUCTION

New Orleans, Louisiana, was the cultural metropolis of the South during the last third of the 19th century. With immigrants from Germany, Spain, Ireland, France, Africa, Italy, French Canada, Haiti, added with people of mixed cultures such as the American Creole (black and French heritages), the musical climate was diverse and broad. One style that crossed most ethnic and national boundaries during this time was New Orleans jazz/Dixieland jazz. Regarded by many as one of America's most celebrated musical styles, this musical art form appealed to the liberal and conservative, the young and old, and the many beautiful cultural and ethnic people. Drawn to its propulsive rhythms and perpetual melodic counterpoint, one is compelled to listen, smile or dance to sounds of New Orleans jazz (also referred to by many as "Dixieland"). Storyville[1], a section of New Orleans where this music flourished, significantly abetted the proliferation of early jazz. Established by Alder Story in 1897 in an effort to confine lascivious activities to a certain section of New Orleans, Storyville (where the French Quarter now lies) was a forty-block area of racketeering, gambling, prostitution, contraband, and music–ragtime, blues, and New Orleans jazz. New Orleans was not the only place where New Orleans jazz was heard. As it became more popular, bands and musicians toured to areas such as California, Chicago, and New York. Noted bands/musicians include:

- Freddie Keppard–established the Original Creole Orchestra (1912). He traveled to the aforementioned areas between the years 1913–1918, ". . . for a while in 1921, both King Oliver's band and Jelly Roll Morton were in Los Angeles."[2]
- Kid Ory's Original Creole Jazz-Band–performed in Oakland and San Francisco, California, ca. 1922.
- New Orleans Rhythm Masters–performed "at the Somerset Club in San Antonio, Texas, in October, 1926."[3]
- The Original Dixieland Jazz Band–often billed as the creators of jazz, took the New Orleans jazz sound abroad, opening in London in 1919.

In New Orleans, there were four basic types of bands: (1) club bands, (2) street bands, (3) marching or parade bands, and (4) dance bands. Club bands played in supper clubs where eating, drinking, dancing, and socializing took place. Street bands, as the word *street* implies, played outdoors. Marching or parade bands were hired for grand openings, parades, Mardi Gras, and so on. The sound of marching music stirs emotions of excitement and patriotism in any soul willing to listen. Characterized by fanfare brass, woodwinds, and a regimented rhythm section all maintained within a strict *tempo di marcia* (marching tempo), marching music was quite distinct from any other style of music during the early 1900s. Despite the fact that many New Orleans jazz bands performed and presented themselves as marching bands, their "front line" performance tradition, discussed later, distinguished their sound from regimented marching music,[4] and are thus more correctly understood as dance bands.

---

[1] "The Big 25, known earlier as Pete Lala's, was Storyville's foremost musicians' hangout . . ." (Keepnews, p. 15).

[2] Keepnews, p. 17.

[3] *Ibid*, p. 25.

[4] See previous chapter, titled "Marching Band Music". By far, John Philip Sousa (1845–1932) was the most influential and prolific composer of march music from the 1890s through WWI. Known as the "March King," Mr. Sousa not only composed march music, but was also the Marine Marching Band's 24th band leader. It is reported that his recording "Semper Fidelis" (1890) was the most popular piece of marching music in America at that time.

Although black musicians such as Charles "Buddy" Bolden, "Bunk" Johnson, Louis "Satchmo" Armstrong, Freddie Keppard, Joseph "King" Oliver, Edward "Kid" Ory, and Sydney Bechet are noted as early creators and innovators of New Orleans jazz, white musicians/bands such as Bix Beiderbecke, Tom Brown,[5] George Brunies, Nick LaRocca, the Original Dixieland Jazz Band, "Papa" Jack Laine, Paul Mares, The New Orleans Rhythm Kings, Leon Roppolo, and Larry Shields were influential as well.[6] Social and racial restrictions on integration during this time prevented black and white musicians from playing together, with some exceptions (e.g., Sidney Arodin). Nevertheless, they were able to hear each other at various informal settings such as after-hours in homes or less socially restrictive environments.

In addition to blacks and whites, Creoles also contributed a great deal to the sound of New Orleans jazz, beginning as early as the late 19th century. An amalgamation of traditions from French and black heritages, Creoles of color developed a culture that became distinctive in its own right. Generally they worked as store owners/managers, professionals, and artisans. With regard to their French heritage, the music forms that are inherent in the *quadrille* and *cotillion* (two popular French dances) had an influence on the New Orleans jazz scene. Also, because of their European heritage, Creoles received music instruction and thus were proficient in reading music. Finally, their African heritage was the probable origin of their desire for improvisation and emphasis on syncopated rhythms. Notable performers included cornet/trumpet players Buddy Petit and Freddie Keppard, clarinetists Sidney Bechet and Jimmie Noone, trombone players Edward "Kid" Ory and Honore Dutrey, and the pianist Jelly Roll Morton.

MUSICAL CHARACTER OF NEW ORLEANS JAZZ

The musical character of New Orleans jazz is unlike any other form of jazz (with the exception of Chicago jazz and to some extent free jazz). Typically performed by a brass band[7] (cornet/trumpet, clarinet, trombone, tuba, banjo, snare/bass drum), its presentation entails two separate parts: front line and rhythm section. The front line instruments–trumpet, clarinet, and trombone–perform a polyphonic texture, while the remaining instruments maintain the harmonic and rhythmic structure. More specifically, the polyphonic texture of the front line is produced by the performance of separate melodies that interweave in a resulting call and response or conversational manner. With regard to the rhythm section, in addition to playing on each count of a quadruple meter, the tuba plays the root pitch of each chord, the banjo strums a chord, and the snare or bass drum maintains the tempo, most often andante (marching). The rhythm section continues playing in this manner even during the solos, which are played individually by all or most of the front line instruments. All of the above characteristics are heard in "Dippermouth Blues" (1923) by King Oliver's Creole Jazz Band, "Cake Walking Babies from Home" (1924) by the Red Onion Jazz Babies, and "Potato Head Blues" (1927) by Louis Armstrong and His Hot Seven.

---

[5] Tom Brown, trombonist, in 1915, brought the first white New Orleans-sounding band to Chicago. They first appeared as a Dixieland Band, then several years later changed their name to Brown's Dixieland Jazz Band.

[6] In 1917, the Original Dixieland Jazz Band made the first jazz recording.

[7] It must be pointed out that this is the typical instrumentation of the brass band. Other instruments such as the piano, guitar, and bass were used, as evidenced by recordings of New Orleans jazz made in the 1920s. As will be discussed in the next part, these instruments, along with the drum set, later became common in Chicago jazz after WW I. Recordings by Jelly Roll Morton will be analyzed to illustrate the difference between New Orleans and Chicago jazz.

TIME	SECTION	INSTRUMENTATION/COMMENTS
00:00	A	Front line instruments (trumpet, clarinet, trombone) illustrating the polyphonic texture
00:42	B	Trumpet solo accompanied by the rhythm section (piano, banjo, and tuba)
01:04	B	Clarinet solo accompanied by the rhythm section
01:45		A brief fill played by the banjo only
01:50	B	Trumpet solo accompanied by the rhythm section, which is playing in "stop time" (i.e., they are playing a chord then resting for a few counts; this is done repeatedly)
02:32	A	Front line instruments (trumpet, clarinet, trombone) continuing with the polyphonic texture

Song Navigator 8.1: "Potato Head Blues" (ca. 1925) by Louis Armstrong, from *His 26 Finest Hot Fives & Hot Sevens 1925–1928* (Nimbus Records); (Genre: New Orleans Jazz)

The performance structure of New Orleans jazz is most often presented in an ABA format. The polyphonic texture exemplifies the A section, while solos occur during the B section. Take, for example, the 1927 recording of "Struttin' With Some Barbecue" by Louis Armstrong and His Hot Five. The A section entails the aforementioned polyphonic texture performed by trumpet, clarinet, and trombone (front line), which are accompanied by the rhythm section–banjo and piano. The B section begins with a clarinet solo, followed by the trombone, and concludes with a trumpet solo–all accompanied by the rhythm section. The A section returns and is performed in the same manner as before. The performance structure in "Potato Head Blues" (1927) by Louis Armstrong and His Hot Seven is the same as the previous song: ABA. The difference lies in the B section. Here, accompanied by banjo, piano, tuba, and drums, the solos are played by the trumpet, followed by the clarinet, a brief solo by the banjo, and then again by the trumpet. The song ends at the conclusion of the A section. Still another example is "Big Butter and Egg Man from the West" (1926) by Louis Armstrong and His Hot Five. In this piece, the trumpet is the only solo instrument. It nonetheless entails the ABA performance structure. To add variety to the solo section, the rhythm section plays either in a continual manner or in what is known as "stop time." In the first, all instruments of the rhythm section play on each count of the measure, each accentuating certain counts. In stop time, however, instruments play certain counts of the measure all together, and "stop playing" (or rest) during other counts. "Dippermouth Blues" by King Oliver's Creole Jazz Band also illustrates this structure. In the B section, the clarinet solo is accompanied by the rhythm section–banjo, piano, spoons–which accentuate one, two, and three all together, and rest on the fourth count, thus illustrating "stop time."

MUSICAL INFLUENCES OF OTHER STYLES ON NEW ORLEANS JAZZ

Although many songs by the aforementioned bands used the word "blues" in their title, and were even blues sounding, they were played in the fashion of New Orleans jazz. Sometimes referred to as New Orleans Blues, songs that employed the performance of the polyphonic texture were in effect, New Orleans jazz. Some examples include:

"Livery Stable Blues" (1917)–Original Dixieland Jazz Band (ODJB).
"Royal Garden Blues" (1917)–ODJB

"West End Blues"–Louis Armstrong
"Dippermouth Blues"–King Oliver's Creole Jazz Band
"Potato Head Blues"–Louis Armstrong and His Hot Seven
"Texas Moaner Blues"–Sidney Bechet
"Franklin Street Blues"–Bunk Johnson

Without question, the coexistence of ragtime, blues, and even stride–a syncopated piano style that combines characteristics of ragtime, blues, and jazz elements–influenced how the popular brass bands performed music, particularly in New Orleans. For example, "Hotter Than Hot" (1927) by Louis Armstrong and His Hot Five uses characteristics and performance practices of all of these. To begin, the structure uses a 32-bar harmonic progression, a common practice in New Orleans jazz. Following the 8-bar introduction, the trumpet and clarinet each perform a solo during the first and second 32-bar progression respectively. Finally, the accompanimental instruments–piano, guitar, and banjo–together provide the harmonic and rhythmic framework.

TIME	SECTION	INSTRUMENTATION/COMMENTS
00:00	Introduction	All instruments: trumpet, clarinet, trombone, piano, banjo, guitar
00:10	Trumpet solo	Trumpet solo accompanied by guitar, banjo, piano
00:45	Clarinet solo	Clarinet solo accompanied by banjo and piano
01:20	Vocal solo	The lead singer (Armstrong) is scatting accompanied by guitar and subtle banjo
01:57	Interlude	Call and response between voice and guitar, no other instruments are playing
02:15	Interlude	Piano only
02:19	Trombone solo	Trombone accompanied by banjo, guitar, and piano
02:36	Coda	All instruments are playing, the trumpet plays while
02:45	Coda	The trumpet plays short passages while the band in performing stop time
02:52	Coda	A brief call & response section between guitar and trumpet

Song Navigator 8.2: "Hotter Than Hot" (ca. 1925) by Louis Armstrong, from *Louis Armstrong: Hot Fives & Hot Sevens – Vol. 2* (2006, JSP Records)

With regard to ragtime influences, their syncopated piano rhythms are played in a similar fashion in many New Orleans jazz pieces. (It should be noted that syncopated rhythms increase in frequency as the song progresses.) In the same piece, the guitar and banjo instruments both play on each count of a quadruple meter. A more in-depth examination shows that the guitar also accents the backbeat (counts two and four), a swing playing style among guitarists. The banjo plays without any accentuations, a tradition in New Orleans jazz. For the third repeat of the 32-bar progression, Louis Armstrong scats an interpretation of the main theme, with the guitar as the only accompaniment. Again, the guitar is playing as it does in swing bands. An interlude follows with Louis Armstrong scatting, which illustrates the call, while Lonnie Johnson responds with vocal-like inflections on the guitar. Performing without a tempo combined with the responsorial manner of the voice and guitar is quite characteristic of the blues. The solo part in the fourth and final full 32-bar progression is evenly divided between the trombone and trumpet. What's interesting here is that while the accompaniment during the trombone solo is identical to the beginning of the piece, the accompaniment during the trumpet solo illustrates New Orleans jazz. Here the distinct New Orleans jazz front line tradition is performed by the trumpet, clarinet, and trombone. The piece concludes with a brief call and response passage performed by the guitar and trumpet without any accompaniment.

As to the influence of blues music, the piece "Franklin Street Blues" by the cornet player Bunk Johnson maintains the 12-bar progression, a specific succession of chords typical of blues songs. The following outline shows the performance of the piece with respect to the front line instruments (cornet/trumpet, clarinet, and trombone). (Note: The heading "Number of Times" refers to the number of times the 12-bar progression is played):

INSTRUMENT(S)	PERFORMANCE PRACTICE	NUMBER OF TIMES
Front line	polyphony	two
Clarinet	improvisational solo	two
Cornet	improvisational solo	two
Front line	polyphony	two

While the Johnson piece is more illustrative of the blues' slow tempo, "Copenhagen" by Bix Biederbecke, which also employs the 12-bar blues progression, is played significantly faster while maintaining the blues character. However, because of the moderately fast tempo, the manner in which the solos are performed, the different progressions with respect to the number of measures, and the harmonic structure, the song emerges with a non-blues character overall. To begin, the tempo is faster than blues and ragtime, which strongly suggests a move from these styles. Following the 16-bar introduction that is subdivided into two equal number of measures played polyphonically by the frontline, the clarinetist plays an improvisational solo once within the 12-bar progression. A saxophone improvisational solo continues once through the 12-bar progression, which is then followed by the frontline playing the same introductory section, and so on. In addition to these points, notice the number of different harmonic structures, as indicated by the letters under the column "Harmony." The following table summarizes these points:

INSTRUMENT(S)	PERFORMANCE PRACTICE	PROGRESSION	# OF TIMES	HARMONY
1. Front line	polyphony	8-bar	two	A
2. Clarinet	improvisational solo	12-bar	one	B
3. Saxophone	improvisational solo	12-bar	one	B
4. Front line	polyphony	8-bar	two	A
5. Trumpet	improvisational solo	8-bar	one	C

6. Front line	polyphony	8-bar	one	C
7. Front line	polyphony	8-bar	two	A
8. Tuba	solo (probably notated)	4-bar	one	D
9. Front line	polyphony	8-bar	one	E
10. Tuba	solo (probably notated)	4-bar	one	D
11. Front line	polyphony	8-bar	one	E
12. Front line	polyphony	8-bar	two	F
13. Front line	polyphony	10-bar	one	A

Based on the foregoing, one could argue that early sounds of what is regarded as New Orleans jazz were in actuality ragtime and blues songs performed in the manner of a late 19th/early 20th century brass bands. Because of the inherent meaning of "bands" versus those instruments, piano and/or guitar, predominantly used in ragtime and blues, more contrasting music ideas and textural flexibility were obligingly exercised. The musical outcome, as evidenced by the piece above ("Copenhagen"), therefore sounded different enough to apply the new term "New Orleans Jazz". The style became even more firmly established by the fact that many songs began using song forms and features, as seen in "Copenhagen," that were characteristically not ragtime or blues.

It is well known that New Orleans jazz was more frequently played instrumentally. On the other hand, because blues–a vocal form–was a favorite style at that time, a number of bands that played New Orleans jazz pieces also included sung songs in their repertoire. For example, the song "Sugar" by Bix Beiderbecke speaks about a wonderful woman he calls "Sugar." "I'm Looking Over a Four-Leaf Clover" is another song performed by Beiderbecke that includes vocals. Although the song is not New Orleans jazz, the section following the sung section incorporates the polyphonic texture, which includes Beiderbecke's improvised trumpet playing against the theme and other subtle parts. Another example occurs near the middle of "Royal Garden Blues" by the ODJB. A singer introduces the front line instruments (trumpet, saxophone, and clarinet) and speaks about how he enjoys their exciting performance style (no doubt referring to the polyphonic texture). The singer continues by making reference to this song as an accompaniment to dancing. Louis Armstrong's "When It's Sleepy Time Down South" is mainly sung throughout. Noted as one of his signature pieces, Armstrong sings this slow ballad as first the trombone and then the clarinet play in counterpoint–a subtle version of the polyphonic texture. Another example is the ballad "Mandy, Make Up Your Mind" by Sidney Bechet that includes a female vocalist.

NEW ORLEANS JAZZ INFLUENCES ON OTHER MUSICAL STYLES

The performance tradition of New Orleans jazz–mainly the polyphonic texture–was also incorporated in other song forms such as ballads (referring to love songs), marches, and music for theatre. The song "I'm Looking Over a Four-Leaf Clover" includes the polyphonic texture as well as singing. Sidney Bechet's version of the Gershwin piece "I Got Rhythm"[8] is performed in the New Orleans jazz tradition throughout the piece. The march "When the Saints Go Marching In" by Louis Armstrong is not only sung, but includes a section performed in the New Orleans jazz style. A similar performance occurs in Louis Armstrong's version of the popular song "Hello Dolly" from the musical of the same name.[9] Following the introduction that includes a rhythmical banjo, Armstrong sings while the trumpet and clarinet play subtle countermelodies during this 32-bar structure. An instrumental rendition of the song (32-bars) ensues that is played in the New Orleans jazz polyphonic texture with clarinet, trombone, and Armstrong on trumpet. Armstrong returns singing the second half of the 32-bar structure against the same subtle trumpet and clarinet countermelodies. The 32-bar structure and the polyphonic texture are also evident in the song "Do You Know What It Means to Miss New Orleans" by Armstrong. The first 32 bars are played instrumentally in the polyphonic texture, while the second is sung with subtle clarinet and trombone countermelodies. The song concludes with yet another polyphonic instrumental 32-bar performance. An additional song noted as part of Armstrong's repertoire is the Berthold Brecht and Kurt Weill song "Mack the Knife." Although Armstrong sings the majority of the song, the polyphonic texture is performed during the final 16-bar chorus.

In closing, the sound of New Orleans jazz is still a hallmark of life and culture in New Orleans, Louisiana. One of the initial impressions of visitors to New Orleans is the city's omnipresent sound of New Orleans jazz. While this sound of jazz is embedded in the soundscape of what was the South's cultural metropolis of the 19th century, it spread and took root in other areas such as Chicago and New York. It is in these two cities, as will be discussed in ensuing chapters, where the sound of jazz continued to evolve, and became a genre that was and continues to be sought after worldwide.

---

[8] "I Got Rhythm" is from the Ira and George Gershwin collaboration of the musical *Girl Crazy* (1930).
[9] *Hello Dolly*, with lyrics and music by Jerry Herman, is credited as a preeminent Broadway show tune. The musical production opened on January 16, 1964, with the person who became associated with the musical, Carol Channing. The film version in 1969 starred Barbra Streisand and Walter Matthau.

CHAPTER NINE

BLUES: FOLK AND CLASSIC STYLES

INTRODUCTION

The 108th Congress of the United States of America declared 2003 as the year of the blues. The resolution reads:

108th CONGRESS

1st Session

H. CON. RES. 13

Recognizing the importance of blues music, and for other purposes.

IN THE HOUSE OF REPRESENTATIVES

January 27, 2003

Mr. Ford submitted the following concurrent resolution; which was referred to the Committee on Education and the Workforce

CONCURRENT RESOLUTION

Recognizing the importance of blues music, and for other purposes.

Whereas blues music is the most influential form of music indigenous to the United States, providing the roots for contemporary music heard around the world such as rock and roll, jazz, rhythm & blues, and country, and even influencing classical music;

Whereas the blues is a national historic treasure, which needs to be preserved and studied for the benefit of future generations:

Whereas blues music documents twentieth-century United states history, especially during the Great Depression and in the areas of race relations and pop culture;

Whereas the various forms of blues music trace the transformation of the United States from a rural, agricultural society to an urban, industrialized country;

Whereas the blues is an important facet of African-American culture in the twentieth century;

Whereas every year, people in the United States hold hundreds of blues festivals, and millions of new or reissued blues albums are released;

Whereas blues musicians from the United States, whether old or new, male or female, are recognized and revered worldwide as unique and important ambassadors of the United States and its music;

Whereas it is important to educate the young people of the United States so that they understand that the music they listen to today has its roots and traditions in the blues;

Whereas there are many living legends of blues music in the United Stets who should be recognized and have their stories captured and preserved for future generations; and

Whereas the year 2003 would be an appropriate time to recognize the importance of blues music since it is the centennial anniversary of when W.C. Handy composed the first blues music to be released throughout the United States; Now,

> *Resolved by the House of Representatives (the Senate concurring),* That the Congress—

(1) recognizes the importance of blues music with respect to many cultural developments in United States history;
(2) calls on the people of the United States to take the opportunity to study, reflect on, and celebrate the importance of the blues; and
(3) requests that the president issue a proclamation calling on the people of the United States and interested organizations to observe the importance of the blues with appropriate ceremonies, activities, and educational programs.

Indeed, the blues are a historical reservoir from which musicians, music enthusiasts, ethnomusicologists, sociologists, anthropologists, and most, if not all, disciplines can explore the intricacies not only of black culture but the American spirit. As a folk literature, blues lyrics specifically identified and substantiated social, political, cultural, economic, and psychological conditions at a time of great importance in America's history, from post-emancipation to WWII. Both then and now, the blues enlightens aficionados–from the extremely limited in musical knowledge to the most advanced–via experiences that can lead to inspirations transcending time and place. In a peculiar way, the musical character of the blues even intrigues those with an antipathetic position due to its lack of, by their standards, musical sophistication. Despite these assertions, the literature's deposits of melancholy, joy, despair, humor, and other personal testaments to the blues illuminate the triumphant nature of the blues songster. From this viewpoint, black bluesmen are cultural heroes as they juxtapose the real-life conditions of an oppressed black culture (*vis a vis* lyrics) with an exuberant and rhythmically invigorating accompanimental playing style.

The notion of expressing testimonials of despair and melancholy through music is certainly not a new idea, nor is it indigenous to the United States. Every culture along with its concomitant subcultures has its own customs or rhetoric for communicating emotions of downheartedness through some means of public display. The blues, however, are a uniquely American manner of expressing these emotions. Commencing with the arrival of the first African slaves, its gradual evolution from field hollers and spiritual vocalization culminated during the last third of the 19th century into a recognizable style of popular music performed by African Americans. A common error among many early researchers was to categorize both this repertoire and its performer as solely melancholy. In reality, it is nearly the antithesis of this, as the blues songster, by virtue of his or her presence, provided testimony to the triumph of character over oppressive circumstances. Indeed, the blues' quintessentially unique harmonic manner of expressing these frequently distressing characterizations becomes therapeutic in

nature, providing a cathartic experience that leaves both performer and listener feeling more optimistic about life.

HISTORICAL BACKGROUND AND MUSICAL COMMONALITIES

Socially influenced in part by post-CivilWar conditions and the effective date of the Emancipation Proclamation in 1865, the blues song, for many, was the vehicle that transmitted aspects of African American culture to the American public. Like folk music, the lyrical content in blues music was revealing with regard to common sentiments expressed by African Americans. Correctly so, for early blues lyrics were generally true in their description of people, places, events, and emotions, and therefore have provided a social, cultural, political, and historical tank of knowledge for researchers, performers, and listeners.

Early blues songs sung by African Americans are quite similar to folk songs that were sung by European Americans. Although the sociopolitical status of blacks and whites was quite different, subject matter in both blues and folk songs originated from the same rural environment. Consequently, topics such as religious consciousness, various love themes, heroic characters, employment, and life's seemingly difficult challenges were common in both styles.

The blues originated concurrently over a wide area–Mississippi, Georgia, the Carolinas, and Texas–during the last third of the 19th century. Due to the earlier occurrence of agricultural development in Mississippi, a greater number of African slaves resided there. Consequently, the strongest influence on the blues heritage came from the Mississippi delta region, giving rise to the term "delta blues."Later Mississippi blues songsters such as John Lee Hooker, Robert Johnson, Muddy Waters, and Howlin' Wolf incorporated particular performance practices in their singing and playing that were, in effect, inspired by the singing stylizations of field hollers and cries among African slaves. Those that earnestly encapsulated the singing traditions of African slaves and placed them within the context of the rural black and his post emancipated conditions were labeled, in retrospect, "country bluesmen." Countless individuals playing on porches or at local markets and various leisure activities accompanied themselves on the guitar or banjo. Testimonials, often very recent, of relationship issues, working conditions, one's level of religious conviction, and social concerns were typical among these blues singers. Indeed, early country blues songsters provided an exuberant "in-the-moment" performance, which became a staple performance practice for all types of blues–country, classic, and electric.

There were three musical commonalities among the many songsters who sang the blues.

1. Though certainly not used in all songs, the 3-line stanza–more popularly known as the **AAB song form**–entails the repetition of the first line followed by a consequent lyrical response. For example:

   I work all day long, and no place to rest my head
   I work all day long, and no place to rest my head
   If I got to live this way, I might as well be dead.[1]

2. Specific harmonies were played on the guitar to support the singer's melodic line. These harmonies are known as tonic, sub-dominant, and dominant, and are generally referred to as the **I–IV–V chords** respectively.

---

[1] Stan Breckenridge. (Performer) (2006.) "Goodbye Blues" from the album *This is My Song* (CA: Stan Breckenridge Music).

3. These chords are organized in a certain manner and played within what is commonly known as the **12-bar progression**, which eventually became known as the 12-bar blues progression. The illustration below shows all three of the aforementioned commonalities:

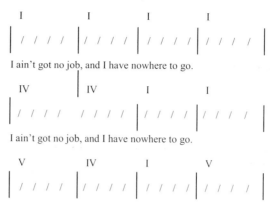

Without question, during the late 19th century, the blues became more entertainment-viable and thus a more popular style than folk singing. Partly due to minstrel-era influences with respect to African American music characterizations, anything having to do with black culture in relation to entertainment had a greater probability of popularity than folk songs. The idea of seeing black performers rather than white imitators of African American culture was becoming more popular. Even more remarkable, for the first time the music stood on its own. Deliberately staged theatrical norms were not mandatory for sustaining interest among an audience of blues fans. A singer could simply accompany himself or herself on the banjo or guitar and provide entertainment for an engrossed audience.

BLUES SONGS VS. BLUES STYLE

The blues song that existed during slavery evolved into the blues style that was evident in the late 19th century. In other words, songs of vocal melancholic expressions of depressed slaves were certainly evident prior to emancipation in 1865, but they were not viewed as a part of an eventual style until after emancipation. Similarities in the lyrical content, vocal articulations, and instrumental accompaniment exist between the blues song and blues style–particularly during the late 19th and early 20th centuries. For instance, both dealt with lyrics that often commented on some miserable situation. Blues songs, or even some Negro Spirituals, spoke about being rejected or being sold into slavery, such as "I've Been Rebuked" or "Goodbye Brother," respectively. Lost love, infidelity, wartime, lost work (e.g., being laid off as a cotton picker due to the infestation of the boll weevil), and prison, although not as miserable as slavery, are depressing lyrics in the blues style. Applying various vocal articulations such as guttural, melisma, bending, falsetto, and bluenotes in order to support and enhance a song's textual meaning is a common practice in Africa, and consequently in these repertoires.

Whether blues song or blues style, this music can be performed with or without an instrument, which occurred more frequently with the blues songs. The greater restrictions among the slaves versus fewer restrictions among the freed slaves clearly influenced the dearth of instruments for accompaniment. In the blues style, it became a common practice for songsters to accompany themselves.

The fiddle,[2] the banjo, and eventually the guitar were the only instruments commonly affordable and consequently these were used by slaves.[3] As a result, they became embedded in African American culture as satisfactory accompanimental instruments for song and dance entertainment after the Civil War.

As time progressed, the blues song evolved into a distinct blues style. It became important to many blues performers to recognize and continue the practice of singing the blues in the fashion set forth by the early songsters.

The early blues were infused with the social conditions (including religious innuendoes) of the songwriter's lifestyle and formulated within the context of secular vocal music. Lyrical content contains reflective, objective, and subjective texts. In addition, lyrics express sadness, love, hate, and even humor–emotions that are experienced by the performer. Artists often comment on the notion that in order to effectively sing the blues, one must have "experienced the blues." Consequently, one sings the blues in order to release oneself from the state of being blues. The singer expresses his or her emotions by utilizing pitch, articulation, volume, duration, and expression to their fullest extent in order to support the meaning and feeling of the text. This is generally presented in an improvisational, interpretational, and/or extemporaneous fashion. Considering all of these points, the singer's presentation of a song, although sung repeatedly, remains quite new and refreshing.

BLUES TYPES

Although most blues songs throughout the decades sound quite similar to the untrained ear, they can be divided into three types: country, classic, and electric (a.k.a. Chicago). The late 19th century marks the beginning of country blues; features of the classic blues came into play after World War I; and World War II denotes the emergence of electric blues. The historical contexts of these temporal parameters greatly impacted and consequently played a definitive role in how the music is played. We begin with country blues, as this type flourished beginning in the late 19th century.

Recognizing the historical significance of notating black music, in 1912 W.C. Handy (1873–1958) became the first person to publish a blues song ("Memphis Blues"), earning him the title "Father" of the Blues." Though he was certainly not the first person to write blues music, he was the first person to musically notate its characteristics and provide the structure of its form. Born in the South (Florence, Alabama), W.C. Handy was familiar with the folk songs, field cries, hollers, and religious music of blacks. Although his father, a respectable local minister, forbade him to engage with what many called lascivious music, at age 22 W.C. Handy became the musical director and bandleader, and played cornet for Mahara's Minstrels until 1903. He studied music and taught at Huntsville College. His first published composition, "Memphis Blues" (1912), was written and titled in 1907 as a rally song for a local politician named "Mr. Crump." The unexpected success of this song as well as the popularity of the term *blues* caused W.C. Handy to rename the song "Memphis Blues." Handy's most notable work titled "St Louis Blues" (1914) inspired Kenneth Adams to write a short story that was based on the lyrics of the song. Filmed by RCA in 1929, Bessie Smith played the leading role as a depressed woman who

---

[2] The fiddle was used because it was a favorite instrument for dancing among the Europeans. (Records indicate that owners of slave ships often secured European fiddlers to entertain the captain and his crew as well as to "dance the slaves"–an event aboard the slave ship where slaves were forced to entertain their captors as well as to exercise in order to avoid rheumatism and other diseases. Because many Europeans believed slaves were musically talented, a gifted slave was often given the task of accompanying European dances using the fiddle.

[3] The African-favored instrument–the drum–was prohibited by most slave masters, as they were aware of its communicative property among the slaves.

had lost her husband/boyfriend. W.C. Handy's other notable songs include "Yellow Dog Blues" (1914), "Beale Street Blues" (1916), "Careless Love" (1921, a.k.a. "Loveless Love"), and "Chantez-Les Bas" (ca. 1922). At the close of WWI, he and Harry Pace[4] formed a music publishing firm named Handy and Pace. Although W.C. Handy is generally not on most Blues enthusiasts' short list with respect to country blues performers, he nevertheless is noted for his many contributions to blues and black music in general. In 1969, W.C. Handy was commemorated with a U.S. postage stamp.

Country/Folk Blues

Characteristics of the country blues style were evident during the latter part of the 19th century and into the early 20th century, as songsters like Blind Lemon Jefferson, Huddie Leadbetter, Lonnie Johnson, Son House, and Robert Johnson were often seen and heard singing on street corners, in barbershops, and at breakdowns and dancehalls. These and many other songsters accompanied themselves on the guitar, banjo, or even, at times, on the bo didley.[5]

Blind Lemon Jefferson (1897–1929) was a major figure in the country blues style of singing and playing. Born in Couchman, Texas, his playing style was of the Texas milieu–a very lyrical manner of singing as compared to the Mississippi delta and North/South Carolina. Born blind at birth, Jefferson learned to play the guitar and was performing as a street singer by his teens. His recording career began on the Paramount label in 1925 with "Got the Blues" and "Long Lonesome Blues." Other songs soon followed, including "The Black Snake Moan" (1926), "Match Box Blues," and "See That My Grave Is Kept Clean" (both in 1927). Throughout his career, Blind Jefferson influenced artists such as Lightnin' Hopkins, Leadbelly, Mance Lipscomb, and B.B. King. The Song Navigator below illustrates the story-telling style of Jefferson.

TIME	SECTION	INSTRUMENTATION/COMMENTS
00:00	Introduction	Guitar
00:12	Verse 1	Lyrics begin with "Hey, ain't got. . . .
00:40	Verse 2	Lyrics begin with "Hm, Black Snake crawlin . . .
01:08	Verse 3	Lyrics begin with "Oh, that must be. . . .
01:39	Verse 4	Lyrics begin with "Mama that's alright. . . .
02:06	Verse 5	Lyrics begin with "Hm, what's the matter . . .
02:32	Verse 6	Lyrics begin with "Well, wonder where . . .

Song Navigator 9.1: "Black Snake Moan" (ca. 1925) by Blind Lemon Jefferson, from *Blind Lemon Jeffereson , Vol. 2 (1927)*, (2005, Document Records); (Genre: Folk/Country Blues)

Leadbelly (1889–1949), born Huddie William Ledbetter in Mooringsport, Louisiana, was a monumental figure in blues and folk song recitations. Taking inspiration from his social and cultural experiences, Leadbelly is regularly credited with the uncanny ability to "tell the story" *vis a vis* songs that placed him above most of his contemporaries. Indeed, his recitations were quite often personal

---

[4] In 1921, Harry Pace formed the first major black-owned-and-operated record label, Black Swan.
[5] A bo didley is a two-or three-stringed instrument constructed on a wall.

Leadbelly. © Photofest

experiences that spoke to every woman and man that wanted to listen. At a young age, he taught himself to play the accordion, guitar, harmonica, and some piano. With guitar as his principal instrument, he was noted for playing in a fashion similar to the barrelhouse piano style–a mixture of blues, ragtime, stride, and some boogie-woogie characteristics. Utilizing a twelve-string guitar, his barrelhouse playing style earned him the title, particularly in Texas, of "King of the 12-String Guitar." His music was so powerful and inspiring that while serving a 30-year sentence for murder in Huntsville, Texas, he was pardoned after serving a little over six years. His plea for freedom was in the form of composed songs that were taken to the governor by John Lomax. Apparently, Leadbelly's sentiments were so poignant that the governor pardoned him with the stipulation that he be released into the care of John Lomax.[6] An enduring musical relationship ensued between Leadbelly and Lomax, which included performing at numerous venues and producing over 200 recordings for the Library of Congress (Folkways label). He also recorded for other notable record labels such as Musicraft, RCA Victor, and Capitol. His performances occurred across the United States with the exception of one tour in Paris, France, during the

---

[6] John and his son Alan Lomax recorded numerous folk, blues, and hillbilly songs among rural Southern blacks and whites beginning in the late 1920s. These are preserved by the Library of Congress on the *Folkways* label.

final year of his life. Some of his more memorable recordings include "Goodnight Irene," "Rock Island Line," "Boll Weevil," "Cotton Fields," and "Pick a Bale of Cotton." Throughout his career, Leadbelly inspired and/or performed with artists such as Woody Guthrie, Pete Seeger, Brownie McGhee, and Sonny Terry. Leadbelly was an excellent composer and performer of songs that represented black culture. In the song "Pick a Bale of Cotton" one can almost feel the task of picking cotton as the singers are incorporating melodic, harmonic, and rhythmic inflections as diversions from the task at hand.

TIME	SECTION	INSTRUMENTATION/COMMENTS
00:00	Verse 1	Lyrics begin with "Great God almighty. . . .; Leadbelly leads off then a group of men join in
00:12	Chorus	Lyrics begin with "Oh Lordy, Pick a Bale . . .; group of men singing; there is evidence of some harmony
00:24	Verse 2	Lyrics begin with "You got to jump . . ."; Leadbelly leads off then a group of men join in
00:36	Chorus	Lyrics begin with "Oh Lordy, Pick a Bale . . . Same as previous chorus
00:48	Verse 3	Lyrics begin with "Well, meet my wife . . . a different male voice (falsetto, other than Leadbelly) leads it off, then the other men join in
00:59	Chorus	Lyrics begin with "Oh Lordy, Pick a Bale . . .; same as before
01:10	Verse 4	Lyrics begin with "Oh, meet my gal . . ., a different male voice (other than Leadbelly) leads it off, then the other men join in
01:21	Chorus	Lyrics begin with "Oh Lordy, Pick a Bale . . .; same as before
01:33	Verse 5	Lyrics begin with "Me and my buddy . . .; a different male voice (other than Leadbelly) leads it off, then the other men join in
01:43	Chorus	Lyrics begin with "Oh Lordy, Pick a Bale . . .; same as before
01:54	Verse 6	Lyrics begin with "me and my partner . . . a different male voice (bass singer, other than Leadbelly) leads it off, then the other men join in
02:04	Chorus	Lyrics begin with "Oh Lordy, Pick a Bale . . .; same as before
02:15	Verse 2	Lyrics begin with "You got to jump . . ."; a different male voice (other than Leadbelly) leads it off, then the other men join in
02:25	Chorus	Lyrics begin with "Oh Lordy, Pick a Bale . . .; same as before
02:36	Verse 1	Lyrics begin with "Great God almighty. . . .; Leadbelly leads it off, then the other men join in

Song Navigator 9.2: "Pick a Bale of Cotton" (ca. 1925) by Leadbelly, from *25 Leadbelly Nuggets, Vol. 1* (2011, Dialogue Recordings); (Genre: Folk/Country Blues)

Born ten days after Leadbelly in New Orleans, Louisiana, Lonnie Johnson (a.k.a. Alonzo Johnson, 1889–1970) was another important figure in the development and dissemination of blues. Unlike previous blues songsters, Johnson's singing style and perhaps more significantly his guitar style placed him among classic blues singers, a type of blues dominated by women. Nonetheless, his characterizations of the blues were similar to the folk or country blues musicians. Learning the guitar (6- and 12-string), violin, and keyboard at an early age afforded him the opportunity to travel to London in 1917, where he joined a musical show. His many instrument talents and performance experiences in Europe allowed him, upon returning to the states in 1921, to play in various theatre orchestras. At age 36, he won a blues contest, which earned him a staff position at the Okeh record label. His first notable recording, titled "Falling Rain Blues," is appealing due to his violin-playing accompaniment. Other recordings include "She's Making Whoopee in Hell Tonight" (1929) and "Why Women Go Wrong" (1930). Having an open mind with regard to new musical ideas and styles, Johnson became involved, unlike the aforementioned blues songsters, in the 1940s urban blues style of singing and performance, and began to play electric guitar. Johnson's playing style throughout his career allowed him to play with artists such as Duke Ellington, Bessie Smith, Johnny Dodds, Victoria Spivey, Louis Armstrong, James P. Johnson (no relationship), Eddie Lang, Don Redman, and many others. He influenced the playing styles of many artists beginning with the country stylizations of Robert Johnson to the urban blues characterizations of B.B. King.

Son House (1902–1988), born Eddie James House, Jr. in Riverton, Mississippi, perhaps epitomizes the country blues songster. Like many, House's vocal style included singing, half-sung, and preaching narration. Regarding the latter, many blues songsters like Son House were influenced by the free-flowing speaking style among African American preachers. During his formative years, Son House was set on becoming a Baptist preacher. But religion was not the only thing attracting this young mind; he was also mesmerized by the rhythmically plaiting sounds of the guitar and its consequent style, namely blues. Aware of the disapproval of blues music among church officials, House nevertheless continued his quest to become a blues songster. His recording titled "John the Revelator" exemplifies both the preaching and blues singing style. Using only his hands as an accompaniment, Son House tells the story of the disciple John and his writing of the Book of the Seven Seals, as found in the Book of Revelations of the *Bible*. Another song that illustrates his vocal style is "Death Letter" (1965).[7] In this song, House sings in a mixture of singing and half-spoken style with a rhythmically strumming accompaniment.

Robert Johnson (1911–1938) was born in Hazelhurst, Mississippi. Though he died young, Johnson recorded 29 songs during his two sessions: San Antonio, Texas in 1936, and Dallas, Texas in 1937. Three well-known songs include "Cross Road Blues," "Come on in My Kitchen," and "Love in Vain." "Cross Road Blues" metaphorically speaks about his difficulty in making a decision. In the end, he feels no one will be able to help him. The song, like many blues strains, shows how the songster calls on the Lord to assist him or her in times of need. Common to the blues is the songster's desire to incorporate religious, which perhaps is a way for him to pay for the sins of leading a less-than perfect religious life. A less serious song is his "Come on in My Kitchen." What is interesting here is that Johnson uses the guitar to emulate the sound of wind. The wind is mentioned because he asks for a woman to "Come on in my kitchen" as it is raining outside. For the male blues songster, women are one of the most common topics. The song titled "Love in Vain" is sung in a melancholy manner as Johnson realizes that a woman whom he has followed to the train station has no affection for him.[8]

---

[7] Son House was rediscovered during the folk, country, and blues revival of the 1960s.
[8] Other early blues songsters include Charley Patton, Fiddlin' Joe Martin, and Willie Brown.

THE TRANSITION FROM COUNTRY TO CLASSIC BLUES

Early notable country blues performers such as Blind Lemon Jefferson (1897–1929), Huddie Ledbetter (1889–1949), Son House (1902–1988), and Robert Johnson (ca. 1912–1938) had their own unique ways of performing. This was exemplified in their use of chord progressions of varying lengths. Since they generally accompanied themselves (a characteristic of country blues), it was difficult to predict the number of measures and lyrical phrasing. Combining these factors with the sociocultural, economic, and psychological conditions after WWI, when this music came to be enjoyed in urban areas by a more diverse audience, and the need for consistency when performing music in ensembles, certain practices came to be regulated, and thus country blues evolved into "classic" blues. Beginning in the 1920s, the 12-bar blues progression, AAB song form, song duration, and lyrical expectancies (particularly for female vocalists) were all practices that became regulated. *classical features*

A few years after the close of WWI, the record industry reported some 25 million copies sold of various recordings. Ragtime, New Orleans jazz, and marching music were the most popular recordings. Capitalizing on people's interests, record labels such as Columbia, Paramount, Victor, and Okeh began to record the foundation of ragtime and jazz music, namely (in retrospect) blues. Despite the fact that the country blues songsters who were performing prior to WWI were predominantly men, we find that recordings began with classic blues singers (mostly women), and were then followed by early bluesmen.

CLASSIC BLUES

Mamie Smith and her 1920 recording titled "Crazy Blues" was the first blues song to be recorded. Following its successful reception, other recordings of women singing blues songs ensued, which, in retrospect, began the classic blues craze. Other notable artists included Gertrude "Ma" Rainey, Bessie Smith, Alberta Hunter, Memphis Minnie, Ida Cox, Ethel Waters, Billie Holiday, and many others. Their recordings were not sung in the manner of early country blues songsters, but rather as singers of blues songs accompanied by small jazz bands. Record labels were capitalizing on the already successful New Orleans-type bands and the emerging big bands by having them accompany women singing blues songs on recordings. The New Orleans staple "frontline" polyphonic texture is heard in the following song.

A distinction needs to be understood between the aforementioned women singers and other women singers of the blues. Singers such as Smith, Rainey, Hunter, and Waters were professional singers who performed for and in a number of different venues. For instance, Smith and Rainey toured with the Rabbit Foot Minstrels (a company of song, dance, and skits); Hunter appeared in *Showboat* in London (1928–1929) and in a UK film titled *Radio Parade of 1935*; and Waters also played an acting role in *Cabin in the Sky* (filmed in 1943) and was regarded as a "pop" singer. These women learned the intricacies of the blues and its traditions and presented them along with their personal experiences in the black community in a professional forum that provided entertainment that most could understand. In this view, the term *classic* is most appropriate for this presentation of the blues. In effect, these vocalists sang the blues as one of several popular styles to become more marketable. There were, of course, many other women singers of the blues who, either by choice or lack of expertise, sang the blues in a less professionally polished and/or effective manner (by music industry standards). Noteworthy singers (listed alphabetically) include Lucille Bogan, Pearl Dickson, Nellie Florence, Mae Glover, Lulu Jackson, Lottie Kimbrough, Lillian Miller, Memphis Minnie, Rosie Mae Moore, Elvie Thomas, and Geeshie Wiley. The following women singers were generally sought out first by record labels to record blues music.

Mamie Smith (1883–1946) from Cincinnati, Ohio, happened to be at the right place at the right time with regard to being the first person to make a blues recording. Sophie Tucker, a popular white

TIME	SECTION	INSTRUMENTATION/COMMENTS
		Instrumentation: Voice, trumpet, clarinet, saxophone, trombone, piano
		Form: The song does not maintain the 12-bar blues progression throughout, instead it uses an 8-bar progression followed by the 12-bar progression
		Texture: The band uses the "frontline" polyphonic texture throughout the song that is characteristic of New Orleans jazz (see Chapter 8)
		Lyrical Content: Her man has left her; he has written her letters; and so on, and now she has the "Crazy Blues."
00:00	Introduction	Instruments only
00:09	Verse 1 – first 8 bars	The singer (Mamie Smith) enters with the lyrics "I can't sleep . . .; the band is playing in a polyphonic manner; the singer uses her natural voice and is applying vibrato;
00:28	Verse 2 – second 8 bars	Lyrics begin with "He makes me feel. . . .
00:46	Verse 3	Lyrics begin with "There's a change . . .; the 12-bar progression begins
01:14	Chorus	Lyrics begin with the title of the song; two 8-bar progressions
01:50	Verse 3	Lyrics begin with "I can read his letter; 12-bar progression
02:16	Verse 4	Lyrics begin with "I went to the railroad . . .; 12-bar progression
02:42	Chorus	Lyrics begin with the title of the song; two 8-bar progressions
03:14	Coda	Slower tempo, then the song ends

Song Navigator 9.3: "Crazy Blues" (1929) by Mamie Smith form the album *Crazy Blues: The Best of Mamie Smith* (1929)

cabaret performer, was initially selected by the Victor label to make the first blues recording, but she had other obligations and could not fulfill the request. Thus, in August 1920, Mamie Smith recorded the first blues song, and its popularity inspired her to record a number of other blues songs. One of her most noted songs is a re-recording of "You Can't Keep a Good Man Down" (ca. 1921).

Gertrude "Ma" Rainey, born Gertrude Pridgett (1886–1939) in Columbus, Georgia, was given the distinguished title of "Mother of the Blues" because of her inspiring lyrical and vocal presentation dramatizing the South in ways to which southerners could relate. Unlike Mamie Smith, who was not solely a blues singer, Ma Rainey's repertoire, although vaudeville- and minstrel-inspired, was primarily the blues. It is reported that her first encounter with the blues came while on tour as a performer with her husband, William "Pa" Rainey, and the Rabbit Foot Minstrels during the very early 1900s. Ma, while in Missouri, became enthralled with both the lyrics of the song and the manner in which a woman was singing about her man who had left her. Soon Ma Rainey incorporated this and other similar songs into her performances. Her 90 recordings occurred on the Paramount label from 1923 to 1929. Some of these include "Jealous-Hearted Blues" (1924), "See See Rider" (1925), "Jelly Bean" (1926), and "Countin' the Blues" (1928).

Bessie Smith. © Photofest

Bessie Smith (1894–1937) was born in Chattanooga, Tennessee, and grew up as an orphan slightly after the turn of the century. Singing on street corners and working with Ma Rainey, she developed an uncanny ability to entertain people of varied musical tastes. Based on her performance ability and her numerous recordings (160 sides) for Columbia from 1923 to 1933, by the late 1920s Bessie Smith became the renowned "Empress of the Blues." Some of her more memorable recordings include "Downhearted Blues" (1923–reportedly selling 780,000 records); "St. Louis Blues" (1925), which was composed and published in 1914 by W.C. Handy; and "Empty Bed Blues" (1925). Of course, Ms. Smith as well as the aforementioned other women singers sang blues songs accompanied by jazz bands.

Alberta Hunter (1895–1984), born in Memphis, Tennessee, was another singer who performed and/or recorded during the classic blues era with many jazz musicians, including Fletcher

Henderson, Joseph Oliver, Louis Armstrong, Sidney Bechet, Perry Bradford, and Fats Waller. Her early recording engagements included songs on the Black Swan record label in 1923, Paramount recording sessions from 1923 to 1924, and the Okeh label in 1924. In addition to her many performances in the United States including USO shows, Ms. Hunter performed in London (periodically from 1927 to 1929), Paris (1929, 1934–35), and Greece, the Middle East, and Turkey (1936–1938). It is interesting that after attaining her own TV show, titled *Debut*, she discontinued music and became a nurse. Ms. Hunter began this new career at sixty-one years of age and continued until she was sixty-six. At that time, she returned to music and continued performing and recording for another twelve years.

Billie Holiday. © Photofest

Billie Holiday (1915–1959) was born Eleanora Fagan Goughy in Philadelphia, Pennsylvania. Most people generally think of Miss Holiday as a performer of blues. While it is true that she did sing and record a number of blues songs, she, like most singers during the 1920s to the 1940s, had to perform a number of different styles in order to achieve success. Consequently, blues and vocal jazz were a singer's most frequently sung styles. Holiday's blues stylizations are evident in the song titled "He's

Funny That Way".[9] Here, her singing style includes the use of bluenoses, bending, *vibrato*, and a some-what sung and spoken manner of articulation. Notice the manner in which she is singing; it is as if she is experiencing these feelings at the moment they are sung. These are some of the most distinguishing features in the stylizations of Miss Holiday.[10]

TIME	SECTION	INSTRUMENTATION/COMMENTS
		Instrumentation: Voice (Billie Holiday), a big band setting (woodwinds, brass, piano, guitar, bass, and drums) Form: AAB song form; 12-bar blues progression Lyrical Content: Her man doesn't love her, as he treats her mean; he seems to, however, make love to her approval
00:00	Introduction	Band
00:12	Verse 1	The singer enters with lyrics the lack of love her man has for her; The band accompanies the singer in the same manner throughout the entire song; the trumpet, more so than any instrument here, plays in response to the singer
00:46	Verse 2	Lyrics about his seemingly unsophisticated way of dressing
01:21	Verse 3	Lyrics about the power of love
01:58	Verse 4	Lyrics about love has the potential, to some, to make one do things unwillingly
02:33	Solo	Lyrics about different levels of love, as the analogy of a hot and cold faucet is used to illustrate this
03:15	Coda	The song ends

Song Navigator 9.4: "Fine and Mellow" by Billie Holiday from the album titled *The Complete Commodore/ Decca Masters*

CLASSIC BLUES LYRICS AND THE 12-BAR BLUES PROGRESSION

Lyrically speaking, in the classic blues genre, women singers predominated. This can be attributed to the rise of women's concerns just before and after WWI, which had infiltrated the private and business sectors in ways that it never had before. Women were being empowered by the unrelenting voices of other courageous women who set precedents for women's rights. Women singers began to be offered opportunities for performances in forums that had generally been discriminatory. Prior to this time, women were certainly well-established in the entertainment world, but not nearly as much as men. Despite the fact that women had the musical talent, they were discriminated against in Tin Pan Alley, vaudeville and burlesque theatre houses, and café and nightclub scenes. The social upheaval that occurred right after WWI was put on notice, as the war's end ushered in societal conflicts. In general, society was very staid and conservative before the war (i.e., women's dresses to the ground, no women

---

[9] "These Foolish Things" appears on the album *The Complete Billie Holiday* on the X5 Music Group label, 2009.
[10] The album titled *Love Songs* by Billie Holiday is a re-mastered album (Verve, 2011) of some of her noted songs that illustrate her versatility outside of blues.

in bars), and comparatively radical after (flappers, short skirts and hair, speakeasies). This social paradigm shift was a major factor in opening people's minds to accepting women's rights and their singing of the blues. Then there was Prohibition–the overreaction to the ultraconservatives' legislation of morality in a desperate attempt to hold onto the values of an era that they could not accept as having passed. During the Roaring Twenties, the social climate shifted significantly. Women became more accepted in many arenas, particularly in the more socially vibrant entertainment scene, and most significantly in the sound recording industry.

The sound recording industry, which had been suspended during WWI, improved technologically and expanded in types of music recorded just after the war. Records replaced sheet music as the most effective way to promote singers and instrumentalists. This was the era of the vinyl record boom. With all of the new attitudes and social changes, a market for women singers materialized. Most significant were blues recordings by African American women. Without a doubt, consumers were being introduced to something different, and before long women became a viable market in the entertainment industry. By the early 1920s, these recordings ameliorated women performers' protestations by effectively terminating the discrimination practices of the various venues.[11] That is to say, in view of the fact that sound recordings were making women increasingly successful in the entertainment industry, proprietors had no choice but to include women in their productions. This in turn demonstrated that the previous protestations of rights and liberties had succeeded in effectively permeating society. Blues songs were regularly performed in various nightclub venues, and certain lyrics were commonplace. For women, songs centered on male and female relationships, with lyrics pointing to both positive and negative characteristics of men. Often, lyrics were highly sexually suggestive. An example is Bessie Smith 1928 recording titled "Empty Bed Blues," which alludes to finding a new man after being abandoned by another. Promiscuous lyrics ensue as she metaphorically refers to a new man as a "coffee grinder." In the third verse, she describes the man as "a deep sea diver." The final verse reveals that this man has been with other women. Billie Holiday's recording titled "Fine and Mellow", describes her man as lacking love, as he treats her mean.

The 12-bar blues progression became a staple of classic blues. As seen below, organizing the primary chords–I, IV, and V–in a specific harmonic succession within 12 bars (measures) contributed to the style's distinctive musical character.

(A)	/	I	/	·I	/	I	/	I	/
(A)	/	IV	/	IV	/	I	/	IV	/
(B)	/	V	· /	IV	/	I	/	I	/

While maintaining this progression or a variation of it in one's mind, the singer strides to fit his/her melodic and lyrical phrases in a manner most suitable to stylistic tendencies of the blues. The AAB song form initiated by country bluesmen became another frequent occurrence of classic blues. As seen above, each letter signifies a lyrical phrase that lasts four measures. In classic blues, it became a standard practice to repeat the first line as well as to rhyme the final words of A and B. For instance, "I went to the store to buy some bread" is the "A" line that is stated twice, and the words, "When I came home you hadn't heard what I said" as the "B" line completes the AAB song form. It was customary to sing four or five verses in this manner; which is also attributed to standard recording lengths at the time. The

---

[11] This is quite analogous to the effect of today's internet. The internet greatly diminishes the chance of discrimination against any person since, generally, people can maintain their anonymity while conversing with others.

following recording of Bessie Smith singing "Empty Bed Blues", recorded around 1926, illustrates the AAB song form that occurred in tandem with the 12-bar blues progression.

TIME	SECTION	INSTRUMENTATION/COMMENTS
		Instrumentation: Voice (Bessie Smith); piano, trombone; the trombone plays in response to the lead singer
00:00	Introduction	Piano and trombone
00:12	Verse 1	Lyrics are about waking up in the morning alone
00:45	Verse 2	Lyrics about finding a new man (coffee grinder)
01:19	Verse 3	Lyrics about her man is a deep sea diver (a sexual euphemism)
01:53	Verse 4	Lyrics about her new man knows how to thrill her
02:26	Verse 5	Lyrics that suggest her new man has other women
02:56	Coda	The song ends at 3:02

Song Navigator 9.5: "Empty Bed Blues" by Bessie Smith from the album *The Complete recordings, Volume 4*

SUBSEQUENT COUNTRY BLUES RECORDINGS

Once the popularity of the classic blues was firmly established in the early 1920s, a search for traditional blues songsters ensued, which took record labels to southern states like Mississippi, Georgia and Tennessee. The Mississippi delta blues was and still is the most widely performed type of blues. Resulting from an oppressively hot, humid climate and the excruciatingly difficult, back-breaking labor that it took to develop the immense body of swamp land, as well as the overbearing oppression and prejudice experienced by black laborers and their families, the social and geographic climate of the Mississippi delta region provided much of the thematic material for the country bluesman. The music born of the feelings that these onerous experiences engendered came from such depths of spirit that this music struck a chord with the American people, generating great interest. This uniquely American music has shaped popular music on a global scale.

As previously mentioned, early country bluesmen performed their songs in a monadic fashion–singing while playing an instrument. Melodic, harmonic, and rhythmic freedom is afforded the singer when music is performed in this manner. Examine, for instance, Robert Johnson's recording titled "Come on in My Kitchen." The singer changes tempo, displays melodic freedom as to lyrical entrances, and chooses to speak rather than sing in one section. In the latter, the singer states with rhythmical freedom: "Can't you hear that wind blowing" and quickly emulates the sound of wind with his guitar. Referred to as "call and response," the country blues performer uses this practice as a way to produce a conversation between the singer (call) and guitar (response). Creating musical conversations through call and response is a blues practice that was influenced by field cries and hollers sung by African slaves during the African Diaspora. Music was, indeed, a way that slaves communicated with one another when all other modes of expression were prohibited. Through numerous vocal articulations such as *melisma*, bending, shouting, guttural sounds, and falsetto, slaves developed a strategy for conversing, which, by and large, permeated musical activities and consequently became a performance practice for many styles of African American music. Many of these features are heard in Robert Johnson's well-known song titled "Cross Road Blues."

TIME	SECTION	INSTRUMENTATION/COMMENTS
		Instrumentation: Robert Johnson is singing while playing guitar (known as monody)
		Form: AAB song form; use of the 12-bar blues progression
		Lyrical Content: Crossroad is an analogy for being undecided about something
00:00	Introduction	Guitar
00:02	Verse 1	Lyrics about arriving at a crossroad; Johnson plays the guitar in response to each lyrical passage throughout the song
00:48	Verse 2	Lyrics about no one seems to want to assist him during this undecided time in his life
01:20	Verse 3	Lyrics about being at this state of mind for a long while
01:52	Verse 4	Lyrics about you can run, but you can't hide; singer uses his falsetto
02:27	Coda	The song ends

Song Navigator 9.6: "Cross Road Blues" by Robert Johnson from the album *The Complete Recordings* (1990, Columbia/Legacy)

For the country bluesman, this practice was transcribed to both the voice and guitar. In some songs, this is not as noticeable when the performer plays the guitar in a less melodic and more rhythmic fashion by strumming it. As one listens to a number of country blues songs, it becomes evident that the guitar accompanies the voice in one of two styles: strumming or picking. Huddie Leadbelly's recording titled "Go Down, Old Hannah" illustrates the first style. Playing in a quadruple meter, Mr. Leadbelly strums the guitar on each count of the measure, accentuating the backbeat (counts 2 and 4), while freely phrasing his vocal melody.

The Leadbelly song is clearly quite different from the picking style displayed in Robert Johnson's "Come on in My Kitchen." Moreover, Mr. Leadbelly departs from the more typical voice vs. guitar call and response performance practice. The call and response occurs within the singer's lyrics instead. The call (antecedent: question), "Go Down, Old Hannah, and don't you ride no more" is responded to (consequent: answer) with "If you ride in the mornin' bring Judgement Day." In either case, the listener is drawn to what the singer is saying by either lyrical conversation or vocal and instrumental conversation.

CHAPTER TEN

COUNTRY: HILLBILLY AND BLUEGRASS STYLES

HILLBILLY

The musical and social influences of folk traditions not only impacted the blues, but also provided the framework, structure, and content of country music as well. In the case of the blues, the field hollers and cries reflecting the African slaves' social conditions greatly contributed to the styles' vocal and lyrical inflections. For the development of hillbilly, the English ballad folk songs and singing styles of the inhabitants of the Appalachian region (often referred to as "mountain people") were of foremost importance. Arising from the British influence beginning in the early 1600s, English ballads represent one of the largest bodies of musical repertoire that had a sustaining effect on the lyrics, function, and manner in which these songs were presented. Later on, the music of Scotch Irish immigrants also became a part of the musical component of people's social activities as early as the 18th century. For amusement, people in rural areas gathered and sang songs and listened to or played fiddle music.[1]

The stylistic term *hillbilly* stems from its reference to people who lived in the mountains who sang folk songs. Also appearing throughout southern states in working-class, white, rural communities, hillbilly music was inspired by vocal and instrumental mannerisms of the people of the Appalachian region. This soon became the favorite music for leisure and social occasions. It is important to note that its designation as country music was not made until the 1940s, when the recording industry was looking for a broader, less explicitly rural stylistic category for the term *hillbilly*. Despite the industry's attempt to segregate the two, with the exception of early folk music of the colonial period, the hillbilly musical style has had the greatest influence on the tradition of country music. One could therefore conclude that the nascence of the country music recording industry was in 1923, when Ralph Peer recorded Fiddlin' John Carson in Atlanta for Victrola (Victor) records.[2] Mr. Carson's recordings included those songs that were popular among the mountain people. As working-class, white citizens (mainly farmers) also manifested a strong interest, Mr. Peer and others in the industry set out to find and record other musicians with similar music. These investigations uncovered two recording artists who have had the greatest influence on the development of country music: The Carter Family and Jimmie Rodgers. Known as the Bristol[3] Sessions, these recordings include folk songs, ballads, and religious songs that were favored by the mountain people and working-class whites.

---

[1] The fiddle was the favored instrument for socializing among the colonists during early colonization in the 17th century.
[2] "Moonshine Kate" is one of the songs recorded.
[3] The city of Bristol lies on the border of Tennessee and Virginia.

The Carter Family. © Michael Ochs Archives/Corbis

The Carter Family (A.P. Carter and his wife Sarah, plus Sarah's cousin Mabel) from Virginia were discovered in 1927. Their success is predominantly due to A.P. Carter's desire to perform/record songs that were exactly like those sung by the people (i.e., mountain and working-class whites). Traveling particularly to the mountain regions, A.P. Carter collected favorite songs and recorded them as true to form as possible.[4] Most songs were accompanied by guitar and centered on two of the three primary chords of western music (I and V). Some of the songs from their 1933–34 recording sessions on Victor include "Faded Flowers," "When the Roses Come Again," "I Loved This Better Than You Knew," "This Is Like Heaven to Me," and "See That My Grave Is Kept Clean." In "Faded Flowers" (1933), the earliest song among these, the title is referring to sorrow resulting from the lost of loved ones. As shown by the timeline (see Illustration 1), the song consists of five verses, with the third verse functioning as the chorus. The song consists of four verses that are sung by a woman soloist with a pick/strum guitar accompaniment. The chorus/verse three is sung in three-part harmony by all members. Although not shown, the harmonic progression consists primarily of the I chord, which is played throughout the first six measures of each eight-measure section (shown in figure). The V chord is played on the seventh measure of each eight-measure section, and returns to the I chord during the final measure. Unlike the previous song, which is performed in duple meter (i.e., time measured by two counts for each stroke),

---

[4] An African American friend named Leslie Riddle—a blues songster—traveled with him to help in remembering the tunes. Such activities show the overlapping of music styles and practices that occurred between whites and blacks.

the song titled "When the Roses Come Again" (heard as early as 1874) is performed in triple meter (three counts for each stroke). Although an uncommon rhythmic meter in today's popular music, triple or waltz meter was frequently used during the colonial period. This song, about the joy of seeing someone during spring, is metaphorically sung with reference to a time when roses are in bloom. As seen in Illustration 2, the song is arranged with a number of verses sung by a soloist (a woman here), a chorus/refrain, and instrumental interludes. In this song, yodeling—a common performance practice among mountain people—is sung in two-part harmony at the end of the chorus section. One of the latest of these recordings titled "This Is Like Heaven to Me" (1903) makes reference to certain experiences in life that resonate the title. (see Illustration 3.) Performed in 6/8, the song has a waltz-like sensation as there is an accent on the first beat of each group of three counts. Unlike the two previous examples, this song makes use of all three of the primary chords, I, IV, and V. Moreover, the arrangement of this song is nearly an equal distribution of all three sections: verse, chorus, and instrumental solo. When performed in the same manner that it was sung by the mountain people, and considering the structure of the previous songs, this piece demonstrates a desire for variety with respect to harmony and song structure.

Despite the fact that Jimmie Rodgers's career lasted only six years as a result of his battle with tuberculosis, he left us with 120 recordings of many of our most beloved early American songs. Although not the first, Mr. Rodgers is often recognized as one of the first to record and consequently popularize the "blue yodel" singing style.

Born in Pine Springs, Mississippi, on September 8, 1897, Jimmie Rodgers was raised in Meridian County—a place known for entertainment—where he learned to play banjo and guitar and received many musical inheritances throughout his early life; some of these include folk and blues songs, vaudeville traditions, plus hobo and railroad songs. Generally, any person living in the southern part of the United States would have come in contact with folk song narratives and blues songsters at some point in his or her life. Vaudeville was the most popular entertainment venue for most Americans during the late 19th century through the beginning of WWI. Staged shows of singers, instrumentalists, dancers, comedians, and a host of other entertainment reflected the many musical tastes of America's diverse cultural heritages. Here is where he, like many others, learned the art of performance and entertainment. With regard to Mr. Rodgers's acquaintance with hobo and railroad songs, his first job as a railroad worker gave him firsthand knowledge of testimonials among people who frequented the railroad. As the result of his battle with tuberculosis, his railroad career ended and music became his second career. Playing in a string band in Asheville, North Carolina, Jimmie Rodgers responded to an advertisement placed by Ralph Peer of Victor records who was looking for performers to record authentic hillbilly music in

SECTION	INTRO	VERSE 1	VERSE 2	CHORUS/ V3	INSTRUMENTAL	VERSE 4	VERSE 5	INSTR.	CHORUS/ V3
Ms.	8	8	8	8	8	8	8	8	8
Part	Guitar	Singer	Singer	All 3 singers	Guitar	Singer	Singer	Guitar	All 3 singers
PP	Pick/ strum	Solo	Solo	3-Part harmony	Pick/strum	Solo	Solo	P/strum	3-Part harmony

Song Navigator 10.1: "Faded Flowers" (recorded 1933–34, The Carter Family)

SECTION	INTRO	VERSE 1	VERSE 2	CHORUS	CHORUS	INSTR.	VERSE 3	VERSE 4	CHORUS	CHORUS	INSTR.	VERSE 5	VERSE 6	CHORUS
Ms.	2	9	9	9	6	9	8	9	9	6	9	Same sequence as before		
Part	Guitar	Singer	Singer	All 3 singers	All singers	Guitar	Singer	Singer	All	All	Guitar			
PP	Pick/ strum	Solo	Solo	3-Part harmony	Yodeling	Melody	Solo	Solo	3-Parts	Yodeling	Melody			

Song Navigator 10.2: "When the Roses Come Again" (recorded 1933–34, The Carter Family)

SECTION	INTRO	VERSE 1	CHORUS	INSTR.	VERSE 2	CHORUS.	INSTR.	VERSE 3	CHORUS	
Ms.	4	8	8	8	8	8	8	8	8	9
Part		Guitar	Singer	All 3 singers	Guitar	Singer	All 3 singers	Guitar	Singer	All 3 singers
PP		Pick/ strum	Solo	3-Part harmony	Melody	Solo	3-Part harmony	Melody	Solo	3-Part harmony

Song Navigator 10.3: "This Is Like Heaven to Me" (recorded 1933–34, The Carter Family)

Jimmie Rodgers. © Photofest

Bristol, Tennessee.[5] In 1927, Jimmie Rodgers recorded "The Soldier's Sweetheart" and "Sleep, Baby, Sleep" and began his short-lived music career. By the end of the year, he had recorded an eventual million seller, namely "T for Texas." Other recordings include "Mississippi River Blues," "Peach Picking Time in Georgia," "Mother, the Queen of My Heart," "Waitin' for a Train," "Jimmie the Kid" and "The Singing Brakeman."

---

[5] Known as the Bristol Sessions.

TIME	SECTION	INSTRUMENTATION/COMMENTS
		Instrumentation: Voice and guitar played by Jimmie Rodgers
		Form: The lyrics are sung using the AAB song form, but the chordal progression is an uneven number of measures (As you recall, the blues often uses the 12-bar progression when the AAB song is present)
		Performance practice: Jimmie Rodgers sings his staple "yodel" (a.k.a. blue yodel) at the end of each verse
		Lyrical Content: A song about his former girlfriend Thelma; Apparently, according to him, someone took his girl; He also mentions his disdain with the negative treatment he receives in Atlanta
00:00	Introduction	Guitar only
00:05	Verse 1	The singer (Jimmie Rodgers) enters with the lyrics of the song title
00:35	Verse 2	Lyrics begin with the words "If you don't want . . .
01:08	Verse 3	Lyrics begin with the words "I gonna buy . . .
01:40	Verse 4	Lyrics "I'm gonna where's . . .
02:10	Interlude	Lyrics are the title of the song; two vocalists sing in harmony
02:18	Verse 5	Lyrics begin with the words "I'm gonna buy . . .
02:54	Verse 6	Lyrics begin with "Rather drink muddy water . . .
03:22	Coda	The song slowly fades out

Song Navigator 10.4: "T. for Texas (Blue Yodel No. 1)" by Jimmie Rodgers from the album *Blue Yodel — His 52 Finest, 1927–1933* (Nimbus Records, 2009)

Mr. Rodgers performed as a soloist, in a string band (fiddle, guitar, and banjo) and even with some instruments of a typical New Orleans jazz instrumentation (trumpet, clarinet, trombone, tuba, banjo, and snare/bass drum), as he had wide-ranging musical tastes. Singing a variety of music, folk songs to vaudeville, sentimental parlor songs, blues lyrics, yodel songs, and popular music hall tunes, Jimmie Rodgers was indeed a representation of folk/rural America. He is often credited with being the first successful country performer to accompany his singing on the guitar. Moreover, his incorporation of the "blue yodel" singing style insured his popularity among the mountain people and consequently became a performance tradition of early country music. Jimmie Rodgers's recordings are an excellent body of work that provide the purist, performer, and listener with early authentic country music. They have inspired a plethora of performers such as Gene Autry, Jimmie Davis, Merle Haggard, Bonnie Raitt, Hank Williams, and Doc Watson.

The popularity of all styles of music spawned so much interest around the country that various consumer product companies found it advantageous to sponsor radio show programs that catered to these musical tastes. In the South, hillbilly music was one of the favorite styles of music. In 1925, a barn dance program, which later became the Grand Ole Opry, at WSM radio in Nashville began operation and soon became the favorite radio show among both southern whites and blacks. WSM's initial radio announcer was George Hay, a popular radio host from Chicago, whose skills contributed to the popularity of the show. In fact, he is credited with naming the barn dance program Grand Ole Opry.[6] By the late 1920s, appearing at the Grand Ole Opry became the ultimate goal of most country musicians. Around 6:00 PM every Saturday evening, the show featured popular hillbilly (eventually country) musicians of the day. As stated by Doc Watson: "There was so much music on the Grand Ole Opry that sooner or later if you were listening on Saturday night you'd heard a group that you'd like" (*American Roots*, DVD).

The first popular performer of the Grand Ole Opry was Uncle Dave Macon. Born circa 1867, Uncle Dave (as he was often called) was a singer, banjo player, and comedian. Influenced by the music of vaudeville and folk songs, Uncle Dave knew the musical desires of his fellow countrymen and women. Singing and playing banjo a few examples include "Buddy Won't You Roll Down the Line" (about the hard life of working in coal mines) and "Shoo Fly, Don't You Bother Me" (a song about not being concerned with other peoples agenda). His experience as a traveling musician afforded Macon to build an impressive repertoire of all sorts. A performance practice among many vaudeville and minstrel performers in the nineteenth entailed humorously speaking about real-life situations. Macon regularly included this practice in a number of his songs. A few include "Sourwood Mountain Medley," "Tom and Jerry," and "Go Long Mule" (he begins the song with the sound of a mule). In the song titled "Tennessee Red Fox Chase" Macon speaks throughout the entire song describing the progression of chasing a fox (a southern past time). Religious nurturing was a mainstay in most hillbilly communities, and singing songs about God was an expected task among hillbilly artists. Macon recorded a number of religious songs; some of which are still popular among numerous congregations like "Are You Washed in the Blood of the Lamb" and "Old Ship of Zion."[7]

Another early star of the Grand Ole Opry was Lee Ford Bailey. Considered to be the first African American performer on the Grand Ole Opry, and perhaps the first black person on radio, Bailey was a favorite harmonica player. By the 1930s, the popularity of the Grand Ole Opry had grown to the point that it was being broadcast nationally. Roy Acuff, a singer and fiddler, became the first national and subsequently featured performer on the Grand Ole Opry and contributed to its development as a truly entertaining venue for a wide variety of people with diverse musical tastes. Seeing the marketability of this radio program, NBC TV began to broadcast a half hour show featuring the Grand Ole Opry beginning in the early 1940s.

Although the Grand Ole Opry garnered an increasingly large number of viewers during the 1940s and early 1950s, it could not compete with emerging styles such as western swing, honky-tonk, rockabilly, and most importantly, rock & roll.

BLUEGRASS

Not all hillbilly performers embraced this new, seemingly organized and more restrictive style of music that became known as country & western, or country. Many of them either continued in the traditional hillbilly manner, whereas others played in a different way that contributed to the establishment of a

---

[6] To many, the Grand Ole Opry is the home of country music.
[7] All the aforementioned songs recorded by Macon are available on the album titled *Uncle Dave Macon: The Very Best Of*, published by Master Classics, released in 2009.

new style of folk/hillbilly music that became known as "bluegrass." If one listens to bluegrass music, recordings of the Del McCoury Band will undoubtedly appear on the playlist. The band was founded by Del McCoury (under the name Del McCoury and the Dixie Pals) in 1967 after his year or so touring with Bill Monroe—the "father" of bluegrass music.

Labeled in the 1950s, bluegrass differed from hillbilly in that the banjo played in a more syncopated fashion and songs were generally faster. Although people danced to bluegrass music, it was also appreciated as music to listen to. Typical instruments included mandolin, fiddle, banjo, and guitar. The mandolin came into play as the result of the musical influences of Bill Monroe. Regarded as the "father" of Bluegrass music, Bill Monroe had the most profound impact on early and contemporary performers of bluegrass. Monroe's greatest contribution to the establishment of bluegrass lay in his ability to sustain the integrity of the folk origins of bluegrass while incorporating different instruments and musical influences. Monroe maintained the tradition of folk songs—the source of bluegrass—by writing and performing songs for people who grew up with similar life situations so that the subject matter was familiar to them. In addition, as the result of his interaction with African American and Mexican culture and music, he was able to compose and perform music that incorporated these styles with his own regional tastes, creating the early foundations of bluegrass.

Born in 1911 in Ohio County, Kentucky, Bill Monroe worked on his parents' farm until he left to meet his brothers in Chicago. While on the farm, Monroe was inspired by his mother's singing around the house, and even fiddling when she had time. His early instrumental influence came from his Uncle Pen, who was the first man Monroe heard on the fiddle. As was the case with most rural families during his time, the Monroes often sang, danced, and/or listened to folk, hillbilly and/or religious music after a family supper. In retrospect, Bill admired the Scottish Irish folk songs Uncle Pen played, such as "Jennie Lynn," "Going Across the Sea," and "Sally Goodin." The intimacy of Uncle Pen's playing style and mannerisms evident in his family gatherings permeated his performances for various country dances in the area as well. Inspired by Uncle Pen's activities, Monroe dedicated a song to him titled "Uncle Pen" (1950).

Unlike some of his older brothers and sisters whose musical influence included shape-note instruction at the singing school at church, Monroe listened to others and played without reading music. Nonetheless, religious music for most people in his area played a major role in their musical development. Exposure to male and female vocal groups as well as to choirs singing in two- to four-part harmony influenced Monroe's harmonic usages in many of his songs.

In the rural South, it was not uncommon to see black musicians playing on their porches and at social occasions. Around the age of 10, Monroe met Arnold Schultz—a black fiddler and guitarist—at a barn dance. Soon afterward, Schultz and Monroe played together at several dances. During this relationship Monroe was inspired by the syncopated rhythms of ragtime and the vocal inferences of blues, and incorporated these stylistic qualities in songs such as "Rotation Blues" and "Lonesome Truck Driver's Blues" (both in 1951), and "New John Henry Blues" and "White House Blues" (both in 1954).

After Monroe's mother's death in 1921 and his father's death in 1927, he, like his older brothers, left the farm to work elsewhere. Playing for various dance and social occasions, Monroe, now 18, finally joined his brothers in Chicago. This is when his indoctrination into the radio business began along with his two brothers, for the "Barn Dance Tour" on WLS radio in Chicago.

Early recordings by Bill Monroe & The Bluegrass Boys[8] include "Bluegrass Special" (1945), "Bluegrass Breakdown" (1947), "Bluegrass Stomp" (1949), and "Bluegrass Ramble" (1950). The latter

---

[8] Members of The Bluegrass Boys at various times have included Jim Shumate, Bobby Hicks, and Charlie Smith (fiddle), Lester Flatt and Connie Gately (guitar), String Bean and Joe Drumright (banjo), and Earl Scruggs (banjo).

Bill Monroe. © Photofest

song features the mandolin as a solo instrument as well as the fiddle. Like early folk songs, bluegrass music, when sung, provides accurate accounts of life situations. For example, Monroe's song titled "I'm on My Way to the Old Home" describes his love for his home state of Kentucky. He mentions listening to the hounds from his old house on a hill and the death of his parents.

With regard to the musical character of bluegrass, its harmonic structure generally disregards embellished chords, but rather uses music's primary chords: I, IV, and V. Despite the virtuosic instrumental playing, the voice, like folk songs, lacks virtuoso singing. This is not to diminish the importance of the voice, as a less-trained voice—characteristic of folk songs—is more appropriate for music that is intended for the "folk." Another feature of bluegrass that is similar to folk singing is the inclusion of other singers during the refrain. Participatory singing encourages camaraderie and community. This was a common activity among the colonists, as they only had each other for socializing and diversion from work. Bill Monroe's "When the Golden Leaves Begin to Fall" (1950) begins with a verse that is sung by Monroe, whereas the refrain is sung homorhythmically by four men.

Camaraderie was a fact of life for those individuals who were exposed to similar environments as Bill Monroe, and playing music formally and informally was a favorite past-time. Two individuals who

TIME	SECTION	INSTRUMENTATION/COMMENTS
		Instrumentation: Voices (lead and background), mandolin, banjo, 2 violins, guitar, bass
		Form: eight-measure sections
		Performance practice: The banjo plays the picking style; violins play legato phrases in counterpoint against the lead singer; mandolin plays in a strumming manner as well as (at times) the picking style; guitar plays in a strumming manner; bass plays quarter notes (i.e., on every count) alternating between root and fifth of each chord
		Lyrical Content: Fond memories of growing up in Kentucky
00:00	Introduction	Instruments only; the banjo plays the lead theme
00:16	Verse 1	The singer (Bill Monroe) enters with the lyrics "Back in the days . . .; the band accompanies throughout the song
00:32	Chorus	Lyrics are the title of the song; two vocalists sing in harmony
00:48	Solo	Two violins are playing in harmony much the same way the two vocalists sing the chorus
01:04	Verse 2	Lyrics "Soon my childhood . . .
01:18	Chorus	Lyrics are the title of the song; two vocalists sing in harmony
01:36	Solo	Mandolin, accompanied by the band
01:50	Verse 3	Lyrics begin with "High in the hills . . .
02:06	Chorus	Lyrics are the title of the song; two vocalists sing in harmony
02:22	Ending	The song ends

Song Navigator 10.5: "I'm On My Way to the Old Home" (1929) by Bill Monroe and The Bluegrass Boys from the album of the same name (1950–1951)

played with Monroe, and who eventually formed their own group are Earl Scruggs and Lester Flatt. Earl Scruggs (b. 1924) with his three-finger picking style is given credit for contributing to the classic features of bluegrass music. Everyone who listened to this music at some time or another heard the quick picking style of Scruggs. Perceived as a minstrel instrument during the Minstrel Era (1820–1870, see Chapter Six), the banjo was, for many, decidedly, associated with a past they wanted to forget. In southern areas, however, it remained integral to the tradition of utilizing those instruments popular among the common folk. When Scruggs joined forces with Monroe, their complimentary playing styles incited further development for Scruggs, from the two-finger to the three-finger picking styles. In addition to Earl Scruggs, Lester Flatt (1914–1979) and his playing and singing style was also central to the tenets of bluegrass music. Joining Monroe's Bluegrass Boys in 1945, Flatt greatly contributed to the sound of the band as an astute musician and singer, who often sang in harmony with Monroe. All solo

TIME	SECTION	INSTRUMENTATION/COMMENTS
		Instrumentation: Mandolin, banjo, violin, guitar, bass
		Form: eight-measure sections
		Performance practice: The banjo plays the picking style; violin plays legato phrases; mandolin plays in a strumming manner as well as (at times) the picking style; guitar plays in a strumming manner; bass plays quarter notes (i.e., on every count) alternating between root and fifth of each chord
		Instrumental song
00:00	Introduction	Instruments only; the mandolin plays the lead theme
00:04	Jam	No one necessarily plays a preeminent theme
00:16	Jam	No one necessarily plays a preeminent theme
00:28	Solo	Mandolin; picking style
01:40	Solo	Banjo; three finger-picking style
00:52	Solo	Mandolin
01:05	Solo	Mandolin
01:18	Solo	Guitar; picking style
01:30	Solo	Violin
01:42		Mandolin
01:54		Banjo plays somewhat of a solo passage a few times, then no one necessarily plays a preeminent theme thereafter
02:08	Coda	Mandolin plays solo passages as the band plays in stop time[9]

Song Navigator 10.6: "Blue Grass Ramble" (1929) by Bill Monroe and The Bluegrass Boys from the album of the same name (1950–1951)

musicians that could rival each other with their virtuoso ability decided to present this on stage live in front of audiences. What emerged was more than excellent music played by virtuoso performers but also a microcosm of camaraderie predicated on the social and cultural milieu that was emboldened by the people who chose to homestead the Appalachian region in the southern part of the United States. The Music Navigator gives an example of virtuoso solos played by Monroe, Scruggs, and Flatt.

Practices that were impeccably set forth by Bill Monroe were imitated by his contemporaries, including Mac Wiseman, Ralph Stanley and the Clinch Mountain Boys, Curly Ray Cline, Jim and Jesse McReynolds, Jimmy Martin, the Foggy Mountain Boys, Earl Scruggs, and the Stanley Brothers.

One cannot deny the wholesomeness of hillbilly, bluegrass, and country & western music. With its folksong vestiges of religious spirituality, committed love, moral consciousness, and non trendy general content, it represents the very nature of America's early beginnings as a religiously conscious

---

[9] Stop time is when all instruments "stop playing" but the time continues on. This may occur several times while an instrument is playing a solo passage (This is also a tradition of new Orleans jazz, see Chapter 8).

society whose goals were often outgrowths of Puritanism. Folk, hillbilly, bluegrass, and country & western songs were interchangeable with respect to sacred and secular lyrics during performances. In other words, one could hear religious songs in a secular context. Such a practice was also common in recording sessions. Bill Monroe typifies this by including songs such as "Lord Protect My Soul," "River of Death," "Swing Low, Sweet Chariot," and "Angel's Rock Me to Sleep" (both recorded in 1950) along with a group of primarily secular songs.

Bluegrass began to lose its popularity during the heyday of rock & roll, beginning with the music of Elvis Presley. The sound of acoustic instruments became outdated. Despite the fact that many bluegrass bands played rock & roll, even with amplified instruments, songs such as Chuck Berry's "Johnny B. Goode" played by these bands did not have the contemporary sound needed to compete with the likes of Bill Haley & the Comets, Little Richard, Chuck Berry, and Elvis Presley. Interest in bluegrass continued in a downward spiral until the folk music revival era of the 1960s. The sociopolitical, cultural, and economic conditions of the 1960s gave rise to a "back-to-roots" movement. Generally precipitated by young people, flower children, and college students, bluegrass bands exemplified the "back-to-roots" movement with its use of acoustic instruments and folk like character. Performed on college campuses and folk music festivals, bluegrass once again found favor among a wider audience whose tastes included other styles of music as well.

Although rock & roll was gaining in popularity, it did not discourage artists from wanting to play or learn bluegrass music. Fortunately, the "back-to-roots" movement of the 1960s, as a result of social and civil concerns among many Americans, renewed interest in folk music, particularly acoustic. Once again, bluegrass music received an injection of public popularity that gave rise to a number of bluegrass bands and performances. Often hosted by bluegrass and folk festivals in countries such as the United States, Australia, Japan, Czechoslovakia, and France, and in college campuses around the world bluegrass bands such as The Seldom Scene, The Osborne Brothers, Allison Krauss and Union Station, Pat Enright and Alan O'Bryant, and the Nashville Bluegrass Band found themselves playing not only for bluegrass listeners, but, as the result of the social climate of the 1960s, for an audience diverse in age, gender, and ethnicity. The entertainment industry capitalized on the cross-marketability of bluegrass to the extent that it developed great potential as film and T.V. music. Consequently, bluegrass music was being heard in films such as *Deliverance* and *Bonnie and Clyde* and was the style used for the popular 1960s sitcom *The Beverly Hillbillies*. Maintaining the traditional instrumentation of string bands—fiddle, banjo, guitar, bass (electric), and mandolin—these and other bands continually disseminate a truly American form of music that has roots embedded in the American spirit.

JAZZ: CHICAGO JAZZ, NEW YORK JAZZ, AND BIG BAND JAZZ

INTRODUCTION

As people migrated from the southern cities of Mississippi, South Carolina, and Louisiana to urban centers like Chicago and New York after WWI, they brought their musical tastes.

Musicians such as Joseph Oliver, Louis Armstrong, Freddie Keppard (all cornet/trumpet players), Sydney Bechet, Jimmy Noone, Johnny Dodds (all clarinet players; Bechet also played soprano saxophone), and Edward Ory (trombone); and band leader/musicians such as Bix Beiderbecke with the Original Dixieland Jazz Band, Fletcher Henderson, Don Redmon, Duke Ellington, and Cab Calloway were all instrumental in the development of the jazz scene in New York, which led to big band jazz. It is apparent that New Orleans jazz begat Chicago jazz and New York jazz, and New York jazz begat big band/swing jazz. In all cases, big cities were havens for dance-inspired music. In Chicago, favored venues included Club Metrepole, the De Luxe Café, Dreamland, the Grand Terrace Ballroom, Moulin Rouge, Pekin, the Plantation Café, the Royal Gardens (which later became Lincoln Gardens), and the Sunset Cafe.[1] New York jazz venues for many bands included the Broadway Roseland Ballroom, Club Alabam, Small's Paradise, the Savoy Ballroom, and the Bamboo Inn (a.k.a. Dunbar Palace). Venues outside of New York that regularly hired jazz bands included the Greystone Ballroom in Detroit, Michigan.

In addition to a few performance practices, differences in these types of jazz lie in their instrumentation. The brass band was common in both New Orleans and Chicago jazz, with a few changes in the latter. New York jazz and its subsequent evolution–big band jazz/swing–consisted of bands where instruments were organized by sections, hence sectional bands/music. The size of bands grew considerably: six members was common among New Orleans jazz bands of the late 19th century; six to nine for Chicago jazz just after WWI; nine to twelve in New York jazz bands (also after WWI); and thirteen to twenty-two for big bands during the early 1920s.

CHICAGO JAZZ

With regard to performance practice differences, while New York jazz focused on sectional alternation and solo melodic lines in an effort to produce the excitement of New Orleans jazz, Chicago jazz

[1] Chicago jazz had a type of jazz known as ". . . South Side style, which meant small-band recordings and jobs at small, rough clubs . . ." (Keepnews, p. 43).

maintained a closer connection to New Orleans jazz. For example, like New Orleans jazz, a number of Chicago jazz pieces exhibited the use of polyphonic texture, regularity of solos by the front line instruments, and "stop time." Differences in Chicago jazz included a faster tempo; the alternation of bass and banjo on counts within a quadruple meter; and, occasionally, variation from the ABA formal song structure. As shown in the illustration below, the 1926 recording titled "Black Bottom Stomp" by Jelly Roll Morton's Red Hot Peppers (recorded in Chicago by the Victor label) exemplifies all of the aforementioned practices. The tempo is quite fast; in fact, it is faster than the typical Chicago jazz piece in 1926. Divided into two general sections (excluding the introduction), the piece basically consists of solos by the front line instruments (including a piano and banjo solo) that are accompanied by the remaining band members. Consisting of piano (Jelly Roll Morton), trumpet, clarinet, trombone, banjo, bass, and drums; all members play the introduction, the first two "A" sections, and the interlude in a chordal fashion (i.e., not featuring a solo or polyphonic texture). The chordal fashion also occurs during the third through fifth "A" sections, but only during the last four measures of each instrumental solo (i.e., trumpet, trumpet, then clarinet). This occurrence is representative of call and response, as the solo instrument calls during the first four measures while the remaining four measures played by the entire band represent the response. The interlude between the final "A" section and the first "B" section functions as a transition. The first "B" section begins with the typical New Orleans jazz polyphonic texture, which is played by the front line instruments (trumpet, clarinet, and trombone). The next four "B" sections consist of individual solos: clarinet, piano, trumpet, and banjo. The piece closes with a return to the polyphonic texture that is played for twice the time of the previous individual solos. In addition to these features, the band plays in "stop time" during the trumpet solo (fourth "B" section), which is a typical practice in New Orleans jazz. The use of a "walking bass" line, which sporadically occurs during the banjo solo, shows Jelly Roll Morton's cognizance of this practice as a driving force in dance styles of the day. Some of the dances included the song's title (Black Bottom Stomp), Charleston, the early Lindy Hop, and the ubiquitous Swing dance of the 1930s.

Another example of the Chicago jazz sound is the piece by Frankie Trumbauer and His Orchestra titled "Riverboat Shuffle" (1927). The instrumentation includes cornet (Bix Beiderbecke)[2], trombone, clarinetist who doubles on baritone saxophone, C-melody saxophone (Frankie Trumbauer), alto saxophone, piano, guitar, and drums. Although the instrumentation is quite different from the previous piece, the sound is nonetheless Chicago jazz. The outline below compares the two pieces.

Similarities
1) Polyphonic texture
2) The polyphonic texture functions as the coda (end or final section)
3) Trumpet and clarinet are featured instruments
4) Trumpet/cornet solo occurs first, then clarinet
5) At least one solo occurs before as well as after the interlude
6) The use of interludes to separate moods
7) The chordal texture occurs at the introduction
8) The banjo/guitar is featured (although briefly)
9) Call and response occurs between a single instrument and the remaining instruments
10) The overall length

[2] Bix Beiderbecke was born 1903 and died 1931. He was admired by his cornet/trumpet contemporaries such as Louis Armstrong and Red Nichols. By age 18, he was performing in professional bands like the Wolverines.

"BLACK BOTTOM STOMP" (1926) JELLY ROLL MORTON'S RED HOT PEPPERS

Practice	Chordal	Chordal	Chordal	tpt/band	cl solo	Chordal	Poly	cl solo	pf solo	tpt solo	bj solo	Poly
Section	Intro	A	A	A	A	interlude	B	B	B	B	B	B
Measures	8	8	8	8	16	4	20	20	20	20	20	40

Song Navigator 11.1: "Black Bottom Stomp" (1926) Jelly Roll Morton's Red Hot Peppers

"RIVERBOAT SHUFFLE" (1927) FRANKIE TRUMBAUER AND HIS ORCHESTRA

Practice	Ch/Poly	Poly	Poly	Poly	Poly	c solo	Ch/Poly	cl solo	Poly	Poly	Poly	Poly
Section	Intro	A	B	A	B1	ABAB1	interlude	ABAB1	A	B	A	B1
Measures	20	8	8	8	8	32	16	32	8	8	8	12

Song Navigator 11.2: "Riverboat Shuffle" (1927) Frankie Trumbauer and His Orchestra

Differences
1) The polyphonic texture appears more frequently in the second piece
2) Solos occur in the middle of the second piece
3) The first piece has more measures (200 vs. 168), but is similar in length due to the faster tempo
4) The second piece has longer solos
5) The first piece consists of eight-measure progressions, while 32-measure progressions are used in the second

As seen above, the similarities between the two pieces far outweigh the differences. The polyphonic texture is a staple in Chicago jazz. Both pieces use the same instruments for the front line. Interestingly, the polyphonic texture occurs at the end of both of the above pieces. This is probably done in an effort to leave the listener with this most jubilant performance practice. With regard to the solos, trumpet/cornet and clarinet are typical solo instruments in most Chicago jazz pieces. The trumpet/cornet is the first featured instrument. Even though the trumpet solo in the first piece occurs more extensively after the clarinet solo (third "B" section), there are two occurrences, as shown, during the third and fourth "A" sections. It can be seen from this how solos play a major role in the performance of Chicago jazz. As illustrated, they occur before and after the interlude, which functions as a midway and transitional section (i.e., to separate moods). With regard to the introduction section, Chicago jazz will frequently begin with all instruments playing in a chordal or homorhythmic fashion. (New Orleans jazz often begins with the polyphonic texture.) Generally, the banjo and/or guitar play in the chordal fashion throughout the pieces. In these two pieces other instruments are added that also play along with the guitar and/or banjo. To add even more contrasting ideas, the banjo/guitar in Chicago jazz will frequently play a solo or in a melodic manner as well the chordal fashion. In "Black Bottom Stomp," the banjo plays a solo, although strumming, just before the closing section, while the guitar is featured in "Riverboat Shuffle." Moreover, in the introduction, the guitar plays the response to the band's call. In closing, as shown by the illustrations, it appears that "Black Bottom Stomp" is longer than "Riverboat Shuffle," 200 vs. 168 measures respectively. This is not the case, as the first piece is significantly faster; 256 bpm (beats per minute) vs. 224 bpm.

NEW YORK JAZZ

Almost simultaneously with the development of Chicago jazz, New York experienced a change with regard to musical approaches to the already popular New Orleans jazz. Aspiring to capture the entrancing nuances of New Orleans jazz, composers, arrangers, and performers in New York jazz approached instrumentation by utilizing the different instrument sections: brass, woodwind and rhythm (or percussion). The goal was to emulate the excitement of the polyphonic texture of New Orleans/Chicago jazz by orchestrating and arranging these instruments in particular ways. Given that the polyphonic texture produces a musical conversation or call and response between instruments, call and response became the underlying practice for performances of New York jazz. The call and response was performed by either a solo instrument against a group of instruments, or between sections (i.e., brass against woodwind). As the first is a common practice and is therefore more easily recognized, the latter will be the focus. Known as sectional alternation, New York jazz pieces were regularly arranged so that the brass and woodwind sections played melodic phrases in a call and response manner, thus in two parts. Moreover, the alternate section/phrase would begin before the first ended, thus producing a seemingly polyphonic texture. Played against the rhythm section, a three-part, front-line-type texture could be produced. Fletcher Henderson's[3] piece titled "The Stampede" (1926), arranged by Don Redman, illustrates this performance practice. During the introduction, the piano plays a phrase, followed by the woodwind, and then brass section. The call and response is then continued by the brass against the woodwind section after the introduction and before the first solo instrument (saxophone).

Also known as sectional music, these bands consisted of nine–twelve members. In fact, Fletcher Henderson–the most influential composer/arranger of early New York jazz–opened in 1922 at Club Alabam with a nine-piece group: piano (Henderson), tuba, drums, two trumpets, banjo, trombone, and two woodwinds.[4] In the "The Stampede," Fletcher Henderson and His Orchestra included piano, trumpet, two cornets, trombone, clarinet, alto saxophone, tenor saxophone, banjo, tuba, and drums. There are also eleven instruments in the piece titled "Dinah" (1929) by Red Nichols and His Five Pennies. Consisting of three trumpets (Red Nichols), two trombones, clarinet (Benny Goodman), tenor saxophone, piano, guitar, bass, and drums (Gene Krupa), sectional alternation also occurs; however, there is more emphasis on the call and response that exists between the solo instruments and the band. As mentioned above, call and response in New York jazz also occurs between a solo instrument and a group of instruments. What is interesting in this piece is that both of these exist in tandem. For instance, in the beginning of the piece, the "call" is played by a trombone solo and the lower brass and woodwind instruments while the upper brass and woodwind instruments perform the response to both the soloist and the lower instruments. With the overlapping of melodic phrases performed by each part against the rhythm section, one can hear vestiges of the New Orleans jazz sound. Moreover, as in Chicago jazz, the polyphonic texture, performed by the typical front line instruments, occurs at the end of the piece. Clearly, this piece shows the relationship and connections between New Orleans jazz, Chicago jazz, and New York jazz.

BIG BAND JAZZ [A.K.A. SWING]

The big band jazz era began at the close of WWI. The term *New York jazz,* whose instrumentation was "big band," was short-lived. By the 1920s, the term *big band jazz* became the most marketable consumer-favored term for jazz. Notable band leaders (listed alphabetically) include Count Basie, Less Brown, Cab Calloway, Tommy Dorsey, Duke Ellington, Benny Goodman, Lionel Hampton, Woody Herman, Fletcher Henderson, Harry James, Stan Kenton, Andy Kirk, Glen Miller, Buddy Rich, and Artie Shaw. A nine- to eleven-piece band was indeed "big," as six members was the common band size prior to this time. The following information, listed chronologically, provides the line-up for a few of the major big bands as well as one recording made by each band during the 1920s.

"The Stampede" (1926) Fletcher Henderson and His Orchestra (11 members)
Russell Smith (trumpet)
Joe Smith (cornet)

---

[3] Fletcher Henderson and Don Redman are given credit for notating the excitement of New Orleans/Chicago jazz for a larger band–hence "big band." Also, the first big band was organized by Fletcher Henderson in 1923.

[4] The term *woodwind* is appropriate here, as it was common for woodwind players to double (play more than one woodwind). In fact, flute, clarinet, and two or more saxophones were frequently played by an individual woodwind player.

Edward "Duke" Ellington. © Photofest

Rex Stewart (cornet)
Benny Morton (trombone)
Buster Bailey (clarinet, alto saxophone)
Don Redman (clarinet, alto saxophone)
Coleman Hawkins (clarinet, tenor saxophone)
Ralph Escudero (tuba)
Fletcher Henderson (piano)
Charlie Dixon (banjo)
Kaiser Marshall (drums)

"East St. Louis Toodle-Oo" (1927) Duke Ellington and His Orchestra (10 members)
Bubber Miley (trumpet)
Louis Metcalf (trumpet)
Joe Nanton (trombone)
Otto Hardwicke (soprano, alto and baritone saxophone)

Harry Carney (clarinet, alto and baritone saxophone)
Rudy Jackson (clarinet, tenor saxophone)
Duke Ellington (piano)
Fred Guy (banjo)
Wellman Braud (bass)
Sonny Greer (drums)

"Dinah" (1929) Red Nichols and His Five Pennies (11 members)
Red Nichols (trumpet)
Manny Klein (trumpet)
Leo McConville (trumpet)
Jack Teagarden (trombone)
Bill Trone/Herb Taylor (tombone)
Benny Goodman (clarinet)
Babe Russin (tenor saxophone)
Arthur Schutt (piano)
Carl Kress (guitar)
Art Miller (bass)
Gene Kruppa (drums)

The popularity of big band jazz (as well as their size) increased during the ensuing decades. Here are some examples of famous big bands along with a recording of each.

1930s

"Moten Swing" (1932) Bennie Moten's
Kansas City Orchestra (12 members)
Joe Keyes (trumpet)
Oran Page (trumpet)
Dee Stewart (trumpet)
Dan Minor (trombone)
Eddie Durham (trombone and guitar)
Eddie Barefield (clarinet, alto saxophone)
Jack Washington (alto and baritone saxophone)
Ben Webster (tenor saxophone)
Count Basie (piano)
Leroy Berry (guitar)
Walter Page (bass)
Willie McWashington (drums)

"Wrappin' It Up" (1934) Fletcher Henderson and His Orchestra (13 members)
Henry Allen (trumpet)
Irving Randolph (trumpet)
Russell Smith (trumpet)
Keg Johnson (trombone)
Claude Jones (trombone)
Buster Bailey (clarinet, alto saxophone)
Hilton Jefferson (clarinet, alto saxophone)
Russell Procope (clarinet, alto saxophone)

Ben Webster (tenor saxophone)
Horace Henderson (piano)
Lawrence Lucie (guitar)
Elmer James (bass)
Walter Johnson (drums)

"Organ Grinder's Swing" (1936) Jimmie Lunceford and His Orchestra (15 members)
Sy Oliver (trumpet)
Eddie Tompkins (trumpet)
Paul Webster (trumpet)
Russell Bowles (trombone)
Elmer Crumbley (trombone)
Eddie Durham (trombone)
Willie Smith (clarinet, alto and baritone saxophone)
Earl Carruthers (clarinet, alto and baritone saxophone)
Dan Grissom (clarinet, alto saxophone)
Joe Thomas (clarinet, tenor saxophone)
Laforet Dent (alto saxophone)
Edwin Wilcox (piano and celeste)
Al Norris (guitar)
Moses Allen (bass)
Jimmy Crawford (drums)

"The New East St. Louis Toodle-O" (1937) Duke Ellington and His Famous Orchestra (16 members)
Wallace Jones (trumpet)
Cootie Williams (trumpet)
Rex Stewart (cornet)
Joe Nanton (trombone)
Lawrence Brown (trombone)
Juan Tizol (trombone)
Barney Bigard (clarinet, tenor saxophone)
Johnny Hidges (clarinet, alto and tenor saxophone)
Harry Carney (clarinet, baritone saxophone)
Otto Hardwicke (alto saxophone)
Duke Ellington (piano)
Fred Guy (guitar)
Hayes Alvis (bass)
Billy Taylor (bass)
Sonny Greer (drums)
Freddie Jenkins (chimes)

"Doggin' Around" (1938) Count Basie and His Orchestra (14 members)
Buck Clayton (trumpet)
Harry Edison (trumpet)
Ed Lewis (trumpet)
Eddie Durham (trombone)

Dan Minor (trombone)
Benny Morton (trombone)
Earle Warren (alto saxophone)
Jack Washington (alto and baritone saxophone)
Herschel Evans (tenor saxophone)
Lester Young (tenor saxophone)
Count Basie (piano)
Freddie Green (guitar)
Walter Page (bass)
Jo Jones (drums)

1940s

"Ko-Ko" (1940) Duke Ellington and His Famous Orchestra (15 members)
Wallace Jones (trumpet)
Cootie Williams (trumpet)
Rex Stewart (cornet)
Joe Nanton (trombone)
Lawrence Brown (trombone)
Juan Tizol (bass trombone)
Barney Bigard (clarinet, tenor saxophone)
Otto Hardwicke (alto saxophone)
Johnny Hodges (alto saxophone)
Ben Webster (tenor saxophone)
Harry Carney (baritone saxophone)
Duke Ellington (piano)
Fred Guy (guitar)
Jimmy Blanton (bass)
Sonny Greer (drums)

"Rockin' Chair" (1941) Gene Krupa and His Orchestra (15 members)
Roy Eldridge (trumpet)
Graham Young (trumpet)
Torg Halten (trumpet)
Norman Murphy (trumpet)
Babe Wagner (trombone)
Jay Kelliher (trombone)
John Grassi (trombone)
Mascagni Ruffo (alto saxophone)
Sam Listengart (alto saxophone)
Sam Musiker (clarinet, tenor saxophone)
Walter Bates (tenor saxophone)
Milton Raskin (piano)
Ray Biondi (guitar)
Ed Mihelich (bass)
Gene Krupa (drums)

Benny Goodman. © Photofest

While it is true that a number of composers, conductors, and directors of big band jazz incorporated even more instruments in their works as time progressed, some bands continued playing with (relatively) smaller line-ups. For example, Coleman Hawkins and His Orchestra's 1939 recording of "Body and Soul" was performed by a nine-member group. That same year, Lionel Hampton and His Orchestra's recording of "When Lights Are Low" utilized ten members. It was also a common practice to perform and/or record as a smaller unit, and feature one or two virtuoso musicians from other bands. For instance, the song titled "I Can't Believe That You're in Love with Me" was recorded in 1940 by The Chocolate Dandies, which featured Roy Eldridge (trumpet)—a regular member of the Gene Krupa orchestra—and Benny Carter (alto saxophone), who was directing his own big band at the time. Other musicians on this recording included Coleman Hawkins (tenor saxophone), Bernard Addison (guitar), John Kirby (bass), and Sidney Catlett (drums). Another example is the 1941 recording of "I Found a New Baby" by the Benny Goodman Sextet, which features Charlie Christian on electric guitar[5] and Count Basie on piano. Other musicians on this recording include Goodman (clarinet), Cootie Williams (trumpet), George Auld (tenor saxophone), Artie Bernstein (bass), and Jo Jones (drums). What is interesting about all of this is that it illustrates musicians' continued desire to perform/record as a small unit (in comparison to big

---

[5] The electric guitar began to emerge selected jazz, blues, country, and rhythm & blues bands at this time.

bands), while continuing their involvement in the more popular larger bands.[6] For instance, even though both Goodman and Basie were each directing a successful big band at the time, they quite frequently made time for performances and recordings as smaller units. Also, Cootie Williams regularly played with Duke Ellington and His Famous Orchestra, and Jo Jones (a regular member of Count Basie's orchestra) also appeared within this smaller unit. These smaller bands allowed musicians more creativity-a departure from the more regimented orchestrations that are inherent with larger bands.

Although the band's size was the most obvious identifier of big band jazz, its musical production was also quite distinctive from previous jazz styles. Rather than performing in the fashion of New Orleans and Chicago jazz where the front line (trumpet, clarinet, and trombone) performed the principal themes, big band orchestrations entailed the performance of themes either by a specific solo instrument and/or by a specific instrument section (i.e., brass or woodwind). With regard to solo instruments, the saxophone, piano, and trumpet most frequently play the main theme and/or an interpretational/improvisational solo. As is the case in most big band jazz pieces, the solo instrument is accompanied by the rhythm section as well as the brass and woodwind sections. In this case, the instruments within the rhythm section (piano, guitar, bass, and drums) maintain the rhythmic and harmonic underpinning of the song's character while the brass and woodwind sections perform periodic or sustaining rhythmic and harmonic phrases. With regard to instrument sections, the melody is played by the brass (cornets/trumpets and trombones) and/or woodwind section (flutes, clarinets, saxophones), and also alternates between them. Known as "sectional alternation" (a.k.a. "melodic sharing"), brass and woodwind instruments share in playing the main theme. As shown by the following Song navigators, melodic sharing also occurs between the brass or woodwind section and a solo instrument. In this instance, the two parts play their respective themes simultaneously. The following Song navigators provide examples of songs where all of the aforementioned performance practices are heard.

TIME	SOLO INSTRUMENT/COMMENTS
	Focus: Solos (cornet, and tenor saxophone); <u>Sectional playing</u>
00:00	Introduction
00:04	Cornet solo
00:12	Cornet solo
00:16	Melody played by sectional alternation between the brass and woodwinds, as well as played by both simultaneously
00:33	Melody played by sectional alternation between the brass and woodwinds, as well as played by both simultaneously
00:50	Tenor saxophone solo
01:28	Cornet solo
02:05	Woodwinds play the melody
02:38	Cornet solo
02:51	Melody played by sectional alternation between the brass and woodwinds, as well as played by both simultaneously

Song Navigator 11.3: "The Stampede" (1926) by Fletcher Henderson and His Orchestra

---

[6] By the end of WWII, the smaller line-up became the typical band that played jazz, namely bebop.

TIME	SOLO INSTRUMENT/COMMENTS
	Focus: Solos (piano, guitar, alto and tenor saxophone, trumpet); Sectional playing
00:00	Piano solo
00:18	Melody played by sectional alternation between the brass and woodwinds
00:27	Piano solo
00:37	Melody played by woodwind section with piano countermelody
00:57	Guitar solo
01:06	Melody played by woodwind section with piano countermelody
01:16	Melody played by brass section with alto saxophone countermelody
01:35	Alto saxophone solo
01:56	Trumpet solo with some piano countermelody
02:15	Tenor saxophone solo
02:24	Trumpet solo

Song Navigator 11.4: "Moten Swing" (1926) by Bennie Moten's Kansas City Orchestra

The piano, saxophone, and trumpet were not the only solo instruments. As heard in "Moten Swing," the guitar (acoustic) was also used. Beginning in the 1940s, the electric guitar became a regular instrument among many big band jazz groups. Although they "only" had six instruments, the Benny Goodman Sextet Featuring Charlie Christian and Count Basie (as well as the same group without Count Basie) successfully played in the big band jazz style. The 1941 recordings by this group titled "I Found a New Baby" and "Breakfast Feud" feature Charlie Christian on electric guitar. Although not as popular as saxophone, trumpet, and piano, the clarinet as heard in "Woodchoppers Ball" by Woody Herman was used particularly when it was the band leader's main instrument. Artie Shaw's phrasing on the melody to "Moonglow" illustrates how the clarinet is still a viable instrument in jazz.

Another instrument that began to emerge in big bands was the vibraphone.[7] Although the spread of its use is attributed to several artists and composers/arrangers, Lionel Hampton is given credit for its popularity as a solo instrument. The recording titled "When Lights Are Low" (1939) by Lionel Hampton and His Orchestra features Mr. Hampton on vibraphone. Hampton's (a.k.a. Hamp) distinctiveness in the big band sound is not only attributed to his incorporation of the vibraphone, but also to the band's youthful and fresh attitude. This is, in part, due to Hamp's obliging and unselfish nature toward young players. Realizing the energetic quality of musicians even before they knew it themselves, Hampton seized the opportunity to have a band member with a unique sound. One particular performer is the saxophonist Illinois Jacket and his "honking" saxophone sound in Hampton's most popular piece titled "Flying Home" (1939).

---

[7] The vibraphone is an instrument very similar in appearance to the xylophone.

Other featured instrumentalists and their respective instruments include Benny Carter (alto saxophone), Coleman Hawkins (tenor saxophone), and Clyde Hart (piano). Lionel Hampton's vibraphone performance, including Illinois Jacket on tenor saxophone, is perhaps most memorable in his band's recording titled "Flying Home" (1940).[8] Even though the alto and tenor saxophone were favored woodwind instruments for solo performances, the clarinet-a favorite in the New Orleans and Chicago jazz styles-also appeared as a solo instrument. The recording titled "Rocking Chair" (1941) by Gene Krupa and His Orchestra features Sam Musiker on clarinet in addition to Roy Eldridge on trumpet. A clarinet solo featuring Benny Goodman, who also conducted his own big band orchestra, also appears in the song titled "Dinah" (1929) by Red Nichols and His Five Pennies.

The use of the boogie-woogie pattern, melodically based on the 12-bar blues progression, was another feature that was used by big band orchestras throughout their productive years. After the decline of the ragtime craze (post-WWI), boogie-woogie became one of the favored piano styles among innovative jazz composers, performers, directors, and conductors. (Stride became the other popular style.) For many vaudeville and musical theatre performers and admirers of notated piano music, ragtime continued as a viable style for public and private entertainment. Where publications of ragtime focused their attention on marketing scores that neatly organized the syncopated right hand part juxtaposed to the strict left hand bass-a chord technique underscoring its readability and ease of playing that was utilized as a marketing strategy-the boogie-woogie piano style, like New Orleans jazz, demanded improvisational skills for a more successful performance. Based on a common blues bass pattern, the boogie-woogie piano style is characterized by a certain melodic or harmonic rhythmic pattern, played by the left hand, juxtaposed with a syncopated theme that is played by the right hand. Played by the left hand, the triplet is the most salient rhythmic pattern. The illustration below provides an example of both the melodic and harmonic boogie-woogie patterns. The first measure of the bass line within a 12-bar "blues" progression is shown, followed by the boogie-woogie pattern that uses the same pitches.

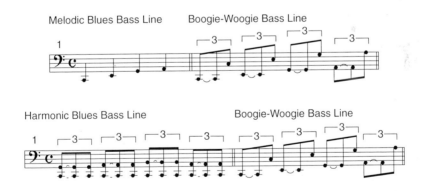

Since the late 19th century, solo pianists had been a fixture on the jazz scene, playing at the multitude of venues in Storyville, rent parties[9], and publishing houses. Employing solo piano players continued through the big band jazz era. Some notable players included Lucky Roberts, James P. Johnson, Fats Waller, Willie "The Lion" Smith, Perry Bradford, Tiny Parham, Jelly Roll Morton, and

---

[8] That same year, the famous vibraphonist Milt Jackson, inspired by hearing Lionel Hampton perform live, played his first professional gig.

[9] A rent party was an evening social gathering of music, dance, and food at an apartment of a person in need of rent money. To enter, everyone paid a small fee in an effort to help pay the person's rent.

Jimmy Johnson. Duke Ellington even played as a pianist upon his arrival in New York from Washington, DC, in 1923. Many of these pianists played in what became known as the Harlem style–ragtime, boogie-woogie, blues, and stride. Fats Waller's 1937 recording of "I Ain't Got Nobody" is performed in a ballad style (i.e., singing-like) that features characteristics of the Harlem style. The following Song Navigator illustrates elements of this style.

TIME	SPECIFIC FEATURE/COMMENTS
	Focus: Harlem Style–piano (ragtime, blues, stride, and boogie-woogie elements)
00:43	**Ragtime-like**: l. h. bass and chord against r. h. syncopated melody
01:37	**Blues-like**: l. h. melodic walking bass line
01:40	**Stride-like**: more fluid r. h.; more melodic l. h. not just tonic (I) and dominant (V) chords like ragtime; chromatic 10th chords played by l. h.
02:20	**Boogie-Woogie**: l. h. plays the harmonic triplet pattern

Song Navigator 11.5: "I Ain't Got Nobody" (1937) Fats Waller

Returning to the discussion of size among big bands, as previously mentioned, white bands were generally larger because they were playing for the larger ballrooms and theatres. To create even more contrasting and innovative ideas to the sound of jazz, bands such as those established by Paul White-man, Jean Goldkette, and Ted Lewis began to incorporate additional instru-

Joe and Venuti and Stephaine Grappelli are noted as the first virtuoso violinists of jazz.

ments such as violins and singers. For example, Paul Whiteman's band had well over 30 members by the 1930s; notable members included singer Mildred Bailey[10], violinist Joe Venuti, and guitarist/banjoist Eddie Lang.[11] The most memorable song of Ms. Bailey's career was the 1932 recording of "Rockin' Chair" with the Paul Whiteman band. Joe Venuti played with the Whiteman band for a year and appeared with the band in the film titled *King of Jazz* (1930). In addition to the aforementioned women singers, some male singers included Bob Eberle (Tommy Dorsey's band, late 1930s/40s) and Frank Sinatra, who sang for the Harry James band in the late 1930s and Tommy Dorsey's band in the early 1940s. For many musicians and consumers, these superfluous additives and approaches to jazz were either not appealing or didn't represent the true spirit of jazz. To suit the purist or at least the more critical jazz listener, smaller bands and solo piano music came to be favored over the sounds of big bands. To suit the public's taste, it became a common practice for conductors/directors to have a small unit (trio to sextet) or solo pianist within the big band. This allowed big bands to perform in a number of acoustically appropriate venues, and thus aided in their popularity, affording a greater opportunity for economic stability.

Whether as small units within a big band or regular small bands, in New York they often played in either the jam session or New York Dixieland jazz style. Although similar in presentation with respect to an emphasis on soloists, they did differ. In the Dixieland style, the omnipresent polyphonic

---

[10] Mildred Bailey was one of the first women singers to regularly sing with a big band, Paul Whiteman's Orchestra (1930s).
[11] Eddie Lang was influential in the change from banjo to guitar for bands during the early 1930s.

Frank Sinatra and Ella Fitzgerald. © NBC/Photofest

texture is the defining feature, while the jam session style represented a more impromptu way of play-ing, similar to performances where musicians would "sit in" during a given song or set.[12] (Of course, musicians would "sit-in" on New York Dixieland jazz songs, but that was not necessarily the norm, as opposed to jam session bands.) Jimmy Ryan's on 52nd Street was one of the most frequently attended and thus celebrated "organized" jam sessions in New York. Venues that featured jam sessions also pro-vided other types of entertainment. For instance, the decorated Stuyvesant Casino on Lower Second Avenue, NY during the 1940s advertised jam session concerts as well as music for dancing.[13] (Jam session bands were also present in other areas such as Washington DC, where Duke Ellington and his Washingtonians were frequently seen.) Whether it was an impromptu jam session or a planned perfor-mance by scheduled musicians, the goal among small groups was to offer a performance that was char-acterized by seemingly improvised individual creativity rather than by restrictions governed by written

---

[12] A "set" was often regarded as 45:15, (i.e., 45 minutes of playing time followed by a 15-minute break).
[13] In 1945, the Stuyvesant was the venue that featured the rediscovery of Bunk Johnson (trumpet), a contemporary of Joseph "King" Oliver.

scores. The recording of "Body and Soul" (1935) by the Benny Goodman Trio illustrates this point. As shown below, the occurrence (i.e., specific section–"A" or "B") of the clarinet and piano solos within the performance illustrates a somewhat spontaneous performance, particularly considering the rigid standard performance practices at that time. For instance, usually the first solo instrument (or singer) performed the entire AABA form without any other solos. In this recording, however, this did not occur. Lastly, the band normally returned to the "A" section after the completion of the second 32 bars. Here, on the other hand, the "B" followed by the "A" section were the final two sections of the piece.

TIME	SOLO INSTRUMENT	SECTION
	Focus: Solos (clarinet and piano)	
00:00	Clarinet	A
00:20	Clarinet	A
00:40	Piano	B
01:00	Clarinet	A
01:20	Piano	A
01:40	Piano	A
02:00	Clarinet	B
02:21	Piano	A
02:41	Clarinet	B
03:02	Clarinet	A

Song Navigator 11.6: "Body and Soul" (1935) Benny Goodman Trio (clarinet, piano, drums)

With regard to the New York Dixieland jazz style, performances were partly due to the innovations of the Original Dixieland Jazz Band. Combining elements of the New Orleans jazz sound such as the occurrence of the front line playing style with the innovative approaches of instrumentation in big band music, they developed a performance tradition that became known as New York dixieland. Fletcher Henderson and Don Redman became the first musicians to capture this sound and notate it for large bands. In 1923, Fletcher Henderson and His Orchestra became the first organized big band in New York. The New York dixieland jazz sound is heard during the final few seconds of the band's 1926 recording titled "The Stampede." Here, trumpets, trombones, and saxophones perform as separate sections. They, in effect, are playing in the manner of solo instruments such as the front line tradition of New Orleans jazz. The rhythm section (piano, guitar, bass, and drums) performs in the same "strict time"[14] manner as does the New Orleans jazz rhythm section (banjo, tuba, snare/bass drum).

New York, Chicago, and New Orleans were certainly "happening" places and environments that functioned as nurturing grounds for many aspiring young musicians. But there is another place worthy

---

[14] *Strict time* refers to maintaining a steady beat with minimal syncopation.

of note in any chronicle of jazz history, namely Kansas City, Kansas. With a very large African American population, all types of jazz–beginning with New Orleans jazz–were being performed throughout the city. Certainly other areas such as Los Angeles, San Francisco, and Houston had significant African American communities, but Kansas City's geographical location provided a convenient route for bands traveling between jazz hubs like Chicago, New Orleans, and St. Louis. With the many musical influences–ragtime, blues, New Orleans jazz, Chicago jazz, boogie-woogie and stride piano styles, and big band jazz–a distinct style arose, namely Kansas City swing.

Although Count Basie was born in New Jersey, he and his orchestra are renowned as having the best representation of the Kansas City swing style. Due to Basie's proficiency in stride and boogie-woogie-style piano playing, he was able to infuse elements of these styles into the omnipresent swing rhythm of the 1930s-40s. The Count Basie Orchestra was just as popular among dancers as well as listeners for Basie's approach to performing ballads. The song titled "Lil' Darlin'" was a favorite among many. Beginning with a brief introduction by Basie on piano, the woodwind and brass instruments perform the melody with lush harmonies that entice the most novice critique of jazz.

While performing in the big band context, Basie was restricted to playing a prescribed arrangement of notes, but in his earlier days and in smaller band settings, he was quite able to demonstrate his proficiency in the extremely intricate, improv-isational stride and boogie-woogie piano styles. Like most pianists of that time interested in these styles, Basie was influenced by the performances of artists such as James P. Johnson, William "The Lion" Smith, and, most significantly, Fats Waller. In fact, while in New York, Basie received instruction from Waller that highly influenced him as a solo pianist. Basie was also known for being a bandman's leader. In other words, musicians saw Basie as "one of the guys"–a person who did not lord his directorship over others.

Beginning with Bennie Moten during the 1920s, and continuing through the William "Count" Basie Band which began in the mid-1930s, the swing style swept the entire country. Even though a number of bands were "swinging" their songs before the 1930s, it was Benny Goodman who was responsible for the nationwide dissemination of swing music during the 1930s. At the same time, Duke Ellington's recording of "It Don't Mean a Thing If It Ain't Got That Swing" in 1932 incontrovertibly established the swing sound, which lasted until the end of WWII. Newcomers such as trombonist Glenn Miller (first band in 1937) and his 17-piece band's 1940 recording titled "Everybody Loves My Baby" continued the exposure of the swing rhythm through WWII. Woody Herman and his band, among others, continued performing big band music for audiences even through the rock & roll craze. His band's 1958 recording titled "Blowin' Up a Storm" begins with a typical Count Basie introduction of a piano solo accompanied by the rhythm section maintaining the swing rhythm. The song gradually builds in texture and volume. During the heyday of swing, some of the more notable jazz band leaders (listed alphabetically) included Count Basie, Cab Calloway, Tommy and Jimmy Dorsey, Benny Goodman, Erskine Hawkins, Woody Herman, Earl Hines, Jimmie Lunceford, Glenn Miller, Lucky Millinder, Artie Shaw, and Chick Webb. Despite the fact that areas such as New York, Chicago, and Kansas City were seen as the popular environments for jazz styles, due to the growing interests in radio broadcasting, the dance craze of the 1920s/30s, and a number of big band jazz circuits, all types of jazz were being heard all over the country as well as in Europe. Thus swing music in particular was not seen as a style with specific geographical origins, but rather as a type of music that was performed by competent musicians throughout the country.

It is important to note that the big band jazz craze spurred the opening or refurbishing of numerous ballrooms, nightclubs, supper clubs, and dance halls. Fortunately, this provided big bands with employment at various venues throughout the country. Cities such as New York, Chicago, and Kansas City were urban havens for the many types of bands. In New York, popular venues included the Cotton Club[15], the Savoy Ballroom, Small's Paradise, the Paramount, Glen Island Casino, the Apollo Theatre, the Strand,

and numerous venues on 52nd Street (a.k.a. "swing street") such as the well-regarded Hickory House and Jimmy Ryan's. In Chicago, some favored venues included the Congress Hotel, the Panther Room, the Royal Gardens, Dreamland, Pekin, Moulin Rouge, the Club Metropole, the Sunset Café, and the Grand Terrace Ballroom. In Kansas City, popular venues included the Reno Club and Kansas City's Fairyland Park. It should be noted that other areas in America also catered to big band jazz. For example, Santa Catalina Island, the Embassy Hotel, and the Palomar Ballroom were popular venues in California; and the Kentucky Club in Washington, DC was a favorite performance venue for many big bands. With these and other entertainment venues, bands were able to sustain a touring circuit throughout the year by spending from a few weeks to several months playing at a number of venues in a given area. Such a performance schedule was beneficial for both the band as well as the audience. For bands, it provided an opportunity to introduce new material or try out different arrangements that could perhaps lead to a recording. For audiences, it provided musical variety as well as new material to evaluate, a chance to hear their favorite singer and/or instrumentalist, and an opportunity to try out new dances with their favorite bands.

As the result of the domestic war effort and so many young men being sent to fight overseas during World War II, there was a significant decrease in the number of available venues. On top of this, with the growing interest in other music styles, the popularity of big band jazz declined sharply after 1946. Groups such as the Count Basie, Duke Ellington, and Woody Herman bands still performed at colleges and theme parks such as Disneyland and Knotts Berry Farm. The emerging youth culture had a tremendous impact on the music industry, precipitating the emergence of a whole new market geared toward them, namely rhythm & blues and rock & roll.

---

[15] Cab Calloway and his band were invited to be the opening band, but declined due to a prior commitment. Instead, Duke Ellington and His Orchestra were hired as the opening band.

PART THREE

A NEW CENTURY AND TWO WORLD WARS: SUMMARY

Key Terms

- Cutting contest
- Ragging
- Syncopation
- Ragtime form: AABBACCDD
- Commercial music
- Tin Pan Alley
- The Great White Way
- Ziegfeld Follies
- Dixieland
- Storyville
- Mardi Gras
- Creole
- Front line performance

- Emancipation Proclamation
- AAB song form
- I–IV–V chords
- 12-bar progression
- Blues song vs. blues style
- Hillbilly
- Blue yodel
- Grand Ole Opry
- Three-finger picking style
- Call and response
- Sectional alternation
- Boogie-woogie

Featured Genres/Styles

- Ragtime
- Marching Band Music
- Musical Theater
- New Orleans Jazz
- Folk and Classic Blues

- Hillbilly
- Bluegrass
- Chicago jazz
- New York jazz
- Big band jazz (a.k.a. Swing)

Featured Songs/Works

- "The Entertainer"
- "Maple Leaf Rag"
- *Treemonisha*
- "Stars and Stripes Forever"
- "After the Ball"
- "God Bless America"
- "White Christmas"
- "Give My Regards to Broadway"
- *Shuffle Along*
- "Lift Every Voice and Sing"
- "Potato Head Blues"
- "Dippermouth Blues"
- "Hotter Than Hot"
- "Franklin Street Blues"
- "Copenhagen"
- "Royal Garden Blues"
- "Memphis Blues"
- "St. Louis Blues"
- "Black Snake Moan"

- "Pick a Bale of Cotton"
- "Crazy Blues"
- "Fine and Mellow"
- "Empty Bed Blues"
- "Cross Road Blues"
- "Go Down, Old Hannah"
- "Faded Flowers"
- "When the Roses Come Again"
- "This is Like Heaven To Me"
- "T. for Texas (Blue Yodel No. 1)"
- "I'm On My Way to the Old Home"
- "Blue Grass Ramble"
- "Black Bottom Stomp"
- "Riverboat Shuffle"
- "The Stampede"
- "Moten Swing"
- "I Ain't Got Nobody"
- "Body and Soul"

Featured Artists

- Thomas "Daddy" Rice
- Scott Joplin
- James Scott
- John Philip Sousa
- Charles Harris
- Irving Berlin
- Victor Herbert
- Florenz Ziegfeld
- George M. Cohan
- Sam, J.J. and Lee Schubert
- Al Jolson
- Sam Lucas
- Bert Williams
- James Weldon Johnson
- James Reese Europe
- Louis Armstrong
- Joseph King Oliver
- Bunk Johnson
- Bix Biederbecke
- Original Dixieland Jazz Band
- Sidney Bechet
- W.C. Handy
- Blind Lemon Jefferson
- Leadbelly
- Son House
- Robert Johnson
- Mamie Smith
- Gertrude "Ma" Rainey
- Bessie Smith
- Alberta Hunter
- Billie Holiday
- The Carter Family
- Jimmie Rodgers
- Uncle Dave Macon
- Bill Monroe
- Earl Scruggs
- Lester Flatt
- Jelly Roll Morton
- Frankie Trumbauer
- Fletcher Henderson
- Bennie Moten
- Fats Waller
- Benny Goodman

Music and Society

- With an emerging middle class who had more time for leisure activities there was a great demand for entertainment: music, dance, and musical theater.
- New Orleans was a cultural metropolis during the late 19th century through WWI. Although people (Blacks, Whites, and Creoles to name some), by and large, segregated themselves the sounds of ragtime, blues, and New Orleans jazz brought them together in districts such as Storyville.
- Southern blacks and whites migrated to cities like Chicago and St. Louis to fill needed labor in the growing factory industry. They brought their music tastes as well that fueled the desire for entertainment.

Discussion Questions

- How did Tin Pan Alley facilitate the sales of sheet music from Musical Theater productions?
- How did American Musical Theater differ from European Musical Theater?
- Why did numerous New Orleans pieces incorporate the word "blues" in their titles?

Learning Beyond the Classroom

- Colleges and universities usually offer musical theater productions every semester. You may have a colleague that is connected to the production in some way or another. Ask if you can attend a rehearsal, but if not go to the production and enjoy yourself. Write about the theme, time period of the story, instrumentation, gender involvement, your opinion as to whether the musical accompaniment supported the story, quality of singing, and character of the songs using terms such as melody, harmony, rhythm, tempo, and form.

- Colleges and universities, as well as professional venues offer performances of big band jazz. Attend a concert to learn how to better identify the interplay of the three main sections (and their specific instruments): woodwind, brass, and rhythm section. Make an effort to identify the following: sectional alternation, accompanimental instruments against the instrument playing solo, accents, tempo changes, and types of dynamics.
- On a large poster board draw a comparison chart of music characteristics and performers between New Orleans jazz, Chicago jazz, New York jazz, and big band jazz.

PART FOUR

Electric Guitar. © Image Source/Corbis

MUSIC AND AMERICAN SOCIETY PRIOR TO AND SLIGHTLY AFTER WORLD WAR II

- CHAPTER TWELVE: Electrified Country and Blues Music (Western Swing, Honky-Tonk, and Electric Blues)
- CHAPTER THIRTEEN: Jazz: Bebop and Cool styles

OVERVIEW

As a result of the war effort, record manufacturing had diminished, but the end of WWII in 1945 gave hope to American capitalism, and the record business again became a viable industry. At the same time, musical tastes were changing. The big band era ended the following year. The production of live barn dance shows sharply diminished. In addition, the use of drums and amplification (electric guitar and bass) was challenging the traditional instrumentation of hillbilly music. The new music on the rise—rock & roll—and its "king", Elvis Presley (a former singer in the hillbilly tradition), incorporated amplification and drums as well as dancing on stage in an effort to appeal to young girls. By the 1950s, with television as the main vehicle for advertising goods and services, America evolved into a visually-based society. The demand for seeing performers such as Elvis Presley, Little Richard, Bill Haley & The Comets, and Chuck Berry grew into a big business for the music industry. Superfluous practices (by country musics standards) such as dancing and theatrical antics like playing on the stage floor were where country musicians drew the line. Despite the fact that country artists such as Bob Wills and His Texas Playboys incorporated amplified instruments into some of their recordings, they could not compete with rock & roll—the new, popular, and first youth culture music. Indeed, the disengaged youth of the Great Depression years had also experienced a "world war." They were consciously or unconsciously aspiring to a sociocultural ideology where their voices could resound as a force toward the revivification of the American spirit and the diminishing of the stain of economic and human disaster. For those in their teens during the late 1940s, their sociocultural and musical desires exploded into America's changing musical tastes, as initiated by the migration of black and white southerners to urban areas, the application of amplification in music, and the revival of the record industry. In addition, these teens were caught up in a sociocultural conundrum. But this time it dealt with race.

Country music is a very broad genre, and continues to influence and be influenced by other styles. Many artists prior to and slightly after WWII made an enormous impact on not only country music, but American music as well. Some of these include The Carter Family, Jimmie Rodgers, Ken Maynard,

Bob Wills, Bill Monroe, Merle Travis, Lefty Frizzell, Kitty Wells, Ernest Tubb, Merle Haggard, Webb Price, Ray Price, Spade Cooley, Hank Williams, Sr., and Johnny Cash. If there were a style that consistently contributed to the forging of the American spirit, country music would certainly stand near the front. Three particular artists who share the honor as inductees to three of American music's most notable organizations–Rock and Roll Hall of Fame, Song Writers Hall of Fame, and Country Music Hall of Fame–are Jimmie Rodgers, Hank Williams Sr., and Johnny Cash. Jimmie Rodgers as well as others will be presented in the discussion of hillbilly music, Hank Williams Sr., and his contemporaries, will be discussed with regard to honky-tonk music, and finally Johnny Cash, who does not fit neatly into either of these categories, will be presented separately.

Often, Nashville, Tennessee comes to mind when considering a place where country music flourished. While this is true today, performances, recordings, and well-known venues of country music flourished as far west as California from the early 1940s to the early 1960s.

Born in Kingsland, Arkansas, Johnny Cash (1932–2003) became a legend in his own time. His first recordings were in 1955 with Sun Records, owned and operated by Sam Phillips.[1] In 1957, Cash recorded two of his most recognized songs: "Folsom Prison Blues" and "I Walk the Line." Cash would go on to experience a healthy, five-decade career.

Lyrics about peoples' social, cultural, and political circumstances; singing with dramatic conviction; and interjections of personal experiences are the tenets of folk music. Seen as a cultural hero to many, the folk musician interprets everyday situations of the common folk.

We will examine popular and not-so-popular approaches to jazz music beginning in the 1940s and ending sometime in the 1970s. These include bebop, cool, free form, jazz rock, fusion, and free. It is essential that we avoid the tendency to categorize performers into the aforementioned styles. While the names Miles Davis and Bill Evans may surface as common names associated with cool jazz, we must never lose sight of the fact that these artists were also active in other styles, such as bebop and even big band (consider the piece titled "Venus di Milo" from Davis's album titled *The Birth of Cool* in 1949). Although the following information provides names of artists commonly linked to a specific style, it should be noted that their performances are not exclusively that particular style.

Prior to rhythm & blues and rock & roll music during the 1950s, popular non-jazz and non-country styles of music included is currently regarded as mainstream or adult contemporary categories. This was the music that came out of the big band jazz era, which gave rise to vocalists.

---

[1] Phillips was the first to record such important artists as Elvis Presley, B.B. King, and Jerry Lee Lewis.

CHAPTER TWELVE

ELECTRIFIED COUNTRY AND BLUES MUSIC

WESTERN SWING

In addition to folk, blues and hillbilly songs (which form America's musical roots), western or cowboy music also constitutes an important tradition in America's musical legacy. America's agricultural and farming beginnings also included the business of livestock ranching. Like agricultural farming, livestock ranching also had its songsters. The cowboy became a significant figure as he sang songs about the experiences one endures while herding cattle, branding livestock, training horses, and so on. While blues and hillbilly were disseminated via radio, film was the vehicle that introduced much of America, and the world, to the "old west" (in retrospect) and subsequent western/cowboy songs.

Ken Maynard–singer, fiddler, and banjo player–was the first person to be noted as a singing cowboy. John Wayne, although not a singer (his singing voice was dubbed), was one of the first major actors of this sort. It was Gene Autry, however, who truly exemplified the western cowboy through singing and movies. Born Orvon Autry on September 29, 1907, in Tioga Springs, Texas, Gene Autry was raised in Texas and Oklahoma environments and was familiar with farming and livestock ranching. Prior to being featured in movies, Mr. Autry was a radio (WLS in Chicago) and recording personality. As the result of an unsuccessful career as a "pop" singer during the 1920s in New York, he eventually discovered that people favored his country style of singing. He soon realized that writing songs about ranching, and then singing and recording these songs in the manner of Jimmie Rodgers, could lead to a promising career. During the Great Depression in 1934, Gene Autry was offered a part in a movie *Phantom Empire*[1] (a12-part science fiction serial) where he sang his eventual first gold record "That Silver- Haired Daddy of Mine." As the result of radio, recordings, and movie appearances, Gene Autry became the biggest star of country music just prior to WWII[2]. Many of the following recordings give one a good sense of the cowboy persona that permeated many western television shows and films during the 1950s and 60s. These include "Back in the Saddle Again," "Tumbling Tumbleweeds," "Mexicali Rose," "You Are My Sunshine," and "A Gangster's Warning." In 1969, Gene Autry was inducted

---

[1] This movie has a scene where Autry and others are performing at a medicine show. Traveling by wagon, a supposed doctor claims to have medicines and potions that cure most ailments. The performer(s)' responsibility is to entice people to the wagon.

[2] As is the case with many popular artists, recording a Christmas album adds to their popularity. For Gene Autry his recordings of "Rudolph, the Red-Nosed Reindeer" and "Frosty the Snow man" are still, to many, Christmas classics.

TITLE	INSTRUMENTATION
"That Silver-Haired Daddy of Mine"	Voice and guitar (Gene Autry), one background singer, slide guitar
"Back in the Saddle Again"	Voice and guitar (Gene Autry), violins, accordion, slide guitar, bass
"Tumbling Tumbleweeds"	Voice and guitar (Gene Autry), two background singers, mandolin, violin, bass
"Mexicali Rose"	Voice and guitar (Gene Autry), violin, 2nd guitar, bass
"You Are My Sunshine"	Voice and guitar (Gene Autry), 2nd guitar, two violins, slide guitar, bass

into the Country Music Hall of Fame. The Following Table provides the instrumentation for several of his popular recordings.[3]

Appearing as a singing cowboy at nearly the same time as Gene Autry was Leonard Slye, better known as Roy Rogers. Born in Cincinnati, Ohio, in 1911, he too was raised in a ranching environment and therefore was attuned to the traditions of the singing cowboy. Arriving in California in 1930, he worked in a peach orchard and as a truck driver. By 1934, he formed his band The Sons of the Pioneers–who wrote many of Rogers's songs such as "Tumbling Tumbleweeds" in 1935. That same year, the band was heard in the film *The Old Homestead*, thus contributing to the establishment of, in many American's ears, the western cowboy sound. Some of Mr. Rogers's films included *Tumbling Tumbleweeds* (1935) and *Under Western Skies* (1938). He is reported to have made over 100 films, most of them as a singing cowboy. After Gene Autry, Roy Rogers was the most celebrated singing cowboy, and by the early 1940s was billed as the "king of cowboys." His last film, *Pals of the Golden West* (1951), was produced by the Western for Republic firm. He and his wife Dale Evans (born Frances Octavia Smith, 1912, Uvalde, Texas)[4] hosted a successful radio show *Saturday Night Roundup* during the 1940s. From the early to mid-1950s, he and his wife starred in their own television series. Some of his most memorable songs include "Hi-Yo Silver" (1938), "Happy Trails To You" (co-written with his wife), "Money Can't Buy Love" ca. 1970), and "Hoppy, Gene, and Me" (1974).

During the 1940s/50s, while certain musicians of country music were gravitating toward bluegrass music, there were also country musicians who approached the genre utilizing other non-country styles of the day. Big band jazz and its musical progenitors such as ragtime, New Orleans jazz, vaudeville, blues, and boogie-woogie influenced many. The popularity of hillbilly and western/cowboy songs heard on the Grand Ole Opry and in various western movies added even more musical heritages to a musician's compositional workshop. Combining musical characteristics and performance practices from these styles and performing them within the context of the Texas milieu produced a style that became known as "western swing." In addition to Gene Autry, performers such as Bob Wills (1905–1975), Spade Cooley (1910–1969), Tex Ritter (1905–1974), and Roy Rogers (b. 1911) truly embodied, albeit in different ways and musicianship levels, this new approach to country music.

---

[3] All songs appear on the album *The Essential Gene Autry* (released by Columbia/Legacy, 1992)
[4] Rogers and Evans married in 1947.

TIME	SECTION	INSTRUMENTATION/COMMENTS
		Instrumentation: Voice (Roy Rogers); spoken voice, group of male singers, guitar, slide guitar, piano, clarinet, bass
		Form: 8-measure sections
		Lyrical Content: The song is about "Silver" (the horse)
00:00	Prelude	Spoken voice saying "Hi Ho Silver . . . away"
00:06	Introduction	Instruments only
00:10	Verse 1	Lyrics begin with the words "Horses come and . . .
00:26	Verse 2	Lyrics begin with the words "Over the trail . . .
00:34	Chorus	Lyrics begin with the words "Giddi' up"; spoken voice say "Hi Ho Silver"
00:50	Solo	Roy Rogers yodels
01:05	Verse 3	Lyrics begin with the words "Cantor along . . .
01:20	Chorus	Lyrics begin with the words "Giddi' up . . . I'll punch . . ."; spoken voice says "Hi Ho Silver"
01:36	Bridge	Group of male voices sing "Hi Ho Silver"
01:48	Verse 4	Lyrics begin with the words "Pick up your heels . . .
02:04	Chorus	Lyrics begin with the words "Giddi' up"; spoken voice say "Hi Ho Silver"
02:18	Coda	Call & response between the lead sing and male group of singers
02:24		Spoken voice saying "Hi Ho Silver . . . away"
02:30	End	The song ends

Song Navigator 12.1: "Hi Ho Silver" by Roy Rogers from the album *Ride Ranger Ride* (released by *Fabulous*, 2001)

James Robert Wills, the first of 10 children, was born in 1905 in Limestone County, Texas. Coming from a family of fiddlers (including his father and grandfather), young Bob was destined to become one of the most influential fiddlers of country music.

Labeled as the "King of Western Swing," his trademark "ah-ha," talking during a song, and uncanny ability to incorporate elements of ragtime, jazz, and blues into country music made Bob Wills one of the most respected musicians of his day. It has been said that his musical performances embody pre-1950 American music. This is attributed to his working alongside blacks in Texas and to his exposure to Mexican mariachi music while in New Mexico, not to mention his experiences in a medicine show.

When Wills was 8, his father, John Tomkins Wills, moved his family of poor farmers to Hall County, Texas in hopes of securing a better life. Working in the cotton fields alongside blacks, little Bob Wills was inspired by black music, particularly the blues, as he heard various vocalities and the use of trumpet and guitar. His 1938 recording "Down-Hearted Blues" displays idiosyncratic vocal features of the blues. The use of the trumpet as the response to his voice was a common practice on black blues recordings such as those by Bessie Smith and Louis Armstrong.

Bob Wills. © Photofest

After his marriage to Edna Porey in 1926, Wills moved to New Mexico and became enchanted with Mexican mariachi music. Mariachi music, among others, was a favorite style of music used for social dances in New Mexico. These occasions undoubtedly had an influence on his life, as the song "Spanish Two-Step" in 1935 became his first original composition. Despite the fact that trumpets are not evident, and Hawaiian guitar is incorporated, the music does indeed resemble mariachi music with its typical cut-time meter, the bass playing on the root and fifth of each chord, and fiddle usages.

In 1929, Bob Wills played in a medicine show that incorporated vestiges of the blackface minstrel era using Jim Crow characterizations. Documents indicate he played the fiddle, danced, and blackened-up—a term referring to putting burnt cork on the face and performing exaggerated imitations of blacks. His recording of "Down-Hearted Blues" with the use of banjo and the ubiquitous polyphonic texture of New Orleans jazz is evocative of the blackface minstrel era.[5]

---

[5] Although New Orleans jazz was not incorporated in minstrel shows, the banjo and piano were used in numerous shows.

As with most performers of the 1920s–1940s, radio played a major role in Wills's economic success. From the late 1920s until the early 1930s, he was a member of the string band called Light Crust Doughboys, a live radio group hired by the Burrus Mill and Elevator Company. After achieving some success with this group, he eventually landed a better live radio job at KVOO in Tulsa, Oklahoma. It is here that the band Bob Wills and His Texas Playboys was established. His popularity spread as this band played for numerous dances and other occasions. Still desiring to compete with the favored mainstream style of the day (big band music), Wills created two bands: a string band of fiddle, banjo, and guitars; and a band that included horns and drums. His 1940 recording "Big Beaver" is clearly in the style of big band jazz. Beginning with sectional alternation between the woodwinds and brass instruments during the introduction, this manner of melodic sharing continues in the A section as the woodwinds play the call with the brass furnishing the responding passages. After the theme is introduced in the A section by the entire band, solos are performed separately by the tenor saxophone and then the trumpet. Throughout the piece, the rhythm section–piano, guitar, bass, and drums–maintains the harmonic and rhythmic structure. Typical in big band jazz, the guitar strums chords on each count of the measure; the bass plays a "walking" bass pattern (although the root and fifth pitches are emphasized); the drummer accents the backbeat on the snare drum while the kick drum plays on one and three; the piano, although subtle, plays in a syncopated manner similar to ragtime and stride styles. The illustration below shows the rhythm section's pattern in a quadruple meter (4/4/):

Db	Db	Db	Db
G	G	G	G
1	2	3	4
Kd	Sd	Kd	Sd

G = guitar
Db = bass
sd = snare drums; kd = kick drum

Bob Wills and his Texas Playboys' 1941 recording of "Liebestraum" (Romantic period piece composed by Franz Liszt) also illustrate the group's passion for big band jazz. This piece begins with homorhythmic passages executed by the brass and woodwind sections followed by the main theme played by the woodwinds with brass responses. A tenor saxophone solo ensues, followed by a restatement of the main theme played by the clarinet, then brass (with woodwind responses), then Hawaiian guitar, then trumpet solo in counterpoint against thematic material by the woodwinds, and finally by all sections. In addition to incorporating performance practices indicative of big band jazz, Bob Wills purposely uses the Hawaiian guitar to add yet another layer to create a musical presentation of contrasting ideas. Another song, "Liza Pull Down the Shades" (recorded in 1938), clearly incorporates music performance practices of big band jazz, particularly swing and ragtime. Beginning with a drum introduction played allegro, the fiddle solo, played by Wills, is followed by the guitar, then the bass, and finally the piano. The piano is clearly playing in the style of ragtime music, as the right hand plays the melody while the left hand plays ragtime's signature bass-chord technique. Also, Wills's incorporation of speaking throughout the song illustrates his fondness for a common practice that was evident in New Orleans jazz/Chicago jazz. When applied correctly, this practice encourages each instrumental soloist during their playing, and consequently contributes to a more exciting performance. The song "Liza Pull Down the Shades" illustrates this practice. Take note of Bob Wills' words of encouragement during the guitar, bass, and piano solos. In addition to performing as both a string and big band, Bob Wills and His Texas Playboys gained increased popularity as the result of the endeavor of various record labels to market his and similar artists' recordings as mainstream music. In the 1940s, record labels opted to produce country as mainstream-type or "pop" music by having popular artists of the day record country music. For Wills, this included the 1941 Bing Crosby recording of his song "San Antonio Rose." In addition, the NAB strike in 1941 aided in broadening America's musical taste as country, along with blues and rhythm & blues was being disseminated to people who otherwise would have ignored it.

TIME	SECTION	INSTRUMENTATION/COMMENTS
		Instrumentation: Voice and violin (Bob Wills); guitar, banjo, piano, 2nd violin, trombone, saxophone, bass, drums voice
		Performance practices: The band is playing in a polyphonic manner, much like new Orleans jazz (see Chapter 8); violin, saxophone, and trombone play in response to the lead singer
		Lyrical Content: The song is about not worrying, as from where he "sits" everything is fine
00:06	Introduction	Two violins
00:10	Verse 1	Lyrics begin with the words "All the summer . . .
00:26	Solo	Trombone accompanied by the band; Bob wills is speaking intermittently
01:00	Verse 2	Lyrics begin with the words "You stole my girl . . .
01:28	Solo	Guitar accompanied by the band; Bob wills is speaking intermittently
01:50	Verse 3	Lyrics begin with the words "Late in the evening . . .
02:18		Though the saxophone plays a brief passage near the end, this section is mainly, however, an instrumental interlude that does not feature any particular instrument.
02:48	Verse 4	Lyrics begin with the words "You see me stealin' . . .
03:12	Coda	Instruments play the final few seconds

Song Navigator 12.2: "Sittin' On Top of the World" by Bob Wills & His Texas Playboys from the album of the same name recorded between the years 1932–1947, (released by *Baierle Records*, 2010)

By the early to mid-1940s, Bob Wills and His Texas Playboys had become a noted band of Country music. His appearance at WSM's Grand Ole Opry radio show solidified his growing popularity, as for the first time and with much reservation from the conservative station, drums appeared on stage in front of a live audience. Inducted into the Country Music Hall of Fame on October 18, 1968, Bob Wills died on May 13, 1975.

Perhaps the most significant performer to rival Bob Wills was Spade Cooley. Nicknamed "Spade" for his penchant for playing cards, he, not Wills, is noted for being the person to be publicly billed as the "King of Western Swing." Born Donnell Clyde Cooley in December 1910, in Park Saddle Creek, Oklahoma, Mr. Cooley had some experience with rural society. By his twenties, he had moved to southern California, playing the fiddle with several bands. His more notable engagements included the Venice

Pier Ballroom (Venice, CA) and the Santa Monica Ballroom (Santa Monica, CA). Despite petroleum rationings due to the war, the Santa Monica Ballroom, as the result of Cooley's popularity, remained successful. Instead of using brass and woodwind instruments (typical for the Bob Wills sound), Cooley favored string instruments such as fiddle, guitar, and harp, and also added the accordion on occasion to his approximately 25-piece band. His popularity grew during the heyday of western swing (early 1940s), and by 1945 he had his first hit recording "Shame on You." Like other country stars at the time, Cooley did some film work for Republic such as *The Singing Sheriff* (1944) and *Square Dance Jubilee* (1949). Spade Cooley's career came to a halt when he was jailed for the murder of his wife in 1961. He died in 1969 during his performance for another artist's benefit concert in Oakland, California.

Another contemporary of Autry, Wills, and Cooley was the singer/actor Tex Ritter. Born Woodward Maurice Ritter in 1905, in Panola County, Texas, he was raised in a ranching environment. Noted for his acting abilities as a singing cowboy, Ritter was employed as a radio host and recording artist, and in Broadway plays and films. As a radio host, he appeared in Chicago, IL and Houston, TX, and after moving from the west coast to Nashville. In 1965, he appeared on WSM (Grand Ole Opry) radio. *Green Grow The Rushes* (1930) was his first successful Broadway play. His first recordings, though unsuccessful, were made under the Decca label. His recording career began to improve after signing with Capitol Records in 1942. He was the first country artist to be signed to that label. His most memorable recordings include "High Noon" (1952) and "I Dreamed of a Highway To Heaven" (1961). Tex Ritter was instrumental in establishing the Country Music Hall of Fame. He was elected to the association in 1964.

HONKY-TONK

Following WWII, southerners migrated to non-farming and urban environments in large numbers. Previously employed in farming and ranching, these people were now working in oil fields, manufacturing, and mining, which afforded many more opportunities for employment. And as is always the case, many social venues arose to divert workers from their arduous tasks. Of particular interest, the honky-tonk became a favored venue among coal miners, oil field and factory workers, and traveling people as a means to dissipate woes. Originating in "dry towns" in Texas, the honky-tonk was a hospitality venue (a.k.a. bar or beer joint) that served food and alcohol, and that provided a place for social dancing. The music coming out of this venue was generally loud (as the electric guitar was favored) and was frequently heard either on the bar's jukebox or performed by a live band. The music played in these venues became known as "honky-tonk." The type of music that was being performed in the honky-tonks ranged from hillbilly to blues-influenced songs. Those songs influenced by the latter are generally categorized under the heading "honky-tonk blues." A number of recordings by Merle Haggard, Webb Price, Ray Price, and even Hank Williams fall into this category.

Singer and guitarist Merle Travis (1917–1983) embodied the experiences of migrant workers through his songs that spoke to the hearts of people engaged in the aforementioned arduous and often dangerous working conditions. Travis was no stranger to these environments. His songs "Way Down in the Mines," "It's Dark as the Dungeon," and "Sixteen Tons," which speak about the dangers of working in coal mines, reflect his personal testaments of being raised among Kentucky coal miners. In addition to his real-life testimonials, his contribution to music includes the guitar finger-picking style. Characterized by playing the bass and rhythm with the thumb and the accompanimental harmony—including the lead notes or melody—with the remaining fingers, this manner of playing allowed the singer to accompany himself without the need for other instruments. While Merle Travis laid the foundation for the spirit of honky-tonk music, it was Ernest Tubb from Texas who encapsulated its traditions and made it more marketable for a wider audience. Regarded by many as the "father" of honky-tonk, his most influential songs spoke about loneliness, drinking, and infidelity. Many of his and other performers' recordings included guitar, fiddle, bass, table guitar, drums, and sometimes piano.

Lefty Frizzell (1928–1975), a singer, guitarist, and songwriter, continued the honky-tonk style but added a vocal style of singing that included bending his notes and adding *melismas*. Take, for example, his song "If You've Got the Money, I've Got the Time." Following a couple of verses, the piano plays a solo in the honky-tonk style. Frizzell returns with a verse, then the violin plays a solo. He again sings a verse, which is followed by an electric guitar solo. Another example of the honky-tonk style is heard in his 1951 release "Always Late (With Your Kisses)." Frizzell begins the song by singing, *a cappella*, the word always in a melismatic manner. The instrumentation includes voice, guitar, slide guitar, piano, bass, and drums. Following Frizzell's second verse and chorus, the slide guitar plays a solo. This followed by the piano honky-tonk solo; the violin solos after this before he returns to the next verse. In retrospect, Frizzell accomplished a major feat, as he had four top-10 hits in 1951 on the country music chart with the songs "Always Late (With Your Kisses)," "I Love You a Thousand Ways," "Mom and Dad's Waltz," and "Travelin' Blues." Such a feat would not occur again until 1964 with The Beatles. In 1972, Lefty Frizzell was inducted into the Nashville Songwriters Hall of Fame. Following his death in 1975, he was inducted into the Country Music Hall of Fame and the Rockabilly Hall of Fame. His singing style influenced artists such as George Jones, Merle Haggard, and even Elvis Presley.

Kitty Wells. © Photofest

Because of the immoral implications of honky-tonk music, it was considered inappropriate by Nashville standards. As public interest continued to grow, however, it eventually became a begrudgingly accepted style of music. With performances by Ernest Tubb on the Grand Ole Opry and his own TV show, other performers such as Kitty Wells and Hank Williams, Sr. emerged on the honky-tonk scene.

Whether hillbilly, western swing, bluegrass, or honky-tonk, performances were dominated by males. However, singer and guitarist Kitty Wells, with her honky-tonk-style recording "It Wasn't God Who Made Honky-Tonk Angels," opened the door for the emergence of women performers in country music. The lyrics to the song (written by Sadie Miller) attempt to vindicate women from a male-influenced portrayal of women as having evil souls. Lyrics with this meaning, sung by a woman, were certainly not mainstream at the time, and in retrospect this song was the first of its type to became a popular hit.

Hank Williams Sr. © Photofest

Hank Williams (1923–1953) was another singer and guitarist that recorded in the honky-tonk style. Raised in a farming environment in Alabama, he was able to capture the heartfelt feelings of southern whites living a rural society. His musical training seems to have been by the black blues and folk street singer Rufe Payne. His first public performance was in the late 1930s and was noted for his singing a blues song concerning the Works Progress Administration.[6] That same year, at age fourteen, Payne formed the Drifting Cowboys, which lasted throughout his short-lived career. As a songwriter as well as a singer, he wrote songs that were eventually recorded by other artists. For example, the song "Six More Miles (to the Graveyard)," was recorded in ca. 1946 by Molly O'Day.[7] At the same time, Hank Williams recorded some of his first written or co-written songs such as "Move It on Over" (a blues-influenced song), "Honky Tonkin'" (a hillbilly-influenced song), and "I Saw the Light" (a religious song). In 1949, his recording "Lovesick Blues" was number one on the country music charts. Like most country artists, Williams's desired to perform at the Grand Ole Opry, this wish became a reality that same year. His most memorable song, "Your Cheatin' Heart," represents a subject matter that was typical of honky-tonk music during the 1940s. On New Year's Day 1953, while traveling to an engagement in Canton, Ohio, Hank Williams died in the back seat of his car. He was inducted into the Country Music Hall of Fame in 1961.

Muddy Waters. © Terry Cryer/CORBIS

---

[6] Also known as the Works Progress Administration (WPA), this agency was formed by President Franklin D. Roosevelt. It lasted from 1935 to 1939, assisting people with employment during the Great Depression.

[7] Molly O'Day, Rose Maddox, and Kitty Wells were popular women country singers during the 1940s and early 1950s.

ELECTRIC BLUES

Also known as "Chicago blues" or "city blues," electric blues is perhaps the most significant name as the sound of the electric guitar could now be heard with other instruments. Due in large part to the Rickenbacker guitar that was invented by George Beauchamp in 1931 and the subsequent founding of Rickenbacker International Corporation by Beauchamp and Adolph Rickenbacker. By 1932 the Rickenbacker guitar became the first electric guitar used for performance. Viewed as an extraordinary invention, guitarists could now be heard in the popular big band setting that was flourishing during the 1920s through the end of WW II. With the popularity of blues on the rise especially in big cities like Chicago and St. Louis, where propulsive electrified sounds were being heard in large clubs, people were mesmerized by the likes of Willie Dixon, John Lee Hooker, Albert King, B.B. King, Sonny Boy Williamson, Memphis Slim, Elmore James, T-Bone Walker, Muddy Waters, and Howlin' Wolf. Muddy Waters, B.B. King, Elmore James, and Howlin' Wolf are regarded in many literary sources as Chicago bluesmen in part because they all came from Mississippi and brought similar blues song traditions liked by many southern blacks who migrated to Chicago after WW I. An interesting tradition in the south, whether in Mississippi or Louisiana, was to incorporate fictional or non-fictional topics centered on what some called "mumbo jumbo" or "voodoo", with colloquial words like "mojo." Examples include "Hoochie Coochie Man" (1954) and "Got My Mojo Working" (1957) by Muddy Waters (1913–1983).

In the first song he sings about various artifacts used for putting spells on someone, in this case women. Furthermore, he is destined for good luck as he was born ". . . on the seventh hour, on the seventh day, on the seventh month . . ." he then asserts to pay attention when the "Hoochie Coochie"

TIME	SECTION	INSTRUMENTATION/COMMENTS
		Instrumentation: voice, guitar is playing the chorus theme harmonica, guitar, piano, bass, and drums
		Form: AAB song form; 12-bar blues progression
00:00	Introduction	Instruments only; the guitar is playing the main theme
00:27	Verse 1	Lyrics begin the song title; Muddy Waters enters with the lead vocal; the guitar is playing in response to the lead singer; the harmonica is playing a riff as well as a passage between verses 1 and 2; the piano is playing a riff
00:52	Verse 2	Lyrics begin with "Going down to Louisiana . . ." Playing style is similar to verse 1
01:17	Chorus	Chorus; "Got My Mojo Working"; the guitar is playing in response to the lead singer while the harmonica is sounding a passage with the lead singer
01:42	Solo	Harmonica solo accompanied by the band; no vocals
02:08	Verse 3	Lyrics about a Gypsy woman. . . .; playing style is similar to verses 1 and 2
02:33	Coda	The song begins to fade out without any singing

Song Navigator 12.3: "Got My Mojo Working" (recorded, 1957) by Muddy Waters from the album *Anthology (1947–1972)*

man comes to town. In the latter song Waters speaks about his "mojo" (a euphemism for charm) being effective on women in Louisiana, yet it doesn't work on a particular woman. Puzzled by this he consorts with a Gypsy woman to see what can be done about this.

Another popular singer and guitarist is Elmore James. As previously mentioned a number of artists from Mississippi now residing and playing in Chicago brought a distinct tradition of singing and playing that thrilled audiences of many social classes, economic status, and varied music tastes in the exciting and booming Chicago city limits. Like King, Waters, and Wolf, Elmore James knew how to appeal to all audiences and that was to just play the blues from one's emotions of personal life experiences, and situations. Born in 1918 in Holmes County, Mississippi, James was familiar with the topics and themes of southern lifestyle, particularly for African Americans. Without doubt his music reflected these themes shared by those in Chicago who probably experienced similar circumstances in Mississippi. Songs like "I Believe" and "I Held My Baby Last Night" speak about an alcoholic woman and a mean-spirited woman, respectively. Adversely Elmore speaks about the common occurrence of women who are treated badly by their man. In the song "It Hurts Me Too" James sings about a man who takes advantage of a particular woman's dedication to him, even through his continued infidelity. In the end James' states when this happens "It Hurts Me Too."

As to Elmore James' music contribution to the electric blues sound he uses the 12-bar blues progression, an emphasis on the guitar, saxophone responses, and an instrumentation that became a staple for this blues style. As stated in previous discussions of blues, the 12-bar blues progression is one of the most salient sounds of any blues style. Coupled with the AAB song form, the 12-bar progression further typifies the unmistakable sound of the blues genre. A hallmark of James' guitar playing is the chordal triplet figure. It occurs at the beginning in songs "Dust My Broom" and "I Believe", while in the song "I Held My Baby Last Night" it occurs within the song. In "Dust My Blues" the chordal triplet figure occurs both at the beginning as well as in a response to the lead singer's vocal line. Playing in a slide manner is another distinct sound of James' guitar playing. This occurs in the songs "Hawaiian Boogie" and at the end of the song "Dust My Broom." James' use of the saxophone is due in part to its popularity in big band jazz which was still popular during this time. The songs "I Held My Baby Last Night" and "I May Be Wrong" both enlist the saxophone playing in response to the lead singer's vocal line. Finally, the instrumentation in many of James' songs includes voice, guitar, piano, saxophone, bass, and drums.

Influenced by country blues songsters such as Lightnin' Hopkins, Blind Lemon Jefferson, Sonny Boy Williamson, Robert Johnson, and others, Chicago bluesmen during the 1940s and on combined music and performance elements of country and classic blues with the electric sound. Additionally, attributed to the social and cultural climate of the 1940s, the music was adjusting and subsequently evolving to suit entertainment needs for people who now had more time and money for leisure activities. Evolving means bluesmen were adjusting what they were doing with instrumentation, instrumental emphasis/solos, instrumental and vocal virtuosos, tempo, lyrics, and a few other performance practices. The goal was to please both the club owner and patrons. Since city clubs were often patronized by a diverse audience it was advantageous to have more than the typical blues instrumentation–voice, guitar, bass, and drums, but other instruments as well. These clubs, already accustomed to big bands, were successful because they provided performances with larger instrumentations such as voice, guitar, piano, bass, drums, harmonica, and a couple of woodwind and/or brass instruments to suit just about everyone's instrument tastes. An example of a person who presently uses a number of instruments is B. B. King (born, 1925).

In his songs "Three O'clock Blues" (released in 1951) and "The Thrill Is Gone" (released in 1970), the instrumentation includes King on voice and guitar, rhythm guitar, piano, synthesizer (emulating strings), bass, drums, trumpet, and saxophones. In the live performance of the latter song, with regard

B. B. King. © Photofest

to a performance practice in electric blues more so than in country/folk blues, dynamics fluctuate from *pianissimo* (very soft) to *forte* (loud), and the tempo accelerates near the end of the song.[8]

In addition to larger bands being used for the electric/Chicago blues sounds, groups lead by piano players who could sing as well as were becoming popular. Artists like Memphis Slim (1915–1988) and his signature song "Every Day I Have the Blues" (1947) could be performed by him on piano and vocals with a drummer, or with additional instruments.

It was by now clear by many that the guitar was the staple instrument for the blues, but the piano added yet another layer of performance so that people were able to segregate this electric style from the established country blues style. The ubiquitous sound of the saxophone in big band jazz, still wide-spread at this time, continued as a popular solo instrument in the electric blues as well. An example of this is heard in the song "Now I Got the Blues" (1946) by Memphis Slim and His 5 House Rockers.

Up to this point it is quite clear the guitar is the most common instrument used by country/folk and Chicago/electric blues musicians. It should be noted that the harmonica is also used within this style of blues music. Like the fiddle, banjo, and guitar the harmonica has roots in America's early period as an instrument that was fairly common among folk communities. After all it was relatively inexpensive, portable, didn't require musical training, and it was fairly easy to produce an adequately pleasing sound. In general, harmonica players in country/folk blues performances played alongside of guitarists who accompanied themselves. In Chicago/electric blues performances the harmonica functioned as a countermelody to the lead vocal line (often sung by someone else) and/or as responses to the lead vocal

---

[8] B.B. King. Live at Montreux, 1993.

TIME	SECTION	INSTRUMENTATION/COMMENTS
		Instrumentation: lead voice and piano (Memphis Slim Taylor), bass
		Lyrical Meaning: A song about having the blues every day
		Form: 12-Bar Blues Progression
00:00	Introduction	Piano and bass; the piano player plays improvisationally with his right hand while the left hand plays chordal style in a shuffle/boogie-woogie rhythm; the bass player in the "walking bass" style; The duo plays the same way throughout the entire song
00:28	Verse 1	Lyrics begin with the title
00:56	Verse 2	Lyrics begin with "Nobody loves me All Night Long. . . .
01:22	Solo	Piano accompanied by bass; Lyrics with "tell . . . crawling Red . . .
01:52	Verse 3	Lyrics begin with "I'm gonna pack. . . .
01:50	Coda	The song ends

Song Navigator 12.4: "Every Day I Have the Blues" by Memphis Slim from the album *The Folkways Years (1959–1975)*

part. An example is the harmonica stylizations by James Cotton in "I've Got My Mojo Working" by Muddy Waters. One noteworthy individual who sang lead and played harmonica between his vocal phrases is Sonny Boy Williamson. His popularity was short-lived but in any case first occurred during the 1950s, about ten years or so prior to his death in 1965. Some popular songs during his performance years include "Don't Start Me To Talkin'," "Fattin' Frogs For Snakes," "Your Funeral and My Trial," and "Bye Bye Bird," to name some.

In big cities with large clubs people congregated to not only socialize and eat, but to dance as well. The bluesman, if he or she wanted to stay working, would often play songs faster to encourage dancing.[9] An example of this is John Lee Hooker's (1917–2000) signature song "Boom! Boom!" (1962). Providing good dance numbers was yet another way the blues was seen as more than music that merely sung about hardships. While a number of artists did indeed speak about lost love, unemployment, social issues, and so on they also humorously pacified listeners with everyday topics as a way to desensitize these topics' seriousness. Furthermore, those who could vocally dramatized with effective inflections the gist of these topics to any gender, nationality, ethnicity, age, or economic status would soon have an admirable following. One such person is T-Bone Walker (1910–1975) and his staple song "Call It Stormy Monday" (1947) where he presents heartfelt descriptions of the progression from the work week's sorrowful beginning to the adulated weekend. Perhaps the most prolific electric/Chicago bluesman that wrote numerous songs on many topics is Willie Dixon (1915–1992). Known for his prolific writing, his music was recorded by artists such as B. B. King, Howlin' Wolf, Koko Taylor, and Muddy Waters, to name some. Dixon was

[9] For club owners, people dancing was usually a precursor for increased revenue, as this would cause patrons to drink more.

able to write about themes most bluesmen shared at some point or another in their lives. Some of his titles include "Bring It On Home," "Hoochie Coochie Man," "I Just Want To Make Love To You," "Little Red Rooster," and "Wang Dang Doodle." The following Music Navigator guides the reader through some of his staple performance practices as heard in the song "Little Red Rooster."

TIME	SECTION	INSTRUMENTATION/COMMENTS
		Instrumentation: voice, guitar, guitar2, harmonica, guitar, organ, piano, bass, and drums
00:00	Introduction	Instruments only; two guitars are playing in response and counterpoint to each other
00:36	Verse 1	Lyrics begin with "I had a Little Red Roster . . .; Willie Dixon enters with the lead vocal; the guitar is playing in response to the lead singer; the harmonica is playing a riff
01:10	Verse 2	Lyrics begin with "Dogs begin to bark. . . .; guitar is playing in response emulating a howling dog sound
01:46	Solo	Harmonica solo accompanied by the band; no vocals
02:21	Verse 3	Lyrics begin with "Now if you see. . . .; the accompaniment is similar to what is being played in verses 1 and 2
02:58	Solo	Piano solo accompanied by the band; no vocals
03:32	Coda	The song ends

Song Navigator 12.5: "Little Red Rooster" by Willie Dixon from the album *Poet of the Blues* (1947)

His song "Spoonful" (first recorded by Howlin' Wolf in 1960) speaks about his need for a little "spoonful" of a particular woman's love and it will ". . . satisfy my soul." Analogies of a spoonful presented in the song include: a spoonful of sugar; a pleasant additive in their coffee and tea; a spoonful of water that can satisfy a person in the desert; and men fight and argue over a woman's spoonful of love. Dixon's song "Wang Dang Doodle" recorded by Koko Taylor (1928–2009) in 1965 helped to reaffirm women's continued involvement in the proliferation of blues music. Like Dixon's "Spoonful", this song maintains the same chord and riff throughout the entire song, thus reaffirming the notion of lyrics and their complimentary rhythms as preeminent.

Another female Chicago blues artist who recorded a Willie Dixon song is the noted Willie Mae Thornton (1926–1984). Her recording of Dixon's "Little Red Rooster" and a song written by her that became popular namely "Ball 'n Chain", along with her most famous song "Hound Dog" all appear on her 1968 album *Ball and Chain*. Though generally categorized as a rhythm & blues artist, her recordings, including "Hound Dog", are comparable to electric/Chicago bluesmen for they display some use of the 12-bar blues progression ("Hound Dog"), themes of undesirable love ("Ball 'n Chain" and "Hound Dog"), and the pervasive guitar sounds and rhythms heard in all three songs.

CONCLUSION

Blues more so than any style has had the greatest impact on a number of different music styles in America. As will be seen in the following chapters, blues has influenced rhythm & blues, rock & roll, folk, fusion, jazz rock, soul, classic rock, psychedelic rock, hard rock, and metal. From the earliest manifestation of the blues through the electric blues, both men and women greatly contributed to its development, character, and delivery.

As we have read, the country blues was primarily nurtured by male performers, while women were the measuring yardstick for traditions of the classic blues. Though women were a contributing factor to the electric/Chicago blues style of the 1940s, it was male-dominated. Partly due to the preponderance of instruments being at least half the character of the blues, men were the instrumentalists and singers, while women who became popular, as evidenced by classic blues, were those that fronted bands as singers. Regrettably music executives, record labels, club owners, and the like were maintaining the status quo regarding society's view of whether women were competent instrumental contenders to their male counterparts. Consequently, male figures were dubbed as the forerunners of the electric blues sound. At the same time the emergence of rhythm & blues (see Chapter 14) was becoming increasingly popular with a generation of youth who either lacked an understanding of the social milieu from whence the blues came or were looking for music that was new, something more conducive to their generation.

CHAPTER THIRTEEN

JAZZ: BEBOP AND COOL STYLES

BEBOP

By the 1940s, the status of jazz had disappointed a number of musicians. Many musicians believed that the superfluous practices of big band jazz were diluting the true character of jazz as set forth by musicians of the first type, namely New Orleans jazz. They were looking to return to the vibrant character of jazz that was so prevalent among bands prior to WWI. While the youth of post-WWII were indulging in their new found freedom of musical tastes, others, particularly jazz enthusiasts, were exploring the new approaches to jazz in New York that were led by musicians such as Charlie Parker, Dizzy Gillespie, Miles Davis, and Thelonius Monk. This new music was bold, aggressive, progressive, confrontational, and intellectual–and it was called bebop.

Charlie Parker © Photofest

With the exception of the ubiquitous polyphonic texture of New Orleans jazz, there are indeed similarities between bebop and other jazz styles. First and foremost is the notion that a significant amount of performance time is placed on the individual musicians rather than the unit. (In big band jazz, the unit is the principal focus). A second difference is the formal structure, namely ABA. The piece titled "Crazeology" recorded by the Charlie Parker Sextet in 1947, illustrates this practice. In both styles, a certain theme occurs in the beginning and end of the piece, while solos are performed between them to allow individual creativity and contrast. The solo instruments were quite similar in both styles as well, namely brass and wind instruments. New Orleans jazz featured trumpet, clarinet, and trombone, while the trumpet, saxophone, and less frequently the piano were featured instruments in bebop. The Gillespie and Parker collaboration titled "Shaw Nuff" (1945) recorded by the Dizzy Gillespie All-Star Quintet features Al Haig on piano, Parker on alto saxophone, and Gillespie on trumpet.

Dizzy Gillespie © Photofest

Bebop was a departure from all styles of jazz to date (i.e., New Orleans jazz and big band jazz) in the following ways:

1) Listening music (versus music designed for dancing)
2) Faster tempo

3) Texture
4) Modality as well as tonality
5) Melodic contour
6) Harmonic/chordal sonorities

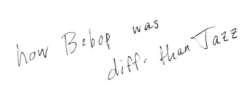

how Bebop was diff. than Jazz

Up to this point, all types of jazz were dance-oriented and were therefore greatly influenced by popular *tempi* of the day. This is not to suggest that all pre-bebop pieces were written and performed strictly for dancing, but as we know, dancing played a major role in their success. For many jazz artists, playing dance music did not allow true artistic expression, as it requires a strict tempo and less rhythmic complexity. Furthermore, music subjected to dance styles and whimsical trends could in no way afford creative and artistic freedom. One approach to eradicating any possibility of dance-oriented music is to play the piece at a tempo that doesn't support any popular dance of the day. Although the jitterbug was often seen in some settings during the performance of a bebop piece, no other dances could compete with the musically challenging *allegro* (fast) tempo of, for example, the bebop piece titled "Koko" recorded in 1945 by Charlie Parker's Re-Boppers. The tempo lies somewhere between 300 to 320 beats per minute!

In regard to texture with respect to thick or sparse, bebop is certainly less sparse than New Orleans jazz. By virtue of the infamous polyphonic texture in New Orleans jazz, there are certainly more parts occurring simultaneously than in bebop. In fact, the three parts that are performed by the members of the front line juxtaposed with the rhythm section playing in strict time totals four simultaneous parts. In bebop, on the other hand, the texture generally consists of two parts: melody/theme juxtaposed with the rhythm section. Generally, the horn section, most often trumpet and saxophone, plays monophonically or homophonically (i.e., different parts that are governed by the same rhythm). Considering the aforementioned ABA form, the monophonic or homophonic playing style most often occurs in the "A" section. The pieces "Koko" (Charlie Parker's Re-Boppers) and "Crazeology" (Charlie Parker Sextet) both illustrate the monophonic playing style, while "Shaw Nuff" and "Klac-toveedsedstene" have passages of both playing styles. Indeed, there are times when the horn section will perform both monophonically and homophonically. The following listening guide illustrates this using the piece titled "Klactoveedsedstene" recorded in 1947 by the Charlie Parker Quintet. (See next page.)

TIME	SPECIFIC FEATURE
	Instrumentation: trumpet, trombone, French horn, tuba, alto saxophone, baritone saxophone, piano, bass, drums
	Focus: Monophonic and Homophonic Playing–Trumpet and Saxophone
00:00	Homophonic playing by trumpet and saxophone
00:08	homophonic playing ends
00:16	Homophonic playing by trumpet and saxophone
00:32	monophonic playing, saxophone solo
02:21	Homophonic playing by trumpet and saxophone
02:52	Homophonic playing by trumpet and saxophone

Song Navigator 13.1: "Klactoveedsedstene" (1947) Charlie Parker Quintet

Most often consisting of piano, bass, and drums, the rhythm section comprises the second part of the two-part texture, which is typical for bebop. The piano supplies the harmonic framework *vis a vis* chords that are played in a "comping" fashion as a way to complement the horn section's or soloist's highly chromatic melodic passages. Due to the often *moderato* to *allegro* tempo, the bassist plays in a "walking bass" fashion, which not only provides the foundation for the harmonic framework but also provides a strict tempo by playing on each count of the (often used) quadruple meter. Similar to the bass and piano players' parts, the drummer supplies the tempo as well as rhythmic accentuations to complement the melodic trumpet and/or saxophone.

Indeed, melodic passages played by the trumpet and/or saxophone were the focus of the performance. Often playing 16th notes in an *allegro* tempo while accenting selected pitches, the melodic contour entails pitches within the modal as well as tonal scales. Without going into great detail about the theoretical differences between the two scale-types, consider the notion that the soloist does not restrict himself or herself to playing pitches within a single key of a given piece.

The melodic contour of bebop jazz also entails the performance of often long antecedent (question/call) and consequent (answer/response) passages. An ability to sustain long phrases while maintaining melodic interest reveals the complexity of bebop. Fittingly, the term *progressive jazz* was also used to identify this music. In other words, musicians were making a concerted effort to extend the musical boundaries of jazz by employing innovative approaches to melody.

To support these melodic passages, the harmony, which was regularly supplied by the piano and sometime guitar, needed to be just as progressive. Because the melody uses tonal, modal, and/or chromatic pitches, the harmony must incorporate similar pitches. In other words, if the melody, in the tonal scale of C, uses a g# (a pitch uncharacteristic of this key), then the harmony/chord will generally include this pitch as well. As a result, the chord (in this case, C, which includes pitches c, e, and g#) becomes altered, hence "altered chord." As a result of the progressive nature of bebop, altered chords were a common occurrence.

Despite the fact that innovation and individuality are important elements of jazz, or any music for that matter, bebop for a number of people-some critics included-had gone too far. The seemingly unrestrictive nature of bebop and its creators had displaced jazz, for some, into a realm of musical ambiguity. By the middle of the 1950s, a different type of jazz was emerging, but this time it was emanating from the West Coast. It was duly named "cool jazz."

COOL JAZZ

Where bebop jazz represented an aggressive move away from the commercialization of jazz seen in big band style, cool jazz in a sense, turned away from the aggressive and internalized performance nature of bebop jazz and began to consider external applications for music performance.[1] *Timbre* or tone color was one such application. This approach to performance involved an emphasis on the type or quality of sound as an endeavor to express the inner quality of a person, subject, or emotion. Cool jazz, like New Orleans jazz and bebop, showed an emphasis on the expressions of the individual artists.

The pursuit of civil rights–equal rights for all people–began to gain momentum during the middle of the 1950s. Cool jazz, as well as other styles, reflected this climate of social injustice. A distinct attitude of individualism and existentialism culminated in an era of experimentation on many different levels.

---

[1] This does not suggest that performers were empty of internal motivation, but rather, as you read on, the antithesis of this; innovative ways to free oneself from the pressures of the outside world was the attitude of the 1950s/60s.

In this view, cool jazz was one of the styles of music used to accompany intellectual discourse, much like the poetic recitations of the Beat Writers concerning existentialistic endeavors and viewpoints.

Covered with smooth-sounding timbre and a flair for inspiring creativity, jazz during the middle of the 1950s was evolving to a more introspective form of art. The term *cool jazz* was given to this introspective style of music, as it exposed the inner personality of the performer, a personality that endeavored to be accepted for itself, whatever that might have been. Being "cool" meant displaying minimal emotion. In some ways, its projection of individuality was to become an exemplum of the existentialistic social behavior among young adults, particularly college students, of the 1960s and 1970s. Grounded in a deep desire to experiment with texture, instrumentation, timbre, the symbiosis of notation and improvisation, rhythm, melodic phrasing, and form were some of the most significant endeavors of cool jazz. The tendency to be engaged "in the moment" while performing was becoming even more obvious during this time. Partly inspired by the individualistic stylizations of solo-playing in bebop, performers of the cool jazz style continued this ideology but without the necessity of having at least half the band playing a solo. (As you recall, this was a common practice in bebop.) In many instances, it was just as fulfilling to hear a single soloist express his or her individual character as it was to hear a number of soloists. After all, beauty was felt and appreciated by the mere aural character of each instrument. For many, such a behavior was a resounding voice in society during the mid 1950s and 1960s.

At the forefront of innovative approaches to jazz during this time included artists (listed alphabetically) such as Chet Baker, Dave Bruebeck, Miles Davis (see photograph at the beginning of the chapter), Stan Getz, Lee Konitz, the Modern Jazz Quartet (MJQ), Gerry Mulligan, and Lennie Tristano. Among these and others, the trumpeter Miles Davis takes prominence. With his 1949–1950 recordings at Capitol Records that were afterwards referred to as *Birth of the Cool*, Davis and his nine-piece band paved the way for new and different approaches to jazz by experimenting with texture, instrumentation, timbre, and written scores and arrangements. Saxophonists Chet Baker, Stan Getz, Lee Konitz, and Gerry Mulligan approached melodic phrases in a manner similar to a singer—what is often referred to as *lyricism*. This was certainly not the first time for this practice. In fact, the saxophonist Lester Young, who played with swing bands in the 1940s like Count Basie and His Orchestra, was perhaps most influential with respect to the production of a soft and subtle timbre. Unlike the audacious and aggressive nature of Charlie Parker's and Dizzy Gillespie's melodic phraseology and timbre as exemplified in bebop, cool jazz took a more restrained and lighter approach to its production. An example of this playing style is heard in the piece titled "Boblicity" (1949) by Miles Davis and His Orchestra. Along with solos by Davis and John Lewis, Gerry Mulligan is featured on baritone saxophone. Pianists Dave Bruebeck's and Lennie Tristano's influences on bebop's melodic phraseology combined with textures that often included counterpoint and chordal style helped solidify the different direction that cool jazz took. Arrangements for instrumentations peculiar to jazz were forged by Miles Davis, Gil Evans, John Lewis (MJQ pianist), and Gerry Mulligan. Scoring for uncommon instruments of jazz, at least for the time, such as tuba, clarinet, and French horn, for example, was broadening the boundaries for jazz orchestration. The reason for music notation was not solely for the purpose of employing uncommon instruments in the jazz performance, but more importantly to combine elements of the classical and jazz traditions. In this view, music notation was employed for several reasons: (1) to experiment with creating balance or symbiosis between notated parts and improvisational parts, (2) to provide notation for bands that featured more than one instrument on a part; and (3) to incorporate classical forms. In the first instance, arrangers such as John Lewis, Miles Davis, Gil Evans, Gerry Mulligan, and Gunter Schuller endeavored to arrange songs where improvisational solos and written parts had the same character. In the second instance, the previously mentioned piece titled "Boblicity" (1949) exhibits an instrumentation that requires notation. This piece also illustrates the symbiosis between the written parts and the soloists, as discussed in the first instance.

TIME	SPECIFIC FEATURE
	Instrumentation: trumpet, trombone, French horn, tuba, alto saxophone, baritone saxophone, piano, bass, drums
	Focus: Instrumentation and Solos (baritone saxophone, trumpet, piano
00:00	All parts
00:57	baritone saxophone solo accompanied by rhythm section
01:25	All parts
01:35	Trumpet solo accompanied by rhythm section
01:42	All parts
02:00	trumpet solo with overlapping horn accompaniment
02:11	Trumpet solo accompanied by rhythm section
02:25	Piano solo accompanied by rhythm section
02:39	All parts

Song Navigator 13.2 "Boplicity" (1949) Miles Davis and His Orchestra

With regard to the third instance, the Gershwin piece from the musical *Porgy and Bess* titled "Summertime," recorded in 1958 by Miles Davis with the Gil Evans Orchestra, uses the theme and variations form. Consisting of a 16-bar (measure) progression, the song is played a total of five times. Miles Davis on trumpet plays the main theme once and four variations of that theme. The cool jazz character is evident here, as the trumpet's melodic phrases begin or end at unpredictable places. In this piece, notice how the variations begin before the end of the 16-bar progression.

TIME	SPECIFIC FEATURE
	Instrumentation: 5 trumpets, 3 trombones, bass trombone, 3 French horns, tuba, alto saxophone, 2 flutes, bass clarinet, bass, drums
	Focus: Theme and Variations (Form)
00:00	Main theme
00:35	trumpet solo improvising
01:10	Same as above
01:46	Same
02:22	Same
02:54	Coda

Song Navigator 13.3: "Summertime" (1958) Miles Davis with the Gil Evans Orchestra

When there appeared to be a concerted effort by composers/performers to incorporate elements of both classical and jazz, the term "Third Stream" was used by some to refer to the sum of the two styles.

The MJQ's piece titled "Django" (1960) employs both classical and jazz elements. John Lewis (MJQ pianist) even experimented with blending stylistic characteristics of cool and third stream. The band's piece titled "Piazza Navonna" exemplifies this point.

As the 1960s drew near, cool jazz ushered in an existential attitude toward music composition and performance that–on one hand–set the trend for jazz during the ensuing decades. On the other hand, cool jazz was merely the embryonic stage of this attitude, as composers/performers such as Ornette Cole-man, John Coltrane, Charles Mingus, Horace Silver, and Cecil Taylor, extended the boundaries of conventions to a seemingly infinite realm. "Free form" or "free jazz" was the eventual term used to describe these approaches to jazz during the 1960s.

It must be understood that it becomes increasingly difficult to distinguish a performer's specific style of jazz after WWII, particularly during the 1960s. Musicians borrowed from the plethora of music traditions: (classical, previous jazz styles, and rock) as well as from world cultures, technological applications, and new, creative ideas. Moreover, with society's focus on equality, among other issues, music crossed racial barriers. Performer attitudes combined with the consumer's desire for less inhibited social mores widened the permeation of diverse styles of music in America.

More than ever before, composers/performers exemplified a sense of musical freedom with respect to melodic contour, harmonic structure, form, timbre, tonality, and instrumentation.

PART FOUR

MUSIC AND AMERICAN SOCIETY PRIOR TO AND SLIGHTLY AFTER WORLD WAR II: SUMMARY

Key Terms
- Walking bass line
- Backbeat
- Honky-tonk
- Electric blues
- City blues

- Comping
- Progressive jazz
- Timbre
- Tone color
- Cool

Featured Genres/Styles
- Western swing
- Honky tonk
- Electric blues

- Bebop jazz
- Cool jazz

Featured Songs/Works
- "That Silver-Haired Daddy of Mine"
- "Back in the Saddle Again"
- "Hi Ho Silver"
- "Liebestraüm"
- "Liza Pull Down the Shades"
- "Got My Mojo Working"
- "Dust My Broom"

- "Every Day I Have the Blues"
- "Little Red Rooster"
- "Wang Dang Doodle"
- "Crazeology"
- "Klactoveedsedstene"
- "Boplicity"
- "Summertime"

Featured Artists
- Ken Maynard
- Gene Autry
- Roy Rogers
- Bob Wills
- Spade Cooley
- Tex Ritter
- Merle Travis
- Lefty Frizzell
- Ernest Tubb
- Kitty Wells
- Hank Williams, Sr.
- Muddy Waters

- Elmore James
- B.B. King
- Memphis Slim
- John Lee Hooker
- T. Bone Walker
- Willie Dixon
- Howlin Wolf
- Koko Taylor
- Willie Mae Thornton
- Charlie Parker
- Dizzy Gillespie
- Miles Davis

Music and Society

- The Works Progress Administration (WPA) aided in providing opportunities for artists of various sorts during this post-Depression era.
- The Grand Ole Opry put aside its objection to honky-tonk's lyrical themes of drinking, dancing, and infidelity and began to broadcast it along with hillbilly, bluegrass, and western swing on national T.V. Mainstream America across the nation was now being introduced to these styles, which led to a greater interest in country music.
- As a result of the need for materials for the war efforts (WW II), manufacturing records slowly declined, thus record sales plummeted after the exuberant beginning of the 1920s.
- Because of the decline of attendance at large supper clubs like the Savoy, Small's Paradise, and even the Cotton Club, adjustments needed to be made to hiring large bands. With the invention of the electric guitar and the popularity of the jump band and its similarly big band style of playing, smaller bands became the mainstay for these and other venues.

Discussion Questions

- What reasons exist today as to the popularity of country music?
- If a solo artist is playing an electric guitar and singing in an AAB song form as well as using the 12-bar progression, is the style folk or electric blues?
- Do you believe bebop jazz pieces provide a natural progression from big band jazz? How is bebop jazz similar to New Orleans jazz?
- Do remnants of bebop and cool jazz exist in today's jazz? If so, identify some music characteristics and/or performance practices.

Learning Beyond the Classroom

- Numerous blues festivals occur across the nation each year. Attend a festival and see if the following are present: AAB song form, lyrical themes, 12-bar progression, acoustic vs. electric guitar, use of bending/sliding, solo vs. group performance, tempo usages, and picking and/or strumming style of guitar playing.
- Though not as frequently evident as blues festivals, try to find and attend a bluegrass festival and take note of the following: instrumentation, string instruments only, banjo/mandolin, guitar picking or strumming style playing, lyrical themes, tempo usages, and acoustic vs. electric instruments.
- On a large poster board draw a comparison chart of music characteristics and performers between the different styles of country music: hillbilly, bluegrass, western swing, and honky-tonk; and blues styles: folk, classic, and electric.
- If you play guitar, write a song using the AAB song form while using the 12-bar progression as an accompaniment. If you don't play guitar, write a song in the AAB song form and ask a friend to sing and play it.

PART FIVE

Antique Radio. © Steve Nagy/Design Pics/Corbis

POPULAR MUSIC IN AMERICA POST WORLD WAR II THROUGH THE 1970s

- CHAPTER FOURTEEN: Rhythm & Blues
- CHAPTER FIFTEEN: Rock & Roll
- CHAPTER SIXTEEN: A Revitalization of American Music: The British Invasion; 1960s Revival Music (Folk, Blues, and Country); and Psychedelic Music
- CHAPTER SEVENTEEN: New Approaches to Black Music: Funk, Disco, and Soul Styles
- CHAPTER EIGHTEEN: Jazz: Free/Free Form, Fusion, and Jazz Rock

OVERVIEW

Styles of popular music that existed between the end of WWII and the mid-60s included country, bluegrass (which was lumped in with country music), rhythm & blues (including boogie-woogie, urban/Chicago blues, and doo-wop), bebop jazz, cool jazz, rock & roll, pops-style rock, soul (basic and Motown), folk and folk rock, and a revival of blues and country music. In the 1960s and early 1970s there also existed market-driven categories like the British invasion and mainstream. The latter category consists of artists and bands of varied musical styles. Some of these include Herb Alpert, Perry Como, The Fifth Dimension, Engelbert Humperdinck, Jack Jones, Tom Jones, The Lettermen, Dean Martin, Johnny Mathis, Dionne Warwick, Andy Williams, and the British invasion. This era also marked the advent of numerous singers who were marketed as soloists who wrote their own material; they were known as singer/songwriters. Some had a regular band that accompanied them, while others did not. Because of the predominance of the emergent youth culture after WWII, the focus here will be on the specific styles that achieved the greatest success among them, namely rhythm & blues, rock & roll, and pop-style rock.

The National Academy of Broadcasters' (NAB) strike against American Society of Composers, Authors, and Publishers (ASCAP) in 1941 for their alleged monopolization of performance on the radio precipitated a need to secure non-ASCAP artists for NAB radio programs. Prior to the boycott, radio broadcasters were airing music mainly from ASCAP's music catalog that included publishing firms that catered to post-Vaudeville, Tin Pan Alley, musical theatre and film songwriters while regularly denying folk, hillbilly, and black music. During the boycott, the newly established (in 1939) Broadcast Music Incorporated (BMI) performance rights agency created by the NAB sought to increase its catalog of non-ASCAP publishers who by and large were not the typical Tin Pan Alley sort. Fueled by a desire to accommodate the musical tastes of those serving in the military during the war as well as both black and white southerners who had migrated to urban areas, and the resultant increased buying power of African Americans, radio broadcasters capitalized on the growing interest in both southern and African American-based music styles. Styles such as rhythm & blues and hillbilly (billed as country music) satisfied these market demands.

The U.S. deployment of the atomic bomb on Hiroshima in 1945 marked the end of WWII, and also the close of the Big Band Jazz Era (1920s–1946). Large venues that promoted these big bands found it increasingly difficult to continue to operate their businesses as they were and still survive. As a result, many venues closed while others stayed afloat by relocating their businesses to smaller rooms and featuring smaller bands. Fortunately, the invention of electric amplification, particularly for guitar and bass, made it feasible for smaller bands to project their music to large audiences. The growing number of migrants to urban areas created a flourish of blues-based artists, who became known as urban blues performers. (See chapter on blues recordings.) In addition, many musicians (particularly younger players) seized the opportunity afforded by this changing climate to create less restrictive approaches to jazz performance, as many of them had become disgruntled with the evolution of jazz up to that time. Artists such as Dizzy Gillespie, Charlie Parker, Thelonious Monk, Bud Powell, Miles Davis, Charlie Christian, Stan Kenton, Jimmy Blanton, and many others began to experiment with different approaches to jazz, which, in a way, was a return to the vitality and character that was so evident in New Orleans jazz. Bebop jazz was born out of these innovatively new ideas.

With the ending of the war and President Harry Truman's issuance of an executive order to put an end to segregated federal buildings in 1945, the rise of bebop jazz seemed to reflect a new black social consciousness. Often regarded as black intellectual music, bebop was indeed a point of departure and a musical expression that signified a new musical and social era. In 1949, the same year that NATO was formed, music trade journals, most significantly *Billboard*, emerged as a viable force in chronicling music activities in America.

The NAB strike and subsequent BMI formation during the 1940s were major contributors to the dissemination of rhythm & blues and country music. Radio broadcasters throughout the nation aired songs in areas to people who had previously disregarded these styles. Although few at first, those broadcasters airing black songs to white teens had a major impact on the future of popular music in the United States. White teens were intrigued by the aggressive, rhythmic, and perceived sensuous nature of a number of rhythm & blues songs. Mainstream America, however, was not enchanted with what they referred to as "jungle music." Nevertheless, the youth culture was gaining momentum as the fastest-growing and, most significant market for music products with regard to record sales. The music industry seized the opportunity to supply this new demand while showing some sensitivity to parental concerns by having white artists record black songs. The term crossover became the eventual label for this practice. Generally, record labels, A & R (artists and repertoires) managers, or producers would select the most popular rhythm & blues songs as evidenced by the music charts (either *Billboard* or *Cash Box)* for their white artist.[1] To please parents, non-threatening white singers would sing edited or what was commonly known as "watered-down" versions of the original songs. To solidify this, the industry made an attempt to disassociate the white crossover versions from black sounding versions, or rhythm & blues music, and therefore elected to label them rock & roll. To some, the year 1951 marks the beginning of the rock & roll era, as Alan Freed, a white disc jockey (DJ), announced on the air "Let's all rock and roll."[2]

---

[1] Since R & B was marketed to the African American consumer, what is ironic is the fact that record labels, A & R people, and producers were selecting songs from the musical tastes of blacks for the white consumer.

[2] "Rock & roll" was a term used by African Americans for sexual intercourse.

The invention of the transistor radio in the 1950s promoted music more readily available for both youth[3] and adult, as it meant that music could be heard in other places besides at home, in the car, or on television. By the mid-1950s, television, as the new advertisement medium, provided the visual link between rhythm & blues/rock & roll music and its performers. The emergence of *American Bandstand* in 1953, hosted by Dick Clark, provided the primary visually based dissemination of this music.

Like rhythm & blues, hillbilly/country music received eventual airing as the result of the NAB strike. In addition, the proliferation of country music was also attributed (in part) to the singing of songs within this genre by "popular" artists of the day such as Nat King Cole, Bing Crosby, Ella Fitzgerald, Patti Page, and Frank Sinatra. In addition, the production of films from the mid-1930s to the mid-1950s depicting the western cowboy lifestyle also popularized various aspects of country music. Through the singing, playing, and/or acting careers of individuals such as Gene Autry, Roy Rogers, Dale Evans, Tex Ritter, Bob Wills, Spade Cooley, and Tex Williams, many Americans were introduced to and eventually became intrigued by country music. The western cowboy and images of driving livestock on the plains lie at the core of the American spirit, of which the American frontier is an inseparable part.

As geographical and social boundaries were being reassessed, so were class, economic, and political limits. Younger citizens were becoming a force to be reckoned with, as they not only were concerned with their own plight, but that of others as well. In unprecedented ways, America's white youth began to explore the black community through its music and issues of class and civil liberties. In many ways these were inseparable to a growing number of white citizens who came to realize the inherent affective qualities of music, particularly black music—soundscapes that are inextricably attached to the culture.

While at first subtle, the voice of the youth culture eventually became a powerful factor in the momentum of the Civil Rights Movement during the mid-1950s. Black and white teens were reassessing their perceptions of race as the perspectives of race and color taught by their parents took a back seat, and rock & roll–the unprecedented youth culture phenomenon–took the front. As different musical tastes were experienced, so were varied cultural traditions. America was being educated by its youth. Exposure to the racism of many whites fueled inquiries regarding the morality of social as well as physical segregation strictly on the basis of color. For many African Americans, it became paramount to participate in relieving their plight, not only by listening to rhetorical affirmations made from concerned European American brothers and sisters, but also through legislative actions that effectively addressed issues of equality and justice. Concern for the ambiguous status of the black American citizen precipitated a "back to Africa" effort during the 1960s. Aroused by this outlook, black people in America began to draw upon and to some extent absorb their African heritages. Evidenced by the "black power" sign of the raised fist, the "afro" hair style, African attire, and so on, black people were making America aware of their dissatisfaction with the current status of their "civil rights." Combined with the previous concerns of the youth culture, these heartfelt and "soulful" concerns were the inspiration for what became known as "soul music." To market soul music to an even wider audience, Barry Gordy, Jr. founded Motown records, where he proceeded to produce more acceptable "watered-down" versions of rhythm & blues performed by African Americans. While Motown recordings made black music palatable to mainstream America, a different type of approach to black music was also brewing during this time–funk. Through rhythmic propensities, funk epitomized the African American's absorption of African culture, representing a definite departure from mainstream music.

Social change was not only shaping certain aspects of black music, but other genres as well. The social climate of the early 1950s was tempered by the McCarthy hearings/trials, which were considered by many to be "witch hunts." A number of Americans of all occupations were brought to trial for

---

[3] During this time, affixing a transistor radio onto one's bicycle was a common occurrence.

their alleged ties to communistic regimes both here and abroad. Folk singers were frequently brought to task because of their typically politically charged lyrics. A number of young white Americans were intrigued by the black call for equality–the tenor of civil rights–and soon began to challenge their parents' views about class structure. Singers such as Bob Seeger were "blacklisted"[4] for their political protestations against American policies.[5]

More than any other decade in 20th century American history, the 1960s represents the largest variety of as well as the most challenging societal conditions. In the eyes of many, the assassinations of President John F. Kennedy (1963), Malcolm X (1965), Dr. Martin Luther King, Jr., and Senator Robert F. Kennedy (both in 1968) thwarted the progressive move toward a greater degree of racial, ethnic, and gender equality. These leaders were the main inspiration for such legislation as the Civil Rights Act (1964) and the Equal Pay Act (1963).[6] Civil rights permeated other facets of society and fueled other emerging or continuing movements, such as feminism, the hippie culture, and gay rights. Folk music provided a vehicle for expressing emotions and contemplating actions during these trying times in American history. Folk rock continued these sentiments but with added musical elements that, in effect, appealed to the younger audience.

Women's continuing struggle to attain equal rights was gaining ground in the 1960s as evidenced by the establishment of the National Organization for Women (NOW) in 1966, whose initial purpose was "to take action . . . to break through the silken curtain of prejudice and discrimination against women . . ."[7] Music reflected these changing times most noticeably in lyrical themes. Indeed, unlike lyrical themes among women singers of the 1950s that centered on the desire for love or on waiting for the return of their man from war, lyrical themes in the 1960s often related to ideologies of empowerment as well as the feminist quest for equal rights. For example, Aretha Franklin's entertaining and honest concerns for reciprocal love are heard in "Respect" and "Think" (both in 1967). These particular lyrics represent but a minute example of women's sociopolitical protestations concerning equality and justice. In addition to love for all humankind, other themes spawned by the hippie movement were also being introduced during this time. On the surface, these themes appeared to be the antithesis of the progressive lyrics heard in many women's songs; such as those heard in "Somebody to Love" (1967) by Grace Slick of Jefferson Airplane. The fact is, however, these lyrics are even more progressive as they show a disregard for social mores of the previous decade.

Inspired by the Beat Movement[8], which started in New York in the 1940s and migrated to San Francisco in the 1950s, white, middle-class, college-educated individuals embarked on a journey during the 1960s, espousing an ideology of peace and love that spawned a subculture of young people whose goal became challenging post-WWII social mores. These individuals, mainly in their mid-20s, instigated the "hippie" movement, which practiced tolerance among people of different races and genders. Hippies were political pacifists and generally protested any war. They experimented with drugs

---

[4] The word *blacklisted* although politically incorrect, was the term used at that time.

[5] Even Aaron Copeland, one of America's most celebrated composers of music, was on trial in 1953 for his alleged political ties with communism. This was absurd, as Mr. Copeland expressed that anti-American sentiments concerning civil liberties, equality, and political protestations meant they were pro-communist.

[6] The Civil Rights Act and related legislation was greatly influenced by the march on Washington D.C. in August 1963, where 250,000 people of many different nationalities and social classes listened to Dr. Martin Luther King, Jr. deliver his famous "I Have a Dream" speech.

[7] NOW 1966 Statement of Purpose from http://www.now.org/

[8] William Burroughs, Allen Ginsberg, and Jack Kerouac were three well-known Beat writers. Their writings discussed and encouraged existentialism, the use of drugs to enhance creativity and embrace tolerance, a non-imperialistic/capitalistic-based mentality, and a disregard for post-WWII social/sexual mores that opposed any of the above.

(LSD and marijuana), and were open-minded toward sex and love (i.e., free love). Also known as "flower children," their viewpoints were public in 1967 when the first "Human Be-In" was staged in Golden Gate Park, San Francisco. In a setting that promoted love and camaraderie, drugs, and poetic readings, many people were introduced to the new music that regularly accompanied such occasions, namely acid rock or psychedelic rock. Gay rights activists also became increasingly vocal, as the 1960s presented an ideal forum for engaging in personal and intellectual discourse on human emotions, opinions, and alternative lifestyles.

While domestic concerns abounded, America's involvement in the Vietnam "conflict," which continued to escalate throughout the 1960s, diverted some attention to American international interests. In 1969, America's interests literally went "out of this world" as the Apollo space shuttle placed the first human being on the moon, adding to the cultural milieu of broadening perspectives/viewpoints. But setting their sights on the moon (as well as broadening perspectives) was rather far-fetched for more conservative Americans. Likewise, tastes in international music were generally assumed to be in the high arts, such as European opera and orchestral music.

A new era was dawning. Inspired by American blues and rock & roll musicians, European youth began to develop their own musical styles. The 1960s became a time when European artists created music that catered to youth. Known as the British Invasion, America experienced a wave of artists such as The Beatles, the Rolling Stones, and Cream, who–among others–inexorably shifted the popularity of foreign music to these new styles for youth as well as adult Americans.

It must be understood that there was a difference between pop-style music and pop-culture music, although for many the two were one and the same. Pop-style music emphasizes certain musical trends with the intent of appealing to a broad audience–young and old, rich and poor, and all ethnicities. The music is generally engaging with respect to its tunefulness, but less controversial with regard to serious social concerns. Because trends are connected to social and behavioral mannerisms, they are subject to deviation and frequent change. Pop-culture music, on the other hand, refers to specific styles or trends of music that are embraced by people who share some of the same ideals, traits, traditions, and customs; hence the word *culture*. It is plausible that a person could enjoy a pop-style song and yet not embrace the ideologies of the pop-culture denoted in that song. For example, a parent during the 1960s may have enjoyed listening to "I Want to Hold Your Hand" (Beatles, 1963), but would have vehemently disavowed any association with pop-culture. Similarly, young African Americans (a sub-pop culture) preferred Willie Mae "Big Mama" Thornton's version of "Hound Dog" (1953) to the pop-style 1956 version by Elvis Presley.

A subcategory of pop-style and pop-culture music was warranted as the result of the marketability of youth music that commenced after WWII. This marked the first time in American history that there was a concerted effort to market music to youth. The category "youth pop music" reflects musical tastes among persons aged 16 to 23. Within this category, considerations relating to pop-style music and pop-culture music should be taken into account.[9]

In order to reach the enormous youth population while maintaining the adult market (e.g., parents), music executives needed to reassess their marketing strategies. To satisfy these growing and varied musical tastes, the music industry took another turn. With regard to music, the 1960s is known as the "Era of the Producer." Some examples include Phil Spector, Lieber and Stoller, and Berry Gordy. Rather than being performed by a rock & roll band, it became commonplace for a performer/songwriter's music to be produced. In many situations, the person who developed the product from an orchestral/ arranger viewpoint then became the focus.

---

[9] Today's youth pop music includes styles such as pop-punk, hip-hop, thrash, underground, alternative, and speed metal, and various pop-style music performers such as Christina Aguilera, Hillary Duff, Beyonce, Jessica Simpson, Britney Spears, and Shakira.

In the 1960s, America experienced a revitalization of its own music creations from interests abroad and from concerns of civil liberties among those at home. Indeed, music groups from abroad such as The Beatles and The Rolling Stones were performing their versions of American-inspired styles such as blues, country, rhythm & blues, and rock & roll. The time was also ripe for legislation regarding the civil rights of all Americans. These concerns were the wellspring from which folk singers drew their inspiration for performances that centered on the well-being of the common person. Existentialism, as sung about by folk singers, inspired musicians to experiment with their own ideas of music and its relationship to their lives. Cues for what became known as "psychedelic rock," existentialism, surrealism, and other aspects of social behavior greatly affected how musicians approached composition and performance. In a nutshell, the invasion of music groups from Britain, folk styles (including blues and country), and psychedelic rock forever changed the music scene in America, underscoring the spirit of American individuality, acceptance, tolerance, and open-mindedness.

August 28, 2005, marked the 42nd anniversary of Dr. Martin Luther King, Jr.'s "I Have a Dream" speech, when a quarter of a million people–black and white, male and female, young and old–congregated on the steps of the Lincoln Memorial and listened to numerous speeches about civil rights in America. Listening to Dr. King deliver this momentous speech, all people, but particularly blacks, felt inspired and empowered. Dr. King had made it clear that when it came to African Americans, this great nation had not fulfilled its basic obligation of guaranteeing equal rights and opportunities to all people. The time was ripe and the stage was set for people of all social classes and ethnicities to confront head-on and eradicate deplorable attitudes toward black people in America. It had been predicted that the march on Washington would precipitate rioting and civil chaos; however, there was not one unruly incident. The event was truly a day of peace, which exemplified what America could be. In the history of the United States, it was the day that made the most significant change with respect to civil rights.

In retrospect, it is no surprise that contemporary music, including lyrics, reflected what was experienced on August 28, 1963. Indeed, an existential mood permeated both rhetorical and poetic recitations, which greatly influenced music performance and composition considerations. From this viewpoint, a song's lyrical content is often real since it represents the experiences and emotions of people. The musical character of many songs supported the lyrics by applying either subtle or overt orchestrations that further engaged the listener. In essence, the intent was to create music that was heartfelt, music that transcended ethnicity, gender, and social status. The goal was to create music that resonated the "I Have a Dream" speech and, ultimately, the American spirit.

Looking at the lyrical content in African American songs previous to the 1960s provides evidence of the powerful effect of the social climate that prevailed during that decade. The music of the 1950s was an outgrowth of the social conditions of male and female relationships during World War II. At that time, couples often coped with life, at least temporarily, without the physical presence of the loved one. As a result, topics of love during the 1950s seem to have a common theme of individuals reflecting on conditions of loneliness like those experienced during the previous decade. As representatives of women with loved ones at war, female soloists often displayed feelings of uncertainty regarding a particular man's love for them. They often conveyed the experience of being broken-hearted. For instance, with the exception of Sarah Vaughan's "Whatever Lola Wants" (1955),[10] the majority of Top 10 hits, such as "I Cried a Tear" (1958) by LaVern Baker and "Broken-Hearted Melody" (1959) by Sarah Vaughan,[11]

---

[10] The popularity of "Whatever Lola Wants" by Sarah Vaughan was due in part to its dissemination via the stage play and movie titled *Damn Yankees*.

[11] Performances by female groups focused their attention on songs that expressed their commitment to a particular man (with the exception of the Chordettes's 1958 hit titled "Lollipop"). Some songs include "Born to Be with You" (1956) and "Just Between You and Me" (1957) by The Chordettes, and "Mr. Lee" (1957) by the Bobbettes.

featured topics about love ambiguities. Male soloists expressed similar feelings. Songs with similar subject matter as those found among female singers include "Unchained Melody" (1955) by Roy Hamilton, "What Am I Living For?" (1958) by Chuck Willis, "Lonely Teardrops" (1958) by Jackie Wilson, and Clyde McPhatter's 1958 hit "A Lover's Question." In this song, McPhatter is rather uncertain as to whether or not the person in question will reciprocate his feelings of love. Desired love was also a topic among male soloists. Some songs include Thurston Harris's 1957 hit "Little Bitty Pretty One," in which a man is asking a woman to talk to him; Bobby Freeman's 1958 hit "Do You Want To Dance?" and Wilbert Harrison's pursuit of pretty women in the 1959 hit "Kansas City." Larry Williams's song "Short Fat Fannie" (1957), a somewhat humorous description of the opposite gender, exemplifies themes given musical expression only by male performers.[12]

Songs by female soloists during the 1960s featured a broader variety of topics when compared to those of the previous decade. Male singers continued to cover a wide range of topics during this time. In addition to singing love songs, female performers sang about dance, a sense of individuality, "speaking out" against men in general, and tropological meanings (that is, words that offer a remedy for moral enhancement). Male singers' topics included love, dance, "speaking out" against a particular type of woman, allegories, religion, sensuality, and survival. The dance craze during the 1950s, fueled by rock & roll music, inspired the use of specific text in song lyrics of the 1960s. A significant number of songs describe how to perform a specific dance. Some examples by female singers include the 1962 hit "The Loco-Motion" by Little Eva, and "Mashed Potato Time" (1962) and "Do the Bird" (1963), both by Dee Dee Sharp. Sharp's "Mashed Potato Time" provides historical information by referring to the point in time when this dance began. She also encourages listeners to dance by referring to the "Mashed Potato" as an easy dance, and furnishes the listener with specific instructions. Dance songs by male singers include Chubby Checker's "The Twist" (1960), "Let's Twist Again," "Pony Time," "The Fly" (all in 1961), plus "Limbo Rock" and "Slow Twistin" (both in 1962). Checker's recording of "The Twist" also furnishes words that describe the movements of the dance called "The Twist." Other male artists who contributed dance songs to this decade include Sam Cooke and Rufus Thomas. Leslie Gore was the only woman who exhibited this type of expression among her peers (she sings about her right to cry) with her 1963 hit "It's My Party." While speaking out against men is not a common subject among female singers, one song by Gore states this with regard to love, namely "You Don't Own Me" (1964).[13] Some male songs display a negative attitude toward an extended family member (such as a mother-in-law) or a soon-to-be family member (such as a wife). Examples include Jimmy Soul's 1963 hit "If You Wanna Be Happy," which comments on the idea that one should not marry a pretty woman, as it will make one miserable. In the 1961 hit "Mother-in-Law" by Ernie K-Doe speaks about his woes as the result of his mother-in-law's personality. Songs with allegorical meanings are evident only among male soloists during this time. An example includes the 1961 hit "Spanish Harlem" by Ben E. King, which speaks about the maturity of a young woman. Another example is Wilson Pickett's 1967 hit "Funky Broadway," which refers to a portion of that famous street of theatres in New York City.

Because both men and women are involved in religious activities, one would perhaps expect to hear religious songs from both genders. This, however, is not the case; this subject matter was only

---

[12] Male groups, like male soloists, address various aspects of love. Some of these include specific joyous moments, metaphorical descriptions of young women and women in general, desire, chivalry, and expressions of teenage situations. Songs that focus on a specific moment will generally employ the word night in their title, such as "Oh, What a Night" (1956) by The Dells and "One Summer Night" (1958) by The Danleers.

[13] It is interesting to note that a European American (Leslie Gore) sings these topics. Songs sung by African American women with this type of subject matter do not appear until the 1970s.

evident among male singers during this time. Songs include the 1961 hit "A Hundred Pounds of Clay" by Gene McDaniels, which talks about God's formation of the earth, man, and woman; and "Little Green Apples" (1968) by O.C. Smith, which talks about the things God has made.

Sensuality is another topic that appears among male singers. One example is the 1965 hit "The Birds and The Bees" by Jewel Akens.

Due to the emergence of the many issues surrounding equal rights, by the mid-1960s, women began not only to speak out but to apply tropological intent to their songs. One singer noted for this practice is Aretha Franklin. Franklin has led the way in providing prescriptions for the enhancement of a man's morals. Songs that appeared in 1967 included "Chain of Fools," which contains protestations regarding her situation as a link in a particular man's chain of women, and "Respect," which speaks about receiving respect from a particular man. In 1968, the Top 10 hit "Think" prescribes the act of thinking as a means of reforming a particular man's improper behavior.

A song that can be interpreted as providing words of encouragement for both men and women, "Only the Strong Survive" (1969) by Jerry Butler was inspired by endeavors that were pursued during the Civil Rights Movement, particularly by African Americans.

CHAPTER FOURTEEN

RHYTHM & BLUES

INTRODUCTION

The end of WWII marked the end of the big band era, when smaller groups became the norm. Because of changing musical trends, a resulting loss of patrons, and a decrease in record manufacturing, many large dance halls and supper clubs found it was not financially viable for them to continue offering dance music by big bands. Consequently, they either closed their doors or downsized. It was at this time that the "jump band" came to the forefront, as they satisfied the public's appetite for big band sounding music, but were in fact smaller bands. Jump bands certainly existed before the mid-1940s, but along with other styles and band types, they were overshadowed by the favored sounds of big band jazz. Consisting of saxophone, trumpet, piano, guitar, bass, and drums, the jump band played in the fashion of big bands, but more frequently incorporated singing, stylistic characteristics specific to the blues, shuffle, and the stylistically categorical "boogie-woogie" rhythms. These characteristics were rooted in the tradition of blues, but took on a different name.

The term *rhythm & blues* came to refer to the urbanized style of blues music. The performance of blues songs was altered from its original folk-style presentation to a more entertaining and thus widely appealing delivery. The performer incorporated varied performance practices to appeal to a number of different musical tastes. Even though rhythm & blues songs and their performers catered to the African American community, people of different nationalities and musical tastes also enjoyed the music. Some of the more salient aspects that shaped early rhythm & blues included a faster tempo that was more conducive to dancing, more playful subject matter, and the use of additional instruments (e.g., saxophone, trumpet, and electric guitar). Greatly influenced by slightly more equal social prospects as a result of WWII, the NAB strike against ASCAP, and the subsequent formation of BMI, and perhaps most significantly, the marketability of music to the rising and economically viable youth culture, a number of artists began performing blues outside of its typical folk-based mode in a manner that catered to the changing tastes of post-WWII conditions. In summary, a whole new social structure was being shaped in America as a result of the following factors:

1. The decline of big band jazz;
2. The increase of African American buying power after WWII;
3. The consequent need for music that catered to them;
4. The search for new music and performers by the newly formed BMI licensing agency; and
5. Strategies that marketed music to a historically younger audience.

The jump band served as the prototype for rhythm & blues, performing music that enticed people to dance the most exciting dance of the 1940s-the jitterbug. Jump bands that could encapsulate vocal melodic recitations and rhythmic dance propensities with the big band sectional style of playing as exemplified by brass and woodwind instruments laid the foundation for rhythm & blues. Jump bands satiated the appetite for the diminishing big band-sounding music while exposing its listeners to a closer connection to African American culture. Most notably, its lyrical content focused on experiences of African American culture and not generalized themes of love as typified by big bands. This resulted in jump band and rhythm & blues music inevitably becoming disassociated with the 1930s/40s big band sound. Subsequently, rhythm & blues- sounding music became a component of the race series-black-sounding music.[1]

The origin of placing songs of specific types on charts as a consumer marketing scheme dates back to the 1920s, when record sales reached over 100 million.[2] Popular styles of music at that time included blues, New Orleans, Chicago, and big band jazz, and gospel.[3] Since all these styles were African American in origin, music executives found it advantageous to categorize them for more effective marketing purposes, including marketing music specifically to the African American community. In doing so, the race series chart explicitly identified that music which was "black sounding."[4] The following list provides names of companies/labels that participated in the race series beginning in the 1920s:

Victor and Bluebird
Columbia and Okeh (recorded the first African American woman)
Brunswick and Vocalion
The A.R.C. labels
Gennett and Champion
Black Patti (African American owned)
Black Swan (African American owned)
Paramount
Merritt

It was a sign of the times that black music was placed into this category — more because of the race of the performers than the style that they played. Blues, jazz, and gospel songs were all placed under the race music series, regardless of their stylistic differences. From the 1920s to the 1930s, approximately 15,000 songs were categorized in this manner, with blues receiving the most sales (10,000), followed by jazz (3,250), then gospel (1,750). Blues artists popular at that time included Mamie Smith,[5] Bessie Smith, Memphis Slim, Big Bill Broonzy, Alberta Hunter, Robert Johnson, Blind Lemon Jefferson, Leadbelly, and Billie Holiday. Popular jazz recording artists included Louis Armstrong, Count Basie, Cab Calloway, Duke Ellington, Ella Fitzgerald, Fletcher Henderson, Earl Hines, Fats Waller, and many others. Gospel recording artists included Mahalia Jackson, Sister Rosetta Thorpe, and the Dixie Hummingbirds. The race series continued through the 1930s and into the 1940s.

In 1942, *Billboard* began charting black-sounding music under the category "Harlem Hit Parade." On October 24th of that year, "Take It and Git" by Andy Kirk & His Twelve Clouds of Joy was the

---

[1] Ironically, the word *black* became a chart category used by *Billboard* to identify black-sounding music.

[2] The 1920s marked the beginning of the vinyl record boom.

[3] Approximately 15,000 songs were placed under the race series from the 1920s to the 1930s.

[4] I have purposely used the phrase "black-sounding music" to imply that the performer does not have to be black. In most cases, however, he or she is.

[5] Mamie Smith was the first African American woman to record a blues song: "You Can't Keep a Good Man Down" and "This Thing Called Love."

number one record. Partly due to the success of this record, *Billboard* became more active in charting black music, and consequently "Harlem Hit Parade" was replaced nearly three years later by the already established and more general black music category "Race Records." Within this category, two chart names were used, "Juke Box" (began February 17, 1945), and "Best Sellers" (began May 22, 1948).

On June 25, 1949 *Billboard* discontinued the use of "Race Records" as a category in favor of "Rhythm and Blues Records," the already popular term being used among African Americans.[6] Like the "Race Records" category, the chart names "Juke Box" and "Best Sellers" were continued, and a third chart category titled "Jockey" was added on January 22, 1955. In addition, the race records tradition of placing all styles or types of African American songs under a single chart name regardless of their stylistic differences continued with the new "Rhythm and Blues" category throughout the 1940s and into the 1950s.[7] To reiterate, rhythm & blues as a stylistic category diminished during the 1960s, and consequently became like rock in ensuing years: an umbrella term used to identify a subculture, an attitude, or music that has inherited its effervescence.

Stylistic features that were evident in rhythm & blues of the 1940s and 50s that truly established a distinct style were, by the mid-1960s, lost in the forest of creative substance. At this juncture, the term *rhythm & blues* functioned much the same as race series-a market-enthused category as opposed to a music-driven style. One only needs to look at the *Billboard* charts with respect to African American music to discern this marketing scheme. The following outline gives the time period and stylistic categories used to identify African American music.

October 24, 1942   Harlem Hit Parade
   "Take It and Git" (1942), Andy Kirk & His Twelve Clouds of Joy
February 17, 1945   Race Records (Juke Box and Best Sellers charts)
   "Choo Choo Cha Boogie" (1944), Louis Jordan & His Tympany Five
June 25, 1949   Rhythm & Blues Records (Juke Box, Best Sellers, and Jockey charts)
   "Hound Dog" (1953), Willie Mae Thornton (urban-type rhythm & blues)
   "Sh-Boom" (1954), The Chords (doo-wop type rhythm & blues)
October 20, 1958   Hot R&B sides (in 1962 renamed to Hot R & B Singles)
November 30, 1963 to January 23, 1965, no "black-sounding" chart was published
   "Remember (Walking in the Sand)" (1964), The Shangri-Las
January 30, 1965   Hot Rhythm & Blues Singles
   "My Girl" (1965), the Temptations
   "Natural Woman" (1967), Aretha Franklin
August 23, 1969   Best Selling Soul Singles
   "Share Your Love with Me" (1969), Aretha Franklin
July 14, 1973   Hot Soul Singles
   "I Wanna Be Your Lover" (1979), Prince
June 26, 1982   Hot Black Singles
   "Early in the Morning" (1982), the Gap Band
   "What's Love Got to Do with It" (1984), Tina Turner
   "Power of Love" (1991), Luther Vandross
December 5, 1992   Hot R&B Singles

---

[6] "Pop" and "Country Western" were the titles of other categories also used at this time by *Billboard*.

[7] As will be discussed later in the chapter, boogie-woogie, urban, and doo-wop types of rhythm & blues were quite distinct during the 1940s, yet they all appeared on the "Rhythm & Blues chart."

2000-Present   Hot Rhythm & Blues/Hip-Hop and Rap
"Work It" (2002), Missy "Misdemeanor" Elliott
"Luv U Better" (2002), LL Cool J
"Love of My Life (An Ode to Hip-Hop)" (2002), Erykah Badu Featuring Common

Although it is commendable that *Billboard* discontinued the racist "race music" chart, from a musico-logical perspective, the replacement category of rhythm & blues is not much of an improvement. Most African American performers, regardless of their stylistic features, were placed on the rhythm & blues chart. Take, for example, the song by Ike and Tina Turner titled "Proud Mary" (1971). Considered rhythm & blues by virtue of their ethnicity, one can clearly hear the rock & roll-type rhythm in this song.

Sadly, because of the arbitrarily constructed, financially motivated category of rhythm & blues, many past and even current listeners are not aware that many other very rich styles of African American music existed during the 1940s.

Three types of music flourished that were categorized and consequently viewed as rhythm & blues music beginning in the late 1940s: boogie-woogie, doo-wop, and urban blues. Boogie-woogie referred to those songs where a distinct *ostinato* (or bass pattern) provided the harmonic and rhythmic founda-tion. Doo-wop songs were mainly performed by male quartets and quintets who harmonized with a two- or three-part linearity. Urban was the type of rhythm & blues that was most frequently heard from the 1940s through the early 1960s. Commonalities found in all three types include the following:

1. Generally sung
2. Voice is preeminent
3. Lyrical themes include dancing, good times, specific black community occasions, women's descrip-tions of men
4. Generally played at a tempo that encouraged dancing
5. Frequently featured a saxophone solo
6. Frequent use of handclapping

DISTINCTION BETWEEN ELECTRIC BLUES AND URBAN RHYTHM & BLUES

That is to say, both styles were being performed in urban settings for adult audiences. In reality, electric blues placed a greater focus on the voice and guitar, while the urban rhythm & blues tradition called for songs that could entice people to dance through the use of infectious and intoxicating rhythms and orchestrations, and/or lyrics. While the two styles were easily differentiated by the discriminating lis-tener, they did share many characteristics.

1. They were both flourishing in larger midwestern, western, and northern cities.
2. The music industry used the term "race music" to categorize nearly all black artists, and therefore many people paid little attention to their musicological differences.
3. Both types incorporated blues elements such as the 12-bar blues progression, AAB song form, use of the shuffle/boogie-woogie rhythm, lyrics pertinent to African American situations and experiences, call and response, similar instrumentations, and vocal articulations such as falsetto, full-throated/guttural sounds, and *melisma*.

The following outline lists a few of the more popular songs of both the electric blues and urban blues, during the 1940s and 50s, which utilize the 12-bar blues progression and the AAB song form:

Electric blues style songs:
"Got My Mojo Workin'" by Muddy Waters
"I Love You" by Arthur "Big Boy" Crudup

"Cotton Crop Blues" by James Cotton
"Three O'Clock Blues" by B.B. King
"Shake For Me" by Howlin' Wolf
"I May Be Wrong" by Elmore James

Urban blues style songs:
"Hound Dog" by Willie Mae "Big Mama" Thornton
"(Mama) He Treats Your Daughter Mean" by Ruth Brown
"Beer Bottle Boogie" by Koko Taylor
"The Thrill Is Gone" by B.B. King
"I'll Play the Blues for You" by Albert King

Although similar in their singing techniques, performance practices, and instrument usages, electric blues and the urban style of rhythm & blues came from very different performance traditions. Whereas electric blues followed an evolutionary progression from country blues through classic blues, urban rhythm & blues exhibited these influences as well as characteristics of gospel and big band. Other aspects that distinguish the urban rhythm & blues style from the electric style include the use of brass and woodwind instruments, lyrical intentions, and perhaps most significantly, the use of (or a much greater use of) women singers, which provide all the attributes specific to women singers such as vocal ranges and timbre, and gender-specific lyrics. Regarding instrumental differences, when more instruments are used, particularly brass and woodwind instruments, any song has the capacity to reach a broader audience. Examples include B.B. King's "The Thrill Is Gone" and Albert King's "I'll Play the Blues for you."

People of different socioeconomic classes, musical preferences, and perspectives about music's function (i.e., listening vs. dancing) are often drawn to large cities and urban environments, which are generally more tolerant of differences (like having women singers) than small towns and cities. Entertainment venues took advantage of this by offering entertainment as diverse as possible to satisfy their clientele.

Whether performed by men or women, urban blues tended to cater to these differences in ways that affected the song's message, tempo, and other performance traditions like adding background singers. With regard to lyrical messages, lascivious lyrics, though also present in urban blues, were referenced covertly or through metaphor. On the other hand, in electric blues songs like Howlin' Wolf's "Rockin' Daddy" or "Rock Me Baby" by B.B. King (marketed as both electric blues and the more youth-inspired "urban" blues), the word *rock*–an African American euphemism for sex–was an overt proclamation to many. In Big Mama Thornton's recording of the Lieber and Stoller song titled "Hound Dog," the lyrics make reference to a type of dog, but the dog is a metaphor for a promiscuous man. This becomes even more apparent when listening to Elvis Presley's version (discussed in Chapter 15).

Certain performance practices and characteristics within the blues tradition have remained constant and pertain to both styles. These are listed below.

1. Male singers generally play an instrument, while women singers are frequently accompanied by instrumentalists.
2. Voice takes precedence over other instruments.
3. The guitar is the principal instrument (second to voice).
4. Lyrical themes focus on hard luck, sadness, personal experiences, and humor.
5. Both listening music and dancing music occur.
6. The song form is generally AAB.
7. The 12-bar blues progression is most commonly performed.

Louis Jordan. © Photofest

RHYTHM & BLUES: BOOGIE-WOOGIE

Also referred to as "jump blues," boogie-woogie rhythm & blues denoted the use of a specific performance style that was played by the bassist and/or the left hand low notes sounded by the pianist. Its lyrical content was more playful, and included more everyday topics that were prevalent in the black community. Some examples include topics of "fish fries (or social hangouts)" and the "speakeasy," as in Louis Jordan & His Tympany Five's recording titled "Saturday Night Fish Fry" (ca. 1944); the topic of the infamous "chicken shack" as another name for a social hangout among African Americans as heard in Clyde McPhatter's ca. 1950 recording titled "Chicken Shack Boogie"; the topic of love in McPhatter's number one rhythm & blues hit titled "Sixty-Minute Man" (1951); and the topic of dance as in the song titled "Elevator Boogie" (ca. 1946) by Mabel Scott.

The boogie-woogie style of playing developed and flourished during the 1920s/30s with pianists such as James P. Johnson, Fats Waller, William Smith, and Pete Johnson. As was the case in other styles of music performed on piano during that time-namely ragtime, blues, and stride-a specific technique played by the left hand gives boogie-woogie its distinct character. This left hand technique provides the rhythmic and harmonic foundation, hence *ostinato*, of boogie-woogie music. (See the illustration below.)

Similarities between the melodic blues and the boogie-woogie bass lines

Harmonic Blues Bass Line   Boogie-Woogie Bass Line

Similarities between the melodic blues and the boogie-woogie bass lines

The boogie-woogie *ostinato* was influenced by the melodic and harmonic bass lines used in blues music. For instance, boogie-woogie inherited the intervallic character of the melodic blues bass line and the syncopated rhythm of the harmonic blues bass line. Looking at the example, the boogie-woogie *ostinato* uses the same intervals as those seen in the melodic blues bass line. The difference lies in the number of times each note is struck. As seen, notes occurring on each count of the measure are struck once in the melodic blues bass line, while in the boogie-woogie *ostinato*, they are struck twice. The rhythmic motion of the harmonic blues bass line, as shown by the illustration above, has the appearance of the triplet figure. However, it is not sensed as such, but rather as a stroke consisting of a "long-short" gesture. This rhythm is the result of the tie that occurs on the second eighth-note. (The tie prevents each note from being stuck three times, thus resulting in a "long-short" gesture.) In addition, in the performance of the boogie-woogie *ostinato* the second note struck within each count is sounded an octave higher; this action performed continuously conveys an impression of jumping. This particular melodic and rhythmic gesture contributed to the development of the "jump blues," which later was referred to as rhythm & blues. During the 1940s the jump blues, empowered by the boogie-woogie style of playing, was performed by small bands (a.k.a. jump bands).[8]

During the 1940s, the jump bands' instrumentation included saxophone, trumpet, piano, guitar, bass, and drums.[9] Early songs with the jump band sound and their respective performers included Louis Jordan-known as the "father" of rhythm & blues-"Is You Is or Is You Ain't My Baby," "Choo Choo Cha Boogie," "Let the Good Times Roll," "Ain't Nobody Here but Us Chickens," and "Saturday Night Fish Fry"; "Good Rockin' Tonight" by Wynonie Harris; "Chicken Shack Boogie" by Amos Milburn; "Rocket 88"[10] by Jackie Brenston with His Delta Cats; and "Elevator Boogie" by Mabel Scott.

During the same time period, there were a number of recordings that used larger bands, such as the Johnny Otis Orchestra and their 1950 recording titled "Cupid Boogie." In this song, trumpets, saxophones, trombones and a four-piece rhythm section accompany the vocal duet (woman and man). A similar instrumentation is used in the recording titled "Elevator Boogie," sung by Mabel Scott. Another example is the song titled "Hey, Ba-Ba-Re-Bop" (ca. 1945) by Lionel Hampton & His Orchestra, whose instrumentation includes trumpets, saxophones, and trombones against a four-piece rhythm section. The song also features a trumpet solo in addition to a soprano saxophone solo. Even though larger bands were used, they still performed in the jump band fashion. For instance, the first two songs employ the typical rhythmic boogie-woogie pattern, while the second song clearly outlines a typical blues-type bass line.

Whether the bands were large or small, the saxophone and less frequently the piano were the solo instruments. In New Orleans jazz, the bandleader was often the lead singer and trumpet player. Rhythm & blues often followed the same pattern, with the lead singer also playing saxophone. Examples

---

[8] The boogie-woogie *ostinato* in a jump band context was played by the bass player.

[9] The trumpet is often the instrument omitted in quintets.

[10] "Rocket 88" was written by Ike Turner while traveling to Memphis to see Sam Phillips, founder of the Memphis Recording Service and the subsequent Sun Record label.

include Louis Jordan and all of his popular songs, and Jackie Brenston who recorded "Rocket 88" (1951). Song Navigator 14.1 gives an overview of solo instruments.

TIME	SECTION	SOLO INSTRUMENT/COMMENTS
		Instrumentation: voice, guitar is playing the chorus theme harmonica, guitar, piano, bass, and drums
		Form: AAB song form; 12-bar blues progression
00:00	Introduction	All instruments except voice
00:18	Verse 1	Lyrics begin with "Heading for the station. . ."
00:34	Chorus	Lyrics begin with title of song
00:45	Solo	Piano solo accompanied by guitar, bass, and drums; no vocals
01:02	Verse 2	Lyrics begin with "You reach your destination. . ."
01:19	Chorus	Lyrics begin with title of song
01:30	Solo	Saxophone solo accompanied by guitar, bass, drums, and trumpet and saxophone playing in response to the saxophone solo; no vocals
01:58	Verse 3	Lyrics begin with "Gonna settle down. . ."
02:14	Chorus	Lyrics begin with title of song
02:26	Coda	Instrumental with some half sung lyrics by Jordan

Song Navigator 14.1: "Choo Choo Cha Boogie" (recorded, 1946) by Louis Jordan and His Tymphany Five

Blues has certainly inspired various performances of the boogie-woogie style. Of the three types of music billed as rhythm & blues during this time, the boogie-woogie style used the 12-bar blues progression more so than the urban and doo-wop styles. Some examples include "Choo Choo Cha Boogie" and "Let the Good Times Roll" by Louis Jordan and His Tympany Five, "Honey Hush" by Joe Turner, "Blues" and "Going Home" by Wynonie Harris, and "Chicken Shack Boogie" by Amos Milburn.

While the boogie-woogie was based around various instrumental qualities, it was generally sung. Whether man or woman, jump band or larger band, or fast or slow, the boogie-woogie type rhythm & blues was usually sung. For example, in the song titled "Cupid Boogie," Little Esther sings about marriage and various expectations that befall a couple. Louis Jordan's "Saturday Night Fish Fry" refers to aspects of a speakeasy.[11] In Milburn's "Chicken-Shack Boogie," the overall structure consists of alternating verses and solos. In addition to the saxophone solos, a piano solo occurs during the next to last solo section. This represents the epitome of the boogie-woogie rhythm & blues, as the voice part alternates with the saxophone and piano playing in somewhat of a dueling performance, which occurs in the introduction as well as the coda section.

RHYTHM & BLUES: URBAN

Unlike Chicago blues, which maintained its connection strictly with blues, performers of urban rhythm & blues borrowed stylistic features of the blues (listed above), gospel, and jazz. The influence of gospel was expressed in the notion of vocal emphasis with its many fluctuations of voice, beginning in the 1920s; and the influence of harmonic, rhythmic, and orchestral tendencies stemmed from the big band jazz tradition.

[11] The speakeasy was a night club during Prohibition.

Dinah Washington. © Photofest

Singers who did not play an instrument created one of the most significant changes to the sound of urban blues and the ensuing evolution of rhythm & blues. As singers, these performers were restricted neither by instrumental tendencies nor by the stylistic propensities of blues and jazz. Instead, their performances reflected more of the vocal stylizations of blues, gospel, and vocal jazz. Performers such as Dinah Washington (the "queen" of rhythm & blues), Ruth Brown, Clyde McPhatter, Willie Mae "Big Mama" Thornton, and Big Joe Turner paved the way for creating a new approach to rhythm & blues, distinguishing it from the traditional urban blues sound.

It is important to note that the term *urban* is generally a way to convey a city environment as opposed to a rural or suburban setting. A city environment, affords more performance opportunities, as its goal is to accommodate a wide audience, one that varies in gender, ethnicity, age, national/international origin, social environment, and so on. Consequently, the urban rhythm & blues performer has to be well prepared for all types of audiences if he or she is to be successful. Due to these and other factors, women performers of this type of music were heard just as frequently as men. Some recordings include "Baby Get Lost" (ca. 1948) by Dinah Washington, "King Size Papa" (ca. 1948) by Julia Lee & Her Boyfriends, and "(Mama) He Treats Your Daughter Mean" (1953) by Ruth Brown. As previously stated urban rhythm & blues artists, particularly women, performed in front of a number of different audiences. In addition to the jump blues instrumentation, women singers were accompanied by larger bands and orchestras as well. For example the song "What a Difference a Day Makes", which includes an orchestral arrangements, was popular with audiences this time as well.

TIME	SECTION	INSTRUMENTS/COMMENTS
		Instrumentation: voice, background singers, strings, guitar, bass, bells, and drums
00:00	Introduction	Begins with cellos, violins, violas, bells, then background singers
00:16	Verse 1	The lead singer is accompanied by strings, bass, and drums; background singers provided a harmonic structure singing with the vowel "ooh"
00:48	Verse 2	The lower strings provide responses to the lead singer's vocal line; the background singers enter just before the next verse
01:18	Verse 3	The lead singer is accompanied by strings, bass, and drums; background singers provided a harmonic structure singing with the vowel "ooh"; lower strings provide responses to the lead singer's vocal line
01:48	Verse 4	The lead singer is accompanied by strings, bass, and drums; background singers provided a harmonic structure singing with the vowel "ooh"; upper and lower strings provide responses to the lead singer's vocal line

Song Navigator 14.2: "What a Difference a Day Makes" by Dinah Washington from the album titled *20th Century Masters: The Millennium Collection* (2002, Hip-O Records)

It is also important to mention that during this time, i.e., just after WWII, rhythm & blues music had such a significant impact on the music industry that its stylistic features became embedded in American popular culture. As the result of a growing interest among European American teens, European American artists also began performing rhythm & blues music, resulting in its description as rock & roll. In other words, early rock & roll is nothing more than rhythm & blues with a European American face. The music industry found it necessary to use the term *rock & roll* to disassociate European American performers from African American music, or what many referred to as "jungle music," so that mainstream parents would not feel as threatened by it. Despite the fact that African Americans used the term *rock & roll* as early as the 1930s as a reference to procreative gestures, to many European Americans it seemed distinct from the term *rhythm & blues*. To promote this disengagement, European American artists were billed as rock & roll performers, while African American artists were viewed as performers of rhythm & blues music. Consequently, European American performers of rhythm & blues were placed on *Billboard's* "Pop" or "Hot" chart, while songs by African Americans appeared on the "Rhythm & Blues" chart. As the 1950s progressed, America started becoming aware that there was not as great a distinction between rhythm & blues and rock & roll as had been alleged by industry executives through their marketing endeavors. A number of African American artists, who by and large performed rhythm & blues music,[12] were categorized as

---

[12] For instance, Mr. Berry was marketed as a rock & roll performer and yet he continually makes reference to "rhythm & blues" in his song "Roll Over Beethoven." Examples are provided near the end of this section.

performers of rock & roll music. A few of the more famous included Little Richard, Chuck Berry, Bo Diddley, and Fats Domino.[13]

RHYTHM & BLUES: DOO-WOP

The doo-wop style of singing was a favorite pastime among African American males as early as the late 1800s. The term *doo-wop*, however, did not come into popular use until the 1950s, as it was associated with the term "doo-wah"—a mechanism used to record singers. Male quartets and quintets (and occasionally trios) performed this type of music, which was categorized as rhythm & blues from the 1940s–60s. Practices include, but are not limited to, a featured bass singer, the performance of numerous vocal nuances sung by background singers, and distinct lead singer and background singers' parts.[14]

The history of 20th century style doo-wop singing originates from the popularity of gospel groups and their performance traditions during the 1930s, 1940s, and early 1950s. By the late 1940s and early 1950s, many male quartet and quintet groups soon emerged performing "secular" music in a similar fashion.

The Cadillacs. © Photofest

[13] Little Richard and Chuck Berry are both recognized as the "father" of rock & roll.
[14] These practices are evident among male groups more so than they are among female and mixed-gender groups. There are instances, however, where some of these practices are heard in female and mixed-gender groups; these will be addressed accordingly.

One of the most significant performance practices exercised by doo-wop groups is the application of three distinct linear parts, as illustrated below. They include lead, background unison/chordal accompaniment, and bass spoken or sung passages incorporated together with or during pauses in the lead and the background singers' parts.

TIME	SECTION	INSTRUMENTS/COMMENTS
		Instrumentation: voice, background singers, guitar, piano, bass, and drums
00:00	Introduction	Begins with bass singer (solo), followed by 3 voices "bah bah dit . . . accompanied by guitar, piano, bass, and drums
00:08	Verse 1	The lead singer enters accompanied by background singers, piano, guitar, bas, and drums
00:32	Verse 2	Lyrics have the words "Don't believe in wasting time . . ."; with the same accompaniment as above
01:03	Verse 3	Lyrics include the title song; with the same accompaniment as above
01:17	Solo	Saxophone solo accompanied by the same as above
01:40	Verse 4	Lyrics include the title song; with the same accompaniment as above

Song Navigator 14.3: "Speedo" by The Cadillacs from the album titled *Doo Wop Classics, Vol. 1* (2003, Rhino)

The division and function of the lead singer's, background singers', and bass singer's parts are seen in either the performance of text, melody, or harmony.[15] Such division is evident in all ensembles, regardless of gender membership. In most male ensembles during the 1950s, the lead singer generally provides the text and melody as his or her principal function, while the background singes' role generally furnishes the vocal harmonic accompaniment. The background singers, consequently, will generally perform the harmonic texture of a song with vocal nuances and less text, so as not to interfere with the role of the lead singer. For example, the background singers in the group named The Dells apply the nuances "ha" (tenor), "ooh" (baritone), and "do" (bass) against the lead singer's part, in their 1956 hit titled "Oh, What a Night." In addition, the background singers continue to sing text after the lead singer has discontinued his passage. Other male ensembles that usually performed in this manner included The Rays in their 1957 hit titled "Silhouettes," and Little Anthony & The Imperials in their 1958 hit titled "Tears on My Pillow." In mixed-gender ensembles during the 1950s, the display of distinct lead and background singers' parts was evident in all of the "Top 10" doo-wop hits. These included "My Prayer," "(You've Got) the Magic Touch" (both in 1956), and "Twilight Time" (1958), all performed by The Platters; "Happy, Happy Birthday Baby" (1958) by The Tune Weavers; and "Sixteen Candles" (1958) by The Crests.

Of particular mention is the bass singer, who became a featured component in male vocal groups during the 1950s.[16] In addition to its harmonic function, this part often provides humorous melodic lines and/or spoken text, such as is evident in the hits "Yakety Yak" (1958) and "Along Came Jones" (1959), both sung by The Coasters. The bass singer also provided solo singing in the introduction to a

---

[15] In some instances, as will be discussed, this will also depend on gender membership.

[16] Some mixed-gender groups contained a bass singer. The function of this part, however, was limited to providing the root note within a harmonic texture that was sung in chordal fashion.

song, such as with the 1958 hit titled "Book of Love" by The Monotones. During the 1960s, with the exception of The Temptations and The Marcels, the practice of featuring a bass singer began to diminish. The bass singer's function became limited to providing the root note of the background singer's texture, sung in either chordal fashion or homorhythmically.

An examination of quartet and quintet groups indicates that a performance can include one or a combination of the following four musical style characteristics.

1. The principal melody of a particular section is sung or spoken by the lead singer with or without background vocal accompaniment. If background singers are present, they generally accompany the lead singer in unison and/or passages in chordal fashion, singing either words of the text or vocables of vowel sounds.
2. All members of the group sing the principal melody of a particular section, in unison, or homorhythmically, or chordal fashion.
3. The principal melody of a particular section is sung or spoken by more than one lead singer with background vocal accompaniment.
4. The presence of three linear parts:
   a. Lead singer
   b. The two background singers who accompany the lead singer with unison and/or passages in chordal fashion, singing either words of the text or vocables of vowel sounds
   c. The occurrence of a spoken or sung part by the bass singer incorporated together with or during pauses in the lead and background singer's phrases.

The song titled "Ain't No Woman (Like the One I've Got)" (1973) by The Four Tops illustrates the first style, as the background singers provide an accompaniment, in unison, to the lead singer's verse. Another example of this is heard in the song titled "Blue Moon" (1961) by The Marcels. In this selection, the background singers provide a harmonic accompaniment sung in a chordal fashion with text, as well as in a homorhythmic fashion applying the vocalizations "di" and "dip" against the lead singer's verse.

There are also instances in which the background singers will accompany the lead singer with a combination of sung and spoken vocalizations. For instance, the song "Young Blood" (1957) by The Coasters exhibits the vocalization "shoo," which is sung to a homophonic texture, and the spoken vocalization "who," performed as a medium-pitched shout.

The preceding musical selections, as examples of the first style, illustrate the common practice concerning unison and chordal background vocal accompaniment during the lead singer's "verse." It is also common to hear, as examples of the second style, a homorhythmic texture within the same song that is sung during the "chorus" and/or "introduction." The songs "Ain't No Woman (Like the One I've Got)" and "Young Blood" furnish examples of this style.[17] The illustrations below provide time lines for each musical example:[18]

Style	N/A	2	1	2	1	2	N/A	2	N/A	2
Section	Intro.	Chorus	Verse1	Chorus	Verse2	Chorus	Vnstr.	Vhorus	Instr.	Chorus
Measure	1–4	5–10	11–22	23–30	31–42	43–50	51–58	59–66	67–70	71

Song Navigator 14.4: Illustrating performance styles in the song "Ain't No Woman (Like the One I've Got)" (1973) by The Four Tops.

---

[17] The singing of the chorus as the introduction to a song is a common practice among most vocal groups (all types and gender combinations).

[18] The purpose of illustrating time lines of entire songs is to show the placement of music examples within an overall structure.

Style	1	2	1	2	1	1	2	2
Section	Verse1	Chorus	Verse2	Chorus	Bridge	Verse3	Chorus	Chorus
Measure	1–8	9–16	17–24	25–32	33–40	41–48	49–56	57–64

Song Navigator 14.5: Illustrating performance styles in the song "Young Blood" (1957) by The Coasters.

Another example of the second style can be heard in the song titled "If You Don't Know Me by Now" (1972) by Harold Melvin & The Bluenotes. This occurs as the singers perform a three-part homorhythmic texture during the chorus.[19]

The third style involves the performance of the principal melody of a particular section, sung by two or more lead singers who are accompanied by background singers. As heard in the song tilted "Oh, What a Night" (1956) by The Dells, the lead singer provides the melody, using texts. The second lead functions as a descant[20] (using the vowel sound in the word night) to the principal lead part. The tenor and baritone singers' parts sustain a two-part chordal accompaniment (with the vocalization "ooh" as well as text), while the bass singer furnishes (with the vocalization "do") an underlying *ostinato* passage.

The third and fourth styles can be heard in the song titled "Yakety Yak" (1958) by The Coasters. The third style is evident as more than one leader sings the principal melody (this occurs at the beginning of the song). Illustrating the fourth style, two members speak a brief passage using words of the title, while the bass singer speaks the response "Don't talk back."

Another example of the fourth style can be heard in the song "Oh, What a Night." This performance involves the presence of three distinctive parts: (1) lead singer; (2) three background singers accompanying the lead singer with a passage in chordal fashion, singing with the vocalization "ooh," as well as the text; and (3) the bass singer providing an *ostinato* passage (using the vocalization "do"), similar to the function of the bass guitarist.

The rhythmic character of doo-wop singing is performed in such as way that its intent is set on emulating the rhythmic propensities of a syncopated horn part (as heard in the background singers' part), and electric bass line (as heard in the bass singer's part). As the result of these practices, it becomes apparent that an instrumental accompaniment is not necessary in a doo-wop performative context. This is due to the fact that the aforementioned parts perform the principal elements of music: melody, harmony (including bass), and rhythm.

Even though male groups typified the doo-wop style of singing during the 1950s, there were some popular women's groups. Some of these groups and their songs include The Chordettes and their well-known songs "Mr. Sandman" (1954), "Born to Be with You" (1956), "Just Between You and Me" (1957), and "Lollipop" (1958); The Bobbettes, who recorded "Mr. Lee" (1957); and the Chantels with their song "Maybe" (1957). By the 1960s, some female groups began to incorporate other nuances in addition to those previously mentioned.[21] An increase in the number of vocal nuances utilized by female performers can be attributed to the enhancement of social, political, and economic conditions for women and minorities during the 1960s. Such conditions affected performances by groups such as The Crystals in their 1963 hit titled "Da Doo Ron Ron," and The Chiffons in their 1963 hit titled "He's So Fine." More prominent, percussive sounds of "do" and "lang" are evident in "He's So Fine"

---

[19] Some notes have more than one singer on a part. Due to the utilization of reverberation and over-dubbing recording techniques, it is difficult to ascertain specifically those notes that are, in fact, doubled.

[20] *Descant* is an upper voice that harmonizes with the lead singer's melody.

[21] Mixed-gender groups continue to utilize the same nuances as those heard in the previous decade.

by The Chiffons. This is the first decade during which a number of female African American groups recorded "Top 10" hits.[22]

Some mixed-gender groups that also sang in the doo-wop style, such as The Tune Weavers ("Happy, Happy Birthday Baby," 1957), The Platters ("My Prayer" and "You've Got the Magic Touch," both in 1956 and "Twilight Time" in 1958), and The Crests ("Sixteen Candles," 1958). Unlike their male contemporaries, these 1950s female performers did not utilize as many nuances. In fact, nuances were limited to the sounds of "ooh," "oh," "do," and "ah." Like women's groups of the 1960s, by the end of the decade mixed-gender groups such as The 5th Dimension and The Friends of Distinction were not subjected to the application of a limited number of vocal nuances as a prerequisite to attaining a popular hit among black and white audiences. In fact, popular recordings by groups such as The Platters (who recorded the most songs of all mixed-gender groups during the 1960s), The Orlons, The Sensations, Ruby & The Romantics, and Gladys Knight & The Pips all exhibited the application of numerous and varied vocal nuances.

In popular female groups during the 1950s, the lead singer and background singers often shared the performance of text, melody, and harmonic texture. The majority of female ensembles during the 1960s, however, began to discontinue the utilization of this practice in favor of the division of roles between the lead singer and background singers.[23] This was even more clearly defined as two of the decade's most popular female groups The Vandellas and The Supremes, became known as Martha Reeves & The Vandellas and Diana Ross & The Supremes, respectively. In retrospect, this was an attempt not only to show change with respect to performance practices but also to fulfill the dream and civil rights of women who wished to be viewed as individuals possessing the same capabilities and aspirations as men. What is most interesting is that while the previously mentioned movements of the 1960s (such as The Civil Rights Movement and the feminist movement) were instrumental in establishing legislature for social change, music was a major catalyst by which many became socially conscious of such changes.

An indication of change, while initially apparent with the enactment and subsequent implementation of legislative decisions, was evident on a more subliminal (and in some ways more effective) level by being intrinsically woven into the display of gender roles through changes in the performances of the lead and background singers' parts. This was exemplified during the 1960s by the first appearance of popular mixed-gender "duets."[24] Indeed, both members of the most popular mixed-gender duet during this decade-Marvin Gaye and Tammi Terrell-possess a principal role in the performance of their songs.[25] This is displayed in the division of verses in their songs, since each member performs an approximately equal number of verses. In contrast, the principal role of female members in mixed-gender groups during the 1950s had been as background singers.

During the 1960s, some of the more popular mixed-gender groups were The Orlons (three women and one man), The Sensations (one woman and three men), Ruby & The Romantics (one woman and four men), Gladys Knight & The Pips (one woman and three men), The 5th Dimension (two women and three men), and The Friends of Distinction (two women and two men). The lead and the

[22] The doo-wop style of singing was a practice that was mainly performed by African American male ensembles during the 1950s. The European American group named The Chordettes recorded the majority of popular hits among female ensembles.

[23] Motown Records was leading the way with innovative practices during this time. The Supremes and The Vandellas were two favored Motown groups.

[24] Within these groups, attention should not only be paid to the role of the lead and background singers' parts, but also to the specific gender assignment.

[25] It is noteworthy to mention that the female vocalist of the duo Peaches and Herb, in their 1957 hit titled "Close Your Eyes" exhibited a subordinate role to the male.

background singers' parts became more interchangeable with the 5th Dimension and The Friends of Distinction. That is to say, there was a lesser distinction between who sang lead and who provided the background accompaniment. Unlike these two mixed-gender ensembles, most male groups during the 1960s maintained a distinct division between their lead and background singers' parts.[26]

In conclusion, by the mid. 1960s, salient characteristics representative of the three types of rhythm & blues were unrecognizable in what was then being called rhythm & blues. The boogie-woogie/shuffle rhythm that was so prevalent during the 1940s and 50s was practically nonexistent during the 1960s. The distinct stylizations of doo-wop that exhibited a lead singer against two or three voices singing homorhythmically and an *ostinato* bass singer were outdated by the mid-1960s. Some characteristics of the urban type of rhythm & blues such as the quintessential backbeat, vocal emphasis, and folk-like lyrics would be, for some, the only connection between rhythm & blues of the 1940s and that of the 1960s. But for many, either the title of Nelson George's *The Death of Rhythm and Blues* or the descriptor "evolving" expressed the status (or lack thereof) of rhythm & blues during the 1960s.

---

[26] The exception to this is the Motown group The Temptations–worth mentioning due to their popularity during the 1960s–70s as well as the fact that their practices influenced groups in later decades. The Motown Record Company was leading the way in implementing innovative approaches to performing music, including The Temptations' different ways of distributing the lead and background parts during the 1960s. This is evidenced by the fact that more than one member sang lead within several of their "Top 10" songs. For example, the songs "You're My Everything" (1967) and "Cloud Nine" (1968) each featured two soloists. Even though the same two or three members of this quintet alternated in the singing of a lead part, the overall performance was distinctly different than that of groups that featured the same lead singer in all their songs.

CHAPTER FIFTEEN

ROCK & ROLL

ROCK & ROLL

When Alan Freed, a disc jockey at WLAC radio in Cleveland, began exclaiming "Let's all rock and roll!" on live broadcasts in 1951, a large number of people were well aware of the type of music this term represented. And certainly, once Ike Turner's piano playing was juxtaposed to Jackie Brenston's screaming saxophone sounds in the 1951 recording of "Rocket 88," rock & roll was here to stay.

Recognized as a style of music that was reflective of the emergent youth culture, rock & roll began to surface among a group of people who until now had no economic staying power. Shrouded in the streams of democracy, youth now had something to call their own. Rock & roll helped to fuel the inherent social behaviors of young people–curiosity and the need for individuality. As we begin to examine the musical content of rock & roll, it should be noted that it was more than music; it also functioned as a medium of expression for young people who had previously had no voice. When contemplating the typical life situations among youth of the 1950s, visions of high school proms, cheerleaders, and athletes come to mind. Fittingly, for the first time in American history a significant number of songs' lyrical contents catered to these very youth experiences. At the same time, in an effort to appeal to the parents, since basically they were still the major source of income for the music industry, the media presented images of typical suburban white families through programs such as *Dennis the Menace, Leave It to Beaver The Adventures of Ozzie & Harriet*, and *My Three Sons*. The way of life portrayed on these shows was the antithesis of what was purported to be the image of rock & roll lifestyles. Some early rock & roll performers who represented the raw, aggressive nature inherent in the music included Little Richard, Chuck Berry, Elvis Presley, Fats Domino, Bo Diddley, Bill Haley & The Comets, and Jerry Lee Lewis.

As rock & roll began to spread throughout the country and abroad, the machine was set in motion. No longer could the music industry, parents, and the media ignore the vibrancy and marketability of teenagers' musical tastes. Some took the time to understand the contents of the music, but others expressed only disgust for this music since it would, in their minds, greatly contribute to the decline in social values and morals. One person accused of exacerbating this moral decline was Sam Phillips, owner and operator of the Memphis Recording Service in Tennessee. Opening his recording service in 1944, Mr. Phillips began recording favored blues artists Howlin' Wolf, B. B. King, and even Rufus Thomas. Experiencing some success, by 1951 he established his own record label, the Sun Record Company. His most significant recording contract was with the young Elvis Presley (1935–1977).

Elvis Presley. © NBC/Photofest

On a break from working as a truck driver in the area, Elvis secured the services of Sam Phillips to record a couple of selections as a gift for his [Elvis's] mother. In the summer of 1953, Elvis recorded his first two songs, "My Happiness" and "That's When Your Heartaches Begin." Recognizing the potential talent of Elvis Presley, including the possibility of his making black music acceptable for white America, Mr. Phillips invited Presley back for an audition, and in January, 1954, brought in some studio musicians to work out some songs with him. After hearing Presley and the band rehearse several songs such as Arthur Crudup's recording titled "That's Alright Mama," Phillips determined that this artist could perhaps accomplish the task of disseminating what he [Phillips] deemed as beautiful music—namely, black music or what was commonly referred to as "race music"—to mainstream American culture. Within a little over a year, Presley had recorded a number of country and blues songs under the auspices of the Sun Record Company. Some of these included "Blue Moon of Kentucky," and the urban blues/rhythm & blues songs "Good Rockin' Tonight," "Milkcow Blues," and "That's Alright Mama." In 1954 the latter song was the one that sparked interest in Sam Phillips, and a few days later it was being played on the radio. The following Song Navigator shows the structure of "That's Alright Mama" (originally recorded in 1946 by Arthur "big boy" Crudup, an African American).

TIME	SECTION	INSTRUMENTATION/COMMENTS
		Instrumentation: Voice (Elvis Presley Rogers); guitar, second guitar, bass, drums
		Form: 9-measure sections
00:00	Introduction	Instruments only
00:06	Verse 1	Lyrics begin with the words the song title
00:27	Verse 2	Lyrics begin with the words "Mama she done told . . .
00:47	Solo	Guitar solo accompanied by the band
01:10	Verse 3	Lyrics begin with the words "I'm leaving town . . .
01:30	Improvisational	Singer begins to scat sing, and sings the words to the title
01:49	Coda	Begins to fade out

Song Navigator 15.1: "That's Alright Mama" by Elvis Presley from the album *Elvis' Golden Records* (1958, RCA Records Label)

Without a doubt, Presley embodied the American spirit, as his music, performances, and attitude resounded with freedom, democracy, and the American way. Even after his untimely death, Presley's music continues to be marketed to each new generation with the same vitality that earned him the title "King of Rock & Roll."

However, there is still debate as to whether Elvis Presley is the true "king of rock & roll." Some believe the crown's rightful owner should be Little Richard, while others believe the crown should be worn by Chuck Berry.

Little Richard. © Paramount Pictures/Photofest

For some, this has created a forum for discussing racism by addressing the inequalities of how white and black performers were marketed to mainstream culture during the 1950s. It is true that black artists received extremely limited radio, television and general market promotions compared to their white counterparts, thereby making it literally impossible for them to be considered equal contenders in receiving accolades similar to those received by their white contemporaries. While the argument may be plausible, it comes down to the use of the word *king*. A king is one who is often favored by his or her subjects and/or a person who is widely known. In this view, I believe there is no argument that Presley is the true king. While this debate will continue for years to come, one cannot ignore Presley's musical contributions and the sheer magnitude of his recordings and performances, which made him stand above all others.

The second important step of Presley's career following his nurturing by Sam Phillips was his introduction to Colonel Tom Parker. In 1954, Presley performed on a radio show in Shreveport, Louisiana called "Louisiana Hayride." As a result of this performance, he was signed to a one-year contract, during which his popularity grew among young country fans. It was here that he met Colonel Tom Parker. Seeing the vitality of Presley, Parker secured a managerial contract with his and Hank Snow's artists' management company, Hank Snow Attractions. In the final months of 1955, Parker secured a more mainstream and powerful contract for Presley at the preeminent record label, Radio Corporation of America (RCA). Presley's career skyrocketed following Parker's perseverance in getting television exposure for him. Presley appeared on the Dorsey Show on CBS, the Milton Berle Show on NBC, and then the Steve Allen Show for ABC. At the time, the Ed Sullivan Show on CBS received the highest TV ratings with regard to the number of viewers. Sullivan had a conservative audience that was less prone to viewing artists who appealed to youth, especially those who gyrated on stage. When Presley appeared on The Steve Allen Show on July 1, 1956, the program earned a higher viewer rating than the Ed Sullivan Show. Sullivan had to concede Presley's popularity and booked him for an appearance. That September, Presley appeared on the Ed Sullivan Show; CBS received over 80% of the viewing public–over 50 million viewers. Colonel Parker believed that Presley's music material and overall demeanor needed to be curtailed in order to reach conservative audiences who were prone to spend their discretionary income on recorded music. Presley's music did indeed evolve, as his cover versions of black songs and the less-than-desirable honky-tonk and rockabilly sound was kept to a minimum.

Musically, rock & roll was initially nothing more than rhythm & blues in "whiteface,"[1] as exemplified by many white performers singing rhythm & blues songs under the pseudonym of rock & roll. During this time of social, cultural, and geographical segregation (principally) between blacks and whites, the term *rhythm & blues* came to be associated exclusively with black people. Mainstream America–particularly white parents–overtly expressed their disapproval of black people's music permeating the minds and hearts, if you will, of young white teens. But by the late 1940s, interest in rhythm & blues or similar sounding music had already pervaded a large portion of the youth culture– of both black and white teens. To satisfy both parents and youth, record labels seized upon the term *rock & roll* as a marketing strategy to dilute the negative connotation of black music that existed in the minds of many people. Even though Elvis Presley's 1956 version of Willie Mae "Big Mama" Thornton's "Hound Dog" in 1953, or Bill Haley and The Comets' 1956 version of Big Joe Turner's original recording of "Shake, Rattle, and Roll" in 1954 were rhythm & blues songs, the identification of these as rock & roll songs was applied to make an attempt to disassociate them from black-sounding music, with great success. One could argue that Elvis Presley, Jerry Lee Lewis, and Bill Haley, for example,

---

[1] Unlike blackface, where whites would perform antics and wear black makeup to pejoratively imitate black slave life, white performers would still imitate blacks, but without the makeup, and, in this case, out of admiration.

all could be categorized as rockabilly performers as their music employs a combination of musical elements from hillbilly and rhythm & blues. The fact remains, however, that the first successful songs of these and other related artists were not hillbilly-inspired music, but rather rhythm & blues. Having said this, instrumental/vocal similarities between rhythm & blues and rock & roll included the typical three- or four-piece rhythm section (guitar, bass, and drums; or piano, guitar, bass and drums) and a singer who generally played the guitar or piano. Musical similarities included the AAB song form, 12-bar blues progression, and lyrical themes that specifically referenced dancing[2] and the rhetoric of love relationships geared more toward youth. When white artists covered a black artist's song, the instrumentation often remained the same. For example, Bill Haley & The Comets cover[3] of Big Joe Turner's "Shake, Rattle, and Roll" included the same instruments. Also, in Elvis Presley's cover version of Big Mama Thornton's recording of "Hound Dog," both the same instrumentation as well as the guitar solo were present. As demonstrated in the following Song Navigators, there are distinct differences between the two versions.

COMMENTS (ORIGINAL VERSION BY ARTHUR CRUDUP)

Instrumentation: voice, saxophones, piano, guitar, bass, drums

Tempo is 176 BPM

The song begins with a four-measure introduction (featuring the piano) followed by V1, V2, V3, chorus, tenor saxophone solo, V4, chorus, V5, chorus

When the chorus is sung (lead singer only) it is sung in a syncopated manner

The saxophones respond to the singer's call

Lyrics are sexually explicit, as they refer to the physical maturity of a young woman

Consistent and pronounced backbeat, which is played by the snare drum and handclaps

Song Navigator 15.2: "Shake, Rattle and Roll" (1954) by Big Joe Turner from the album *Big Joe Turner: Greatest Hits* (2005, RCA Rhino Atlantic)

As the Song Navigators above demonstrate, despite the contention that rock & roll is synonymous with rhythm & blues, there are a few differences between them. In addition, white musicians tended to favor the guitar, while black musicians placed more emphasis on the piano and saxophone. These tendencies were derived from previous styles associated with each category (i.e., white and black). For example, country music, a style generally perceived as being performed by whites, regularly included the guitar as its focus; whereas jazz, a style that was recognized as a black creation, generally featured saxophone, trumpet, and piano solos. Thus, the major white influence on rock & roll was the ubiquitous presence of the guitar, while the piano appeared more frequently than other instruments among black performers of rock & roll (but the black musicians were labeled as performers of rhythm & blues). Another difference lies in the approach to tempo. Black performers regularly performed songs in a moderate tempo, while white performers played songs moderately fast.[4]

---

[2] Hillbilly music was meant for dancing, even though the song's lyrical content did not reference specifically dancing.

[3] The meaning of *cover* during this time implied that a white artist would record a version of a song by a black artist that had already achieved popularity among black audiences.

[4] This still exists today, as the tempo in styles such as r & b/hip-hop and rap are performed moderately slow to moderate, while typically white styles such as post-punk, rock, and alternative are performed moderately fast to fast.

Bill Haley. © Columbia/Photofest

COMMENTS (COVER VERSION BY BILL HALEY & THE COMETS)

Instrumentation: voice, background singers, saxophones, piano, guitar, bass, drums

Tempo is 192 BPM

The song begins with a four-measure introduction (featuring saxophones), followed by V1, chorus, V2, chorus, instrumental by saxophones, V3, V4, chorus

The chorus is sung by both the lead singer and background singers; when this occurs, there is less syncopation as words are sung "on the beat"

The saxophones respond to the singer's call

Lyrics refer to a particular woman's failure as a mate; lyrics are not sexually explicit like the original vesion

Consistent and pronounced backbeat, which is played by the snare drum and handclaps

The rhythm is more of the shuffle style, as evidenced by the piano playing on the upbeats

Song Navigator 15.3: "Shake, Rattle and Roll" (1956) by Bill Haley & The Comets from the album *The Best of Bill Haley & The Comets Joe Turner: The Miliillenum Collection* (1999, Geffen)

Artists such as Fats Domino (born 1928), Chuck Berry (born 1926), and Bo Diddley (born 1928) helped to bridge the gap between rhythm & blues and rock & roll by presenting atypical performances of rhythm & blues. Fats Domino's music, in addition to using typical rhythm & blues structures and

COMMENTS (ORIGINAL VERSION BY WILLIE MAE THORNTON)

Instrumentation: voice, guitar, piano, bass, drums, hound dog sounds

The tempo is 176

The form is chorus, V1, chorus, guitar solo (plays the 12-bar blues progression three times through), V2, chorus

Guitar solo with the singer speaking in a recitative manner during the guitar solo

Lyrics clearly refer to the singer's disgust with a person (presumably a man, although she never mentions a gender)

Consistent and pronounced backbeat, which is emphasized by hand claps

The bass player's rhythm in combination with the drummer's rhythm (played on the tom-toms) produces a Latin-type rhythm

Song Navigator 15.4: "Hound Dog" (1953) by Willie Mae Thornton from the album *Elvis And the Originals* (2010, Ideal Music)

COMMENTS (COVER VERSION BY ELVIS PRESLEY)

Instrumentation: voice, background singers, saxophones, piano, guitar, bass, drums

The tempo is 192

The form is chorus, V1, chorus, guitar solo (plays once through the 12-bar blues progression), V2, guitar solo (same as before), V2 (same lyrics as previous verse), chorus.

Background singers sustain harmony on the vowel "ah" during the guitar solo (both times)

Lyrics refer to the singer's disgust with a dog and not a person (although it could be interpreted as such)

Consistent and pronounced backbeat, which is played by the snare drum; hand claps do not occur on the back beat but rather in the same rhythm as the bass player's

The bass player's rhythm combined with the drummer's rhythm (played on the tom-toms) produces a Latin-type rhythm

Song Navigator 15.5: "Hound Dog" (1956) by Elvis Presley from the album *Elvis And the Originals* (2010, Ideal Music)

Chuck Berry = unlike typical Black

progressions, also incorporated nonconforming arrangements. His 1955 song titled "Ain't That a Shame" departs from the I – IV – V 12-bar blues progression and the three-line stanza format–distinct features that are characteristic of rhythm & blues. He also displayed a less-intimidating personality than, for example, Little Richard. Chuck Berry, unlike many other black performers of his day, was not nurtured by the likes of Muddy Waters or Elmo James, but rather by artists such as Frank Sinatra and Pat Boone. Indeed, Berry grew up in a white neighborhood, where his father owned a restaurant. It is not that Chuck Berry purposely or consciously made an attempt to sound similar to Sinatra and/ or Boone; these and similar artists were simply his early influences. Bo Diddley was another black

Chuck Berry. © Photofest

artist who appeared to mainstream culture. This is supported by the fact that he was the first African American to appear on the conservative Ed Sullivan Show (1955). Hits during the mid-1950s such as "Bo Diddley," "Hey Bo Diddley," and "Who Do You Love" received good reviews from both black and white audiences. The syncopated rhythms appealed to blacks, while the danceable and less aggressive lyrics appealed to whites.

Elvis Presley's raw and eccentric energy was too aggressive for country music fans, particularly those of the conservative Grand Ole Opry; and among blacks, his vocals were recognizably not black. Caught between sociocultural and parental attitudes, by 1955 the initial optimistic view of Presley's career had reached a plateau (i.e., elevated but flat on the top and lacking the resources to promote nationally). Recognizing this and seizing upon the RCA record label's interest in Presley's contract, Sam Phillips opted (without regret) to sell Presley's contract to RCA in late 1955 for approximately $35,000. Under the tutelage of Colonel Tom Parker, the singer's image was purposely commercialized in an effort to appeal to mainstream America. Although he was still influenced by and recording country and blues songs, the commercialized, "watered-down" versions of Presley's songs were less threatening to white parents and country audiences. Moreover, since RCA marketed Presley's music to the much larger white market, there was no concern about black audience reactions.

Following the release of Presley from Sun Record Company, Sam Phillips discovered another eccentric artist, the piano player Jerry Lee Lewis.

Like Presley, Lewis had been brought up listening to southern gospel music, blues, rhythm & blues, honky-tonk, and rockabilly stylizations. Despite the fact that he was pressured from an early age to become a minister, the secular styles of the day were pulling him in another direction. After securing a recording contract with the Sun Record Label, Lewis immediately gained significant success with Big

Jerry Lee Lewis. © Photofest

Maybelle's 1955 recording titled "Whole Lotta Shakin' Goin' On" in 1957. One of the greatest distinctions between Jerry Lee Lewis and other white artists at the time was the fact that his presentation was not watered down to suit mainstream America. Footage of him performing this song shows him gesturing to an imaginary woman to shake her body for his pleasure. Between 1957 and 1958, experienced much success with songs such as "Great Balls of Fire," "Breathless," and "High School Confidential." In 1958, his career came to a screeching halt after it was discovered that he had married his young teenage cousin while still married to his second wife. Although he continued to record in the 1960s, the rock & roll craze had subsided as artists such as Paul Anka, Fabian, Connie Francis, Pat Boone, and The Four Seasons were promoted to fight against the socially unacceptable, immoral behavior that had overtaken a number of rock & roll performers. By the late 1960s and into the 1970s, Jerry Lee Lewis returned to his roots in country music and recorded a number of songs that reached the top of the charts. Some of those included "To Make Love Sweeter for You," "Would You Take Another Chance on Me," "Chantilly Lace," and "Me and Bobby McGee."

Other artists marketed as rock & roll stars with country roots and a flair for incorporating blues/rhythm & blues characteristics in their performances included Eddie Cochran (1938–60), Buddy Holly

(1936–59), Carl Perkins (born 1932), and Gene Vincent (1935–71). Some of their music activities are outlined below.

Eddie Cochran (singer and guitarist)
"Milk Cow Blues" (1957)
"Summertime Blues" (1958)
"Teenage Heaven" (1958)
"Sittin' in the Balcony" (1958)
"C'mon Everybody" (1958)
The Girl Can't Help It (1956 film)
Untamed Youth (1957 film)
Go Johnny Go (1958 film)
Buddy Holly (singer and guitarist)
"That'll Be the Day" (1957)
"Oh Boy" (1957)
"Not Fade Away" (1957)
"Peggy Sue" (1957)
"Every Day" (1957)
Carl Perkins (singer and guitarist)
"Movie Mag" (1955)
"Let the Juke Box Keep Playing" (1955)
"Blue Suede Shoes" (1956)
"Pink Pedal Pushers" (ca. 1958)
"Pointed Toe Shoes" (ca. 1958)
"Country Boy's Dream" (ca. 1966)
"Shine, Shine" (ca. 1966)
Gene Vincent
"Woman Love" (1956)
"Be-Bop-A-Lula" (1956)
"Dance to the Bop" (1958)

As previously stated, the rock & roll craze began to diminish by the late 1950s. Little Richard walked off stage one night and decided to dedicate his life to God. Elvis Presley was in the army from 1958 to 1960. The untimely early deaths of Eddie Cochran, Buddy Holly, and Gene Vincent dampened the momentum of rock & roll. In addition, Chuck Berry spent two years in jail on a conviction that involved a teenage girl's employment at his nightclub in Indiana, and of course, Jerry Lee Lewis's marriage to his teenage cousin left a negative stain on youth-inspired music.

POP-STYLE MUSIC

Rock & roll music during the 1950s produced feelings of repugnance in many American parents. Lyrics with sexual innuendos, songs that regularly featured drums,[5] and musical tendencies that some believed precipitated inappropriate behavior all suggested that rock & roll was contributing to the decline of American youth. Moreover, the fact that a growing number of youth, particularly white teens, were

---

[5] I once had a conversation with a person of about 50 years of age who remarked, "Music went to hell when drums entered this country."

buying into the sounds of rhythm & blues/black music or "jungle music" (as it was referred to by many white Americans) caused great concern for many parents regarding the plight of American values and social mores. To satisfy parental concerns as well as continue to market music to an ever-growing youth culture, music executives found it advantageous to produce less-threatening music, namely pop-style rock.

Pop-style rock is regarded as music that tends to focus more on the artists' visual appeal and/or songs with lyrics that are less threatening to mainstream society. This music does not contain lyrics that are politically charged, promiscuous, or negatively aggressive toward parents. Instead, it contains lyrics about innocuous subjects such as young-love relationships ("Be My Baby," 1963 by The Ronettes), surfing ("Surfin' Safari," 1962 by The Beach Boys), and dancing ("The Twist," 1961 by Chubby Checker).

Pop-style rock–a term used in the 1950s/60s–generally referred to recordings with mass appeal. During this time and even today, a pop-style artist's presentation is inoffensive, by mainstream standards, to any gender, age, ethnicity, or political perspective. As a result, the performance is often watered-down, sugar-coated, and less exceptional musically. Watering-down or sugar coating songs was strictly a market-enthused scheme, as it generally involved the editing of lyrics and the performance of less African American-inspired vocal nuances. Specific styles and strategies that were used to market pop-style rock included advocating surf music and publicizing the terms *pop* and *teen idol*.

POP-STYLE ROCK: POP

During the late 1950s and early 1960s, the word *pop* (referring to "popular") was used to identify music that consisted of soundscapes that required a minimal understanding of music and that featured and/or less thought-provoking lyrics. The music was often very tuneful. Indeed, those music producers and executives pursuing industry success regularly favored recordings that were singable (easy to sing). Such appeal is achieved by composing songs that are melodically and rhythmically easy to learn and then sing or hum. An example of singability is The Beach Boy's recording titled "Surfer Girl" (1963). During the chorus, the melody is sung on each count of the measure. Even though the melody is vocally harmonized throughout the chorus, the melody predominates since it is the highest note of the homophonic texture. Whereas the melody in the chorus to "Surfer Girl" is sung with quarter notes, even subdivisions of the quarter note rhythm (or eighth notes), which are easily sensed, are used in the song titled "Venus" by Frankie Avalon. In this case, each verse begins with four eighth notes followed by a held note. Another example is the title song of the 1961 film *Where the Boys Are*.

The original recording by Connie Francis employs a tuneful melody consisting of a combination of non-syncopated long and short notes.

Performers in this category and some of their popular songs are listed in the table below.

ARTIST	POPULAR SONG
Sonny and Cher	"I Got You Babe"
The Association	"Cherish"
The Association	"Windy"
Grass Roots	"Midnight Confessions"
The Foundations	"Build Me Up Buttercup"
The Box Tops	"The Letter"

Connie Francis. © MGM/Photofest

POP-STYLE ROCK: TEEN IDOLS

In general, *pop* songs of this type were recorded by European American youths who were marketed as young people who shared similar ideals and morals as parents of young teens. The idea was to set an example of the wholesomeness and moral integrity that parents felt should be embraced by America's youth. Some specific artists who were naturally suited to and thus were promoted as an integral part of this endeavor included Pat Boone, Connie Francis, Frankie Avalon, Annette Funicello, Fabian, Ricky Nelson, and Brenda Lee. These performers were often labeled "teen idols."

At the outset, an attempt was made to produce young artists singing songs that had previously been recorded by pre-1950s crooners and jazz artists such as Bing Crosby, Frank Sinatra, Ella Fitzgerald, Mildred Bailey, and Nat King Cole. In 1960, Connie Francis recorded "Who's Sorry Now" (written ca. 1923), which had previously been recorded by singers Ella Fitzgerald and Nat King Cole and played by big bands such as those led by Benny Goodman and Benny Carter. Another example was Fabiano Bonaparte's (popularly known as Fabian) recording of the old standard "It Had to Be." Previously recorded by noted earlier artists such as Billie Holiday, George Shearing, Doris Day, Artie Shaw, and Tony Bennett, Fabian's recording was intended to be a more contemporary version sung at least twice as fast as the original. The same strategy was employed in Ricky Nelson's recording of "Am I Blue," Which had been sung by early artists such as Billie Holiday, Betty Carter, and Nat King Cole. Nelson's version is faster with a typical rock & roll instrumentation: guitar, bass, drums, and voice.

When producing prerecorded songs failed to create the sales generated by record executives, the next (extremely successful) tactic involved the production of songs recorded by young singers singing about topics like love in a youthful, naive, and innocent manner. A good example was Frankie Avalon, whose songs were intended to elicit youthful love sensations without implying promiscuity. Some examples included "Diana," "Bobby Sox to Stockings," and his staple song "Venus." The most suggestive song among Avalon's repertoire was titled "Teacher's Pet," in which he expressed the desire to be with a certain person for reasons other than to be the "teacher's pet." With her recording titled "Where the Boys Are," Connie Francis came to represent the ultimate example of society's portrayal of women as possessing the innate desire for wanting nothing more in life than male friendship and eventual marital commitment. An all-too-common theme before and slightly after the WWII, women, through mainstream songs, were portrayed as individuals who had little to say about their status other than speaking of their love. Ms. Francis' recording titled "Stupid Cupid" expresses, among other messages, that even when a woman does not desire a love relationship, "stupid Cupid" knows better. A closer examination of the lyrics reveals that the woman (Ms. Francis) does not mind the sensations experienced by the particular man in question. While the theme of the wonderful sensations of love was certainly the norm among teen idol recordings, there were a few recordings about the pain of love. One example was the song "Lipstick on Your Collar" by Ms. Francis. Discovering a red lipstick stain on her boyfriend's collar, she divulges that

Pat Boone. © Photofest

her lipstick is pink while her best friend's is red. Another example is Ms. Francis's song titled "Frankie," which deals with the pain of a former love who has found another. The idea of youthful romance is stretched to the limit of appropriateness in Fabian's hit song titled "Tiger." The general message revolves around his tiger-like proclivities when near a particular young woman. Nevertheless, the song was his biggest hit; much more so than his more innocuous hit titled "Turn Me Loose."

Pat Boone was a singer who captured the hearts of both young European Americans as well as their parents and who was highly marketed to sneer at the purportedly raw, aggressive, falsely advertised, morally destructive rock & roll music. Born Charles Eugene Patrick Boone in 1934, his singing stylizations with respect to rock & roll of the 1950s and 60s were marketed as rock & roll made palatable to conservative mainstream American society. Several of his many famous recordings included "Ain't That a Shame," which was originally recorded by the rhythm & blues artist Fats Domino; and Little Richard's "Tutti Frutti." By and large, however, Boone's recordings were reminiscent of the vocal stylizations of his idol, Bing Crosby–a popular crooner of the 1930s and 40s. Some recordings similar to Crosby's style included "I'll Be Home," "April Love," "Don't Forbid Me," and "Love Letters in the Sand."

Dick Dale. © Photofest

POP-STYLE ROCK: SURF SOUND

During the 1950s and 60s, surfing became a favorite pastime not only for youth residing in beach cities, but for inland dwellers as well. A dedicated surfer who found solace riding the waves and playing music for his peers sparked a movement that gave rise to surf rock.

Known as the "King of Surf Guitar," Dick Dale, born Richard Monsour to a Lebanese father and Polish mother, helped to shape a sub-culture that lived for the almighty wave and music that catered to its constituents. Dale's use of reverb, sliding, and his guitar picking style led a revolution that inspired others to follow. Dale's song titled "King of the Surf Guitar" provides a good example of his playing style, lyrical content (including the identification of specific California cities), and singers paying homage to his title. Like many other artists of other styles, Dale used the 12-bar blues progression as the basic format for his songs "Surf Beat" and "Let's Go Trippin'." Using his staple guitar sound, Dale played in a fast tempo with a rock beat the 12-bar blues progression, creating an interesting "surf beat."

Popular surf music, or for that matter most popular songs geared toward the youth culture of the 1950s and 60s, usually featured vocals. However, The Ventures inspired record producers and musicians alike to take stock in the notion of producing instrumental pieces for popular consumption. Still considered the number-one group in rock history to have the most instrumental hits, The Ventures' success began with their self-produced hit titled "Walk, Don't Run." Other popular songs that followed include the 12-bar blues progression-based songs titled "Yellow Jacket" and "Twisted," plus other songs such as "No Trespassing," "Perfidia," and "Driving Guitars (Ventures Twist)." Though The Ventures spread the surf sound worldwide, their popularity during the 1960s paled in comparison to that of The Beach Boys.

The Beach Boys. © Photofest

Formed in Hawthorn, California in the early 1960s, the group primarily consisted of family members: Brian Wilson, Carl Wilson, Dennis Wilson, Mike Love, and their friend Alan Jardine. With Brian Wilson as the group's main music producer, The Beach Boys created a number of popular songs that continue to appeal to today's youth. One appealing aspect is their radio-friendly lyrics encapsulated by tuneful melodies and close harmonies. Some of these include "Wouldn't It Be Nice," "Good Vibrations," "Surfin' USA," "California Girls," and "Surfer Girl." The latter song consists mainly of a harmonized melody in four parts that moves along in a melodious manner. Historically, The Beach Boys' songs provided a tapestry of American society. It told listeners, whether nationally or internationally, about "California Girls" and it described cars such as "Fun, Fun, Fun." The teen surfing craze in America was immortalized by songs such as "Surfin' USA," "Surfer Girl," and "Surfin' Safari."

Lyrics were such an important aspect of The Beach Boys' song productions that by 1966, nearly five years after their formation, they made history by recording rock music's first thematic album. Titled *Pet Sounds*, the songs are thematically linked by romantic lyrics. With the exception of instrumental tracks six and twelve, "Let's Go Away for a While" and the title track "Pet Sounds," respectively, all songs exhibit typical themes of shared love. For instance, topics can be assumed by the title of the first five tracks: "Wouldn't It Be nice," "You Still Believe in Me," "That's Not Me," "Don't Talk (Put Your Head on My Shoulder)," and "I'm Waiting for the Day."

In closing, the pop-style rock scene of the 1960s was short-lived, as groups from Britain such as The Beatles, The Rolling Stones, The Yardbirds, The Kinks, Gerry and The Pacemakers, The Animals, Cream, Herman's Hermits, and Freddie and The Dreamers were slowly invading America with their cross-Atlantic approach to rock & roll–a style drawn out of the American spirit.

CHAPTER SIXTEEN

A REVITALIZATION OF AMERICAN MUSIC: THE BRITISH INVASION; 1960s REVIVAL MUSIC (FOLK, BLUES, AND COUNTRY); AND PSYCHEDELIC MUSIC

INTRODUCTION

In the 1960s America experienced a revitalization of its own music creations from interests abroad and from concerns of civil liberties among those at home. Indeed, music groups from abroad such as The Beatles and The Rolling Stones were performing their versions of American-inspired styles such as blues, country, rhythm & blues, and rock & roll. The time was also ripe for legislation regarding the civil rights of all Americans. These concerns were the wellspring from which folk singers drew their inspiration for performances that centered on the well-being of the common person. Existentialism, as sung about by folk singers, inspired musicians to experiment with their own ideas of music and its relationship to their lives. Cues for what became known as "psychedelic rock," existentialism, surrealism, and other aspects of social behavior greatly affected how musicians approached composition and performance. In a nutshell, the invasion of music groups from Britain, folk styles (including blues and country), and psychedelic rock forever changed the music scene in America, underscoring the spirit of American individuality, acceptance, tolerance, and open-mindedness.

BRITISH INVASION

While youth-inspired American music (particularly African American styles) was gaining ground during the 1960s, some music executives began looking at the music scene across the Atlantic. The intention was to satisfy those European American parents who were disgruntled about the effect that the American youth music scene was having on their teenagers. These parents looked to what the "mother" country had to offer as a substitute for, in their view, the deplorable state of American music. This and other circumstances paved the way for many music groups from Europe, particularly Britain, during the 1960s. Regarded as "the British Invasion," some of the new arrivals included The Beatles, The Who, Gerry and The Pacemakers, The Searchers, and The Rolling Stones. Capitalizing on America's fascination with Western European culture, European groups challenged the American spirit's creation–rock & roll–with their own flavor of youth culture music. Ironically, most of these groups were inspired by American popular performers of the 1950s like Chuck Berry, Buddy Holly, Little Richard, Bill Haley, and Muddy Waters, and sold cover versions of these artists throughout Europe and America. Furthermore, as European groups recorded more and more songs by American artists, their overall performance practices became progressively more Americanized. In effect, Americans were being sold what they had already created. Nevertheless, many Americans were charmed by the fact that these performers were from their motherland–the continent of their ancestors. Many American performers were concerned that The Beatles and other European groups would saturate the market of youth culture music. Performers such as Jerry Lee Lewis, The Shirelles, The Beach Boys, and Ben E. King were all anxious about their musical careers once The Beatles had landed.

Regarding groups from Europe prior to their invasion of America, there were three areas in England where youth-culture music was flourished: London, Liverpool, and Manchester. Liverpool groups included The Beatles and Gerry and The Pacemakers; The Rolling Stones originated in London; and Herman's Hermit's and Freddie and The Dreamers hailed from Manchester. (The Rolling Stones are discussed in detail in the section on blues revival groups from Britain.) London was where trend-setting styles emerged, including fashion and an inerest in American blues and country music. Similar to American youth subcultures in the 1950s like the beatniks in New York,[1] London gave rise to the mods and rockers. With respect to musical tastes, the more trendy Mods favored the current styles of the day such as Motown and jazz (bebop and cool), while the Rockers cheered the older groups that played 1950s rock & roll-type music such as Buddy Holly, Little Richard, and Chuck Berry.

In addition to American music, British youths in the 1950s and early 60s were listening to their own breed of folk music called "skiffle," which featured voice, guitar, bass, drums, and homemade instruments such as the washboard and washtub bass. Lonnie Donegan (born Anthony Jones Donegan in Glasgow, Scotland) is considered to be the earliest influential skiffle musician. The song titled "Does Your Chewing Gum Lose Its Flavor on the Bedpost Overnight" was an American favorite. Combining elements of blues, jazz (particularly New Orleans jazz), and dance-influenced rhythms, Donegan helped to create a style of music that became the bedrock for many groups such as Gerry and The Pacemakers, The Searchers, The Animals, and The Beatles–all of whom went on to become popular in America.

In 1962, prior to arriving in America, The Beatles (Paul McCartney, John Lennon, George Harrison, and Ringo Starr) recorded "Love Me Do" and "PS. I Love You," igniting their career in London, and leading to the album *Please Please Me* in 1963. By the following year, The Beatles were the craze throughout Western Europe. Looking to enter the American market–where most European groups had failed–in 1964 their producer George Martin produced a song written by Paul McCartney and John Lennon titled "I Want to Hold You Hand." Attempts were made in 1963 to gain a foothold with the American audience, first with Vee Jay Records, and then with Swan label, but these failed. Even getting an airing of their song on *American Bandstand* that year produced little excitement among teens. By the end of the year, however, their music slowly began gaining ground in America. Beginning February 9, 1964 with three consecutive appearances on the weekly *Ed Sullivan Show–the* most widely watched TV variety show in America–The Beatles could no longer be ignored by mainstream media. Soon Beatlemania was sweeping the United States. While visiting New York Martin commented, "You would see middle-aged men walking around with Beatles wigs on their heads. No matter where you turned your dial on the radio, at any time of the day, you would hear a Beatles song. It was complete saturation."[2]

---

[1] On the east coast from the mid. to the late 1960s, there were two general groups: the "greasers" and the "rahs." The greasers wore black leather; the girls teased their hair in beehives, and they tended to be the tougher crowd. The rahs wore madras shirts, listened to Gerry and The Pacemakers, and were the more popular, well-mannered, upper-middle-class types.

[2] Time Life Video and Television. *The History of Rock N' Roll,* 2004.

The Beatles. © CBS/Photofest

Why did so many Americans become so enthralled with The Beatles so quickly? After all, as stated by John Lennon, "America has all the great music, why should they want to listen to European groups sing their music?"[3] First of all, parents regarded the mother country as more conservative, stable, and the source of their Victorian morals. They saw Europe as the place of origin for high art, and thus believed that music generated there would be culturally uplifting for their children. The Beatles initially appeared to be just what American parents were seeking, with their clean-cut, looks as well as their innocuous lyrics and performance practices. They were non-threatening, and thus parents did not try to hamper their teens' enthusiasm. Their manager Brian Epstein and producer George Martin had carefully crafted their public image to appeal to the broadest possible mainstream audience, marketing them and selecting and producing their music to appeal to young teenage girls in particular, who overzealously responded.

---

[3] *Rock & Roll* [videorecording]/senior producer, David Espar; BBC series producer, Hugh Thompson; a co-production of WGBH Boston and the BBC, South Burlington, VT: WGBH, c 1995.

The Beatles filled a void in the popular music world that had been created with the end of the initial rock & roll craze of the 1950s. Most of the groups that had followed, while socially acceptable, were pale reflections of the raw energy of the original sound. The Beatles struck a chord. People had not known what they were missing, but they surely recognized it when it appeared. The Beatles were an amalgamation of all that had come before, combing rhythm and blues, rock & roll, and folk elements. In the final analysis, it was not the accoutrements that captivated the mind, hearts, and ears of the world, but their charisma. They had a genuineness that touched people.

[handwritten margin note: Beatles combined all sounds]

Under the tutelage of Brian Epstein the Beatles entered America in 1964, and their consequent success marked the first time a European group to invaded *Billboard's* pop charts. During the week of April 4th of that year, The Beatles held an unprecedented top five spots on the *Billboard* Hot 100 chart with the following songs:

CHART LISTING	SONG TITLE
#1	"Can't But Me Love"
#2	"Twist and Shout"
#3	"She Loves You"
#4	"I Want To Hold Your Hand"
#5	"Please Please Me"

The musical character of their earlier songs, such as "Love Me Do" and "I Want To Hold Your Hand" shows their proclivity to record tuneful, radio-friendly love songs, which also contributed to their tremendous appeal to teenage girls.

By the mid 1960s, Beatles' phenomenal success made it possible for McCartney and Lennon to embark on a compositional journey that would place them among some of the most gifted tunesmiths and poets of all time. Greatly inspired by the writings of Bob Dylan, the song writing team moved beyond basic chord progressions and surface modes of expression such as "I love you" and "He/she loves me" to musicality and lyrics that would engage and provoke thought at a deeper level. The song "Yesterday" is an example of this. Written by McCartney in 1965, the song moves away from the typical harmonic progressions–centered strictly on the tonic, sub-dominant, and dominant harmonies[4]–of rock music at the time to harmonies that cleverly weave through relative minor and major tonalities. That same year, songs on the album titled *Rubber Soul* incorporated Indian influences such as George Harrison's fascination with the sitar. It was the synergy between all the members of this group that made them truly remarkable. They were very sensitive to each other and the world around them, and this was reflected in the evolution of their music. They were greatly affected by their exposure to the hippie culture in San Francisco, where they performed their last live performance at Candlestick Park in 1966.

Early June 1967 marks what some regard as their most significant contribution to rock music–*Sgt. Peppers Lonely Hearts Club Band.* Freed from the rigors of touring, they had spent uninterrupted time in the studio developing their creative ideas, which they expressed in unprecedented ways by taking advantage of technological advancements in electronics and recording. For instance, the song titled

---

[4] The tonic, subdominant, and dominant harmonies are synonymous with the I – IV – V chord progressions–basic harmonic structure in Western music.

"Lucy in the Sky With Diamonds" uses effects such as varying the speed of tracks; "When I'm Sixty-Four" uses reverberation and tape reversing; and "Being for the Benefit of Mr. Kite" features various circus-type organ sounds. With this album the Beatles became spokespersons for the younger generation. They promoted peace and love among all people with songs like "All You Need Is Love" (1967) and "Revolution" (1968), which were part of the albums they went on to record: *Magical Mystery Tour* (1967), *The White Album* (1968), *Abbey Road* (1969), and *Let it Be* (1970). Not only did The Beatles' music have such a tremendous impact on popular music in America, but their movies did as well. Their movies—*A Hard Day's Night* and *Help!*—were precursors of music videos. Prior to The Beatles, concerts had been in smaller venues, holding up to only a few thousand people. Tickets were relatively inexpensive, since the primary purpose of the concert was exposure of the groups to sell records. The Beatles were the first to fill sports arenas to capacity, allowing producers to see the potential profit in concerts themselves.

Once the doors to America were unlocked by The Beatles, a flood of British groups followed. Gerry and The Pacemakers was another group from Liverpool that was also managed by Brian Epstein. One of their most successful recordings titled "Don't Let the Sun Catch You Crying" (1964) was written by Gerry Marsden as the result of a recently failed relationship with his girlfriend. Fortunately, their relationship rekindled after his girlfriend discovered it was written for her, and they eventually married. Like Gerry and The Pacemakers, the group named The Animals (formed in Newcastle, a city outside London) was influenced by American artists and their singing styles, such as Sam Cooke's recording "Bring It on Home to Me" (1958). It is reported that following their acceptance on the Chuck Berry UK tour in 1964, the group's keyboard player (Alan Price) wrote the arrangement for one of their most celebrated hits titled "House of the Rising Sun" (1964). Knowing they could not compete with Chuck Berry's driving rock & roll rhythms, The Animals were able to capture their fans with this song about a bordello in New Orleans, sung in a sultry voice by their lead singer, Eric Burdon. Another group

The Who. © Neal Preston/CORBIS

that competed with these two groups was Herman's Hermits. Formed in Manchester and marketed as a clean-cut group, their first major hit in America was "Mrs. Brown You've Got a Lovely Daughter" (1968). The Who was another group that entered the American market music scene following the success of The Beatles. Centered around Pete Townshend's songwriting and the band's proclivity for drama on stage, they became a favorite for their songs as well as their performances. Their career catapulted with the 1965 release *My Generation* with hits such as "My Generation" and "I Can't Explain." In many ways, The Who was paved the way for the incorporation of theatricism, as evidenced in their music performances, particularly the work titled *Tommy* (1969). Although not an opera in the classic tradition, with respect to costumes, scenery, and recitative singing, it is, however, a multi movement work.

1960'S REVIVAL MUSIC: FOLK, BLUES, AND COUNTRY

For many, the 1960s represent the most socially, culturally, and politically challenging decade in American history. Seen as a canvas for painting colors of varied tones, stylistic tendencies, and social, cultural, and political commentaries, society embraced that music which reflected their personal petitions for humanitarianism. There was a renewed interest in the ideals of civil liberty, which sparked a wave of activity among musicians of many sorts. More than any other time in American history, musicians within a particular genre began to borrow musical elements from each other, and from many different styles as well. Consequently, it became increasingly difficult to characterize an artist as belonging to a specific stylistic category. For example, The Byrds not only performed folk rock, but their earlier recordings also demonstrated their appetite for blues music. The Rolling Stones song titled "(I Can't Get No) Satisfaction" (1965) was recorded by white and black artists. The Animals original song and recording of "The House of the Rising Sun" (1964) was performed by artists of varied styles such as Bob Dylan (folk–1962) and Charlie Byrd (bebop–1963). The Marshall Tucker Band performed some songs that are similar to jazz rock, and even funkesque. To provide a point of reference to the reader, the ensuing performers have been placed in their principal genre.

FOLK

Folk music is a style that is used to raise people's level of social consciousness; it conveys important messages and emotions in ways that more effectively reach the "folk." Using music's inherently appeasing and tranquilizing qualities, the folk singer is looked upon as an individual who strives to clarify the aesthetic character of his/her subject. For instance, Woody Guthrie's songs titled "Roll On, Columbia" and "Grand Coulee Dam" (both 1941) were commissioned by the Department of the Interior to musically enlighten the beauty of the Columbia River and a federal dam, respectively. Historically, the folk singer has been heralded as the spokesperson for humanity; a troubadour who speaks out against inequities in culture, gender, social class, and so on. Although folk singers have been present during every decade in American history, they did not become an active political voice until the 1940s with the innovations of Woody Guthrie and Pete Seeger.[5] They as well as less-known folk singers, became a political vehicle for communicating concerns of humanity to governments and political regimes. They inspired a number of folk singers such as Bob Dylan, Joan Baez, Peter, Paul and Mary, Simon and Garfunkel; Crosby, Stills and Nash, Phil Ochs, and the Kingston Trio. During the 1960s, these artists addressed issues such as Vietnam, civil rights, racism, women's rights, violence, and social injustices.

---

[5] Guthrie and Seeger combined efforts, resulting in the formation of the Almanac Singers, which also include Lee Hays and Millard Lampell. Later, Seeger helped to form and was a member of the Weavers.

The musical performance of folk music places great emphasis on the lyrics rather than the superficial, nonmusical gimmicks employed for mass-marketing purposes. Vocal virtuosity is not necessary to attract listeners. Rather, the singer captivates audiences with a vocal recitation style that illuminates the lyrical message. Accompanied by acoustic instruments such as guitar, fiddle, banjo, and/or harmonica, the singer transforms lyrics into social pronouncements, commentaries, and protestations that reflect a specific group–women, farmers, civil rights activists, and others.

As evidenced by Woody Guthrie's recording titled "This Land is Your Land" (1940), folk music also encourages people to be proud of their surroundings, and to understand that the beauty to be found in nature is for all people, not just a select few. Beginning with the recurring melodic theme refrain, Guthrie describes the various beautiful parts of America such as New York City, the redwood forest, and the gulf waters. In the first verse, he alludes to the endless sky, and the extensive countryside. He gives us personal accounts of his travels as he talks about the desert, and the wheat fields, all the while telling the listener, as he was told by a voice, "This land is Your land." Accompanying himself on acoustic guitar, Guthrie employs repetitious sonorous sounds that effectively engage the listener. It is important to note that the avoidance of melodic complexity is a tradition of folk music.

One of the most prolific songwriters of the 1960s was the Duluth, Minneapolis-born Robert Allen Zimmerman, better known as Bob Dylan. Born May 24, 1941, Mr. Dylan's inspirations included Dylan Thomas (after whom he was named), Woody Guthrie, and Lonnie Johnson. In his teens, Dylan traveled the countryside playing guitar and singing at numerous venues; it was in these places that he experienced the "true" American. Whether in rural European American or African American communities, Dylan learned the frustrations of "Americans" and transformed these emotions into anti-war and civil rights songs such as "A Hard Rain's Gonna Fall" and "Blowin in the Wind" (both 1963) respectively. In the former, Dylan begins by describing the emptiness of beauty while traveling. His travels include

Bob Dylan and Joan Baez. © Photofest

mountains, highways, forests, and a graveyard. He continues describing the devastation of life after war and destruction, in which society is filled with selfishness, death, hatred, hunger, poisoned water, and abandoned children. Dylan's eschatological recitation calls upon the listener to pay attention to social concerns. In "Blowin' in the Wind" Dylan speaks about the omnipresence of social and cultural inequities during the 1960s. He encourages people to stop the pretense surrounding the issue of civil rights, and states that the answer is "Blowin in the Wind." In both songs, Dylan accompanies himself on the acoustic guitar. In the latter, he adds the harmonica in an instrumental solo.

Joan Baez is one of the most well-known folk singers of the 1960s. As described by Leslie Berman,

> "[Joan Baez is] the first folk phenomenon to reach the general public's consciousness . . . whether singing transcontinental British folk ballads or New World gospel, modern antiwar or protest songs, or the poetry of Robert Zimmerman's American arcane, Baez's signature vibrato and outspoken politics assured her the undivided attention of legions of rapt folk crowds . . ."

Like Dylan and other folk singers of the day. Baez (who also accompanied herself on the acoustic guitar) sang about war and peace. In her song titled "Last Night I Had the Strangest Dream" (1963), she recounts dreaming about the signing of a document by men among many countries that agreed to end war. In a great room filled with men standing, holding hands, and praying, much joy and happiness abound. The joy and peace continued outside the room where it permeated throughout all societies, where weapons and duties of war were all laid down. The song titled "Where Have All the Flowers Gone" (1963) is yet another example of the war and destruction theme. The song describes the absence of young women and men as the result of war and death. Baez and others also sang light-hearted songs such as "She's A Trouble Maker" (1963), which jokingly speaks of a young woman who sets out to break men's hearts. Another Baez song titled "The Water Is Wide" (1963) also talks about love, but in a more serious manner. Here, Baez uses metaphors such as the power of an oak tree and a bush with thorns to describe love and its many joys and heartbreaks.

The group known as Peter, Paul, and Mary were also extremely popular performers of the folk music revival scene of the 1960s. Some of their popular songs include "If I Had a Hammer" (1962), "Puff (The Magic Dragon)," "Blowin' in the Wind" (both 1963), "Leaving on a Jet Plane" (1967), and "Kisses Sweeter Than Wine" (1966). With two guitars and three people, Peter, Paul and Mary were able to present folk songs in a variety of ways. For instance, two guitars can produce a thicker texture by playing different rhythms and in different registers (high vs. low sounds). Vocally, they frequently sang in three-part harmony such as in the songs "If I Had a Hammer," "Puff (The Magic Dragon)," and "Kisses Sweeter Than Wine." In the first song, Mary sings the lyrics while the two male singers provide vocal accompaniment using the nuance "ooh." Songs about peace and love, "If I Had a Hammer" and "Puff (The Magic Dragon)" are fine examples of folk music's endeavor to present themes that are melodically singable. In fact, during live concerts singing was encouraged during these types of songs. In this way, the song's tunefulness captivates listeners, imprinting them with the lyrical meaning.

Simon & Garfunkel were another popular folk duo during this time. Some of their most famous songs include "Mrs. Robinson" (1968), "The Sounds of Silence" (1964), and "Bridge Over Troubled Water" (1970). Unlike their contemporaries, Simon & Garfunkel used additional instruments such as the drums and bass in "Mrs. Robinson." Following the first verse, which includes only voice and guitar,

Peter, Paul, and Mary. © Photofest

in "The Sounds of Silence," the drums and bass are added and continue throughout. In "Bridge Over Troubled Water," only the piano is used to accompany the vocal line.[6] These and other features set the stage for the crossing over of some folk songs into the rock music genre as well as the folk revival in general providing inspiration for many rock musicians.

Simon & Garfunkel. © Photofest

---

[6] The electric bass is added during the final four measures.

FOLK ROCK

On the whole, folk rock is electrified folk music without the political poignancy that was so prevalent in the folk revival of the 1960s. The person who took the helm of this marriage of folk and rock elements was Bob Dylan. Sometime between 1964 and 1965, Dylan was making the transition from folk to folk rock performances. In 1964, he released the album *Another Side of Bob Dylan,* which included songs performed in the traditional folk manner (singer accompanied by an acoustic guitar). The following year, Dylan released two albums, *Bringing it All Back Home* and *Highway 61 Revisited* that both included instruments uncharacteristic of folk music such as electric guitar, bass, and drums. *Bringing it All Back Home* includes songs such as "Subterranean Homesick Blues," "She Belongs to Me," and "Maggie's Farm" that use electric guitar, bass, and drums as accompaniment to Dylan's voice. Dylan was not, however, fully removed from the traditional folk song performance scene as songs like "Mr. Tambourine," "Gates of Eden," and It's Alright Ma (I'm Only Bleeding)" are performed in the traditional folk song manner. Dylan's staple harmonica playing is also used in "Mr. Tambourine Man." The song titled "It's All Over Now, Baby Blue" instrumentally falls somewhere between folk and folk rock, as the instrumentation includes voice, guitar, harmonica, and electric bass. While *Another Side of Bob Dylan* is exemplary of folk, and *Bringing it All Back Home* is illustrative of the transition from folk to folk rock, *Highway 61 Revisited* is securely in the folk rock style. Including the popular song "Like a Rolling Stone," the songs "Ballad of a Thin Man," and "Queen Jane Approximately" all use organ, electric guitar, piano, bass, and drums. The remaining songs all use the electric guitar, bass, and drums. Even a whistle sound is used in the song "Highway 61 Revisited."

Although Bob Dylan made the transition from folk singer to folk rock artist (albeit with reluctant acceptance by his folk-purist fans), the mood of this new style of music was more fitting for groups like The Byrds, The Mamas and the Papas, Barry McGuire, Paul Simon, and even the singer/songwriter team of Crosby, Stills, Nash and Young. While instrumentally they definitely fell within the precepts of rock, lyrically many of their songs were more in keeping with folk singing, as exemplified by their 1970 recording titled "Ohio," which speaks about the shooting of students at Kent State University by the National Guard.

The inauguration of folk rock was marked by The Byrds release of Dylan's "Mr. Tambourine Man" in 1965. Featured in their album titled *Mr. Tambourine Man* (1965), both this song and others were played with rock music's instrumentation and danceable *tempi*. Without question, The Byrds epitomized the early sound of folk rock. Immersed in the matrix of the 1960s, where social change and music borrowing flourished, The Byrds recorded/performed songs that represented multiple styles. For instance, "Mr. Tambourine Man" appealed to both traditional folk and folk rock fans. The sounds in "All I Really Want To Do" (also from the album *Mr. Tambourine Man*) characterize the pop-styled rock scene as evidenced by the light-hearted lyrics of love as well as the non intrusive singing style. The character of folk music continued in 1966 in their next album titled *Turn! Turn! Turn!* in the song "Turn! Turn! Turn! (To Everything There is a Season)." The song speaks about a turn for all things in life, such as love, peace, war, tears, and hate. That same year the song titled "Eight Miles High" (released on the album titled *Fifth Dimension)* emulated the psychedelic rock sound with its use of modes representative of East Indian music, the 12-string guitar that could produce a polyphonic texture similar to the Indian sitar, and surrealistic lyrics and metaphors of being "high."

The distinction between folk and folk rock lies in how the music is performed. Folk places more emphasis on what is being said, resulting in less elaborate harmonic and rhythm events. On the other hand, musicians of folk rock, though the lyrics are important, also desire to appeal to the listener by adding various musical ideas. The outline below illustrates this point.

FOLK	FOLK ROCK
Acoustic instruments	Electric instruments
Tempo is generally slower	Tempo is generally faster
Does not use drums	Uses drums
Intended for listening	Listening and dance
Less focus on vocal virtuosity	More focus on vocal virtuosity
Less focus on harmonic textures	More focus on harmonic textures

BLUES REVIVAL

One could certainly argue that there is no need to establish a category such as blues revival since the blues have never gone dormant. Beginning with recordings in the 1920s, music characteristics of the blues continue to permeate many styles of music. Some of these styles and their recordings include New Orleans jazz ("West End Blues" by Louis Armstrong and His Hot Five), early gospel ("Precious Lord" by Thomas Dorsey), big band jazz ("Woodchoppers Ball" by Woody Herman), and numerous rhythm & blues/rock & roll such as "Hound Dog" by Willie Mae "Big Mama" Thornton, and a later version by Elvis Presley, "(Mama) He Treats Your Daughter Mean" by Ruth Brown, "Shake, Rattle, and Roll" by Big Joe Turner and a later version by Bill Haley & The Comets.

Indeed, by the late 1950s and early 60s, the effect of rhythm & blues/rock & roll was being felt globally, most significantly within American and Western European communities. By the 1950s, British groups became even more interested in music that was blues based, which subsequently sparked a surge by numerous groups to perform and record rhythm & blues/rock & roll in addition to the more traditional blues music. The blues revival coincides with the British Invasion (early 1960s) with respect to musical interests and songs produced. As a result of record sales and the enthusiastic interest in Europe, the music industry in America acknowledged the fact that there was a market for blues records in its own country.

Some early bands in Britain that played blues-based music during the 1960s included The Rolling Stones, The Yard birds, ZZ Top. The Allman Brothers, and Cream (See Chapter Eighteen.) Following The Beatles invasion of America, The Rolling Stones was regarded as the most popular band in all of Western Europe. The Rolling Stones, first album, titled *The Rolling Stones* (1964), contained many cover versions of popular American hits such as "Not Fade Away" (by Buddy Holly), "Route 66" (recorded by many artists such as Nat King Cole, Rosemary Clooney, and Chuck Berry), "You Can Make It if You Try" (by Yvonne Fair with James Brown), "Can I Get a Witness" (by Marvin Gaye), "Walking the Dog" (by Rufus Thomas) and "I'm a King Bee" (versions by Muddy Waters and Slim Harpo). Without question, the album contained more elements of blues man any other style. For instance, the songs "Route 66," which is sung, and the instrumental piece that features a harmonica and guitar solo titled "Now I've Got a Witness," both use the 12-bar blues progression. The AAB song form and the 12-bar blues progression are evident in the song titled "I'm a King Bee." Moreover, a harmonica solo (this instrument is commonly used by blues musicians) is also added to further emulate the delta blues sound. The song titled "I Just Want to Make Love to You" uses the 12-bar blues progression and the AAB song form, and its original author is the preeminent Chicago blues musician Muddy Waters. The song is rhythmically played in the fashion of the Waters version, including the harmonica emulating James Cotton. Although played faster, the Stones' version of James Cotton's song titled "Honest I Do" is emphatically sung with African American dialect. The harmonica is also played in a manner similar to Cotton's version. The song titled "Little by Little" uses the 12-bar blues progression, but extends each harmonic section by a factor of two. Below is the standard 12-bar blues progression.

The Rolling Stones. © Photofest

```
 I            I            I            I
|/ / / /|    |/ / / /|    |/ / / /|    |/ / / /|
 IV           IV           I            I
|/ / / /|    |/ / / /|    |/ / / /|    |/ / / /|
 V            IV           I            V
|/ / / /|    |/ / / /|    |/ / / /|    |/ / / /|
```

The Rolling Stones version is played in the following manner:

```
 I            I            I            I
|/ / / /|    |/ / / /|    |/ / / /|    |/ / / /|
 I            I            I            I
|/ / / /|    |/ / / /|    |/ / / /|    |/ / / /|
 IV           IV           IV           IV
|/ / / /|    |/ / / /|    |/ / / /|    |/ / / /|
 I            I            I            I
|/ / / /|    |/ / / /|    |/ / / /|    |/ / / /|
 V            V            IV           IV
|/ / / /|    |/ / / /|    |/ / / /|    |/ / / /|
 I            I            I            V
|/ / / /|    |/ / / /|    |/ / / /|    |/ / / /|
```

Of all the American performers who influenced European bands, Chuck Berry is at the top of the list. The Rolling Stones and other groups such as The Animals were proud to be on Berry's UK tour in May 1964. The Stones' version of Berry's "Carol" shows a proclivity for his rock & roll sounds. With the exception of playing a faster tempo, the song is identical to Chuck Berry's version, including Berry's staple of rhythmically strumming the guitar during the introduction. The influence of the blues continued in their next album titled *12 × 5,* released in the same year as *The Rolling Stones.* Of the twelve songs on the album, "Around and Around," "Confessin' the Blues," and "Good Times, Bad Times" all used various aspects of the blues. The Stones' next album, titled *The Rolling Stones Now!* (1965) features the blues hit "Little Red Rooster" by Howlin' Wolf. The song that catapulted them to fame in the United States was their hit "(I Can't Get No) Satisfaction" from their 1965 album titled *Out of Our Heads.* The phenomenal success of this song paved the way for their triumphant appearance in America in 1966.[7]

Unlike The Beatles' comparatively clean-cut and broadly appealing image. The Rolling Stones' "bad boy" image made their music appear to be less marketable to mainstream American culture. One reason for this perception among record producers was their proclivity for the blues, an African American style of music, which by mainstream American standards during the early 1960s was considered lewd and inappropriate for European American youth. During this same time, however, the Civil Rights Movement was positively affecting the American image of African American culture, which was gradually becoming an integral part of American mainstream society. This incipient acceptance included music like the Motown sound. Fortunately for them. The Rolling Stones' entrance on the American music scene occurred at a time when its young people, the main targeted audience, were becoming socially conscious of the values and mores that represented their individual tastes and were questioning the values imposed on them by their parents.

Examples of songs from other blues revival performers included "It's Not My Cross to Bear" (1969) by The Allman Brothers, "Brown Sugar" (1970) by ZZ Top, "The Nazz Are Blue" (1966) by The Yardbirds, and "Sleepy Time Time" (1966) by Cream.

COUNTRY REVIVAL

From the beginning of the music record industry, country music (like blues) has been a vibrant force. Due to the emergence of other styles of music, however, it is often overshadowed by new or different musical trends. During the early 1970s, however, mainstream interest in country music re-emerged as a byproduct of the soul searching that occurred in folk and blues music of the 1960s, which encouraged going back to nature and seeking one's cultural roots, both of which are amply reflected in country music. In addition, blues and country music are closely related, so southern musicians would have grown up with exposure to both styles and would naturally incorporate them into their music. This would not have happened with European performers, since country music was not nearly as popular as the blues in Europe. Consequently, as these American groups were developing their sounds, all of these elements would converge. All this incited what was commonly known as the "country music revival." Some of the more popular artists during this time included the Charlie Daniels Band. The Eagles, The Allman Brothers, The Outlaws, Lynyrd Skynyrd, and The Marshall Tucker Band.

Country music initially emerged on a nationwide scale during the 1930s. Later musical trends established during the 1950s and 60s (particularly blues and rock & roll) affected the evolution of country music characteristics and performance practices during the country revival era. Some of these practices included more elaborate productions, enhanced vocal harmonies, the strong presence of drums,

---

[7] It is interesting to note that, in this same year, The Beatles gave their final American performance, which took place in San Francisco.

and broader lyrical themes. In examining country music at this time, it becomes clear that there were two general approaches to this style: southern rock and country-style rock.

COUNTRY REVIVAL: SOUTHERN ROCK

A distinguishing characteristic of southern rock is that the lyrics frequently refer to a particular geographical area: "The Hills of Arkansas" (1971) by Black Oak Arkansas, "Sweet Home Alabama" (1974) by Lynyrd Skynyrd, "Georgia" (1975) by The Charlie Daniels Band (CDB), "Mississippi Kid" (1973) by Lynyrd Skynyrd, and "Virginia" (1975) by The Marshall Tucker Band (TMTB). In addition to geographical locations, southern rock artists speak about cultural practices found in the the United States. For instance, the song titled "Hillbilly" (1973) by The Marshall Tucker Band speaks of dancing to a hillbilly-sounding band–a southern band. It also talks about southern-type activities such as drinking moonshine and corn liquor, *do-si-do* square dancing, and guitar blues picking/chicken-picking time.[8]

In addition to lyrical themes that were common to the southern rock sound, specific instruments were used in addition to rhythm and lead guitar, slide guitar, piano (on occasion), bass, and drums. Some examples include the mandolin, such as in the song "See You Later, I'm Gone" (1973) by TMTB, the harmonica and mandolin in "Mississippi Kid" (1973) by Lynyrd Skynyrd, and the fiddle in "The South's Gonna Do It Again" by CDB.

COUNTRY REVIVAL: COUNTRY-STYLE ROCK

With regard to the country-style type of country revival music during the early 1970s, some performers included The Eagles, The Band, The Byrds, Linda Ronstadt, Poco, and Crosby, Stills, Nash, & Young. While some of these bands did not exclusively perform country-style music, they have all recorded hit songs in this genre.

Country-style music performance practices were more market-driven, emphasizing music features such as more vocally controlled phrasing as in the song titled "Most of Us Are Sad" (1972) by The Eagles, and smooth-sounding harmonies in their song titled "Nightingale" (1972). The group named The Band also recorded some songs with country music influences, such as the slide guitar in the song "Caldonia Mission" (1968), and the tunefulness and non rhythmic complexity of their song "The Weight." The Byrds (like many groups) recorded some songs representative of country-styled rock. For example, the song titled "I Trust" (1971) uses the slide guitar and harmonies, sung by a choir, similar to what one would find in African American gospel music. Poco also recorded some country-styled songs such as "Pickin' Up the Pieces" and "You Better Think Twice" (both ca. 1970). This group's smooth harmonic textures are quite similar to the early recordings of The Eagles. With the addition of Neil Young to the group, some of Crosby, Stills, Nash, & Young's recordings took on a distinctly country-style rock style, as exemplified in the omnipresent slide guitar in the song "Helpless" (1970).

Among women performers, Linda Ronstadt recorded a number of country-style rock songs such as the gospel-like "Rock Me on the Water" (1972), which speaks about people's need for God and personal salvation. While the use of the fiddle in her love song titled "Crazy Arms" (1972) creates an illusion of southern rock, the more vocally produced melodic phrasing, smooth sounding harmonies, rhythmic non complexity, and the use of slide guitar clearly establishes it as a country-styled rock song.

---

[8] "Chicken pickin'" is a lead guitar style or technique used in country music where the plucked strings are pulled outward by the fingers of the right hand and the note played immediately dampened by decreasing the pressure of the left hand finger on the fret (See Terry Burrows, *Play Country Guitar*. Dorling Kindersley Limited. London, 1995).

Since the country revival of the early 1970s, there continues to be great interest in country music. Some of the early 21st century top country performers include Shania Twain.[9] Faith Hill, Alan Jackson, Tim McGraw, Dixie Chicks, Lee Ann Womack, Leann Rimes, Kenny Chesney, and Garth Brooks.

In closing, one can see how musicians are affected by the culture and the times, and how the culture is in turn affected by the music they create. Art and culture are inextricably interwoven in the circle of life. The British Invasion subsided in America in the late 1960s, as their taste was being influenced by the likes of David Bowie, The Doors, Jimi Hendrix, and a sense of theatricism. Studio-produced recordings with orchestral arrangements and sound effects could not be effectively reproduced live, and therefore their shows were becoming outdated. International and domestic interests in the revitalization of folk, blues, and country music reassured Americans of the many contributions made and produced by numerous talented and creative musicians and producers, respectively. The beginning of technological contributions to music performance of the 1960s helped give rise to the public interest in emerging musical styles like art/progressive rock, disco, and glitter and glam.

PSYCHEDELIC

Inspired by the Beat Movement,[10] which came to San Francisco from New York in the 1950s, white, middle-class, college-educated individuals during the 1960s embarked on an ideology of peace and love that spurred youth culture whose goal was to challenge post-WWII social mores. These individuals, mainly in their mid-20s, practiced tolerance toward people of different races and genders; were political pacifists and generally protested any war; experimented with drugs (LSD); and were open-minded toward sex and love (i.e., free love). Known as the "hippie culture," their viewpoints were made public in 1967 when the first human "be-in" was staged in Golden Gate Park, San Francisco. During an event that promoted love and camaraderie, drugs, and poetic readings (such as those by Jack Kerouac, 1922–1969), many people were first introduced to a new music: acid rock or psychedelic rock. The Monterey International Pop Festival in 1967 provided a forum for both the performer and consumer to come together in an environment where music would generate an atmosphere of peace and love. Occurring for three days from June 16–18, the festival attraced over 200,00 people who viewed such diverse acts as The Who, Otis Redding, Janis Jopin, and Ravi Shankhar. Some important psychedelic rock performers included the Grateful Dead, Jefferson Airplane, and Jimi Hendrix.[11]

Psychedelic rock, beginning in the late 1960s, represented an existentialistic approach to music, which emphasized the self rather than the concerns or pressures of the outside world. Musically, this involved a disregard for certain musical rules and conventions, particularly those governing popular music of the day, such as the three minute and 23-second song duration, typical chord progressions, standard melodic and harmonic structures, and typical lyrical themes. Because the music focused on self-expression, time was needed to develop and expose ideas. Resulting typically longer songs. In light of this, bands preferred to perform their songs live, as the recording studio environment was too

---

[9] Shania Twain's 1997 album titled "*Come On Over*" sold more than 34 million copies worldwide, making it "the most successful album of all time by a female solo artist" (*Billboard*, Nov. 2002, p. 55).

[10] William Burrougi, Allen Ginsberg, and Jack Kerouac are well known Beat writers. Their work discussed and encouraged existentialism, the use of drugs to enhance creativity and tolerance, an antiimperialistic and anticapitalistic mentality, and a disregard for post-WWII social mores that opposed any of the above.

[11] It should be pointed out that the music industry uses other terms to categorize these and other groups. For example. The Grateful Dead are sometimes referred to as performers of jam rock, while Jimi Hendrix is noted as a performer of acid rock. In both cases, the adjective that precedes *rock* is a synonym of *psychedelic*.

stagnant and there was no audience encouragement. Because time was not a factor, bands incorporated many improvisations in their performances. Studio recordings were generally shorter versions of songs from their live performances such as the Grateful Dead hit "The Golden Road (To Unlimited Devotion)" from their *The Grateful Dead* album released in 1967. There are many songs that illustrate this group's proclivity to play extended music such as "Viola Lee Blues" (1967) and "Black Peter" (ca. 1970), 10:09 and 7:30 respectively. The Grateful Dead are known for borrowing musical elements from styles such as country, blues, and rhythm & blues. For instance, their recording of "Sitting on Top of the World" from *The Grateful Dead* album was originally recorded in the 1950s by the Western swing country artist Bob Wills & The Texas Playboys. On the same album, the song "Good Morning Little School Girl" is played in the blues style. The use of the harmonica during the introduction sets the blues mood for this song.

Jefferson Airplane was a group that was formed in the mid-1960s. Like The Grateful Dead, they made San Francisco their home. Signe Toly Anderson was the lead singer prior to Grace Slick joining the band. Grace Slick (born 1939) was a model before becoming a singer. She was so inspired by Jefferson Airplane after seeing them perform in Los Angeles that she formed a band to open for them. Soon she became a member of Jefferson Airplane, becoming one of the first women of rock music. She now resides in Los Angeles where she spends time painting in acrylic, and watercolor. When asked why she did not paint in oils in an interview aired on April 27, 2003, Slick replied, "I'm 63 years old and oil [paint] takes too long to dry." Her full-throated manner of singing complemented the band's raw character and their desire to explore facets of the mind through performing music that was not only unrestrictive musically, but lyrically as well. Such a mind set was put to task Slick expressed her confusion regarding social mores in the song titled "White Rabbit" (1967). This piece is a spoof on the various experiences of Alice in the book *Alice's Adventures in*

Jefferson Airplane. © Photofest

Wonderland (1865) by Reverend Charles Lutwidge Dodgson (a.k.a. Lewis Carroll). Slick's reference to Alice's experiences of chemical substances such as pills, marijuana, and mushrooms are illustrative of, in Slick's opinion, contradictions in life. On one hand, children are taught "Say no to drugs" while this book and a Disney film by the same name show Alice indulging in these mind-altering substances. On the same album, the group scored another hit titled "Somebody to Love." Fortunately for their label and radio-friendly airplay, this song was more acceptable to mainstream culture.

James Marshall Hendrix (1942–1970) is perhaps the most instrumental musician in furnishing a transition from rock & roll to rock. The raw rock & roll sounds of the 1950s were slowly declining, and British groups were waiting in the wings to enter and forever change American music. And indeed they had, as rock & roll characteristics such as the 12-bar blues progression, three-line verse form, and a garage-band sound were becoming passé. Electric guitar effects such as distortion and feedback and theatricism were slowly becoming a reality for large concerts. The age of experimentation was knocking at the door, combined with the urge for many American artists to gain reputations as innovators of musical style, particularly of a type that appealed to the youth culture. Though Hendrix may have had little concern about this, his performances displayed a sense of virtuoso authority for American breed styles such as blues, rhythm & blues, and rock & roll. For example, as heard in his recording titled "Red House" from the *Are You Experienced* (1967, The Jimi Hendrix Experience) album, Hendrix continued the use of blues traditions as important music elements and fused them with distortion and feedback. To be specific, the song is sung in the three-line song form (AAB) and uses the 12-bar blues progression.

Jimi Hendrix. © Photofest

TIME	SECTION		COMMENTS
			Instrumentation: voice, guitar, bass, drums
00:00	Introduction		Begins with guitar and singer saying the words, "Ah yea"
00:50	Verse 1	(A)	The first line of AAB song form begins with "There is Red House . . ."
00:59	" "	(A)	Repeat of the first line
01:14	" "	(B)	Third line starts with "I ain't been home . . ."
01:29	Verse 2	(A)	Lyrics begin with "Wait a minute . . ."
01:44	" "	(A)	Repeat of the above line
01:58	" "	(B)	Lyrics begin with "I have a bad . . ."
02:13	Solo		Guitar solo with the singer speaking some words extemporaneously
02:57	Verse 3	(A)	Lyrics of this verse begin with "Well I might as well . . ."
03:13	" "	(A)	Repeat the above line
03:28	" "	(B)	Lyrics of this verse begin with "Guess my baby don't . . ."

Song Navigator 16.1: "Red House" by Jimi Hendrix Experience from the album *Are You Experienced* (released 2010, Legacy Recordings)

Additionally, as heard in the music of blues artists such as Robert Johnson, Memphis Minnie, B.B. King, and Muddy Waters, Hendrix plays the guitar in response to his vocal lines. "Purple Haze," from the same album, displays his rhythm & blues-sounding vocal passages combined with his guitar virtuosity while playing few chord changes–a characteristic of rock & roll. Hendrix would go on to record numerous popular songs throughout his brief career, such as "All Along the Watchtower," "Foxy Lady," and "Manic Depression." His performance of "The Star Spangled Banner" at the Woodstock Music and Art Festival in 1969 is one of music's most memorable moments.[12]

Janis Joplin (1943–1970) was another favorite psychedelic rock performer. Like The Grateful Dead, Joplin was influenced by folk, country, and blues revival music during the 1960s. Her recording titled "Me and Bobby McGee" (1971) is reminiscent of southern country, as she incorporates a reference to a southern state (here Kentucky). In addition, the slide guitar, organ, and honky-tonk-style of piano playing all suggest her country influences, Joplin's blues influences can be heard in the 1968 version of "Ball and Chain" (originally sung by urban blues singer Big Mama Thornton). Performed in the typical AAB blues song form, 12-bar blues progression, and vocal dramatization, Joplin's deliverance is similar to what one would hear in a blues song. She is accompanied by instruments that incorporate distortion and feedback, which makes it characteristic of psychedelic rock. Her performance of this song, as a member of the Big Brother and Holding Company, on June 18, 1967, at the Monterey Pop Festival contributed to the group's success. Her performance at Woodstock with the Kozmic Blues

---

[12] Due to weather conditions, Hendrix's performance actually occurred on Monday, August 18th.

Janis Joplin with Big Brother and the Holding Co. © Warner Brothers/Seven Arts/Photofest

The Doors. © Electra Records/Photofest

Band was another important point in her career, not necessarily because of the band's success but rather by virtue of its appearance at what is known as the most successful rock music festival in U.S. history. We see another stage in her career with the posthumously released *Pearl* album in 1971. The album features two of her most popular songs: "Me and Bobby McGee" and "Mercedes Benz."

The Doors, formed by UCLA film students Jim Morrison and Ray Manzarek in the mid-1960s, picked up the psychedelic sound. While neither a Monterey Pop Festival performer (too early, as the band was formed in 1965) nor a Woodstock performer (it was thought Morrison would disrobe), their contributions to psychedelic performances are immeasurable. From Morrison's often-dramatic performance to Manzarek's use of a synthesized organ, The Doors performances inspired artists like Iggy Pop. David Bowie, and Lou Reed. The group's niche of theatrical vignettes through music performance was enhanced by their diverse repertoire and extended live music performances. In songs such as "The End" and "Light My Fire," both in 1967, "Spanish Caravan" in 1968, and "When the Music's Over" in 1970, the band displays a proclivity to create music drama. The latter song continues for over sixteen minutes and incorporates improvisations (guitar and synthesized organ) and distortion and feedback–all characteristics of psychedelic rock. Like other psychedelic groups, The Doors were also influenced by styles of the day, namely blues and rhythm & blues. Their songs titled "Riders on the Storm" and "The Changeling" from the album titled *L.A. Woman* (1971) show the group's roots in rhythm & blues-type music as evidenced by the rhythm guitar and electric piano accompanimental passages. Additionally, in "Riders on the Storm" the presence of the bass guitar playing subdivisions of each count throughout the entire song is similar to what one heard in disco music at the time. Moreover, as mentioned previously, The Doors were making strides in creating musical drama as demonstrated in "Riderson the Storm" as well. The Song Navigator below illustrates all these as well as a few other interesting aspects of the song.

TIME	SECTION	COMMENTS
		Instrumentation: voice, guitar, piano, bass, drums
00:00	Introduction	Begins with storm and lightning sound effects
00:20	" "	The bass begins the even subdivisions of each beat accompanied by the drums; the electric piano is added; storm and lightning effects occur intermittently
00:50	Verse 1	Lyrics begin with title of song; the guitar playing is playing in response to the lead vocal line
01:16	Verse 2	Lyrics begin with ". . . There's a killer . . ."; Piano solo accompanied by guitar, bass, and drums
01:45	Solo	Guitar solo accompanied by piano, bass, drums, congas (very subtle), and storm and lightning effects
02:18	Verse 3	Lyrics begin with "Girl you gotta love . . ."; accompanied by guitar, piano, bass, and drums
02:47	Solo	Piano solo accompanied by guitar, bass, drums, congas, and storm and lightning effects occurring intermittently

04:36	Interlude	Piano, and storm and lightning effects only; the song has the appearance of ending but continues after about 10 seconds
04:46	Introduction	Similar to the introduction at 20 seconds, but with a greater presence of congas
05:04	Verse 1	Same as Verse 1, with the exception of storm and lightning effects that occur here
05:33	Coda	An instrumental section where the guitar plays a melodic line that is imitated by the lead singer
05:51	" "	The singer imitates the previous guitar line as mentioned above; this section also features the piano and guitar playing improvisationally
06:30	" "	A distinct tempo diminishes as the piano, guitar, and storm and lightning effects sound in an improvisational manner; the song ends at 7:07

Song Navigator 16.2: "Riders on the Storm" by The Doors from the album *The Very Best of The Doors* (2001, Rhino/Elektra)

Morrison's untimely death on July 3, 1971, ended The Doors' steady progress as a performing band, but not the remaining members' interest in consulting on projects related to the band's history such as the Oliver Stone film in 1991 titled *The Doors*.

CHAPTER SEVENTEEN

NEW APPROACHES TO BLACK MUSIC DURING THE 1960s: FUNK, DISCO, AND SOUL STYLES

INTRODUCTION

August 28, 2005, marked the 42nd anniversary of Dr. Martin Luther King, Jr.'s "I Have a Dream" speech, when a quarter of a million people–black and white, male and female, young and old–congregated on the steps of the Lincoln Memorial and listened to numerous speeches about civil rights in America. Listening to Dr. King deliver this momentous speech, all people, but particularly blacks, felt inspired and empowered, Dr. King had made it clear that when it came to African Americans, this great nation had not fulfilled its basic obligation of guaranteeing equal rights and opportunities to all people. The time was ripe and the stage was set for people of all social classes and ethnicities to confront head-on and eradicate deplorable attitudes toward black people in America. It had been predicted that the march on Washington would precipitate rioting and civil chaos; however, there was not one unruly incident. The event was truly a day of peace, that exemplified what America could be. In the history of the United States, it was the day that made the most significant change with respect to civil rights.

In retrospect, it is no surprise that contemporary music, including lyrics, reflected what was experienced on August 28, 1963. Indeed, an existential mood permeated both rhetorical and poetic recitations, which greatly influenced music performance and composition considerations. From this viewpoint, a song's lyrical content is often true since it represents the experiences and emotions of people. The musical character of many songs supported the lyrics by applying either subtle or overt orchestrations that further engaged the listener. In essence, the intent was to create music that was heartfelt, music that transcended ethnicity, gender, and social status. The goal was to create music that resonated the "I Have a Dream" and, ultimately, the American spirit.

Looking at the lyrical content in African American songs previous to the 1960s provides evidence of the powerful effect of the social climate that prevailed during that decade. The music of the 1950s was an outgrowth of the social conditions of male and female relationships during World War II. At that time, couples often coped with life, at least temporarily, without the physical presence of a loved one. As a result, topics of love during the 1950s seem to have a common theme of individuals reflecting on conditions of loneliness like those experienced during the previous decade. As representatives of women with loved ones at war, female soloists often displayed feelings of uncertainty regarding a particular man's love for them. They often conveyed the experience of being brokenhearted. For instance, with the exception of Sarah Vaughan's "Whatever Lola Wants" (1955),[1] the majority of Top 10 hits, such as "I Cried a Tear" (1958) by LaVern Baker and "Broken-Hearted Melody" (1959) by Sarah Vaughan,[2] featured topics about love ambiguities. Male soloists expressed similar feelings. Songs with similar subject matter as those found among female singers include "Unchained Melody" (1955) by Roy Hamilton, "What Am I Living For?" (1958) by Chuck Willis, "Lonely Teardrops" (1958) by Jackie Wilson, and Clyde McPhatter's 1958 hit "A Lover's Question." In this song, McPhatter is rather uncertain as to whether or not the person in question will reciprocate his feelings of love. Desired love was also a topic among male soloists. Some songs include Thurston Harris's 1957 hit titled "Little Bitty Pretty One," in which a man is asking a woman to talk to him; Bobby Freeman's 1958 hit titled "Do You Want To Dance?" and Wilbert Harrison's pursuit of pretty women in the 1959 hit titled "Kansas City." Larry Williams's song titled "Short Fat Fannie" (1957), a somewhat humorous description of the opposite gender, exemplifies themes given musical expression only by male performers.[3]

Songs by female soloists during the 1960s featured a broader variety of topics when compared to those of the previous decade. Male singers continued to cover a wide range of topics during this time. In addition to singing love songs, female performers sang about dance, a sense of individuality, "speaking out" against men in general, and tropological meanings (that is, words that offer a remedy for moral enhancement). Male singers' topics included love dance, "speaking out" against a particular type of woman, allegories, religion, sensuality, and survival. The dance craze during the 1950s, fueled by rock & roll music, inspired the use of specific text in song lyrics of the 1960s. A significant number of songs describe how to perform a specific dance. Some examples by female singers include the 1962 hit titled "The Loco-Motion" by Little Eva, and "Mashed Potato Time" (1962) and "Do the Bird" (1963), both by Dec Dee Sharp. Sharp's "Mashed Potato Time" provides historical information by referring to the "Mashed Potato" as an easy dance, and furnishes the listener with specific instructions. Dance songs by male singers include Chubby Checker's "The Twist" (1960), "Let's Twist Again," "Pony Time," "The Fly" (all in 1961), plus "Limbo Rock" and "Slow Twistin" (both in 1962). Checker's recording of "The Twist" also furnishes words that describe the movements of the dance called "The Twist." Other male artists who contributed dance songs to this decade include Sam Cooke and Rufus Thomas. Leslie Gore was the only woman who exhibited this type of expression among her peers (she sings about her right to cry) with her 1963 hit titled "It's My Party." While speaking out against men is not a common subject among female singers, one song by Gore states this with regard to love, namely "You Don't Own Me" (1964).[4] Some male songs display a negative attitude toward an extended family member (such as a mother-in-law) or a soon-to-be family member (such as a wife). Examples include Jimmy Soul's 1963 hit titled "If You Wanna' Be Happy," which comments on the idea that one should not marry a pretty woman, as it will make one miserable. The 1961 hit titled "Mother-in-Law" by Ernie K-Doe

---

[1] The popularity of "Whatever Lola Wants" by Sarah Vaughan was due in part to its dissemination via the stage play and movie titled *Damn Yankees*.

[2] Performances by female groups focused their attention on songs that expressed their commitment to a particular man (with the exception of the Chordettes's 1958 hit titled "Lollipop"). Some songs include "Born to Be with You" (1956) and "Just Between You and Me" (1957) by The Chordettes, and "Mr. Lee" (1957) by the Bobbettes.

[3] Male groups, like male soloists, address various aspects of love. Some of these include specific joyous moments, metaphorical descriptions of young women and women in general, desire, chivalry, and expressions of teenage situations. Songs that focus on a specific moment will generally employ the word night in their title, such as "Oh, What a Night" (1956) by The Dells and "One Summer Night" (1958) by The Danleers.

[4] It is interesting to note that a European American (Leslie Gore) sings these topics. Songs sung by African American women with this type of subject matter do not appear until the 1970s.

speaks about his woes as the result of his mother-in-law's personality. Songs with allegorical meanings are evident only among male soloists during this time. An example includes the 1961 hit titled "Spanish Harlem" by Ben E. King which speaks about the maturity of a young woman. Another example is Wilson Pickett's 1967 hit titled "Funky Broadway," which refers to a portion of that famous street of theatres in New York City.

Because both men and women are involved in religious activities one would perhaps expect to hear religious songs from both genders. This, however, is not the case; this subject matter was only evident among male singers during this time. Songs include the 1961 hit titled "A Hundred Pounds of Clay" by Gene McDaniels, which talks about God's formation of the earth, man, and woman; and "Little Green Apples" (1968) by O.C. Smith, which talks about the things God has made.

Sensuality is another topic that appears among male singers. One example is the 1965 hit titled "The Birds and The Bees" by Jewel Akens. Due to the emergence of the many issues surrounding equal rights, by the mid-1960s, women began not only to speak out but to apply topological intent to their songs. One singer noted for this practice is Aretha Franklin. Franklin has led the way in providing prescriptions for the enhancement of a man's morals. Songs that appeared in 1967 included "Chain of Fools," which contains protestations regarding her situation as a link in a particular man's chain of women, and "Respect," which speaks about receiving respect from a particular man. In 1968, the "Top 10" hit titled "Think" prescribes the act of thinking as a means of reforming a particular man's improper behavior.

A song that can be interpreted as providing words of encouragement for both men and women, titled "Only the Strong Survive" (1969) by Jerry Butler was inspired by endeavors that were pursued during the Civil Rights Movement, particularly by African Americans.

SOUL MUSIC

Within the African American community, the aforementioned lyrical expressions were encapsulated by and referred to as "soul" music. Performed in a manner that communicated heartfelt emotions—grounded in love, peace, equality, freedom, and ethnic tolerance—soul was more than music; it was an outgrowth of human experience. As we further examine the social climate of the 1960s, we see that soul music emerged from and reflected a time of civil unrest in America that had a particularly powerful effect on African Americans and women. Not only was there civil unrest, but this decade also witnessed events that affected American social conditions. These events included the invasion of British popular groups (e.g., The Beatles, The Who, and The Rolling Stones); three assassinations (Kennedy, King, and Malcom X); the Flower Children/Hippie Movement; the Vietnam War; the psychedelic drug scene; and the Apollo moon landing. In some ways, the 1960s represented a second renaissance of black culture (the first being the Harlem/Black Renaissance from 1921–1933) as a number of inspirational African American songs were directed to the black community. Specific concerns that dealt with love as a re-dedication of black pride and respect for each other were paramount, as exemplified by songs such as "Hold on to What You' ve Got" (1965) by Joe Tex, which speaks to men and women about giving honor and respect to the one you are with; and the many songs of Aretha Franklin, who in essence was the voice of women struggling for self-respect and equality. She sings about honor and respect for women in songs such as "Do Right Woman—Do Right Man" (1967), "Respect," and "Think."

With respect to marketing, soul music can be regarded as the next evolutionary stage of rhythm & blues. In this view, one could conclude that it did not matter whether the chart name was "Soul" or "Rhythm & Blues." It was still deemed "black-sounding music." Fortunately, the improving social conditions of the 1960s contributed to the emergence of hundreds of African American performers. With integration legislatively mandated, people who had not been exposed to African Americans and their

Aretha Franklin. © Photofest

music were now appreciating it, helping contribute to its proliferation as droves of black performers took to the stage.

In general, soul music combines certain music characteristics and performance practices of gospel (such as the 1964 song titled "Mercy, Mercy" by Don Covay & The Goodtimers) and rhythm & blues (all three types). An example is the singer Sam Cooke. As a former member of the gospel quintet named The Soul Stirrers, Cooke became one of the group's favored singers among the public, which prompted him to embark on a solo career. Although some African Americans displayed their disapproval of Cooke's career switch to the secular music world, he nonetheless continued to pursue a career in popular music. Some of his popular songs included "You Send Me" (1957), "(What a) Wonderful World" (1960), and "Cupid" (1961). Despite the fact that these songs do not feature a gospel-inspired sound most suited to the taste of African Americans, the public found their subject matter to be most appealing.

Soul music is often viewed as secular gospel music because of its inheritance of gospel characteristics such as numerous vocal articulations, instrumentation, extemporaneous and improvisational presentations, and an emphasis on emotionalism. Rhythm & blues influences on soul music include the use of brass and woodwind instruments as a common component of a song's accompaniment, instrumental solos (saxophone, piano, and guitar) within a sung performance, and the emphasis on current social themes.

As common as these features were in many songs, there nonetheless were two distinct approaches to composing/performing soul music, henceforth to be referred to as "basic soul" and "Motown soul." In general, basic soul maintained a closer connection to vocal stylizations similar to gospel music, whereas Motown fused vocal and instrumental stylizations of current styles and trends, which tended to be more mainstream sounding.[5] The following discussion of musical selections of basic and Motown soul will provide a greater understanding of soul music during the 1960s. The purpose of differentiating the two styles is to describe how, based on societal conditions, they do indeed differ from one another, and not to imply that one is superior to the other. The most important point is that together, both approaches to African American music during the 1960s brought about a greater exposure to and consequent understanding of African American culture by the general public. Also, in both types, the voice is preeminent and therefore singers are emphasized in the music.

SOUL: BASIC

Basic soul encapsulates a wide range of performers and distinctive performance practices that were mixed and matched by performers within the genre. Performers such as Aretha Franklin, Ray Charles, and Otis Redding displayed a high degree of gospel-type vocalizations; Sam Cooke and The Shirelles were primarily known as popular mainstream artists; and lyrically speaking, the sounds of James Brown were decidedly pro-black. Be that as it may, the influence of gospel music (to a greater or lesser extent) can be detected in all basic soul music. Regarding mixing and matching elements, an artist such as Aretha Franklin may best be known for her inflections of gospel while at the same time will have a recording more representative of the mainstream-type sound. Therefore, the ensuing discussion is merely a general guide to understand the scope and breadth of basic soul. Lyrically, basic soul catered to African American culture with such themes as love, racial pride, civil rights, and feminism. The combination of these themes with the seriousness of gospel music resulted in a greater display of emotional presentations. In the aftermath, the music was not "watered down." Singers did not compromise the usage of typical aspects of black music such as the importance of vocables, lyric interpolations, a seemingly extemporaneous presentation, being full-throated, a less smooth-sounding vocal tone quality, and syncopation as ways to further a song's lyrical meaning. For example, James Brown frequently used these features, as evidenced in his song titled "Say It Loud–I'm Black and I'm Proud" (1968). The vocal nuance "uh" opens the song and his use of lyric interpolations (an added word between phrases) help to illustrate an ability to perform extemporaneously. Ray Charles's 1955 hit titled "I've Got a Woman" is similar to gospel music, utilizing extemporaneous presentations with interpolated words, vocables, and a less restricted structure with respect to the song's organization. Each verse contains very few different lyrics, but rather a restatement of the same lyrics that includes a few words at the end to complete the thought. Both Otis Redding in his recording titled "Try a Little Tenderness" (1967) and "I Thank You" (1968) by Sam and Dave display this gospel-influenced manner of singing.

---

[5] By no means does this suggest that Motown is inferior to basic soul music. In fact, if it were not for its innovative approaches to African American music, many non-African Americans would not have been exposed to African American music.

Ray Charles. © Photofest

Their guttural vocal productions are similar to what can be heard among some preachers in the African American church experience.

Guttural sounds are not specific to any gender. Aretha Franklin–regarded as the "queen" of soul–frequently uses a full-throated/guttural sounding voice, which can be heard in the songs "Respect," "Chain of Fools' (1968), "Think," and "(You Make Me Feel Like) A Natural Woman" (1968). There is no doubt about the significance of the voice in soul music, as it has several responsibilities. For example, it is used to establish a song's tempo and/or emotion, such as the singing of a vocal incipit (a sung introductory statement) in "I've Got a Woman" by Ray Charles and "Do Right Woman—Do Right Man" by Aretha Franklin, respectively.

With regard to instrumentation, basic soul focused more on vocal ingenuity and placed less emphasis on using strings and other types of orchestral arrangements, which gospel music relied upon due to its "lyrical" focus. For example, in "Do Right Woman—Do Right Man," minimal accompaniment is provided because it is not needed against the more skillful vocal presentation. Voice, background singers, saxophones, trumpets, and trombones are usually found in recordings of basic soul. However, this is not always the case as exemplified by the song titled "Natural Woman" by Aretha Franklin, in which strings are included in the instrumental accompaniment. In general, however, basic soul songs such as "Knock on Wood" by Eddie Floyd and "Tell It Like It Is" by Aaron Neville use

Otis Redding. © Tony Frank/Sygma/Corbis

saxophones, trumpets, and trombones along with a four- or five-piece rhythm section (piano, guitar, bass, drums, and often organ).

Basic Soul Artists With a More Gospel-Type Presentation include the following.

PERFORMER	SONG TITLES
Ray Charles	"I've Got a Woman"
Aretha Franklin	"Respect," "Think," "A Natural Woman"
Impressions, The	"Amen," "It's Alright"
Wilson Pickett	"Na Na Na Na," "Funky Broadway," "Mustang Sally"
Otis Redding	"Try a Little Tenderness," "These Arms of Mine"
Righteous Brothers, The	"(You're My) Soul and Inspiration"
Sam and Dave	"Soul Man," "Hold On! I'm Comin'," "I Thank You"
Jackie Wilson	"Baby Work Out," "(Your Love Keeps Lifting Me) Higher and Higher"

Recordings by these artists display various vocal and instrumental elements similar to gospel music such as incipit (a very brief vocal lead in), use of religious words within a generally secular song, full-throated voice, falsetto, and so on. As previously mentioned, Ray Charles's vocal incipit as an introductory statement in the song "I've Got a Woman" is a technique used in gospel music. The lyrical content in the song "Amen" by The Impressions is an example of the fondness for religious music held by the African American community. Their song "It's Alright" speaks specifically to black people about temporary tribulations that will eventually be "alright." Wilson Pickett's full-throated vocal production as heard in the song "In the Midnight Hour" emulates a gospel tradition. On occasion Mr. Pickett uses the phrase "in the gospel hour," a lyrical expression in the gospel music tradition. The seemingly improvisational manner in which Jackie Wilson sings the song "(Your Love Keeps Lifting Me) Higher and Higher," particularly with extemporaneous inflections throughout the song, without doubt exhibits the gospel tradition. Otis Redding sings his recording titled "These Arms of Mine" in 6/8 meter-a rhythmical measuring unit found in blues and gospel.[6]

Basic Soul Artists With a More Mainstream-Type Presentation include the following

PERFORMER	SONG TITLES
Brooke Benton	"Rainy Night in Georgia," "The Boll Weevil Song"
Chubby Checker	"The Twist," "Let's Twist Again," "Slow Twistin'," "Limbo Rock"
Chiffons, The	"He's So Fine"
Sam Cooke	"You Send Me," "What a Wondeful World," "Cupid"
Crystals, The	"He's a Rebel," "Da Doo Ron Ron," "Then He Kissed Me"
Dixie Cups, The	"Chapel of Love"
Drifters, The	"Save the Last Dance for Me," "Under the Boardwalk," "Up on the Roof"
Little Anthony & The Imperials	"Goin' Out of My Head," "Hurt So Bad"
Marcels, The	"Blue Moon"
O'Kaysions, The	"Girl Watcher"
Peaches & Herb	"Close Your Eyes"
Ronettes, The	"Be My Baby"
Ruby & The Romantics	"Our Day Will Come"
Shangri-Las, The	"Leader of the Pack," "Remember (Walkin' in the Sand)"
Shirelles, The	"Will You Still Love Me Tomorrow," "Soldier Boy," "Mama Said"

---

[6] The 6/8 meter refers to counting either six beats for each measure, while experiencing an emotion of counting two sets of three (e.g., *1.2.3 4.5.6*).

Sam Cooke and The Soul Stirrers. © Photofest

These artists were just as marketable as Motown artists. Their lyrical and vocal inflections were just as appealing to mainstream tastes as they were to African American taste. Songs such as "The Twist" and "Let's Twist Again" were simply about encouraging people to dance. Sam Cooke's recordings titled "Cupid" and "You Send Me" were tuneful and radio-friendly songs of love that were welcomed by mainstream culture. Moreover, similar to the productions of many Motown songs, the addition of the orchestra to the instrumental accompaniment in the song "Cupid" is an attractive sound to a mainstream music audience. Although topics of promiscuity and "bad girl" images were not typical themes with America's general public, a few songs became popular nonetheless. These include "Will You Still Love Me Tomorrow" by The Shirelles, addressing a young woman's concern about the continuity of a man's feelings for her after a night of love and romance; as well as bad girl-type groups such as The Crystals with their song "He's a Rebel" and The Shangri-Las' "Leader of the Pack."

Basic Soul Artists With a Pro-Black Presentation are best represented by James Brown. Without question the song titled "Say It Loud–I'm Black and I'm Proud" (1968) exemplified the mood of black culture in the face of racism and civil rights issues. Such a mood was also evident in the song "Get Up, Get Into It, Get Involved" (1971) by Brown. Combining these pro-black lyrics with danceable and very syncopated rhythms, Brown was able to get his message of soul power across to people of varied national and ethnic backgrounds. Moreover, the song titled "Soul Power" (1971) reinforces the notion of "people power" as a way for people to look at themselves for solutions of racism and discrimination. Rightly so, James Brown earned the title "Soul Brother No. 1."

SOUL: MOTOWN

While Motown soul used gospel-like vocal qualities, it approached black music differently than performers of basic soul. Started in 1959 and totally dominated by founder and owner Berry Gordy, Motown Records' approach to soul music was to refine performance practices (including instrumental practices) as well as to refine the overall demeanor and behavior of young African American performers. This was done in an effort to appeal to a wider audience. To accomplish this, Mr. Gordy needed to disassociate his groups from styles and/or music practices that tended to denote African American usages, or "jungle music," as it was pejoratively referred to at that time. While this transpired with many of Motown's performers, there was an exception, namely Marvin Gaye. After the death of Tammi Terrell, his singing partner in their popular duets,[7] Gaye embarked on a solo career with Motown Records. His gospel-like singing manner became more pronounced during his solo career. With recordings such as "Pride and Joy" (1963), "How Sweet It Is to Be Loved By You" (1964), "Ain't That Peculiar" and "I'll Be Doggone" (both in 1965), "Too Busy Thinking About My Baby" and "I Heard It Through the Grapevine" (both in 1968), and "That's the Way Love Is" (1969), his presentation reflected features closer to basic soul. Gordy set out to produce groups of variety sizes: Stevie Wonder and Mary Wells as soloists; Marvin Gaye and Tammi Terrell as duets; The Supremes as a trio group; quartets such as Gladys Knight and The Pips, The Four Tops, Smokey Robinson & The Miracles, and Martha & The Vandellas; and The Temptations as a quintet group. Within a year, Motown scored its first top hit, namely "Shop Around" (1960) by Smokey Robinson & The Miracles.

Since the presentation of vocal groups within Motown soul was an important consideration, many performances entailed crafty, and in many ways less rhythmic complexity when compared to basic soul. An example is the song titled "Come See About Me" (1964) by The Supremes with its very marketable, well-polished and smooth-sounding performance that greatly appealed to America's musical taste. Another example is "My Girl" (1965) by The Temptations. Performed in the rhythm & blues doo-wop tradition, the harmonies incorporate vocal nuances and words to support the lead singer's part. The Four Tops also recorded many tuneful songs with a harmonically complimentary accompaniment.

Syncopation and rhythmic complexity seem less apparent in Motown soul than in basic soul. Again, this is an example of Mr. Gordy's endeavor to get mainstream America to listen to more performances of African American music, and simplifying the rhythm is one way of doing this. Furthermore, Mr. Gordy was concerned with producing more music that could accompany popular dances of the day, such as the jerk, mashed potato, philly dog, watusi, pony, hitchhike, temptation walk, skate, monkey, and many others. Because he was catering to mainstream America and its diverse levels of dancing ability, less complex rhythmic patterns were employed to help novice dancers stay on the beat. Consequently, accents generally occurred on every count of the measure such as handclaps in "Come See About Me" by The Supremes, or a strong backbeat (counts two and four) such as finger snaps heard in both The Temptations' "My Girl" and "Baby I Need Your Loving" (1964) by The Four Tops, and the use of

---

[7] Some popular songs of Tammi Terrell and Marvin Gaye included "Ain't Nothin' Like the Real Thing," (1968) and "If I Could Build My Whole World Around You" (1967).

The Supremes. © Photofest

handclaps on the back beat in the song "Quicksand" (1964) by Martha & The Vandellas. As examples of a rhythm not typically used in Motown songs, the Percy Sledge song "When a Man Loves a Woman" (1966) and "Tell It Like It is" (1967) by Aaron Neville both employ the 6/8 meter. Although a typical meter in black music styles such as blues, gospel, and doo-wop rhythm & blues, the 6/8 meter seldom occurred in popular Motown hits. To Mr. Gordy's credit, Motown helped change the overall sound of black music. To accomplish this, producers avoided typical aspects of black music, and rhythm, due to its distinctiveness in black music, was an effective element to modify.

In addition to using a less-syncopated rhythm to market black music to mainstream culture, Motown frequently used orchestral arrangements in many of its recordings. In a way this practice gives the impression that an instrumental presentation is equal in importance to the vocal performance. Again, this reflected an intent on the part of Motown to appeal to a wider audience. In "My Girl," there is interplay between the string section and the vocal and horn parts. The use of the baritone saxophone in "Quicksand" demonstrates a proclivity to use an instrument that was favored among big band jazz enthusiasts. "Baby I Need Your Loving" uses strings in the introduction, each time the chorus is sung,

The Temptations. © Photofest

and during some verses. The Mar-velettes' recording titled "My Baby Must Be a Magician" (1967), in addition to the typical instruments (piano, guitar, bass, and drums), uses other instruments including organ and strings as well as an unusual guitar effect performed sporadically.

Inasmuch as the number of female groups (particularly African American) increased ten-fold from the previous decade, ensembles who recorded popular hits utilizing the doo-wop style of singing was slowly diminishing. For Motown, the doo-wop style of singing was the most conspicuous black-sounding aspect, and consequently, among women groups, the utilization of numerous vocal nuances was minimized to achieve a less Afro-centric presentation. Mr. Gordy's emphasis on refinement proved to be supremely successful, since his female groups recorded over 50% of the "Top 10" hits during the 1960s. Motown's ideology was also evident with productions among male ensembles. Its three principal male groups who were making popular recordings during this time were The Miracles, The Four Tops, and The Temptations. The Temptations was the only group out of these three who frequently incorporated more vocal nuances than "ooh," "ah," "do," and "oh" in their performances. Even then, however, the number of these usages was significantly less than those heard among groups from the previous decade.

FUNK

Funk music emerged during the middle of the 1960s and continued well into the 1970s. The social climate of the 1960s was reflected in the aggressive and rather unconventional approaches to instrumentation, rhythm, text, and compositional practices of youth-culture music, whatever the style. From a philosophical perspective, funk music reflected the individuality of African Americans, as this music contained musical individualism within a group context—something not evident to such a great degree in the previous decades. Despite the fact that existentialism and individualism were common themes during the 1960s, the overall musical presentation of funk emphasized the togetherness promoted on by the hippie movement. This was the result of many artists' desire to perform a mix of melodic, harmonic, and rhythmic riffs (brief melodic/harmonic/rhythmic patterns). This desire became commonplace among funk performers to the point where getting to the core or groove became paramount during performances. The use of riff exists *ad infinitum* in funk music. One of the earliest examples of this that became the staple for many funk songs is the James Brown recording of "Cold Sweat" (1967).

Funkadelic. © Photofest

When listening to songs such as "One Nation Under a Groove" (1978) by Funkadelic, "Atomic Dog" (1982) by George Clinton, or "Bootzilla" (1978) by Bootsy Collins, there is no question that rhythm is the most interesting musical element in funk. The rhythm is characterized by the performance of riffs by all parts: voice (lead singer and background singers), bass, keyboard, drums, guitar, brass and woodwind instruments, and tambourine. In effect, the combination of each part's riff is what produces a song's groove (or harmonic and rhythmic foundation). An example is Sly & The Family Stone's song titled "Thank You (Falettinme Be Mice Elf Agin)" (1970). The song begins with drum, bass, and guitar, each playing its own riff. A horn riff and a second guitar riff are added after the first four measures of the introduction; this is done to help establish the song's groove prior to either the singer or the main theme's entrance. The following Song Navigator provides a visual overview of these and other practices of funk music. James Brown is one of the most interesting performers to listen to in this regard, as he takes full advantage of the excitement produced by combining various riffs. In "Say It Loud—I'm Black and I'm Proud" (1969), both a drum and a vocal riff introduce the song's groove. During the first verse, a four-piece rhythm section and an extended riff played by the horns supports Brown's vocal line.

TIME	SECTION	COMMENTS
		Instrumentation: voice, background singers, trumpets, saxophones, trombone, guitar, piano, bass, drums, and strings
00:00	Introduction	Bass, drums, and guitar riffs
00:10	" "	Horns and a 2nd guitar riff are added; a rhythmic spoken part using vocables
00:19	Verse 1	Vocalists sing in unison; horns play sporadically accompanied by the entire band
00:37	Verse 2	Same as Verse 1; horns play sporadically
00:55	Chorus	Vocalists sing in a homophonic fashion accompanied by the entire band
01:13	Interlude	Instruments only; guitars play the lead riffs
01:22	Verse 3	Same as Verse 1
01:40	Verse 4	Same as Verse 1
01:58	Chorus	Same as Chorus above
02:17	Interlude	Same as Interlude above
02:26	Verse 5	Same as Verse 1
02:44	Verse 6	Same as Verse 1
03:02	Chorus	Same as Chorus above
03:21	Verse 7	Same as Verse 1
03:40	Chorus	Same as Chorus above

Song Navigator 17.1: "Thank You (Falettinme Be Mice Elf Agin)" (1970) by Sly & The Family Stone

Rhythm is such an important aspect of funk that vocal sounds are frequently used as a contribution to the song's rhythmic continuity. James Brown does this rather successfully in many songs. Using vocal stylizations such as full-throated/raspy and guttural sounds, numerous vocables, and shouts. Brown continues rhythmic continuity in songs such as "Say It Loud—I'm Black and I'm Proud," and "I Got You (I Feel Good)" (1965). In addition to rhythmic continuity, Brown uses shouts as a way to direct the band, such as telling them when to change to a different musical section. For instance, in "Say It Loud—I'm Black and I'm Proud," Brown shouts each time just before the bridge section.

With reference to the tempo, songs range from moderately slow to moderately fast. For instance, a moderately slow song is "Tell Me Something Good" (1973) by Rufus, featuring Chaka Kahn; the song "Play That Funky Music" (1976) by Wild Cherry is moderately fast by comparison.

While rhythm is indeed a defining aspect of funk, the lyrical content of many of the songs must be considered. Never in the history of black music have there been lyrics that toy with science fiction and silliness as those heard in funk. One can attribute this to the growing individuality of youth as well as to the existential-istic attitude of the 1960s that affected black culture even to the point

James Brown. © Photofest

of non conventionalisms. In other words, it seems up to this point that a good number of musicians played it safe by composing and performing within the fashion, tradition, and, more importantly, acceptance of African American culture. One only needs to listen to songs such as the already-mentioned "Atomic Dog" and "Bootzilla," and also "Mothership Connection Starchild" (1978) by George Clinton, and "Supergroovalis-ticprosifunkstication" (1976) by Parliament. To add to this, during the 1970s art rock and glitter and glam era, George Clinton went on tour presenting a theatrical show whereupon after the landing of a spaceship, Dr. Funkenstein emerged from the ship to give "funk" to the planet earth.

In general, groups performed funk. Bands consist of voice (lead and background singers' parts), four-piece rhythm section (organ/synthesizer both played by one person, guitar, bass, drums), and a brass and woodwind section (often trumpets and saxophones, and sometimes trombones). Other instruments sometimes included congas, timbales, tambourine, and other types of percussion sounds. It is important to note that an ensemble generally performed funk (as opposed to a solo singer who was accompanied by a band) In funk, the focus was more frequently on the entire band as a unit. Songs such as "Get the Funk Out Ma Face" (1976) by the Brothers Johnson, "What Is Hip?" (1973) by Tower of Power, "Pick Up the Pieces" (1974) and "Cut the Cake" (1975) by AWB all present songs in ensemble fashion. The music is sung or can be played instrumentally. When sung by one person there is often a background singers' part that is sung by approximately three to five singers. An example of this is in the song "Say It Loud—I'm Black and I'm Proud." When more than one person sings the melody, it can be presented in a monophonic or homophonic fashion. In many funk songs, the melody is also presented by a group of singers in a homorhythmic manner. Some examples include "Jungle Boogie" and "Hollywood Swinging" (both 1974), and "Funky Stuff" (1973), all by Kool & The Gang. This is also audible in the song "Up For The Down Stroke" (1974) by Parliament. For instance, the monophonic texture occurs during the first chorus, while the homophonic texture happens during the second half of the next time the chorus is sung. Texture is used in this style of music to create contrast. For example, in "Thank You (Falettinme Be Mice Elf Agin)," the verses are sung in unison, while the chorus section is homophonically sung by a group. In addition to these textures, the polyphonic texture is also performed. For example, in "Up For The Down Stroke," during the last eight measures of the bridge section, the lyrics of the chorus section are added to the existing bridge lyrics. Because they are sung at the same time but with different rhythms, this produces a polyphonic texture.

Still another defining characteristic of funk was its different approach to the bass. Not only was there a more active bass line with respect to the number of notes played and complex syncopated riffs, but also a new way of playing the instrument. This new technique was called "slapping," where one physically "slaps" the bass with the thumb. The technique also involved periodically pulling the strings, thus producing a "popping" sound. Larry Graham of Sly and The Family Stone is given credit for developing this new technique to playing the bass. The song "Thank You (Falettinme Be Mice Elf Agin)" illustrates this performance technique.

Because composers of funk often approached the creation of new songs with capricious attitudes, the incorporation of other non-traditional instrumental sounds became commonplace. For example, in "Up For the Down Stroke," there are several different synthesizer sounds as well as a "wah-wah" sound played by the guitarist. In "Thank You (Falettinme Be Mice Elf Agin)," the "wah-wah" sound is played as a guitar riff. In creating a party atmosphere, performers were less inclined to have drastically contrasting sections within a song. Some examples include "Bustin Loose" (1979) by Chuck Brown & The Soul Searchers, "Loose Booty" (1973) by Sly & The Family Stone, "Shake Your Rump to the Funk" (1976) by The Bar-Kays, "P. Funk" (Wants To Get Funked Up)" (1976) by Parliament, and "Fight the Power" (1975) by the Isley Brothers. Since dancing was a main social activity within this environment, performers were very creative in producing recordings that best suited their listeners' tastes. Fortunately, improvisation was a characteristic of funk music. Although this aspect was not necessarily noticed on recordings, live performances often showcased artists' ability to be extemporaneous. While this is true, funk was also performed in a predictable manner. For instance, songs regularly consisted of an introduction, verses, chorus, and bridge/interlude. This structure helps the listener as well as the band get into the "groove" or "flow" of the song. The chorus section was the most important as it was used as the introduction and the closing section.

Funk showcases the individuality of artists and had a proclivity for using rhythm as the underpinning for composition. In the aftermath, funk along with disco, became the most influential features in the later development of hip-hop music.

DISCO

In the early 1940s, the National Academy of Broadcasters' (NAB), in retrospect, rightfully argued its opposition to airing records over live performances of musicians, as doing so would put a lot of musicians out of work. Interestingly true, this had now permeated the nightclub dance scene as club owners hired disc jockeys to play "records" rather than live bands. The club scene at this time also hosted non-stop dance material to sooth the taste for group dances such as the hustle. To fulfill this desire, for many club owners it seemed more effective, not to mention profitable, to hire a deejay who could seamlessly string together popular songs in order to produce nonstop dance music. After all, a band's repertoire could not compare to the vast number of songs available to the deejay. He or she could easily provide music for any occasion and any audience. Moreover, the average consumer generally preferred to dance to the original recording, as songs often incorporated certain sections for audience participation.[8] What club owner or venue entrepreneur could ignore the advantage of paying a single individual versus a band that could produce dance music?

The dance craze during the 1970s was an inevitable occurrence; the popularity of dance resurfaces every 15 to 20 years, much to the delight of adolescents and young adults. The previous dance craze of the 1950s/early 1960s saw the emergence of dances such as the twist, mashed potato, jerk, skate, monkey, pony, and swim, all accompanied by what was popularly known as rock & roll. The dance craze before then gave birth to the charleston, swing, the two-step, and the lindy hop, which were danced to the music of the big bands. New York City's cosmopolitan environment during the 1970s greatly inspired the musical, social, and dance practices of the disco scene. Moreover, the effects of the civil rights social scene in the previous decade helped to fuel the emerging gay community. In New York City, three groups in particular gave rise to the disco music social dance scene: blacks, Latinos, and gays.

Beginning in the 1970s, the deejays became a permanent fixture in music. Spinning (playing) records for dance clubs, wedding receptions, bar mitzvahs and bat mitzvahs, holiday parties, or other social gatherings, the deejay provided musical entertainment to appeal to anyone's appetite.

While deejays were increasingly being used to supply dance music, a number of people during the beginning of the 1970s favored live dance bands that performed songs by popular groups like Kool & The Gang, K.C. & The Sunshine Band, Donna Summer (see photograph at the beginning of the chapter), The Bee Gees, the Village People, Earth, Wind and Fire, and many others.

---

[8] An example would be the motioning of the letters "YMCA" in the song "YMCA" (1978) by The Village People, or the "ya-hoo" sound in the song by Kool & The Gang titled "Celebration" (1980).

The Village People. © Associated Film Distributions/Photofest

While funk music was popular with a number of different audiences, it was not the preeminent style of the 1960s. It could not compete with the invasion of British groups, and was too aggressive for the still racially segregated American society. Disco, on the other hand, was neither too black or nor too white; it was grey, which for many meant that music which reflected the changing times of social and racial integration. For others, "grey" meant the digression of music, which was empowered by technology, glitter, and glam theatrics, and characteristics that were inferior to those present in previous styles of American music. However one sees it, disco was the new mainstream music of the 1970s. While funk music sought to produce nonstop syncopated dance music during the 1960s/70s, disco music satisfied the hunger for simpler dance rhythms. Popular recordings such as "Shame Shame Shame" (1974) by Shirley and Company, "The Hustle" (1975) by Van McCoy and The Soul City Orchestra, and "Boogie Oogie Oogie" (1978) by A Taste of Honey featured engaging dance rhythms. For many people, the syncopated rhythms of funk music-particularly the synchronized bass and kick drum passages-was not the best accompaniment for dancing. Disco rhythms accentuated the basic counts of each measure of a quadruple meter, including an emphasis on the backbeat (counts two and four). Unlike the syncopated riffs of funk music, disco furnished a simpler rhythm to facilitate the 1970s dance craze.

Disco music's presentation can be divided into two categories: (1) ensemble or orchestra, and (2) disc jockey, who combines (called a "mix") danceable parts (called "breaks") of favorite 1960s "funk" music. In the first category, there were two types of ensembles or orchestras that presented disco music: (1) a vocalist or group of vocalists who did not play an instrument accompanied by a rhythm section, and a supplemental unit-brass, woodwinds, and strings; and (2) a band consisting of a rhythm section, trumpet player, trombonist, and saxophonist, each of whom might sing some portion of the melody and/or harmony. Songs such as "Never Can Say Goodbye" (1974) by Diana Ross, "I Will Survive" (1979) by Gloria Gaynor, and "Last Dance" (1979) by Donna Summer all represent the first type where a soloist is the featured performer. I should note that there are a few exceptions to the first type, with respect to the singer playing an instrument. An example is the singer and pianist Barry White. Some of his recordings include "I'm Gonna Love You Just a Little Bit More, Baby" (1973), "Can't Get

Enough of Your Love" and "Never, Never Gonna Give Ya Up" (both in 1974), and "You're the First, the Last, My Everything" (1977). Returning to the first category, examples include "YMCA" (1978) by The Village People, "Disco Inferno" (ca. 1978), by The Trammps, and "Love Train" (1972) by the O'Jays. The second type of disco presentation is exemplified in the recordings of "Shake Your Booty" (1976) by K.C. and The Sunshine Band, and "Celebration" (1980) by Kool & The Gang.

An advantage of having a larger group is the ability to create a number of contrasting ideas with the inherently different sounds of instruments. Fueled by a desire to create non-stop dance music many songs were orchestrated and arranged with elaborate and/or extended introductions. Disco songs are often organized using sections, such as an introduction, verses, chorus, and bridge/interlude. A good majority of disco song opens with an introduction. This performance practice announces the tuneful music in an effort to entice people to want to dance. Additionally, every song ends with a repetitive chorus as a way to leave the dancer/listener with celebratory and joyous feelings. Song Navigator 17.2 features the song "Celebration" by Kool & The Gang illustrates these points.

TIME	SECTION	COMMENTS
		Instrumentation: voice, background singers, trumpets, saxophones, trombone, guitar, piano, bass, drums, and strings
00:00	Introduction	Opens with Drums and Rhythm Guitar; Voices speaking in a celebratory fashion; Guitar line leads more band members
00:09	" "	Trumpets, saxophones, and trombone are added to the band
00:17	" "	Band plays their own riffs; voices sing a homophonic vocable ("yah-hoo"); solo voice responds to the group of voices; Kick drum and Bass play on every count, while the snare drum plays the back beat
00:33	Chorus	Lyrics begin with the song title
00:49	Verse 1	Lead vocalists enters accompanied by the band
01:05	Verse 2	Group of singers and lead singer sing in an alternating fashion; There are minimal lyrics
01:20	Bridge	Solo singer, followed by a group of singers; this section also includes strings
01:33	Interlude	This section is the same as the last part of the Introduction, and storm and lightning effects only; the song has the appearance of ending but continues after about 10 seconds
01:49	Chorus	Same as chorus above
02:04	Bridge 2	This is a second Bridge section that functions as a Coda (ending section)
02:20	Verse 2	Same as Verse 2 above
02:36	Interlude	Same as previous Interlude above
02:52	Chorus	Same as chorus above

Song Navigator 17.2: "Celebration" (1980) by Kool & The Gang from the album *Celebration* (1987, Island Def Jam)

Donna Summer. © Photofest

Donna Summer was the undisputed "queen" of disco music during the 1970s and early 1980s. This title is the result of her having a repertoire of popular dance songs that lyrically spoke to teens and young adults about love, sexuality, and the empowerment of women. Her songs include the following:

"Love to Love You Baby" (1976)
"I Feel Love" (1977)
"Last Dance" (1978)
"Dim All the Lights" (1979)
"Hot Stuff" (1979)
"Bad Girls" (1979)
"She Works Hard For the Money" (1983)

While disco supplied dance music at a time when knowing how to "disco dance" was often a requirement for the trend-minded young adult, it was short-lived. This was due, in part, to a diminishing of the dance craze and a return to musical styles that were often blues-based, such as hard rock and heavy metal. But disco did not end without exerting some influence on styles such as art rock and glitter and glam rock—styles that incorporated theatricism and multi movement. Moreover, it seemed that many non-disco artists found it advantageous to jump on the disco bandwagon, which led to some notoriety. Some examples include "Dancing Queen" (1976) by ABBA, "Miss You" (1978) by the Rolling Stones, "Da Ya Think I'm Sexy" (1979) by Rod Stewart, "9 to 5" (1982) by Dolly Parton, and "The Magnificent Seven" (1988) by The Clash.

CHAPTER EIGHTEEN

JAZZ TRADITIONS: FREE FORM/FREE JAZZ, FUSION, AND JAZZ ROCK

FREE FORM/FREE JAZZ

Up to the 1960s, jazz often borrowed music characteristics and performance practices from its predecessors. During the mid-1960s, however, jazz musicians began to approach jazz composition with seemingly little regard for jazz conventions, with the exception of improvisation, and focused more on existential perspectives. This approach avoided a distinct scale or mode, harmonic structure, rhythmic cohesiveness, theme from which to improvise or interpret, and so on. In this context, the "performance" is an engagement of individual ideas that progresses through time and space and ultimately seeks to illuminate an emphasis on the course of action rather than the action alone. In other words, attention is placed on how members go about developing their own ideas against the ideas of others. Having said this, you might find this to be more revealing while attending a performance rather than listening to a recording, as body movement is often an essential part of the presentation. In any case, this is called "free-form jazz." It is noteworthy that other terms such as "third stream," "avant-garde," and "free" also labeled this new approach to jazz composition and performance during this time. The following discussion examines a few pieces that might be categorized as free form or free jazz.

In general, free jazz avoids any melodic, harmonic, and rhythmic cohesiveness. When listening to, for example, the piece titled "Free Jazz" (1960) by the Ornette Coleman Double Quartet, some questions may arise:

1. What are they doing?
2. Why are they playing in this manner?
3. What should one look for in a performance of this type?

To answer these questions, one must avoid comparing the music characteristics and performance practices of this piece with that of any other style of music. In other words, do not try to find a melody, harmonic structure, rhythmic cohesiveness, or formal structure, as this approach will lead you straight to the nebulous zone. To make matters even more confusing, the instrumentation is unique to namely, a double quartet. Further examination of the instrumentation, however, may be one's gateway to getting to the core of this performance. For instance, do not try to discern the playing of eight instruments. Rather, try to visualize two separate quartet bands, each with a two-piece woodwind unit accompanied by a two-piece rhythm section–bass and drums. The performance involves the interaction of the woodwind players and the rhythm section of each quartet playing in an improvisational fashion. After distinguishing the two entities, make an attempt to hear them perform simultaneously. It creates a very interesting sound. In summary, the "process" is what is most significant about a performance of free jazz. Free form is different from free jazz in that the song's "form" is usually unrestricted, while melody, harmony, and rhythmic cohesiveness are maintained by the instrumentalists.

John Coltrane. © Photofest

The recording of "Alabama" by John Coltrane in several ways represents the antithesis of the previous piece ("Free Jazz"). For instance, at the beginning of the piece you will hear a distinct melody, played by the tenor saxophone (Coltrane), juxtaposed with a harmonic succession of chords, which establish a distinct tonal center. There is also rhythmic cohesiveness throughout the piece as the accompaniment (piano, bass, and drums) supports the saxophonist's different *tempi*. Given these particular features, what factors are used to categorize this piece as free form? I believe that Mr. Coltrane presents an introspective musical performance that represents his perturbation at of the segregation laws against African Americans, particularly children, while on a visit to Alabama. This type of meditative thought is common among musicians who present a performance of free jazz. For this reason alone, "Alabama" is categorized as free form.

In summary, bebop, cool, jazz rock, fusion, and free were all specific approaches to jazz from the 1940s through the 1970s. They were not the only approaches to jazz, but as one examines the movers and shakers of jazz music, these were the styles frequently performed.

FUSION

While jazz rock, rock styles, and funk forms of musical practices and eventual forms of jazz were the order of the day (1970s), there continued a "mainstream" of the jazz tradition. Despite the fact that bebop, cool, and hard bop were coexisting with mainstream, they were not the norm for music marketing among the record labels; instead, big band jazz was still favored. Partly due to paying homage to the greats of pre-WWII big band jazz, statistics showed that the other forms of jazz, as previously mentioned, were not as appealing to the consumer who experienced pre-WWII music activities, as well as the emerging youth culture. Although, as previously mentioned, big band jazz came to a screeching halt as the most marketable music at the close of WWII there nonetheless were performances by some of the pre-WWII big band greats. Some of these included (listed alphabetically) Count Basie, Duke Ellington, Woody Herman, Stan Kenton, Buddy Rich, and Woody Herman. Some albums include Woody Herman's *Giant Steps* (1973), Stan Kenton's *Live at the Redlands* (1970), and *Rich in London* (1972) by Buddy Rich's band, to name a few. While these and other musicians were continuing the tradition or "mainstream" of jazz during the 1970s, it was the eclectic nature of fusion that was becoming more intriguing to the broad-based music listening public.

To begin, there was without doubt a symbiosis of societal conditions and music activities that greatly affected composers and performers of jazz during the 1970s. Social and cultural conditions of the 1960s (civil rights, sociopolitical issues, Vietnam, and the sexual revolution) combined with certain musical approaches of the 1960s provided the impetus for musical changes that were occurring. The social and cultural confrontations of two ethnic groups–black and white–during the 1960s provided a forum for dealing with integration and consequently interaction and exchanges of social issues that had not occurred to this degree in the history of American society. These social and cultural exchanges affected music activities in the United States in several ways. First, composers and performers were became more open to fusing characteristics of styles that historically were marketed to dissimilar audiences. Second, consumer musical tastes began to broaden as the result of this different approach to music. For instance, as the result of being exposed to different social and cultural issues in America, a number of Americans became more unified in their quest for civil liberties and equality. Such a viewpoint was reflected in music as songs displayed in their lyrics a greater level of social consciousness, and an inclusive approach to combining formerly segregated social and ethnic issues. Finally, as the result of the aforementioned effects, the music industry began to seriously consider these changes in their marketing strategies. No longer were the majority of consumers oblivious to the social, cultural, and political climate that prevailed in America at this time. The music industry followed the trend of social-based songs, and marketed music to the emerging broad-based public.

Indeed, social and cultural confrontations led to a preponderance of musical audiences that possessed a wide variety of musical tastes. As a marketing strategy encouraged by record labels and record producers to "sell" jazz to newcomers to the style, musicians borrowed musical characteristics and performance practices from classical styles, funk, rock, rhythm & blues, bebop, and cool in an attempt to appeal to such broad musical tastes. Along with other conditions, this led to the "fusing" of music features of varied styles, which produced what we now regard as *fusion*, and more specifically jazz rock and jazz funk. In the 1970s, jazz was again becoming popular; it had not experienced such popularity since the big band jazz era–1920s through early 1940s. Again, it was the consumer-friendly approach to jazz that contributed to its popularity. One examples is Herbie Hancock's album titled *Head Hunters*, which reached the top 20 on *Billboard's* pop chart, eventually achieving platinum status. The

album featured two songs– "Chameleon" and "Watermelon Man"[1]–that have become jazz standards among today's jazz performers. The album titled *Birds of Fire* (1972) by the Mahavishnu Orchestra also reached *Billboard's* top 20 status. It must be understood that fusion, to some jazz enthusiasts and critics, was nothing more than the commercialization of jazz.[2] Such a belief was held for the simple reason that those music styles where musicians take stock in composing and performing music for the sake of its consumer-friendly appeal generally do not leave lasting musical impressions.

Musically, the innovative approaches to jazz led principally by Miles Davis with his recordings *Birth of the Cool* (1949–50), *In a Silent Way* (1969), and *Bitches Brew* (1970), had the greatest influence on musicians who composed in the fusion format beginning in the 1970s. Although there existed other pioneers of fusion such as the bands Lifetime (formed by former Davis drummer Tony Williams), Dreams, and The Fourth Way, and musicians such as Larry Corywell and Mike Nock, Miles Davis employed some of the most gifted musicians of the day. Some of the most notable performers on Davis's albums who later formed their own groups include (listed alphabetically) Chick Corea (piano), Herbie Hancock (piano), John McLaughlin (guitar), Wayne Shorter (saxophone), and Joe Zawinul (piano). Some of the earliest fusion groups of the 1970s were Return to Forever (formed by Chick Corea), the Mahavishnu Orchestra (formed by John McLaughlin), and Weather Report (formed by Wayne Shorter and Joe Zawinul). These and other musicians were influenced by Davis's musical approaches, and created or extended the ideological and aesthetic qualities inherent in his music. Appealing to a generation of music listeners with limited experiences in jazz who nevertheless possessed an awareness of the "good" in pursuing ethnic tolerance and equality for all, a significant number of musicians borrowed from several idioms–classical, jazz, and rock–that coexisted during the 1970s.

Chick Corea founded his group, Return to Forever, in 1970. As a pianist, he was able to incorporate the use of synthesizers into his compositional and performance ideas. Utilizing syncopated and even rhythms of various rock styles as the basis for the rhythmical drive, juxtaposed with a synchronized harmonic progression as the underpinning of virtuosic melodic themes and improvisational solos, Corea's music, in essence, catered to both the jazz and rock enthusiast. Some of his recordings are *Return to Forever* (1972) *Musicmagic* (1977), *Light Years* (ca. 1979), and *Eye of the Beholder* (1988).

TIME	SECTION	INSTRUMENTATION/COMMENTS
		Instrumentation: Piano, voice, flute, bass, drums
00:00	Introduction A	Piano only
00:40	Introduction B	Piano, voice, and flute all perform the same melodic line, some percussion effects are used
01:16	A	Piano establishes a moderato tempo, drums are added, then voice and flute (that perform the same melodic line)
02:25	Flute solo	Flute solo accompanied by piano, bass, drums
02:27	Piano solo	Piano solo accompanied by piano, bass, drums
03:58	A	Similar to A section above
04:33	Interlude	No tempo, bass performs a brief fill, use of bird sounds

---

[1] "Watermelon Man" appears on this album as a rewrite from Mr. Hancock's first album, Crossings (1971).
[2] The commercialization of music is the process by which a song's melodic, harmonic, and rhythmic tendencies are compromised for the sake of consumer appeal. Phrases such as "watered-down" and "sugar-coated" are analogous to commercialization.

04:45	Introduction B	Similar to what is played in Introduction B above
05:57	A	Allegretto tempo, piano, bass, flute, and voice all play improvisational passages from time to time
07:28	Piano solo	Piano solo accompanied by the band
09:24	Piano solo with vocal inflections	Piano solo accompanied by the band, an increasing use of vocal sounds
10:02	Piano, voice, flute	Piano starts a melodic line, voice joins in followed by flute, these instruments become increasingly dissonant
10:41	Interlude	No tempo as B above
10:54	Introduction B	Similar to Introduction B above

Song Navigator 18.1: "Return to Forever" by Chick Corea from the EP Return to Forever, (1972, ECM)

About the same time that Chick Corea formed Return to Forever, John McLaughlin formed the Mahavishnu Orchestra. Like Corea, McLaughlin was a virtuoso performer. His innovative approach to jazz during the 1970s was attributed to his rock guitar playing style. As heard on the group's recordings *Inner Mounting Flame* (ca. 1972), *Birds of Fire* (ca. 1972), and *Between Nothingness and Eternity* (ca. 1972), McLaughlin's British rock-influenced guitar stylizations helped create the distinct sound of the group and added to the solidification of fusion during the 1970s.

Still another group, Weather Report, was setting new approaches to jazz during the 1970s that led to eventual trends in fusing characteristics of jazz and rock. Formed by Joe Zawinul and Wayne Shorter in 1970, the group eventually moved toward compositions that emphasized rock and funk-based grooves underneath a colorful soloist. One of their more popular songs, "Birdland," from their *Heavy Weather* album (1977), illuminates funk-like syncopated rhythms as played by the bassist Jaco Pastorius.

A host of other competent musicians continued the trend of fusing music characteristics and performance practices from the "well" of music sources. As rock music entered the arena of more pop-oriented sounds, so, too, did musicians with extensive jazz backgrounds or those new to the jazz world with interest in the concept of fusion begin to blend elements of pop in their music. For instance, the song titled "Breezin'" (1976) by guitarist and singer George Benson achieved crossover appeal, as it appeared on the jazz, soul/rhythm & blues, as well as pop charts. One negative aspect from the viewpoint of the jazz enthusiast is the fact that pop music typically has only a minimally lasting effect on the music world, and therefore would relegate jazz to even further obscurity. On the other hand, in view of the quickly changing pop scene and its fresh ideas, fusing its elements with jazz stylizations could also engage fans of the pop scene as well as introduce some form of jazz to the consistently emerging youth population. Some of the more popular musicians who experimented with many ideas of jazz, rock, and pop during the late 1970s included saxophonists Michael Brecker, David Sanborn; trumpeters Randy Brecker, and (brother of Michael), and Chuck Mangione; guitarists George Benson, Al DiMeola, Stanley Jordan, and Pat Metheny; the bands Spyro Gyra and Yellowjackets; and the multitalented Quincy Jones.

JAZZ ROCK

The era of experimentation during the 1960s not only influenced artists to consider new approaches to their music within their own style, but also to look at the possibility of combining musical elements from various styles. The rock & roll scene of the previous decade had enough on its hand in with dealing with the explosion of youth culture music and, by some views, the possible deterioration of social morals. Moreover,

the music taste of many bands in the 1960s tended to avoid the trendy and the less musically challenging rock & roll style. Instead, these bands favored the musical sophistication of jazz. Because bands such as Blood, Sweat and Tears, Tower of Power, and Chicago did not come from the same jazz tradition as Miles Davis, John Coltrane, or Charlie Parker, their idea of jazz was geared toward the music currents of the day. These included rock & roll and its evolutionary rock style, blues, soul, funk, and jazz. With more interest in jazz elements and the desire to attract a younger audience, the aforementioned bands began to combine elements of these styles to create what became known as "jazz rock." It should be noted that the term *rock* in "jazz rock" was the favored word as its usage was more current, and generally referred to youth-inspired music. But the word rock in this instance in effect encompassed elements of rock & roll, blues, soul, and funk. Therefore the musical character was viewed as rock music with jazz elements.

Musical elements of jazz used by jazz rock bands included an emphasis on brass and woodwind instruments, the swing rhythm, and instrument solos with similar melodic jazz phraseology. To support this, bands were larger than most bebop and many cool jazz bands. In jazz rock, the instrumentation usually consisted of lead singer, guitar, piano, bass, drums, saxophone, trumpet, and trombone. Rock elements included rock drum rhythms, a singing style similar to soul (such as the use of *melisma* and full-throated sound), and a general emphasis on the instruments as more than merely accompanimental. An example of this is heard in the song titled "God Bless the Child" in 1969 (a Billie Holiday favorite), by Blood, Sweat, and Tears (BS&T). The song begins with a brass and woodwind introduction played in a hymnal fashion. Following this, the meter is compounded, which in effect combines a triple and quadruple meter, more commonly known as the 12/8 meter. The triple is more common in jazz (and blues), while the quadruple is standard for rock music. As seen below, it can be counted in two ways:

Triple	**1**	2	3	**4**	5	6	**7**	8	9	**10**	11	12
Quadruple	**1**			**2**			**3**			**4**		

A little past the midway point, the band plays an instrumental section that vacillates between a Latin rhythm and a swing rhythm. Here, instrumental solos are played beginning with the trombone (Latin rhythm), trumpet (swing rhythm), and saxophone (Latin). When the singer returns to the final verse, the harmonica plays in response to his passages. The song concludes in a manner similar to how it begins.

TIME	SECTION	INSTRUMENTATION/COMMENTS
		Instrumentation: Voice, guitar, organ, trumpets, saxophones, trombone, organ, guitar, bass, drums
00:00	Introduction	Brass and Instruments only
00:15	Introduction	The tempo begins, played within a 12/8 meter, The entire band is playing with no vocals
00:32	Verse 1	Lyrics begin with the words "Them that's got . . .
01:08	Interlude	Instruments only featuring brass and woodwinds playing accents
01:16	Verse 2	Lyrics begin with the words "And the strong seem . . .
01:52	Interlude	Instruments only featuring brass and woodwinds playing accents
02:00	Bridge	The tempo changes to a 4/4 meter

02:20	Interlude	No tempo, lead vocal accompanied by brass and woodwind instruments
02:29	Verse 3	Tempo and meter returns to the same as Verse 1; Lyrics begin with the words "Rich relations made give you . . .
03:04	Instrumental section A	Tempo is faster; the style of playing is similar to what one hears in Latin music
03:44	Instrumental section B	Tempo is a little faster; the style of playing is similar to what one hears in swing music
03:53	Instrumental section A	Same as A above
04:02	Instrumental section B	Same as B above
04:12	Instrumental section A	Same as A above
04:20	Bridge	Same as Bridge above but with the organ accompanies (as opposed to brass and woodwind instruments) the lead singer
04:48	Verse 3	Same as Verse 3 above, and the harmonica is added to the band accompaniment
05:27	Coda	No tempo, a return to what is played in the introduction – brass and woodwind instruments play in a hymnal manner, the lead singer also closes with "Every child . . .

Song Navigator 18.2: "God Bless the Child" by Blood, Sweat & Tears from the album Blood, Sweat & Tears (1969, Columbia)

Another example is the BS&T song titled "Spinning Wheel" (1969). Halfway through the song, the band plays a swing rhythm that is melodically colored by a trumpet solo. BS&T's version of the first movement of "Variations on a Theme" (1969) by Erik Satie (1866–1925) further illustrates their diverse musicality. Another group that exemplifies the jazz rock sound is Three Dog Night (TDN). Their recordings do not use distinct jazz traditions like those found in BS&T, but elements of soul and rock do surface in the song "Joy to the World" (1970). In this recording, the lead singer uses *melisma* and shouts and screams much the same way as did singers of soul music such as Aretha Franklin and Otis Redding. (In fact, the lead singer performs Redding's original song titled "Try a Little Tenderness" in a similar manner.) The drummer's kick drum rhythm in "Easy to Be Hard" (1969) resembles that used by funk bands at the time, a rhythm that is highly syncopated. The songs "One" (1969) and "Mama Told Me (Not to Come)" (1970) display the group's use of soulful background singing with their often-called "classic rock" as well as jazz rock sound.

Another group that exhibited some aspects of jazz rock is the band Chicago. An example is their song titled "Does Anybody Really Know What Time It Is?" (1969). The song begins with solo jazz piano stylizations performed without a tempo that continue for nearly 25% of the song. When the tempo is established, a trumpet solo precedes the singer's first verse. The bass lines to Chicago's "Free" (1971) and Tower of Power's "What Is Hip" (1973) are similar to what one would hear in funk. To be sure, bands that played jazz rock were quite different from their fusion counterparts.

PART FIVE

POPULAR MUSIC IN AMERICA POST WORLD WAR II THROUGH THE 1970s: SUMMARY

Key Terms

- Jump bands
- NAB
- ASCAP
- BMI
- Race records
- Ostinato
- Rock & roll
- Doo-wop
- Sun Record Company
- Pop-style
- Teen idols

- Folk
- Human Be-In
- Flower children
- Existentialism
- Theatricalism
- Jungle music
- Slap bass technique
- Wah-wah sound
- Dee jay
- Payola
- Cover version

Featured Genres/Styles

- Rhythm & blues
- Boogie-woogie
- Urban
- Doo-wop
- Rock & roll
- Pop-style
- Surf sound
- British invasion
- Skiffle
- Folk rock
- Blues revival

- Country revival
- Southern rock
- Country-styled rock
- Psychedelic
- Soul: Basic and Motown
- Funk
- Disco
- Free/Free form
- Fusion
- Jazz Rock

Featured Songs/Works

- "Choo Choo Cha Boogie"
- "Chicken Shack Boogie"
- "What a Difference a Day Makes"
- "Speedo"
- "Ain't No Woman (Like the One I've Got)"
- "Young Blood"
- "Oh What a Night"
- "Yakety Yak"
- "That's Alright Mama"
- "Shake Rattle and Roll"
- "Hound Dog"
- "Stupid Cupid"

- "Lipstick on Your Collar"
- *Pet Sounds*
- "Love Me Do"
- *Sgt. Peppers's Lonely Hearts Club Band*
- "Blowin' in the Wind"
- "White Rabbit"
- "Ball and Chain"
- "Riders on the Storm"
- "Say It Loud, I'm Black and I'm Proud"
- "Thank You (Falettinme Be Mice Elf Again)"
- "Celebration"
- "Free Jazz"

Featured Artists

- Louis Jordan
- Amos Milburn
- Dinah Washington
- The Cadillacs
- The Coasters
- The Four Tops
- The Dells
- The Chordettes
- Sam Phillips
- Elvis Presley
- Bill Haley
- Big Joe Turner
- Willie Mae Thornton
- Chuck Berry
- Bo Diddley
- Jerry Lee Lewis
- Eddie Cochran
- Buddy Holly
- Carl Perkins
- Gene Vincent
- Connie Francis
- Pat Boone
- Dick Dale
- The Ventures
- Beach Boys
- Lonnie Donegan
- The Beatles
- Gerry and The Pacemakers
- The Who
- The Rolling Stones
- Woody Guthrie
- Bob Dylan
- Joan Baez
- Peter, Paul and Mary
- Simon and Garfunkel
- The Byrds
- The Grateful Dead
- Jefferson Airplane
- Janis Joplin
- The Doors
- James Brown
- Aretha Franklin
- Otis Redding
- The Supremes
- The Temptations
- Sly & The Family Stone
- George Clinton
- Kool & The Gang
- Donna Summer
- Ornette Coleman
- Chick Corea
- Weather Report
- Blood, Sweat and Tears
- Chicago

Music and Society

- The U.S. deployment of the atomic bomb on Hiroshima in 1945 marked the end of WWII, and also the close of the Big Band Jazz Era (1920s–1946).
- Though the U.S. wasd still by and large a segregated nation, white teens were becoming increasingly interested in rhythm & blues or black music.
- For the first time in America, music executives were pursuing a younger market in the 1950s, due in large part to the baby boomers, but also to the growing concern to diminish the stain of racism. For young people, rhythm & blues and rock & roll signaled a change not only for music but for human-istic concerns as well.

Discussion Questions

- How did the McCarthy Trials affect music?
- Discuss how the Civil Rights Act, Equal Pay Act, founding of the National Organization for Women impact music during the 1960s and the ensuing decades.
- What was the role of the producer in the 1960s? Has it changed today?
- Discuss reasons for America's fascination with British groups such as The Beatles, Rolling Stones, and The Who.

Learning Beyond the Classroom

- Attend a rock concert and see if you can discern music characteristics from previous styles such as blues, country, rhythm & blues, rock & roll, folk, folk-rock, funk, disco, psychedelic, and hard rock.
- View films such as *Rock Around the Clock* (1956), *Beach Blanket Bingo* (1965), and *Mr. Rock & Roll: The Alan Freed Story* (1999) to learn more about teen music and the social climate during the 1950s and 1960s.
- Take a poll of family, friends, and colleagues and ask them to draw distinctions between rock & roll and rock music. You might be surprised by what people say.
- Initiate a conversation with a family member or acquaintance that lived in America beginning in the 1950s. Inquire about their experiences and activities with music and how it reflected the social climate at the time.
- Visit the Rock & Roll Hall of Fame in Cleveland, Ohio to get a multimedia experience of music and pertinent activities beginning in the 1950s.

PART SIX

Lollapalooza. © Rob Grabowski/Retna Ltd./Corbis

POPULAR MUSIC IN AMERICA FROM THE 1970s THROUGH PRESENT DAY

- CHAPTER NINETEEN: Rock Music and Theatricalism: Art Rock and Glitter and Glam Rock
- CHAPTER TWENTY: Hard Rock and Heavy Metal
- CHAPTER TWENTY-ONE: Socio-Political Activism Music: Reggae, Punk, and Hip-Hop
- CHAPTER TWENTY-TWO: Yesteryear's Mainstream and Alternative Rock
- CHAPTER TWENTY-THREE: Popular Music in the 21st Century

OVERVIEW

In an effort to create new ideas or at least use different approaches to better express a song's lyrical or musical meaning, a number of musicians in the late 1960s began to explore the possibilities of incorporating distortion and feedback in their songs. Aided by a number of electronic gizmos such as phase shifters, fuzz tones, wah-wah, and a plethora of effects, guitarists in particular took advantage of these mechanical devices along with distortion and feedback to boost the overall effects in a song.[1] The instrumental output of these innovations was more powerful sounding in volume, and consequently impacted how artists composed music. Lyrical themes, vocal production, melodic phrasing, rhythmic tendencies, and various musical characteristics were all affected by distortion and feedback. Music employing these effects became known as "hard rock" and "heavy metal" (or simply "metal").

Musicians who played hard rock and heavy metal made an attempt to disassociate themselves from the "soft rock" styles of the previous decades by increasing the volume, using distortion, and playing aggressively (or hard). These performance practices were built on the stylistic tendencies of blues, psychedelic rock, and, for some bands, classical music. For example, "Four Until Late" (1967) by Cream makes use of both the 12-bar blues progression and the AAB song form—both of which are explicitly blues. In their 1967 recording "Sleepy Time Time," Cream's blues characteristics are evident by the

---

[1] A phase shifter transfers sound from one speaker to another (e.g., left to right channel). The fuzz tone distorts a pitch so that it sounds like several pitches. A wah-wah sound is similar to the fuzz tone, but does not distort sound, and vacillates between two pitches.

use of 12/8 (4/4) compound meter, the adagio tempo, the walking-bass line, and blue notes as sung by the band's lead singer, Eric Clapton. The first half of Steppenwolf's song "Power Play" (1972) strictly follows the 12-bar blues progression, using the typical I, IV, and V chords. The blues influence is demonstrated in the walking bass riff played in a slow tempo in Led Zeppelin's "Dazed and Confused" (1969) as well as in the use of the 12-bar blues progression and the harmonica in the beginning of their song "Bring It on Home" (1969). The improvisational guitar solo in "Dazed and Confused" exemplifies a characteristic of psychedelic rock—applying minimal restrictions to improvisational solos. The improvisational solo combined with the accompaniment in Cream's "I'm So Glad" (1967) is quite similar in character to psychedelic rock. The overt Bach-like melodic counterpoint sounded on the organ in the beginning of Iron Butterfly's[2] song "My Mirage" (1968) clearly reflects the influence of classical music. The application of quite distinct movements (or moods) in the song "Bohemian Rhapsody" (1975) by Queen reveals the influence of classical music's multi movement formal structure. Orchestral arrangements throughout various sections of Bad Company's "Weep no More" (1975) demonstrates that typical classical instrumentation could be an effective tool to build upon the rock styles of that time.

Unlike soft rock bands, which had radio play to help generate large revenues, hard rock and heavy metal bands (particularly the latter) had to rely on persistent touring schedules to make their money and subsequent chart appearances. There were reasons for their exclusion from the music charts. The sheer power or volume produced by groups such as Black Sabbath, Deep Purple, Blue Cheer, Blue Oyster Cult, and Led Zeppelin, as well as many of these groups' non mainstream lyrics, initially prevented them from receiving the level of radio and TV coverage furnished to their soft rock counterparts.

While the categorization of groups is truly a personal preference, there are some differences in the musical presentation of hard rock vs. heavy metal that will ultimately lead to a more comprehensive understanding of music activities during the late 1960s and 1970s.

The socio-political climate of the 1960s and 70s was such that individuals felt compelled to express their stance on politics, government policy, and social behavior. In reggae music, the Rastafari religious movement[3] of the 1930s and its belief in fairness to all people played a major role in developing a sociopolitical viewpoint. Not only did punk musicians write about unfairness for the economically deprived and America's governmental policies, they also embraced reggae musicians' stance on "power to the people." Moreover, some punk bands utilized various reggae (or a variation of) music characteristics such as the guitar playing on the backbeat (counts two and four of a quadruple meter). Examples are the songs "Concrete Jungle" (1979) by The Specials and "London Calling" (1988) by The Clash. Punk is an American-bred style that also found favor among European audiences. The Sex Pistols and their recordings "Anarchy in the U.K.," and "God Save the Queen" achieved success in America. At the same time, rap music became the voice for many young urban blacks who felt that America was leaving them behind. "The Message" (1982) by Grandmaster Flash and The Furious Five was a protestation about the hideous living conditions of many urban blacks.

The existence of the youth culture as a potential viable market during the 1950s exploded during the 1960s. The prevalence of existentialism and social concerns that permeated society during the 1960s was reflected in the existence of a revival not only of humanistic concerns but of music as well.

---

[2] Iron Butterfly members included Ron Bushy (drums), Lee Dorman (bass), and Doug Ingle (organ)—spokesman and founder of the band. They were an underground band in the Los Angeles music scene beginning in the latter third of the 1960s.
[3] The Rastafari Movement was supported by working-class Jamaicans who believed that Haile Selassie I, a former emperor of Ethiopia, was God incarnate.

The Apollo moon landing and even Woodstock in 1969 signaled the close of an era and the dawn of a new decade decorated with glitz, flamboyancy, and superfluous attitudes. This led to music endeavors such as disco, glitter and glam rock, theatrical music productions, and the continuation of funk. The 1970s ushered in ideals that seemed to stifle the "flow" of the urgency of political reform and civil liberties of the previous decade. By the late 1970s, the music industry was capitalizing on the growth of a culture that exhibited a mundane appetite for music. Fortunately, there were a number of singer-songwriters that offered an alternative to the routine sounds of disco and similar styles.

Prior to WWII, when singers who also played an instrument were generally associated with a specific style of music such as big band, Chicago blues, and country, performers of this sort from the 1970s are more difficult to categorize. Known as singer-songwriters, some of these include (listed alphabetically) Jackson Browne, Jimmy Buffett, Harry Chapin, Phil Collins, Jim Croce, John Denver, Neil Diamond, Dan Fogelberg, Billy Joel, Elton John, Carole King, Van Morrison, Randy Newman, and Stevie Wonder. Because of the impact of these artists, information is provided in Chapter Twenty-Two about their musical career and contributions to the well-spring of composers who also perform their own music.

The bulk of this chapter presents styles and types of music and their respective artists that were popular in the 21st century. Present day terms used to chart popular music can be seen in a couple of ways. First, present day professional music trade journals, like *Billboard*, organizes popular songs into five general categories: 1. Overall popularity, 2. Breaking & Entering 3. Genres, 4. International, and 5. Web. Second, from a musicological standpoint, within the aforementioned categories popular songs fall into two basic groups: *style* and *category*. Stylistic terms include rock, rhythm & blues/hip-hop, Latin, rap, country, folk, jazz, Christian, gospel, blues, and several others. Categoric terms include hot 100, radio songs, digital songs, digital albums, pop, social 50, dance/club, ringtones, heatseekers, alternative, adult contemporary, and others.

As discussed in previous chapters, popular music is the result of sales and airplay. And beginning in the last third of the previous century, sales in today's market encompasses hard copy, and digital downloads or streaming, while airplay includes internet radio as well as the traditional format. Sales and airplay results are based on, in addition to the music's substance, functionality and quality as discussed in Chapter 1, other factors such as marketing schemes, social media, and the artist's personal drive and motivation.

In today's scheme of creating success of an artist, selling recordings is still an important vehicle for accomplishing this, but less of an economic factor. Indeed, economic gains are achieved less by the recordings and more by endorsements, merchandise sales, and live performance sales. It is no wonder that an artist accepts engagements, for example, at the yearly Super Bowl half-time shows without their usual monetary compensation; allowing their songs to be performed on very popular music programs such as *Glee* and *American Idol*; or appearing in popular video games like *Guitar Hero* and *Red Fraction*.

Without question, technology continues to play a major role in determining the popular music scene in the 21st century.

CHAPTER NINETEEN

ROCK MUSIC AND THEATRICALISM: ART ROCK AND GLITTER AND GLAM ROCK

The Moody Blues. © Hulton-Deutsch Collection/CORBIS

ART/PROGRESSIVE ROCK

Art rock/progressive rock received its stylistic name as the result of new musical trends set by musicians who desired to focus more on music-driven (artistic focus) than market-enthused (industry perspective) creations. Fueled by the ever-expanding ability to fully express ideas by selecting specific elements from the plethora of musical tools, devices, and technological advancements that were available, musicians were enthralled with the many possibilities of musical composition and expression. Up to this point, the incorporation of musical elements of classical music had not noticeably permeated rock. When listening to the many different styles of rock music that existed during the 1970s, one soon notices some salient musical practices with respect to elements of classical music that were not evident in the 1960s. Many songs began to have a more formal structure, particular instrument usages, orchestral arrangements, a compositional tool such as leit motif, and expression and dynamic usages. The Beatles' completely unique 1967 album titled *Sgt. Pepper's Lonely Hearts Club Band*, and the "rock opera" album titled *Tommy* by The Who in 1969, represented the formation of an avant-garde rock or, at the least, new music creations demonstrating that rock could be more than trendy music for the youth pop culture. This, in turn, led to the application of the stylistic titles "progressive" or "art rock" being applied to this new type of music.

At the outset, progressive and art rock were one and the same, as each appeared to be displaying an urgency to legitimize the significance of rock music. In general, this resulted in several approaches:

1. Incorporating elements of classical music, as it is considered a "legitimate" style;
2. Utilizing new technology to demonstrate its applicability to making music, for example with the use of computers-a viable measurement of intellectuality, thereby increasing the status of rock music; and
3. Embellishing on typical musical characteristics of rock music (as well as creating new ones) to the extent of spawning a new, somewhat avant-garde sort of art.

To make a distinction between the two styles, the first two approaches above exemplify progressive rock, while the third is characteristic of art rock. This is not to suggest that some bands of art rock did not incorporate technology, and that embellishing on musical elements is solely an art rock practice. Overlapping certainly occurred between the two styles, but the elements that predominated determine in which area a particular group belongs.

Progressive rock, which emerged from Britain, was somewhat of an extension of the psychedelic scene. Groups that enjoyed the flavor of psychedelic rock, with its improvisational nature and its open approach to new ideas, include The Moody Blues *(Days of Future Passed,* 1967), The Nice *(The Thoughts of Emerlist Davjack,* 1967), Procol Harum *(A Salty Dog,* 1969), and King Crimson *(In the Court of the King Crimson,* 1969). By the 1970s, major forces in the progressive rock realm included Pink Floyd, Yes, Emerson, Lake & Palmer, Genesis *(Foxtrot,* 1972 and Wind & Wuthering, 1976), and Jethro Tull *(Living in the Past,* 1972).

A common usage in classical styles of music involves the creation of distinct movements (moods) within the context of a song. Regarded as multi movement works, a movement can be attributed to melodic changes, tempo and/or meter changes, the existence of acoustic and electric instruments, the juxtaposition of a typical rock band with symphony orchestra, lyrical and instrumental sections, and textures-movements producing an engaging presentation that expands the listening experience. The song titled "Roundabout" (1971) by Yes incorporates these and other elements. In general, the song contains three distinct sections. Each section is distinguished by a certain tempo, rhythmical differences, and texture. The illustration below provides an overview of the song and its movements from the perspective of the aforementioned musical distinctions.

Movement 1 (A)
Introductory statement
Synthesizer against the acoustic guitar performing in a *rubato* manner
(The singer is added when this sections recurs; also, there is a distinct tempo)
Movement 2 (B)
The singer produces a number of verses, and a repetitive chorus
The accompanimental instruments include guitar, bass, drums, and organ
Movement 3 (C)
Latin rhythm (including more percussive instruments), a different mood
The drums and percussion section are play twice as fast as the layered vocals
Guitar and bass play a riff; vocals enter singing in a homophonic manner
Movement 4 (D)
Organ and guitar solos
A different mood exists here even though there is a chordal progression that is similar to one used during Movement A

Since musicians were looking to extend and "develop" their musical ideas, more time was needed to accomplish this. At the time, popular styles of music in the 1960s were confined to presenting a song within a three minute and twenty-three second time allowance, with the exception of psychedelic rock and various types of jazz such as cool and fusion. In the mid-1960s, some record labels allowed their artists more freedom with respect to the length of a song. The Moody Blues was one of the earliest groups to take advantage of this. A band from Birmingham, UK with interest in rhythm & blues and psychedelic rock, their earlier recording with Decca Records, proved to be unsuccessful. Sometime between 1966 and 1967, the band was offered a contract with Deram Records to record a rock version of Antonin Dvorak's *From the New World Symphony*.[1] The band eventually embarked on the task to compose an album with a particular concept. Record executives reluctantly agreed to give the group artistic freedom. This effort produced their most successful concept album titled *Days of Future Passed* (1967). As seen by the titles listed below, the concept deals with specific periods and times of day. Each of the seven songs is longer than the standard 3:23 time frame; the total album time equals that of a typical album of the day consisting of twelve songs-approximately 40 minutes, 30 seconds.

What is most significant about this album is its use of a rock band—The Moody Blues—in combination with a symphonic orchestra—the London Festival Orchestra—incorporating all of its advantages of instrumentation, dynamics, and textures as a way to develop the concept.[2] The song titled "Nights: Nights in White Satin" is album's most celebrated song. Utilizing the classical-music influenced movement idea, the song progresses in the following manner.

---

[1] Decca Records was responsible for the formation or Deram Records, which generally promoted alternative artists.
[2] When The Moody Blues were touring as a band, the orchestra sounds were played by the mellotron—a keyboard instrument that has prerecorded orchestral sounds attached to each key. Each recorded sound lasts about eight seconds; it can produce sounds by pressing one key after another.

SONG TITLE	LENGTH OF SONG
"The Day Begins"	5:51
"Dawn: Dawn Is a Feeling"	3:49
"The Morning (Another Morning)"	3:56
"Lunch Break: Peak Hour"	5:32
"The Afternoon: Forever Afternoon . . ."	8:24
"Evening: The Sunset/Twilight Time"	6:40
"Night: Nights in White Satin"	7:24

Movement (Section)	Instrumental or Vocal	Ensemble Type	Featured Instrument(s)
Introduction	Instrumental	Orchestra	Flute
Verse 1	Vocal	Band	Singer
Verse 2	Vocal	Band & orchestra	Singer & strings
Chorus	Vocal	Band & orchestra	Singer & mellotron
Verse 3	Vocal	Band & orchestra	Singer & strings
Verse 4	Vocal	Band & orchestra	Singer & strings
Chorus	Vocal	Band & orchestra	Singer & mellotron
Solo	Instrumental	Band	Flute & orchestra
Verse 5	Vocal	Band & orchestra	Singer & strings
Verse 6	Vocal	Band & orchestra	Singer & strings
Chorus	Vocal	Band & orchestra	Singer & mellotron
Chorus	Vocal	Band & orchestra	Singer & mellotron
Bridge	Instrumental	Orchestra	Strings
Bridge 2	Vocal & instrumental	Orchestra	Spoken voice
Coda	Instrumental	Orchestra	Orchestra

Song Navigator 19.1: "Nights in White Satin" by The Moody Blues

Although "Nights: Night in White Satin" was their most widely played song, one should not over-look the sensation received by the experience of listening to the album in its entirety, particularly if the listener is familiar with the aforementioned *From the New World Symphony*.[3]

The group named Queen also effectively used the idea of multi movement works as evidenced in their song titled "Bohemian Rhapsody" from the 1975 album titled *A Night at the Opera*. The song progresses in the following manner.

Movement (Section)	Instrumental or Vocal	Ensemble Type	Featured Instrument(s)
Introduction	Vocal	Voice and Piano	Voices
A	Vocal	Band	Singer and Piano
B	Vocal	Band	Singer
C (Solo)	Instrumental	Band	Guitar
D (Bridge (operatic style)	Vocal	Band	Voices
Solo (tempo change)	Instrumental and vocal	Band	Guitar and singer
A'	Vocal	Band	Singer

Song Navigator 19.2: "Bohemian Rhapsody" by Queen

Another group that was influenced by psychedelic rock and enjoyed tremendous success as a progressive rock band was Pink Floyd. The band formed in Cambridge, England in 1965. Their debut album, titled *Piper at the gates of Dawn* (1967) illustrates their progressive mindset with their eclectic mix of psychedelic music ("Interstellar Overdrive"), British-type theatre singing style ("The Gnome" and "The Bike"), a dash of surf-sounding guitar riffs ("Astronomy Domine"), and various creative ideas using different chord progressions and sound effects. Unlike The Moody Blues' late 1960s recordings, Pink Floyd does not use the symphonic orchestra or the complete concept of a multi movement work. In 1973, however, Pink Floyd recorded what has become their most successful musical contribution to the progressive/art rock scene. The album, titled *Dark Side of the Moon*, is less obscure sounding than their earlier albums, which were not as radio-friendly as this album. Like the album *Days of Future Past* by The Moody Blues, *Dark Side of the Moon* should be listened to from beginning to end. The album begins and ends with the sound of a beating heart in the songs "Speak to Me/Breathe" and "Eclipse," respectively. In the first song, the combination of the slide guitar, tuneful vocalizing, and the use of the Hammond B-3[4] sound with some jazz influences all contribute to a radio-friendly appeal. The notion of progressive rock is evidenced by the use of effects as heard in the song "On the Run" which features

---

[3] *From the New World Symphony* was the result of Antonin Dvorak's second visit to America during the late 19th century. Moved by America's landscapes and soundscapes—indigenous people, immigrants, and Africans—Dvorak composed a piece that im-parts the impression of the formation of a "new world."
[4] The Hammond B-3 was a common type of organ used by many bands of varied styles during the 1960s and 70s.

phase-shifting (sound moving from the left to the right ear); the use of clock sounds in the song "Time"; and the sound of a cash register in their most celebrated song titled "Money." While "Money" is indeed one of Pink Floyd's most popular songs, one should not stop without listening to the song titled "Us and Them." Not only does this song seem to exemplify the album's title with its lyrics that deal with two separate entities where one is no greater than the other, but its use of a saxophone solo, gospel-like singing style, spoken text, and organ, all produce visual eclectic images of the *Dark Side of the Moon-a* place of ambiguity.

GLITTER AND GLAM

Similar to pop-styled rock performers of the 1960s, there was a greater focus on the visual among glitter and glam groups during the 1970s. Categorized by their flamboyancy with elaborate stage costumes, and a sense of boldness leaning towards sexuality, these bands utilized the stage as a forum to act out fantasies that appealed to a growing culture in need of something to claim as their own.

The term "glam rock" often applied to British bands such as David Bowie, T. Rex, Roxy Music, Mott Hoople, Gary Glitter, Slade, and Sweet. "Glitter rock" was the American term for similar music performed by bands such as Alice Cooper, Iggy Pop, and Lou Reed.

The analogy that art rock is to performer as glitter and glam is to entertainer is certainly appropriate. As previously discussed, performers were more inclined to focus on their musical talents/gifts and therefore are less concerned with appealing to an audience with superfluous antics. This does not necessarily imply that groups who favored glitter and glam theatrical productions were inferior musicians, but they did have an appetite for music production rather different from their art or progressive rock contemporaries. David Bowie is a prime example of this. Born David Robert Jones in London, Bowie was intrigued by British theater, including advant-garde and mime, and had a desire to perform American music. His first album, titled *David Bowie* (1967), includes an eclectic mix of music. The song titled "Uncle Arthur" is reminiscent of a musical accompaniment for an Irish jig mixed with progressive harmonic structures underneath Bowie's somewhat theatrical recitation. Songs titled "Sell Me a Coat," "Love You Till Tuesday," "There Is a Happy Land," "When I Live My Dream," and "She's Got Medals" consist of an easy listening mix of band with orchestra that is similar (on a simplistic level) to what art rock groups used to explore the possibility of developing their musical ideas. "Rubber Band" opens with an instrumental fanfare section and continues with a marching band-type accompaniment against Bowie's very fluid vocal line. The song "We Are Hungry Men" begins with a synthesized sound against a spoken part and progresses through various influences, including the American country revival scene of the 1960s, brass fanfare, and a touch of psychedelic texture and harmonic structure. The song "Come and Buy My Toys" is produced with acoustic and electric bass as the only accompaniment to his vocal line. The influence of American styles on Bowie is evident in the song titled "Join the Gang." This piece employs a brief funk-style drum riff; a bluegrass mandolin picking style; a blues-type piano riff; a walking swing bass section; a hard rock-type section featuring the bass guitar; and an ending section of sound effects. The song "Maid of Bond Street," which includes band, orchestra, and accordion played in a 6/8 meter and Bowie's theatrical recitative vocal line, produces an assorted mix of sounds and images. The final song on the *David Bowie* album, titled "Please Mr. Gravedigger," is even more of an eclectic production as the sound of a gong, thunder, rain, bird sounds, a person walking on what appears to be wet leaves, and Bowie's half-sung and spoken voice that emulates a person with nasal congestion are used to describe the duties of the town gravedigger. While the album is rather illustrative of Bowie's influences and many different soundscapes, the album failed to attract the attention it hoped would result. In 1969, however, Bowie's many talents became noticed with the album *Space Oddity*.

David Bowie. © MTV Networks/Photofest

Due in part to the album's single of the same name that coincided with the Apollo 11 moon landing in 1969, Bowie experienced his first bout with fame. Although the song is about a fictitious astronaut who is lost in space, it nonetheless was associated with the monumental feat of landing on the moon and the reality of humans in outer space.

To support the music's "out-of-this-world" image, Bowie needed to present these and other images in a grand theatrical production. Seeing the feasibility of marketing Bowie for large audiences, architects and engineers were contracted to create stages with an array of spectacular visual effects, glitter, and glam. To further suit the growing desire for outrageousness, Bowie, who from the start was fascinated with the idea of creating different characters, created the androgynous person Ziggy Stardust who existed roughly between the years 1969–1973. Ziggy Stardust is a messiah who comes to rescue the earth from its blandness and replace it with the 1970s hippie movement agenda of peace and love. Ziggy is further characterized as a rock star who indulges in illegal drugs and sexual promiscuities that eventually overcome him, causing him to be destroyed by his own kind. Fittingly, Ziggy Stardust recorded the album *The Man Who Sold the World* in 1970, and its success was likely the result of the newly created character. Though the album was not successful with the American audience (since its cover features Bowie lounging on a couch wearing a dress with hair arranged in the manner of women's hairstyles of the 1970s), it did demonstrate Bowie's boldness in wanting music and theatre to function as one. The title track of the same name includes the combination of electric and acoustic guitar, bass, drums, organ, and percussion instruments—guiro and maracas—and again shows Bowie's proclivity for merging elements of varying styles and instrumentations. The songs "The Width of a Circle" and "All the Madmen" employ the hard rock style, lending power of sound that was needed for staged shows. The song "Black Country Rock" utilizes riffs as played by the electric guitar and electric bass.

The album released in 1972 titled *The Rise and Fall of Ziggy Stardust and the Spiders from Mars* includes musical elements that show Bowie's earlier music influences of rhythm & blues, soul, and psychedelic rock. Following this album, he went on to record numerous albums that showed his creativeness over quite a long period of time.

The glam rock band T. Rex, originally known as Tyran—nosaurus Rex, was formed by Marc Bolan in the mid-1960s. After the band's initial gig, they disbanded and became an acoustic duo for a while featuring Bolan on vocals and guitar and Steve Took on bongos. Willard Manus's book titled *Mott The Hoople* became the name, as changed by producer Guy Stevens, for the glam rock band of the same name. "All the Young Dudes," written by David Bowie, is one of their more popular songs. Released in 1972, the single did well in Britain and the U.S.

As previously mentioned the American equivalent of British glam rock was commonly known as "glitter rock." Like glam rock, theatricism was the norm for performances as it helped to provide major productions for the visually-enthused fan. The group named Alice Cooper exemplifies this: it set out to act out childhood-like fantasies of horror and death. Formed by Detroit-born Vincent Damon Furnier, group took the name Alice Cooper after considering a number of different band names. Their 1971 album titled *Love it to Death* featured the song tiled "I'm Eighteen." The song reflects certain experiences of being eighteen, such as the ambiguous emotion associated with being somewhere between a boy and a man. That same year, their release of "Killer" from the album of the same name was a seven-minute production of experiences from killing to receiving a death sentence. The listener is not spared the sound effects of death: screaming sounds follow the instrumental solo (about four minutes into the song). An audio representation of the moment before an execution is symbolized by the drummer's death, the use of organ, and a recitation of Latin words by a priest. The song concludes, about 25 seconds from the end, with footsteps and the sound of electricity that crescendos into oblivion. By 1972, the group sealed their stardom with the song "School's Out" from the album of the same name. Clearly a song that rivals the early hard rock and metal bands, all the instruments (voice, organ, lead and rhythm guitar, bass, and drums) extend their playing to the fullest.

Iggy Pop, another glitter-type performer, was born James Newell Osterberg, Jr. in Muskegon, Michigan. The 1977 release tilted "Lust for Life" from the album of the same name features a theme common to several of his later albums, such as *Nude and Rude: The Best of Iggy Pop* and *Naughty Little Doggie* (both 1996), and the 1997 release *Heroin Hates You*, where these embodied the notion of self-gratification. Like many glam and glitter bands, Iggy Pop had a musical relationship with David Bowie. They co-wrote the songs "China Girl" and "Tonight," from the albums *The Idiot* (1977) and *Lust for Life*, respectively. The former song speaks about being in love with a "China Girl." A keyboard melodic passage playing in a certain scale is used to emulate the sound of Chinese music. The song "Tonight" is a prayer from a man as he kneels at the bedside of a loved one who has turned blue. Basically, he believes that everything will be all right "Tonight."

Lewis Allen Reed, better known as Lou Reed, was born in Brooklyn but grew up in Long Island, New York. Although not a performer of glitter and glam with the flamboyance of someone like David

Bowie, Reed's stage acting, "real-life" lyrics, and association with Iggy Pop and Bowie places him near this category. Following his graduation as an English major at Syracuse University, he became a part of the Velvet Underground from 1965 to 1970. He sang and wrote songs about non mainstream situations such as drug life, prostitution, and various sexual scenarios. Reed's debut album titled *Transformer* (1972) contains what has become his signature song, namely "Walk on the Wild Side." The song is about New York City, where there exists over-the-top activities such as transvestism, prostitution, and hustling. Although the Velvet Underground continued through 1973, Reed embarked on a solo career two years following his departure from the group, where he released the album titled *Berlin* (1973). The single titled "Berlin" begins with a mixture of sounds such as speaking, hand clapping, and cheering, a group singing "Happy Birthday," and a blues-style piano playing. All sounds except the piano subside as Reed enters, singing about being at a café in Berlin, his surroundings being what he calls "paradise." The romantic theme in "Berlin" is a far cry from the song titled "Carolina II." Here, the story is about a woman who is not afraid of dying as the result of being beaten by a person she doesn't love. Death also prevails in the song titled "The Bed," which is about the "place" where a woman has committed suicide by slitting her wrists. The following year, Reed released the album titled *Sally Can't Dance* (1974). The single of the same name is a dance song that combines elements of rock and funk. Similar to "Sally Can't Dance," the song titled "Animal Language" is a dance number that incorporates typical rock & roll rhythm and woodwind and brass sounds similar to those found in funk music. The song is about the activities of a dog and a cat.

In closing, art/progressive rock and glitter/glam rock reflect a time when consumer desire for music concerts that incorporated theatricism was at an all-time high. Additionally, the "pop art" movement that began in the 1950s became an embodiment of mass culture themes such as business, marketing, comic books, etc. It sought to focus more on art for the general consumer as opposed to the aesthetics of expressionism, which was often abstract at the time. Also known as neo-dada (the contemplative aspects that lie at the core of this art), its earliest figures include Richard Hamilton, Jasper Johns, and Andy Warhol. Warhol was perhaps the most influential artist on those musicians looking for ways to express real-life situations in a more unconventional manner. Born in Pittsburgh, PA. Andy Warhol (1928–1987) was of Ruthenian heritage. Warhol's works included paintings of basic aspects of American culture: celebrities Judy Garland, Diana Ross, and Elizabeth Taylor; money; and his most memorable works featuring products from the Coca-Cola and Campbell's corporations. As for music inspiration resulting from Warhol's works, the work titled "The Exploding Plastic Inevitable" (1965), which is labeled performance art, is most significant here. A multimedia presentation of canvases, people as part of the art work, and music by the Velvet Underground inspired musicians such as Lou Reed, Iggy Pop, David Bowie, and many others. Whether art/progressive rock or glitter/glam rock, musicians were looking for new ways to convey their ideas and/or expressions of life. They did this by adding theatricism, creating songs that were multi movement works, incorporating rock instrumentation combined with symphonic orchestra, and projecting lyrics that either spoke about taboo subjects or were a far cry from the mundane, mainstream-inspired vernacular.

CHAPTER TWENTY

HARD ROCK AND HEAVY METAL

HARD ROCK

Some noted hard rock performers during the 1970s included Cream, Free, Bad Company, Boston, Bon Jovi, Pat Benatar, Heart, and Steppenwolf, Asia ("Heart of the Moment", "Only Time Will Tell", both in 1982), Foreigner ("Feels Like the First Time", 1977, "Waiting For a Girl Like You", "I Want to Know What Love is", both 1981), Aerosmith ("Gypsy Boots", 1985 "Rag Doll" 1987), Motorhead ("The Watcher", "Motohead", both in 1977), ZZ Top ("La Grange", 1973, "Gimme All Your Lovin", 1983).

Hard rock differed from heavy metal in the following ways:

1. More frequently used acoustic instruments;
2. Differences in thematic lyrical material;
3. Conscious emphasis on vocal virtuosity as well as vocal harmony;
4. Borrowed music characteristics from folk-rock, soul/funk, country and blues revival, and psychedelic rock.

The British band Cream–one of the earliest bands labeled as hard rock–was regarded as a "power trio," as each member frequently played his instrument to the extreme.[1] The song "Toad" on their 1967 album *Fresh Cream* illustrates this point. The song begins with a rock & roll like character, but then evolves into a more "hard" sound as the guitarist (Eric Clapton) added distortion to his solo. The drummer continues the power sound with an extended solo playing a number of stylistic rhythms, which lasts for nearly the entire song. The song concludes with a restatement of musical material from the beginning section. "Cat's Squirrel" (1967) by Cream is another example of the power trio sound. Beginning with guitar, then bass, then drums, all instruments continue to play to their fullest with respect to range and rhythmic complexity. At this stage of rock musical development or innovation, this type of texture was produced as the result of performing individual riffs. While the song "Cats' Squirrel" illustrates a melodic riff played in unison by the lead guitar and harmonica, the song "Sunshine of Your Love" (1967) supplies a thicker texture as the result of counterpoint between the voice and the instruments.

Although riffs like those played by the guitar and bass in the song "Sunshine of Your Love" (1967) were frequently employed to create a powerful sound, this particular song's overall aggressive presentation is conveyed through the use of counterpoint between the voice and the instruments. The song

---

[1] Cream includes Eric Clapton on guitar, Jack Bruce on bass, and Ginger Baker on drums.

opens with a riff played in unison by guitar and bass. The drummer plays at the end of this opening riff, and eventually establishes the tempo as the guitarist plays in a chordal manner. The vocal and instrumental counterpoint occurs at this juncture as one singer sings two phrases that are continued in a responsorial fashion by another singer. It is interesting to note the main riff in this song is rhythmically similar, although faster, in Steppenwolf's song "Move Over" (1972).

Hard rock groups regularly employed acoustic as well as electric guitar, with distortion, in their songs. For example, Boston's recordings "Foreplay Long Time," "Let Me Take You Home Tonight," "More Than a Feeling" and "Peace of Mind," (all in 1976) make use of both acoustic and electric guitar. The acoustic guitar is incorporated throughout Bon Jovi's song "Wanted Dead or Alive" from their album *Slippery When Wet* (1986). Despite the existence of an electric guitar solo with some distortion, the acoustic guitar sound nonetheless supports the exemplary "American West or cowboy" character. Most songs on Heart's[2] album *Dreamboat Annie* contain acoustic guitar, two of which– "(Love Me Like Music) I'll be Your Song" and "Sing Child"– incorporate an acoustic string section. (The latter also uses the flute.) Acoustic guitar and piano are both used in the album-titled song "Dreamboat Annie." Other examples include the introduction to "Call on Me" that uses acoustic piano and "Shooting Star," which uses acoustic guitar, both from Bad Company's 1975 album *Straight Shooter*. Steppenwolf's "Monster" (1972) makes use of the acoustic guitar during the song's verses. (Electric guitar is used during the section before and during the chorus.) The harmonica also appears in the song. Their song "Fag" employed the acoustic piano throughout the song. It is interesting to note that acoustic guitar is often used in conjunction with romantic lyrics, due to the quality of the sound it produces.

Romantic lyrics appeared more frequently in hard rock than in heavy metal. Indeed, hard rock bands used a wide array of themes with respect to romantic lyrics. These included desired love, commitment, happiness or euphoria, lost love, etc. For example, the song "Dreaming" (1967) by Cream clearly refers to the desire to be with someone, as the singer portrays a man who is hoping that a person will reciprocate love. Boston's 1976 song "Let Me Take You Home Tonight" explicitly refers to the desire to experience the comfort and company of another, as a man has been watching a woman for a while. Their song "I Feel Free" (1967) makes reference to a person who has a complete feeling of happiness or euphoria in the company of another. A sense of a love commitment is expressed through Boston's song "More Than a Feeling." Here, as the title suggests, a person has "More Than a Feeling" for another. Another example is Free's "All Right Now," in which the singer expresses his ideas of love after meeting a woman who seems to be smiling at him. Love is an emotion that cannot be fully understood without knowing its antithesis. That said, the songs "Four Until Late" and "Rollin' and Tumblin'" (both in 1967) by Cream talk about the sorrowful or painful character of love. In the first, the singer talks about the sorrows of his woman, and that it will take a good man to calm her. In the latter song, the singer portrays a man who has awakened and discovered that his woman has left. Free's song "Fire and Water" also illustrates this as the singer divulges his pain at leaving a woman who shows, according to him, little or no emotion for him. The title "Fire and Water" refers to the woman's parents, who have caused their daughter to have a heart as cold as ice. Pat Benatar's song "Hit Me with Your Best Shot" makes it clear that even though the pain of love hurts, she (in this case) is willing to take on a man who has broken many hearts. Finally, the British originated band Foreigner and their debut album of the same name in 1977 sold millions of copies in the U.S. of their love song "Feels Like the First Time." The Song Navigator below outlines the sections and characteristics of hard rock.

---

[2] Ann and Nancy Wilson are the sustaining members of Heart, which has changed membership quite often.

TIME	SECTION	INSTRUMENTATION/COMMENTS
		Instrumentation: Voice, back-up singers, guitars, organ, bass, drums
00:00	Introduction A	Guitars only
00:09	Introduction B	Piano, bass, and drums are added
00:27	Verse 1	Lyrics begin with "I would climb . . .
00:45	Verse 2	Back-up singers singer is accompanied b
01:04	Chorus	Lyrics begin with the title of the song accompanied in a major tonality
01:20	Verse 3	Similar to A section above
01:39	Verse 4	Same as Verse 2 above
01:56	Chorus	Sung using lyrics of the song title, but is accompanied with a minor tonality
02:38	Chorus	Same as the Chorus section above
02:56	Bridge	Focus on guitar playing a syncopated riff, the singer interjects some lyrics
03:14	Chorus	Same as the Chorus section above

Song Navigator 20.1: "Feels Like the First Time" by Foreigner from the album *No End in Sight: The Very Best of Foreigner* (2010, Rhino)

Hard rock bands also spoke about taking life easy, happiness, success, and peace of mind. For example, taking life easy is the topic of Cream's songs "Sleepy Time Time" and "Sweet Wine" (both in 1967). In the first, the singer views life as the enjoyable experience of rest and peace of mind. In "Sweet Wine," the singer is not in favor of city life and all the hustle and bustle of making money, exhorting that those sorts of things can wait. Whether experiencing it or being in pursuit of it, happiness is something that cannot be bought. Cream's 1967 song "N.S.U." speaks about this and takes it a step further by contemplating the mystery of happiness. The singer also mentions that the guitar is the only thing that makes him happy. In Boston's song "Rock & Roll Band," the singer talks about his band's early experiences, with the focus on happiness and the success by their appealing music. In their song "Hitch a Ride," the stated desire to get to New York City could be construed as a reference to heaven or at least to euphoria. Finally, their song "Peace of Mind" talks about the trials and tribulations of life. The singer encourages the listener to look beyond the struggle to succeed to discover a place of "peace of mind."

The music of the 1960s placed an emphasis on singers and vocal virtuosity. In an attempt to present thought provoking lyrics–particularly romantic themes–in combination with vocal virtuosity, singers within many hard rock bands beginning in the late 1960s took stock in the idea of vocal tastefulness by pursuing contrasting ideas. Above all, the singer's part was generally louder or at least more audible than the other instruments. In those cases where the singer's part was comfortably audible, and yet the volume was insignificant between the vocal and instrument parts, the clarity often lies in the performance of each part. Take for example, "Livin' on a Prayer" by Bon Jovi. The voice, drums, bass, and synthesized sounds are all nearly equal in volume, and yet the singer's lyrics are quite audible. In part, clarity is accomplished by the performance of specific melodic/harmonic and rhythmic lines that coexist in a complementary way. Each linear passage (voice, drums, bass, and synthesizer) embraces the melodic/harmonic and rhythmic character of all performed parts. Bon Jovi generally used the voice in a traditional fashion. The function of voice, for them, was to present the lyrics using typical vocal characteristics. On the other hand, the voice in many heavy metal bands functioned more like an instrument, i.e., a guitar using distortion or sound effects. In addition, hard rock bands regularly incorporated simple to complex vocal harmonies. For example, Boston's 1976 recording "Something About You" displays some very interesting and appealing homorhythmic phrases.

Some hard rock bands incorporated elements of current styles of the day. For instance, Bad Company's "Feel Like Makin' Love" (1975) makes use of vocal and instrumental harmonic and rhythmic tendencies that resemble country songs of the 1970s.[3] With regard to vocal harmony, the background singers bend their notes on certain words in response to the lead singer's lyrics–a typical practice in country music. Similar rhythmic gestures (including tempo) are also evident in this song. The guitar solo in the middle of the song leans more toward country in its use of suspended chords played in a less-than-syncopated fashion. These characteristics are not typical of hard rock. Hard rock's use of distortion and unison guitar and bass riffs distinguish it from country music. In this song, these features occur during the chorus as the response to the lead singer's lyrics. With the exception of the guitar solo, played in the fashion of hard rock, their song "Shooting Star" (1975) uses all of the country music and hard rock features already mentioned.

Steppenwolf. © Photofest

---

[3] Hard rock and heavy metal coexisted with the revival of country music during this time.

Steppenwolf (see heavy metal section) is another band that borrowed features from other styles, partly due to a concurrent revival of country and blues music. In their 1972 song "Monster," tempo and rhythmic gestures used in the blues are incorporated into the song's first tempo change. The influence of soul/funk music of the 1960s/70s is exhibited in the vocal and instrumental tendencies in their 1972 song "What Would You Do (If I Did That to You)." The syncopated bass line and drum groove in the introduction combined with the riffs of the conga and Hammond B-3 organ are typical practices of soul music. The women background singers' homorhythmic phrasing is another typical practice of soul music. A portion of the song's lyrics strongly advocate equality–a civil rights issue of the 1960s–as a verse makes reference to a man's prejudicial statement regarding the atypical appearance of another. In an effort to illustrate this attitude as a divisive mannerism with respect to humanity, the lead singer inquires "What would you do (if I did that to you)?" The lyrical message combined with the aforementioned music characteristics not only illustrates Steppenwolf's familiarity with typical features of soul, but also and perhaps more importantly, with an awareness of social injustices that plagued American society.

These and other groups laid the foundation for hard rock and, perhaps unwittingly, were setting the stage for its metamorphosis into heavy metal.

TRANSITION: HARD ROCK TO HEAVY METAL

For many songs there is a fine line between those that are hard rock or heavy metal. It becomes even more problematic when a group such as AC/DC (alternating current/direct current), a hard rock band on the cutting edge of stylistic features that became staples in heavy metal, regards itself as rock & roll. While musicians may not have been much concerned about this, record label executives with their marketing strategies view it another way however. Seeking to introduce the next big thing in music is usually the order of day for producers and record labels. Since the development of hard rock precedes heavy metal the focus was now on marketing their artists to neatly fit into the latter, thus new style or music category, regardless if the song is truly that. In retrospect, early heavy metal songs were those that

AC/DC. © Atlantic/Photofest

incorporated either something different or an extension of one or more existing features of hard rock. Take for example the song "Back in Black" (1980) by AC/DC.[4] The song consists of guitar distortion–a feature of hard rock, while the lead singer's vocal shouting singing style is less characteristic of hard rock and more of the emerging heavy metal style. Two of their songs prior to "Back in Black" such as "T.N.T" form the album of the same name (1975) and "High Voltage" also from the album of the same name (1976), were very much in the style of hard rock. By this time AC/DC was the most popular band in Australia, and there was a concerted effort to focus on entering the American music scene. By the early 1980s AC/DC had a number one album–*For Those About to Rock We Salute You*– in the U.S. The title song of the same name, with its guitar distortion, vocal full-throated and shouting, firearms going off, and virtuoso guitar solo, clearly shows the bands proclivity to contribute to the sounds of what became known as heavy metal.

HEAVY METAL   *early 70's into 80's*

With the exception of a few bands during the early 1970s, there was not a large distinction between hard rock and heavy metal, which became the favored style during the 1980s. Bands such as Iron Butterfly, Blue Cheer, and Black Sabbath built on hard rock performance practices through volume, lyrical themes, and in many cases musical virtuoso tendencies. Beginning in the late 1960s and early 1970s, bands in Britain and America took advantage of the aforementioned practices and presented them in theatrical productions. Propelled by the public's fascination with power via volume and distortion, the occult, and certain band members' musicality, heavy metal eventually became the style of choice.

The band Steppenwolf predated heavy metal bands and was generally labeled as hard rock even though they were the first to use the term "heavy metal" in their song "Born to Be Wild" (1968).[5] Their experimentation with lyrical themes of spirituality and the supernatural, as well as singing about drugs in ways others during their time had not paved the way for groups like Black Sabbath. Hard rock bands such as Heart, Boston, Pat Benatar, and Bon Jovi rarely included these subject matters on their recordings. In Steppenwolf's 1973 *Greatest Hits* album the songs "For Ladies Only," "The Pusher," "Jupiter's Child," "It's Never Too Late," "Screaming Night Hog," "Snowblind Friend," and "Tenderness (For Ladies Only)" all make reference to spirituality or the supernatural. Just as chemical substances were subject matter in psychedelic rock and related styles during the mid-1960s, they continued to be dealt with musically at this time. Steppenwolf's overt message portrays "The Pusher" (drug dealers) as a monster, insensitive to the value of human life. Their song "It's Never Too Late" talks about a man who has all the right stuff, but doesn't know what to do. He is depressed and has suppressed his emotions, hurting family and friends in the process. It asserts that one should want to do something positive before dying. Furthermore, it implies that this individual's behavior is uncharacteristic in a person who has been nurtured in a healthy environment. Overall, the covert message is for people, particularly their listeners, to avoid mind-altering chemical substances.

Steppenwolf's musical tendencies were just as progressive as their subject matter. In their song "Screaming Night Hog," the band uses guitar, bass, organ, and harmonica riffs that are played in unison or harmonic counterpoint with overlapping parts (i.e., a polyphonic texture) against a rhythmically supporting drummer. Against the rhythm guitarist playing a riff in a chordal fashion in the song The Pusher," the lead guitarist enters with distortion that appears to emulate the mind-altering effect of chemical drug substances. This performance practice also occurs quite frequently as the response to the

---

[4] The album Maximum AC/DC (released 2000, Chrome Dreams) is a collection of interviews about AC/DC.

[5] Steppenwolf's "Born to Be Wild" (1968) is the first song that uses the words "heavy metal."

lead singer's lyric call, "The Pusher." In their most popular song, "Born to Be Wild," each instrument (including the voice) "pushes the envelope" with respect to volume and rhythmic tendencies.

Like hard rock, the instrumentation of heavy metal bands consists of lead guitar, rhythm guitar, bass, drums, and frequently the organ. These bands continued as well as increased the intensity of the aggressive playing started by hard rock bands. If one needed to select a band that clearly drew the line between hard rock and heavy metal styles, Black Sabbath would stand at the forefront.

Black Sabbath. © Photofest

Their intoxicating musical characteristics, theatrical productions, sound effects, lyrical themes, and sheer power and volume raised the bar for aggressive hard rock/heavy metal bands. While hard rock and psychedelic rock were the first styles of rock music to consistently incorporate distortion and power, Black Sabbath became one of the first groups to relentlessly expand it even further. Their songs "War Pigs," "Sweet Leaf," "Rat Salad," and "Electric Funeral" on their *Paranoid* album all begin with the guitar using heavy distortion. Distortion is particularly effective for this group, as it is used to support the diabolical nature of the group's display of black magic, sorcery, spiritualism, the supernatural, and themes centered on science fiction. Indeed, this group's theatrical performance was explicitly supported by their musical performance practices such as powerful sounds, change of tempo, varied textures, improvisatory guitar solos with heavy distortion, the singer's sung and spoken-like melody, and sound effects or nonmusical sounds, all of which could occur within the same song. All of these are heard in Black Sabbath's eight-minute 1971 recording War Pigs." The assessment or judgment of inconsiderate people who regularly favor war is acted out on stage through a myriad of musical activities. The song begins in a slow tempo all instruments with playing within the 6/8 meter. The sound of sirens (sound effect) enters and diminishes just before an abrupt tempo change, which is twice as fast.[6]

---

[6] The sound of sirens is also in the introduction to their recording of "Hey Joe," which was also originally recorded by the Leaves (Los Angeles-based group) and subsequently covered by Jimi Hendrix in 1967 (but without the sirens).

Entering at this moment, the singer (Ozzy Osbourne) adds another layer to the performance, while the texture remains sparse as the drums, guitar, and bass only play and accent on every eighth beat while the singer presents combined sung and spoken-like phrases between them. (Even though the drummer is playing the high-hat during the singer's phrases, the focus is clearly on the singer.) The power of the song is produced by the guitar (including its distortion) and the bass playing in unison. After several sequences of this alternating pattern, the tempo changes again for a short instrumental interlude and then changes again to a funk-like groove underneath the singer's lyrical phrases.[7] A guitar solo with heavy distortion follows, concluding with the singer's re-emergence (which is similar to the singer's first entrance). The coda section includes the guitar, bass, and drums each playing to their fullest with respect to volume and the "filling-up" of sonic space, and closes with five seconds of music that quickly accelerates to high pitch. (This was produced by manipulating the tape recording machine.)

In addition to Black Sabbath, other heavy metal bands in Europe included Deep Purple, Judas Priest, Iron Maiden, Def Leppard, Scorpions, Motörhead, UFO, Led Zeppelin, and AC/DC (from Australia). After first trying the names Polka Tuck and then Earth, in 1969 the name Black Sabbath became the mainstay for members Ozzy Osbourne (lead vocalist), Tony Iommi (guitarist), "Geezer" Butler (bass), and Bill Ward (drums). Originally a blues-based band from Birmingham, England, Black Sabbath was by far the most popular band that consistently performed specific features of heavy metal. The line-up for Deep Purple included Ian Gillan (lead vocalist), Ritchie Blackmore (guitar), Roger Glover (bass), Jon Lord (keyboard), and Ian Paice (drums). Because of the keyboard–an instrument not typical of rock bands at this juncture–and other innovative ideas such as the incorporation of musical elements indicative of classical music, Deep Purple seemed to vacillate between art rock and heavy metal. Indeed, their work *Concerto for Group and Orchestra*, which included a performance with the Royal Philharmonic in 1969, clearly shows their interests in a broad range of musical traditions. Most probably because art rock was losing ground in popularity to heavy metal and also because it was somewhat restrictive in its usage of the classical tradition, Deep Purple moved toward making heavy metal their favored style. This is particularly evident in their use of lyrics that deal with spirituality or the supernatural. In the song "Chasing Shadows," (1969) a person who is lying in bed hears an inner voice that may be leading him to a "place" of darkness (which could mean death). In their song "Why Didn't Rosemary," (1969) Deep Purple is referencing Rosemary's baby–Satan. In essence, they are stating that life would be better if Rosemary had taken the pill.[8]

If flirting with the occult seemed to propel bands to success, Iron Maiden wasted no time in taking advantage of this marketing device. Deriving their name from the medieval torture device, they presented themselves as a band that favored images of the occult. With sustaining members Dave Murray (guitar) and Steve Harris (bass), Iron Maiden continued their media-pegged image as a satanic group with the release of their album *The Number of the Beast* in 1982. With Bruce Dickinson as their lead singer, this album became a favorite among the American occult-music audience.

While occult themes were the focus for many heavy metal bands, Led Zeppelin used these less frequently as a promotional tool. In fact, their musical interests lay in several other styles such as hard rock or at least a crossover from hard rock to heavy metal. These interests were largely due to the efforts of guitarist Jimmy Page, who actually produced the majority of their albums. Formed by Jimmy Page (guitar) and Robert Plant (voice) in 1968, Led Zeppelin was one of the most popular bands in Britain (after the Beatles and the Rolling Stones). Other members included John Paul Jones (bass), and

---

[7] The term *funk-like* refers to the synchronization that exists between the drums and bass–a definitive characteristic of funk music in the 1960s.

[8] *Rosemary's Baby*, 1967, is a novel by Ira Levin. The novel was adapted for film in 1968, which was directed by Roman Polanski.

Led Zeppelin. © Neal Preston/CORBIS

John Bonham (drums). As the result of technology, a move toward theatrical shows, and the desire to expand on hard rock, heavy metal soon became the style of choice for many bands. Led Zeppelin was one of the early bands that embraced these new approaches to hard rock and consequently contributed to the proliferation of heavy metal. Their song "Stairway to Heaven" from the album *Led Zeppelin IV* (1971) is the most requested FM song of all time worldwide, and has sealed their place as one of the greatest bands in modern history.

As the opening band for Led Zeppelin's 1977 U.S. tour, the British audience appeared disenchanted with the idea that the American audience was experiencing Judas Priest after its nurturing years in England. Eventually, however, the British audience accepted them as truly one of their own. Their most significant musical contribution to heavy metal, as evidenced by their debut album *Rocka Rolla* (1974), was their use of two lead guitars. Not only does this add even more power through volume and distortion, but also another layer of sound that is expanded by melodic counterpoint, thereby producing a thicker texture. Although the membership changed over the years, staple members of the quintet included K. K. Downing (lead guitar), Rob Halford (lead vocalist), Ian Hill (bass), Glen Tipton (lead guitar), and John Hinch (drums).

While it is true that hard rock used acoustic instruments more frequently than heavy metal, the latter did occasionally employ acoustic instruments as well, especially among those bands with either art rock influences or those that were otherwise influenced by traditions of classical music. This was particularly evident in Deep Purple's song "April" (1972). The introduction begins with the organ, followed by acoustic piano and guitar playing the main theme in unison. The organ takes over the main theme while the guitar and piano supply their own harmonic accompaniment. Eventually, timpani are added to accent the end of certain phrases. In the middle of the piece, an orchestra typical of the classic/romantic period plays an unrelated theme. The band, with lyrics, returns to the original theme. Other examples include Steppenwolf's 1973 recording It's Never Too Late," which incorporates the acoustic piano. As the first purely heavy metal band, Black Sabbath clearly defined the differences between the hard rock and heavy metal genres. One such distinction is made by the fact that their 1970 album *Paranoid* omits almost all acoustic sound (with the exception of voice and drums).

Outlined below, Led Zeppelin's recording "Dazed and Confused" from the album *Led Zeppelin* (1969) brought them favor throughout Britain.

"Dazed and Confused" (6 minutes, 26 seconds) —

1. "A" section begins with a bass riff.
   a. Guitar enters with distortion, as the sound vacillates between the left and right channels.
2. 1st verse–Voice enters powerfully with a full-throated, somewhat bluesy sound production, almost in a screaming manner.
   a. Counterpoint ensues between the bass and voice while the guitar plays in a responsorial manner against the voice.
   b. Drummer enters at the close of the first verse; guitar joins the bass player's riff.
3. 2nd verse–the accompaniment subsides prior to the voice entering, and the guitar comes in playing the same riff as the bass player.
   a. Close of the 2nd verse–the drums, bass, and guitar play powerfully, exemplary of the power trio; the same guitar and bass riff continues unabated, with the drummer adding awe-inspiring fills.
4. 3rd verse–the instruments play louder and more forcefully than the previous verse.
5. "B" section–instrumental call & response occurs between the distorted guitar (call) and voice (responding in vocables as an instrument); the bass and drums supply the rhythm by playing their own riffs. This section has a floating, surreal feeling to it.
   a. The guitar becomes more improvisational, still using distortion and phase shifting, and plays more notes.
   b. The tempo abruptly shifts to being twice as fast. The guitar continues as the featured instrument with the singer emitting vocables at times. The guitar solo evolves into a series of very rapid notes.
   c. The mood shifts to a fuller texture, with the guitar strumming chords and the singer improvisationally inserting phrases in the background like "Oh, don't leave me so confused now." Although the singer is present, the instruments are much louder.
   d. The playing briefly becomes almost jazz-like, with a lot of syncopated drumming.
6. Return to "A" section at the original slow tempo, with the "A" section bass riff being re-introduced as a lead-in to verse 4.
7. 4th verse–the instruments are playing in the same manner as the 2nd verse. The singer's lyrics can now be heard.
8. A return to the "B" section with a minimal amount of call & response between the bass and the drums.
   a. The singer begins to moan "oh" on every count and therefore does not function as a response to any part
   b. The tension and volume build up to a climax, and the song ends with a resounding guitar chord that gradually fades away.

Song Navigator 20.2: "Dazed and Confused" by Led Zeppelin

Like many bands at this time, various elements indicative of the blues were incorporated in Led Zeppelin's songs. In their song "Bring It on Home" (1969), the introduction includes guitar with harmonica–the two main instruments used by country blues songsters. Other blues features in this song include the eighth-note triplet (first two notes are tied) gesture that is played by the guitar; the presence of the 12-bar blues progression including the use of I– IV– and V chords in part of the song; and call and response passages performed between the singer and the harmonica player respectively. Following the guitar and harmonica introduction, the singer enters with extemporaneous nuances and then uses lyrics. At this juncture the band moves in another direction as they play in a rhythmical manner more typical of rock than blues. When all is said and done, the song returns to the introduction (although brief), using blues-based characteristics. The omnipresent 12-bar blues progression including its signature chords, I– IV– and V, is rather inescapable when playing blues-like music. Zeppelin's song "Moby Dick" begins with a bass and guitar riff playing within a strict 12-bar blues progression as follows: I7 / I7 / I7 / I7/ IV7 / IV7 / I7 / I7 / V7 / IV7 / I7 / I7 //, against a rock rhythm. The song differs from traditional blues as a result of the use of distortion by the guitarist. The blues character remains present, however, as the 12-bar blues progression plays underneath the soloist.

In 1971, Zeppelin recorded what many consider to be their finest work, namely "Stairway to Heaven." Written by the lead singer Robert Platt, the lyrics seem to reflect a sense of spirituality. A multi-movement piece that changes with different tempi, rhythms, textures, volume, and vocal executions, "Stairway to Heaven" shows its similarity with art/progressive rock of the early to mid-1970s.

American bands that were contributing to heavy metal concurrently with their British contemporaries included Iron Butterfly, Blue Cheer, Alice Cooper, Blue Öyster Cult, Aerosmith, Kiss, Van Halen, and Guns N' Roses. The song "In-A-Gadda-Da-Vida" (1968) by Iron Butterfly was Atlantic Record's best-selling recording. Led by organist Doug Ingle, initial group members included Danny Weis (guitar), Darryl deLoach (guitar), Jerry Penrod (bass), and Roy Bushy (drums). Often noted as one of the loudest hard rock trios in America, Blue Cheer members Bruce Stephens (guitar and vocals), Richard Peterson (bass and vocals), and Paul Whaley (drums) formed in Boston, Massachusetts, in 1967.

Alice Cooper. © Warner Bros. Records/Photofest

The group Alice Cooper featuring Alice Cooper (born Vincent Furnier, lead vocalist), Glen Buxton (guitar), Michael Bruce (keyboards and guitar), Dennis Dunaway (bass), and Neal Smith (drums) was one of the earliest groups to use a great amount of make-up and theatricalism.

Like some British bands, the New York band Blue Öyster Cult also incorporated elements of art rock and heavy metal in their performances. Founders Richard Meltzer and Sandy Pearlman were initially critics writing about rock music. Their weekly critiques afforded them the opportunity to objectively examine the inadequacies in certain rock styles and consequently discover ways to better appeal to public tastes. Experiencing various name changes during the late 1960s, the name Blue Öyster Cult came about in 1971 during their record contract with Columbia. By that time, band members included Donald Roser (guitar), Allen Lanier (keyboards), Joe Bouchard (bass), Allen Bouchard (drums), Meltzer (occasional vocals), and Pearlman (manager/producer). The wave of heavy metal bands had begun by the early 1970s.

Following Blue Öyster Cult's record contract, Columbia signed a group from New Hampshire the next year, namely Aerosmith. Formed in 1970 by Steve Tyler (lead vocalist) and Brad Whitford (rhythm guitar), they added Joe Perry (lead guitar), Tom Hamilton (bass), and Joey Kraemer (drums) and performed, (or as are in the business say "chopped wood" or "paid their dues") in various nightclubs. While *Get Your Wings* (1974) was their debut album, *Toys in the Attic* (1975) was their first album to sell over a million copies.

Whereas the Rolling Stones and Yardbirds inspired Aerosmith's somewhat traditional rock persona, other groups were inspired by the personas of superhero comic book characters. In 1977, Marvel Comics published a book on the group Kiss, and the animated film *Kiss Meets the Phantom of the Park* was televised the following year. Founding members Gene Simmons (bass) and Paul Stanley (guitar) added Ace Frehley (guitar) and Peter Criss (drums), and presented theatrical productions of sheer power acted out in comic book-type characterizations. Simmons was a "monster," Stanley a clown, Frehley a spaceman, and Criss a cat.

Van Halen (reportedly discovered by Simmons of Kiss) was the first major American heavy metal band to extend the notion of power to also include virtuoso performances, mainly by guitarist Eddie Van Halen. Formed by brothers Eddie and Alex (drums) Van Halen circa 1972, the rest of the members included David Lee Roth (lead vocalist) and Michael Anthony (bass). The skillful guitar work of Eddie became a distinguishing feature of the band, separating them from many of their contemporaries. His creative musical approaches, such as the use of a synthesizer, combined with his guitar mastery made him a sought-after guitarist.[9] Roth's articulate singing style combined with his sexually overt antics served to make him a good "front man" for the group. The album *1984 (MCMLXXXIV),* released in 1984, included the hit single "Jump," which was their biggest selling release.

While Alice Cooper and Kiss were seen as bands that freely expressed themselves on and off stage, the group Guns N' Roses took this to an even greater height. A 1980s Los Angeles-based group, their debut album *Appetite for Destruction* (1989) was one of the top 10 albums of the year. Guns N' Roses riled their audiences with, for some, real-life matters such as racism and sexuality. The song "One in a Million" makes pejorative references to African Americans and homosexuals. Their song "Welcome to the Jungle" is the band's signature song. They were popular from the late 1980s to early 1990s. Lead singer. Axl Rose is currently the only original member.

---

[9] He played the guitar solo in Michael Jackson's "Beat It" in 1982.

CHAPTER TWENTY-ONE

SOCIO-POLITICAL ACTIVISM MUSIC: REGGAE, PUNK, AND HIP-HOP

INTRODUCTION

The socio-political climate of the 1960s and 70s was such that individuals felt compelled to express their stance on politics, government policy, and social behavior. In reggae music, the Rastafari religious movement[1] of the 1930s and its belief in fairness to all people played a major role in developing

The Sex Pistols. © Photofest

---

[1] The Rastafari Movement was supported by working-class Jamaicans who believed that Haile Selassie I, a former emperor of Ethiopia, was God incarnate.

a sociopolitical viewpoint. Not only did punk musicians write about unfairness for the economically deprived and America's governmental policies, they also embraced reggae musicians' stance on "power to the people." Moreover, some punk bands utilized various reggae (or a variation of) music characteristics such as the guitar playing on the backbeat (counts two and four of a quadruple meter). Examples are the songs titled "Concrete Jungle" (1979) by The Specials and "London Calling" (1988) by The Clash. Punk is an American-bred style that also found favor among European audiences. The Sex Pistols and their recordings titled "Anarchy in the U.K.," and "God Save the Queen" achieved success in America. At the same time, rap music became the voice for many young urban blacks who felt that America was leaving them behind. The song titled "The Message" (1982) by Grandmaster Flash and The Furious Five was a protestation about the hideous living conditions of many urban blacks.

REGGAE

With the many cultural influences evident in Jamaica—the birthplace of reggae—its music appeals to a number of different people and cultures. Indeed, with customs and traditions of Cuba, Africa, Spain, the United Kingdom, and even America, Jamaica displays an amalgamation of ideologies that intrigues even the purist. Some people have the notion that reggae is a style of music that was created on American soil. Although reggae borrowed musical elements of popular styles in America such as certain horn riffs in rhythm & blues, and specific vocalities of gospel music, it nonetheless developed in Jamaica.

Ska and rock steady—popular styles in the 1960s—were precursors to reggae. With regard to ska, the music combines musical aspects of *mento,* calypso, and rhythm & blues. A further investigation shows that *mento* music draws from African traditions, while calypso stems from music traditions of Tobago and Trinidad. *Mento,* a folk music, comes from the Spanish word *mentar,* or "to say or speak." In this view, the music can be seen as a vehicle for personal political viewpoints as well as expressions of love and social situations.

Ska is characterized by rhythmic vocal melodies accompanied a degree of woodwind and brass involvement, and a typical ska rhythm section—bass, guitar, keyboard, drums. It often combined elements of the calypso rhythm with rhythm & blues-type riffs colored by instrumental solos, often played by the saxophone, trumpet, piano, and guitar. Ska bands were known for performing instrumental versions (in the ska style) of well known songs. An example of this is one of the most influential bands named The Skatalites, and their recording of the "James Bond Theme." The song begins with melodic sharing by brass and woodwinds instruments. This section is followed by solos in the following order: trumpet, saxophone, trombone, saxophone, and guitar. In the mid-1960s The Skatalites recorded some of their best known songs: "Guns of Navarone" (circa. 1964) and the Grammy nominee titled "Hi Bop Ska" (1995). The group was short lived, in part due to band member Don Drummonds' murder conviction in 1965. The group reformed for a concert in 1983, and due to great success continued performing thereafter.

The sound of rock steady is similar to what one would hear by combining gospel-type harmonies with a calypso or Latin rhythm played in a moderate to moderately fast tempo. Unlike ska, where extended instrumental solos was the norm, especially in those songs performed by The Skatalites, rock steady regularly featured vocal singing. One early group that helped to establish the rock steady sound is The Maytals. Their album titled *Monkey Man/From the Roots* (1970) includes these features in songs such as "Loving Spirit" (about God's spirit in one's soul), "The Preacher" (emulates the recitative manner of a preacher), and "Revival Reggae." God as love is the subject matter of the latter song, which is supported by three-part homorhythmic[2] singing. The group's gospel sound is attributed to the leader, Frederick "Toots" Herbert. Herbert was influenced by his experiences and participation in singing gospel music in a church in Maypen, Jamaica. Other topics in the album include promiscuity ("Peeping Tom"), creation "("Gold & Silver"), and regional fables ("Monkey Man"). Their single release in 1968 titled "Do the Reggae" is said to be the first time the word reggae is used with respect to music. Because of the song's popularity, the term *reggae* became commonly used among followers of this type of music.

Sometimes seen with its correct spelling–raggae–the music is rooted in syncopated rhythms with an emphasis on the back-beat (counts two and four of a quadruple meter). Reggae differs from both ska

Bob Marley. © Photofest

and rock steady with its slower tempo. Additionally, the distinct calypso rhythm in both ska and rock steady is not as salient in reggae. Reggae's greatest disseminator outside of Jamaica is Bob Marley. Born Robert Nesta Marley (1945–1981) in Saint Ann, Jamaica, he became a singer and songwriter and a voice for socially, politically, and economically deprived Jamaicans. His activist attitude stemmed from

---

[2] *Homorhythmic* refers to different vocal parts singing in a very rhythmic manner.

his belief in the Rastafari Movement. Early Marley songs that embody his sociopolitical views and/or a sense of spirituality included "Soul Rebel," "Corner Stone," "Jah[3] is Mighty," and "400 Years" (all in 1970s). Marley's career began as a member of a group that eventually became known as The Wailers. A few years after their formation in 1966, only three original members remained: Bunny Livingston, Peter McIntosh, and Marley. Sometime thereafter, Marley teamed with Lee "Scratch" Perry and his studio band named The Upsetters. To many, Perry helped to influence Marley's reggae style, particularly since he afforded Marley and others the ability to experiment with their creativity in his studio, named The Black Ark. Marley would go on to record and produce numerous albums during his short life. Some of his more popular songs included "Stir It Up," "Concrete Jungle," "Get Up, Stand Up," and "I Shot the Sheriff." Jimmy Cliff was another popular reggae artist during the early reggae years. Some of his popular songs included "Many Rivers to Cross," "Hurricane Hattie," "Waterfall," "Wonderful World, Beautiful People," and "Vietnam."

PUNK

The beginning of punk can be traced to Andy Warhol's 1965 traveling art show titled *The Exploding Plastic Inevitable*, when The Velvet Underground premiered as the accompanimental music to this artistic presentation.

It is interesting to note that punk artists often receive respect from their fans when record sales are low and their songs don't appear on Billboard charts. This idea supports the notion that the true tradition of punk lyrics and performances place less of an emphasis on mass-market appeal strategies. Instead, artists tend to focus on social issues confronting their, regularly, young consumers. These issues include their disgust with alleged governmental actions such as minimal concern for people and more concern for interests abroad. Political issues are not the only protestations of punk artists Everyday life situations such as manhood, parental issues, and relationships are also a focus of punk music.

General music characteristics include fast tempo and distortion and feedback. The vocalist usually sings in a full-throated and often shouting manner, the musical structure often includes an introduction, any number of verses and a refrain, and frequently uses only a few chord changes. Not considered mainstream music, punk bands found it difficult to present their songs to a willing audience. A place in the Bowery District of Harlem, New York, named Country, Bluegrass, and Blues and Other Music for Uplifting Gormandizers became the mainstay for many early punk bands. Popularly known as CBGB's, in 1973 owner Hilly Kristal took a chance on creating a haven for bands that were not signed to record labels. Although bands such as Wayne County and Suicide were two of the earliest punk bands to perform there, it wasn't until the band Television that CBGB's became a refuge for punk bands. Following their debut on April 14, 1974 at CBGB's, punk bands such as The Ramones and Blondie appeared later that year.

The Ramones (Joey, Dee Dee, Johnny, and C.J.) play songs that are considerably short. Their Rhino Record release in 2004 titled *Loud, Fast, Ramones* consists of 30 songs! It contains a number of hits that exemplify their career, beginning with their formation in 1974 in Forest Hills, Queens New York. As listed on the album, these songs include:

"Blitzkreig Bop"
"Beat on the Brat"
"Judy Is a Punk"
"Gimmie Gimmie Shock Treatment"
"Glad to See You Go"
"Pinhead"

---

[3] *Jah* is Rastafarian for God incarnate.

The Ramones. © Photofest

"Rockaway Beach"
"We're a Happy Family"
"Shenna Is a Punk Rocker"
"Teenage Lobotomy"
"I Wanna Be Sedated"
"I'm Against It"
"I Wanted Everything"
"I Just Want to Have Something to Do"
"Rock 'N' Roll High School"
"Do You Remember Rock and Roll Radio"
"The KKK Took My Baby Away"
"Psycho Therapy"
"Outsider"
"Highest Trails Above"
"Wart Hog"
"Mama's Boy"
"Somebody Put Something in My Drink"
"I Wanna Live"
"Garden of Serenity"
"I Believe in Miracles"

The majority of songs are satires on some situation in life. Such songs include "We're a Happy Family," "Teenage Lobotomy," and "I Wanted Everything." Most songs are played at a similar fast tempo. Other commonalities include the following.

1. No more than a few chords are played
2. The introduction is frequently played by all instruments (guitar, bass, and drums).

3. Most songs include some singing or shouting (such as "Blitzkreig Bop" and "Teenage Lobotomy"), and normally the refrain is played by all band members.

4. Usually there are no solos (a brief guitar solo appears at the beginning of "Somebody Put Something in My Drink" and near the end of "I Believe in Miracles").

5. The 16th note (i.e., four taps for each count) is the typical rhythm for all instruments (in a quadruple meter the drummer plays, in addition to 16th notes on the cymbal, the kick drum counts one and three and the snare on counts two and four). See illustration below:

Cymbal	....	....	....	....
Counts:	**1**	**2**	**3**	**4**
Kick drum	x		x	
Snare drum		x		x

6. Use of sound effects (see discussion below).

Aspects of some songs do not fit into the above commonalities. The song titled "Pinhead" begins with drums and the vocalist singing in a half-sung, shouting voice. Reminiscent of what one would hear from the Beach Boys, three-part harmony, uncharacteristic for The Ramones, occurs in "Rockaway Beach," "Sheena Is a Punk Rocker," and "Rock 'N' Roll High School."

Sound effects also appear in a few songs. People talking, a crying baby, and a barking dog are included at the end of "We're a Happy Family." The song "Pinhead" also includes nerdy-type talking at the song's close. Talking followed by a ringing bell appears at the beginning of the song "Rock 'N' Roll High School." In "Do You Remember Rock and Roll Radio?" the song begins with the sounds of a radio changing channels. Sirens appear, along with the band, at the beginning of "Psycho Therapy."

Some songs such as "I Wanna Be Sedated" and "I Just Want to Have Something to Do" are played slightly slower (moderately fast) than most songs. No songs are played with a slow tempo, which is often used for love ballads. Although love ballads are not common for The Ramones, the collection above, in any case, includes a few exceptions such as "I Just Want to Have Something to Do" and "Pinhead." The latter title certainly does not suggest a love song, but the lyrics reveal that the singer is in love with a nurse and does not want to be a "Pinhead" anymore.

With regard to other instrument usages, an organ and brass and woodwind instruments are incorporated in "Do You Remember Rock and Roll Radio?"

In most songs, the vocalist uses a more conventional manner of singing where the lyrics can generally be understood. The singer's melody in "Wart Hog," however, is sung in a more shouting fashion. Although not quite the same as "Wart Hog," the melody in the song "Somebody Put Something in My Drink" is sung in a more full-throated and shouting manner than the majority of songs in this collection.

At times, The Ramones did more than make political statements by identifying a specific entity and its unnerving persona. For instance, the song "The KKK Took My Baby Away" speaks about a person who is frantically searching for his/her baby, even to the point of phoning the President and the FBI. Although the songs generally steered away from speaking about killing and spirituality, the collection does include a few exceptions. The songs "Psycho Therapy" and "I Wanna Live" make reference to using a gun to kill someone. In "Garden of Serenity," references are made to the end of life, and "I Believe in Miracles" speaks about the singer's belief that a better world exists.

Like the Ramones, Blondie was also formed in 1974. Group members were Chris Stein (guitar), Deborah Harry (vocalist), Clem Burke (drums), and Jimmy Destri (keyboard). In 1977, they released their first album titled *Blondie,* which was somewhat well received. That same year they released their second album *Plastic Letters,* which led to an international tour to Europe and Asia. In 1978, they released their third album titled Parallel Lines. From this album, the song "Sunday Girl" reached number 1 in the U.K. "Heart of Glass" (1979) (initially sung in a reggae manner) reached Number 1 in the United States and sold extremely well in the U.K. It became evident that Blondie wanted to include something new for each album. Their fourth album, titled *Eat to the Beat,* also included a full-length video. Its video appeal perhaps inspired film directors to incorporate some of Blondie's songs in film. In 1980, the song "Call Me" appeared in the film titled *American Gigolo.* Deborah Harry's charm led to an appearance on *The Muppet Show* that same year. Along with *Eat to the Beat,* their fifth album titled *Autoamerican* reach platinum sales. Media attention seemed to focus on Harry, reinforced by her appearances on the popular TV program *Solid Gold,* and she released her first solo album titled *Koo Koo* in 1981. This stint, as is quite common among groups, led to the band's final album, namely *The Hunter.* Deborah Harry continues to perform and periodically appears in films. Other members are involved in different music projects.

The Dead Kennedys originated in San Francisco, California, in 1978. The original group consisted of Eric Boucher (lead singer), Carlos Cadona, (rhythm guitar), Geoffrey Lyall (bass), East Bay Ray (lead guitar), and Bruce Slesinger (drums). Their albums *In God We Trust, Inc.* (1981), *Plastic Surgery Disasters* (1982), *Franken Christ* (1985), *Bedtime for Democracy* (1986), *Mutiny on the Bay* (2001), and *Give Me Convenience or Give Me Death* (2004) along with their pictorial covers, illustrated the group's sociopolitical stance toward American culture. Songs from the first two albums listed above include:

"Advice from Christmas Past"
"Government Flu"
"Terminal Preppie"
"Trust Your Mechanic"
"Well-Paid Scientist"
"Buzzbomb"
"Forest Fire"
"Halloween"
"Winnebago Warrior"
"Riot"
"Bleed for Me"
"I Am the Owl"
"Dead End"
"Moon Over Marin"
"Religious Vomit"
"Moral Majority"
"Hyperactive Child"
"Kepone Factory"
"Dog Bite"
"Nazi Punks F*** Off"
"We've Got a Bigger Problem Now"
"Rawhide"

Many of these songs are a satire on some political daily life situation. Examples include "Trust Your Mechanic" (which speaks about being taken advantage of); "Forest Fire" (about the excitement of starting a fire); "Winnebago Warrior" (about people and their gas hogs leaving their debris behind); "We've Got a Bigger Problem" (their disgust with Ronald Reagan politics); and "Moral Majority" (a satire of a caring preacher).

Known for playing extremely fast, the songs "Religious Vomit," "Hyperactive Child," "Dog Bite," and "Nazi Punks F*** Off" all illustrate the group's ability to maintain a fast tempo. As seen by the titles, the fast tempo of these songs (which last from 37 seconds to a 64 seconds) supports the songs' assumed content. Unlike recordings by The Ramones as previously discussed, where all instruments usually played the introduction, many of the Dead Kennedys' songs begin, though briefly, with one or two instruments. Some examples include the following:

"Terminal Preppie"–brief bass introduction
"Well-Paid Scientist"–brief bass introduction
"Buzzbomb" drum roll solo as introduction
"Forest Fire"–bass introduction
"Halloween"–bass introduction
"Winnebago Warrior"–bass introduction
"Riot"–drum introduction, bass enters, guitar effects, then solo guitar,
"Bleed for Me"–brief bass introduction, then cymbals, then guitar
"I Am the Owl"–bass introduction, then drums and guitar solo
"Dead End"–guitar introduction, then bass, then drums
"Kepone Factory"–guitar introduction
"We've Got a Bigger Problem Now"–bass introduction

A number of songs incorporate spoken words at the beginning. For instance, "Advice from Christmas Past" begins with a woman who is speaking satirically about her desire for the finer things in life. "Moral Majority" begins with women's voices humming the melody to the religious hymn titled "Rock of Ages" underneath a male spoken satire imitating a preacher who is out for no one but himself. The vocalists sing the opening to the Disney song "Mickey Mouse."

Finally, the Dead Kennedys added a little more variety with regard to tempo. In the songs "Government Flu," "Forest Fire," "Riot," "Bleed for Me," and "Moral Majority," a fast tempo follows the slower introduction. The song "Trust Your Mechanic" begins with a fast tempo, but abruptly plays more slowly just before the midway point, then after 15 seconds or so returns to the original fast tempo.

Another punk group is The Dead Boys from Ohio, formerly known as Frankenstein. Members include vocalist Stiv Bators (Steve Bator), lead guitarist Cheetah Chrome (Gene O'Connor), rhythm guitarist Jimmy Zero (William Wilden), bassist Jeff Magnum (Jeff Halmagy), and drummer Johnny Blitz (John Madansky). Former art rock performers in the mid-70s, they decided to move toward punk. They signed a contract with Sire Records and recorded their first album titled *Young, Loud, and Snotty*. Playing in the fashion of punk caught the eye of concert producers, and by *1977,* The Dead Boys were opening for Iggy Pop (in the United States) and The Damned (in England). That same year they recorded their second album titled *We Have Come for Your Children.*

In addition to those already mentioned, other notable punk groups include Murphy's Law, The Dictators (the starting band consisted of seven members), The Bay City Rollers, Patti Smith, The Specials ("Concrete Jungle"), The Clash ("London Calling" and "White Riot"), The Offspring ("Kill the President" and "It'll Be a Long Time"), The Virus ("The Time Is Now"), The Dickies ("Eve of Destruction" originally by Barry McGuire), The Damned ("Born to Kill"), Sex Pistols ("God Save the Queen"), Buzzcocks ("Ever Fallen in Love?"), Naked Aggression ("Killing Floor"), Green Day ("The Grouch"), D.O.A. ("Race Riot"), American Head ("Pushing the Envelope"), The Bullys ("Damn"), The Boys ("Cop Cars"), Pissant (Los Angeles), ZLO (Estonia), Outtareach (El Monte, CA), The Mud City Manglers, and many more. Even artists such as Lou Reed and Iggy Pop are known for indulging in the punk craze.

HIP-HOP

In an article in *Business Week* dated October 27, 2003, and titled, "The CEO of Hip-Hop: Impresario Russell Simmons," Susan Berfield writes:

> *Hip-hop music and its signature style, rap, emerged from mostly impoverished largely African-American urban neighborhoods, grew into an entire way of life, and today dominates youth culture. It's not about race or place. It's an attitude, a state of mind. Marketing experts estimate that one-quarter of all discretionary spending in America today is influenced by hip-hop. Coke, Pepsi, Heineken, Courvoisier, McDonald's, Motorola, Gap, Cover Girl-even milk: They all use hip-hop to sell themselves.*"[4]

Snoop Doggy Dogg and Tupac Shakur.
© Mitchell Geber/CORBIS

---

[4] *Business Week*, October 27, 2003, p. 92.

No other style of pop youth-culture music has survived as long as hip-hop. Indeed, styles such as punk, rock & roll, disco, new wave, heavy metal, soul, and even rhythm & blues (traditional) have not influenced pop culture as much as hip-hop. Why is this so? To begin, it is important to realize that hip-hop is more than a musical style; it is also a subculture. Viewing the youth culture during the inception of hip-hop provides some interesting facts not only about the music, but about the evolving urbanization of the African American community. The outstanding research by Dr. Tricia Rose titled *Black Noise: Rap Music and Black Culture in Contemporary America* provides an excellent understanding of the inception of and the socialization of hip-hop music. She states:

> *Rap music is a black cultural expression that prioritizes black voices from the margins of urban America. Rap music is a form of rhymed storytelling accompanied by highly rhythmic, electronically based music. It began in the mid-1970s in the South Bronx in New York City as a part of hip-hop, an African-American and Afro-Caribbean youth culture composed of graffiti, breakdancing, and rap music. From the outset, rap music has articulated the pleasures and problems of black urban life in contemporary America. Rappers speak with the voice of personal experience, taking on the identity of the observer or narrator. Male rappers often speak from the perspective of a young man who wants social status in a locally meaningful way. They rap about how to avoid gang pressures and still earn local respect, how to deal with the loss of friends to gun fights and drug overdoses, and they tell grandiose and sometimes violent tales that are powered by male sexual power over women. Female rappers sometimes tell stories from the perspective of a young woman who is skeptical of male protestations of love or a girl who has been involved with a drug dealer and cannot sever herself from his dangerous life-style. Some raps speak to the failures of black men to provide security and attack men where their manhood seems most vulnerable: the pocket. Some tales are one sister telling another to rid herself from the abuse of a lover.*"[5]

It is in the inner cities of these areas where youth continually endure trying socioeconomic situations and consequently have developed a lifestyle of particular social activities: DJing, break–dancing (a.k.a. B-boying), graffiti art, and rap (a.k.a. MCing). DJing refers to the process by which a disc jockey displays his/her skill in playing and mixing songs for listeners, and most importantly dancers. Breakdancing was a style of dance that frequently occurred during an event/party where rap/hip-hop and/or funk music was played for listeners. With reference to the graffiti art scene, artists received their inspiration from the metropolitan environment in New York and the emerging hip-hop culture. Rap music, like black music since the 1600s, is a folk literature that informs, articulates, and inspires people, in this case young people in the African American community. I should also point out

---

[5] See T. Rose, *Black Noise: Rap Music and Black Culture in Contemporary America*, 1994, p. 2.

that the practice of "beatboxing" (i.e., rhythmic/groove competition) is becoming a fifth recognized element of the hip-hop scene.

Havelock Nelson and Michael Gonzales conducted an interview with Fab 5 Freddy of Yo MTV Raps, and noted the interview in their book titled *Bring the Noise: A Guide to Rap Music and Hip Hop Culture*. I have included a small but poignant and relevant portion regarding DJing:

> *DJs in my neighborhood would come out with their*
> *sound systems when I was coming up-people like*
> *Frankie D, Master D, Pete 'DJ' Jones and*
> *Grandmaster Flowers 'who inspired Flash to add*
> *Grandmaster onto his name'. Them bringing music*
> *out into parks and shit gave me something to do in*
> *the summer, something to keep me out of trouble. I*
> *used to follow these guys, and I would go asking*
> *things like, 'Yo, where's the jam, where they at-what*
> *park? St. John's, Albany, where"? I got the bug and*
> *was real curious when I saw those turntable*
> *techniques go down, I used to be one of those kids as*
> *a jam who used to stand in front of the DJ all the*
> *time. I would party a little bit, but I was more like,*
> *Damn what is going on with the DJ? You know, like*
> *what's that record that he's playing? Or why does it*
> *sound like that? Or how come I ain't hearing this*
> *record nowhere else in my life? I used to ask them,*
> *and they would say, 'Yo, it's the Uptown sound!" I*
> *started taking train rides into Manhattan trying to*
> *find the shit. Eventually I met some graffiti guys that*
> *had some fourth or fifth generation tapes of Flash*
> *back in the early, early days. Man, they're so scratchy*
> *it's like trying to tune in Flash on shortwave. But*
> *I used to listen to that shit and go 'Yeah, this is*
> *the real shit!"*[6]

Breakdancing indeed displays phenomenal acrobatic feats and excellent body control, but the idea of dancing on a portable stage in front of other dancers or curious onlookers is not new. In fact, it pre-dates the Civil War.

> *In the north there was frequent mention of dances*
> *performed by Negro slaves. In New York there were*
> *accounts of Dutch burghers traveling in form the*
> *countryside to see Negroes dancing. Many of these*
> *dances took place in New York's Catherine Market*
> *where, after the day's business was concluded, the*
> *slaves would regularly celebrate by dancing, their*
> *efforts being rewarded by onlookers. The slaves*
> *carried with them large boards, some six feet square,*

[6] See H. Nelson and M. Gonzales, *Bring the Noise: A Guide to Rap Music and Hip-Hop Culture*, 1991, p. vi.

*which served as portable dancing areas for the
jigs and breakdowns which were the popular dance
forms. Music—or rather, rhythm—was provided
by various parts of the body, the thighs and torso,
and hand-clapping."*[7]

As mentioned, dancers often performed as a way to gain notoriety or—in the 1970s black and Latino urban communities in New York—to earn respect. Where dancers during the 1800s would construct a portable platform (often wood) for dancing, in contemporary American black ghettos where young teens would dance outdoors, cardboard was often used to execute one's breakdancing skills. In both cases, this was referred to as a "break down"—a dance event that frequently utilized a portable stage/ platform. It is interesting to note that in hip-hop culture there exists a symbiosis between "break down" and "breaks." In this context, *break* refers to the most danceable section in a given song. As imagined, rap music and other styles such as funk, go-go, and funky-disco supplied the accompaniment to these occasions.

It is reported that the proliferation of breakdancing is credited to a former member of the Black Spades gang, namely Afrika Bambaataa (founder of The Universal Zulu Nation and Godfather of the hip-hop culture), as a way to curtail gang violence. He aimed to stop the killings in black and Latino urban communities by encouraging gang members to breakdance as a way to compete for their seemingly inevitable need for respect and territorial control. If such a courageous venture could save the life of one human being, then it would be a success; and indeed it was, as a number of gang members laid down their guns, knives, and chains in favor of participating in breakdancing events. Such an event was brought to the international stage by way of Michael Jackson's videos and song titles of the same name: "Beat It" (1983) and "Bad" (1987). These use choreographed dancing to emulate gang-type fighting.[8] In its more social setting, breakdancing events or parties, which were frequently outside, involved dancers showing off their new or interpretive dance moves in the middle of a circle of onlookers and young hopefuls.[9] It could involve spinning on one's head or hand with the body raised in the air; doing specific dances such as the robot or electric boogaloo; or flipping the body in a seemingly infinite number of ways to display masterful body control.

With regard to graffiti art, it is viewed as a form of artistic expression through painting that reflects one's social, cultural, economic, and political environment. It began in the early 1970s with a young man of Greek heritage named Demetrius, who artistically wrote his name in subways as he traveled throughout various districts. A number of young people became intrigued by his remarkable artistic ability. Eventually other young artists began a similar quest, which evolved into creating elaborate designs, colors, shapes, and styles. Soon this became known as tagging—an artistic exhibit of one's territory and subsequent style. By the mid- to late-1970s some artists such as Fab 5 Freddy and Jean Michel Basquiat received recognition and had their work displayed in galleries and museums in exclusive downtown New York art galleries.

As is the case with music in African culture, social music, music making, dancing, and expression are not segregated from everyday life or from each other. Similarly, DJing, breakdancing, graffiti art, and rap music formed a cohesive bond that contributed to the formation of an American subculture

---

[7] See E. Thorpe, *Black Dance*, 1990, p. 38.

[8] The late Michael Peters, a former member of the Alvin Ailey American Dance Theatre, choreographed several of Mr. Jackson's successful videos. His most popular and influential work is the choreographed dancing in Jackson's video for his 1984 hit, "Thriller."

[9] There is a similarity between this event and what was discussed regarding Place Congo in Chapter 2.

of hip-hop. While rap music was more socially inclusive for black and Latino urban communities in New York, it was socioculturally exclusive to other communities. New York's hip-hop culture was rap to most external communities. As a result, listeners in these external communities were uninformed about rap music's function and intention. (See previous quote by Dr. Rose.) Therefore, in order for the music to appeal to mainstream America, the subject matter had to be either diluted, or be made generalizable to all youth experiences and thus non threatening.

Despite the fact that rappers such as Afrika Bambaataa, DJ Kool Herc, Grandmaster Flash, Kurtis Blow, Lovebug Starski, Roxanne Shante, and many others were heavily involved in rap music's formation, it was the group Sugar Hill Gang and their recording titled "Rapper's Delight" (1979) that brought rap to national attention.[10] The following year, "The Breaks" by Kurtis Blow became the first gold rap single, and by 1984, rap music saw its first gold album, *Run DMC* by the group of the same name. Two organizations are noteworthy for their popularization of B-Boy culture worldwide; Rock Steady Crew and the Electirc Boogaloos. From the mid-980s through the early 1990s, a plethora of MC/rap artists received significant commercial success. Some of these include (listed alphabetically by the first word of the artist):

A Tribe Called Quest
Beastie Boys
Big Daddy Kane
Biz Markie
Boogie Down Productions
De La Soul
Digital Underground
Dimples D.
DJ Flowers
DJ Hollywood
DJ Jazzy Jeff & The Fresh Prince
DJ Starchild
Doug E. Fresh
Dr. Dre
EPMD (acronym for Eric and Parrish Making Dollars)
Eric B. & Rakim
Fat Boys
Ice Cube
Ice-T
Jimmy Spicer
Jungle Brothers
Kenny Gee
Kid Frost
Kid 'N' Play
Kool Moe Dee
KRS-ONE (acronym for Knowledge Reigns Supreme Over
Nearly Everyone)
L.L. Cool J.

---

[10] Grandmaster Caz, the lead rapper in the group Col Ruch Brothers, wrote the song "Rapper's Delight," although he is not credited with doing so.

Marley Marl
MC Lyte
Monie Love
Naughty By Nature
Neneh Cherry
N.W.A. (acronym for Niggas With Attitude)
Poor Righteous Teachers
PM Dawn (PM refers to ". . . from the darkest hour comes the light."[11])
Public Enemy
Queen Latifah
Salt 'N' Pepa
Slick Rick
The D.O.C.
3rd Bass
Wanda Dee
Whodini
Yo-Yo

Because hip-hop is still evolving, it may be premature to categorize much of its substance based on what we have thus far. However, to facilitate continued analysi of the music, here is a list of performers and their songs representative of the genre.

ARTIST	SONG TITLE
Arrested Development	"Mr. Wendel"
Biz Markie	"Just a Friend"
Bone, Thugs, & Harmony	"Crossroads"
Bubba Sparxx	"Ugly"
Cash & Computa	"Ground Zero"
De La Soul	"Me, Myself, and I"
De La Soul	"The Magic Number"
DJ Quick	"Trouble"
Eve	"Me Me"
Eve	"You Had Me, You Lost Me"
Eve Featuring Gwen Stefani	"Let Me Blow Your Mind"
Foxy Brown	"Broken Silence"
Fugees	"Oh La La La"
Junior Mafia	"Need You Tonight"
Lauryn Hill	"Sweetest Thing"

---

[11] Steven Stancell, *Rap Whoz Who: The World of Rap Music*, (NY: Schirmer Books, 1996), p. 222.

Lil' Kim Featuring Sisco	"How Many Licks"
LL Cool J	"Mama Said Knock You Out"
Mary J. Blige	"Family Affair"
Mary J. Blige	"Real Love"
Mary J. Blige	"Where I've Been"
Missy 'Misdemeanor' Elliot	"One Minute Man"
Naughty By Nature	"Hip Hop Hooray"
Nelly	"Ride wth m"
NWA	"Straight Out o Compton"
Kris Kriss	"Warm I Up"
The Roots	"Silent Treatment"
Salt N' Pepa	"Shoop"
Snoop Doggy Dogg	"Wrong Idea"
Tag Team	"Whomp–There It Is"
TLC	"Waterfalls"
Tone Loc	"Funky Cold Medina"
Tupac	"To Live and Die in L.A."
Vanilla Ice	"Ice Ice Baby"

CHAPTER TWENTY-TWO

YESTERYEAR'S MAINSTREAM AND ALTERNATIVE ROCK

SINGER SONGWRITERS

Jackson Browne was born in 1948 in Heidelberg, Germany (his father was an American soldier stationed there at the time). His songwriting talent was influenced by his membership (vocal, guitar, and songwriter) in Los Angeles band The Nitty Gritty Dirt Band in the mid-1960s. Moving to New York shortly thereafter, he released his solo album *Jackson Browne* (December 1971). The album contains two songs–"Doctor My Eyes" and "Rock Me on the Water"– that are currently played on classic rock and easy listening radio stations. The song "Running on Empty" from the album of the same name released in 1978 is his most popular song to date.

Jimmy Buffett, born in 1946 in Pascagoula, Mississippi, is best known for his song t "Margaritaville" (1992). His professional music career began as a country artist, with his first album *Down to Earth* (1970). Prior to that, Buffett was awarded a B.A. degree in journalism from the University of Southern Mississippi in 1969. Following his first album, Buffett recorded a number of albums that illustrated his flair for country music. For instance, the song "The Great Filling Station Holdup" from the album *A White Sport Coat and a Pink Crustacean* (1973) embodied country music characteristics such as sliding guitar, harmonica, and lyrics about spending time in jail for two years following a robbery at a gas station. The song "Door Number Three" from the album *A-1-A* includes slide guitar, harmonica, acoustic guitar, and piano, and features the typical minimally syncopated country rhythm. Browne is also known for incorporating other instruments such as the marimba in the song "A Pirate Looks at Forty" from the album *A-1-A* (1974).

Harry Chapin (1942–1981) was no stranger to the New York club scene as a performer in the early 1970s. As is often the case for performers, performing live at venues helps to build character and musicality. In 1972, Chapin recorded his first album *Head and Tales*. The song "Taxi" received some acclaim among critics and consumers. Although he wanted to pursue a career in documentary film-making, he decided to continue with music due to his early success. It is interesting to note that the song "Taxi" illustrates Chapin's desire to create music stories. Contrasting approaches such as acoustic guitar versus orchestral accompaniments, voices with reverberation, natural voice versus full-throated sound production, and a woman's alto voice in counterpoint with violin all help to maintain interest in the song. Chapin took advantage of orchestral instruments as a way to create music stories as seen in the song "Short Stories" (ca. 1973) from the album of the same name. "Cats in the Cradle" (1974) from the album *Verities & Balderdash* is his best known song to date.

Phil Collins, born in 1951 in London, was the drummer and sang background vocals in the group Genesis during the 1980s. Somewhat like Harry Chapin, Collins seemed set on having a career as an actor. He even played as an extra in *A Hard Day's Night* (1964), starring The Beatles. His first solo album, *Face Value* (1981) contains such hits as "In the Air Tonight" and "If Leaving Me Is Easy." In retrospect, the album shows Collins's orchestral and producing ability. For instance, the song "Thunder and Lighting" contains brass and woodwind passages similar to what one would hear in the groups Earth, Wind, and Fire[1] and Blood, Sweat, and Tears. The joining and arrangement of voice, background singers, synthesizer, congos, strings, acoustic guitar, bass, and drums illustrate his conscious effort to allow space for each instrument in the song "This Must Be Love." The 1985 album *No Jacket Required* contains the dance hit "Sussudio" and the rhythm-driven song "Take Me Home." In 1990, Collins received a Record of the Year Grammy for the song "Another Day in Paradise" (1989). Currently Phil Collins is also known for his music in films such as the Disney movie *Tarzan* (1999) which features the song "You'll Be in My Heart."

Jim Croce (1943–1973) was a singer and guitarist who grew up in Pennsylvania. Like Harry Chapin, he developed musical stamina for tough crowds in Pennsylvania. In 1972, Croce recorded what many consider to be his finest "lyric" creation, namely "Time in a Bottle." That may be the case, but the song "Bad, Bad Leroy Brown" (1973) is by far his biggest seller; it went to Number one on the *Billboard* chart.

John Denver (1943–1997) was born Henry John Deutschendorf, Jr. in Rosewell, New Mexico. He adopted the name Denver as it was his favorite place. As a singer and guitarist, Denver recorded many songs. Nearly half of them were his own: "Leaving on a Jet Plane"[2] (1970s), "Take Me Home, Country Roads" (1971), "Rocky Mountain High" (1973), "Rhymes and Reasons" and "Thank God I'm a Country Boy" (1975). Some of his seminal albums include *Poems, Prayers, and Promises* (1971) and *An Evening with John Denver* (1975). Denver's awards include Entertainer of the Year in 1975, his recognition by the Country Music Association, and his induction into the Songwriters Hall of Fame in 1996.

Neil Diamond, born in 1941 in Brooklyn, New York, is a singer, guitarist, and songwriter with a career that extends over four decades. Whether listening to an early release such as *Velvet Gloves & Spit* (1968) or a current album such as *12 Songs* (2005) Diamond's singing style–sung-spoken-like–and vocal timbre, to his credit, have not changed. Though the former album has no songs that have lasted until today, the album has a variety of styles. For instance, "The Pot Smoker's Song" is a satire about one's desire for pot. The song includes spoken testimonials from those who offer reasons as to why they chose to indulge in marijuana. The song "Brooklyn Roads" includes Diamond's guitar picking combined with a symphony orchestra as the accompaniment to his signature singing. By the next year, Diamond scored a couple of hits from the album *Sweet Caroline-Brother Love's Traveling Salvation Show* (1969). These include "Sweet Caroline (Good Times Never Seemed So Good)" and "Brother Love's Traveling Salvation Show." His popularity continued with *Tap Root Manuscript* (1970), an album that contains the popular songs "Cracklin' Rosie," and "He Ain't Heavy, He's My Brother" (also recorded by The Hollies that same year). Since then, Diamond has recorded a number of popular songs such as "Song Sung Blue," "Cherry, Cherry," and "Solitary Man" (1972); a duet with Barbra Streisand "You Don't Bring Me Flowers" (1978); a few hits from *The Jazz Singer* (film soundtrack, 1980) "America," "Love on the Rocks," "Hello Again"; and "Heartlight" (1982) from the album of the same name.

---

[1] Phil Collins produced Philip Bailey's (Earth, Wind and Fire's, a.k.a. EWF, lead singer) album titled *Chinese Wall* in 1984. He sang a duet with Bailey titled "Easy Lover." Collins also worked with the brass and woodwind members of EWF in the 1980s.

[2] In 1971, the folk trio Peter, Paul, and Mary recorded what has become the most popular version of Denver's "Leaving on a Jet Plane."

Dan Fogelberg, born in 1951 in Peoria, Illinois, is a singer, guitarist, and songwriter. He began to receive some notoriety following the hit "Part of the Plan" from his *Souvenirs* album in 1974. Fogelberg presents intriguing three-part homorhythmic singing in the well-received song "The Power of Gold" from his *Two Sons of Different Mothers* album (1978). In the same album, he also displays his musical creativity by recording a piece with counterpoint–between piano (Fogelberg learned to play at a young age) and flute (played by the popular flutist Tim Weisberg)–in the song "Twin's Theme." The song "Longer" from the album *Phoenix* (1978) is a favorite for the acoustic purist, as the piano, acoustic guitar, and strings complement this song of love commitment. Most of his songs are played in a quadruple meter. The song "Run for the Roses" from *The Innocent Age* album (1981), however, is performed in a triple meter. Often, this meter is used for folk-type music such as folk, blues, and country. The use of slide guitar, harmonica, and words that describe aspects of the South ("here in Kentucky") classifies this as a country song. The album also includes the popular song "Hard to Say," which is currently played on certain classic rock and country radio stations.

Billy Joel, born in 1949 in New York, is one of the most prolific and successful songwriters of the modern day era. He is perhaps most known for his piano playing style in the major hit "Piano Man" (1973) from the album of the same name. A waltz tempo combined with folk instruments such as harmonica, accordion, mandolin, and lyrics that speak about the average person made this song appealing to a broad audience. Moreover, Joel's presentation as a piano player in a bar setting where he describes characteristics of various people is typical for "piano bar" entertainers and patrons, thus adding to the song's popularity. His quick arpeggio playing in the song "Everybody Loves You Now" from the album *Cold Spring Harbor* (1972) illustrates his ability as a competent player. The album contains a favorite titled "She's Got a Way." At times, Joel's lyric inspiration was the result of dissatisfaction with his treatment from record label executives. In the song "The Entertainer" from the album *Streetlife Serenade* (1974), he makes reference to record executives' restrictions on song production and marketing strategies. In 1977 Joel released the album *The Stranger*, which contains two of his most memorable songs: "Just the Way You Are" and "She's Always a Woman to Me." Considering the album's disco-like title track ("The Stranger") and "Movin' Out (Anthony's Song)", released at a time when disco music was still popular, one may have the impression that Joel was making an attempt to join the disco bandwagon. Despite this, the remaining songs are far removed from anything reminiscent of disco. Following the album *The Stranger*, Joel released *52nd Street* which contains another favorite, "Honesty." Other popular songs include "Don't Ask Me Why" and "You May Be Right" (both from *Glass Houses*, 1980), "An Innocent Man," "Tell Her About It," and "Uptown Girl" (all from *An Innocent Man*, 1983). Selling millions of records, in 1992 Billy Joel was inducted into the Songwriters Hall of Fame.

Elton John, born Reginald Kenneth Dwight in 1947 in Pinner, England, is a singer, pianist, and songwriter whose success encompasses more than four decades. His many songs (discussed below) for television and film include the theme song to the sitcom *Friends* and "Circle of Life" from the Disney film titled *The Lion King*. John's musical talents are extensive. If one wonders why he spends tens of thousands of dollars on flowers as stage props, it is probably because he can. Also seen as a glitter rock artist of the 1970s, Elton John's p performances feature outrageous costumes and a level of theatricals that rivals any glitter band. His songs, too numerous to list here, feature a wide variety of musical approaches and lyrical statements. Following a couple of earlier albums, the 1971 release *Madman Across the Water* includes the favorites "Tiny Dancer" and "Levin." The 1972 release *Honky Chateau* contains the popular hit "Rocket Man (I Think I'm Going to Be Gone a Long Time)." To many, John's *Yellow Brick Road* (1973) is one of his most creative albums. It contains the popular songs "Funeral for a Friend (Love Lies Bleeding)," "Candle in the Wind," "Bennie and the Jets," and the title track "Goodbye Yellow Brick Road." The album *Too Low for Zero* (1983) contains the

Elton John. © NBC/Photofest

popular songs "I'm Still Standing" and "That's Why They Call It the Blues." Other favorites include "Daniel" (1973), "Don't Let the Sun Go Down on Me" "Your Song," "Honky Cat," and "Rocket Man," (all in 1974), and "Nikita" (1985). Elton John was inducted into the Songwriters Hall of Fame in 1992.

Carole King, born in 1942 in Brooklyn, New York, is a pianist and songwriter. Because of the history of social restraints placed on women, there were a significantly fewer number of women songwriters during the 1950s–1970s. Although other women songwriters who also performed such as Roberta Flack ("The First Time Ever I Saw Your Face," 1969 and "Killing Me Softly," 1973), Joni Mitchell ("Both Sides Now," 1968 and "Big Yellow Taxi," 1970s), and Carly Simon ("Anticipation," 1971 and "You're So Vain," 1972) had success, they did not receive as much as their male counterparts. Carole King, on the other hand, along with Gerry Goffin, her husband at the time, wrote a number of songs that became hits by various performers. Some of these include:

"Will You Still Love Me Tomorrow" (1961) The Shirelles
"Take Good Care of My Baby" (1961) Bobby Vee
"The Loco-Motion" (1962) Little Eva
"One Fine Day" (1963) The Chiffons
"Up on the Roof" (1963) The Drifters
"Chains" (1963) The Cookies
"(You Make Me Feel Like) a Natural Woman" (1967) Aretha Franklin

Following a divorce with Goffin, King went on to establish her solo career as a songwriter and performer. Her most successful solo album to date is *Tapestry* (1971). It includes songs such as "I Feel the Earth Move," "So Far Away," "It's Too Late" and "You've Got a Friend."

Carole King. © Photofest

Barry Manilow (b. 1943), one of the most prolific pop tunesmith artists during the 1970s and 80s, still experiences popular status with such evergreen titles as "Could It Be Magic" (1973), "Mandy" (1974), "I Write The Songs" (1975), and "Can't Smile Without You" (1978), to name some. Noted for his ability to create memorable melodies, Manilow should be remembered for a few of his timeless commercial jingles such as for McDonalds ("You deserve a break today . . .), State Farm Insurance ("Like a good neighbor . . .), and Band-Aid (I'm stuck on band-aid cause...). His illustrious career includes a T.V. show, recipient of many music awards, involvement with legislation concerning intellectual property rights with respect to music, benefit concerts for those in need, and several other remarkable achievements. Manilow performs as a soloist (voice and piano) as well as with various types of instrumental accompaniment. Currently, he does approximately ten concerts each month throughout the U.S. and Canada with regular performances at the Paris Hotel in Las Vegas.

Van Morrison, born in 1945 in Belfast, Ireland, is a singer, pianist, and songwriter. Another Songwriter Hall of Fame inductee (2003), Morrison's songwriting and performing extends beyond four decades. His first musical success occurred as a member of the U.K. group named Them, and their song "Gloria" (1966). He left the group to embark on a solo career where he scored favorably on the *Billboard* charts with the single "Brown-Eyed Girl" from his album *Blowin' Your Mind!* (1967). Although not a hit, the song titled "Ballerina" from the album *Astral Weeks* (1968) displays Morrison's interest in vocal *melisma*[3], a characteristic of much of African American music at the time. In the 1970s, Morrison recorded his most popular song to date, namely "Moondance," from the album of the same name. The album also contains the rhythm & blues and gospel-sounding song "Crazy Love."

Randy Newman, born in 1943 in Los Angeles, California, is a singer, pianist, and songwriter. From songs such as "Laughing Boy" (1968) and "Sail Away" (1972) to scores for films such as *Toy Story* (1995), *A Bug's Life* (1998), and *Monsters, Inc.* (2001), Newman's musical scope is very broad. Although he and his family moved to New Orleans during his formative years, he is no stranger to the music and film scene, as he returned to the West Coast and received a degree from the University of California, Los Angeles. Newman is also known for his at times over-the-top satirical lyrics about racism embodied in the songs "Rednecks" (1974) and "Short People" (1977). In 1983, Newman's recording "I Love L.A." from his *Trouble in Paradise* album placed him among some of the most popular songwriters of the era. Other successful singer-songwriters during the 1970s included Barry Manilow ("Mandy," 1974),[4] Cat Stevens ("Peace Train, 1971), and James Taylor ("Handy Man," 1977).

Carly Simon (b. 1945), a singer, guitarist and pianist, began her music experience with sisters Lucy and Joey (Simon Sisters), then with just Lucy. Following Lucy's marriage in the mid. 1960s, Carly pursued a solo music career. Experiencing numerous circumstances with managers, boyfriends, musicians, record labels, performances and other situations she scored her first hit in 1971 "That's The Way I've Always Heard It Should Be." This was followed by "Anticipation" that same year, and her most successful hit two years later "You're So Vain" form her enormously popular album *No Secrets*. Carly Simon was inducted into the Songwriter Hall of Fame in 1994.

Stevie Wonder, born in 1950 in Saginaw, Michigan as Stevland Judkins is a singer, songwriter, pianist, and harmonica player. Singing with Motown Records at the age of thirteen, Wonder scored his first hit "Fingertips (Pt. 2)" in 1963. Featuring Wonder's extemporaneous singing and his unmistakable harmonica playing, this paved the way for a plethora of hits, awards, and recognitions as one the 20th century's greatest songwriters. His early recordings were straight-ahead dance songs such as "Uptight (Everything's Alright)" (1968), "I Was Made to Love Her," "Signed, Sealed and Delivered" and "My Cherie Amour" (all in 1970). Through his works from the early to mid-1970s, Wonder displays a compositional period that is set apart from the previous, danceable period to a more contemplative style. His albums *Talking Book* (1972), *Innervisions* (1973), and *Songs in the Key of Life* (1976) illustrate his development as a performer, songwriter, recording artist, and producer. *Talking Book* has such hits as "You Are the Sunshine of My Life," "You and I," and "Superstition." Having an innovative mind for creating interesting tone colors, Wonder was ahead of his contemporaries in his use of synthesized sounds, as evidenced in the latter two songs. Wonder's creativity for recording sounds, including voices, continued through his *Innervisions* album. His synthesized bass, different keyboard sounds, and effects on his singing during the song "Too High" displays his musical inventiveness. Nearly every song on the album incorporates similar considerations, such as "Living For the City," "Golden Lady," and "Higher Ground." The thought-provoking songs "He's Misstra Know-It-All," "Jesus Children of America," and "All in Love Is Fair" in retrospect, set the groundwork for what is now evident in neo-soul: that is, stimulating lyrics with religious undertones that encourage us to stay committed to loving those around us as well as ourselves. The album *Songs in the Key of Life* has a number of songs that are

---

[3] *Melisa* refers to singing from several too many pitches for each syllable.

[4] Many assumed Barry Mani low wrote his recording titled "I Write the Songs," but it was actually written by the Beach Boy Bruce Johnson in 1975.

Stevie Wonder. © ABC/Photofest

present in various media such as jingles, athletic games, and the popular competition program seen on television, *American Idol*. Some of these songs include "Sir Duke," "I Wish," "Another Star," and "Isn't She Lovely." Wonder is still a vibrant artist as evidenced by his duet performance with Aretha Franklin at *Super Bowl XL* in 2006.

By the 1980s, label executives and consequently producers intuitively and categorically prognosticated public taste by marketing music as either mainstream or alternative, the former being suitable for all, while the latter appealed only to specific sects. Obviously, as with any business that pursues monetary gains, the industry chose mainstream music marketing to increase their profit. As technology in the 1980s became more feasible for music creation, production and dissemination, there was less demand for musicality on the part of potential performers. The role of the producer became a permanent fixture, and record labels were more willing to produce individuals as long as there was evidence of their marketability.

Through the 1980s and into the 1990s, numerous styles and approaches to music were marketed as mainstream or alternative. For instance, early hip-hop was not considered mainstream music until the late 1980s and early 1990s. Early punk was considered alternative until terms such as *pop punk* in the 1990s made it somewhat mainstream, with artists such as Ashley Simpson and Avril Lavigne.

ROCK MAINSTREAM (A.K.A. MAINSTREAM)

"Rock mainstream" is not a stylistic category but rather a label to identify the many types of performers and performances that fall under the category of rock (as opposed to hip-hop, Latin, R & B, etc.). This chapter will look at musical activities among some of the popular artists during the 1980s to the 21st century. Mainstream rock during the 1980s was more radio-friendly than its antithetic style, alternative rock. In the former, music was more marketable, thus appealing to a wide audience. In this view, music characteristics and performance practices included lyrics that centered on love, relationships, and certain life experiences. It had a danceable rhythm, and an attained level of musicianship (vocalists and instrumentalists), and it was frequently studio-produced. In general, mainstream rock with respect to popularity included those performers who were marketed to a wide audience; in other words they were "crossover" performers–marketed on different charts such as Pop, Top, Hot, R & B, Adult Contemporary, and others. Examples included Prince, Madonna, and Michael Jackson. On the other hand, those performers who were generally listed on only one chart such as Country and R & B were considered potential crossover material. Some examples included Dionne Warwick, Velvet Underground (late), and Afrika Bambaataa.

MAINSTREAM ARTISTS: 1980s and 1990s

Carlos Santana. © NBC/Photofest

Without doubt, Carlos Santana (b. 1947) and his long-established career place him well above many artists. Not only is he one of the biggest selling Latin artists but also of general music marketing. Voted among the top 20 of the most prominent 100 guitarists by Rolling Stone Magazine, Carlos Santana's distinctive sound is imbued with salsa, blues, fusion, and various elements of rock music that has greatly added to his success. Forming the group named Santana in the late 1960s was perfect timing as they were able to appear in America's major music festival, namely Woodstock in 1969. Some of his most recognized recordings and music contributions with other artists include the following:

"Evil Ways" (*Abraxas*, 1970)
"Black Magic Woman" (*Abraxas*)
"Oye Como Va" (*Abraxas*)
"Smooth" featuring Rob Thomas (*Supernatural*, 1999)
"Maria Maria" collaboration with The Product G & B[5] (*Supernatural*)
"The Game of Love" featuring Michelle Branch (*Shaman*, 2002)
"Just Feel Better" (*All That I Am*, 2005)
"I'm Feeling You" featuring Michelle Branch (*All That I Am*)

Right along with Carlos Santana, Tina Turner is an icon in her own right as she transcends time and continues to evolve with the music scene. Born Anne Mae Bullock in 1939, Tina Turner began her

Tina Turner. © Photofest

---

[5] The Product G & B (acronym for Ghetto Blues) is a male duo consisting of Sincere and Money Harm.

music career in the 1950s with her soon-to-be husband Ike Turner. Following her traumatic emotional circumstances as a result of spousal abuse prior to their divorce, Ms. Turner went into hiatus but soon returned triumphantly with a rendition of Al Green's song "Let's Stay Together." The following year her remarkable release *Private Dancer* (1984) includes the popular songs "Private Dancer," "I Can't Stand the Rain," "Better Be Good To Me," and what became a massive hit, namely "What's Love Got To Do With It." The album appeals to mainstream as well as the rock audience as her vocal inflections and instrument performance practices are similar to what one finds in hard rock music of the 1980s. Her 1986 album *Break Every Rule* didn't do as well as the previous album but it did include a song that became a popular hit, namely "Two People." The same is true of her next album, *Foreign Affairs* (1989) where only one song–"The Best"–became popular among the mainstream audience. However in 1994 her appearance in the film *Mad Max Beyond Thunderdome* featured her voice in the theme song "We Don't Need Another Hero," and consequently was released as a single and became an enormous hit. Still performing and presenting her staple improvisational dance routines, Tina Turner is indeed a diva.

Prince Rogers Nelson (b. 1958), more commonly known as Prince, was one of the most widely received rock stars during the 1980s and 1990s. Attributable in part to his ability to combine music

Prince. © Michael Ochs Archive/Corbis

characteristics and performance practices of rhythm & blues, funk, soul, classic rock, psychedelic, disco, techno, and new 1980s rock trends, Prince appealed to audiences of all sorts. One could argue that his persona, musical philosophy and ideology are similar to the 1960s/70s performer Sly Stone (of Sly & The Family Stone, 1960s/70s).[6] His music was indeed attractive to admirers of dance music, traditional as well as contemporary styles, audiences of different nationalities and sociocultural levels, both genders, and a wide age range (early teens through mid-30s). Prince learned to play guitar, piano, and drums without any formal music training, and by his teens had formed a band called Grand Central and then changed the name to Champagne. While still in his teens, he signed a recording contract with Warner Brothers, and by age 20 he had recorded an album *For You* (1978) in which he played all the instruments. Known for his lascivious lyrics in albums such as *Dirty Mind* (1980), *Controversy* (1981), and *Lovesexi* (1988), and songs such as "Do It All Night," "Head," and "Jack U Off," Prince was not afraid to explore topics of sexuality. This is also evidenced by his 1984 film *Purple Rain*, which catapulted "I Would Die for U," "Let's Go Crazy," "Purple Rain," and "When Doves Cry" to the top of the charts.

Madonna. © NBC/Photofest

---

[6] Sly Stone was an African American performer during the 1960s/70s who successfully combined musical elements of black and white popular styles, and thus was appealed to both black and white audiences.

Madonna (b. 1958) is regarded as the 1980s mainstream rock queen. Her provocative lyrics, mass-produced recordings, marketing strategies, and excellent dancing ability secured her as one of the most successful rock stars during this time. Born Madonna Louise Vernon Ciccione in Rochester, Michigan, her first indoctrination to the performance world began as a dancer. (She received a scholarship to study dance at the University of Michigan.) Moving to New York at age 20, she briefly danced with the well-known dance companies Alvin Ailey American Dance Theatre and Pearl Lange. She appeared in a musical in Paris, then returned to New York where she began to pursue music, first playing drums and then singing lead in various bands. At age 24, she signed a recording contract with Sire and recorded disco-flavored songs such as "Burning It Up." By 1985 Madonna was marketed as a sexy performer with provocative visual appeal. The album *Like a Virgin* (1985) catapulted her to international recognition, though not without controversy. As is the case with many musicians, Madonna began to appear in films. These include *Desperately Seeking Susan* (1985), *Shanghai Surprise* (1986), and *Who's That Girl* (1987). She gave a critically acclaimed performance in *Evita* (1996). Madonna's recording success is marked by numerous top hits such as "Holiday" (1982), "Material Girl" and "Crazy for You" (both in 1985), "Papa Don't Preach" (1986), "Express Yourself" and "Cherish" (both in 1987). One could easily devote entire chapters to the music careers of Prince, Madonna, and Michael Jackson.

Michael Jackson. © David Lefranc/Kipa/Corbis

Born in the same year as Prince and Madonna (1958-June 25, 2009), Michael Joe Jackson's music career also flowered in the 1980s. Like Prince, his music interests began at a very early age as a member of his family group named The Jackson Five. With his display of vocal control and extreme giftedness as a dancer, Jackson soon became an appealing figure in the music industry. The song "Ben" (1971), which was the theme song from the movie *Ben*, was his first major hit. With marginal success through nearly the end of the 1970s, his early stardom status as a soloist didn't commence until his appearance in the film *The Wiz* (1978)–an African American version of *The Wizard of Oz*. With music produced by Quincy Jones–a leading arranger, orchestrator and producer in the music industry–Jackson was allowed to examine music on yet another level. With mutual admiration for each other's talents, their collaborative efforts contributed to the production of Jackson's first major solo album, *Off the Wall* (1979). Its success was measured by the fact that no fewer than five songs reached the top of the charts. Some of these were "Don't Stop (Till You Get Enough)," "Rock with You," and "She's Out of My Life." He achieved even greater success with the 1982 album *Thriller*. Of the nine songs, six were major hits. Some of these included "Beat It" (which featured a guitar solo by Eddie Van Halen), "Billie Jean," and the title track "Thriller." In addition to the elite musical production directed again by Quincy Jones, Jackson's outstanding dancing abilities were featured in a short video of the title track. Choreographed by Michael Peters, the *thriller* video set the trend for a number of MTV- aired videos of various performers. Other collaborations included duets with Paul McCartney on songs such as "The Girl Is Mine" (1982) and "Say Say Say" (1983). Jackson co-authored (along with Lionel Richie) the song "We Are the World" (1985)–the USA for Africa charity song. His entrepreneurial efforts were no less astute. In 1984, he signed a multimillion dollar contract with Pepsi, bought the publishing company (ATV Music) in 1985 that held the rights to the majority of The Beatles' songs, and in 1986 starred in a short science fiction film, Captain *Eo*, which was only shown at Disneyland in Anaheim and Disney World in Florida. The following year he released the album *Bad*, which had several top hits such as "Black or White," "Dirty Diana," "The Man in the Mirror," and "The Girl Is Mine."

The enormous popularity of Michael Jackson during the 1980s seems to shun most other artists from scoring on the popular charts. However Gloria Estefan's second album titled *Primitive Love*,[7] released 1985 had two songs that reached the mainstream charts, namely "The Words Get in the Way" and "Conga."

Another popular artist who was marketed as mainstream material was Whitney Houston. Some of her recordings included:

"Greatest Love of All" (1985)
"How Will I Know" (1985)
"Saving All My Love for You" (1985)
"You Give Good Love" (1985)
"Didn't We Almost Have It All" (1987)
"So Emotional" (1987)
"I Wanna Dance with Somebody" (1987)

The boy-band, vocal quartet/quintet craze of the 1980s with groups like New Kids on The Block and New Edition, continued through the 1990s with additional groups NSYNC, Boyz II Men, and Backstreet Boys (discussed in the following section). New Kids on the Block and New Edition were both assembled/guided in Boston by producer Maurice Starr, and both continue to perform to date, though with some membership changes and a hiatus or two. The former has recorded seven albums with *The Block* (2008) being their most recent. They began to achieve notoriety in 1988 with songs from their second album *Hangin' Tough*. Song titles from this recording include "Please Don't Go Girl," "You Got it (The Right Stuff)," "I'll Be Loving You (Forever)," "Cover Girl," and a rerelease of The Delfonics' hit "Didn't I (Blow Your Mind This Time)." The latter group has recorded eight albums with *Candy Girl 25th Anniversary Edition* (2008) being their most recent to date.

---

[7] Gloria Estefan's first album is titled *Eyes of Innocence*, released in 1984.

As the result of a newspaper advertisement Metallica was formed in 1981 by James Hetfield (lead vocalist and guitarist) and Lars Ulrich (drums). One of the interesting facts about this band is that even though a number of members have come and gone it has maintained a fairly successful career since 1982. For example, lead guitarist Lloyd Grand appears on their first demo in 1981. The following year, he was replaced by David Mustaine. That same year, Ron McGovney entered as the bass player who was, within less than a year, replaced by Cliff Burton. In 1983 David Mustaine was replaced by Kirk Hammett as the lead guitarist. Following the death of bass player Cliff Burton as the result of an accident while on tour in 1986, Metallica then recruited Jason Newsted as bassist. After good success with songs such as "Enter Sandman" and "Nothing Else Matters" (both in 1991), Newsted left the group for personal reasons and was replaced by Rob Trujillo. Throughout their many years of success, Metallica has been categorized as heavy metal, speed metal, and now rock mainstream, which is perhaps due to their early start. Lyrical topics include civil rights, justice, insanity, religion, relationships, and war.

Janet Jackson. © Fox/Photofest

Michael Jackson's sister Janet Jackson was another mainstream artist of the 1990s. Her first album release *Janet Jackson* occurred in 1982 and achieved a #6 rating on the *Billboard* rhythm & blues chart, but her popularity was certainly not at the level of her later years. Also, the competition with her brother Michael as a pop star prevented her from becoming a mainstream artist. In addition, Jackson widely popular up to this point, was more popular as a young and emerging TV personality in shows such as

Good Times and *Different Strokes* in the late 1970s and early 1980s. Some of her hits during the late 1980s included "Nasty," "When I Think of You," "Control," "What Have You Done for Me Lately" (all in 1986), "Let's Wait a While" (1987), and "Miss You Much" and "Rhythm Nation" (both in 1989). Her popularity continued in the 1990s, catapulting her to preeminence among women artists to record the greatest number of singles. These include:

"Come Back to Me" (1990)
"Alright" (1990)
"Black Cat" (1990)
"Love Will Never Do (Without You)" (1990)
"Escapade" (1990)
"The Best Things in Life Are Free" (1992)
"That's the Way Love Goes" (1993)

Noted by many as America's first major Latin "Pop" singer, Selena Quintanilla (1971–1995) brought the sounds of Latin music, and more specifically and initially Tejano music to mainstream

Selena. © EMI/Photofest

America. Her short-lived music career began with her first album *Selena,* released in 1989. The album mostly includes songs performed in the Tejano style – Texas-Mexican music. This music was first popular among Mexican Americans in Central and Southern Texas. Born in Lake Jackson, Texas, Selena was no stranger to Tejano music. She absorbed its lyrical meanings, popular themes used among the Mexican American community, and distinctive music characteristics such as the cut time (Polka rhythm) tempo, brass response passages to the lead singer, and the strict time played by the drums. These traditions imbued with contemporized music performance practices allowed her to reach a wider Mexican American and American audiences. The instrumentation of Tejano music includes voice, brass instruments, accordion, guitar, bass, and drums. As heard in her first studio release, Selena mainly sings, with the exception of the song "My Love", in Spanish and in a number of songs the use of the synthesizer adds to the music's contemporized sound and hence crossover appeal. The following year Selena released the album *Ven Conmingo* (*Come With Me*) that includes songs played in the Tejano style as well as popular music at the time. Specifically, the song "Aunque No Salga El" (Even if the sun is not out) uses finger snaps, the 1990s omnipresent Yamaha Full Tines keyboard sound, the anthem-like tempo, an acoustic guitar solo accompanied by more "real" sounding strings. In "Enamorda De Ti," (literally, Enamored of you) its sound is reminiscent of a number of songs by Madonna in that Selena's vocal production includes her natural and at times full-throated voice. Like Madonna's dance songs, this song also includes a snare drum playing the backbeat (accenting the 2nd and 4th counts of a quadruple meter), thus supporting the song's dance-ability. Perhaps her most successful album is *Dreaming of You*, posthumously released in 1995. Of the fourteen songs six were previously unreleased. These include "I Could Fall In Love," "Captive Heart," "I'm Getting Used To You," "God's Child (Baila Conmingo)," "Dreaming Of You," and "Tu Solo Tu." With the exception of the latter song, sung and performed in the Tejano style, all are sung in English and use music production techniques of contemporary styles at that time such as orchestral underpinnings, melodically syncopated guitar and bass parts, and background singer responsorial passages, to name some. One of the appealing aspects of Selena is her embracing and performing of contemporary stylistic tendencies without neglecting her ethnic identity and consequent music characteristics. For instance, in "I Could Fall In Love" she sings in English while delivering spoken text in Spanish in the middle of the song. The use of brass passages in Tejano is effectively incorporated in the contemporary rhythm & blues song "I'm Getting Used To You." Finally, "God's Child (Baila Conmingo)" is sung by David Byrne in English, while Selena provides corroborating verses in Spanish.

A favorite among a wide audience is a former member of the boy band Menudo, named Enrique Martin Morales, better known as Ricky Martin. Born December of 1971 in San Juan, Puerto Rico, following his membership in Menudo, Martin embarked on a solo career in 1991. His live performances of theatricalism and non-stop choreographed dance routines combined with a charming onstage personality propelled him to international fame by the late 1990s. Prior to then he was a moderate actor in Mexico and the U.S. Perhaps his most notable acting part was playing a singer in the popular soap opera *General Hospital* in 1994. His early music releases were sung in Spanish, but in 1999 he received wide acclaim with his Spanish-English release *Ricky Martin* with the subsequent hit "Livin' la Vida Loca." The following year the song "She Bangs", from the album *Sound Loaded,* became his other staple song which earned him the recognition as one of the most popular artists to incite the emerging Latin music craze of the 1990s.

Ricky Martin. © Photofest

Noted for her singing and writing abilities, Mariah Carey began to achieve success in 1990 with her first studio-produced self-titled album. Co-authoring all eleven songs on the album, five became major hits, namely "Vision of Love," "There's Got to Be a Way," "I Don't Wanna Cry," "Someday," and "Love Takes Time." At age twenty-three her success continued with the 1993 release *Music Box*. With the exception of "Without You", Ms. Carey co-authored the remaining nine songs, four of which, in addition to "Without You", were massive international hits. These include "Dreamlover," "Hero," "Anytime You Need a Friend," and "Never Forget You." In all Mariah Carey has recorded 13 albums and there seems to be no slowing down in writing, singing, performing, and producing.

The 1990s represent another instance of the boy-band craze, similar to the 1960s with male quartet/quintet groups like The Temptations and The Four Tops. Two noteworthy groups in the 1990s include NSYNC and Backstreet Boys. Both were formed in Florida during the mid. 1990s as quintets, and both started receiving recognition during the end of the decade. Their recordings consisted of

Mariah Carey. © ABC/Photofest

heart-throb songs geared towards girls in their tweens through late teen years.[8] Live performances included intricate vocal harmonies accompanying the lead singers' often melismatic singing style with highly synchronized dance routines. Longevity is the main difference between these two groups. While Backstreet Boys continue to record and perform,[9] NSYNC on the other hand officially shut down its website in 2006.

NSYNC's most popular songs include "Bye Bye Bye," "It's Gonna Be Me," and "This I Promise You", all from their 2000 album *No Strings Attached*. The group recorded three additional albums with their final one in 2001 *Celebrity*. The Backstreet Boys first received notoriety from their album *Millennium* (1999). Songs that became popular from this album include "Larger Than Life," "I Want It That way," "Show Me the Meaning of Being Lonely," and "The One." The group has recorded seven albums, with their latest *This is Us* (2009).

---

[8] Both groups' popularity was also due to the sale of dolls, for young girls, with striking resemblances some each member.
[9] Kevin Richardson, one of the original members, left the group in 2006.

NSYNC. © Photofest

ALTERNATIVE ROCK STYLES

Similar to the inspiration for thematic material that was used by a number of heavy metal bands, performers of what became known as "gothic rock" served picturesque perceptions of what they believed represented medieval through Renaissance life situations. It appeared to some that these periods were characterized by gloom, coldness, and castle-like environments. Several bands made an attempt to convey these images by incorporating drone sounds in their music, the use of minor more so than major tonalities, and prognosticative lyrics that frequently expressed gloom. The song "Wasteland" by The Mission UK is an example of this. Also from the same album, *God's Own Medicine* (1986), the song "Garden of Delight (Hereafter)" offers an optimistic view of a better life. The group Linkin Park is categorized here due to their "nu metal" sound mixed with rap and electronics. The sextet consisting of Chester Bennington (lead vocals), Mike Shinoda (keyboards and guitar), Brad Delson (guitar), Dave Ferrell (bass), Joe Hahn (DJ), and Rob Bourdon (drums), was formed in Los Angeles, California. Also known by some as rap-rock, groups like Linkin Park are also alternative by virtue of drawing diverse audiences: rock and rap. The song "Papercut" from their *Hybrid Theory* album, released in 2000, illustrates their mix of metal sounds with rap–poetic rhythm and rhyme schemes.

CHAPTER TWENTY-THREE

POPULAR MUSIC IN THE 21st CENTURY

Beyonce. © NBC/Photofest

INTRODUCTION

By the time of this publication, a number of today's popular artists may have become second-ary or overshadowed by the "new big thing." Fortunately, however, a good number of artists and their music presented in this book's previous edition are still performing, and many remain quite popular. In any case, there are numerous new popular artists as well as those who were at the cusp

377

of becoming recognized in the previous decade that have received enormous attention in today's market. Therefore information within this chapter is organized into two parts with regard to popular music and artists: First decade of the 21st century; and the beginning of the 2nd decade of the 21st century.

Today there exist numerous genres, styles, types, and approaches to music. At times it seems a pointless task in distinguishing stylistic characteristics of these genres in an effort to draw conclusions and subsequently categorize them. As in some ways, many of these genres contain stylistic tendencies present in other genres, but on the other hand still seem to have their own distinctiveness. Even so, there are unique music features that aid in our seeming need to categorize music, and consequently artists. But to what end? Though there are quite a few, I offer two explanations. One, from an ethnomusicological point of view, musical development and its significance to a society is a magnifying glass that can reveal intrinsic facets of its social, cultural, economic, and political philosophy and ideology. Secondly, from a marketing stand point people and those in the music business can best understand songs by linking them with similar songs and those dissimilar as well in reviewing music charts. Hence music charts play a vital role in abetting both the consumer and the music profession in this regard and therefore will be used as the basis for this chapter.

THE TURN OF THE 21ST CENTURY MUSIC

Modern Rock, Nu Metal, Alternative Metal, Emo, Pop, Pop Punk, Mainstream, Alternative, Rhythm & Blues/Hip-Hop, Neo-Soul, Country Music, and Latin Music

This section briefly discusses the terms and artists of modern rock, nu metal, alternative metal, emo, pop punk, mainstream, alternative rock, rhythm & blues, neo-soul, contemporary country music, contemporary religious music, and Latin music.

The term "rock" is distinct from the term "classic rock" of the 1960s and 70s. It is used to describe the continuance of the rock music tradition to present day. Rock songs are often distinguishable by their marketability as a specific style, such as metal, nu metal, emo, to name a few. This allows for the music to be marketed to radio stations that support specific styles.

Modern Rock is a stylistic category that continues the use of performance practices as set forth by rock bands as early as the 1960s. For instance, the song "Hate Me" by Blue October uses spoken text, sound effects, and is a multi-movement song, to name a few features. All these features are evident in art rock/progressive rock of the 1970s. The fast tempo, vocal full-throated singing, guitar and bass distortion in The Foo Fighters 2005 release of "No Way Back" is reminiscent of punk songs of the 1970s. The list below includes *Billboard's* Top 10 Modern Rock hits during the week of May 5, 2006.

In a sense the term modern rock is used to describe those songs that have a proclivity to incorporate "modern-day" characteristics, particularly from other styles as well as its own stylistic features. The list below includes some of these artists in the first decade of the 21st century that used characteristics of other styles, such as rapping alongside of its own stylistic tendencies, namely distortion and feedback.

With advantages of the Internet and podcasts, including various devices to listen to music, the 21st century consumer is exposed to any number of genres and types of music. Fortunately for label executives, these technological advances allow the marketing of a wide array of artists and styles. Moreover, music festivals such as *Lollapalooza*[1] (began in the 1990s, see Chapter 3) provides a forum for

---

[1] *Lollapalooza* means "something of a peculiar nature."

Artist	Popular Song
Red Hot Chili Peppers Fighters	"Dani California"
Tool	"Vicarious"
Pearl Jam	"World Wide Suicide"
Blue October	"Hate Me"
Panic! At the Disco	"The Only Difference Between Martydom . . ."
The Raconteurs	"Steady, As She Goes"
Angels & Airwaves	"The Adventure"
Foo Fighters	"No Way Back"
Hawthorne Heights	"Saying Sorry"
Artic Monkeys	"I Bet You Look Good on the Dance Floor"

Figure 23.1 Top 10 Modern Rock, *Billboard* week of May 5, 2006.

Artist	Popular Song
Black-Eyed Peas	"Let's Get It Started"
Breaking Benjamin	"So Cold"
Chevelle	"Leading Us Along (Vitamin R)"
Dashboard Confessional	"Vindicated"
Franz Ferdinand	"Take Me Out"
Green Day	"Green Day"
The Killers	"Somebody Told Me"
Avril Lavigne	"My Happy Ending"
Linkin Park	"Breaking the Habit"
Lost Prophets	"Make a Move"
Moroon 5	"She Will Be Loved"
Ashlee Simpson	"Pieces of Me"
Slipknot	"Duality"
Three Days Grace	"Just Like You"

Figure 23.2 Top 10 Modern Rock who used aspects from other styles of music.

performances of a number of different styles such as punk, nu metal, rap, and alternative. For instance, the song "So Cold" (2004) by Breaking Benjamin is considered **alternative metal** and **emo**. Because the song also contains a somewhat emotional expression about certain aspects of life, it is also regarded as "emo"–short for emotional– that is a subcategory of "indie rock."[2] From the same album titled *We Are Not Alone*, the song "Simple Design" is about having patience and intends to not give up on someone. Because alternative metal is regarded as a 1990s approach to metal, which combines elements of **nu metal,** grunge, and hip-hop, the music can be marketed to a broader audience. An example is Linkin Park's song titled "In the End" (2000). Considered a group usually associated with the nu metal sound, in this song they incorporate rapping, which has the potential to introduce rap to non-rap listeners. Both terms alternative and nu metal are consequences of heavy metal style that was first popularized during the late 1960s early 1970s. Nu metal bands like Tool, Slipknpot, Jane's Addiction, Nirvanna, and others, borrowed heavily from heavy metal using features such as distortion and feedback, power chords, and performed at high volumes, to name some main features.

Pop punk is a term that is used to describe those groups that use punk music characteristics such as fast tempo, 16th notes, few chord changes, distortion and feedback, but write less politically charged songs. Some examples include "American Idiot" by Green Day (2004) and "Pretty Fly (For a White Guy)" (1998). For some pop punk artists the music generally does not set out to make any social or political statement, but rather is often about love. Examples include "Pieces of Me" (2004) by Ashlee Simpson and "Complicated" (2002) by Avril Lavigne.

Mainstream music is generally the most marketable category next to pop. As the result of a wide array of public tastes, it encompasses many genres and styles. These performers are also marketable in the global market. The following list includes those current-day artists that are marketed in countries such as the UK, Spain, and Germany in addition to the United States.

Black-Eyed Peas. © CR: Ray Mickshaw/FOX

---

[2] Independent record labels (Indies) are generally responsible for promoting new and/or alternative music styles such as punk, rap, metal, and grunge.

Artist	Song Title
2PAC & Elton John	"Ghetto Gospel"
Anastacia	"Left Outside Alone"
The Black-Eyed Peas	"Don't Phunk with My Head"
Mariah Carey	"We Belong Together"
Kelly Clarkson	"Since U Been Gone"
Coldplay	"Speed of Sound"
D12	"My Band"
Avril Lavigne	"My Happy Ending"
Gwen Stafani	"Hollaback Girl"
Twista	"Slow Jamz"
Usher	"Yeah"

Figure 23.3 Top artists that also favored well in other countries besides the U.S.

Alternative can refer to several stylistic approaches to music, in general, however, it is a term used when nothing else seems to encompass its character.

There are times when the terms **mainstream** and **alternative** are loosely defined, as the result of those groups that seek to make their songs a more marketable, thus mainstream sound. The group Audioslave is an example of this. Consisting of Chris Cornell as lead singer and the instrumentalists of Rage Against the Machine, their first album of the same name, released in 2002 combines the raw and powerful vocals of Cornell against the metal style of playing by Tom Morello on guitar, Tim Commerford on bass, and Brad Wilk on drums. Alternative rock is exemplified by the heavy metal sounds in the songs "Cochise," "Bring Em Back Alive," "What You Are," and "Light My Way." The song titled "Like a Stone" is more characteristic of mainstream as the result of its lyrics about patient love, the use of less guitar distortion, and a vocal line that is more easily sung than some of the other selections. Although the electric guitar solo that appears slightly after the midway point uses distortion and some effects, it is followed by the use of the acoustic guitar against the lead singer's voice.

Chevelle, started by the Loeffler brothers–Joe (drums), Pete (guitar), and Sam (bass)–released their first album titled *Point #1* in 1999. In 2002, they released their next album titled *Wonder What's Next*. After releasing their self-produced album in 1996, Staind toured Europe and sold nearly 2000 copies. Attracting attention with their album sales as well as sharing the concert bill with Limp Bizkit, the four-man group (lead singer, guitar, bass, and drums) signed a record deal the following year. Green Day is another group that is making waves in the modern rock world today. Generally performing punk, the band consists of Billie Joe Armstrong (lead voice and guitar), Mike Dirnt (bass), and Tré Cool (drums). They are a California-bred band that began performing in the late 1980s as teens. With a number of performances in various areas throughout the state, they recorded what is to date their most successful song titled "America Idiot." Some say the group Three Days Grace from Toronto, Canada is somewhat similar to the band Trapt and Saliva. One thing certain is their heavy metal influences. As evidenced in their popular song titled "Just Like You," lyrics of despair about failed guidance are supported by the use of sheer power from the guitar, including distortion, a rhythmically similar bass part, and drums that stand almost equal in volume to the vocal line. Another group, Slipknot, is being recognized as a top band that is performing a mixture of heavy metal, punk, and some rap elements. About ten years after forming in Iowa during the mid-1990s, Slipknot scored well with the song titled "Duality." The song is reminiscent of a *Star Trek* or *Twilight Zone* episode where one is caught in a nebulous zone and sees the future as if it were the past. In any case, like the band Linkin Park, Slipknot is drawing a somewhat broad audience of punk, metal, and rap fans as they combine powerful guitar and bass riffs, screaming vocals, and a deejay with staged horror-type costumes. The group named The Killers is somewhat reminiscent of the band New Order of the 1970s. And like New Order, this group uses disco-like drum accentuations as heard in the song "Somebody Told Me." Here, the drummer plays accents particularly with the high-hat cymbals opening on the up-beat of each count. The band Dashboard Confessional is credited for exemplifying the "emo" song style in their popular song titled "Vindication," which speaks about attained and lost love.

Latin Music (First Decade of the 21st Century)

Latin music is a genre that entered America during the 1960s, but it did not become widely accepted until the late 1980s and early 1990s. Its minimal attention during the 1960s is the result of being over-shadowed by numerous other styles at the time such as psychedelic rock, soul, funk, folk, and folk rock that catered to dominant music society–mainly white, and secondarily black.

The success of such artists as Carlos Santana, Selena Quintanilla, and Ricky Martin in the 1990s propelled the popularity of other performers of Latin music into mainstream America at the turn of the 21st century. Some of these include Enrique Iglesias, Shakira, Juanes, Las Ketchup, Los Tigres del Norte, Ricardo Arjona, Jennifer Pena, Jerry Rivera, Luis Miguel, Jon Secada, Chayanne, Paulina Rubio, and Cristian. The following information includes a discussion of some of these artists.

Enrique Iglesias, the son of famous singer Julio Iglesias, released his first album (self-titled) in 1995, however much of his success appeared at the turn of the millennium. Prior to the new century Enrique was noted as the most popular male Latin pop artist, who sung in Spanish, among Hispanics. His first three albums *Enrique Iglesias*, *Vivir*, and *Cosas Del Amor*, 1995, 1997, and 1998 respectively are all sung in Spanish. The following album in 1999 titled *Enrique* produced two particular songs that became popular, namely "Be With You" and "Bailamos." The song "Hero" from the album *Escape* (2001) earned him yet another number one song that also sold well in other countries. The song begins with acoustic strings and guitar buttressed by his breathy sound that affirms his conviction of being someone's hero. Enrique is still recording and scoring popular songs such as "Cuando Me Enamoro" and "I Like It" (featuring Pitbull) from his 2010 album *Euphoria*. The popularity of the latter song is due in part to its danceable tempo.

Shakira, like Enrique Iglesias, experienced popularity among Hispanic audiences in the late 1990s with her first two albums *Pies Descalzos* and *Shakira MTV Unplugged*, 1996 and 2000 respectively. By her third album in 2001 titled *Laundry Service*, the song "Whenever, Wherever", first released in English with some Spanish vocables, became a massive hit among mainstream audiences. Since then it received a Spanish release as well. The song's appeal is due to its danceable rhythms, the use of panpipes (a popular instrument in Latin American countries), and Shakira's rhythmic sensitivity with respect to her voice within the space of the other instruments.

Shakira. © ABC/Photofest

The popularity of artist Juanes is perhaps due to his personal experiences. As a songwriter, his lyrics of social injustices and violence are attributed to his family situations: the deaths of his cousin and friend as the result of gunfire, and the loss of his father due to cancer as mentioned in the song titled "Fotografia" (2003).

Another Latin group that has done well in many countries but has yet to do as well in America is the sister group Las Ketchup. Their summer of 2002 hit titled "Asrejé" is the story of a young man named Diego, who is a Rastafarian gypsy that loves to dance and listens to hip-hop. With regard to their inability to do well in America, it could perhaps be due to the use of the musical accompaniment of Sugar Hill Gang's "Rapper's Delight" (1979) in the aforementioned song.

Rhythm & Blues/Hip-Hop and Neo-Soul (First Decade of the 21st Century)

For the first time in the history of Billboard's charting of popular music, during the week of September/ October 2003, the Top 10 songs on the Hot 100 chart were all rhythm & blues/hip-hop or "black-sounding" music.

Although rhythm & blues as a distinct style of music gradually diminished during the 1960s, its musical ideology continues to vibrate strongly in American popular music culture.

Funk or disco was the music that was regarded as rhythm & blues or "black-sounding" during the 1970s. Even more confusing is the fact that from 1969–1982, the term *soul* was used by *Billboard* as the chart category for this music. Furthermore, many of these songs had crossover appeal and consequently

Artist	Song Title
Mariah Carey	"We Belong Together"
Destiny's Child	"Cater 2 U"
Snoop Dogg	"Ups & Downs"
Bow Wow	"Let Me Hold You"
Pretty Ricky	"Grind With Me"
112	"Your Already Know"
Fantasia	"Free Yourself"
Ludacris	"Pimpin' All Over The World"
Game	"Dreams"
Jermaine Dupri	"Gotta Getcha"
Darius Brooks	"Your Will"
Luther Vandross	"Think About You"
Kem	"I Can't Stop Loving You"
Laha Hathaway	"Forever, For Always, For Love"
Dr. Charles G. Hayes	"Jesus Can Work It Out"
Kindred The Family Soul	"Stars"
Basic Black	"Special Kind of Fool"
"Yeah"	Usher
"Make Her Feel Good"	Teairra Mari
"Lose Control"	Missy Elliot
"Hollaback Girl"	Gwen Stefani
"Must Be Nice"	Lyfe Jennings
"Oh"	Ciara
"Get It Poppin"	Fat Joe
"Pon De Replay"	Rihanna
"Just a Lil Bit"	50 Cent
"Let Me Hold You"	Bow Wow Ft. Omarion

Figure 23.4 Top artists placed under the rhythm & blues/hip-hop chart.

appeared on *Billboard's* pop chart. Whether on the soul or pop chart, or of funk or disco styles, the music was deemed rhythm & blues in nature. A similar occurrence is understood as the term *hot black* replaced *soul* in 1982 as the category for rhythm & blues. A return to the term rhythm & blues as the chart name occurred in 1988. Presently, the term "rhythm & blues/hip-hop" is the stylistic category for what was originally known as rhythm & blues. In any event, performers of black-sounding music generally fell into one or more categories during the 1970s: rhythm & blues, funk, disco, and soul. Therefore, one should be prudent when attempting to categorize performers into one specific style, particularly from the 1970s to present day. The list below provides some of the more popular songs and their respective artist that were categorized under the heading rhythm & blues/hip-hop.

Though clearly these songs follow the similar presentation of African American music, even so there needs to be some understanding of that music which is distinct from traditional rhythm & blues (1940s-early 1960s), soul (1960s–1970s), disco (1970s), and hip-hop/rap (1970s-present day). Currently, as previously mentioned, *Billboard* uses the category "rhythm & blues/hip-hop," which, in general, functions as a way to identify popular African American artists. Some of these include Floetry, Glen Lewis, Erykah Badu, D'Angelo, Musiq, Jill Scott, Tweet, Angie Stone were top hit makers on the rhythm & blues/hip-hop chart. And even a few years from this were seasoned rhythm & blues artists who appeared on the then "rhythm & blues" chart name that eventually became the "rhythm & blues/hip-hop" chart. Some of these artists include Anita Baker, Peabo Bryson, Whitney Houston, and Luther Vandross, to name some. At the same time, however, the term *hip-hop* is used, particularly by East Coast and socioculturally aware individuals and music business people to identify what people regard as "rap." At this juncture, the terms *rhythm & blues* and *hip-hop* become problematic. One possible solution to this seeming conundrum is to implement yet another term. It appears that the term **neo-soul** is most fitting for the categorization of the aforementioned newer artists. These performers have a tendency to combine elements of rhythm & blues, soul, hip-hop, and to some extent jazz. Considering the list provided on the ensuing page, a slightly greater number of women performers, are moving in the direction of neo-soul.

Jill Scott is one of the premier artists in this stylistic category. Some of her albums include *Who Is Jill Scott: Words and Sounds, Vol. 1* (2000); *Experience: Jill Scott* (2001); and *Experience Words and Sounds 1* (2001). The song titled "Exclusively" from her *Who Is Jill Scott: Words and Sounds, Vol. 1* CD includes jazz-type chordal progressions juxtaposed with her poetic recitation. The song is rather reminiscent of stylistic presentations heard in cool jazz of the late 1950s through the 1960s. From the same album, the song "Do You Remember" uses a vocal harmonic accompaniment that features a rhythmic passage quite similar to what one would find in soul music of the 1960s/70s. The sparse instrumental accompaniment of bass, drums, and a synthesized piano/bell sound strongly illustrates the focus on the singing–a typical characteristic of 1960s basic soul music. Additionally, the syncopated and pronounced bass part is akin to funk music of the 1960s. From her live album titled *Experience: Jill Scott*, the song titled "Love Rain" uses a sparse accompaniment–keyboard, bass, and drums–that complement her poetic recitation. The melodic phrasing in the song titled "Slowly Surely" displays a vocal virtuosity that consists of chromatic and rhythmic passages and truly separates Scott from hip-hop-type artists. This is not to suggest that neo-soul artists are vocally superior to hip-hop singers. It merely references the fact that the former displays a performance where vocal phraseology is not based on singing stylizations that are evident in mainstream songs. Such singing is clearly evident in the album's song, titled "One Is the Magic #." Here, the singer is using specific pitches that are not within the tonal structure, thus evoking an emotion of atonality. Moreover, she is singing in a dramatic style that is similar to an art song. The album's introductory song titled "Show Intro" uses an instrumentation, particularly with the muted trumpet, that shows an influence of jazz, particularly cool jazz.

Alicia Keys. © ABC/Photofest

Alicia Keys is another singer who is responsible for a greater understanding of neo-soul. Her ability as a singer, pianist, and songwriter allows her to contribute to neo-soul characteristics and performance practices in a fuller way. Take, for example, the song titled "Fallin'" from her debut album *Songs in A Minor* (2001). Her *melismatic* stylizations executed with syncopated rhythms against her piano accompaniment, orchestrated with strings playing in a *legato* and *pizzicato* manner furnish some interesting contrasting sounds. Moreover, the homorhythmic singing in the background singers' part adds another layer of musical texture, which, combined with the other aspects, brings the listener to the point of the most important aspect of the song, the message of love. Like other neo-soul artists, the symphonic orchestra is used to further the stimulating lyrics of love. An example is the song "A Woman's Worth" from the same album, which begins with strings underneath a trumpet, followed by Keys's lyric of "A Woman's Worth." The thought-provoking lyrics of commitment, the piano accompaniment, and Keys' vocal dramatization in the song titled "If I Ain't Got You" from *The Diary of Alicia Keys* album released in 2003 places her within the shortest possible list of not only neo-soul artists but women artists as well. This song is the first of its kind by a woman to remain on the *Billboard* charts for over one year.

Interesting instrumentations are also evident on Floetry's CD titled *Floetic* (2002). Floetry is a female duet that features Marsha Ambrosius as lead singer and emcee Natalie Stewart. In the song titled "Ms. Stress," a cello plays as counterpoint to the rap phraseology. Another example is the song titled "Sunshine," which utilizes a string section that is orchestrated similar to a number of songs in the 1960s. In addition, the Hammond B-3 organ sound and the lower brass instruments, playing *portamento*, are quite reminiscent of soulful love songs of the 1960s.

Several songs on the CD titled *Southern Hummingbird* by Tweet also exhibit similar instrumentations and orchestrations. Without doubt, certain music characteristics in such songs as "Complain" and "Always Will" are moving in a different direction than today's rhythm & blues music with regard to instrumentation/orchestration, arrangement, and/or harmonic counterpoint. For example, in the former song the instrumental accompaniment–consisting of acoustic guitar, slide guitar, organ, bass, and drums–provides complementary tone colors for the singer's numerous lyrical circumstantial analogies to not complaining if a certain love is not returned. A spiritual emotion occurs as the result of the instrumentation and specific placement of instrumental parts (i.e., orchestration), such as the organ entrance during the first occurrence of the chorus (i.e., the song's title). Furthermore, words such as *soul*, *spirit*, and *death* are juxtaposed with the organ sound (with the 1960s infamous tremolo sound of the frequently used leslie speaker)–a typical instrumental usage in black gospel music. The use of the slide guitar, an instrument more frequently evident in country music, also contributes to the song's atypical sound in today's black popular music, not to mention the song's crossover appeal. The song titled "Always Will" by Tweet is yet another song that is undeniably contributing to the identified neo-soul genre. Complemented by a three-part texture played by the acoustic guitar, bass, and string section, Tweet lyrically furnishes scenarios and assurances (such as a soul connection), in first person, as to why there will be longevity in their relationship. Decorated by a background singers' part that furnishes homorhythmic passages in three- and four-part harmonies, the harmonic texture is further enhanced. The artist India.Arie is also using other approaches to instrumentation in black sounding music. The song titled "Ready for Love" includes acoustic guitar, cello, piano, and bass as accompaniment to the vocal line. From the same album, titled *Acoustic Soul*, the song "Nature" exemplifies the neo-soul sound as the mainly acoustic orchestration of guitar, bells, strings, and drums with electric bass complements the singer with sparse and thick textures.

The lyrical content is the most salient aspect of neo-soul. It is indeed soul-like in that it does not require any musicological understanding. Angie Stone, among others, exemplifies this in her CD titled *Mahogany* (2001). The song titled "Soul Assurance" provides eschatological recitations regarding the pitfalls of being addicted to chemical substances. She makes an interesting correlation between staying true to righteousness and having knowledge of "soul music." From the same CD, the song titled "Brotha" speaks respectfully and specifically to and about black men. She dispute's society's too-often frequent negative portrayal of black men as the lyrics provides descriptions of his beauty, strength, courage, and respect. She reassures him with her and perhaps other women's expressions of love and faith. As was the case during the 1960s Stone also speaks about some black men's insecurity and their proclivity for being upset in the song titled "Pissed Off." Of course, songs with similar messages at that time were used to convey tropological insights. One interesting musicological point about this CD is the music accompaniment to the song titled "Easier Said Than Done." Here, the instrumental accompaniment to The O'Jays 1972 hit titled "Back Stabbers" is used for Stone's message about true love and friendship and its often painful results.

Country Music (First Decade of the 21st Century)

Today's country music, as opposed to that of post-WWII, is experiencing the highest gains in record sales, revealing its increased popularity. This is partly due to its crossover appeal that is attributed to 1) The existence of rhythmic propensities that are uncharacteristic of early country songs; 2) The use of certain studio-produced effects; 3) Instrument/sound effects that are characteristic of other styles; and 4) Marketing a significant number of its performers as attractive individuals. Though this began before the turn of the recent millennium we really begin to hear this in songs in the first decade of the 21st century. The song "Complicated" from the album titled *Let Go* by Avril Lavigne (born in 1985 in Napanee, Ontario) includes all of the musical features previously mentioned. In this song, the introduction begins with guitar and spoken lyrics by Lavigne. The rhythmic simplicity provided by the snare drum, high hat, and kick drum during the last four measures of the introduction is also found in styles such as hip-hop. Scratching–a distinct feature of hip-hop–occurs just before she begins the first verse. The electronic simulation placed on her voice during her opening verse is not an effect that was characteristic of country music before the 1990s. The synthesized sound that is ascending and descending through a scale during the pre-chorus section is another feature uncharacteristic of earlier approaches to country music. The rhythmic groove of the kick drum and bass guitar–sounding a low pitch that is not within the range of typical bass tuning–is typical of r & b and hip-hop styles. Scratching occurs again just before the third verse. More electronic vocal simulation occurs during the third verse. The melodic guitar riff and a more rhythmic bass line during the fourth verse are similar to r & b and hip-hop songs. Many of these features occur through the end of the song. In addition to these features, the singer incorporates others that are prominent in most country songs.

"My Front Porch Looking In" (2003) by Lonestar (four male members) is another example of a country song that has contemporary elements. Adding to its country sounding vocal dialect, folk-like lyrics, and use of table guitar, banjo and fiddle–instruments typical to country–the artist uses contemporary sounding guitar distortion, as well as a performance where most of the instruments actively contribute to the song's overall presentation. Without a doubt, these are noteworthy as appealing aspects to a wide audience. These and the following popular artists have all greatly contributed to the continuance of country music as a main stay in American popular music.

Artist	Song Title
Toby Keith (duet with Willie Nelson)	"Beer for My Horses"
Lonestar	"My Front Porch Looking In"
Jimmy Wayne	"Stay Gone"
Brooks and Dunn	"Red Dirt Road"
Brad Paisley	"Celebrity"
Montgomery Gentry	"Speed"
Alan Jackson and Jimmy Buffett	"It's Five O'Clock Somewhere"
Dixie Chicks	"Wide Open Spaces"
Kenny Chesney	"No Shoes, No Shirt, No Problem"
Jeff Bates	"The Love Song"
Shania Twain	"Forever and for Always"

Figure 23.5 Top artists that have contributed to the continuance of country music.

Also in the first decade of the 21st century, country music maintained its folk-like character by addressing some of the more sentimentally social issues. Perhaps the most startling event on American soil is the terrorist attack that occurred in New York City, September 11, 2001.

As a result of this, many country singers recorded patriot albums, such as *Courtesy of the Red, White, and Blue (The Angry American)* (2003) by Toby Keith, in remembrance of the victims. One of the more popular songs on the album, titled "Beer for My Horses," makes reference to the fact that evil should not be tolerated and people should pay consequences for committing crimes. The specific reference to "Beer for My Horses" describes victory over evil, and people along with their horses are in a celebratory mood. The young Jimmy Wayne's recording titled "Stay Gone," and the song titled "Red Dirt Road" (2003) by Brooks and Dunn continue the tradition of country music as a vehicle for addressing moral issues. In these songs, the lyrics make reference to personal memorable social situations that are juxtaposed with religious orientations. While many country songs are of a serious nature with respect to social situations, there are also those that involve satire about common social

Toby Keith. © ABC/Photofest

situations. For instance, Brad Paisley's song titled "Celebrity" (2003) satirically pokes fun at celebrity lifestyles.

BEGINNING OF THE 2nd DECADE OF THE 21st CENTURY

In the second decade of the 21st century there exist numerous styles and types of popular music. Because of the many opportunities for marketing products such as film, T.V., radio, video games, athletic events, and so on, and the large number of baby boomers who now make up the bulk of discretionary spending, music styles include those songs from the 1950s to the present. For instance one episode of the sitcom *Without A Trace*, a mystery drama program about missing persons, used the song "Little Green" (1971) by Joni Mitchell to convey the main point of the episode (and song)–a mother giving up her child.

One of the most effective ways to understand today's popular music scene is to examine the many genres and market-driven chart names (see Chapter 2) used by *Billboard*. General headings include "Overall Popularity," "Breaking & Entering," "Genres," "International," and "Web." Each of these headings consists of specific stylistic or market-driven names that list popular songs and their respective artists. This section includes a discussion of the first three of these headings as they relate to popular songs and artists. In so doing, these headings and chart names will serve as the basis for learning about popular music in the second decade of the 21st century.[3]

Overall Popularity

Overall Popularity	Number 1
Hot 100	"Rolling In The Deep" (Adele)
Billboard 200	*21* (Adele)
Radio Songs	"E.T." (Katy Perry, feat. Kanye West)
Digital Songs	"Rolling In The Deep" (Adele)
Digital Albums	*21* (Adele)
Social 50	*Lady Gaga* (Lady Gaga)
Uncharted	DJ B13nd
Ringtones	"E.T." (Katy Perry, feat. Kanye West)

Figure 23.6 Overall Popularity chart, *Billboard* week ending May 28, 2011.

As seen in the list above uses the category "Overall Popularity" to identify those songs and albums that are most popular within a wide spectrum, including those songs on radio, the digital domain, social trends, popular ringtones, and even those songs that are "uncharted." Without a doubt this list of artists are among the most popular, not only in the U.S. but in other countries as well, and all the number one spots, with the exception of one, are held by women artists. Furthermore, two of them appear in more than one category, with the most popular being Adele.

Adele. © NBC/Photofest

---

[3] That this book is about popular music and not necessarily what this author deems as most representational of the genres and styles discussed within, it is extremely important to know these songs were selected as the result of sales and web and radio airplay.

Born Adele Laurie Blue Adkins, she is a singer songwriter from the U.K. According to sources she is the only U.K. artist, following The Beatles, to have two top five hits appear concurrently on the U.K.'s *Official Singles Chart* and *Official Albums Chart* within the same week. Reportedly the last time this happened was in 1964 with the most popular group to emerge from England, The Beatles. Their two singles "I Want To Hold Your Hand" and "She Loves You" and their respective albums *Meet The Beatles* and *Please Please Me*, both released in the U.K. in 1963, accomplished this major feat. Adele reached this milestone in 2011 with her songs "Someone Like You" and "Rolling In The Deep" from the album *Adele*.

Katy Perry. © Sayre Berman/Corbis

Katy Perry, born Katheryn Elizabeth Hudson in Santa Barbara, CA, was nurtured in a religious household which thus influenced her first self-titled Christian/Gospel album titled *Katy Hudson* (2001). Drawn to the likes of artists such as Alanis Morissette, Madonna, and Queen, Ms. Perry embarked on a secular music career. As a young singer-songwriter engaged in a number of projects with various artists and song-writing/production teams she received initial acclaim with the 2007 single titled "UR So." This was followed by her first major hit titled "I Kissed a Girl" in 2008 from the album *One of the Boys*. Popular in some 20 countries coupled with her appearances with the Warped Tour in the summer of 2008, this song helped to push other songs from the album to big hits as well. These include "Hot N Cold," "Thinking of You," and "Waking Up in Vegas." Ms. Perry is solely responsible for writing "Thinking of You," "One of the Boys," and "The Mannequin", and co-wrote all other songs from the album. Her next album titled *Teenage Dream*, released in 2010, has scored four major hits, namely "Teenage Dream," "E.T.," "Firework," and "California Girl" (featuring Snoop Dogg).

Lady Gaga. © FRANCK ROBICHON/epa/Corbis

Born on March 28, 1986 and a little over two years after Katy Perry, Stefani Germanotta, better known as Lady Gaga (taken from the Queen song "Radio Ga Ga"), began getting attention among music executives with her 2008 single release titled "Just Dance." The album, titled *The Fame*, was released that summer and the song "Poker Face" became another major hit. *The Fame Monster*, released the following year, was to be a re-release of *The Fame*, but it was decidedly released as its own album. There exist several similarities in the music of Lady Gaga and Katy Perry. These include co-writing (with some solo writing by Ms. Perry) all songs on at least one of their albums, their albums feature energetic songs intended for the dance club, their live performances entail highly choreographed dance routines, and they are noted for flamboyant and extravagant regalia–sometimes off stage, more so however by Lady Gaga. It should be noted, as mentioned in Chapter 2, that Gaga's marketing team allowed a one-day sale of $.99 cents for a MP3 digital download, through Amazon, of the entire album. Without question the queen goddess's little monsters (Gaga fans) were ecstatic by this move as it continues to add to her image as a performer who cares about her fans. Such dedication has not gone unnoticed among music executives, writers, her peers, and fans, as stated in an article "[Gaga] reshaped pop in her image, telling kids it's cool to be gay and freaky or unpopular, that they're born that way: a message that's largely been absent from the charts since Nineties alt-rock's outcast chic.[4]

Breaking & Entering

Heatseekers Songs	Heatseekers Albums
"Hello" by Martin Solveig & Dragonette "Hustle Hard" by Ace Hood	*Strange Negotiations* by David Bazan *Demolished Thoughts* by Thurston Moore
"Homeboy" by Eric Church	*Pala* by Friendly Fires
"Barefoot Blue Jean Night" by Jake Owen	*Back Burner* by For The Fallen Dreams
"Rise Above 1" by R. Carney, feat. Bono/ Edge "Pumped Up Kicks" by Foster The People	*Scary Monsters and Nice Spri . . .* by Skrillex *Frankie Ballard (EP)* (self-titled)
"Donald Trump" by Mac Miller	*Halfway to Heaven* by Brantley Gilbert
"Far Away" by Marsha Ambrosius	*Pickin' Up The Pieces* by Fitz & The Tantrums
"Crazy Girl" by Eli Young Band	*Megalithic Symphony* by AWOLNATION
"I Smile" by Kirk Franklin	*The Head And The Heart*

Figure 23.7 Heatseekers Songs and Heatseekers Albums *Billboard,* June 2011

The Breaking & Entering category, as seen above, lists those recordings that are either rising to a higher rating, or songs that are entering the chart at a high rating. Songs are organized into two subcategories: **Heatseekers Songs** and **Heetseekers Albums**. The former chart includes songs whose topics range from addressing the epidemic of suicide as in "Far Away" by Marsha Ambrosius; having a casual good time with friends as heard in the song "Barefoot Blue Jean Night" by Jake Owen; Eric Church's song "Homeboy" about one brother that wishes another would stop getting in trouble and come "home"; "Hustle Hard" by Ace Hood reveals the fact that, for his environment, every day may indeed be a new day but he still needs to "Hustle Hard"; The Eli Young Band's recording of "Crazy Girl", which is about the love of a person who to some may seem crazy; and Kirk Franklin's song titled "I Smile" that speaks about having faith in God, and when times get tough he says, "I Smile."

It is interesting to note that the top 10 albums on the second subcategory of Breaking & Entering, namely Heatseekers Albums, consist of completely different artists than the aforementioned "song" chart. Furthermore, a good number of these artists are fairly new and/or from abroad.

---

[4] Brian Hiatt, (June 9, 2011), *Rolling Stone,* p. 42.

Genres

Genres	
Pop Songs	"E.T." (Katy Perry, Feat. Kanye West)
Adult Contemporary	"Firework" (Katy Perry)
Adult Pop Songs	"Rolling In The Deep" (Adele)
Dance/Club Play Songs	"Till The World Ends" (Britney Spears)
Dance/Electronic Albums	*The Fame* (Lady Gaga)
R&B/Hip-Hop Songs	"Sure Thing" (Miguel)
R&B/Hip-Hop Albums	*Goblin (Tyler, The Creator)*
Rap Songs	"Look At Me Now" (Chris Brown Feat. Lil Wayne)
Rap Albums	*Turtleneck & Chain* (The Lonely Island)
Rock Songs	"Rope" (Foo Fighters)
Rock Albums	*Hot Sauce Committee Part Two* (Beastie Boys)
Alternative Songs	"Rope" (Foo Fighters)
Alternative Albums	*Hot Sauce Committee Part Two* (Beastie Boys)
Hard Rock Albums	*Wasting Light* (Foo Fighters)
Folk Albums	*Helplessness Blues* (Fleet Foxes)
Country Songs	"Heart Like Mine" (Miranda Lambert)
Country Albums	*My Kinda Party* (Jason Aldean)
Bluegrass Albums	*Paper Airplane* (Alison Krauss & Union Station)
Jazz Songs	"Contact" (Boney James)
Jazz Albums	*Crazy Love* (Michael Buble)
Blues Albums	*10 Great Songs* (George Thorogood)
Classical Albums	*The 99 Most Essential Gregorian Chants* (Various Artists)
Latin Songs	"You" (Romeo Santos)
Latin Albums	*Drama y Luz* (Mana)
Regional Mexican Songs	"Te Amo y Te Amo" (La Adictiva Banda San Jose de M.)
Regional Mexican Albums	*Los Huevos Racheros* (Joan Sebastian)
Latin Pop Songs	"Lluvia Al Corazon" (Mana)
Latin Pop Albums	*Drama y Luz* (Mana)
Tropical Songs	"You" (Romeo Santos)
Tropical Albums	*Prince Royce* (Prince Royce)
Christian Songs	"Glorious Day (Living He Loved . . .)" (Casting Crowns)
Christian Albums	*Born Again* (Newsboys)

Gospel Songs	"I Smile" (Kirk Franklin)
Gospel Albums	*Hello Fear* (Kirk Franklin)
Independent Albums	*Goblin (Tyler, The Creator)*
Catalog Albums	*19* (Adele)
Reggae Albums	*Live Forever: September 23 . . .* (Bob Marley And The Wailers
World Albums	*Songs From The Heart* (Celtic Woman)
New Age Albums	*Truth of Touch* (Yanni)
Comedy Albums	*Turtleneck & Chain* (The Lonely Island)
Kids Albums	*Lemonade Mouth* (Soundtrack)
Soundtracks	*Lemonade Mouth* (Soundtrack)
Tastemaker Albums	*Helplessness Blues* (Fleet Foxes)

Figure 23.8 Genres and a Popular Song/Artist, *Billboard* week of June 4, 2011.

The heading titled Genres enlists the largest number of charts that include some categories that have been staples since *Billboard* first began charting songs and albums, namely pop, country, and rhythm & blues. Today there exist numerous marketing terms to appeal to public tastes, some are stylistic while others are categorical charts. Stylistic charts include those with distinct music characteristics such as rhythm & blues/hip-hop, rap, rock, hard rock, folk, country, bluegrass, jazz, blues, classical, regional Mexican, gospel, and reggae. All others, however, are categorical (and as previously mentioned, market-driven). That is to say, they are not a recognized style but rather useful terms to categorize those songs with various commonalities. For example, the term *pop*, as discussed in Chapter 1, refers to those songs considered to be most popular among a wide audience, which receives the most attention in sales and airplay in a given week. Looking at *Billboard's* **Pop Songs** chart of the week ending June 4, 2011, some popular songs include "E.T" by Katy Perry featuring Kanye West, "Just Can't get Enough" by The Black Eyed Peas, "Rolling in the Deep" by Adele, "Till the World Ends" by Britney Spears, and "On the Floor" by Jennifer Lopez featuring Pitbull. Though all have some similarities, (perhaps less in Adele's song), they are quite different nevertheless. For example, "Rolling in the Deep" presents more vocal melodic passages, thus illustrating the singer's vocal ability that subsequently evokes greater meaning from the lyrics, while the songs "Till the World Ends" and "On the Floor" both stress short vocal repetitious passages in order to suit the songs' dance character.

At first glance (See Figure 23.9) the chart names **Adult Contemporary** and **Adult Pop Songs**, two other names of the heading Genres, which seem redundant, but further listening reveal some differences in these two chart categories.

The lyrical content in the **Adult Contemporary Songs** chart, more so than the other, entails less frivolous statements of love. Moreover, a significant number of these songs convey a sense of being unwanted, unloved, and that dreadful feeling of loneliness. For instance, the lyrics in "Secrets" by OneRepublic is about a man willing to reveal all his secrets in order to win the heart of a desired woman. In the song titled "Marry Me" by Train, the lyrics evoke feelings of loneliness without having someone to love or to be loved. A similar song titled "Mine" by Taylor Swift is about a certain man being the first and best thing that is truly hers. Prior to these feelings she reminisces, as a child, about her parents and others who seem to argue to the point of breaking up. The lyrics in the number one song on this chart is

Adult Contemporary	Adult Pop
"Just The Way You Are" by Bruno Mars	"Rolling in the Deep" by Adele
"Firework" by Katy Perry	"F**kin' Perfect" by Pink
"September" by Daughtry	"For the First Time" by The Script
"Marry Me" by Train	" E.T." by Kath Perry
"Rhythm of Love" by Plain White T's	"F**k You" by Cee Lo Green
"F**kin' Perfect" by Pink	"Never Gonna Leave This Bed" by Maroon 5
"Mine" by Taylor Swift	"I Do" by Colbie Caillat
"Rolling in The Deep" by Adele	"Keep Your Head Up" by Andy Grammar
"Secrets" by OneRepublic	"Good Life" by OneRepublic
"Hold On" by Michael Buble	"Grenade" by Bruno Mars

Figure 23.9 Adult Contemporary and Adult Pop Songs charts, *Billboard* week ending June 4, 2011.

perhaps what everyone desires to hear from a husband, wife, friend, or a parent and that is to be loved . . . "Just The Way You Are" by Bruno Mars. A similar theme is heard in Pink's song titled "F**kin' Perfect", where one may have feelings of undesirability, but to another they are, using a euphemism among today's young adults, "F**kin' Perfect." The lyrics in the song titled "Rhythm of Love" by Plain White T's, seek to endorse the fact that love is a natural phenomenon that transcends time and it is a part of the rhythm of life.

Regarding the **Adult Pop Song** chart, the song "For the First Time" by The Script is about the notion of losing contact with your loved one, so one needs to regroup and do things that in the end will encourage the euphoric feeling of meeting "For the First Time." A significant amount of the music production stays within "pop" performance practices such as the lead vocalist singing a subtle brief rap passage (two times), which is a practice one expects to hear in songs representative of the pop-youth culture (See Chapter 2). With respect to instrumentation, the recording reveals an emphasis on power guitar and drum sounds. Even though a string section is used, which occurs at the coda, the overall appearance of the song places more focus on the voice, and the power guitar and drums sounds. Similar to the performance of "pop" sounds in "For the First Time", is the song titled "Never Gonna Leave This Bed" by Maroon 5. Here even more power guitar and drum sounds are coupled with rhythmic synchronization passages of the kick drum and bass guitar (a performance practice in funk music). These practices could certainly explain why they appear on the Adult Pop chart as it seems the goal is to appeal to an adult audience while still maintaining a youthful "sound" character.

While this may be true, one cannot overlook the fact that of these top 10 songs, two songs appear on both charts. These include "F**nkin Perfect" by Pink and "Rolling in the Deep" by Adele. Though one may expect profane words to be used more casually among a "pop" audience, the use of the "four letter word" does not appear to bother a more "reserved" audience as well. Perhaps the presence of "Rolling in the Deep" on both charts is due to the singer's vocal virtuosity, its lyrical content, and non-expected "sound" appearance (i.e., a white artist who sounds black). Additionally, her popularity could be due to another phenomenon coming from across the Atlantic Ocean (Beatles being the first), or maybe the pleasure of having an outstanding marketing team. Whatever reasons, in addition to two of the same songs appearing on both charts, there are four artists who appear on both charts as well, namely Katy Perry, Pink, Adele, and OneRepublic. As already discussed, two of these artists, Pink and Adele, have the same song on both charts. From a marketing standpoint the remaining two, Katy Perry and OneRepublic, are reaching a wider audience by virtue of having different songs on each chart. Though both of Perry's songs deal with supernatural subjects, the song "Firework" is more desirable, and perhaps believable. Speaking about the power that exists in everyone to inspire, change, motivate, while at the same time believing in ourselves is a verity. Regarding OneRepublic's song "Good Life", a significant amount of the music production stays within "pop" performance practices such as the power drum sound and whistling that occurs during each chorus. In closing, in addition to love as a dominant theme on the Adult Contemporary Songs and Adult Pop Songs charts, the notion of empowerment is also noted as a preferred lyric among this audience as evidenced by the songs "Just The Way You Are," "Firework," "F**kin' Perfect," and "Keep Your Head Up."

Kanye West. © NBC/Photofest

There was a time when the **Rhythm & Blues/Hip-Hop** chart was more reflective of the Adult Contemporary and to some extent Pop Songs chart. Currently however that does not seem to be the case. Present day popular songs and their respective artists of the rhythm & blues/hip-hop chart may suggest a return to somewhat segregated listening audiences. Artists who typically scored among the top 10 on the rhythm & blues/hip-hop chart like Beyonce, Mary J. Blige, Lauryn Hill, Usher, to name some, were also just as popular subsequent to their high rating on the pop/hot and adult contemporary charts. Today's rhythm & blues/hip-hop artists are not scoring as high on these other charts. Nevertheless some popular artists include Miguel, Nicki Minaj, DJ Khaled, featuring Drake, Rick Ross & Lil Wayne, Beyonce, Lil Wayne, Rihanna, Chris Brown, Kelly Rowland, featuring Lil Wayne, Trey Songz, featuring Drake, Jill Scott, featuring Anthony Hamilton, Jay-Z & Kanye West, featuring Otis Redding, Wiz Khalifa, featuring Too Short, and Big Sean, featuring Chris Brown.

Rihanna. © ABC/Photofest

Performance practices in some of today's popular rhythm & blues/hip-hop songs include a focus on the vocalist part (whether singing or rapping), the instrumental accompaniment uses synthesized sounds along with drums and bass, a number of songs have overt sexual lyrics, and songs speak about the here and now. Though this music analysis is not intended to represent an exhaustive study, there, in any event, are some curious findings. With regard to the voice being the central aspect, the volume of the singer is almost always above the instrumental accompaniment. Though a majority of songs on this chart are sung, rapping can occur anywhere from a minimal amount to 50% of the song. Examples of those that include at least 50% rapping are "I'm One" (DJ Khaled, featuring Drake, Rick Ross & Lil

Wayne), "Unusual" by Trey Songz, and "Sure Thing" by Miguel. Polyphonic vocal textures continue to be a staple among singers of rhythm & blues, which dates back to the doo-wop singing style of the 1940s. The songs "How To Love" by Lil Wayne, "Super Bass" by Nicki Minaj, and "She Ain't You" by Chris Brown are all illustrative of two to three vocal parts that overlap thus producing a polyphonic texture. Finally, with regard to the vocal part, performers present rhythmical singing and rapping passages that show this music's proclivity to feature rhythm as one of its central tenets.

As for instrumental accompaniments, there exists a minimalistic approach to providing instrumental support of the singers' part. A number of songs use one to three synthesized parts, along with most always, drums and bass. To bridge the vocal lead with the instruments a number of songs incorporate rhythmical vocal background singing parts that highlight the lead singer's phraseology. Songs like "How To Love" and "Super Bass", to name two, include minimal instrumental accompaniment yet even so, because of each song's rhythmic character, seem to use just enough to engage the listener to this type of music.

Regarding lyrical themes among popular songs on the rhythm & blues/hip-hop chart, they include love, commitment, infidelity, partying, profanity (few or many words), and make overt or allegorical sexual statements. Songs like "Sure Thing" and "How to Love" provide positive views of how a man feels about and treats his loved one, hence committed love. In the latter, Lil Wayne explains that due to a particular woman's previous experiences with men she is not at fault as to her uncertainty of "How To Love." Beyonce's "Best Thing I Never Had" speaks to the fact of discovering her man as not being as wonderful as she had previously believed. Rihanna's song "Man Down" stirred controversy regarding its possible inappropriateness in suggesting that women who have been raped should take revenge (in this case killing) on her perpetrator. Chris Brown's "She Ain't You" is about a man's infidelity, as he desires to be with someone else. Party-type songs include "I'm On One" and "My Last." Some songs with overt sexual references are "Super Bass" which references a woman's heart going "boom boom" as the result of a man's physical stamina in love making, and "Motivation" that overtly speaks about her motivational encouragement to ensure her man sexually pleases her.

The **Rap Songs** chart is still one of the most marketable genres to date. In is noteworthy to mention that some songs on the rhythm & blues/hip-hop chart, as mentioned above, contain "rapping" and therefore appear on the Rap Songs chart as well. A few of these are "Super Bass" by Nicki Minaj, "My Last" by Big Sean featuring Chris Brown, and "I'm the One" by DJ Khaled featuring Drake, Rick Ross & Lil Wayne. Some other popular artists and their songs include "Party Rock Anthem" by LMFAO featuring Lauren Bennett & GoonRock, "Out of My Head" by Lupe Fiasco featuring Trey Songz, "Give Me Everything" by Pitbull featuring Ne-Yo, Afrojack & Nayer, "Lighters" by Bad Meets Evil featuring Bruno Mars, "Marvin & Chardonnay" by Big Sean featuring Kanye West & Roscoe Dash, and "Look at Me Now" by Chris Brown featuring Lil Wayne and Busta Rhymes. When listening to a number of these songs one quickly notices the minimalistic approach to instrumental accompaniment. In many songs the drums and two or three synthesized sounds, along with some intermittent effects provide the accompaniment to the rappers phrasing. In songs like "Party Rock Anthem" and "Give Me Everything" the chorus section is sung while the verses consist of rapping. In most songs on this chart, even though it is for the rap audience, singing occurs anywhere from minimal to a significant portion of the song. Perhaps in the near future there may not be a major difference with respect to music characteristics in this and the rhythm & blues/hip-hop charts. However, a difference in lyrical content does exist in these two charts. As previously discussed above, popular rhythm & blues/hip-hop songs were about love, commitment, infidelity, partying, profanity (few or many words), and make overt or allegorical sexual statements. A number of popular rap songs include these themes as well but present them in an explicit manner, often with a forceful delivery.

Foo Fighters. © NBC/Photofest

The **Rock Songs** chart within the Genres heading, include many artists who have been in the business for quite a while and may or may not have scored a Top 10 rating. The Foo Fighters is one of the groups listed on the discussion of modern rock at the turn of the 21st century. This is not to suggest other artists have not achieved a Top 10 rating between the beginning of the 21st century through today, however, achieving a Top 10 rating in any case is no easy task.

Artist	Popular Song
Foo Fighters	"Rope"
Rise Against	"Help Is On The Way"
Seether	"Country Song"
Mumford & Sons	"The Cave"
The Black Keys	"Howlin' For You"
Cage the Elephant	"Shake Me Down"
Incubus	"Adolescents"
Papa Roach	"Burn"
Linkin Park	"Waiting For The End"
Sick Puppies	"Rip Tide"

Figure 23.10 Top 10 Rock Songs Chart, *Billboard* for the week of May 14, 2011.[5]

---

[5] *Billboard*, (see http://www.billboard.com/bbcom/charts/)

When listening to numerous songs today under the genre heading "rock" there is no question music characteristics and performance practices of previous approaches to rock music as early as the 1970s are still evident in today's songs. These include the lead singer's powerful deliverances, a similar instrumentation, distortion as effects, use of power chords, short melodic or harmonic rhythmic patterns (a.k.a. riffs), an emphasis on guitar soloing and sounds, a dichotomy with regard to volume in the vocal part versus the instrument accompaniment, staccato and sustained chords as accompaniment to the lead singer, use of moderate to fast tempi, and meter changes.

The lead singer's ability to deliver a compelling and often powerful vocal performance is one of the tenets of rock music. For example, the lyrical content in the song "Help is on the Way" by Rise Against speaks about "black gold" (oil) and its disastrous effect on society. The lyrics satirically affirm that "Help is on the Way." In order to evoke a greater meaning of these lyrics about this ecological devastation the singer delivers the song using his full-throated voice. Furthermore, after the second time the chorus section is sung the singer delivers the lyrics with a powerful screaming voice. Invoking powerful vocal sounds in this song suggests the importance and subsequent urgency to take action rather than waiting for someone else to solve this problem. Another example of a powerful vocal performance is heard in the song titled "Burn" by Papa Roach—a song about a person who believes they were mistreated, scorned, rejected, and so on by another, and therefore takes pleasure in watching them "Burn." The aforementioned hurtful words are reinforced by the singer's full-throated and sometimes shouting vocal production, along with powerful guitar chords and their accompanying distortion affects. Still other examples of full-throated singing are heard in the songs titled "Country Song" and "Broken" (featuring Amy Lee) by Seether, and "My Body" by Young the Giant. In many songs the lead singer delivers the lyrical meanings with his natural voice. Examples of this manner of singing can be heard in today's popular songs like "Rip Tide" by Sick Puppies, "Through Glass" by Stone Sour, and "So Far Away" by Avenged Sevenfold. At times the lead singer needs to employ a spoken-like part to a phrase or section in order to offer an additional layer of dramatic contrast. This is evident in the bridge section of "Shake Me down" by Cage the Elephant. A rock band or artist will also integrate a number of vocal deliveries in a song. An example is "Waiting for the End" by Linkin Park. In this song the introduction begins with a voice speaking in a rap manner, followed by the first verse being presented in harmony with the singers' natural voice. The next section features a melodically melancholy-type falsetto voice, followed by a bridge section that includes a harmonized-type rap section.

In songs such as "Rope" (Foo Fighters), "Shake Me Down" (Cage the Elephant), "Adolescents" (Incubus), "Lies of the Beautiful People" (Sixx: A.M.), and "Country Song" (Seether), distortion is used similarly to evoke a greater meaning of the lyrics and is a performance practice that distinguishes this genre from others. Rock music beginning with artists and groups of the late 1960s such as Jimi Hendrix, Led Zeppelin, AC/DC, and Jefferson Airplane, and The Who, to name some, without doubt were characterized by using powerful chords, played by the guitar, as the basis for distortion effects. Additionally, synchronized guitar and bass riffs were staples in songs like "Dazed and Confused" by Led Zeppelin and "Sunshine of Your Love" by Cream. These same usages are also evident in "Rope" and "Lies of the Beautiful People." Also apparent is an emphasis on the voice and its relationship to the instruments. In a number of today's rock songs a dichotomy exists with respect to volume between the singer and instruments, but this should not suggest the singer is subordinate to the instrumental part. Whereas in most genres when the volumes of the vocal part is equal to or lower than the instruments it is often perceived as less important than the instrument, this is not the case in rock music. Because the voice is also seen as an "instrument", and that instrumental innovation is the basis of the music, the notion of an egalitarian presentation overrides this perception. Examples include "Rope" where even at times the guitar seems to be louder than the singer. In the song "Burn" by Papa Roach, a dichotomy regarding volume exists in the chorus section when the singer sings the word "Burn" against guitar power chords with distortion, bass, and drums all accenting against the singer's part. Rise Against comes very close to achieving a dichotomy vocal and instrument presentation in their song "Help Is on the Way."

Today's songs under the auspices of rock have also inherited yesteryear rock music's proclivity in using vocal harmonies, a doubling of the lead singer's part, and polyphonic vocal textures. Generally one can expect vocal harmonies, sung by band members, to occur during the chorus. Occurrences of this are heard in "Cosmic Love" (Florence & The Machine), "Howlin' For You" by The Black Keys, and "Help is on the Way" to name some. In most genres with representative popular songs the chorus is what most consumers remember, as it is often tuneful thus singable, and lyrically encapsulates the reason for the story itself (presented by the verses). In rock music, whether from the 1970s or presently, the chorus is further bolstered with accompanimental sustaining (*legato*) chords, rather than short and detached chords (staccato)–which occur during the verses. For instance, the songs "Rope," "Help is on the way," "Lies of the Beautiful People," and "Rip Tide" by Sick Puppies all illustrate this continued performance practice of rock music. In addition to background singing during the chorus section rock bands also incorporate this practice during verses. Examples include the songs "Adolescents" and "Waiting for the End" by Linkin Park. In the latter recording the group also includes a harmonized rap-like section.

Rock music is a genre that entails power chords, distortion, natural to full-throated vocal deliverances, background harmony, and an instrumental component nearly equal (or equal) to the vocal part. Moreover, the "attitude" of rock music is such that it entails an approach to music that surely doesn't disregard genres prior to its existence, but has, however, a tendency to appease young audiences by playing songs fast. That said, tempo, normally performed from moderate to fast, is another very important characteristic of rock music. An aggregate of today's rock songs in any given week will most definitely reveal they are not played slowly. Of course there are exceptions, but by and large rock music is about energy, power, quick changing moods, and circumstances about today and tomorrow–and not yesterday.

Similar to art/progressive rock of the 1970s, today's rock artists continue to record and perform songs in a multi-movement form. With the intent to soothe its audience's desire for energy, power, and moods, music tools such as tempo and/or meter changes are a couple of salient practices. The songs "Help is on the Way," "Adolescents," and "So Far Away" by Avenged Sevenfold all have at least three different movements, hence moods.

While today's rock bands have embraced rock music's heritage of distinctive performance practices they are also including other features as well. Some of these new or at least more salient features include the doubling of the lead singer's part during one or more verses. This is evident in songs "Adolescents" by Incubus, "Rope" by Foo Fighters, "You Are a Tourist" by Death Cab for Cutie, and "So Far Away" by Avenged Sevenfold. In the latter song, the doubling of the lead singer's part an octave apart, following the guitar solo section, functions as a dramatic element that further engages the listener. Using synthesized sounds and effects is certainly not new in rock music, as one can hear these in earlier rock songs like "Money" by Pink Floyd and "Space Oddity" (1990) by David Bowie. Currently, this seems to be used to a greater degree in a number of songs. For instance, in "Howlin' For You" by The Black Keys a synthesized sound (string-like) riff is played nearly throughout the entire song. In "Shake Me Down" a siren-like sound appears two-thirds into the song, "Waiting for the End" has a synthesized riff at the beginning of the song, and the introduction to "Lowlife" by Theory of a Deadman has in addition to guitar, bass, and drums, a synthesized sound as well. A few songs end with some sort of synthesized sound such as "You Are a Tourist" by Death Cab for Cutie and "Cosmic Love" by Florence & The Machine. In the latter song a synthesized heartbeat sound is used in response to the lead vocalist singing the word "heartbeat." Additionally, the song ends with an *arpeggio* played by the harp, which is then concluded with a synthesized sound.

Another interesting aspect in today's rock music is that musicians do not feel bound to adding instruments that are usually not associated with rock music. For instance the song titled "The Cave" by Mumford & Sons incorporates the banjo that gives one the sensation of bluegrass music. Also, the song's use of piano, and trumpets playing in a fanfare manner, are not necessarily evident in today's rock music. And in "Cosmic Love" by Florence & The Machine the use of harp contributes to the song's esoteric sonority.

The **Country Songs** chart, under the Genres heading, lists some of today's most popular artists. They include Sara Evans, Miranda Lambert, Brad Paisley featuring Alabama, Rascal Flatts, Kenny Chesney, Keith Urban, Jerrod Niemann, Taylor Swift, The Band Perry, Ronnie Dunn, Toby Keith, Luke

Taylor Swift. © ABC/Photofest

Bryan, Easton Corbin, Chris Young, Jason Aldean, Dierks Bentley, Martina McBride, Ashton Shepherd, and others. Looking at country music at the beginning of the second decade of the 21st century, we find the continuance of previously stated contemporary performance practices nestled within the context of early country music expectations. An example is the recording titled "Dirt Road Anthem" (2011) where the artist, Jason Aldean, implements extended "rap" phases (he even uses the phrase "my hood"–a frequent usage in rap music). This song which clearly shows country musicians proclivity to embrace, or at least experiment practices typical of other genres in an effort to stay dynamic. Another example is the song titled "I Won't Let Go" (2011) by Rascal Flatts (Gary LeVox, Jay DeMarcus, and Joe Don Rooney). The gist of the song is an expression of commitment to never giving up on someone. In addition to these comforting lyrics the song has crossover appeal as LeVox's (lead singer) dynamic vocal *melismas* continue to place the band's cutting edge sound of country music on other charts as well.

It is interesting to note that of the twenty top country songs on the *Billboard* charts during the week of May 28, 2011 only six are sung by women artists. ("Just a Kiss" is a female and male duet sung by members of Lady Antebellum.) These include "Heart Like Mine" by Miranda Lambert (#1); "A Little Bit Stronger" by Sara Evans (#3), "Mean" by Taylor Swift (#6); "You Lie" by The Band Perry (#8); "Teenage Daughters" by Martina McBride (#18); and "Look It Up" by Ashton Shepherd (#19). Three songs deal with a personal romantic relationship, two deal with infidelity, and the other is about an emotional break-up. The remaining three entail individual topics. The number one song on the country music charts is sung by Miranda Lambert. She is speaking about her many experiences, both good and bad, but in the end Jesus will understand, as she believes He has a "Heart Like Mine." "A Little Bit Stronger" chronicles the singer's process of slowly feeling better after an emotional break-up. The song titled "Mean" is about encouragement to those who are picked on by mean people, as ultimately they will be successful. "You Lie" by The Band Perry is about this particular man's proclivity to lie. "Teenage Daughters" is about parents' experiences of having a teenage daughter. An experience alluded to in the song is previously being your child's best friend and cool, but then as the singer states, ". . .we are just mothers and fathers." The song "Look It Up" is about an unfaithful man who is being told to look up the meaning of the words faithful, forever, easy, liar, good-bye, get gone, get lost, so long, sober, baby, and forgiveness. According to Ms. Shepherd, had her husband/boyfriend known the meaning of these words he wouldn't be her "ex" husband/boyfriend.

In the song titled "A Little Bit Stronger" (2011) by Sara Evans, like other contemporary country songs, the use of guitar distortion and accentuating drums help to facilitate its crossover appeal. There is no question that the lyrical content of the song is something many people can relate to as the singer is dealing with an emotional break-up, but each day she is able to feel "A Little Bit Stronger."

Another aspect that connects these songs and thus forges their identification as country music is the use of a similar instrumentation that was also apparent in early country music (namely hillbilly). In "A Little Bit Stronger" instruments include voice, background singers, banjo, mandolin, slide guitar, bass, drums, piano, and organ. A similar instrumentation is present in the song titled "You Lie" by The Band Perry, which includes voice, guitar, piano, fiddle, mandolin, bass, and drums. Taylor Swift's song titled "Mean" uses voice, banjo, mandolin, fiddle, slide guitar, guitar, bass, and drums. Keith Urban's song titled "Without You" begins with some of these same instruments–guitars and banjo, then eventually fiddle—as well as using the typical rhythm section, namely guitar, bass, and drums.

As previously mentioned, the idea of country music's crossover appeal is well-established in the song titled "Live a Little" by Kenny Chesney. The introduction does not reveal this as a country song, as during its 56-second duration it uses a minimalistic guitar passage, accenting drums, and a distorted guitar sound. The song "Heart Like Mine" by Miranda Lambert has crossover appeal to a Christian audience as she presents a personal perception of her existence as it relates to a Christian way of life. In a live performance Miss Lambert prefaces the song by conveying her Christian up-bringing that was followed by joining a band and learning about the secular world. At the end of the day she believes Jesus would understand as she states Jesus has a, "Heart Like Mine." The song includes Lambert on lead vocal and rhythm guitar, who is accompanied by rhythm/lead guitar and acoustic bass.

Like what has been addressed previously, country music is perhaps the most recognized style of music that continues the notion of the American Spirit (see Introduction) with its lyrics about the circumstances of everyday people, as well as its religious convictions, that at the end of the day one will prevail with hard work and perseverance. As an exemplum of the American Spirit its longevity as viable popular music is attributed in large part to songs about family and its foundation such as topics of love, friends, and religious conviction. As was the case with the progenitors of the "country" daily life and consequently hillbilly music, religion played a major role in people's lives. Whether people consciously or subconsciously imbued religious words in both a secular as well as a sacred context, for many artists this is what they knew and consequently what they did, and still do. In addition to "Heart Like Mine" by Miranda Lambert as discussed above, Justin Moore's song titled "If Heaven Wasn't So Far Away" (2011) provides another example of the interjection of one's religious ideology. Here, he speaks about the loss of his grandfather, losing three friends in high school, the loss of a friend to drugs, and the loss of a friend in Vietnam. He resolves that he would go see them if "Heaven Wasn't So Far Away."

In continuing country music's sense of wholesomeness, Chris Young's single titled "Tomorrow" (2011, #11) speaks about letting a love go "Tomorrow", but right now he is going to enjoy and embrace her strong in his arms. The song "Bleed Red" (2011, #12) by Ronnie Dunn, is a song about the many things we as people go through like cry, hurt, regretful words, fall down, etc. The video representation begins with the singer's daughter expressing the pain and hurt following a break up. Following this many beautiful and catastrophic moments are shown like cemeteries, tearing down the East German wall, a baptism, the destroying of Sadam Hussein's statue in Iraq, seeing the heartbeat of a life while in a woman's womb, war, Mother Teresa, Dai Lama, soldiers coming home and being greeted by loved ones, the bombing of the twin towers on September 11, 2011, and a few others.

Finally, country music is noted for encapsulating nostalgic moments about southern living. In the song "Old Alabama" by Brad Paisley, he pays tribute to the group that, in his view, exemplifies the southern way of living, particularly in Alabama. Paisley does this by singing about the things that a particular girl is not "turned on" by, such as a fancy dress, or singers like Frank Sinatra or Barry White. Instead she gets excited by listening to the group Alabama while driving through Tennessee and other southern areas. An interesting part of the song features members of Alabama whose lyrics are about singing from the heart, which is where music and soulful feelings and emotions really originate.

The Genre heading also identifies the charts **Latin Songs, Latin Albums, Regional Mexican Songs, Regional Mexican Albums, Latin Pop Songs**, and **Latin Pop Albums**. Certainly one could argue that all these categories each have distinguishable music characteristics. For instance Latin holds specific traditions such as specific rhythmic gestures, sung in Spanish or a combination of Spanish and English, specific instrumentation, an emphasis on certain instruments, and so on. Examples include "You" by Romeo Santos, "Me Encantaría" [I would Love You] by Fidel Rueda, and "Corazon Sin Cara" [A Heart Without A Face] by Prince Royce to name a few. Some commonalities in all songs include: 1.They all are sung in Spanish, with some occurrences of English (spoken text) in "You" and "Corazon Sin Cara"; 2. The use of a Latin type syncopated rhythm including an emphasis on either the congas or timbales. Of these three songs, "Me Encantaría" represents a minimal influence of Western music and more of the Mexican music tradition. This is evidenced by the use and performance manner of certain instruments, namely trumpets, clarinets, saxophones, trombones, and tuba. The many rhythmic passages played by the brass and woodwind instruments, and the doubling of the bass guitar part with tuba are characteristics one would find in Latin music more so than in any other present day popular style.

Looking at today's **Latin Songs** versus **Latin Pop Songs** charts, there seems to be minimal differences. Further examination reveals that both charts have five songs in common, and four of these reside in the upper five ratings (see Figure 23.11).

It is curious to note all of these, with the exception of "Ven A Bailar" by Jennifer Lopez, are by male artists. And even in Ms. Lopez's song, the first 40 seconds are presented by Pitbull–male artist– who also speaks and makes sounds intermittently throughout the song. The majority of songs are sung in Spanish which suggests one or both of these points: 1.These artists are appealing to a mainstream English-speaking audience without giving up an important component of their ethnic (Spanish-speaking) identity, and/or 2. There exist such a large number of Hispanics who statistically boost sales and streaming/radio airplay of certain artists to the point of high volume recognition and thus their popular

Latin Songs	Latin Pop Songs
"Taboo" by Don Omar	"Give Me Everything" by Pitbull, feat. Ne-Yo, Afrojack & Nayer
"Give Me Everything" by Pitbull, feat. Ne-Yo, Afrojack & Nayer	"Amor Clandestino" by Mana
"You" by Romeo Santos	"Ven A Bailar" by Jennifer Lopez feat. Pitbull
"Ven A Bailar" by Jennifer Lopez feat. Pitbull	"Gritar" by Luis Fonsi
"Amor Clandestino" by Mana	"Taboo" by Don Omar
"Di Que Regresaras" by La Original Banda el Limon de Salvador Lizarranga	"Dia De Suerte" by Alejandro Guzman
"Te Amo y Te Amo" by La Adictiva Banda San Jose de Mesillas	"You" Romeo Santos
"Olividame" by Julion Alvarez Y Su Norteno Banda	"Tan Solo Tu" by Franco De Viata, feat. Alejandro Guzman
"Cuanto Me Cuesta" by La Arrolladora Banda el Limon	"Rabiosa" by Shakira, feat. Pitbull
"Prometi" by Intocable	"Mi Corazon Insiste" by Jencarlos Canela

Figure 23.11 Latin Songs and Latin Pop Songs charts, Billboard week of August 13, 2011

status. The song "Give Me Everything" by Pitbull, featuring Ne-Yo, Afrojack & Nayer ranks the highest as it appears in either the number one or number two position on these charts. The song's dance-like character is reinforced with lyrics that speak about the sorts of activities that accompany going out dancing as well as what the title suggests.

Regional Mexican Songs and **Regional Mexican Albums** are chart names intended for the Hispanic culture in America. They include the music styles Banda, Mariachi, Norteña, and Ranchera. The Banda (band) style of music is popularized by bands that incorporate brass and woodwind instruments in their songs. The music is almost always sung in Spanish as it seeks to cater to the Mexican population, which is where it started. Stylistic features include a lead singer who is accompanied by background singers, brass and woodwind instruments, tuba which replaces and emulates a bass guitar, congas, and drums. Examples include popular songs in 2011 such as "Di Que Regresaras" [Tell Me You Will Be Back] La Original Banda el Limon de Salvador Lizarraga and "Te Amo y Te Amo" [I Love You and I Love You] by La Adictiva Banda San Jose de Mesillas. While both apply a similar instrumentation the former song uses the I– VI– II– V chord progression–a harmonic progression incorporated in numerous doo-wop style vocal groups of the 1940s and 50s. Banda bands sometimes referred to as Norteña (Spanish for Northern) bands also play Ranchera music. A style of folk music of Mexico that initially featured a singer who accompanied himself, ranchero music is a favored style of music among inhabitants in a ranch environment. Presently Ranchero music is played by a soloist as well as bands such as the group Los Cardenales de Nuevo León in their 2005 recording titled "Falsa Ilusion" (False

Illusion). The song consists of a lead singer as well as a harmonizing second vocal part, accordion, guitar, bass, and drums. Of all the accompanimental instruments the accordion plays a more significant part as it responds to the lead singer's part. The waltz rhythm (triple meter) is another feature of this song that is typically Ranchero.

Christian Songs is yet another Genre Heading on the *Billboard* charts. In previous years this chart was titled contemporary religious music. Because of the increased popularity of religious music, more specifically under the auspices of Christian music, *Billboard* publishes its charts as Christian Songs and Christian Albums. The names Gospel Songs and Gospel Albums also appear as published charts, but will not be discussed here.

A relatively recent development in religious music first appeared in the 1980s. Of particular interest is the praise & worship type of participatory presentation. The concept behind "praise & worship" is to prepare the heart in order to receive the Word."[6] In a church service or worship setting, songs are sung while the congregation is entering the environment and/or sung between parts of the worship service. Singing occurs in an effort to provide a certain level of spiritual consciousness among the congregation prior to the pastor's message. Presented by a small group of singers who are accompanied by a band–piano, synthesizer,[7] guitar, bass, and drums–songs contribute to the mood of spirituality and to the establishment of an environment of righteousness and brotherhood. In many cases, the leader commonly noted as the Worship Pastor or Music Minister, may play the piano, compose, teach, and direct the small praise & worship team and congregation. Some early influential artists include Fred Hammond, Donny McClurkin, Kirk Franklin, Don Moen, and Tommy Coombs. These and other artists write songs and perform them in such a way that one feels encouraged to participate. This does not suggest any compromising with respect to the song's musicality, as much attention is placed on composing songs that are musically intriguing and spiritually nourishing to the novice and advanced singer alike. Kirk Franklin's song titled "Hosanna" provides a good example of the aforementioned features among praise & worship type songs.

With regard to the **Christian Songs** chart, the music employs music characteristics heard in current secular styles of music such as the use of powerful guitar chords, pronounced drums, use of orchestral arrangements, an emphasis on guitar and piano accompaniments, use of a large choir, and lyrics that stress the significance of God. A couple of songs that illustrate most of these features include "The Way" (2011) by Jeremy Camp and "You Love Me Anyway" (2011) by Sidewalk Prophets. Christian artists also encourage others to have a relationship with God by fashioning their music in an even more secular manner. For instance, the song "Move" by MercyMe is played in a fast tempo quite similar to punk music, and uses a guitar and bass riff along with intrinsically performed vocal harmonies that give the song a dance-like character.

In closing, popular music at the beginning of second decade of the 21st century is as vibrant as it was at the turn of the recent millennium. One salient aspect of today's popular music is not only the presence of more women artists, but the number of women maintaining high levels of popularity in many stylistic or market-driven genres. During the 1950s-60s women artists were frequently neglected as substantial rock performers. This is due in part to the social climate of that time when women were still being viewed as caretakers and/or the root of the family structure and not seen as movers and shakers of popular music. Fortunately, due to the achievements of many women composers and performers such as Wanda Jackson, Gertrude Rainey, Bessie Smith, Dinah Washington, and Kitty Wells, and

---

[6] Personal communication, J. Michael O'Neal, 2004.

[7] The synthesizer is used to produce a fuller sound by emulating organ, brass, woodwind, and string sounds.

many others, present day women artists are attaining popularity in unprecedented numbers.[8] Because of the innovations of early women artists present day artists (listed alphabetically) like Adele, Beyonce, Mariah Carey, Lady Gaga, Alicia Keys, Jennifer Lopez, Nicki Minaj, Katy Perry, Rihanna, Shakira, Britney Spears, and Taylor Swift, to name some are scoring high in record sales, airplay, merchandizing, and touring. In the latter part of the previous century women artists like Paula Abdul, Mary J. Blige, Blondie, The B 52's, Cher, Taylor Dayne, Destiny's Child, Whitney Houston, Janet Jackson, Madonna, LeAnn Rimes, Selena (Quintanilla), Tina Turner, TLC, and many others were continuing the progress of women in music and society as set forth by those who came before them. And today other artists like Selena Gomez, Avril Lavigne, and Demi Lovato are looking to secure their place as viable women in this enormous industry of male dominated figures.

Another recognizable aspect in today's music scene is the popularity of Latin music. With popular artists like Carols Santana, Julio Iglesias, and Gloria Estefan making recordings that became mainstream hits, a greater foundation was being forged to help pave the way for ensuing artists like Enrique Iglesias, Ricky Martin, Selena (Quintanilla), and Shakira.

Finally, with the dawn of social media like Facebook, Twitter, YouTube, MySpace, and others, a song and its respective artist has the potential to become popular in a matter of minutes. No longer do artists and record labels have to wait for a physical pressing of their product or for radio disc jockeys to air their music. All that is needed is to upload to one of the aforementioned or other similar social media and a song or album has the prospect of exponentially reaching consumers, often in the tens of thousands at nearly the same time. Because of this and other evolving innovative mechanisms (e.g., iCloud) for getting music to the people, popular music has become even more liquid as we continue in the 21st century.

---

[8] An exhibit titled Women Who Rock recently opened in Ohio.

PART SIX

POPULAR MUSIC IN AMERICA FROM 1970s THROUGH THE PRESENT DAY: SUMMARY

Key Terms
- Music-driven
- Market-enthused
- Multi-movement
- Mellotron
- CBGB's
- B-boying
- MC-ing
- Rap
- Graffiti art
- Breakdancing
- Dj-ing
- Tejano
- Overall popularity chart
- Breaking and entering chart

Featured Genres/Styles
- Art/Progressive Rock
- Glitter and Glam
- Theatricalism
- Ska
- Reggae
- Punk
- Hip-hop
- Rock mainstream
- Tejano
- Alternative rock
- Modern rock
- Nu metal
- Alternative metal
- Emo
- Pop
- Pop punk
- Mainstream
- Rhythm & blues/hip-hop
- Neo-soul
- Country
- Latin music
- Regional Mexican music

Featured Songs/Works
- "Roundabout"
- *Days of Future Passed*
- "Bohemian Rhapsody"
- *Dark Side of the Moon*
- *Space Oddity*
- "I'm Eighteen"
- *Lust for Life*
- "Walk on the Wild Side"
- "Toad"
- "Sunshine of Your Love"
- "Livin' On a Prayer"
- "Feel Like Makin' Love"
- "What Would You Do (If I Did That to You)"
- "Back in Black"
- "Born to Be Wild"
- *Paranoid*
- "Dazed and Confused"
- "Bring it on Home"
- "I Wanna Be Sedated"
- *Private Dancer*
- *Purple Rain*
- *Like a Virgin*
- *Thriller*
- *Teenage Dream*
- *Born This Way*

Featured Artists

- Yes
- Antonin Dvorak
- The Moody Blues
- Queen
- Pink Floyd
- David Bowie
- Ziggy Stardust
- Alice Cooper
- Iggy Pop
- Lou Reed
- Andy Warhol
- Cream
- Bon Jovi
- Bad Company
- Steppenwolf
- AC/DC
- Black Sabbath
- Deep Purple
- Led Zeppelin
- Blue Öyster Cult
- Van Halen
- Guns N' Roses
- Skatalites
- The Maytals
- Bob Marley
- The Wailers
- Lee "Scratch" Perry
- The Ramones
- Blondie
- The Dead Kennedy's
- Afrika Bambaataa
- DJ Kool Herc
- Grandmaster Flash
- Kurtis Blow
- Jackson Browne
- Jimmy Buffett
- Harry Chapin
- Phil Collins
- Jim Croce
- John Denver
- Neil Diamond
- Dan Fogelberg
- Billy Joel
- Elton John
- Carole King
- Barry Manilow
- Van Morrison
- Randy Newman
- Carly Simon
- Stevie Wonder
- Carlos Santana
- Tina Turner
- Prince
- Madonna
- Michael Jackson
- New Kids on the Block
- Metallica
- Janet Jackson
- Selena Quintanilla
- Ricky Martin
- Mariah Carey
- NSYNC
- Backstreet Boys
- Breaking Benjamin
- Chevelle
- Enrique Iglesias
- Shakira
- Jill Scott
- Alicia Keys
- Tweet
- Adele
- Katy Perry
- Lady Gaga
- Miranda Lambert
- Rascal Flatts
- Taylor Swift
- Kenney Chesney

Music and Society

- The socio-political climate of the 1960s and 70s was such that individuals felt compelled to express their stance on politics, government policy, and social behavior. These circumstances were reflected in music styles such as folk, soul, psychedelic and progressive rock.

- In today's society, the Internet has greatly influenced how people listen to music. Moreover, purchasing individual songs as opposed to full albums (CDs) has caused songwriters, performers, and record executives to rethink marketing strategies to deliver their products with the highest possible return.

Discussion Questions
- What similarities are evident in reggae, punk, and hip-hop?
- What advantages/disadvantages exist when an artist offers a song or complete album for free?
- Do you believe digital downloads (vs. hard copy sales) will become the norm in the near future?
- In your opinion, is there a need to continue to use chart names like Latin or Regional Mexican? Do these continue to segregate one group from another?
- What factors govern how you purchase music?
- Music or club scenes in a number of science fiction films often show musicians playing an eclectic mix of styles with several interesting-looking instruments. What do you believe music might sound like 30 years from now? What types of instruments will people be using? Or perhaps you might think music will be played by some type of electronic gadget.

Learning Beyond the Classroom
- Visit a music store that carries vintage albums to read liner notes, examine album art, or ask the owner/employee about their experiences with these and other vintage albums.
- Visit a college, university, or local library and explore the many recordings available. In most cases, one can listen to these recordings in private settings.
- Attend a music festival that has performances of a diverse number of styles and examine not only the different artists, but those in attendance as well. Also, take note of the many merchandizing booths.

BIBLIOGRAPHY

Ahrens, Frank. "Four Students Sued Over Music Sites: Industry Group Targets File Sharing at Colleges." *Washington Post*, April 4, 2003.

American Federation of Musicians, www.afm.org/

Baskerville, David. *Music Business Handbook and Career Guide*. 6th ed. Thousand Oaks, CA: Sage Publications, Inc., 1995.

Billboard. New York: Billboard Magazine.

Berfield, Susan. "The CEO of Hip-Hop: Impresario Russell Simmons." *Business Week*, October 27, 2003, p. 92.

Bonnaroo. Retrieved on June 18, 2011 from www.bonnaroo.com/about.aspx

Calmia, Matthew. "Cloud Services May Help Curb Piracy." Retrieved on June 24, 2011 from www.mobiledia.com/news/93159.html.

De St.-Méry, Moreau. *Danse*. NY: Dance Horizons, 1976.

Dickens, Charles. *American Notes*. (First printed in 1842; reprint published by NY: Modern Library), 1996.

Dinnerstein, Leonard, Nichols, Roger L., and Reimers, David. *Natives and Strangers: Blacks, Indians, and Immigrants in America*. NY: Oxford University Press, 1990.

Douglass, Frederick. *Narrative of the Life of Frederick Douglass: An American Slave*. NY: Signet Classic, 1968.

Dunn, Richard S. *Sugar and Slaves: The Rise of the Planter Class in the English West Indies, 1624–1713*. VA: University of North Carolina Press, 1972.

Emery, L.F. *Black Dance: From 1619 to Today*, 2nd ed. NJ: Princeton Book Co., 1988.

Epstein, Dena. *Sinful Tunes and Spirituals: Black Folk Music to the Civil War*. Urbana, IL: University of Illinois Press, 1977.

Equiano, Olaudah. *The Interesting Narrative of the Life of Olaudah Equiano or Gustavus Vassa the African*. NY: W. Durrell, 1791.

Fletcher, Tom. *100 Years of the Negro in Show Business*. New York: Da Capo Press, 1984.

Franklin, Benjamin. *The Autobiography of Benjamin Franklin*. NY: Macmillan Press, 1962.

Garofalo, Reebee. *Rockin' Out: Popular Music in the USA*. 2nd ed. New Jersey: Prentice Hall, 2002.

Halperin, Shirley. "American Idol: 5 Theories Why Pia Toscano Was Eliminated." *Hollywood Reporter*, April 8, 2011.

Hardy, P. and D. Lang. *The Farber Companion to 20th Century Popular Music*. Boston, MA: Farber and Farber, 1990, p. 357.

Henderson, Amy, and Dwight Bowers, *Red, Hot & Blue: A Smithsonian Salute to the American Musical*. Washington, DC: Smithsonian Institute Press, 1996.

Hickins, Michael. "Facebook Backs Obama Anti-Bullying Campaign." *The Wall Street Journal*, March 10, 2011.

Hitchcock, H. Wiley. *Music in the United States: A Historical Introduction*. New Jersey: Prentice-Hall, Inc., 1969.

Jackson, David. "Obama's Day: Campaign Against Bullying." *USA Today*, March 10, 2011.

Keepnews, Orrin, and Bill Grauer, Jr. *A Pictorial History of Jazz: People and Places from New Orleans to the Sixties*. NY: Bonanza Books, 1954.

Kenney, William H. "James Scott and the Culture of Classic Ragtime." *American Music*, 1991, Vol. 2, p. 149–182.

Kimball, Robert. [Producer]. *Shuffle Along*. Recorded Anthology of American Music, Inc. Library of Congress Card No. 75-751056, 1976.

Kinnard, J. "Who Are Our National Poets?" *Knickerbocker Magazine* 26, 1845.

Knopper, Steve. "Youtube." *Rolling Stone*, March 31, 2011, p. 17.

Krasilovsky, M. William, and Sidney Shemel. *This Business of Music: The Definitive Guide to the Music Industry*. NY: Billboard Books, 2002.

Labat, Père. *Nouveau Voyage Aux Isles de l'Amerique*. Paris, 1722, Vol. II, p. 52.

Ligon, Richard. *True & Exact History of the Island of Barbados*. London: Printed for H. Moseley, 1657.

Morgan, T., and W. Barlow. *From Cakewalks to Concert Halls: An Illustrated History of African American Popular Music from 1895 to 1930*. Washington, D.C.: Elliott & Clark Publishing, 1992.

Music Notes. "Popular Digital Sheet Music Downloads." Retrieved July 3, 2011 from www.musicnotes.com/

Naggar, David, esq. The Music Business: Explained in English. Revised. San Francisco, CA: DaJe Publishing, 2006.

National Organization for Women. Statement of Purpose from http://www.now.org/

Nelson, H., and M. Gonzales. *Bring the Noise: A Guide to Rap Music and Hip-Hop Culture*. New York: Harmony Books, 1991.

Nielson Soundscan, November 2002.

Parales, Jon. "The Cloud That Ate Your Music." *The New York Times*, June 22, 2011.

Passman, Donald. *All You Need to Know About the Music Business*. NY: Simon & Schuster, 2000.

Pomerantz, Dorothy. "The Celebrity 100." *Forbes*, May 18, 2011.

Pomfret, John E. and Shumway, Floyd M. *Founding the American Colonies, 1583–1660*. NY: Harper & Row, 1970.

"Prelude to the Century: 1870–1900." *Time-Life Books*. Alexandria, Virginia: Time-Life Books, 1990.

Rachlin, Harvey. *The Encyclopedia of The Music Business*. N.Y.: Harper & Row Publishers, Inc., 1981.

Rancilio, Alicia. "The Glee Project' Looks For New Glee." *Associated Press*, June 24, 2011.

Randel, Don Michael (Editor). *The New Harvard Dictionary of Music*. Cambridge, Mass.: Belknap Press of Harvard University Press, 2003.

Rock & Roll. Producer David Espar. Videocassette. Hugh Thompson, a co-production of WGBH Boston and the BBC, South Burlington, VT: WGBH, 1995.

Rose, Tricia. *Black Noise: Rap Music and Black Culture in Contemporary America*. NH: University Press of New England, 1994.

Sisario, Ben. "In Lady Gaga's Album, Evidence of a New Order." *New York Times*. June 1, 2011.

Smithsonian Collection of classic jazz. Producer Martin T. Williams. Compact Disc. CBS Records, 1987.

Southern, Eileen. *Music of Black Americans*. 3rd ed. NY: W.W. Norton, 1997.

Stancell, Steven. *Rap Whoz Who: The World of Rap Music*. NY: Schirmer Books, 1996.

Stoutamire, Albert. *Music of the Old South: Colony to Confederacy*. Rutherford, NJ: Fairleigh Dickinson University Press, 1972.

Takaki, Ronald (editor). "Colonized and Immigrant Minorities" in *From Different Shores: Perspectives on Race and Ethnicity in America*. 2nd ed. NY: Oxford University Press, 1994.

Talley, Thomas. *Negro Folk Rhymes*. Knoxville TN: University of Tennessee Press, 1991.

Taylor, William. *Inventing Time Square: Commerce and Culture at the Crossroads of the World*. New York: Russell Sage Foundation, 1991.

The History of Rock n' Roll. Videocassette. Time Life Video and Television, 2004.

Thompson, Kay C. "Lottie Joplin." *Record Changer 9* (October):8, p. 18, 1949.

Thorpe, Edward. *Black Dance*. New York: The Overlook Press, 1990.

Toll, Robert C. *Blacking Up: The Minstrel Show in Nineteenth-Century America*. New York: Oxford University Press, 1974.

Twain, Mark. *The Autobiography of Mark Twain*. NY: Harper, 1959.

United States Copyright office at http://www.copyright.gov/forms/

Verstegen, Richard. [Engraving]. *Théâtre des Cruautez des Hérétiques de notre temps*

Wong, Sterling. "MTV Joins Obama's Anti-Bullying Campaign With New Movie." Retrieved on March 10, 2011 from MTV.com.

Zeidler, Sue. "Music Industry Sends Warning to Swappers." *Reuters* April 30, 2003.

a cappella   A song performed without an instrumental accompaniment.

accelerando   To gradually sing or play faster

accent   To place an emphasis on a sung or played note or group of notes

accompaniment   Harmonic and rhythmic support of a melody or theme

adagio   To play a musical passage slowly.

Aerophone   A classification for wind instruments

allegro   To play a musical passage fast.

alto (voice)   The female voice that sings notes below a soprano but above a tenor; This term is also used to identify a particular range of notes, and therefore can include male singers as well

arrangement   The organization of sections within a song; notation of specific parts and passages for singers and instrumentalists

backbeat   Emphasis is placed on counts 2 and 4 of a quadruple meter

bandsman   A band member who has equal status among other band members. This person is a regular member of the band (as opposed to a sideman, who is only hired for a specific engagement).

baritone (voice)   A term for a male singer who sings notes just above the bass singer but below the tenor

bar   Also referred to as measure, the space on the music staff that is used to organize durations into a specific meter

bass (voice)   A male vocalist who sings the lowest among singers.

bending   To sing or play a pitch just below or above the actual pitch.

blue notes   To play a lowered 3rd and 7th from a major diatonic scale; a common feature of blues music

boasting   A term among music and hip-hoppers that entails bragging about oneself

bo didley   A two or three string instrument constructed on a wall

boogie-woogie   A style of music developed by African American pianists during the late 1920s/30s; it became more popular during its usage in rhythm & blues music, which occurred in the 1940s

brass instruments   Cornet, trumpet, French horn, trombone, tuba, and euphonium

break (performance)   A technique where all members stop playing in order to allow an expressive solo or to create contrast

break (hip-hop)   The most danceable part of a song

bridge   A section of a piece that is distinct from the verse or chorus that creates contrast yet combines (hence bridges) elements of both the verse and chorus sections

call and response   A performance practice that entails a sung or played antecedent (question) and consequent (answer)

choir   A group of at least 10 or more singers; used on occasion to indicate a group of instrumentalists

chord   Two or more notes sounded simultaneously

chord progression   A succession of specific chords played repeatedly

Chordophone   A classification for string musical instruments

chorus (song form)   A section within a song distinct from the verse and bridge; generally the most tuneful section of a song

chromatics   To play half-steps or semitones

claves   Two wooden instruments that are struck together, producing rhythmical patterns within the rhythm section of a band

coda   The section of a piece that brings it to a close

combo   A band including from two-four members (e.g., piano and bass; singer, piano, bass; guitar, bass, drums, etc.).

comping   Chords played in a rhythmical manner by the pianist and/or guitarist as an accompaniment to a soloist, horn section, or to the band as a whole

congas   Tall, waist-size drums.

contralto (voice)   The female voice in the tenor and sometimes the baritone ranges

contrast   Compositional and/or performance techniques used to create excitement in a musical piece

cool jazz   A style of jazz developed by African Americans during the 1950s

cover songs   Originally, a practice that entailed recording of popular African American songs by European American artists for a European American audience; currently, refers to any time a group records a previously recorded song by another artist

Creole   An African/African American person with French or sometimes Spanish ancestry

crescendo   To gradually increase in volume

crossover   When a song is bought by an audience that generally doesn't buy music of the sort

cutting contest   A vocal or instrumental competition among individuals or bands; occurred as early as the performance of ragtime during the late 1800s

diminuendo   To gradually decrease in volume

doubling   A term for woodwind players that refers to playing more than one instrument

double time   To play a piece twice as fast; this performance practice generally occurs within the context of a song

duple meter   The song is counted, and subsequently felt in two

ensemble   In general, denotes a medium-sized vocal or instrumental group

extempore   An improvised lyric

falsetto   Refers to a man who sings in the alto and sometimes in the soprano ranges

field holler   A vocal expression, outcry, or protestation uttered by African slaves while working on plantations in America during the slave period

flat   To lower a pitch by a half-step

form   The organization of sections within a song

forte   To play a musical passage loudly

fortissimo   To play a musical passage very loudly

front line   The principal instruments of a band; term was first used by New Orleans jazz bands that referred to the cornet, clarinet, and trombone as the "front line"

groove   For musicians, a state of euphoria as the result of musical parts that complement each other

harmony   The coming together of two or more entities

head   A term used in performances of jazz where the main theme of a song is learned without musical notation

head voice   A specific term used for women singers, refers to the placement of air in a certain resonating area that allows them to sing high notes

high-hat   The two small cymbals of a drum set. The drummer strikes the high-hat with the drumstick and opens and shuts it by pressing on a pedal

homophony   Two or more parts that are governed by the same rhythm

hook   The most tuneful part of a song (sometimes referred to as the chorus)

horn section   Woodwind and brass instruments within a group

Idiophone   A classification of musical instruments that entails the production of a pitch as a result of being struck

improvisation   To create music instantaneously

instrumentation   The specific instruments within a work

interlude   A short passage that functions as a melodic, harmonic, or rhythmic bridge between sections, its function is similar to a bridge, but much shorter in time

interpolation   The extemporaneous insertion of words or vocables between intelligible text

interpretation   An adaptation of an existing melody with personal musical influctuations

jam session   An informal performance of vocalists and instrumentalists; it also functions as a social gathering of musicians and friends

key   The tonal center of a song

key signature   The place on a musical staff, located at the beginning of the song, which indicates the key of the song; it generally contains a number of flats or sharps relative to a specific key

kick   An accent that is emphasized by the majority or the entire band

measure   Also referred to as bar, the space on the music staff that organizes durations into a specific meter

melisma   A vocal practice that entails the singing of three or more notes per syllable of a word

melody   A set of pitches that constitutes a musical statement

Membranophone   A classification of musical instruments that designates various types of drums

meter   In general, rhythms are organized in to patterns of two, three, or four

mezzo forte   To play a musical passage moderately loud

mezzo piano   To play a musical passage moderately soft

moderato   To play a musical passage moderately

monophony   The singing of the same notes by a group of singers

motive   A brief theme that is used for the basis of a longer statement or the entire work

movement   A section of a larger work distinguished by its melody, harmony, rhythm, etc., which produces a particular "mood"

musical alphabet   A-B-C-D-E-F-G

octave   In Western theory, tones that are 8 notes apart (higher or lower)

orchestra   A group that consists of a combination of sections, such as woodwinds, brass, percussion, and strings

ostinato   A repetitive bass pattern

overdubbing   To record parts over other sounded parts

passage   A musical statement

performance practice   A common occurrence of something in a performance that is not generally written down

phrase   A musical statement that consists of an antecedent (question) and consequent (answer)

piano (dynamic)   To sing or play a musical passage softly

pianissimo   To play a musical passage very softly

pitch   An audible tone

polyphony   Two or more different parts occurring simultaneously

presto   To play a musical passage very fast

quadruple   The song is counted and the mood is felt in four

recitative   A vocal performance tradition that involves the singing (or partly sung and partly spoken) of a passage in a rubato fashion

refrain   A section of a song that is repeated; in popular music, the chorus

rhythm   The result of an arrangement of sounds with particular durations that creates a pattern of movement in time

rhythm section   The core of a group. A three-piece rhythm section includes piano or guitar, bass, and drums; a four-piece includes all four of the above instruments

riff   A brief melodic, harmonic, and/or rhythmic pattern

ritardando   To gradually sing or play slower

root note   The lowest note of a chord

rubato   To play a musical passage at no specific tempo

sampling   To digitally record the sound of something

sacred song   Religious words

scale   An intervallic arrangement of pitches that produce a certain tonality (such as major and minor)

scatting   In its traditional sense, the singing of vocables that emulate a musical instrument

scratching   Technique, peculiar to hip-hop, involving the forcing of the turntable and vinyl record in a forward and backward motion, which subsequently "scratches" against the needle. This is done as a way to produce very rhythmic accompanimental sounds.

secular song   Non religious words

sharp   To raise a pitch by a half-step

sideman   A person that is hired for a onetime engagement; unlike the bandsman, the sideman is not a regular band member

slap bass   A performance technique on the electric bass where one plucks the strings and strikes the bass with the thumb in an accented manner. Larry Graham is given credit for developing this technique.

snare drum   The drum of a drum set that plays the backbeat (emphasis on counts two and four)

soprano (voice)   The highest female voice

standards   Songs are regarded as regular selections within ones repertoire of popular hits

stop-time   Instrumental performance technique that entails stopping by all band members on certain beats of the measure

string instruments   Violin, viola, cello, contra (string or upright) bass

swing   Can refer to a type of rhythm, dance (1930s–40s), style of music (big band swing, 1930s–40s), and an era (1930s–40s)

syncopation   In technical terms, the combination of weak and strong beats or short and long durations that produces uneven percussive sounds

tag   Often refers to playing the last 4 or 8 measures of a piece several times

tempo   Rate of speed.

tenor (voice)   Male voice above bass but below alto; can also refer to female voice lower than alto voice (See contralto.)

texture   Refers to layers of sound

theme   The principal tune of a piece

timbre   The tone quality of a voice or instrument

time signature   A time measuring unit that organizes durations

toasting   A term among music and hiphoppers that exalts someone

trading twos or fours   The alternation of instrumental solos in a two- or four-measure pattern.

triad   A three-note chord

triple   The song is counted and the mood is felt in three

triplet   Three notes of equal value within a count

twelve-bar blues   A specific succession of chords within 12 measures

unison   To sing or play the same pitch either at the same octave or an octave apart

vamp   To play a passage repeatedly until cued for the next section or to end the song

verse   That part of a song that "tells" the story, it generally consists of different words set to the same melody

vibrato   A minimal fluctuation of pitch performed by a singer

walking bass   A bass technique that involves the playing of step-wise notes on each count of the measure

woodwind instruments   Oboe, flute, clarinet, bassoon, and saxophone

INDEX